the cultural
territories of race

the

edited and with an introduction by michèle lamont

CULTURAL

TERRITORIES

RACE

of

black and white boundaries

the
university of
chicago press
chicago and
london

russell sage
foundation
new york

MICHÈLE LAMONT is associate professor of sociology at Princeton University. She is the author of *Money, Morals, and Manners,* and editor of *Cultivating Differences: Symbolic Boundaries and the Making of Inequality,* both published by the University of Chicago Press.

The University of Chicago Press, Chicago 60637
The University of Chicago Press, Ltd., London
© 1999 by The University of Chicago and the Russell Sage Foundation
All rights reserved. Published 1999
08 07 06 05 04 03 02 01 00 99   1 2 3 4 5
ISBN: 0-226-46835-6 (cloth)
ISBN: 0-226-46836-4 (paper)

Library of Congress Cataloging-in-Publication Data

The cultural territories of race : black and white boundaries / edited and with an introduction by Michèle Lamont.
    p. cm.
   Includes bibliographical references and index.
   ISBN 0-226-46835-6 (cloth : alk. paper).—ISBN 0-226-46836-4 (pbk. : alk. paper)
    1. United States—Race relations.   2. Ethnicity—United States.   3. Afro-Americans—Race identity.   4. Whites—United States—Race identity.   I. Lamont, Michèle, 1957–
E185.615.C85   1999
305.8'00973—dc21   98-48863
                                     CIP

♾ The paper used in this publication meets the minimum requirements of the American National Standard for Information Sciences—Permanence of Paper for Printed Library Materials, ANSI Z39.48-1992.

contents

Acknowledgments / vii

Introduction: Beyond Taking Culture Seriously
MICHÈLE LAMONT / ix

part one: dealing with racism

The Social Situation of the Black Executive: Black and White
Identities in the Corporate World   ELIJAH ANDERSON / 3

Navigating Race: Getting Ahead in the Lives of "Rags to Riches"
Young Black Men   ALFORD A. YOUNG JR. / 30

Explaining the Comfort Factor: West Indian Immigrants Confront
American Race Relations   MARY C. WATERS / 63

Is Racial Oppression Intrinsic to Domestic Work? The
Experiences of Children's Caregivers in Contemporary America
JULIA WRIGLEY / 97

part two: class and culture

Above "People Above"? Status and Worth among White and Black
Workers   MICHÈLE LAMONT / 127

"There's No Shame in My Game": Status and Stigma among
Harlem's Working Poor   KATHERINE S. NEWMAN AND
CATHERINE ELLIS / 151

Meanings and Motives in New Family Stories: The Separation of
Reproduction and Marriage among Low-Income Black and White
Parents   MAUREEN R. WALLER / 182

part three: education and the politics of race

Friend and Foe: Boundary Work and Collective Identity
in the Afrocentric and Multicultural Curriculum Movements
in American Public Education   AMY BINDER / 221

Multiculturalism as a Moving Moral Boundary: Literature
Professors Redefine Racism   BETHANY BRYSON / 249

Education and Advancement: Exploring the Hopes and Dreams of
Blacks and Poor Whites at the Turn of the Century
PAMELA BARNHOUSE WALTERS / 268

part four: ideology and the politics of race

"You're Too Independent!": How Gender, Race, and Class Make
Many Plural Feminisms   JANE J. MANSBRIDGE / 291

"Dis Beat Disrupts": Rap, Ideology, and Black Political Attitudes
MICHAEL C. DAWSON / 318

Affirmative Action as Culture War
JENNIFER L. HOCHSCHILD / 343

epilogue: the future of racial classification

The Possibility of a New Racial Hierarchy in the
Twenty-First-Century United States   HERBERT J. GANS / 371

About the Contributors / 391
Index / 397

acknowledgments

This volume was initiated as part of an agenda-setting and stock-taking series of books sponsored by the Culture Section of the American Sociological Association and edited by former chairs of the section. The previous volumes are those of Diana Crane (*Sociology of Culture: Emerging Theoretical Perspectives*, London: Blackwell, 1994) and Elizabeth Long (*From Culture to Cultural Studies*, London: Blackwell, 1997). Proceeds from these publications are donated in part to the section. I thank Diana Crane and Ann Swidler for convincing me to include this book in the series, with the hope that it will make a difference.

The collective endeavor I shared with my collaborators was made possible by a grant from the Russell Sage Foundation and the intellectual support of its president, Eric Wanner. Each chapter benefited in various ways from the opportunity afforded by this grant to bring together authors at a crucial stage in the preparation of their chapters.

This project was also made possible by the John Simon Guggenheim Memorial Foundation and the Russell Sage Foundation: their fellowships freed me from my teaching duties and allowed me to focus my energies on this and other projects for an extended period in 1996 and 1997. The months I spent at the Russell Sage Foundation were beneficial in so many ways that I cannot begin to enumerate them. The volume was completed at a time when I enjoyed the peaceful hospitality of the School of Social Science of the Institute for Advanced Studies, and it is with pleasure that I acknowledge this "in-kind" contribution to my scholarship.

Doug Mitchell of the University of Chicago Press and David Haproff of the Russell Sage Foundation are terrific editors. To be able to work with both simultaneously has been a privilege, and I want to thank them for making the process so enjoyable. Nubia Alexander, Sarah Caban, Cheryl Seleski, and Donna DeFrancisco also made a difference in this direction, and it is with gratitude that I acknowledge their technical assistance, professionalism, and good humor.

Now that the time to draw the curtain has come, I offer the contributors to this volume my warmest thanks for their responsiveness and intellectual commitment to the project. My single regret goes toward scholars whose work I would have liked to include, but could not due to space limitations. I hope that this project will inspire colleagues to commit themselves to parallel endeavors aimed at exploring the cultural territories of race from a multiracial or comparative perspective.

introduction: beyond taking culture seriously

michèle lamont

In the last few years, the dynamic between white and black cultures has taken hold of our collective imagination and captured the attention of growing numbers of scholars, artists, citizens, and cultural consumers. Essays on black popular culture and articles on black intellectuals appear regularly in influential publications such as *The New Yorker* and *The Atlantic Monthly*.[1] Movies on race and identity and philosophical debates about community and multiculturalism multiply and shape debates in the public sphere.[2] Cornel West's *Race Matters* (1993) sold two hundred thousand copies while the hardback edition of *The Bell Curve* by Herrnstein and Murray (1994) attracted inordinate coverage, selling over four hundred thousand copies.[3] Social scientists also engage the topic in large numbers. While race, like immigration and other "social problems," remains more than ever the bread and butter of sociology, more anthropologists turn their attention toward their own society to address race and ethnicity (e.g., Gregory and Sanjek [1994]; Lamphere [1992]; Ong [1996]). Despite differences in intellectual style, the interests of political scientists, social psychologists, and historians also often converge as they focus on black/white dynamics.[4] Hence, issues of race and cultural identity are now firmly at the forefront of disciplinary and interdisciplinary agendas.

Cultural arguments have always been integral to the study of racial inequality, although they have often been received critically. Following in the footsteps of the Moynihan report (1965), which influenced political and academic discussion early in the War on Poverty, Thomas Sowell (1994) and neoconservative authors (Mead [1986] and D'Souza [1996] in particular) have returned to values to explain differences in economic attainment, reiterating the "culture of poverty" thesis. This thesis identified pathological and self-perpetuating subcultures as the main cause of racial inequality and was sharply criticized for "blaming the victim" and for being unable to look at alternative cultures on their own terms. Like the literature on racial prejudice, it was also accused of downplaying the structural determinants of racial inequality.[5] Critics promoted "institutional racism" as a more adequate explanation of racial inequality: they argued that this conceptual term better renders the systemic character of American racial discrimination.[6] Another theory with a strong cultural bent, assimilation theory, has also been rejected by writers from the "new immigration" literature for downplaying the contribution of ethnic and racial groups to American sociology.[7]

Now, culture is back in full force as an important descriptive or explanatory analytical dimension, not only in the field of ethnic and racial studies, but in the discipline of sociology at large.[8] Among scholars working on racial inequality, it is center stage even for such influential (though not always converging) structural thinkers as William Julius Wilson, Douglas Massey, and Nancy Denton. Indeed, in *When Work Disappears* (1996, chap. 3), William Julius Wilson explains the persistence of poverty among blacks by pointing to available cultural scripts and habits, drawing on the work of cultural sociologist Ann Swidler (1986). In *American Apartheid* (1993, chap. 6), Massey and Denton dedicate a chapter to discussing the oppositional culture of poor African-Americans. Ethnicity scholars such as Morawska (forthcoming) also draw on sophisticated tools developed by cultural sociologists (e.g., Sewell [1992]) to open new vistas in the literature on ethnic identity and assimilation: instead of positing a dualism between structure and culture or between attitudes and behavior often present in earlier writings, she discusses scripts of collective ethnic identity as cultural structures and promotes a research program having their historical constitution as its focus. More broadly speaking, immigration scholars increasingly center their attention on rules for cultural membership and boundary work (Brubaker 1992; Favell 1997; Feldblum forthcoming) while the challenges raised to national identity by postnational citizenship and transnationalism are coming under greater scrutiny (Soysal 1993). Within and outside of the confines of sociology, the social construction of race and other aspects of identity is the topic of an ever-growing number of theoretical essays, as scholars turn their attention to exploring how the self is defined through publicly available categories, including those pertaining to race.[9] Fortunately, the empirical literature is also growing, although at a slower pace. Ethnographers—anthropologists and sociologists—are multiplying their terrains of inquiry (e.g., Fernandez-Kelly [1995]; Espiritu [forthcoming]; Park [1996]). Using different tools, survey researchers continue to elaborate models of ever-increasing sophistication to address difficult issues pertaining to the nature of American racism (e.g., Bobo, Kluegel, and Smith [1997]; Dawson [this volume]).

At a minimum, the present collection is grounded in the conviction that it is possible to use the tools developed by cultural sociologists and cultural anthropologists productively to move beyond the "politicized dichotomies of structure vs. culture" (to use Mary Waters's phrase in this volume; also Newman 1992 and Reed 1991). A growing number of scholars working in these fields have come to conceive of cultural tools as systemic, structural properties of the environment, or as available repertoires or scripts.[10] This has important implications for the examination of the cultural dimensions of race: If culture consists of scripts, to say that the underprivileged (whether as members of a class or a racial group) have cultural understandings that help to reproduce their status does not blame the victim nor is it necessarily conservative. Furthermore, to understand racist beliefs as shaped by available grammars of arguments points to the systemic character of racism.[11] Of course, these theoretical shifts do not reduce class or racial inequality the way the creation of good, stable jobs would. However, they can make a difference by providing a more complex understanding of the cultural territories of race: they focus our attention on the place of repertoires of strategies of action, symbolic boundaries, cognitive classification, scripts of personhood and collective identity, and developing ideologies in the reproduction of racial inequality. Hence the importance of giving a substantive push in this direction and of focusing our attention on studies such as those included in this volume, which, although they generally do not address directly the presumed structure/culture divide, do take culture seriously.

However, these essays go further than "just" taking culture seriously: all share the goal of moving the theoretical agenda beyond hollow reaffirmation of the constructed character of identity.[12] Some of the recent literature on identity—not only racial identity, but also sexual, gender, ethnic, class, and national identities—encourages the production of theory in a vacuum.[13] This volume offers a counterweight to this trend: all the authors are preoccupied with gaining theoretical leverage from a close "corps à corps" with their data. Hence, all the essays included here draw on systematic and careful empirical work in their examination of the cultural territories of race. Furthermore, most focus on an aspect of boundaries, or on the relational dimension of racial identities and positions, that have become a mainstay in the literature (Barth 1969; also Jenkins 1994). These aspects are (1) differences among blacks in how they deal with whites and are treated by whites (chapters by Anderson, Waters, and Wrigley); (2) boundaries among blacks (and between categories of blacks such as African-Americans and West Indians) based on how they relate to one another given their relationships with whites (chapter by Waters) and their market position (chapter by Newman and Ellis); (3) boundaries among blacks based on how they relate to one another given their relationships with black culture (apropos of Afrocentrism, rap, and other issues) (chapters by Binder and Dawson); (4) differences among blacks and between whites and blacks in their understandings of various aspects of social life, including education, family, class cultures, reproduction, marriage, and feminism (chapters by Young, Lamont, Waller, Walters, and Mansbridge); (5) boundaries among whites based on their attitudes toward blacks (chapter by Bryson); (6) how whites use issues of race to promote particular political positions (chapter by Hochschild). With one or two exceptions, chapters report on larger, still unpublished research projects.

Some readers will be concerned with our almost exclusive focus on blacks and whites in the context of the increasingly multiracial character of American society. Racial polarization in the United States has long pitted blacks and whites against one another, although the intensity of the conflict varies regionally and historically. This conflict has been repeatedly described as having played a very distinctive role in the making of American society (Smith 1997). There is growing evidence that these two racial groups live in very different cultural worlds; recall that 85 percent of blacks, compared with only 34 percent of whites, agreed with the decision of the jury in the case of O. J. Simpson's criminal trial (Hochschild 1996, xi).[14] Such findings might remind us that even in a multiracial America, the black/white dynamics remain absolutely crucial and deserve special scrutiny. Of course, more research is needed on boundaries that oppose other racial groups than whites and blacks and on the ways in which black/white relationships are shaped by other racial groups. We do not pretend to "do it all" in the pages that follow. The initiative is in the hands of colleagues who wish to examine these issues in monographs and future edited collections.

The volume is divided into several parts, each dealing with one aspect of the ways in which culture intersects with racial inequality. The overall movement is from racism and class cultures to education and ideology. The first part concerns the experience of racism. Deploying the same ethnographic talents that characterizes his earlier studies, Elijah Anderson analyzes how black executives manage their stigmatized identity in the workplace by negotiating their relationships with other blacks, with whites, and with the mainstream culture of the corporation. Drawing on Goffman's writings on the self and identification, his chapter provides a rare glimpse of the cultural impact of affirmation action, responding to Jennifer Hochschild's call (in this volume) for more study of this type. For his part, Alford Young Jr. offers a few cases of young African-Americans as analytic exemplars of cultural strategies of action available for negotiating the constraints that black men meet on their way from rags to riches. His description of their folk theories of the social order and their understanding of the available scripts and appropriate ideologies for success (including impression management and avoidance of repression) illuminates important realities that have remained largely unexamined to date. Mary Waters presents results from her large-scale study comparing how African-Americans and West Indies immigrants deal with race relations. She suggests that each group's life experience provides different ways of dealing with whites (such as the ability to create for whites a "comfort zone"), which shapes their expectations and market positions. Using her findings, she develops an insightful critique of the culture/ structure dualism that, as suggested above, too often characterizes the American literature on race. Finally, Julia Wrigley compares how white, Latino, and black (African-American and West Indian) caregivers are treated by and deal with their white employers. Her poignant interviews illuminate important racial differences in the amounts of stigmatized work they do and the amount of social distance their employers maintain toward them. These four contributions point to the importance of analyzing responses to racism as part of the worldviews embedded in the life experiences of individuals and emerging from the environments that surround them and from the scripts and cultural repertoires of action available to them.

The second part addresses various dimensions of class cultures, focusing on the solid working class, the working poor, and low-income groups. Drawing on interviews conducted with stable working-class men living in the New York suburbs, my chapter analyzes the relationship that whites and blacks have with people located above them in the social structure. Contrary to prevailing arguments, it shows that workers have considerable distance from middle-class values and the American dream and adopt moral criteria of evaluation that allow them to position themselves above "people above." Paradoxically, a larger number of black interviewees than white interviewees are attached to middle-class values, but blacks who oppose such values draw stronger boundaries against them than whites do. Katherine Newman and Catherine Ellis turn our attention to the precarious world of the working poor as it exists in the fast-food industry in Harlem. Drawing from Newman's massive study, they describe how these young people draw on resources provided to them by the broader American culture, by the workplace, and by their social network to create and maintain their mainstream identity as workers against the stigma of flipping burgers for a living. This involves stressing commonalities with the rest of the working world by drawing strong boundaries against people below, just as some working-class men draw boundaries against people above. Finally, Maureen Waller analyzes how white and black low-income parents living in Trenton, New Jersey, understand and explain unmarried parenthood. She finds more homogeneity in black accounts than in white accounts, which she explains by available cultural repertoires and the conditions in which individuals experience the growing separation between marriage and reproduction. Considered together, these contributions illustrate how theoretical tools developed by cultural anthropologists and cultural sociologists can raise new questions and provide new tools for the study of racial inequality.

The third part concerns education and the politics of race. Like Anderson, Amy Binder focuses on boundaries among African-Americans, analyzing the dynamic between proponents of Afrocentrism and multiculturalism within the context of the school reform movement in three states. She shows that the process of collective identification of blacks is driven by their collaboration with or opposition to whites. Bethany Bryson also focuses on boundaries, but among whites as they fight to redefine the meaning of racism. She draws on interviews with English professors at four universities to analyze how one's position toward multiculturalism can become a basis for exclusion within academia. She shows that this type of exclusion is more frequent in elite than nonelite universities. Finally, Pamela Barnhouse Walters's chapter brings an important historical dimension to the volume, using archival data to tackle an issue akin to that taken on by Alford Young Jr.: the meaning of education in the strategies of mobility of poor blacks. Unlike Young, she focuses on racial differences. She finds that at the turn of the century, northern immigrants and poor blacks prized the right to education as a symbol of their Americanness and social citizenship—which was not the case for poor southern whites, for whom citizenship was not at issue. Because of its mandatory and collective nature, the educational system is the territory par excellence where groups engage in identity politics. Hence the importance of examining how racial identity is shaped by and constructs this environment, as illustrated by the three rich contributions included in this part of the volume.

The fourth part of the book deals with race, politics, and ideology. Political theorist Jane Mansbridge looks at the meaning that white and black women give to feminism in the context of broader normative worlds. Drawing on rich interviews and survey data, she analyzes the signification and salience of "independence" in these women's daily lives, revealing what differences tell us about the specific challenges that both groups face in their struggle for dignity, equality, and justice. She shows that the existence of plural feminisms is linked to the inescapable cultural differences that shape the lives of white and black women. Also drawing on survey data, Michael Dawson addresses the very important question of the political uses of black popular culture, and of rap particularly, dissecting its relationship with political ideologies such as feminism and black nationalism. He provides much-needed empirical knowledge on the effects of exposure to and attitudes toward rap on general political attitudes, homophobia, sexism, and black nationalism, finding a strong connection between rap and community nationalism. He also draws normative conclusions about the place of rap in the making of a more vigorous black public sphere. Finally, Jennifer

Hochschild explains the dearth of empirical knowledge concerning affirmative action and its implementation by the primarily symbolic use that politicians and policy makers have made of it in struggles to impose particular definitions of what it means to be an American. Together, these three contributions connect racial differences to the broader political processes and ideas that shape American society.

Herbert Gans's speculative essay on likely changes in the racial classification system is the epilogue to the volume. Gans returns to issues of stigma addressed in several chapters to describe these changes. Patterns of group mobility and racial discrimination are bringing forth a major racial realignment: again, the dominant polarization to come is one that will move from a dual hierarchy pitting whites against blacks to one that will pit all nonblacks against blacks, with Asians and Latinos being increasingly categorized with whites in the nonstigmatized group.

In conclusion, I want to stress that the articles presented here are also offered with the hope that they will generate more qualitative studies of the world inhabited by victims of racism and inequality, and eventually, will inform policy makers and others who seek to address such problems. The efforts of talented interviewers have taught us much about teenage mothers, welfare recipients, victims of racism, racists themselves, and so-called deadbeat dads.[15] These researchers have produced the type of detailed analysis of under-studied cultural worlds that is particularly useful in an environment where economists often dominate policy-making. It is imperative that cultural analysts not abandon this turf, for what we have to contribute can truly shape the way our societies understand the worlds of victims of inequalities of all types: our intellectual labor can amplify voices that remain too often muted in American public discourse.

Notes

This introduction has benefited from very helpful comments from Karen Cerulo, Herbert Gans, and Wendy Griswold.

1. Influential essays on black popular culture include Rose 1994. Michael Dawson (this volume) provides a review of this literature, focusing on rap music. Essays on black intellectuals include Anderson 1994, Berube 1995, and Boynton 1995.

2. On independent African-American films, see for instance Watkins 1998. On community and multiculturalism, see Taylor 1992.

3. Personal communication with a former editor at Free Press.

4. In political science, see in particular the literature on symbolic racism (most recently, Kinder and Sanders 1996) and the work of younger scholars such as Gilens (1996) and Mendelberg (1997). Recent studies by social psychologists include Sidanius et al.

1996; Hogg 1996; Lott and Maluso 1995; and Brown 1995. In history, see in particular the literature on whiteness (Roediger 1991) and multiculturalism (Hollinger 1995).

5. Moreover, this literature was criticized for its theoretical functionalism and for underplaying internal differences among the poor. Good statements of these critiques are available in Hannerz 1969; Liebow 1967; Stack 1974; and Valentine 1968.

6. In the words of Stephen Steinberg (1997, 110), a strong proponent of structural approaches to racism, "'Institutional racism,' coined by Stokely Carmichael and Charles Hamilton in their book *Black Power,* was the most important conceptual innovation to emerge from the cross-fertilization of racial militancy and radical politics during the 1960s. It challenged the prevailing paradigm within social science that reduced racism to the racial beliefs and practices of individuals instead of focusing on the systemic basis of racism and the imperative for attacking racism systematically. Indeed, affirmative action policy is predicated on the argument that the exclusion of blacks from coveted job sectors was ipso facto proof of institutional racism. By implication, racism was to be measured by results, not attitudes."

7. For a summary of this debate and a defense of the concept of assimilation, see Alba and Nee 1997 and Rumbaut 1997. For a useful statement on the uses of the concept of assimilation in the study of immigration, see Portes and Bach 1985. For a treatment of the normative status given to white culture, see Frankenberg 1993.

8. Within American sociology, this return to culture is demonstrated by the rapid growth of the Culture Section of the American Sociological Association. Created in the mid-eighties, by the mid-nineties this section had grown to be the fourth largest section of the ASA, with more than eight hundred members. Cultural arguments enjoy growing centrality in a number of subfields of the discipline, including network analysis, organizations, economic sociology, social movements, and political sociology, to mention only a few.

The renewed attention to culture can be accounted for by social and intellectual factors endogenous to the discipline (including generational shifts and dissatisfaction with social-structural explanations), by interdisciplinary factors (such as the vitality of cultural history and cultural anthropology under the influence of scholars such as Darnton [1984] and Geertz [1973]), and by exogenous social and cultural factors, such as the growing influence of multiculturalism in popular culture and frequent discussions of family values in the media.

9. Although citing a few authors is to do an injustice to many, the theoretical influence of Omi and Winant (1986) and Gilroy (1987) is worth mentioning. An excellent review of literature on identity is available in Cerulo 1997.

10. This literature includes Hall 1988; Lamont 1992; Sewell 1992; Swidler 1986; and Wuthnow 1987. On culture as script, see DiMaggio 1997. If we have learned anything from sociological theory, cultural anthropology, and cultural sociology in the last decades, it is that microphenomena—including individual values—are often instantiations of aspects of the macrostructural realities and can have systemic structural properties (see in particular Bourdieu 1977). This point is as central to the Durkheimian tradition as it is to poststructuralism. For illustrations, see Lamont and Fournier 1992.

11. As do Steinberg 1997 and Di Leonardo's (1992) essay on racial differences between whites and blacks.

12. Constructivism has long been an established—if sometimes embattled—perspective in the sociological literature. Calhoun 1994 provides a comparison of the sociological, feminist, and postmodernist literatures on identity. See also Hogg, Terry, and White 1995 for a comparison of the sociological and social-psychological literature on identity.

13. For a critique of the intellectual habitus found in some (but not all) cultural studies quarters, see Schudson 1997.

14. We will recall that Massey and Denton (1993, 160) showed that in 1980, the average black person in the ten largest U.S. cities lived in a neighborhood that was at least 80 percent black and that the vast majority resided in areas that were 100 percent black. Spatial isolation leads to social isolation, which means that blacks are less likely than members of any other groups to report friendship with anyone else but members of their own group. There is a genuine lack of social connection with mainstream society that translates into growing cultural autonomization.

15. These skilled interviewers include several contributors of this volume, as well as other sociologists, such as Duneier (1992); Edin and Lein (1997); Feagin (1991); Luker (1996); and Wellman (1993).

References

Alba, Richard, and Victor Nee. 1997. "Rethinking Assimilation Theory for a New Era of Immigration." *International Migration Review* 31:826–74.

Anderson, Jevis. 1994. "The Public Intellectual." *New Yorker,* January 17, 39–49.

Barth, Fredrik. 1969. *Ethnic Groups and Boundaries.* London: George Allen and Unwin.

Berube, Michael. 1995. "Public Academy." *New Yorker,* January 9, 53–70.

Bobo, Lawrence, James R. Kluegel, and Ryan A. Smith. 1997. "Laissez-Faire Racism: The Crystallization of a 'Kinder, Gentler' Anti-Black Ideology." In *Racial Attitudes in the 1990s: Continuity and Change,* edited by Steven A. Tuch and Jack K. Martin. Westport, Conn.: Praeger.

Bourdieu, Pierre. 1977. *Outline of a Theory of Practice.* Cambridge: Cambridge University Press.

Boynton, Robert S. 1995. "The New Intellectuals." *Atlantic Monthly,* March, 53–70.

Brown, Rupert. 1995. *Prejudice.* Oxford: Blackwell.

Brubaker, Rogers. 1992. *Citizenship and Nationhood in France and Germany.* Cambridge: Harvard University Press.

Calhoun, Craig. 1994. "Social Theory and the Politics of Identity." In *Social Theory and the Politics of Identity,* edited by Craig Calhoun. Cambridge: Blackwell.

Cerulo, Karen. 1997. "Identity Construction: New Issues, New Directions." *Annual Review of Sociology* 23:385–409.

Darnton, Robert. 1984. *The Great Cat Massacre and Other Episodes in French Cultural History.* New York: Basic.

Di Leonardo, Micaela. 1992. "Boys on the Hood." *Nation,* August 17–24, 178–86.

DiMaggio, Paul. 1997. "Culture and Cognition." *Annual Review of Sociology* 23:263–87.

D'Souza, Dinesh. 1996. *The End of Racism.* New York: Free Press.

Duneier, Mitchell. 1992. *Slim's Table.* Chicago: University of Chicago Press.

Edin, Kathryn, and Laura Lein. 1997. *Making Ends Meet.* New York: Sage.

Espiritu, Yen Le. Forthcoming. "The Discourse of Morality: Family, Culture, and Gender among Second-Generation Filipinas." *Gender and Society.*

Favell, Adrian. 1997. *Philosophies of Integration.* London: Macmillan.

Feagin, Joe R. 1991. "The Continuing Significance of Race: Antiblack Discrimination in Public Places." *American Sociological Review* 56:101–16.

Feldblum, Miriam. Forthcoming. *Reconstructing Citizenship.* New York: State University of New York Press.

Fernandez-Kelly, Patricia. 1995. "Towanda's Triumph: Social and Cultural Capital in the Urban Ghetto." In *The Economic Sociology of Immigration: Essays on Networks, Ethnicity, and Entrepreneurship,* edited by Alejandro Portes. New York: Sage.

Frankenberg, Ruth. 1993. *The Social Construction of Whiteness.* Minneapolis: University of Minnesota Press.

Geertz, Clifford. 1973. *The Interpretation of Culture.* New York: Basic.

Gilens, Martin. 1996. "Race and Poverty in America. Public Misperceptions and the American News Media." *Public Opinion Quarterly* 60:515–41.

Gilroy, Paul. 1987. *There Ain't No Black in the Union Jack.* Chicago: University of Chicago Press.

Gregory, Steven, and Roger Sanjek, eds. 1994. *Race.* New Brunswick: Rutgers University Press.

Hall, John R. 1988. "Social Organization and Pathways of Commitment: Types of Communal Groups. Rational Choice Theory and the Kanter Thesis." *American Sociological Review* 53:679–92.

Hannerz, Ulf. 1969. *Soulside.* New York: Columbia University Press.

Herrnstein, Richard J., and Charles Murray. 1994. *The Bell Curve.* New York: Free Press.

Hochschild, Jennifer L. 1995. *Facing Up to the American Dream.* Princeton: Princeton University Press.

Hogg, Michael A. 1996. "Intragroup Processes, Group Structure, and Social Identity." In *Social Group and Identities: Developing the Legacy of Henri Tajfel,* edited by W. Peter Robinson. Oxford: Butterworth Heinemann.

Hogg, Michael A., Deborah J. Terry, and Katherine M. White. 1995. "A Tale of Two Theories: A Critical Comparison of Identity Theory with Social Identity Theory." *Social Psychology Quarterly* 58:255–69.

Hollinger, David A. 1995. *Post-Ethnic America.* New York: Basic.

Jenkins, Richard. 1994. "Rethinking Ethnicity: Identity, Categorization, Power." *Ethnic and Racial Studies* 17:197–223.

Kinder, Donald R., and Lynn M. Sanders. 1996. *Divided by Color.* Chicago: University of Chicago Press.

Lamont, Michèle. 1992. *Money, Morals, and Manners.* Chicago: University of Chicago Press.

Lamont, Michèle, and Marcel Fournier, eds. 1992. *Cultivating Differences: Symbolic Boundaries and the Making of Inequality.* Chicago: University of Chicago Press.

Lamphere, Louise, ed. 1992. *Structuring Diversity.* Chicago: University of Chicago Press.

Liebow, Elliot. 1967. *Tally's Corner. A Study of Negro Streetcorner Men.* Boston: Little Brown.

Lott, Bernice, and Diane Maluso, eds. 1995. *The Social Psychology of Interpersonal Discrimination.* New York: Guilford.

Luker, Kristin. 1996. *Dubious Conceptions.* Cambridge: Harvard University Press.

Massey, Douglas S., and Nancy A. Denton. 1993. *American Apartheid.* Cambridge: Harvard University Press.

Mead, Lawrence. 1986. *Beyond Entitlement.* New York: Free Press.

Mendelberg, Tali. 1997. "Executing Hortons: Racial Crime in the 1988 Presidential Campaign." *Public Opinion Quarterly* 61:134–57.

Morawska, Ewa. Forthcoming. "Ethnicity as the Double Structure: A Historical-Comparative Approach." In *Cultural Analysis and Comparative Research in Social History,* edited by Willfried Spohn. Opladen: Budrich and Leske.

Moynihan, Daniel P. 1965. *The Negro Family.* Washington: Office of Policy Planning and Research, U.S. Department of Labor.

Nagel, Joane. 1996. *American Indian Ethnic Renewal.* London: Oxford University Press.

Newman, Katherine. 1992. "Culture and Structure in the Truly Disadvantaged." *City and Society* 6:3–25.

Omi, Michael, and Howard Winant. 1986. *Racial Transformation in the United States from the 1960s to the 1980s.* New York: Routledge.

Ong, Aihwa. 1996. "Cultural Citizenship as Subject-Making: Immigrants Negotiate Racial and Cultural Boundaries in the United States." *Current Anthropology* 37:737–62.

Park, Kyeyoung. 1996. "Use and Abuse of Race and Culture: Black/Korean Tension in America." *American Anthropologist* 98:492–99.

Portes, Alejandro, and Robert L. Bach. 1985. *Latin Journey.* Berkeley: University of California Press.

Reed, Adolph. 1991. "The Underclass Myth." *Progressive,* August, 18–20.

Roediger, David. 1991. *The Wages of Whiteness.* London: Verso.

Rose, Tricia. 1994. *Black Noise.* Hanover, Conn.: Wesleyan University Press.

Rumbaut, Ruben G. 1997. "Assimilation and Its Discontents: Between Rhetoric and Reality." *International Migration Review* 31:923–60.

Schudson, Michael. 1997. "Cultural Studies and the Construction of Social Construction: Notes on Teddy Bear Patriarchy." In *From Sociology to Cultural Studies,* edited by Elizabeth Long. New York: Blackwell.

Sewell, William H., Jr. 1992. "A Theory of Structure: Duality, Agency, and Transformation." *American Journal of Sociology* 98:1–29.

Sidanius, J., F. Pratto, S. Sinclair, and C. Van Laar. 1996. "Mother Theresa Meets Genghis Khan: The Dialectics of Hierarchy-Enhancing and Hierarchy-Attenuating Career Choices." *Social Justice Research* 9:145–70.

Smith, Rogers M. 1997. *Civic Ideals.* New Haven: Yale University Press.

Sowell, Thomas. 1994. *Migration and Cultures.* New York: Basic.

Soysal, Yasemin Nuhoglu. 1993. *Limits of Citizenship.* Chicago: University of Chicago Press.

Stack, Carol. 1974. *All Our Kin*. New York: Harper and Row.

Steinberg, Stephen. 1997. "The Role of Racism in the Inequality Studies of William Julius Wilson." *Journal of Blacks in Higher Education* 15:109–17.

Swidler, Ann. 1986. "Culture in Action: Symbols and Strategies." *American Sociological Review* 51:273–86.

Taylor, Charles. 1992. *Multiculturalism and "The Politics of Recognition."* With commentary by Amy Gutman, Steven C. Rockefeller, Michael Walzer, and Susan Wolf. Princeton: Princeton University Press.

Thompson, J. Phillip, III. 1998. "Universalism and Deconcentration: Why Race Still Matters in Poverty and Economic Development." *Politics and Society* 26:181–220.

Valentine, Charles A. 1968. *Culture and Poverty*. Chicago: University of Chicago Press.

Watkins, Craig. 1998. *Representing*. Chicago: University of Chicago Press.

Wellman, David T. 1993. *Portraits of White Racism*. 2d ed. New York: Cambridge University Press.

West, Cornel. 1993. *Race Matters*. Boston: Beacon.

Wilson, William Julius. 1996. *When Work Disappears*. New York: Knopf.

Wuthnow, Robert. 1987. *Meaning and Moral Order*. Berkeley: University of California Press.

part one
dealing with racism

the social situation of the black executive: black and white identities in the corporate world

elijah anderson

Blacks in executive-level positions in the United States today must deal with extremely complex social dynamics. Although as blacks they are identified first and foremost as members of a historically stigmatized group, as executives they are also identified as members of an elite and powerful class in today's corporate world. An examination of their problems, and the manner in which they have been resolved or left unresolved, will yield insights into the situation of minorities generally.

In preparing to "enter the field," I requested complete access to the people of one work setting within the company, a major financial service corporation in center city Philadelphia. Such access would have afforded me the opportunity to follow and observe the subjects of the study in their daily activities and to question them at will. I would have liked to have engaged in intensive participant-observation, an ideal situation for generating "slice of life" portrayals of the work setting and for gleaning important insights into the corporate culture generally and the social situation of minority employees of the company more particularly. This plan was declined by the company. Instead, I was permitted to roam the premises and interview persons referred to me by the vice president for employee relations, who is himself black.

The representation here is therefore based both on observation of the social setting and on intensive ethnographic interviews with a small sample of executive-level "minority" employees including blacks, Jews, and women. Accordingly, the resulting observations are not meant to be representative but rather suggestive of the quality of experience within the company. Over the course of six months, the interviews were conducted on the work premises or at area restaurants during the workday, and they frequently extended to ninety minutes.[1] The company was generous in providing office space as well as time for employees to be interviewed, and the interviewees were most helpful and quite candid in their discussion of questions put to them by me. The interviews were open ended and informal in an attempt to elicit information and insights into the personal lives of employees and their situation within the organization.

Historical Basis of Affirmative Action

An adequate assessment of the present-day situation of executives in this company, and in the American corporate world in general, requires some historical perspective on black mobility. Such a viewpoint is important since social change within this corporate environment is related to important changes in other major institutions of American society.

Over the past half century, American society has changed profoundly in the area of race relations (see Myrdal 1944; Drake and Cayton 1962; Cox 1948; Hacker 1995; Wilson 1980, 1987, 1996). Largely as a consequence of affirmative-action programs, black Americans, long segregated in ghettos and treated as second-class citizens, have only recently begun to participate in the wider society in ways previously restricted to privileged members of the white majority group. This process of racial incorporation signaled the beginning of the still very slow decline of the American caste-like system of race relations, and it may be traced to certain general sociohistorical developments. The most dramatic changes were spurred by the civil rights movement, the subsequent major civil disorders, and the social and political responses to these new and provocative developments (see Kerner et al. 1968).

Major policy responses included the civil rights legislation of 1964, 1965, and 1968. Perhaps most important for the subject of this essay was the executive order issued and signed by President John F. Kennedy and then revised by President Lyndon Johnson in 1964 prescribing "affirmative action" as an important remedy for racial discrimination, social injustice, and the resulting inequality. At the time, public support for these remedial measures was widespread and overwhelming but by no means unanimous. Some critics have argued that because of the overarching concern of government, business, and academia for social peace, these policies were simply desperate measures to "cool out" the "long hot summers" in particular and alienated black Americans and their white allies more generally. I believe that while there was concern on the part of policy makers to prevent further outbursts of violence and disorder in American cities, there also appeared to be a genuine national consensus to make the socioeconomic system more equitable, particularly to members of the national black community. But also important was the provocative international specter of black Americans being whipped and beaten daily in their efforts to obtain the basic civil right to vote in the "world's leading democracy." This image was simply too much of a contradiction for many Americans, including policy makers, to bear, particularly with the emergence of so many newly independent "colored" nations of Africa and other parts of the third world at once trying to decide whether to follow in the orbit of the Soviet Union or the West in the midst of the cold war.

Whatever the reasoning or intentions of policy makers, American social life has moved toward equality for blacks since that time. Moreover, to a significant degree, the events that provided increased mobility for blacks also did so for other minority groups. Blacks, women, and members of other minority groups, including newly arrived immigrants, have become the beneficiaries of significant civil rights legislation, including affirmative action, which has been strictly enforced by successive federal administrations, with the exception of those of Reagan and Bush. As a result of such policies, members of these groups, most notably white women, are now participating in the American occupational structure at levels inconceivable a few decades ago.

Consistent with these trends, the black middle class has expanded in both size and outlook and appears to be in the process of transforming from a class of small business operators and professionals serving the black community almost exclusively to one that is increasingly economically independent of that community (see Frazier 1957; Wilson 1980; Landry 1987; Collins 1997). With such developments, members of this group appear increasingly involved in the corporate and business sectors of society at large. Even to the casual observer, black Americans appear to be considerably more fully included in American life than ever before. Largely shut out from becoming bankers, stockbrokers, corporate executives, and responsible government agents before the social upheaval brought on by the civil rights movement (see Stryker 1953), blacks have become increasingly visible in such occupations, although very few move beyond the middle levels to areas of major influence.

Beginning in the 1960s, as part of the general movement toward greater black incorporation, an impressive number of African-Americans began attending predominantly white colleges and universities, from which they were previously excluded, at times by law; and the number of black professors, particularly those teaching at predominantly white institutions, also increased. This general process of incorporation did not bypass the corporations, some of which gladly recruited blacks; others, though, needed to be pressured into establishing affirmative action programs to remedy past underrepresentation and discriminatory behavior.

However, as African-Americans have become ostensible beneficiaries of affirmative action, leading to a growing presence of middle-class blacks in major social positions, especially in corporate life, growing numbers of white Americans began to feel highly threatened. In an era of deindustrialization and corporate downsizing and the resulting insecurities of the American workforce, policies that were once indulged and viewed as noble efforts against racial discrimination became increasingly viewed negatively as so many "race preferences" for blacks. In these circumstances, such efforts to include blacks worked to create a growing backlash and resentment among a number of those whites with whom individual black beneficiaries would share work settings. Indeed, many whites, and some blacks, have gone so far as to mount legal and ideological challenges to affirmative action programs, arguing "reverse discrimination" (see Glazer 1987, 1997; *Regents of the State of California v. Bakke,* 1978; Skrentny 1996; Bearak 1997). All this has culminated in a growing nationwide movement to legally dismantle affirmative action programs through state initiatives. Proposition 209 has outlawed affirmative action in California, foreshadowing what could happen throughout the United States.

Ironically, along with the apparent growth of black representation and participation in various areas of American life, but particularly the workplace, fewer citizens can see a need for affirmative action. With such visible black participation, as well as a growth of the presence of other minorities in the workplace, including white women, it becomes increasingly difficult to make the argument that racism is the sole factor denying opportunities to blacks; that the system itself is racially exclusionary. In these circumstances, race is prematurely degraded as a powerful explanation of inequality. In essence, the power of the concept has been weakened by the proliferation of symbolic elements that contribute to the appearance of inclusiveness—particularly successful blacks—in the corporate workplace; by their presence and high visibility, they strongly imply that the occupational structure is open and egalitarian, if not meritocratic.

Nevertheless, black executives often express their doubts. While it is clear that social conditions have improved considerably for many middle-class blacks and their progress toward attaining social parity with middle-class whites has given many hope, it must be pointed out that racial inequality continues to be endemic to American society, and that tremendous numbers of blacks as well as other people of color remain segregated in ghettos, are poor, and continue to be treated as second-class citizens (see Massey and Denton 1993; Feagin and Sikes 1994; Cose 1993). In fact, as improvements in the condition of the black middle class become more pronounced, a social and economic split between members of the black middle class and the black lower class becomes more discernible. The initiatives and policies mentioned above had their most direct and immediate effect on blacks who were well-prepared and poised to take advantage of any opportunity that arose in the occupational system. In this scenario, the lower class was largely ignored at a time when the jobs upon which this class depended started to be lost due to automation, deindustrialization, and the rise of the global economy (see Wilson 1980, 1987, 1996; Anderson 1990; Rifkin 1995). This historical context is important for understanding aspects of the social life of the company on which this report is based.

After President Johnson issued his executive order prescribing affirmative action, the company I studied instituted its programs to recruit and train blacks. Without such pressure and the initiatives that followed, the number of blacks working and being promoted within the company would have been significantly smaller.

To be sure, affirmative action has produced conflicting results in this corporate setting. A few blacks have indeed been highly successful, occasionally reaching upper-level management positions. But many others are frustrated, feeling strongly that they have been detained and kept from rising because of an invisible "job ceiling" for blacks; they believe there are certain jobs that blacks will never obtain and others into which blacks are being channeled. Moreover, it is difficult for them to feel and act as if they are accepted as full participants in the organization (see Cose 1993).

Since skin color, particularly its social and political significance, appears to be such a problematic issue for the personnel of the organization, it would be conceptually useful, following Goffman (1963), to consider its relationship to the concept of stigma, or "spoiled identity." Goffman distinguishes three categories: "the own," "the wise," and "the normal." The own represents the stigmatized group in society. This group consists of a collection of individuals with a similar "negative" difference. Within the group, there is a discrepancy between each person's "virtual" and "actual" social identities, which can be seen as the difference between his or her "good," "virtuous," and "positive" qualities and "negative" attributes. Stigma thus is a matter of degree and perhaps best viewed as a product of social interaction; in effect, it is a transaction between those who are stigmatized and those who assign stigma (see Becker 1973). For Goffman, those who assign stigma include the normals (those members of the organization who feel essentially that corporate life is fair to them and others and have few complaints) and the wise ("normal" people who have the capacity for empathy toward outsiders and who tend to extend themselves to the "own" to assist them and make them feel welcome within the organization) as well as members of the own themselves.

However, it is important to keep in mind that much has happened in the politics of difference since Goffman advanced his position. Today, Goffman's view of stigma appears rather absolutist insofar as he has a generally clear conception of what does and does not constitute stigma in life. In this view, the one person in our society without stigma is the young, married, white, urban, northern, heterosexual Protestant father, college educated, fully employed, of good complexion, weight, and height, and a recent record in sports (Goffman 1963, 128). All others, we are to presume, are in some way compromised and would really rather be "normal"; they would be more than ready to trade in their status and identity as "stigmatized" if that were possible. With respect to the "tribal" stigma of race, such an analysis is weakened by the fact that, since the beginning of the civil rights and black (cultural) nationalist movements that have culminated in today's Afrocentrism, many black people, but not all, appear increasingly black and proud and would cringe at the thought of giving up their blackness for promises of racial inclusion or assimilation. Such positions have their parallels among feminists, gays, and various ethnic groups. In fact, in present-day America there seems to be an emerging concern with valuing one's differences, playing up one's particularity, be it ethnic, racial, or sexual, and attempting to compete effectively for place and position among so many others who make up our pluralistic society (see Rose 1990; Schlesinger 1992; Feagin and Sikes 1994; Glazer 1997). Nevertheless, Goffman's typology, taken as conventional commentary on race and difference, provides us with a conceptually useful, if ideologically conservative, benchmark from which to approach the social situation of the black executive.

The Own

Within the organization I studied, the own may be characterized as a loosely knit collection of black employees. Such people may at first glance appear, especially to outsiders, to be a monolithic, tightly knit, "self-interested" group. The actual situation, however, is more complicated than that. Membership in the own is usually involuntary and, because it is determined by skin color, persistent, although in reality its members at times may "fade" in and out of the association. To a certain degree, this is a matter of perception, and putative members become more or less closely affiliated with the own depending upon the issue at hand and the attendant social circumstances. Moreover, individuals with observable phenotypical features identifiable by all Americans but especially by blacks as "black" or black African in origin are automatically made eligible for membership in the own. During social interaction and instances of sociability, fellow blacks in effect claim them, and whites readily associate them with the own.

Among some blacks in the organization, the sense of affiliation with the own can be situational, while for others it can be a full-time preoccupation. At the same time, however, the frustrations of black employees resulting from an awareness of the job ceiling and other indications of negative differential treatment, mixed with hurt but often hidden feelings, may work to set them apart from others in the company, including other minorities. Many feel strongly that their experiences in the American occupational structure are unique and that other minorities—women, Asians, Jews, and Hispanics—do not confront the same personal and social problems within the company. They come to see their skin color and the social significance it has acquired over the centuries as their chief and lingering problem, not just in the workplace but in society in general (see Cose 1993). Hence, for a large number of blacks in the organization, skin color is *the* persistent issue, a conspicuous and observable characteristic that often makes them subject a priori to negative consideration and treatment. But they tend to keep such views to themselves or to share them mainly with fellow blacks who they think are trustworthy or, rarely, with whites who have earned their confidence.

At the same time, many of those blacks who are doing well in the organization have found it necessary to distance themselves from the own and to present themselves as individuals who have struggled despite great odds and made it. Indeed, for them, it is generally considered bad form to define oneself as publicly preoccupied with race, as a "race man" or "race woman," or as one who promotes "the race" over others (see Drake and Cayton 1962; Goffman 1963; Anderson 1997). In this context, at times with deep ambivalence, some feel it prudent to tone down their enthusiasm for company policies that appear to favor "the race" (see Steele 1990; Carter 1991; Kennedy 1997). For instance, such people may feel they must publicly distance themselves from the concept of affirmative action, even though without this policy and the accompanying governmental pressure, many of them probably would not hold the positions they do, because many white executives engaging in business as usual would simply have overlooked the many talented blacks they now count, occasionally with displays of pride, among their number.

Accordingly, it is not uncommon to hear some of these blacks voice complaints about the wisdom of affirmative action programs and quotas. These complaints often stem from a complex psychological need to identify publicly with a corporate culture that at times denies them full participation. In working to resolve this dilemma, many have internalized conceptions of the organization as a virtual meritocracy, while others are left embittered by what they see as a sham of equal opportunity. But generally in their daily behavior at work, most find themselves enacting their versions of the corporate orientation, a clear commitment to organizational rules and values that their white counterparts and superiors readily sanction. To enact such a role effectively strongly implies that the individual him- or herself is included as a standing member of that system. But in terms of feeling fully included, most are left with reservations. It may be that at least some of this acceptance of the corporate orientation has to do with the felt need to present oneself as a "team player," or they may hope to benefit—or at least to cover themselves—by "going along to get along," while offering up the classic caveat about not selling out and "remembering where you came from."

It is conceptually useful to divide the black executives into two groups: the core own and the peripheral own. The core own may be identified as those blacks who have recently emerged from traditional, segregated black communities or who maintain a strongly expressed or a racially particularistic sense of identity, while the peripheral own are often the products of less racially isolated backgrounds and tend to be more universalistic in outlook (see Anderson 1990, 40–42). Generally speaking, the core own tends to be organized around the belief that American society is irredeemably racist and that relationships with whites are to be entered into with a certain amount of suspicion, if at all, and such relationships are best understood as being primarily of an instrumental nature. Hence, those of this position tend to interact with whites only on a formal level; and their friendships are mainly with other blacks who are "black enough," meaning those with an orientation that places race first and emphasizes solidarity with the African-American community.

The peripheral own, on the other hand, tend toward a more cosmopolitan orientation, while regarding the problem of American race relations as difficult but hopeful. In deference to norms of racial caste, they tend to engage other blacks for close friendships, but are open to friendships with whites and others. Imbued with values of social tolerance, such blacks tend to be comfortable in relationships with various kinds of people, and tend to see them as individuals first and people of a certain race second. As a result of these differential identifications, the core and the peripheral own tend to have different corporate experiences. Complicating the picture, however, is the fact that certain coworkers, black and white alike, will lump all blacks together into something of a single group. For such people, the member's skin color and physical attributes help define the person's special relationship with the company. Members of the own, who are generally expected to acknowledge, befriend, and support one another on the basis of skin color, thus assume a common social and cultural history with respect to the white American norms of racial prejudice and discrimination toward blacks (see Hughes 1945; Blumer 1958; Wellman 1977; Pettigrew 1980; Feagin and Sikes 1994; Hacker 1995). These assumptions serve as an important organizing principle for the own.

When brought to the organization, the core own's identity and its related values become sharpened by the distinctions they draw between themselves, the peripheral own, and other coworkers, who tend to be white and of middle-class background. Therefore, a core own member whose sense of identity is threatened by the everyday vicissitudes of life within the organization, particularly by the extent to which he or she is required to interact closely with whites, often gravitates to others who are black and have similar social attitudes and values. These individuals then find racial solidarity particularly valuable as a defense because of what they view as a generalized pattern of bad treatment at the hands of whites and, by extension, of white oppression of black communities. In these circumstances, many of the black employees are reminded of the strong adversity their people traditionally experienced in their everyday dealings with whites; when the experience is not personally remembered, it may be socially reconstructed by members of the own.

Collectively, the own, particularly those in the core, tend to subtly define the present situation as a hostile one, thus making it ever more difficult for them to trust white coworkers and easier to trust fellow blacks. This oversimplified view further encourages association on the basis of color and as a result contributes to the reification of a racial division of labor, while working to undermine comity and goodwill among blacks and whites in the workplace.

Among themselves, functionally "backstage," members of the own commune and commiserate with one another. Here they may "talk black," both articulating the frustrations they experience in working among insensitive whites and identifying the work-related issues they believe are racially based. They may greet one another as "sister" and "brother," invoking feelings of familial solidarity.

On these occasions, members of the own appear relatively relaxed, but often they may not fully be so. For many feel they must be alert and aware of those who might turn on them, selling them out to those in authority. Highly motivated to succeed, they feel competitive not only with their white coworkers but at times with their black colleagues as well. As the issue becomes survival, they learn to watch and protect their backs, at times from one another. Yet, as they meet and talk, and to a degree collude, they learn to trust and find themselves socializing, often on the basis of race unity. Here, not only do they make small talk, perhaps discussing what was on television last night, they also discuss public issues of the day, particularly issues that impact on the lives of blacks in corporate life. They pass around relevant news clippings and through sociability gain perspective on the corporate world. But equally important, it is in these gatherings that members of the own compare notes on experiences with their white colleagues, at times collectively distinguishing between "enemies" and "friends," or the "wise," in the general organization and discussing issues pertinent to their jobs. It is here also that some might complain about problematic supervisors or about an errant white secretary who shows too little respect for blacks, or might even single out peripheral own members who have shown themselves to be outside the fold or have blatantly violated the rules of the own.

As a group, the peripheral own tend to have a more cosmopolitan orientation and in general are better educated than their core own counterparts. They thus tend to occupy a higher status in the organization. For such blacks, there is a strongly felt need to believe they are present in the organization not solely because of the color of their skin but because of their own excellence in the general business world. Furthermore, in cases where racial particularism among blacks might be invoked to favor a black or other minority individual, and for some of the complicated reasons mentioned above, those blacks who occupy positions of authority might hesitate to offer such endorsements. Rather, they sometimes bend over backward to judge an individual not on the basis of color but with regard to the issue at hand and on their own perceptions of that person's merit. A major reason for this hesitancy and the attempt to neutralize racial particularism in public has much to do with the standing power relationships within the organization as well as feelings of insecurity experienced by members of this group. As indicated above, one way of dealing with such feelings is through acts of overcompensation by strongly embracing the corporate culture, including the meritocratic norms of the organization, and by demonstrating their team loyalty and worthiness at every opportunity.

Such norms may be strongly affirmed through close attention to presentational rituals in the areas of dress, speech, and manners. But if such behavior promises the approval of corporate higher-ups, such rituals may put off members of the core own, sharpening the division between the two groups. For, compared with others in the company, both whites and blacks, the members of the peripheral own appear utterly "polished." The men usually dress in stylish fashions, wearing expensive "corporate" outfits tending toward dark pinstriped suits; their appearance seems carefully chosen to conform to some handbook on dressing for success. The black women often appear glamorous, not limiting themselves to the dark and subdued colors worn by the white women of their corporate status. In general, those of the peripheral own tend to be "impressive looking" to their white coworkers, particularly for persons of their color-caste. Moreover, their use of language suggests that they have been well educated; over the phone they are at times mistaken for educated whites.

As indicated above, not only do they seem to feel at ease in the company of whites, but their demeanor in the presence of whites seems almost casual and certainly confident. During such interactions, they leave no doubt that they are the social and intellectual equals of their white coworkers. Moreover, they give the impression of having had personally satisfying interactions and positive experiences with whites, and they are mostly willing to blame whatever bad experiences they may have had on errant individuals, not on whites generally.

In managing the various and sundry issues of the corporate world, members of the periphery like to appear to be colorblind, indicating that race plays a limited role in their understanding of the social world, but they display some ambivalence in this regard, particularly as the conservative political establishment effectively assaults the very basis of their existence: by actively questioning affirmative action and other policies they feel have provided blacks with opportunities in the corporate world. Strikingly, such actions and news reports give them pause, causing them to reserve judgment and to hold on to a racial analysis of the social and corporate world. It is such reservations, and the dynamic tensions they create, that allow race to continue to play an important role in their work and personal lives. But it may well be just such ambivalence that encourages some of these individuals to simply defer to the powers that be, at times playing along with what they think their white colleagues would like to think. It is in just such sets of circumstances that such individuals experience most acutely the racial "twoness" of which Du Bois spoke almost a century ago (Du Bois 1995). Some others, to be sure, less ambivalent but well-schooled by the dominant system and its ideology of egalitarianism, individualism, and merit, embrace the corporate culture more fully. It is with such ambivalences and reservations that, on a social basis, the peripheral own tend to fraternize with both blacks and whites, often believing they are making little distinction on the basis of skin color, yet doing so all the while. It is within this context, from this benchmark, that they project a kind of cosmopolitan ideal. Yet, as indicated above, in reality, when it comes to most issues affecting them personally, they do make distinctions based on color. Moreover, because of their class position, and sense of privilege flowing therefrom, the activities the peripheral own pursue during time out are likely to be those the core own most often associate with whites: such activities as golf and tennis as well as occasional evenings at the symphony, the opera, or the theater, at times in the company of white coworkers and friends. During backstage sessions, the core own sometimes jokingly accuse them of selling out or of being co-opted by the system. While these barbs may seem humorous, they sometimes hit home. According to one male black senior vice president with whom I discussed my analysis:

> In terms of their lifestyles, some do the opera thing and the art museum thing. But all black executives will also do the jazz. They also do the house party. They wouldn't do it with the core group, but it would be a high-class house party. You'd have some where you'd do some socializing and you'd bring a few whites into it. But the ones that were really serious parties were kind of isolated. You'd have two different sets of agendas: one where you'd want to create some cohesion with some of the whites so they could see how nice you could socialize, but where you'd really want to let yourself go and get down and talk about issues, then it would be blacks only. The core would never do that [invite whites to a party].
>
> And they play golf, play tennis. About ten, twelve years ago, my wife

bought me some golf clubs for Christmas. I never thought about playing golf before that. She said, You need these to be a part of the team. So I took up golf. I bought her golf clubs the following Christmas. And I play several times a year. Before that, whenever we would go on a company retreat, there was always some free time, and there would be some golf and some tennis and some volleyball. And I would be in the volleyball game because I didn't have the skills to play tennis—I wasn't too good at that—and I never touched a golf club. And those folks are into a different group. I think that whole thing's gonna change twenty years from now because of Tiger Woods. We'll still have exclusive clubs because of the money but it will be less so. So it won't be as prestigious because everybody's out there doing it.

To members of the peripheral own, such experiences support their values of openness to new social experiences and to social relationships more general than those bounded by color and race. Bent on upward mobility, they usually have some plan for realizing success, and to a degree most have already experienced it within the firm. However, because of their ambivalent relationship with the own, they run a distinct risk of becoming for some whites the subject of ambiguity. This question of their place in the structure becomes especially acute when members of this group are seen by whites congregating or fraternizing closely with other blacks. There are times when outsiders might interpret such close associations as a violation of organizational etiquette regarding the relationships between superiors and subordinates. Such members thus harbor a certain ambivalence with respect to the own as they are haunted by the concern that associating closely with the own may seriously impair their own chances of advancing in the organization. Yet, for reasons noted above, they feel some obligation to engage in such association.

As indicated above, when blacks rise in the company, they tend to move away from the core own to the more loosely knit peripheral own. A person whose status changes may easily be accused of disavowing membership in the own, for his or her behavior, including styles of interacting with white associates, can suggest a certain distancing from more ordinary black employees. As this occurs, depending on his or her status and behavior, the individual may be subject to sanctions by the loosely knit group of the own; to deal with such an individual, members of the own may come together. Their sanctions may amount to expressions of hostility—including angry looks and gossip—and the threat of ostracism from the own. It must be remembered, however, that, because of the professional nature of business occupations, these sanctions are usually of a mild and somewhat indefinite kind. Their real impact is negated by the possibility that the person being sanctioned at one moment may be needed for support at another. Instead of forcing issues, some people simply "stew" and gossip when they observe one of the own violating group norms.

When stewing does occur, it may take the form of pouting, and it usually goes on behind a person's back, not to his or her face. Thus, the complaints often remain subtle and only marginally effective. In general, the own becomes and remains something of a shadow group, emerging when it or one of its members is being or is feeling threatened; seldom, if ever, does it strike out as a major force.

The basis for the club of the own often has to do primarily with the insecurities of its members about their standing in the wider group. This standing is thought to be strongly affected by their blackness and its meaning within a predominantly white firm; the members of the own believe skin color has a direct impact upon the way they are regarded within the firm. Many have the recurring feeling of being persecuted or "on" when in the presence of whites, a sense that someone is always watching and "just waiting to get something on me." There is also a general belief that although individuals may be unsure of themselves, the members of the own may be able collectively to do something about their situation. There is a sense that they are strangers in hostile territory and that the formation of this informal club is in part a matter of self-defense. Hence, "unity" becomes an important social value, if not a major principle of social organization.

Yet some of the own, particularly those on the periphery, are not sure how much legitimacy the group deserves. Accordingly, those seriously attempting to negotiate the organizational ladder tend to be careful about the racial and political implications of their public associations, particularly when on the job. They are cognizant of the fact that they have to avoid compromising themselves in the eyes of the powerful members of the organization. It is this set of issues that operates to confuse and somewhat frustrate certain members of the own, thus contributing to their worries about appearing "too black" in one set of circumstances and "too white" in another. Whites are inclined to see these ambivalent blacks one way, and fellow blacks are inclined to see them in another. Many of the whites may become disturbed by what appears to be insincerity on the part of a trusted black friend and colleague. But often this "insincerity" is an outgrowth of the black person's attempts to successfully manage the various and sometimes conflicting demands placed on him or her by color and by its social meanings within the organization. The own and the larger white group are deeply implicated in the black executive's mode of operation.

The members of the own appear to understand and to be somewhat tolerant of the black executive's excesses, appreciating this member's need to deal with his or her white colleagues. In the words of one executive, it is acceptable to be "white"—but only to a degree. To venture beyond the acceptable degree of association—and thus of perceived identification—is to risk the already discussed sanctions of the own. It is important here to understand that such limits on behavior are in reality a matter of social negotiation and, depending on the executive's social resources in the situation, he or she may thus be able to get away with more or fewer transgressions in the face of the own. The executive's behavior may be interpreted simply as competence on the job and not as a conscious attempt (without good reason) to approximate "white" ways.

On the other hand, when the person negotiates effectively with the own group, he or she runs the distinct risk of alienating white coworkers and superiors. Given the political realities of this situation, the black executive often resolves the conflict by risking his or her relationships with other members of the own, assuming those other members lack real power and influence in comparison with supervisors and other higher-ups, who tend to be white. From this perspective, fellow blacks are relatively politically expendable, whereas the upper-level whites are not. The understanding of this reality creates tolerance in members of the own for the "deviance" of their members. In the words of the senior vice president referred to earlier:

The [peripheral] own was like a support group. At the same time, I went to great lengths to keep a good relationship with the core own. I couldn't do everything that they would do because some things I didn't think were correct or politically savvy in terms of progressing. One of the issues is [as a member of the peripheral own] you can go along with the core and do everything they do, but the end result is you have no influence with the company. So by doing that you hurt the core. So even though the more astute ones will say what he's doing is OK, some of the core folks say that if you don't act the way I act, you've sold out. But some of them give the peripherals slack, because they understand you have to do that to stay in the good graces and have some kind of minimal power, marginalized power, whatever it is. So they don't call it acting white necessarily; it varies by the individual.

Some folks who were black executives whom I saw in that vein, whom I saw identifying a lot less than I did with blacks—at the bottom line, I also found out that they were doing things, low-key things, that would improve the plight of the black employees, but they just weren't raising the banner about it. They were keeping a low profile. I think it's a rare black executive who has no conscience about reaching back and doing something for his people. Some will go out of their way to relate, mentor, and coach, etc. Others will keep a distance. But even with that distance they will do things as the opportunity arises. And the thing is that the further you stay away from the core, the more power you have to make things happen. You might meet with the core privately, but some of these folks didn't meet with the core at all, didn't want to be seen with them.

I could see those things being played out. For the most part, I got very positive feedback [from the core], but I'm sure there were some folks saying,

He sold out. He's not one of the brothers. So even with myself I think it was a negative reaction [at times], but those folks who got an even more negative reaction were the very same folks who had the ability to make change. Those people would never socialize with the core [although] they would say hi. They would take the company position on issues. They would not assume that everything was racist. They [the peripheral own] would ask questions as if they were objective arbitrators versus somebody who's going to defend their race to the end. So they would do things that would come across as being conservative or not understanding. And I think they were going through the process of trying to appear to be superobjective even to the point of being overly so and making you prove your case. I think in their heart, in small settings among the club, you'd hear what was really happening. But they would behave as if the structure was correct. And that would give them coin [leverage] with the power structure.

I had a lot of positive feedback but just reading it as a possibility that there were folks who thought I sold out was painful. [But] in your heart you know you're doing good things and you're trying to do the right thing and you're doing what you need to do to not assimilate but at least have people not be concerned about you in terms of wanting to cut you out of any kind of power, decision-making process. In terms of who's going to be downsized, you need to act in a certain civil manner so they'll say, This guy, he's part of the group. You're never really part of the group but you're close enough that you can sit in the room.

And the thing is that once you get on that management track, either you change right away and you start wearing different suits and different clothing or you never rise any higher. They're never going to envision you as being a white male, but if you can dress the same and look a certain way and drive a conservative car and whatever else, they'll say, This guy has a similar attitude, similar values. He's a team player. If you don't dress with the uniform, obviously you're on the wrong team. I've talked to young guys who are becoming managers about the dress, the style, and why it's important. The way I would always put it to them would be, It's a choice. You don't have to do what they do, but let me tell you what you're giving up. You dress like this [in a flamboyant, stereotypically black way], you're not part of the team. It shouldn't be important, but these are the rules. And so they can make conscious choices.

People [the normals] won't reach out to you if you don't at least look like you're trying to act like them. Because they are afraid of people who are looking like that [flamboyant]. I can be in a suit and tie and still be a threat, but a guy like that is really a threat. He might remind them of a drug dealer or somebody. He might pull out his knife if he doesn't like you. So the peripheral own dress in the conservative style, Brooks Brothers.

At the same time, for the larger organization, the members of the peripheral own often serve (although sometimes their role is unacknowledged) as cultural brokers of a sort, working to bridge the social gap between members of the minority community and management (see Collins 1997). And, in fact, such peripheral blacks often informally see themselves as communication links between people of their own racial background and the predominantly white firm. In informal conversations, they sometimes attempt to edify and sensitize their white colleagues about black life. They are sometimes successful in this regard and thus are often highly valued by those of the enlightened management group who increasingly must come to terms with minority issues. But because of this communication function and because blacks are so poorly represented at the higher reaches of the organization, the black executive runs the further, and often debilitating, risk of becoming all-consumed by this role.

Sensitive to the risks involved, many black executives strongly resist this feature of their positions, at least formally. They would much rather see and identify themselves as persons with more general roles (or with roles they view as more central to the mission of the organization) than that of managing the minority community. When they feel themselves being used simply as communication links and representatives of blacks, many feel themselves seriously compromised and complain that they are unable to do the work for which they have been trained. They worry that they may be seen as tokens, and they often begin to question the roles they play in the organization. For some, this perception leads to demoralization, cynicism, or deeper questions concerning their real value to the organization. This role can also create difficulties for them within the own. Although whites may view their role as mainly helping expand the horizons and influence of blacks within the company and as leaders and role models, members may enact it somewhat grudgingly.

In general, however, the members of the peripheral own tend to display a positive attitude about life in the company and may become spokespersons for the company. This outlook is enhanced by their perception of the individual as master of his or her own destiny. If they have complaints, they take them to those in authority, as individuals, not as members of the own, thereby creating fewer tensions with white leadership. Also, with their presentation of self, including their dress and demeanor and general social outlook, they are the ones who seem most able to seek and to gain effective relationships with white mentors or with white political allies in the company.

For members of the general organization, however, the distinctions between the core own and the peripheral own are often invisible. Rather, "the blacks" signify a reference group, although whites and blacks see the significance and meaning of the group quite differently (see Shibutani 1961; Merton 1957). When whites think of blacks, they may find it conceptually convenient to consider the individual as part of the black group. Although some whites may pride themselves on seeing and treating blacks as individuals, blacks often remain unconvinced of their ability to do so.

The Wise

This brings us to "the wise." The wise are people in the organization who are privileged in some respect (usually upper-middle-class) but who, because of their upbringing, education, or general life experiences, have developed a deeply sympathetic or empathetic orientation toward people they define as unfortunate victims of social injustice. The members of the wise have an appreciation of the special background of the own and so bring a unique brand of social awareness to the corporate setting. This awareness, mixed with their own intelligence and their understanding of the corporate world, generates in them a rare ability to appreciate the contributions of minorities to the corporation and to society in general. Combining this sense of appreciation with a real sensitivity to life within their own caste and its relation to the minority caste, such persons have developed a certain wisdom mixed with a sense of tolerance in the area of human relations. Compared with others in the organization, the executives in the wise are particularly strong in the field of human affairs.

The wise are often made up of Jews, women, successful blacks (members of the peripheral own), and other minority members who occupy high-status positions within the firm. Significantly, liberal Jews tend to be overrepresented in this category. Because of the Jews' long history as victims of prejudice and discrimination at the hands of the majority group, such people are often in a position to observe and to appreciate the plight of blacks in American society in general and in the corporation in particular. Because of their own group and personal experience with prejudice and discrimination or because they have simply taken a liking to the member of the own whom they work with, the wise are often able to empathize with the dilemmas of the black executive, particularly if he or she is young and located low on the corporate ladder.

Occupying positions of authority and influence, as well as having a certain independence, these executives have a chance to do something to alleviate the problems they see. They often go on record to demonstrate their empathy for the plight of blacks and other minorities in the organization. Among the own, such persons may be identified and spoken of as allies. With an understanding of the ways of both whites and blacks, the wise are able to express their special identity in ways that other whites might not notice but that are unambiguous to many blacks. They may demonstrate this quality by assisting a black employee during a difficult period or by associating closely with blacks at certain corporate functions, by showing a real and sincere interest in issues important to minorities, by displaying a tolerant manner toward minorities, or by appreciating contributions of the own and other minorities of the company. Of all the whites of the organization, in the minds of members of the own, the wise are viewed as the most likable and trustworthy. Because of these abilities, the wise more readily appreciate contributions of the own and other minorities to the company.

While members of the wise are usually privileged and white, they may be located almost any place within the organization. In addition, blacks on the corporate ladder sometimes report how they have been befriended by a black janitor or doorman; in their encounters with such individuals, they discover how much more they have to discuss with them than with white peers or superiors who are not members of the wise. At times, a lower-level white person may serve a similar purpose. The main quality all such persons have in common with the member of the own is their perception of him or her as "alone," as needing social support, or simply as "approachable." Key features of members of the wise are their ability to understand the situation and their general receptivity to members of the own.

Because of their openness, the well-connected members of the wise often provide valuable connections for the upwardly mobile members of the own, particularly people who tend to make up the peripheral own. By developing this connection into a social relationship, the own member can gain even more mobility as well as a rare and useful perspective on the hierarchy of the organization and on how it may or may not be negotiated. Opportunity for a protégé-mentor relationship often grows out of such connections. One male black executive had such an experience:

> My first mentor in the corporate world was a Jewish man, and he helped me quite a bit. This man helped me, and after he left our company, when he still stayed in contact, my brother lost his job. I reached out to him, and he hired my brother. My brother was desperate. But he had the power to bring people in. If he said it would happen, it would happen. So he said to my brother, Based on my knowledge of your brother, I know you must have some of the same qualities. So you're hired.
>
> Normally you don't have that kind of leverage, that kind of ability to reach out and say, Hey, would you mind so-and-so, and have somebody help. He could really shut the door, but I had nurtured this relationship with him for several years at one company. Then when he left, he was there to help. And again, this was a Jewish man. I wouldn't call him racially sensitive, where he was on top of all the issues, but he was a fair-minded man.
>
> The relationship [between us] started when I was having a problem. I was I guess pretty much full of myself and I knew I was good at what I did. If I

was at a meeting and somebody wanted to do something that was bureau-cratic or would slow me down or whatever, I would say that. And this person would not raise an issue at the meeting, but they would go behind my back and undermine what I was doing behind the scenes. So this Jewish guy came to me and told me what was happening: You need to learn how to not wear your emotions on your sleeve. It was the first time I thought about that, but he was right. He played cards quite a bit. He was talking about, It's like playing poker and you're gonna gain and everybody else is holding their cards and you can't see what they are, but your cards are lying face up on the table. And I was used to being straight out and honest—this is how I feel. A lot of people wouldn't come out with it, but if they had some agenda, they would go about taking care of it. And I learned that. He explained it to me, how you need to mellow out and not be face to face in terms of how you address issues and how you dealt with people. I guess the expression he used was that you have enough enemies in the corporate world without creating new ones. And it may not even be obvious that they're going after you, they're gunning for you. But he said, if you put somebody down, say some-thing ugly at a meeting, and the person has the opportunity to hurt you, they will. My attitude at the time was, because I'm good at what I do and I know what I'm doing, I could just say what I felt like saying. But that was not really the case at all.

So we would socialize. I played golf with him. We played racquetball to-gether several times. He had my wife and me over to his house. I had risen to middle-management just acting a certain way. So since that carried me that far, why change? He explained to me why change, because it would hinder you as you went forward. And I used that same logic in terms of choosing your battles with my children, family, friends, other employees, whatever. I explained to them I had the wisdom that I picked up and used and now I was passing it on to them.

At the same time, the member of the own has a chance to mentor the wise and even sometimes the "normal" person. Michelle is a case in point. A black manager who considers herself a member of the peripheral own, she in fact transcends all three categories while maintaining links to all of them. She has used her considerable understanding to get on in the corporation and in the process has herself become wise in its ways. She has become a strategic actor (see Goffman 1961) who can in turn edify and assist members of the various categories with their problems in the organization. As such, she reverses the model by mentoring normals in the ways of the own and in their sensitivities to race issues. In return, she can wield a certain amount of power by helping people perform better for the organization. Unlike the male executive quoted earlier, Michelle is not ambivalent about her intermediate position between the core own and the normals; she is not concerned about being seen by the core as selling out because she is convinced that her style of behavior benefits all blacks.

First of all, when I joined the department, I was basically the only black professional. There was one other black person who was, as far as they were concerned, the typical ghetto negro, because she came from there. She lived in North Philadelphia, made no bones about it, she looked as the stereotype, she behaved as the stereotype. And I wanted to create my own positive image, not just as a black person but as a person who is committed to professionalism but who happens to be black. So that my blackness would not be the only thing that they're concerned about.

I would always deal with people in a way that respected who they were so that I would get the respect that I was demanding by my behavior. I also reported to someone who was a bright, young, Catholic male, who went to a Jesuit school and recognized that we have something in common in that he was Catholic and I was Catholic. He was young. He came to the position of course because of his father. And he certainly recognized that, so he took pains to always tell me how hard he worked and how he worked from the mail room up to where he is, which was not true—he spent maybe two minutes in the mail room of his entire career. And he was made in charge of the department very young, probably at the age of thirty something. And he was not in a sense filled with all the old traditional tapes of people who would think about black people in a certain way. To him it was something that you looked at sort of funny or joking or whatever, but he was not punitive. If he did it, it would not be what I consider malicious. He would have done it based on what I think most white people have a problem with, and that is not by *comm*ission but by *om*ission, by not realizing what it means. If confronted with it, which I constantly did, he was always, Oh, I didn't realize. Oh, I'm sorry.

There was another manager who was there who was also Italian, that he tried to be buddy-buddy with, but this Italian person had been with me for a long time so he knew me. So he would also share with me what they shared in the bathroom that he didn't tell me. He told me, Michelle, a lot of decisions are made in the bathroom. So he would tell me. So I had this other relationship with this other person that sort of helped me deal with the boss.

My boss let me hire one other professional person [a black man] and he also put me in charge of the word-processing pool, and I made sure that I hired people of color. So I changed the complexion of the pool.

Even today, I'll tell you something else: when our jobs [hers and the Italian manager's] were downsized, I went and interviewed for a job at Merrill

Lynch, and it was clear to me they didn't want a woman because how could a woman know anything about financial stuff? So he had a job he didn't like. So I called him and said, Why don't you go and apply for the job? He got the job and eventually became a vice president. Now he's still at Merrill Lynch and I call him frequently, and he still calls me for advice. And every once in a while I have lunch with him and I make him pay for it and I say, You still owe me.

In my organization, I must say that there were a number of white people who were friends; when I say "friends," I mean work friends. The white women were not hostile to me or the other blacks, as long as they did their work, as long as they felt they were competent. A lot of the white women came to me for advice about how to deal with their boss, how to deal with situations, because they saw how I handled things.

Ironically, members of the core own group, because of different styles of communication that are compounded by the social distance that normally exists between the core own and whites, have relatively little opportunity to make positive impressions on members of the wise. Members of the core group, more sensitive to race than the colorblind peripheral own, are likely to perceive such a wise person as white first, making him or her ineligible for trust. In an important sense, the members of the core own appear handicapped by their inability to make distinctions among whites, to trust whites, or to conceive of a white person being able to go out of his or her way for a black person. For the core own, all relationships with whites tend to be instrumental, whereas the peripheral own are able to establish and sustain expressive friendships and associations with white people.

The Normals

The last group, the "normals," are people who make up and identify with the majority in the corporate culture. Handicapped by their close identification with the majority, they are generally oblivious to the special situation and plight of blacks and other minorities in the company. Even when they understand the special problems minorities encounter, many tend to be unsympathetic to them; they often feel the workplace has done enough for minorities. They may feel this way in part because they have been conditioned to perceive the minority person as a threat to their own interests; many such people emerge from a situation without advantages, and they are inclined to look upon a black person or another minority group member as a competitor within the organization, even when there is no basis for such thinking. Furthermore, many are of the opinion that the company has already done enough or too much. These people often believe that blacks and other minorities, assisted as they are by government programs to remedy past prejudice and discrimination, do not deserve to be employed by the company, particularly when there are so many well-qualified normals around.

This outlook is at times shared, perhaps to an increasing degree, by some of the minority employees of the corporation themselves, including a number of the blacks. Such beliefs reflect an ethos that emphasizes homogeneity in a culture where white skin color and male gender predominate. There exists a need for all members of the corporation to present themselves as and to pass as normals. Blacks, women, Jews, and other minorities with conspicuous and observable differences find passing difficult. Those who more readily approximate the dominant standards and values, including language, dress, and style of self-presentation, may find it easier to pass. This group includes white minorities, particularly when their members are almost indistinguishable from the white majority. In such an environment, certain minorities in pursuit of status within the organization may assume the supposed posture of the majority, including a degree of indifference to the special needs of minorities within the company. Some minority individuals may consciously sever all connections with their respective groups. And given what has become an increasingly competitive context, striving minorities may find some reward—psychological or otherwise—in ignoring or deemphasizing the importance of the special concerns of blacks and others.

Because of a certain dissonance that results from being caught between the poles of fully accepting this position and identity as members of the own, blacks are more sensitive to the shortcomings of this outlook. Thus, most blacks find themselves working to reshape the corporate ideology and culture to allow their own incorporation. Such actions ultimately place them outside of the normal group. Those minority group members who are white may not suffer the same dissonance and, because of their own group's divergent interests within the corporation, they may find it difficult to display a tolerance of blacks and others who may be viewed as outsiders within the corporation.

In their efforts to embrace the normal identity, such people may show their annoyance with the black presence by actively discrediting blacks whenever possible. They seldom facilitate the hiring of blacks in their immediate surroundings and may be heard telling sad tales of the last one who failed to work out, stories that the wise and the own must often suffer through. In their conversations on the subject, they like to emphasize "standards." Members of the own, being aware of such implicit charges against their competence and integrity, are then encouraged, if not required, to be more formal, distant, and guarded with whites in general. Such experiences, and the responses to them, help solidify the own's generally negative working conception of life in the company. The prevalence of such experiences encourages an ambivalent stance by the members of the peripheral own as they try to negotiate the organizational ladder of the company.

Conclusion

A major result of this country's civil rights movement of the 1960s was the incorporation of large numbers of blacks into the American occupational structure. Since then, through antidiscrimination legislation, including affirmative action, the black middle class has grown; it presently amounts to roughly a third of the black population. In addition, with the arrival of "fair housing" legislation, it has gravitated away from the inner-city black communities. Over the years, in effect, middle-class black people have begun to participate in the broader society in ways that would have astounded their predecessors.

However, a primary instrument of this incorporation process, affirmative action, is now being seriously challenged, becoming increasingly untenable ideologically and politically. Strikingly, the process, at least in part, is being undermined by its seeming success: the apparent proliferation of blacks, and other minorities of color, in the professions, academia, business, and government, at a time when the workplace is becoming increasingly competitive. In effect, the advent of "diversity" seems to have been the political price required by affirmative action to survive. In addition, the appearance of such diversity serves as impressive evidence that the system is open, fair, and egalitarian, while restrictions of race become obscured. With such ostensible success, the former participants and their allies (the wise) in the civil rights movement recede, feeling they have little left to fight for, especially when preferences are severely criticized as "racially based," in the current social and political context. Moreover, deindustrialization, corporate downsizing, and increased immigration have led to a highly competitive workplace in which established but insecure workers tend to be much less generous in their support of social programs of almost any kind, but particularly those viewed as favoring one race over another. In these circumstances, many former liberals question their earlier support for remedial measures like affirmative action as a tool for achieving equal opportunity.

In this context, they simultaneously degrade racism as an explanation for a black person's inability to succeed, a position strongly held by powerful and well-organized conservatives. Moreover, conservative activists have been successful in challenging and outlawing affirmative action policies in California, and are presently waging similar campaigns in other states. Their goal is to ideologically redefine affirmative action as a beatable menace that is inimical to the interests of whites and others who view their rights as threatened, if not abrogated, by such policies. If successful, such campaigns will have important implications and consequences not just for colleges and universities throughout the land, but for the American workplace as well. As black presence in such settings seriously declines, the struggle for black equality is set back, further alienating many black people.

In the organization I studied, before affirmative action policies were initiated, there were almost no black people present. In the average firm of thirty years ago, when present at all blacks were most often found in the lowliest positions, including those of janitor, night watchman, doorman, elevator operator, secretary (at times required to work out of sight), or an occasional assistant director of personnel. With the arrival of affirmative action policies, the situation began to change, as the workplace became more inclusive. Accordingly, top executives and supervisors began to actively recruit blacks, providing them with a new kind of racial coin. This development enabled blacks to negotiate not only with their talents, including education and "people skills," but also with their skin color. Thus, one of the important effects, if not a goal, of affirmative action was to place a premium on black skin color, negating its historical demerit.

Traditionally, the racial system had provided preferences to those with white skin color, but now the tables would be somewhat turned. For many corporate, political, and civic leaders, the social "good" of racial incorporation, at least for a time, outweighed the ambiguous, if sometimes arbitrary, invocations of "meritocratic" standards.

During the tensions of the civil rights movement, and later the civil disorders occurring in many cities, business and government leaders encouraged racial peace and social progress, creating incentives that strongly motivated their organizations to absorb and use black workers. Strikingly, many who were now being recruited as corporate employees had once been involved or sympathized with the college student and "black power" movements of their day. Now they were upwardly mobile, residing outside the ghetto, driving "nice" cars, sporting expensive dress, lunching in upscale restaurants with white colleagues, and at times discussing business strategy with high corporate officials. In time, these direct beneficiaries of affirmative action, particularly members of the peripheral own described in this essay, gravitated from group concerns long associated with liberating subjugated blacks to more individualistic concerns associated with personal economic well-being. In general, theirs was often a socially tense passage through a kind of nether world, fraught with risks, including taunts and criticisms of being an "oreo," a "sellout," or an "Uncle Tom." Most dealt with their dilemmas with ambivalence, either by forging a strong relationship with the own, or by actively distancing themselves from it. Regardless, such tensions and choices took their toll on black unity.

Here, as suggested throughout this essay, many executives occupied an ambiguous position, which was at times resolved superficially by "code switching." Depending on the issue and the audience at hand, they might behave in a racially particularistic manner in private, while embracing more mainstream behavior in public (see Du Bois 1905). Most had the strong desire to be included as full participants in the organization, and to effectively meet the standards that "everyone else" was expected to meet. Yet, on their jobs, many have experienced all manner of reaction to their presence in the organization—from effective mentoring and acceptance with "open arms" to "cold stares" and "hostile" receptions and persistent racial discrimination.

Presently, with the increasingly effective assaults on affirmative action policies, many black executives become disillusioned and insecure. Over time alienation takes a toll, and people become more isolated in the workplace, gravitating to what I call the "core own." Here, in response to perceptions of an unreceptive work environment, they may keep to themselves, looking inward, while becoming racially energized to collaborate in the outright racial polarization that infuses so many work settings today (see Cose 1995).

But for such behavior, a social cost is sometimes exacted that works to compound the initial problems at work. In the corporate setting, blacks who become so isolated often remain a group apart, inhabiting a social ghetto on the lower rungs of the corporate ladder. From this perspective, frankly, when the occasional black person achieves success, the promotion may be met by cynicism among certain black peers rather than unqualified praise; ambiguity often rules. Among those strongly associated with the own, depending on how he/she wears success, epithets like "token" or "sellout" may be whispered behind their backs. Although government pressures and policies have enabled many blacks to land executive positions in major corporations—and most perform their duties with real competence—many have been unable to attain the corresponding informal social power, along with relative feelings of security, taken for granted and enjoyed by many of their white counterparts in the workplace.

Moreover, in the changing economy and the increasingly competitive workplace, uncertainty often prevails, negating feelings of generosity and empathy with those who are most often marginalized and excluded. Therefore, accomplishing the unfinished business of equal opportunity, and the full incorporation of blacks, promises to be extremely difficult. The task at hand cannot be fully achieved without the support and active engagement of the wise—enlightened normals with the strong capacity for empathy with outsiders—who willingly go about the sometimes daunting social task of reaching out to blacks in the firm, recruiting, welcoming, befriending, and carefully mentoring them. In actively supporting the prevailing levels of black presence in the workplace, such socially liberal people were at times actively engaged as though they were on some kind of mission, and many were: their collective if unstated goal was to move our society forward by creating black access to meaningful positions in the workplace, furthering the process of incorporation and racial equality. Ironically, in the present socially and politically competitive context, enacting such roles may seem inappropriate, even quaint, a throwback to the "do gooder" era of not so long ago. Such people who once reached out to blacks are much less visible in today's workplace.

Hence, for the laudable goal of equal opportunity, the real challenge is that of somehow edifying, encouraging, cultivating—in essence, "growing" the wise, including blacks who have risen in the firm. All this, at a time when many feel the economic pie to be shrinking, when often ambiguous notions and tests of "merit" are invoked, and when blacks are at times portrayed as unworthy and undeserving of close mentoring or a "hand up." Without the full engagement of such allies in the struggle for racial justice, blacks and other minorities will remain marginalized, creating ever more tension in the workplace. Thus, a major task is that of growing the wise and bringing them together with the own in spite of unrelenting social forces that are hard at work to create fewer of their collective number.

Notes

I would like to take this opportunity to thank Victor Lidz, James Kurth, Kenneth Shropshire, John Skrentny, Harold Bershady, Acel Moore, Nancy Anderson, and Christine Szczepanowski for helpful comments on this work.

1. In order to build on this primary research experience, I have been informally interviewing a variety of black and white, male and female executives of organizations throughout the Philadelphia area over the past ten years.

References

Anderson, Elijah. 1990. *Streetwise.* Chicago: University of Chicago Press.
———. 1997. "The Precarious Balance: Race Man or Sellout?" In *The Darden Dilemma,* edited by Ellis Cose. New York: HarperCollins.
Bearak, Barry. 1997. "Between Black and White." *New York Times,* July 27, sec. 1, p. 1.
Becker, Howard S. 1963. *The Outsiders.* New York: Free Press.
Blumer, Herbert. 1958. "Race Prejudice as a Sense of Group Position." *Pacific Sociological Review* 1:3–7.
Carter, Stephen L. 1991. *Reflections of an Affirmative Action Baby.* New York: Basic Books.
Collins, Sharon M. 1997. *Black Corporate Executives.* Philadelphia: Temple University Press.
Cose, Ellis. 1993. *The Rage of a Privileged Class.* New York: HarperCollins.
Cox, Oliver. 1948. *Caste, Class, and Race.* New York: Doubleday.

Drake, St. Clair, and Horace Cayton. [1944] 1962. *Black Metropolis*. New York: Harper and Row.

Du Bois, W. E. B. 1995. *The Souls of Black Folk*. New York: Dutton.

Feagin, Joe R., and Melvin P. Sikes. 1994. *Living with Racism*. Boston: Beacon.

Frazier, E. Franklin. 1957. *The Black Bourgeoisie*. New York: Free Press.

Glazer, Nathan. [1975] 1987. *Affirmative Discrimination*. Cambridge: Harvard University Press.

———. 1997. *We Are All Multiculturalists Now*. Cambridge: Harvard University Press.

Goffman, Erving. 1961. *Strategic Interaction*. Indianapolis: Bobbs-Merrill.

———. 1963. *Stigma*. Englewood Cliffs, N.J.: Prentice-Hall.

Hacker, Andrew. 1995. *Two Nations*. New York: Ballantine.

Harrison, Bennett, and Barry Bluestone. 1988. *The Great U-Turn*. New York: Basic.

Hughes, Everett C. 1945. "Dilemmas and Contradictions of Status." *American Journal of Sociology* 50:353–59.

Ignatiev, Noel. 1995. *How the Irish Became White*. New York: Routledge.

Kennedy, Randall. 1997. "My Race Problem, and Ours." *Atlantic*, May, 55–66.

Kerner, Otto, et al. 1968. *Report of the National Advisory Commission on Civil Disorders*. Washington: Bantam.

Landry, Bart. 1987. *The New Black Middle Class*. Berkeley: University of California Press.

Massey, Douglas S., and Nancy A. Denton. 1993. *American Apartheid*. Cambridge: Harvard University Press.

Merton, Robert K. 1957. *Social Theory and Social Structure*. New York: Free Press.

Myrdal, Gunnar. 1944. *An American Dilemma*. New York: Harper and Row.

Pettigrew, Thomas, ed. 1980. *The Sociology of Race Relations*. New York: Free Press.

Regents of the State of California v. Bakke. 1978. 438 U.S. 265.

Rifkin, Jeremy. 1995. *The End of Work*. New York: Putnam.

Rose, Peter I. [1973] 1990. *They and We*. New York: Random House.

Schlesinger, Arthur M., Jr. 1992. *The Disuniting of America*. New York: Norton.

Shibutani, Tamotsu. 1961. "Social Status in Reference Groups." In *Society and Personality*. Englewood Cliffs, N.J.: Prentice Hall.

Skrentny, John David. 1996. *The Ironies of Affirmative Action*. Chicago: University of Chicago Press.

Steele, Shelby. 1990. *The Content of Our Character*. New York: St. Martin's Press.

Stryker, Perrin. 1953. "How Executives Get Jobs." *Fortune*, August, 117ff.

Wellman, David T. 1977. *Portraits of White Racism*. New York: Cambridge University Press.

Wilson, William Julius. 1980. *The Declining Significance of Race*. Chicago: University of Chicago Press.

———. 1987. *The Truly Disadvantaged*. Chicago: University of Chicago Press.

———. 1996. *When Work Disappears*. New York: Knopf.

navigating race: getting ahead in the lives of "rags to riches" young black men

alford a. young jr.

Introduction

In *Ain't No Making It: Aspirations and Attainment in a Low-Income Neighborhood,* a study of the future orientations of young black and white men, author Jay MacLeod (1995) provides the following remark from Derek,[1] one of his African-American respondents:

> If you really want something in life, you gotta go for it because it's really not that hard to make money. If you really want something, you just gotta go for it. Too many people I know don't realize that; it's their own fault, I guess. . . . If these people would really commit themselves, they could have anything they wanted. And I don't know of anyone who could tell me different. . . . There are too many opportunities out there, too many people that are willing to do things for you. Hell, they can even get a federal loan and get something out of their lives, but they don't want it. (217)

MacLeod reports that Derek attended an elite elementary school with external financial support. He seemed destined to reap social and financial rewards that seemingly were unattainable for most, if not all, of his neighborhood peers. However, later in his work MacLeod reveals that Derek never attained the status that seemed his destiny. Instead, Derek chose to attend a public high school in his neighborhood, declining the opportunity to pursue elite, private secondary education. Thereafter, Derek's life history included service in the navy while trying to support his infant son and wife. He went AWOL following an unsuccessful attempt to resolve a salary discrepancy, and then served time in military prison for his action. At the end of MacLeod's account, Derek was working as an hourly wage earner at an airport.

In considering his life experiences, one can imagine why Derek proclaimed that mobility was a possibility for anyone in American society. He knew that public support was available because he received it. He also knew that a better life was available because he experienced a milieu that provided direct entry into it. Finally, he regarded his inability to further his mobility as due to nothing more than his own decision making in the midst of a range of options and possibilities. The simple thesis of Derek's life is that access to avenues that can improve one's social mobility also may lead to a diminished sense of external constraints on mobility.

Compare his remarks to those of Nelson, a respondent in a study that I conducted on black males' conceptions of their life chances. At the time of my fieldwork, Nelson was attending a prestigious graduate institution that established the expectation, if not the foundation, for his permanent location in an elite social station in life:

> There is less opportunity for people to get ahead because the system is all locked up and the power base . . . is pretty sewn up. You can't see it and touch it, and so you can't change it. . . . There are some people that have to make it through in order for us to believe that the system is really functioning and it's something that we all can participate in. For instance, I think it's really a big myth if I came to try to make a million dollars. I think I would have to do everything in my power to make it, but it may not necessarily come because there is a limit. Everybody can't be millionaires that wants to be.

Other than geographic and temporal differences, Nelson's early life had much in common with that of Derek.[2] Nelson grew up in a low-income family in Chicago. He was raised by his mother, and also received intermittent support from two male figures who resided in (and, in one case, married into) the household at different times in his youth. However, after similar early childhood familial conditions, only contrasts remain in the subsequent life experiences of Nelson and Derek. Nelson continued to progress along an upwardly mobile trajectory. More importantly—and unlike the case of Derek—Nelson did so while developing a worldview about the structures and processes of social mobility in American society as being restrictive, unequal, and unfair. What Derek could not recognize, and what is not sufficiently recognized by many who are

interested in the mobility trajectories of those who began from positions of socioeconomic disadvantage, is that a potential consequence of experiencing extreme upward mobility is the realization of the ubiquity of external constraint.
In fact, those who have experienced significant mobility over the course of their
lives may be more aware of the pervasiveness of such constraint than those who
have not.[3]

The ensuing argument is predicated on the claim that the difference in opinion between Derek and Nelson may be due, at least in part, to the fact that
Nelson has been more successful in negotiating the transformation of his social
status (and thus increasing his mobility prospects) over his lifetime. Therefore,
he has experienced greater exposure to constituencies that possess social power
in addition to those that are subordinate. This range in experience mattered for
his ability not only to interpret external constraint, but to maneuver around it
in order to engage upward mobility.

Not surprisingly, Nelson's experience of encountering and attempting to circumvent constraint is similar to that of many who belong to the contemporary
African-American middle class. Research on this group has brought forth a co-
gent understanding that individuals may realize quite well that durable external
constraints impinge upon their ability to engage upward mobility even as they
manage to achieve at least some measure of success in their efforts.[4] This claim
will not be challenged in this chapter. Instead, the objective is to uncover how
these realizations emerge out of the experience of moving from positions of
disadvantage to ones of upward mobility. The achievement of this task necessi-
tates further consideration of the work of Jay MacLeod.

The intent of MacLeod's work is to offer an understanding of the effects of
life experience on interpretations of one's own future prospects. In doing so, he
provides an expanded empirical consideration of habitus, in his view moving
beyond Bourdieu's employment of the term. His effort involves taking into
account ethnicity, educational history, peer associations, neighborhood social
ecology, demographic characteristics, and other points of consideration that
have been implicated in Bourdieu's definition of habitus, but, as MacLeod
states, not rigorously accounted for in actual empirical analysis (MacLeod 1995,
137–38). Moreover, MacLeod asserts that broader social events, circumstances,
and forces provide the cognitive and discursive capacities for individuals to form
interpretations about themselves and social life.[5]

This chapter is a response to the fact that, after taking into account the contributions of Jay MacLeod and the findings in research on middle- and upper-
class black Americans' thoughts about personal mobility, an underexplored domain of inquiry remains. This domain concerns the situations of individuals who
have experienced a transformation in their status from socioeconomic disadvantage to upward mobility (hereafter regarded as the "rags-to-riches" phenome-

non). This chapter explores two issues that pertain to this matter. The first is how patterns of life experience facilitate interpretations of racial constraint for rags-to-riches young black men. The second is how racial constraint is negotiated by these men as a consequence of their assessments of it. In addressing these issues this chapter applies the analytical frame employed by MacLeod, which provides a general account of how worldviews emerge from life experiences. MacLeod pays specific attention to the spheres of family and schooling in this process. This chapter emphasizes these spheres because they are the foci for much of the men's discussion about constraint. Keep in mind that the objective is not to ascertain the relative importance of each site, but how manifold factors concerning these sites connect to facilitate distinct interpretations and ideologies concerning mobility. Through a reappropriation of MacLeod's approach, this inquiry demonstrates more precisely how the general findings elucidated in research on the views of the black middle and upper classes came to be. More importantly, it also encourages a new means of considering the relationship between individuals' conceptions of constraint and their preparedness to engage upward mobility.[6]

The Research Questions, Method of Inquiry, and Framing of the Data

This research effort is part of a larger inquiry on how black men in their early to mid-twenties conceive of their future life chances (Young 1996). At the time of the fieldwork, the four men ranged in age from twenty-four to twenty-seven.[7] They were selected from a data set of nine "rags-to-riches" cases that, together with fifty-two less mobile men, composed a two-year engagement in fieldwork centering on how urban-based black men from low-income parentage conceive of their future life chances.[8] In the data set, half of the men have experienced some degree of upward mobility, ranging from consistent minimally skilled employment to the point of near entry into the white-collar professional world. The other half have remained in poverty, in most cases having no education beyond high school, and having worked no more than a few weeks in their adult lives.

The fact that the cases selected for this inquiry fall at the upper end of the mobility divide is not the sole reason for their inclusion here. More importantly, each of these cases reflects the most extreme movement of the men from their socioeconomic positions at the point of early childhood to where they found themselves at the point of early adulthood. Furthermore, each of the cases selected for this analysis reflected a distinct ideology of personal mobility that included a logic for navigating race-specific external constraint. The other five rags-to-riches cases reflected minor variations or amalgamations of the ideologies exhibited by the cases explored here. Thus, the four cases serve as distinct analytical exemplars. In presenting four case studies, I put on hold the quest for generalizability in favor of carefully documenting and dissecting the ways by which past experience informs the development of worldviews and ideologies. Future research (including that to be conducted by this author) should explore the potential diversity and convergences in patterns of life experience and belief systems that are maintained by individuals who occupy the same structural positions. For now, the preoccupation will remain with four distinct depictions of this process.

Of course, one would not be surprised that each of these men, having experienced higher education (including the pursuit of advanced degrees) in elite institutions, would hold views that starkly contrast with those of Derek. Most people who benefit from such experiences would attribute greater significance to structural constraint. However, it is not simply that these men provide counternarratives to Derek's that makes this inquiry important. It is the ways by which they call upon their life histories, and the content of those recollections, that lend significance to this preoccupation with them.

Each of these four men found himself tracked for upwardly mobile strata some time prior to his early twenties. The fact that these men were headed toward greater mobility, but had not yet experienced much personal history as upwardly mobile individuals, suggests some contextual points to consider. Having only some early adult experience at making their lives better meant that they had no prolonged encounters with constraint. Therefore, their proposed and actual methods for dealing with constraint had not yet failed them, yet they also had not stood a very long test of time. Thus, the events that make up the life experiences of these men enabled them to formulate conceptions of mobility that were based at least as much on imaginations of social processes and outcomes as on actual experience with them.

As table 1 indicates, each man was a product of a single-parent household and experienced limited interaction with his father. In two cases (Nelson and Danny) it is clear that the mother improved her socioeconomic status in the course of her son's life. Much of this activity occurred well after the birth of the sons, so that greater socioeconomic security for these households was not achieved until these two men were close to achieving that status for themselves. The fact that two of the mothers experienced great mobility might appear to validate an individual-initiative thesis as the pivotal force for generating increased mobility outcomes. Consequently, it would appear to be less significant to concentrate on external impediments. However, there remains more complexity to this process than might be immediately apparent. The following commentary makes clear that intrafamilial dynamics must be assessed alongside the men's encounters with the external environment in order to make sense of their rags-to-riches evolution.

TABLE 1   PROFILE OF THE CASE STUDIES

Characteristics	Bruce (26)	Reggie (24)	Nelson (27)	Danny (24)
Community of rearing	Midwestern urban (pop. 250,000)	Midwestern urban (pop. 300,000)	Midwestern urban (pop. 1,000,000)	Midwestern urban (pop. 1,000,000)
Household composition	Mother, older sister (2 years), baby brother	Mother, seven brothers and sisters (8 to 32 years of age)	Mother, two brothers (25 and 14 years of age)	Mother, no other children
Mother's employment status during son's youth	Semiskilled, followed by public assistance	Public assistance, followed by semiskilled employment	Semiskilled (attended school through son's youth, now Ph.D. candidate)	Semiskilled, later became a schoolteacher
Father's employment (none resided in the household)	Minimal employment; died when Bruce was eleven	Minimal employment; died when Reggie was eight	Entertainer, virtually no contact with Nelson; died when Nelson was twenty-two	Teacher, sees Danny "maybe once a year"
Education	Public elementary, public high school, small liberal arts college	Public elementary, public high school, Ivy League college	Public elementary (two years private), public high school, small liberal arts college	Public elementary, public high school, Ivy League college
School activities	Football (high school)	Football and wrestling (high school), basketball (elementary)	Basketball (college)	Tennis (elementary, high school), swimming (high school, college)
Aspiration	Higher-education administrator	Professor	Professor or civic affairs	Neurosurgeon
Current status	Graduate school in a social science field	Graduate school in a social science field	Graduate school in a social science field	Medical school
Philosophy of mobility	Strategic negotiation	Symbolic interaction	Hard work ethic	Avoiding oppression

Beyond the contrast in household status, much of the background circumstances for the four men are similar.[9] Each was active in school-based athletics (as we shall see, another crucial point) and each made the transition from early experiences in public school to elite private-school education. Additionally, each aspired for a white-collar occupation that requires graduate study, thus necessitating that they acquire credentials far beyond those that many upwardly mobile individuals obtain.

Perspectives on Racial Constraint in the Mobility Process

Each of the men held a similar point of view concerning American social structure and the processes of social stratification, social mobility, and social inequality. None of them regarded American society as an open one with respect to
possibilities for upward mobility. They also did not believe that meritocracy was
a factor in determining who got ahead in American society, arguing instead that
severe social constraint on personal mobility was a basic fact of life, especially
for black Americans and low-income individuals. However, they could not provide specific arguments about how race or class operate independently as strati-
fying mechanisms in American society.[10] Instead, both categories were incorporated into their discussions of the hows and whys of disenfranchisement in
American society. In an example of the sentiment shared by all of the men,
Reggie commented:

> I can't even begin to say how many types of divisions we have, clothes, [ways
> of] talking, sports. . . . I don't see just static boundaries when I look out
> there. I just see overlapping boundaries and however they are mobilized in
> a given incident is what I see. I mean, because I can see racial boundaries at
> one moment and then you know, class boundaries at the next, you know, just
> all different types.

In a comment that reflected the views of the other men, Reggie went on to
explain how various bases for social difference created rigid boundaries in society. He said, "I think jobs, jobs have characteristics. . . . [I]f the characteristics
of your social category doesn't [sic] match the characteristics of the job then
you've got a problem."

Reggie pointed out that social categories were not the same as categories
of skills needed for job performance. In his view, social categories comprised
attributes such as race, ethnicity, and gender. He stressed that people come to
define appropriate positions for others in occupational and social spheres by
attending to social categories first, which sets the parameters for how others
draw conclusions about task-related skills or competencies. In summing up his
views on the foundations of inequality in the mobility process Reggie said, "It's
not necessarily just racial. . . . There's just a divide, there's a divide. There is a
divide between the people who are going to make it in this society and the
people who just aren't. There is no position for them."

It is clear that both Reggie and Nelson (evidenced by his earlier remark)
considered mobility in American society to be circumscribed by factors beyond
individual talent or ability. This was also the case for Bruce and Danny. Each

of the men was immediately able to point to circumstances and events in his life experiences to substantiate these claims. When pressed to elaborate on what kinds of people they believed were the greatest victims of inequality and unfairness in the mobility process, race, class, and gender depictions were invoked in varied and cross-cutting ways. Each of the men articulated that white men almost always were in superior positions in the social order. They also felt that black women faced particular constraints due to their being both black and female (i.e., victims of racial and gender discrimination), but their dual status sometimes could be a relative benefit.[11] In the same line of thought, they also believed that black men faced unique constraints in contemporary American society. In fact, throughout our discussions the most vivid depictions of the convergence of race, class, and gender came out of considerations of the case of black men. The attention that the men gave to this issue underscored an important conditional effect concerning this study—that of the crisis of black men in contemporary American life.[12]

Each of the four men acknowledged that black men were in a grievous social condition. In a remark that captured the sentiments of the others, Bruce said, "Mainstream society has painted a picture that African-American males are threatening and violent and these other people are not . . . or maybe not as threatening or violent, so therefore I think that reduces the life chances of African-American males."

Additionally, Reggie stated that the public image of black men is a "social negative" that underpins any other perceptions about them held by others. Therefore, as victims of a severely negative societal regard for them, black men were inhibited from achieving extreme mobility. In discussing how race and other attributes overshadow judgments of skill and capability Reggie said:

> That whole premise [of meritocracy] is based upon the fact there are these perfect evaluators of information, and I've just given you like a thousand reasons why that just isn't the case. I could never really evaluate you, you know what I mean? There are so many other things that are going to prevent me from evaluating the skills that you have.

Reggie stressed repeatedly that individuals were evaluated by factors that may have little or nothing to do with actual performance. For him, the very case of being a black male meant that accurate evaluations of abilities or competence would be undercut by the more immediately devalued public status of black men. In the end, each of the men came to terms with his views on racial constraint in ways similar to that of Nelson, who said, after a lengthy commentary on his personal history:

> I think I have an understanding of the limitations of American society, and therefore not to expect more than what I really get from day to day, which is racism. . . . I think that if you don't have any understanding of that you take a chance of risk [of being frustrated further with life].

In summary, the men claimed that the social outcomes in American society were tainted such that not all people, and clearly not all African-Americans, who deserved to got ahead in life. Moreover, the men could not discern exactly who directed this process, but each of their references to it implied or made explicit the greater access to social power that whites, and white men in particular, acquired than black men as a result of the systemic order in American society. Now that their general vision of constraint in the mobility process has been made clear, it is appropriate to consider how family and schooling experience facilitated their realizations.

Family and Schooling in the Realization of Constraint

Each of the men came to realize how constraint factored in social life, and his life more particularly, at a different point in his youth. For each, the points of realization involved some kind of exposure to social environments predominantly occupied by non-African-Americans. While this exposure took place at different moments in their personal histories (ranging from Reggie's kindergarten experience to Bruce's experience in college), each set of encounters allowed the men to begin to crystallize their conceptions of the durability of racial constraint. With the exception of Danny, schooling and family experiences were the significant sites for when and how understandings of racial constraint were formulated. In Danny's case, a non–school based athletic program was pivotal. For all four cases, however, what was realized or observed in one sphere (family, schooling, or otherwise) was reinforced or clarified by interaction and discussion that occurred later on in their lives in the context of family or school.

Bruce discussed his schooling experience as the source of his realizations that he was a victim of racial inequality. He reported that throughout his elementary- and high-school years he was a consistent, but not superlative, performer. When he reached his college years, he began to recognize that a consistently solid performance was no indication of having received a high-quality education. Moreover, as he matured he came to view his frustrations with his elementary- and high-school learning experiences not merely as a personal issue, but as a consequence of the inequitable structure of educational opportunity.[13] Bruce stated that he proceeded through elementary school while being tracked in regular classes. He remembered school as a positive social experience. However, as far as his academic experience was concerned he desired to be placed in honors classes, but never attained this objective. The result, he said, was that "I was very unhappy a lot of the time in my classes."

As Bruce recalled, he recognized his disappointment at that time as a private dilemma that he was unable to resolve. However, his skill in athletics and the guidance of teachers and other institutional figures helped him to continue through school and gain admission to an in-state residential college.[14] Upon entering college, Bruce began to recognize the extent of the differences between his exposure to educational opportunity and that of other students. He said:

> I realized that when I went off to college I had a decent education but inadequate compared to my peers, compared to the ones that I had to compete with, in terms of writing skills. My verbal skills weren't as developed, just a knowledge of different things. So I was just kind of disappointed. I probably wouldn't put my child through what I went through.

More importantly, he began to frame his own experience of educational access as part of a larger social phenomenon concerning hierarchy and status. In the midst of recalling his increased awareness of privilege and disadvantage in society, he said:

> [Before college I was caught up in] the immediate, in a very micro-localized sense. . . . [W]hen I went to college, though, I started meeting people from different parts of the world and that's when it started to open up. That's when the macro-thinking started, when I got to college.

The macro-thinking that Bruce referred to pertains to his increased awareness of hierarchy, privilege, and access to societal resources. In essence, Bruce's college years became his opportunity to recognize how structural constraint shaped his life. He explained that he began to understand that personal effort alone did not, and could not, guarantee an acquisition of the best options and rewards that society could offer. Instead, he saw that external effects were crucial regulating forces in life. In explaining his convictions about external constraint, he spoke of his having to experience primary and secondary education in a less enriched inner-city public-school environment. He felt that he was denied greater academic opportunity because he was a young black male of low-income status.

Whether Bruce was accurate in his assessment of how he was located throughout his schooling experiences is not of concern for this analysis. What is important in his case, as well as the others discussed in this chapter, is how such assessments created a sense of the durability of racial constraint in social life. Bruce's sensibility about his schooling history was a bedrock for his emerging worldviews about the structure of opportunity in American society and the obstacles inherent in that structure.

Reggie's worldviews began to emerge much earlier in his life than did Bruce's. Like Bruce, Reggie's initial recognition of racial constraint occurred in the schooling context. The contrast between the two was that schooling experiences did not initially lead Reggie toward a vision of how larger structural inequalities concerned race. Instead, Reggie's schooling experiences led him to emphasize micro-level dynamics. More specifically, he focused on how race-specific power differentials became manifest through social interaction.

Reggie explained that he attended over a half-dozen elementary schools because he had to relocate very frequently throughout his childhood. The general absence of family resources necessitated that he live with relatives and friends at times when his mother could not support him. In the course of discussing his schooling experiences, Reggie explained that he failed the first grade. Thereafter, he was an inconsistent academic performer (until his high-school years, where he began to perform quite well).[15] Reggie recalled that during these early years of inconsistent performance his teachers would often comment to the students that physical attributes affected scholastic ability. He mentioned that race was one such attribute that was implicated in their explanations. This led to his understanding that his racial background could be an overriding basis for how others responded to him. Reggie's experiences in school led to his developing a worldview about racial constraint that prioritized interactive contexts. The following is an example of the type of schooling experiences that led him to these realizations:

> When I was in kindergarten it was time for break, I mean naps, and so when we take our little naps, the carpets, we lay them out, and white students turned to me, and there were three or four black students in kindergarten, and they said, "No black students over here. You guys can't lay over here." So, you know, we all pack up our little, you know, rugs and were moving, right, and they say, "Not you, Reggie. You're not black, you're brown." So, so I was basically laying in between the other black students and the white students, and that's been my experience.

Reggie's skin color is chocolate-milk brown. He stated that the other black students in his kindergarten classroom were darker than him, and while he said that this incident confused him at the time that it occurred, it also informed him quite directly that race mattered in public space. For Reggie, the enduring effect of this and other encounters that he experienced in school was that arbitrary perceptions of him could often be made that concerned his racial background, and these perceptions could be profoundly consequential for his ability to maneuver in life. Reggie makes this clear in the following remarks about other school experiences:

[I]n junior high a few friends of mine, we all played basketball, and two of my friends dated white women, and the coach was white. . . . [He] said that if you date a white girl you would not play basketball, you would not start on this team. It was just understood. And it was kind of an uproar because both of these guys were pretty good and they probably should have been starting ahead of me, but I didn't have no white girlfriend so I was starting. . . . It was like, "Well, black guys can't date white girls. . . ." And then the debate took a turn. It was like, "Well, who could date a white girl?" you know. And people were like, "Well, Reggie could date a white girl. . . . Yeah, Reggie, yeah it would be all right if Reggie dated a white girl. You're really smart. . . ." And then the coach pulls me aside and said, "Well, Reggie," this is like later on in the day, "Reggie, if you want to date a white girl, it would be all right, you could still play basketball."

This was yet another experience that left Reggie feeling very insecure about the ramifications of interacting with whites in school. He went on to say, "I didn't even hang out with the white people [in high school] because I couldn't, you know what I mean. I didn't want to create that type of tension, you know, there was enough tension already. So I didn't really hang out with them."

Again, Reggie recounts a tale of how race was made to be a guiding factor for how others chose to interact with him. This and other accounts that he provided portrayed how racial circumstances placed him in the ambiguous position of realizing that race mattered in public, but not always knowing exactly why and how he was being situated by others in a specific encounter.

Reggie's additional comments about his past indicated that race continued to be important for him in the ways previously described. These perceptions were enriched further as class distinctions became more apparent for him after he began interacting with his more financially secure college peers.[16] Again, the emergent theme for Reggie was one of his not knowing exactly how to fit into the larger social pattern. As he said:

[Ivy University] was a wild deal. . . . I really couldn't fit in with the black students, because most of them came from money, and me and my friend . . . we didn't come from that, you know. We were there and it was just like, you know, we just felt like strangers in strange lands. It was funny because we didn't expect that. . . . But once we got there it was all little racial islands, and the racial islands were stratified along class lines and status, you know, if you didn't dress right, if you weren't in the right [fraternity], you know.

For Reggie, racial constraint became manifest in his repeated experience of being evaluated by virtue of his race and not by factors that he felt legitimately pertained to the situations at hand. Therefore, in addition to forming the same general worldview of racial constraint in the American mobility process that was articulated by the other men, Reggie's early experiences with constraint resulted in his development of an acute consciousness of his status in public, and to the specific relevance of race and class in determining that status. Reggie's disposition corresponds very clearly to his personal ideology for engaging upward mobility—an approach that I labeled in table 1 as "symbolic interaction." This will be made clearer in the following section.

Unlike what was revealed in the accounts of Bruce and Reggie, Nelson explained that he came to realize the existence of racial constraint as a consequence of discussions with his mother and his observations of her efforts to complete her schooling while striving to support him and his brother. He did not mention school as an important site for him primarily because he was not very committed to or involved in the social and educational aspects of school (whereas Reggie, another poor performer early on, showed a great interest in the social aspects of school and took stock of peer and student-teacher interaction). Nelson described his precollegiate schooling years as a time when he lacked focus and motivation. In talking specifically about high school he stated, "I just kind of walked through there like a zombie in my own world, stumbled through there, all the way through there. Academically I don't know how I made it."

Although Nelson spent most of his early years in Midwestern inner-city public schools, he also spent a year in a northern California public elementary school while his mother obtained a master's degree. During that time the family persisted on meager resources, with Nelson and his brother often accompanying their mother to school in the late afternoons because child care was not affordable. Upon returning to the Midwest, Nelson spent some time in a Montessori school that he felt was regressive for his academic development. He then attended a Catholic elementary school for a year. There he experienced conflict with the administration over a program in religious studies. Then came his less than stellar performance in public high school. In discussing his lack of excellence there, Nelson explained that the schooling environment was as counterproductive for him as was his personal predisposition toward schooling:

I saw guys with guns in the building. . . . I got robbed, you know, all kinds of stuff like that. A guy got shot on campus, and those were negatives early on. It didn't turn positive until I was in my junior year and established some friendships, even though they weren't around the academic part of the school.

Nelson credits his mother's encouragement of him and her commitment to her own upward mobility as the basis for his eventual quest for greater mobility. He also referred to her interaction with him as the source of his initial awareness of socioeconomic constraint on mobility, which later evolved into a more focused understanding of how race functioned as a constraining factor. He spoke of how his mother went from a low (and often non) wage earning high-school graduate when he was a child to a Ph.D. candidate during his late adolescence. Although he recalled little specific conversation about his school-work while he was growing up, he remembered his mother being very supportive of him in general and very committed to informing him about the societal limits on personal opportunity. He also remembered paying careful attention throughout his youth to her efforts to confront and overcome her own initial obstacles to mobility. He began to see her experiences as indicators of what social life was like in general for low-income African-Americans. He attributed this to his mother's effort to convey to her sons clear messages about how she maneuvered around the situations and obstacles that came upon her. Reflecting on his early years, Nelson said:

> I don't know how she did it. She tells me now stories when she had to steal hot dogs to feed us, and that touches me, you know. . . . We couldn't say, "I can't" around the house. We'd say, "I tried. . . ." She thought that that was very important, there was no hope or any other way without it. And I think that was from her realization that the American Dream kind of thing wasn't open [to everyone] anymore.

Later, this chapter will make the connection between the messages that Nelson received at home and the ideology that he elucidated for circumventing racial constraint in his life. At present, the emphasis will be on the interaction in Nelson's household that led to his realization of the pervasiveness of external constraint in the mobility process. Nelson not only attended to his mother's messages about limited access to opportunities. His commentary indicated that he also observed his mother's daily efforts as a basis from which to formulate his worldview. Indicative of the types of experiences that he had with his mother that allowed him to develop his understanding of racial constraint is this:

> I was going to go to fifth grade and I wanted to get out of the Montessori school. My mom missed work [to take me to a new school]. . . . My mom [wants to] take me up to a school that's one block out of our district. . . . [S]he calls first and she sets it up and she tells where we live. [The school official] says, "That's OK, we should be able to accept." And my mom is pretty articulate and may sound to some people like she could be Caucasian, occasionally,

I don't know. And we walk up there and it's a white principal and he says, "Oh, we're sorry. He lives out of the district." And I remember my mom walking me home and she just cried. And it really, really was a powerful experience for me. It tells me that no matter what you do, no matter how hard you work, sometimes people are going to slap you in the face. And that's what I meant by not being picked in the lot [referring to earlier comments about limitations on who gets ahead]. She worked all the time to get me where I was and couldn't quite map it down.

This and other events provided for Nelson a basis for realizing constraint in the same ways that within-school encounters did for Bruce and Reggie. The fact that Nelson emphasized the household as the principal site was due to his mother's experiences. As she went about acquiring the capital needed for her own upward mobility, her exposure to a more diverse social world (and her increasing security in knowing how to maneuver in it) provided her with the capacity to share with her son information and experiences about constraint and obstacles.[17] Neither Bruce's nor Reggie's mother acquired such a capital base. Therefore, formal schooling—the first site of substantive interaction outside of the household—was their principal venue for recognizing racial constraint on mobility.

The final case is that of Danny. He reported that he came to understand important distinctions in social power as a consequence of a tennis program that he participated in when he was a young boy. Unlike the others, Danny pointed to an arena other than family or schooling as his initial source of realizing racial constraint. Nevertheless, his experiences in the tennis program first emerged out of a family context in which his mother encouraged and exposed him to social groups that served neighborhood youth. During his childhood, his mother's life experience was similar to that of Nelson's. His mother completed her education during his youth, and eventually became a schoolteacher. Danny stated that her involvement in education facilitated her awareness of the better schooling options in his community, and she ensured that he was exposed to them. Consequently, Danny did not experience the turbulent academic encounters that befell the other men. Indeed, with the exception of experiencing economic constraint, Danny's early life was quite unlike those of the other men. He reported that he was a consistent high performer in school, and he experienced little overt social conflict with other students, or with faculty and administrators. Danny said that he did not discuss with his mother his schooling or his career goals in any depth, nor did she attempt to foster intense dialogue with him. The consistently high performance in schools that were overwhelmingly populated by black Americans, and the absence of substantial discussion at home, indicates why neither site was especially relevant for his cognizance about racial constraint. However, the household context was the site where he was encouraged to pursue experiences that would allow him to attain that cognizance.

The tennis program was run by a neighborhood resident who was interested in exposing low-income and working-class African-American youth to recreational options not usually available in their community. On weekends, Danny traveled with his peers to suburban communities to compete against other teams. He and his teammates played with inexpensive rackets and equipment, while the opponents had "all that expensive stuff." His involvement in tennis, which evolved into competitive play in high school, created a broader social exposure for Danny that allowed him to frame his worldviews on mobility and opportunity. Through tennis, he not only encountered individuals of elite social status, but also ventured into their communities such that he acquired a visual sense of their quality of life. As Danny explained:

> Tennis gave me an opportunity to go outside [of his community of residence]. Before that I had no reason [to leave]. Baseball, basketball, all that was within walking distance. School was basically . . . only twenty minutes from where I lived. To me, [tennis] was an opportunity to get outside [the neighborhood] since most of the people who played were in the suburbs.

Thus, tennis did for Danny at an earlier age what the college experience did for Bruce and Reggie—it created a means of informing and then enhancing his understanding of power and status differentials, the good life, societal rewards, and the meaning that all of this had for understanding his own mobility prospects. Most importantly, Danny's introduction to privileged communities at an early age allowed him to begin to contemplate how access to such terrain could occur for himself. Danny reported that he began to make comparisons and contrasts between his life in the city and the quality of life in the suburbs. He quickly made sense of the disparities in wealth and status between his peers and his competitors. As he stated, while in elementary school he associated elitism, privilege, and material comfort with whites, and deprivation, despair, and subordination with blacks, particularly those living in the inner city, thus racializing his vision of stratification in American society.

Danny's perspective on status and power differentials was enriched by his college experience. In talking about that period Danny stated that he began to understand how his vision of extreme privilege and economic comfort could appear to those that possess it as regular accoutrements in life. He talked of seeing parents "writing a check for their kids to go to school, no problem, and then buying them a car and buying a house [while their kids were] in college."

Danny had nothing to say about interpersonal racial conflict or strife. Instead, he emphasized how he first identified, and then came to understand more fully, privilege and disadvantage as structural features of life. Within that larger vision Danny learned and accepted that racism was, as he put it, "a universal problem" that caused fundamental divisions in society. As we shall see, his means of confronting this involved making choices that he believed would lessen the impact of this problem in his personal life.

As each of the men continued his schooling experiences, and continued increased interaction with social elites, he grew more convinced that he was a subject in the American social order who faced specific constraints while pursuing his future desires. However, each was also convinced that he could maneuver in specific ways in order to potentially achieve those objectives. Their ability to do so emerged not only out of their capacity to imagine the means for reaching their goals, but also by the fact that their life experiences involved their accumulating enough diversified forms of capital such that they could maneuver in certain ways to attain their ambitions.

Family and Schooling in Ideologies for Personal Mobility

In large part, the ideology that each man endorsed as a means of enhancing his mobility prospects was rooted in his perception of the importance of circumventing the consequences of the negative public image of the black male. It was stated earlier that their worldviews concerning racial constraint centered on their contention that being a black man was a liability in public life. Each of them understood that his individual efforts could not mitigate this public image. Consequently, their ideologies consisted of ideas about either maneuvering around racial barriers, partially succumbing to them, or attempting to minimize their pervasiveness in their own lives. In investigating them more precisely, some caveats and supplementary factors that make clear how these patterns emerged will be introduced.

First, each of the men endorsed a set of general tenets concerning self-advancement. They stressed education, both for the purposes of increasing their stock of knowledge and skills and for its value as a credential. They also asserted that commitment to hard work, determination, and focus on desired objectives were all essential for getting ahead. Essentially, their ideologies incorporated what often is regarded as a mainstream value or normative system. However, their life experiences taught them that mainstream ideologies would not be enough to ensure upward mobility. Thus, a more provocative understanding of their ideologies for personal mobility must take into account the additional values and beliefs that were incorporated into their orientations as a result of their vision of race, and black masculinity in particular, as a basis of constraint in their lives.[18]

In considering more specifically the relevance they placed on being black men, each spoke about the challenge of navigating "the system" in order to attain his objectives. They were not explicit in defining "the system." Instead, they employed the term as a referent for the composite of individuals, materials, ideas, and circumstances that constituted the environment within which they were striving to make the best life possible for themselves. In discussing the system, each emphasized the problematic situation of black men (and black Americans more generally) in that milieu, and how they took that circumstance into account not only in interpreting external constraint, but in enacting their plans for mobility. The last row of table 1 identifies the ideology maintained by each of the men.[19] We will now explore each case in greater depth.

Bruce's ideology is described as one of strategic negotiation. Throughout our discussion he emphasized the importance of impression management as the best approach for him to achieve his life goals in the face of a social world that was hostile to black men. His comments made clear that he came to this approach as a result of early family-based interaction. In talking about his parents, Bruce said that he learned from them the importance of being conscientious about his own public behavior and demeanor and of learning how to function effectively in public interaction. He said, "They've had a big impact because they have taught me how to deal with people, and I think that more than anything is the key component with me doing well, having a bright future in this country."

Although his father never lived with him, Bruce did have some consistent interaction with him. He talked about the conversations that he had with his father while he was a young child, as well as the observations that he made of his father's style of socializing and interacting with others. In speaking about the role that his father played in reinforcing his sense of the importance of this practice Bruce said:

> He had this certain mysticism about him that just impressed me. . . . I could just say that when he was sober I saw the way he dealt with people. And I always wanted to get that. I mean that's why I'm good with people now. I got that from him, I would say.

Bruce explained that his father was an alcoholic. He eventually died from his addiction. Bruce's exposure to his father's public persona ended when he was still a child. However, he learned enough to appropriate this approach and apply it later in his life. In addition to his adherence to mainstream values and norms, Bruce's personal ideology included a stress on the ability to appear assertive without being threatening, to make people feel comfortable in his presence, and to develop social ties with influential people so that he could learn about their styles of interaction as well as accrue whatever benefits came from interacting with them. Each of these practices was important for him in his quest to counter the pernicious consequences of his being a black male. This is evident in Bruce's response to a question about his sense of personal skills and abilities:

> I can at least negotiate and get what I want to move ahead because I've been a part of the system that the mainstream society deems as the necessary thing to do in life and I've been able to do well in that system. That's how I've been able to survive. . . . The best way for me to get ahead in American society is to learn from people who have, as I've said, worked the system. . . . [T]hey have a better understanding than me of how to get things out of it. . . . If you know how to interact with people and you're good at getting what you want, then you can move up through the classes.

Bruce stated that his neighborhood peers (most of whom he did not consider to be close friends) provided his initial testing ground for cultivating and exercising the skills that he learned about from his father. He claimed that in his interaction with them he learned how to "judge character," meaning how to interact comfortably with a wide range of social types. Discussing his neighborhood associations, he said:

> I may have learned something from them that I didn't put them in my inner circle of close friends . . . that I've learned in my interaction with them. So I can say, "Well, how do you look out for this other personality? . . ." They are sort of like my practice ground for my learning how to negotiate.

In summary, Bruce took ideas that were cultivated at home and began to employ them in other spheres of his life. Having maintained a strong sense through personal experience that structural inequality was a vivid reality, and that being a black male made for additional difficulties, he bridged family messages with schooling experiences to conceive of a personal ideology for securing his mobility quests. That ideology was predicated on realizing that although the larger social context was inalterable, his own status within it could be manipulated by strategic interaction.

Reggie's ideology was similar to that of Bruce in that Reggie also prioritized the interactive context. The distinction is that instead of emphasizing proactive interactive techniques, Reggie stressed the reactive posture of discerning how others felt about him as a gauge for how he should conduct himself in order to achieve his desired objectives. Earlier, this chapter argued that Reggie's worldview about racial constraint emerged in large part from his history of encounters that reified the social significance of race for him. His remarks made clear that those experiences also fostered his ideological orientation toward mobility. In talking about the requisites for getting ahead, Reggie said:

> You have to know what other people think of you. If you know that then you can use that to your advantage. . . . That's what I constantly get from brothers who work on Wall Street and in firms, that you have to be aware of what they expect you to do, and use that to your advantage.

A little later in the discussion, Reggie made it clear that the "brothers" that he was talking about were his peers in college. By his college years, he began to consider how he could influence the impressions others had of him. He said that he began paying careful attention to the differences in race-specific perceptions of him in diverse contexts such as the classroom, the street corner, and the athletic field. He felt that each setting involved different readings of him as a black male that could create constraints as well as possibilities in different circumstances.

While many black men may share such an understanding of black masculinity, Reggie built upon it to formulate an ideology for personal conduct. In summarizing his views Reggie said:

> [T]here are times when it is definitely advantageous to be an African-American male. I mean there are sometimes that I benefit from other people's perceptions of me . . . when I'm walking down the street and I grit, when I'm looking [hard] at someone, there's no problem. If I was a white dude walking down the street at night and looked at some of the brothers, they'd be like, "Who is this clown?" you know what I mean. There are definitely times when there is a benefit to being a brother, you know. [But at other times] people will still think less of you in other situations.

For Reggie, the perceptions of others about him became a crucial point of reflection about how the social world operated, and consequently how he could operate within that world. He grew up in a low-income—yet predominantly white—urban community. Much of Reggie's experience with interracial interaction shaped his increasing consciousness of how he was made to feel different. Thus, having been located by others as different for reasons that were consequential, if not always sensible to him, Reggie worked to transform this condition into a resource in his preparation to engage upward mobility. This was a logical approach for someone who increasingly came to view himself as a marginal being throughout his rise in social status and broadening social exposure.

Unlike Bruce and Reggie, Nelson's ideology lacked a first-order emphasis on the social context. Instead, Nelson's grew out of his view that uncertainty was a core feature of social life for black Americans. Hence, he felt that they should not commit much mental energy toward trying to establishing certainty about desired outcomes. Nelson argued that putting forth his best effort was all that he could do in the quest to secure a better future.

> I feel that people that work hard and avail themselves of the variety of resources have the best chances for getting ahead. And that's because you have to expend energy to succeed. And the people that expend energy increase their chances of being chosen out of the lot. . . . You have to hope that some opportunity comes along. But you have to never despair and bust your ass as long as you have to before you can get it.

To locate more precisely the source of his ideology, keep in mind that Nelson recalled many occasions involving the difficulties that his mother experienced in making a better life for herself. He viewed her life experience as one of steadfast hard work in the midst of uncertainty and sometimes unforeseeable obstacles (recall the effort to get Nelson admitted to a school outside of their residential district). Despite a less than stellar academic performance, Nelson was admitted to a local small college.[20] It was during his college years that Nelson came to understand that hard work, coupled with access to appropriate opportunities, could benefit him as well. He explained how his basketball coach helped him realize this:

> My first term I had a GPA of o.88. . . . I wasn't playing basketball at the time [but] he took me in and was my father basically because he'd come to the room and tell me, "Get off the phone." [He'd] tell me I should go to bed at times, tell me, "Your mother didn't send you up here to play around." And the next quarter I was off academic warning. . . . I think that nurturing and that father image there did a great deal for me in terms of getting myself together, and then the other positive factor was my involvement in basketball. . . . I took it upon myself to work hard, and basketball turned out to be a great discipline exercise for myself.

After finding initial success with this, Nelson channeled this understanding into a more general ideology for his life. The commitment to hard work emerged out of his interaction with his eventual basketball coach, who first came into his life as an academic adviser. Upon making the basketball team, Nelson quickly realized the benefits of hard work.

> I'd have to say that basketball for me has been a power builder. . . . I was around other black men that said, "Look, man, you got to get aggressive, you got to work harder, you got to play. Quit being so wimpy." And if you turn

that into something else, that's your approach to everything. You know, if you want something then you have to be aggressive, you can't be wimpy about it.

Nelson transferred that approach to other matters in his life. He became a diligent student and an active participant in student organizations on campus. By the time he finished college, he was admitted to a law school of moderate standing. He was dismissed from that institution after his first year because he chose to forgo academics while committing himself to organized involvement in redressing racial issues on campus. A few years later he was admitted to a master's program in an urban university under academic warning, and then began a pattern of exceptional academic performance that continued through his admission to a premier program in graduate studies (he matriculated a few weeks prior to our conversation).

Nelson's ideology was appropriated directly from his mother, and further informed by experiences with other supportive individuals. His family remained the principal sphere for his realizations about racial constraint and his personal ideology for navigating it. The educational arena became a site for him to experience success. Thus, schooling became meaningful only after he endorsed an ideology that allowed him to begin succeeding.

I know that no matter how much I bust my ass, no matter how much intelligence I have displayed . . . somewhere I could be missed. . . . The flip side of that is that it doesn't matter if I'm going to be missed. I have to spend my life doing it because if I don't there is only despair, nothing else.

In the end, although Nelson first applied his ideology in a predominantly white setting, and found success there, he did not surrender his claim that racial constraint remained a pervasive force in the social world.

Finally, Danny's approach for securing his desired options in life can be described as an ideology of avoiding oppression. Danny took oppression to mean virtually any social force or condition that placed limits on personal mobility.

[G]angs and violence and stuff like that [are a form of oppression]. . . . You shouldn't have to worry about innocent-bystander stuff. . . . Rent is a form of oppression, teachers telling you you can't do this is a form of oppression, peers trying to get you to go out when you should be studying is a form of oppression. . . . Worrying about material things is a form of oppression. Worrying about what people say that's not really relevant to your personality is a form of oppression. Like "He can't dress too well," or certain things like "He's a nerd," or all that other stuff. . . . People who don't value education as much is a form of oppression. People who don't avoid drugs on principle alone. . . . You know, accepting things that shouldn't really be accepted [are forms of oppression].

Danny's conception of oppression emerged directly out of his early exposure to both more privileged suburban communities and the lower-income environment in which he was reared. He drew from both contexts in order to identify what he saw as oppressive circumstances concerning personal mobility. In responding to a question concerning his approach to continuing to improve his future Danny said, "The main way I go through life is to avoid oppression. You try to learn what it is and try to avoid it, and that helps out a lot. And it helps out with opportunity."

Danny had a more consistent and prolonged exposure to the contrasting surroundings of his neighborhood and more privileged communities than the other three men. During his interview he referred to his neighborhood as a source of oppression more frequently than did the other men, who were also much more matter-of-fact in discussing the attributes of their communities. A number of circumstances contributed to his ability to do so. His demeanor (soft-spoken and nonassertive), style of dress (what might be considered preppy), and favored activities (tennis and swimming) differed from those of many young men in his community.[21] His previous comment indicates that these differences mattered in how he drew distinctions between himself and his neighborhood peers. Other comments about avoiding oppression further illustrated the extent to which he coupled these experiences with those in more advantaged neighborhoods in order to come to an understanding of external constraint. He believed that he began to identify avoidance of oppression as a means for personal mobility as early as the seventh grade.

You kind of see things that are holding other people back. And then you go on to racism, that's a whole other issue itself. But things that our black community still holds, values we still hold that are oppressive to us, those are things that I think if we could overcome that, that's a giant step because I think that there will always be racism. You know, people will always tend to stick with their own, you know, there will always be racist people. That's my view. It's been like that for the history of the world. But if we can kind of overcome the oppressions we set on ourselves then that would be a giant step for ourselves.

In discussing how he planned for college and his assessment of his college years, Danny provided evidence of how sophisticated his approach to avoiding oppression had become.

[Ivy University was] where people were more politically correct and even though it wasn't in their hearts to like black people they tried to accept them or something, you know. Everywhere else [other schools that he visited] they were like, "Why are you worthy of being here?" You have to always prove yourself. . . . So I kind of chose [Ivy] for those reasons. . . . [I]f they were, you know, kind of racist, they wouldn't let it show. They tried not to let it show because you could always point it out [to the administration] and say, "You're doing this and this and this." And [Ivy] is in a community where they will critique it, whereas at [a rival Ivy League school] you could do outrageous shit and get away with it. . . . [T]here were some problems [at Ivy], like "They only got in because they were black" and stuff like that, and that is a universal thing too, something you have to deal with as a country, not just [Ivy]. . . . [Ivy] wasn't that bad compared to what it could have been like.

Danny began to formulate his ideology for personal mobility much earlier in life than did Nelson. However, much like Nelson, Danny first tested it in an educational milieu (albeit in very different ways from Nelson), then adopted it as a general approach to life. Danny's adherence to this ideology was made explicit in his discussion of his career planning. He explained that he desired to be a neurosurgeon. His particular interest was in radiation oncology, and, as he explained, that choice was predicated on his vision of durable race-specific constraint and how to circumvent it.

I was looking for opportunities for blacks in terms of doing something I like but having some kind of power; some kind of field where I could do a lot of, I could be diversified, do a lot of things. . . . So, the best thing I thought of was being a doctor. I thought that being a doctor would allow me to reach my potential more than I could if I were in any other situation that relied on other people. . . . [Y]ou really don't need anyone else. It's just your brain. People come to you when they're sick and don't really need to rely on other people. . . . So with the field that I'm going into I don't really feel that I'm at any disadvantage because I'm black.

Danny was very much convinced that certain careers in medicine would allow him to function with the kind of independence that other occupational spheres would not. After taking into account the greater material rewards available in the field of surgery, Danny explained that he decided to pursue radiation oncology because he believed that it would provide a larger percentage of African-Americans in need of his services than would other specialties. In the midst of discussing his career interests, Danny drew comparisons between medicine and business, the latter being more restrictive in his view because it required greater social interaction, cooperation, and trust in order to achieve positive results. He believed that medicine, especially surgery, was a more independent venture. Therefore, one could achieve prominence in the field not through collaboration or reliance upon others (which could lead to forms of oppression such as social pressure, conflicts, and misjudgments of one's character) but as a result of independent effort.

One may question the validity of Danny's claims about race and social interaction in the medical profession. However, for this analysis we must attend to the way in which race-specific obstacles were reconciled in the process of developing a career goal. Unlike the other men, Danny's ideology emerged not from much proximate experience with constraint, but from a careful consideration of how to avoid it. The irony in his case is that although he was introduced to the most extreme differentials in power and status of any of them, his comments make him appear to be less personally wounded than the others because he did not offer any accounts of direct discrimination or racial conflict in his past.

Clearly, the accounts of how the distinct ideologies emerged for each man illustrate that perceptions of racial constraint could persist in the midst of successful engagement of upward mobility. Their mobility was ensured by the capital they garnered from their affiliations with certain institutions (e.g., educational institutions) and from particular social experiences (e.g., the styles and content of family-based interaction, exposure to those with more socioeconomic privilege). Moreover, these encounters provided them with intimate exposure to differences in social power and access to societal rewards. Consequently, they were able to utilize some of their capital to conceive of personal ideologies for mobility that included methods for confronting racial constraint.

Conclusion

The general objective of this chapter was to provide evidence for understanding how the life experiences of individuals can shape their capacity to make profound perceptions of external constraint yet also conceive of great personal prospects. In prioritizing family and schooling, this chapter depicted, through an emphasis on the construction of meaning throughout lived experience, how these two settings became relevant for the construction of interpretations and ideologies concerning mobility. Accordingly, by attending to the means by which experience in specific settings helped the men to formulate interpretations and ideologies (two categories of meaning), it became possible to discern how the same experiential contexts produced simultaneous visions of problems and possibilities.

For Bruce and Reggie, schooling was the setting where they came to view racial constraint as a significant factor for the mobility process. Bruce used the family context to devise a means of negotiating race. Reggie, on the other hand, continued to focus on schooling as a site for devising his approach toward that end. Nelson emphasized the family as the relevant sphere for his realization of both racial constraint and a personal ideology for confronting it. However, schooling maintained a place of importance because it became the testing ground for that approach. Danny emphasized an alternative setting as the relevant sphere for his realizations about racial constraint, yet schooling also served for him as an initial testing ground for his ideology about personal mobility.

Of course, an account of interpretations and ideologies alone does not convey how the men's prospects emerged. As the testimony of the men conveyed, social networks, support mechanisms, and other resources attained throughout their lives allowed the men the capacity to engage mobility. Through exploring the type of encounters that the men experienced it became clear how they were socialized into networks that increased their capital not only for dealing with the schooling environment, but in life more generally. Their encounters not only exposed them to situations and resources that enriched their sense of future prospects, but also better informed them of how to perceive the complexities of certain obstacles and to plan to overcome them. For instance, their exposure to white, upwardly mobile individuals provided them with the means to consider how these individuals could affect, positively or negatively, their own mobility quests. Thus, they acquired a more profound understanding than might low-income black men who had little interaction with more socioeconomically secure white Americans. Finally, it allowed each of them to develop a logic for engagement in the social world that was more complex than would have been the case had he remained in the low-income social context in which he was born.

This chapter makes clear that research should be pursued on the varied conceptions of capital and how they relate to the capacity of individuals to make sense of and plan action in the social world. Such research should account for the relevance of more than the two spheres of life experience considered here because the concept of capital accounts for a variety of resources that emerge from diverse spheres, social experiences, and social encounters.

Taking this into account, there remains much merit in choosing to ground this chapter in the spheres of family and schooling. The merit is that it resulted in an analysis that does not altogether refute, but must be situated alongside, some core arguments in empirical work on family and schooling in low-income environments and in theoretical work in social and cultural reproduction. Much of the research on low-income black American families and children explores the extent to which these families value education and encourage the children to pursue schooling as a route to secure future employment.[22] Clearly, this chapter did not provide any precise assessments of child-rearing practices. It merely conveyed what these men recalled about the messages that parents and significant others transmitted to them, either orally or through behavioral patterns, that affected their worldviews. However, by doing so this chapter emphasized that it is not simply the values transmitted to the men, but the meanings they formulated based upon their experiences, that were crucial for orienting them toward success and cultivating their awareness of the particular difficulties that accompanied their pursuits. An important point of emphasis for future studies of the relationship between African-American family life and schooling is the category of meaning. Such an emphasis extends the prospects for cultural analyses beyond the boundaries established by the focus on values or norms concerning schooling and mobility.

This chapter also extends the parameters of the discussion in research in the area of social and cultural reproduction. Like the present work, this line of research is preoccupied with the issue of meaning. As Jay MacLeod (1995) has indicated, contributors to this area of research agree that the maintenance of subordination is largely predicated upon the process of individuals interpreting their life situations such that subsequent actions are taken that often reinforce their condition. In working from this general thesis, social and cultural reproduction theorists have pursued different points of emphasis in their work, some of which has led to contrasting claims about the ways that social structure and agency connect in the promotion of inequality.[23]

Again, this chapter does not refute the general line of reasoning in research on social and cultural reproduction. Instead, the evidence provided here offers interpretations of life experience that result in visions of constraint, obstacles, or uncertainty concerning future outcomes that do not necessarily result in the reproduction of subordination. Additionally, this evidence also speaks to how barriers and bridges to mobility may be formed, re-formed, redefined, or overcome in unique ways. All of these processes, once enacted, make up the foci of findings of much traditional ethnography on mobility.[24]

The evidence in this chapter signifies that if sufficient capital is accumulated (including, but not restricted to, social networks, social experiences, and material resources) such that individuals are enabled to make interpretations as well as enact certain kinds of behaviors, then subordination may be overcome instead of reinforced. Clearly, there are issues that must be carefully addressed concerning this claim because it may facilitate an understanding that individual-level adaptations are the locus for changing the social outcomes of the disadvantaged. One must keep in mind that the capacity of individuals to accumulate sufficient capital is predicated in the first place upon the structural conditions that create very different patterns of access to that capital. Therefore, too much attention to the question of how individuals may better maneuver in social life omits recognition of the durability of the structural context. Larger-scale social change emerges from something more than urging that disadvantaged individuals "see" a way through their situations in order to improve their lives. However, this does not detract from the importance of critical consideration of what people see and why they see it as they do because, as this study of individuals who have moved across black and white social boundaries has revealed, such an effort is crucial for advancing our understanding of lived experience.

Notes

I would like to thank Carla O'Connor, the other contributors to this volume, and the anonymous reviewers for their suggestions.

1. The names used in MacLeod's study, as well as those in this chapter, are pseudonyms.

2. Clearly, the geographic and temporal differences are significant contributors to such divergence in opinion. Indeed, aspects of those differences will be explored as a basis for understanding how Nelson's views on mobility and opportunity could emerge as they did.

3. In this chapter, *external constraint* refers to those impediments on mobility that are beyond the control of the individual. Most often, these constraints are constructed by social groups or maintained as a result of certain social conditions. These include any effects that race, gender, or class status have on access to material resources that enhance upward mobility (e.g., being both black and poor may result in greater exposure to inferior schooling due to one's residential location or inability to afford better options) or that stigmatize individuals such that mobility is inhibited (e.g., being regarded as incompetent because of race, gender, or class background).

4. A rich overview of research that has conveyed this point can be found in the work of Jennifer L. Hochschild (1995). Some of the more prominent studies on the issue of perceptions of racial constraint by the African-American middle class include Collins 1997 and Feagin and Sikes 1994. Some personal accounts on this matter include Carter 1991 and Cose 1993.

5. Consequently, MacLeod argues that many of the realizations made by the men in his study occurred because they were reared in the immediate post–civil rights era. Thus, he argues that the creation of new patterns of access vis-à-vis government policy and other initiatives enhanced the capacity of his black respondents to misinterpret race as a virtual noninhibitive factor for their personal mobility quests.

6. Toward this end this chapter reflects its author's more comprehensive research agenda, which is to document and analyze how individuals create coherent systems of meaning about themselves and objects in the social world that pertain to upward mobility. This objective is a supplement to that branch of qualitative work that either focuses upon actions or behaviors concerning mobility (a comprehensive overview of which can be found in Horowitz 1997), or is concerned with how actors attempt to interpret or reconstruct their identities so that they are in accord with their mobility pursuits or aspirations (an example of which is offered by Karp 1986).

7. Like most of the additional rags-to-riches cases, my exposure to and regular association with these four men predated my involving them in the larger research initiative. I first met them between six and twelve months prior to conducting fieldwork. Therefore, without employing formal ethnographic analysis per se, I was able to evaluate their comments against both prior and subsequent interaction with them and casual observation of them.

8. The data collection technique employed in this study was the structured, open-ended interview, commonly known as the "long interview" (McCracken 1988). This data collection method was employed because of its utility in securing narrative commentary that preserves the ambiguities, contradictions, and subtleties extant in an individual's worldview. The first portion of each interview centered on my asking each man questions about his family life while growing up. Thereafter we discussed their schooling and labor force experiences, peer associations, and hobbies and general interests. The next section concerned the views that each individual held about American social structure and how they believed that mobility, stratification, and inequality functioned within their constructs. The final set of questions focused on each man's sense of his own life chances, as well as how each thought that he could attain his life goals.

9. Nelson was the only one who had ever held a full-time job (he was employed for two years as a social worker prior to entering graduate school for the second time). All four experienced brief employment experiences as youths, and none of them reported that such experiences were pivotal in his developing worldview. They stated that their jobs simply provided them with some disposable income.

10. In his discussion of how race is the modality through which class experience is lived, Stuart Hall (1980) deciphers how and why individuals conflate class and race in discussing their life experiences. Undoubtedly, race was a modality through which the men in this study experienced social life. However, they also experienced significant change in their class location over time. Their being educated in elite milieux was the first encounter with this change. Thus, their experiences allowed them access to settings where they could intensely and critically reflect upon how much their original class status might matter as much as the more visible category of race (some of these moments will be discussed more fully in this chapter). In the end, this contributed to the ways in which they fused race and class in their discussions of constraint and the structure of opportunity in American society.

11. Here the men spoke of black women as not appearing as threatening in social life as did black men, thus privileging them in a unique way for attaining upward mobility. They also spoke of black women as being generally more oriented toward success than were many black men because, as they argued, in recent times black women began to acquire greater familiarity with success than black men.

12. In the past twenty years, the troubled situation of African-American men has been a focal point in academic research and popular commentary (see Anderson 1990; Dyson 1989; Gary 1981; Gibbs 1988; Glasgow 1980; Herbert 1994; MacLeod 1995; Majors and Billson 1992; Majors and Gordon 1994; Mauer 1990, 1995; Monroe 1995; Staples 1982; Sum and Fogg 1990; Wilson and Neckerman 1984). Some of this work also has stressed the despondency in young black men's thoughts about their future

prospects, and the increased public image problems that black young men face in the urban public space, where their very presence and demeanor have often been construed by others as a social problem.

13. The evolution of Bruce's thought reflected what C. Wright Mills (1959) discussed as the transformation of private troubles into public issues. As Mills claimed, this transformation occurs when social structure and history are made relevant to individual circumstances such that people begin to view their life situations as artifacts of more expansive social contexts.

14. Bruce credits his mother (and his father for the time when he was living) with continually asserting to him that he and his sister had the capacity to be unlike the children in their community. At least as important, however, was the fact that Bruce had a role model in an uncle who was the first in the family to attend college, and who paid careful attention to Bruce throughout his childhood. Additionally, Bruce was the favored nephew of an aunt who was also upwardly mobile. Thus, his mobility quest was fueled by his celebrity status in his extended family, and the intimate understanding that individuals from his circumstances (e.g., his uncle) could get ahead.

15. Reggie attributed his eventual academic success first to his mother, who stressed order and discipline in her children, because, as he argued, she lacked those attributes in other parts of her life (e.g., the ability to maintain a socioeconomically secure household). Reggie explained that he persisted in school following the guidelines of his mother and other adults who framed their own life experiences of nonachievement as counterexamples for him. Additionally, he benefited from social contacts in athletics. It was a happenstance meeting with a football coach at his eventual college of choice that led him to apply in the first place. The coach was stranded in town, spent the afternoon watching Reggie's team practice, spoke to Reggie afterward, and later sent him an application. Without that encounter, Reggie claimed he would have followed the path of most of his peers and pursued the local state institution.

16. Although students in American higher education appear to be much more liberal than do many other sectors of American society, this did not diminish the ways by which college attendance heightened the racial awareness of these men. First, the college experience involved daily interaction with individuals who were of more privileged socioeconomic standing. More often than not these were Caucasian students. Thus, the college experience provided a specific context for associating race with social power. Furthermore, and as will be made explicit later in this chapter, while Caucasian college students may express more liberal views, this does not account for how black students read their actual interactions with them. It often was in the course of interaction with majority students that these men developed a more keen sense of how race mattered in social life.

17. My use of the term *capital* is informed by Pierre Bourdieu's (1986) discussion of its multifaceted definition (social, human, and cultural capital). Taken together, these acquisitions constitute a stock of resources that can be employed to achieve a desired outcome. In the case of Nelson, his mother's increasing stock of capital helped facilitate his own emerging views on mobility and external constraint and what was required to overcome it.

18. My attention to the incorporation of generic "mainstream" orientations about

mobility with factors that concern one's specific situation in social contexts is informed by the work of Carla O'Connor (1996). There she argues for attentiveness to conarratives, or the coupling of mainstream *and* individual-level or situation-specific values, norms, and beliefs concerning how individuals in low-income circumstances make sense of their views of the world and their behavior within it. While the present work considers conarratives about mobility, the point in O'Connor's work is that conarratives can be constructed concerning any dimension of an individual's life.

19. First, it appears that Bruce and Reggie shared an Erving Goffman–like perspective on how to maneuver in order to enhance their mobility prospects. In essence, each argued for an approach that placed the interactive or social context above an emphasis on personal resources or skills (the latter illustrated by Nelson and Danny). The crucial difference is that while Bruce emphasized *self-initiative* in social interaction, Reggie privileged the *interpretation* of the interactive context as pivotal. Hence, whereas Bruce appears more Goffman-like in his disposition, Reggie exemplifies a Blumerian brand of symbolic interaction (to explore the contrast in each scholar's perspective see Goffman 1959 and Blumer 1969).

20. His admission was due in large part to his mother's initiative. Her lengthy involvement in schooling not only fostered an intimate sense of its importance in the household, but created a very proximate model of how to pursue schooling while contending with the extreme burdens and obstacles of raising children with limited resources. Therefore, as Nelson reported, after his mother told him, "You got two options: you can get your ass out of here and get a job, or get your ass out of here and go to school," he had more than enough vicarious exposure to education to enable himself to find a way to continue his schooling. Additionally, his mother's familiarity with higher education was helpful in acquiring financial aid.

21. While the same might be said for the other men in this analysis given their access to elite educational institutions, it was clear that such differences were registered more consciously by Danny. An indication of why this was so is that he competed in sports that were less familiar to most African-American men, whereas the others played sports, and thus fostered social identities, that are traditionally associated with black males.

22. See, for example, Aschenbrenner 1975; Clark 1983; Jarrett 1994, 1995; Rainwater 1970; Stack 1974.

23. In providing a short but insightful summary of these similarities and differences, Jay MacLeod (1995) discusses the different degrees of emphasis on structure, culture, and agency found in the work of scholars such as Paul Willis (1983), Pierre Bourdieu (1977), and Henry Giroux (1983).

24. Although emphasizing class, Ruth Horowitz's (1997) review of qualitative research on mobility acknowledges much of the literature that precedes the work of Jay MacLeod. In this review she investigates the relevance of culture and community to the responses and reactions of people who are contending with obstacles to mobility. The present chapter focuses on the construction of meaning, and thus directly addresses only a small part of the larger cultural terrain that pertains to mobility and human action. Horowitz provides important commentary on the larger cultural landscape and the myriad qualitative approaches utilized to interrogate it.

References

Anderson, Elijah. 1990. *Streetwise*. Chicago: University of Chicago Press.

Aschenbrenner, Joyce. 1975. *Lifelines*. New York: Holt.

Blumer, Herbert. 1969. *Symbolic Interaction*. Berkeley: University of California Press.

Bourdieu, Pierre. 1977. "Cultural Reproduction and Social Reproduction." In *Power and Ideology in Education,* edited by Jerome Karabel and A. H. Halsey. New York: Oxford University Press.

———. 1986. "The Forms of Capital." In *The Handbook of Theory and Research for the Sociology of Education,* edited by John G. Richardson. New York: Greenwood.

Carter, Stephen L. 1991. *Reflections of an Affirmative Action Baby*. New York: Basic.

Clark, Reginald M. 1983. *Family Life and School Achievement*. Chicago: University of Chicago Press.

Collins, Sharon M. 1997. *Black Corporate Executives*. Philadelphia: Temple University Press.

Cose, Ellis. 1993. *The Rage of a Privileged Class*. New York: Harper Collins.

Dyson, Michael Eric. 1989. "The Plight of Black Men." *Zeta Magazine,* February, 51–56.

Feagin, Joe R., and Melvin Sikes. 1994. *Living with Racism*. Boston: Beacon.

Gary, Lawrence, ed. 1981. *Black Men*. Beverly Hills: Sage.

Gibbs, Jewelle Taylor. 1988. *Young, Black, and Male in America*. Dover, Mass.: Auburn.

Giroux, Henry A. 1983. *Theory and Resistance in Education*. London: Heinemann Educational Books.

Glasgow, Douglas. 1980. *The Black Underclass*. New York: Random House.

Goffman, Erving. 1959. *The Presentation of Self in Everyday Life*. Garden City, N.Y.: Doubleday Anchor.

Hall, Stuart. 1980. "Race, Articulation, and Societies Structured in Dominance." In *Sociological Theories: Race and Colonialism*. Paris: UNESCO.

Herbert, Bob. 1994. "Who Will Help the Black Man: A Symposium." *New York Times Sunday Magazine,* November 20, 72–77, 90–92, 109–10.

Hochschild, Jennifer L. 1995. *Facing Up to the American Dream*. Princeton: Princeton University Press.

Horowitz, Ruth. 1997. "Barriers and Bridges to Class Mobility and Formation." *Sociological Methods and Research* 25:495–538.

Jarrett, Robin. 1994. "Living Poor: Family Life Among Single-Parent, African American Women." *Social Problems* 41:30–49.

———. 1995. "Growing Up Poor: The Family Experiences of Socially Mobile Youth in Low-Income African American Neighborhoods." *Journal of Adolescent Research* 10:11–135.

Karp, David A. 1986. "'You Can Take the Boy Out of Dorchester, But You Can't Take Dorchester Out of the Boy': Toward a Social Psychology of Mobility." *Symbolic Interaction* 9:19–36.

MacLeod, Jay. [1987] 1995. *Ain't No Making It: Aspirations and Attainment in a Low-Income Neighborhood*. Boulder, Colo.: Westview.

Majors, Richard, and Janet Mancini Billson. 1992. *Cool Pose*. New York: Lexington.

Majors, Richard, and Jacob U. Gordon, eds. 1994. *The American Black Male.* Chicago: Nelson-Hall.

Mauer, Marc. 1990. *Young Black Men and the Criminal Justice System: A Growing National Problem.* Washington: Sentencing Project.

———. 1995. *Young Black Men and the Criminal Justice System: Five Years Later.* Washington: Sentencing Project.

McCracken, G. 1988. *The Long Interview.* Newbury Park, Calif.: Sage.

Mills, C. Wright. 1959. *The Sociological Imagination.* New York: Oxford University Press.

Monroe, Sylvester. 1995. "America's Most Feared." *Emerge,* October, 20–28.

O'Connor, Carla. 1996. "Optimism Despite Limited Opportunity: Schooling Orientation and Agency Beliefs amongst Low-Income African American Students." Ph.D. diss., University of Chicago.

Rainwater, Lee. 1970. *Behind Ghetto Walls.* Chicago: Aldine.

Stack, Carol. 1974. *All Our Kin.* New York: Harper and Row.

Staples, Robert. 1982. *Black Masculinity.* San Francisco: Black Scholars Press.

Sum, Andrew, and Neal Fogg. 1990. "The Changing Fortunes of Young Black Men in America." *The Black Scholar* 21 (January–March): 47–55.

Willis, Paul. 1983. "Cultural Production and Theories of Reproduction." In *Race, Class, and Education,* edited by Len Barton and Stephen Walker. London: Croom Helm.

Wilson, William Julius, and Katherine Neckerman. 1984. "Poverty and Family Structure: The Widening Gap Between Evidence and Public Policy Issues." Paper presented for the conference "Poverty and Public Policy: Retrospect and Prospects," December, Williamsburg, Virginia.

Young, Alford A., Jr. 1996. "Pathways, Possibilities, and Potential: Young Black Men and Their Conceptions of Future Life Chances." Ph.D. diss., University of Chicago.

explaining the comfort factor: west indian immigrants confront american race relations

mary c. waters

Authors from Ira Reid in the 1930s to Glazer and Moynihan in the 1960s to Thomas Sowell most recently have described West Indian immigrants as more successful than American blacks and have devised a number of theories to explain why. Some of those who tout West Indian success argue that this shows that racism and discrimination are not an explanation for the relative lack of success of African-Americans in the United States (Sowell 1978). Other authors have questioned the "myth" of West Indian success, or questioned the theories put forward to explain that success (Steinberg 1989). Lately the debate has become more technical with academics arguing about whether black immigrants do in fact do better than African-Americans (Model 1991, 1995; Kalmijn 1996).

This is a politically charged debate and the explanations for West Indian success tend to map onto political differences. Conservative writers such as Thomas Sowell tend to stress cultural explanations. Liberal writers such as Stephen Steinberg tend to stress structural explanations. In this chapter I survey one aspect of West Indian immigrants' culture—their attitudes and behaviors around race relations. I argue that there are some cultural differences in the ways in which West Indians and African-Americans deal with race relations. Through an examination of the experiences of working-class and middle-class West Indian immigrants, I show the ways in which their approach to race relations can lead to positive labor market outcomes, especially in the service economy. I attempt to move beyond politicized dichotomies of structure vs. culture as explanations for West Indian success by showing the ways in which immigrants' culture is dynamically shaped by structural conditions in both West Indian and American society.

Perhaps the best known of the analyses of West Indian success is Thomas Sowell's argument that first- and second-generation black immigrants' occupational and educational success shows that "[c]olor alone, or racism alone, is clearly not a sufficient explanation of income disparities . . . between the black and white populations" (Sowell 1978, 43). Sowell cites the success of various black luminaries in the United States who are actually immigrants or the children of immigrants including Marcus Garvey, James Weldon Johnson, Claude McKay, Stokely Carmichael, Shirley Chisholm, Malcolm X, Kenneth Clark, James Farmer, Roy Innis, W. Arthur Lewis, Harry Belafonte, Sidney Poitier, and Godfrey Cambridge. To this list one could add the most admired black American, according to opinion polls, Colin Powell, who is the son of Jamaican immigrants.

Sowell argues that West Indians have always been overrepresented among successful black Americans, as measured by their higher incomes, education, occupational status, and higher business ownership (Sowell 1978, 41). He also cites the lower crime rates and birth rates of West Indians. Even controlling for geographic residence, Sowell finds that in 1969 American Negroes made less than West Indians. Although the two groups had the same amount of education, African-Americans had fewer people in the learned professions and in professions in general and a higher percentage of laborers.

Sowell also uses 1970 census data on birth place of parents to analyze the relative success of second-generation West Indians. He found that second-generation West Indians in New York City, who were unlikely to have an accent that would enable a white employer to distinguish them from native blacks, "exceeded the socioeconomic status of other West Indians, as well as that of native blacks—and of the United States population as a whole—in family income . . . , education . . . , and proportion in the professions" (Sowell 1978, 44). He concludes that this relative success of West Indians "undermines the explanatory power of current white discrimination as a cause of current black poverty" (Sowell 1978, 49).

Sowell was not the first scholar to note the remarkable achievements of West Indians or to use those achievements to draw unsubstantiated conclusions about the experiences of black Americans. The argument that foreign-born blacks are more successful in American life than American-born blacks can be traced back to the work of Ira Reid, a sociologist who conducted a study of foreign-born blacks in the 1930s, published as *The Negro Immigrant: His Background Characteristics and Social Adjustment 1899–1937*.[1] Reid's work was the source for Glazer and Moynihan's (1963, 35) oft-quoted argument that the success of West Indians was because "the ethos of the West Indians, in contrast to that of the Southern Negro, emphasized saving, hard work, investment, education."[2]

More recent academic debates have centered on whether the post-1965 immigrants and their children can also be called a "black success story." Researchers have examined data from the 1970, 1980, and 1990 U.S. censuses to answer the question: Do black immigrants outperform African-Americans? Data from the 1970 census gave a resounding yes as the answer. In a multivariate study that controlled for background characteristics Chiswick (1979) concluded that foreign-born blacks who had been in the United States at least ten years had higher annual earnings than native-born blacks. Analyses of 1980 census data did not find an earnings advantage when foreign-born and native-born blacks with the same background characteristics are compared, but these analyses did find an employment and an occupational advantage (Butcher 1994; Farley and Allen 1987; Model 1991).

In an analysis of 1990 census data, limited to urban blacks, both native and foreign born, ages twenty-six to sixty-four, with positive annual earnings in 1989, Kalmijn (1996) finds that black immigrants from English-speaking Caribbean countries and their descendants are more educated, more likely to be married, and have higher-prestige occupations and higher earnings than native-born African-Americans with no Caribbean ancestry. They are also less likely to be on public assistance than comparable African-Americans (Model 1995). These differences do lend some support to Sowell's and other earlier writers' arguments about the cultural superiority of West Indian over American blacks, for as Kasinitz (1988, 177) points out, "[I]f propensity towards education and two income families are not cultural traits, what are?"

Authors who stress cultural differences between African-Americans and West Indians as explanations for the latter's success point to a difference in the historical conditions of slavery and freedom in the Caribbean and the United States. For instance, Reid (1939, 84) argues that the higher ratio of Africans to slaves born in captivity in the Caribbean led to a higher degree of resistance and a stronger sense of family among the Caribbean slaves and their descendants and that the lack of a population of poor whites in the islands led to slaves and free blacks being trained in skilled work there, whereas in the American South the black codes and other restrictions led to less skilled workers among the American slaves and their descendants.[3] Forsythe (1975, 65) argues that West Indians do so well in the United States because they have the Protestant ethic, which he defines as including: "a strong belief in self, discipline, drive and determination." This ethic developed, he argued "because of the West Indians' schooling in the British educational system, their majority status in the Caribbean and the wider 'role frontier' available there." Others argue that majority status provides role models and leads West Indians to grow up believing that "anything was possible" and that their dreams could be fulfilled if only they work and try hard enough (Parris 1981, 10).

Of course, cultural explanations for differences in outcomes between groups are hard to pin down. They often rely on impressionistic accounts of how the groups differ, which are enormously influenced by stereotypes that affect how the analyst interprets behavior and beliefs.[4] This debate has often relied on stereotypes about native-born blacks not valuing education, being less ambitious for their children, and being less likely to believe in the American dream. Careful analysis of an exhaustive amount of survey data on this topic has disproved many of these stereotypes about African-Americans (Hochschild 1995, 160). Model (1995) argues that class differences in the Caribbean have created very different cultures within societies, and historical differences across islands have also led to different cultural adaptations. Which of these many Caribbean cultures, she asks, is the culture supposedly brought with all of the immigrants and responsible for all of their successes?

Those who stress structural explanations for West Indian success tend to focus on the selectivity of immigration, the psychological and structural consequences of immigration, and the taste some employers reportedly have for foreign-born over native-born blacks. Immigration is a selective process in a number of ways. Legal restrictions on who can immigrate have selected for literacy in earlier years, and since 1965, for certain occupations, especially nurses coming from the West Indies (although most immigrants in the post-1965 era come in under family reunification and not occupation immigration categories).

Immigration is also selective in ways that are less easily measured. Even when immigrants and those who stay behind do not differ on measurable characteristics such as education or skill level, one still has to factor in the reality that immigrants are the ones with the ambition and drive to move to a place where they think opportunities will be better. The personality characteristics this selects for might not be measurable in large data sets, but they could easily lead to aggregate differences across groups.

The psychological and structural consequences of immigration have strong effects on the social organization of immigrant communities in the United States. These structural conditions can have consequences that can also explain some of the differences between American blacks and West Indians. Immigrants are more likely to accept low-wage, low-status jobs than natives in a country because the immigrant's sense of self is not as bound up with the job as is a native's (Piore 1979). Immigrants will judge jobs based on comparisons with the opportunities available to them in their own country. In that case low pay and the conditions in secondary labor market jobs look good to them. They also do not perceive the same stigma attached to low-status jobs as do natives—because their sense of self is tied to a status system in the home country.

Immigrants are also embedded in networks that can provide information and referrals to job opportunities in a way that natives often are not. Since immigration proceeds along chains of networks, most immigrants in an established stream have a chain of contacts that can bring them valuable information and referrals (Portes 1995; Tilly 1990). Both of these factors—the ready-made networks and the lack of an aversion to low-status jobs—go a long way toward explaining the much higher labor force participation rates among unskilled low-educated West Indians relative to unskilled low-educated native-born blacks.[5]

Finally, discrimination in favor of the foreign born on the part of white employers can certainly be a factor. Analysts of the situation of West Indians in the United States starting with Reid have documented the belief of West Indians that they are treated better by whites when it is known that they are foreign born (Reid 1939; Lowenthal 1972; Stafford 1987; Foner 1987; Sutton and Makiesky-Barrow 1987). Bryce-Laporte (1972, 46) writes:

> The white landlord, the white shopkeeper, and the white boss will also tell them of their moral superiority over the American black and distinctiveness of their accent, and if British, the grammatical correctness of their English or American—leaving them to believe that they are the recipients of exceptional favors.

Indeed our interviews with white employers for this study showed a sharp preference for West Indians over American blacks in hiring decisions. This leads to the hypothesis that West Indians in the United States do not suffer from the same degree of discrimination as American blacks—and that some portion of their better outcomes can be traced to this.

While all of the factors discussed above can plausibly account for some of the observed characteristics of West Indian immigrants, I focus in this chapter on one factor that is implied by many authors but has never been systematically analyzed—a distinct West Indian–American set of attitudes and behaviors concerning relations with white Americans.

The Study

In 1990–92 I conducted a study in New York City of black immigrants to the United States from the Caribbean. The overall study was designed to explore the processes of immigrant adaptation and accommodation to the United States, to trace generational changes in adaptation and identification, and to explore the reactions of immigrants and their children to American race relations. Interviews with black and white Americans who interacted with the first and second generations were included in order to understand the dynamic and interactive processes of self- and other-identification and the development of ethnic attitudes and stereotypes. The 212 in-depth interviews conducted in-cluded 72 first-generation immigrants from the English-speaking islands of the Caribbean, 27 native-born whites, and 30 native-born blacks, as well as 83 ado-lescents who were the children of black immigrants from Haiti and the English-speaking islands of the Caribbean. The first generation, who are the focus of this chapter, were drawn from two work sites, unskilled workers at a food ser-vice company in downtown Manhattan (given the pseudonym American Food), and middle-class schoolteachers in the New York City school system. At Ameri-can Food a sample of black American coworkers and white American employers (all of the whites who worked at American Food were in management) were interviewed. Samples of black American and white American teachers were also interviewed. The in-depth life history interviews lasted between one and two hours and were conducted by me, a white female, and a team of three research assistants, two of whom are second-generation Caribbean-Americans (one fe-male and one male) and one a black male American.

The set of cultural practices and ideologies about race that the immigrants described for us stem from two major influences—the fact that they are volun-tary immigrants to this country, and the culture of race and race relations that has evolved in the Caribbean. This West Indian–American cultural response to race relations helps to foster social mobility for many first-generation immi-grants. But cultures—as patterned ways of dealing with the environment—change when the environment changes.[6] The West Indian's notions of race and behaviors about race change over time in the United States as the beliefs they hold that race will not hold them back, and as the expectations they have about encounters with whites, come up against a reality in which race is still a potent boundary in American society.

The Culture Associated with Being an Immigrant

West Indian societies were originally founded on a base of slavery and colonial exploitation. Blacks were brought to the West Indies involuntarily as slaves to work on sugar plantations. West Indians who come to the United States, on the other hand, come as voluntary immigrants. As voluntary immigrants in the United States, West Indians display certain psychological and cultural reactions to American society that are closer to other voluntary immigrants than to African-Americans who were absorbed into the United States involuntarily. John Ogbu (1978, 1990) makes a distinction between immigrant "voluntary mi-norities" who have chosen to move to a society in order to improve their well-being, and castelike "involuntary minorities" who were initially brought into the society through slavery, conquest, and colonization, which is very helpful in understanding West Indian immigration.

Because they use their home country and culture as a frame of reference, voluntary migrants who are subject to discrimination and exclusion "did not measure their success or failure primarily by the standards of other white Americans, but by the standards of their homelands. Such minorities, at least during the first generation, did not internalize the effects of such discrimination, of cultural and intellectual denigration" (Ogbu 1990, 150). They develop "immigrant identities" that _differ_ from the identities of the dominant group in societies, but are not necessarily _opposed_ to those identities.

The coping responses that different groups develop for dealing with problems of racism and discrimination thus reflect the different histories and social psychologies of the groups. Ogbu (1990, 152) argues that voluntary migrants "acquiesce and rationalize the prejudice and discrimination against them by saying, in effect, that they are strangers in a foreign land [and] have no choice but to tolerate prejudice and discrimination."

Involuntary minorities do not have a homeland with which to compare their current treatment, or to root their identities in. Thus, Ogbu argues, they do not see discrimination against them as a temporary barrier to be overcome. Instead, "Recognizing that they belong to a subordinate, indeed, a disparaged minority, they compare their situation with that of their white American peers. The prejudice against them seems permanent, indeed institutionalized" (Ogbu 1990, 153). This understanding of their situation leads the involuntary minorities to conclude that solidarity and challenges to the rules of the dominant society are the only way to improve their situation. Ogbu describes the psychological orientation that develops among involuntary minorities as being "oppositional" in nature.

These oppositional identities mean that the involuntary minorities come largely to define themselves in their core identities in terms of their opposition to the dominant group. For blacks in America, Ogbu asserts, the very meaning of being black involves _not_ being white. The strong value put on solidarity and opposition to rules perceived as being against them means that when a member of the group is seen as cooperating with the dominant society's institutions, his or her very identity is called into question. In Ogbu's work, the young black student who tries to achieve in school is accused of "acting white."[7]

Assimilation is thus doubly threatening to the involuntary migrants—they must adopt some cultural practices such as language and styles of interaction that are not only different from what they are used to, but are perceived as antithetical to their own culture and language. These "secondary cultural differences," as Ogbu describes them—cultural differences that developed over historical periods of interaction between the dominant and minority groups—are thus seen as intimately tied to the involuntary minorities' sense of group identity. Because involuntary minorities see the rules of the game as so stacked against them and permanent, their "folk theory" of how to make it in society stresses collective effort and group challenges as the ways to overcome barriers set up by whites. Thus individuals who attempt to assimilate and to achieve as individuals often run into strong pressure not to:

> Crossing cultural boundaries, behaving in a manner regarded as falling under the white American cultural frames of reference, is threatening to their minority identity and security, but also to their solidarity. Individuals seeking to behave like whites are discouraged by peer group pressures and by affective dissonance. (Ogbu 1990, 155)

Jencks notes this difference between European immigrants and African-Americans, both of whom faced discrimination, but with different psychological consequences:

> For Europeans who came to America because they were dissatisfied with their homeland, assimilation has often been difficult, but it has not for the most part been intrinsically humiliating. European immigrants come with no animus against America and they had reason to believe that if they learned to act like Americans they would be accepted as such. . . . In order to become fully assimilated into white America blacks must to some extent identify with people who have humiliated and oppressed them for three hundred years. Under these circumstances "assimilation" is likely to be extraordinarily difficult. (Jencks 1992, 129)

West Indians are a group Ogbu uses to compare with African-Americans to show the difference between involuntary and voluntary minorities. West Indians are described as voluntary immigrants who do not experience the same degree of disillusionment and cultural inversion and oppositional identities as do African-Americans. But West Indians are also the descendants of slaves. Why is it that their initial incorporation into their own societies as involuntary migrants does not create an involuntary minority attitude toward whites in the United States when they arrive?

Part of the answer lies in the discussion of differences in racial cultures between the two societies I will describe, but the other important variable that explains West Indian racial beliefs and practices is their immigration status. Judging from the responses of the people we interviewed, the movement to the United States does seem to provide the immigrants with a "foreign status" that makes their reactions to discrimination and prejudice more likely to resemble those of other voluntary immigrants in the United States than those of black Americans. (It also leads whites to respond differently to the West Indians than to African-Americans, as long as the whites see the West Indian's master status as "immigrant" rather than "black.") If, as Cornell (1999) argues, ethnicity can be understood in part as a "narrative" we tell ourselves about our history and our world and our place in that world, the act of immigration tends to erase the slave narrative and replace it with an immigrant narrative. That immigrant narrative includes an optimism about the immigrants' life chances in the United States, even though the immigrants are far from naive about the degree of racial discrimination they expect to encounter. A sixty-two-year-old Trinidadian female teacher who has been in the United States fifteen years expresses this opinion:

> You see I'm not American, and I do not see myself as having been deprived by the whites of America. To the contrary, I came here, I was accepted, I was acknowledged for what I knew and I am in a position now where I am earning a good salary. I do not view myself in the light of black Americans.

The immigrants we spoke to all had a very rosy picture of race relations at home—reflecting the "erasure" of the involuntary narrative of ethnicity, as well as the stark contrast between the race relations they remember and the pervasiveness of race and racial conflict they encounter in the United States. This is in spite of the fact that the islands have had their share of race problems. Jamaica has long been a source of black power ideas. Marcus Garvey was a Jamaican, who developed his ideas of black power and pride during his time in the United States and brought those ideas back to Jamaica. Barbados has a long history of brutal relations between its small white population and its large black population. Trinidad and Guyana are both countries with sizable East Indian populations. They have both seen bloodshed over their racial divisions in the last thirty years.

Nevertheless, you would be hard put to find much description of any of these ideologies or problems in the description of their home countries our respondents provided. For West Indians in New York, race relations at home are recalled through rose-colored glasses. If you took everything the respondents we spoke with said at face value, you would believe the Caribbean is the perfect society for peace and harmony between blacks, whites, and other groups.[8]

Q: Did you expect white people to behave a certain way before you came to the United States?

A: Well, to be honest, it's new. In Trinidad—there are white people in Trinidad, but, the white people in Trinidad is like they all accept you. . . . When I was growing up, we didn't have this prejudiced thing. I never knew what prejudice was. So as far as the way white people were supposed to react, I didn't know. (Thirty-six-year-old Trinidadian female supervisor, in United States nineteen years)

While the official slogan of the Jamaican government—"out of many, one"—attempts to foster an image of multiracial harmony, Jamaica can perhaps be described as the West Indian country with the highest amount of black power ideology and concern with "racialism." (This concern with racial oppression has been fueled by growing poverty and unemployment in the Kingston slums and by the heavy prevalence of tourism on the island, which brings very rich whites into contact with very poor blacks.) But among the Jamaicans we interviewed there was little sense of difficult race relations back home. Even this thirty-seven-year-old Jamaican worker whose only reference point for describing race relations at home is black domestic household workers interacting with white employers describes the interactions and relations in glowing terms:

A: Well, because up here, you know, this racial—racist business different from back home, you know. Different from back home. Back home, mostly blacks always work with whites. In the residential area you mostly find the black people, they always work the white. Washes them clothes, clean them house, you know. And they always say the white people handle them so good. People always say that. Yeah, sometime, a lady in my house, she used to work with white lady, and she said the white lady handle her like her own color. Yeah, she told me that. But being up here, everybody is so, you know, different. Like certain streets you can't walk on up here cause it's white and, you know, not back home. (Thirty-seven-year-old Jamaican female worker, in United States three years)

There were some class differences in how respondents recalled race in their home countries. The middle-class teachers gave a more nuanced view of race relations at home. They described race relations in the Caribbean far more positively than race relations in the United States, but more of them than the working-class respondents described the complexities of the intersection of race and class in their home countries:

Q: What were race relations like in Jamaica?
A: We did not have race, we had class. Yeah, we have class. We have class among black people. The class that we have out there was who was the parents, where do you live? What kind of school did you attend, that kind of thing out there. You could live any four corner of the island if you have the money for a certain area and even if you're not white, you can live there if you can afford to. So there was no area that you cannot live. So we have that among

ourselves, class amongst black people, in Jamaica. (Forty-one-year-old Jamaican male teacher, in United States five years)

Like other voluntary immigrants West Indians are likely to see prejudice and discrimination in the United States as more isolated occurrences, and as temporary barriers to be overcome, rather than as permanent, pervasive symptoms of a society that has overarching enmity toward them. A West Indian, we were told repeatedly in the interviews, treats individual whites as individuals and does not react to whites purely on the basis of skin color. But a West Indian also does not put up with "racist" nonsense when it does occur.

When I came here, I didn't meet too many of them [whites] in the beginning. Very few, you know. But I'm a person who takes everybody—how you present yourself to me, that's how I take you. I don't judge, I don't prejudge. I don't look at the color and say, Oh, white! Maybe he expects this, maybe he expects that. You know? Then, when we start to interact, however you interact with me, that's the way I'm gonna interact with you. So, however you deal with me, that's how I'm gonna deal with you. I have met some who were very nice. I have met some who were awful. The awful ones, I deal with them awful too. And the nice ones, I deal with them nice. . . . Just the way you deal with me, that's how I'll deal with you. Black or white. (Thirty-six-year-old Trinidadian female supervisor, in United States nineteen years)

This concern with "racialism" and differentiating true racism from imagined racism reflects a particular experience with race that the West Indian immigrants have brought with them.

The Culture the Immigrants Bring with Them

Patterson (1989) has described the difference in how racial relations are organized in the Caribbean and the United States as a critical difference between a society in which there is racism (the Caribbean) and a chronically racist society (the United States). What is this critical difference? While both societies were founded to a great extent based on slavery, the "American slave society was unique in the complexity and sophistication of the culture of slavery that it developed and in the extraordinary role slavery and the slave culture played in that development" (Patterson 1989, 478). Contrasting these two types of societies, Patterson argues that in many countries where racism exists, such as England, France, or the Caribbean, "many people there, perhaps the majority, believe in the inherent superiority of whites over nonwhite peoples. Yet they are not racist cultures because this ideology is a minor component in their systems of belief; it serves no indispensable cultural or socioeconomic functions and is not a critical element in the way people define themselves physically and socially. Not so in America" (Patterson 1989, 478). The culture of slavery that existed in the United States from the founding until the civil rights movement, and whose legacy persists in the very core of American culture currently, means that black Americans do have it much harder psychologically in dealing with white cultural values, which fundamentally disvalue them. It is a much larger part of the core American culture, in a way it could never be in the Caribbean, where the numbers of white people who hold such a culture was never great. So Patterson (1972, 39) argues that a key difference between the Caribbean and the United States is that the United States is "more terrifying in the all-pervasive presence of the white group and white culture, and the crushing sense of racial isolation and despair" that develops. This is a common theme in the interviews we conducted: the immigrants sense something overwhelming in the culture of America about race—something that they argue has affected African-Americans in a very fundamental way.

> I'm very disappointed in black Americans because I think they've allowed others to make them feel that they're not important, or it's as if they act the part that has been put on them. They limit themselves because people say that blacks are limited. They limit themselves and they live like that and I don't believe that. (Thirty-seven-year-old Jamaican female teacher, in United States ten years)

Reid (1939, 55) noted that the black immigrants he studied all reported that the whites they encountered in the Caribbean were nothing like the American whites in their degree of racial hostility and contempt. That this contempt and hostility takes a toll is incontestable; a number of studies document the feelings of rage and sadness African-Americans endure every day because of white behaviors and attitudes.[9] Indeed Cornel West (1991, 224) has called the results for the poorest African-Americans of living in such a racialized society "black existential angst," which derives from

> the lived experience of ontological wounds and emotional scars inflicted by white supremacist beliefs and images permeating U.S. society and culture. These wounds and scars attack black intelligence, black ability, black beauty, and black character daily in subtle and not so subtle ways. . . . The accumulated effect of these wounds and scars produces a deep-seated anger, a boiling sense of rage, and a passionate pessimism regarding America's will to justice.

The way in which this difference between the two societies is described by the immigrants is that they see Americans, both white and black, obsessed with "racialism." "Racialism" was the word used to refer to a heightened sensitivity to race, a tendency to racialize situations and relations between people. The overarching concern with race among Americans was shocking to the immigrants when they first arrived. It was so different from what they were used to back home. Mary, a thirty-eight-year-old teacher who immigrated in 1981 at age twenty-nine, reported that she was used to dealing with whites because there were whites in Jamaica, and that she did not expect there to be problems in the United States:

> You heard about crime but you didn't hear that you come here and you would be bombarded with this racial thing. And even to this day, sometimes, it's difficult to see things from a race perspective. I still see it as people against people. I find that American blacks, they talk about it, they see it in every incident that happens, it has to be race why this happens. . . . You become much more sensitive to it because the television and the radio, they pick it up, they say, Don't you see that, don't you see that? And then you start becoming aware that there is something that's going on, you know.

Many people we spoke with, both working class and middle class, were especially concerned that their children would develop this attitude:

Q: Are there any things that you've tried to tell your children as they're growing up about how to be black, or how to get along with white people?
A: Well, no, I've never really told [my children] because of black this and black that. Eventually you will start to become racial. At least I feel that. You see, I feel that it doesn't matter the color of your skin. And you know, the minute you will start to look at, oh, he's white, they're black, and this black isn't going to do this, you know, eventually it becomes you and humbles your thinking and everything. You know, like they would say up here is racial. . . . But you know, for me to tell them that you're black, you're this, you're that—no, I don't. (Thirty-eight-year-old Guyanese female worker, in United States nine years)

The perception that black Americans are too quick to cry race is intimately tied to the immigrants' belief that opportunities exist in the United States and that their own black skin has not, and will not, prevent them from taking advantage of those opportunities. It is this belief that racism, while it might exist, can surely be overcome with determination and hard work that propelled the immigrants to move from a majority black society to the United States in the first place.

We're not saying that there is not racism, we're not saying that there's not prejudices. We're not saying that there are not certain jobs where they put a token black man. We're not saying that. But you don't have to be negative all the time. I just cannot understand because I came here, I didn't have a high-school diploma from this country. You understand? But—I mean, I love my job, I'm doing what I like to do. If anybody tell me they was going to take my job from me, I would probably die. Because I love what I do. I may complain a little doing it. You know? And it's like, I'm more or less satisfied. My next step after this will be to have my own catering business. And that is what I'm working towards now. You know? So, don't tell me I can't do it. I could do it. [I say to African-Americans], Why you can't do it and you're right here? (Thirty-six-year-old Trinidadian female supervisor, in United States nineteen years)

The idea that while racial prejudice might keep the group down, it will not stop them from succeeding as individuals reflects a long-standing tradition among West Indian immigrants—they fight individually, not collectively, for their rights (Reid 1939, 122). Indeed, scholars who studied earlier waves of immigration described how West Indians often stressed their British ties and their foreign status as ways to combat discrimination.[10] In psychological terms West Indians have often dealt with the stigmatized nature of the black race in United States society through a strategy of "exit" rather than "voice." While black Americans generally perceive little possibility for individuals to succeed by exiting the category of black people, and thus tend to develop a collective strategy to give voice to their lack of equality, West Indians, especially in the first generation and especially when they first arrive, believe that by evoking their foreign status, working hard, and avoiding racialism and by challenging true racism with loud cries of protest, they can exit from the stigmatized black category.[11]

These beliefs that individual effort can overcome racial barriers do not mean that West Indians deny the existence of racism (a charge that African-Americans often make and that the immigrants vehemently deny). Rather, the immigrants argue that they are very vigilant in noticing attitudes or behaviors that might keep them from achieving socioeconomic mobility. The immigrants often see racism on the job and in society and they think that racism should be challenged. In fact, the foreign born pride themselves in being more likely to stand up to whites when "real" situations occur. Yet their lack of racialism was often pointed to by the immigrants to explain why they thought they got along with whites better than African-Americans. This manager believes that whites are more at ease with him because he does not react to them based on their race.

I think—I am a Caribbean-American. I see what a person is, right? And if I need something from you, I'm going to ask for it, regardless of who you are. And like, I'm a person. I mean, color and nationality is secondary and I think that most Caribbean people focus on that point of view. And I think this helps people to get along. You know, if you don't have any preconceived notions. I have no problem with white Americans and I think that from that perspective they treat you differently. In conversations with other black Americans—not all, mind you, some—I see that some of their basic concepts are so strange, that it keeps them back. You know, their values. (Forty-two-year-old Grenadian male manager, in United States nine years)

Several respondents consciously tied this difference between West Indians and African-Americans to what they perceive as the Americans' preoccupation with the historical experience of slavery. This Jamaican teacher argues that African-Americans see slavery in job hierarchies that are merely job hierarchies:

I would think [that West Indians get more opportunities and more breaks than African-Americans from white people in New York], but I don't think it's because of the whites. I think it is because of the blacks. The attitude of the blacks, I see it everyday. And that's—for example, some people will say you are subservient, you are just accepting of everything. It's not a matter of accepting, it's a matter of the work ethic. That a white person is set over you—it's not who is set over you, but you came here with a certain work ethic. Somebody is set over you and you do what you are told to do. It's not that you don't have any backbone or that you are subservient or anything, it's just that you are in the workplace and somebody has to be the boss. I think we accept that quicker than American blacks, much more readily than American blacks. American blacks say he's white and he's set over me, that is slavery and he tells you to do that and it's still the slavery thing continuing. (Forty-one-year-old Jamaican female teacher, in United States seven years)

Thus the cultural beliefs and practices West Indian immigrants bring to the United States reflect two influences—their status as voluntary immigrants, which leads them to expect hard work and ambition to conquer discrimination; and their experiences in Caribbean society, which lead them to expect racial discrimination, but to see it as a relatively contained part of life, not one that suffuses every encounter between black and white. These expectations are severely challenged by the immigrants' experiences in American society.

Encountering the Reality of American Race Relations

The expectations that the immigrants have about race relations in the United States do not prepare them well for their experiences here. Most respondents report surprise at the racial situation they encounter; many report deep shock. This is because the immigrants come expecting to encounter what I call *structural racism*—blocked mobility for blacks in the society and a hierarchy in which whites have political and economic power. When they encounter this kind of racism the immigrants are able to handle these situations well—mainly by challenging the situations they encounter—doing things like applying for jobs and housing that they feel they deserve, even if they feel whites are trying to prevent their mobility.

But almost everyone we spoke to was unprepared for the degree of *interpersonal* racism they encountered in the United States—the overarching concern with race in every encounter, the constant role race plays in everyday life, the subtle experiences blacks have every day in the United States that are tinged with racial suspicions and overtones. The immigrants' encounters with each of these forms of American racism will be examined in turn.

STRUCTURAL RACISM. Before they leave home, the immigrants tend to base their expectations of the racism they will encounter in the United States on the race relations they have seen in the Caribbean. Back home whites and light-skinned blacks were more likely to be in higher socioeconomic positions, and it was very rare to see a white person at the bottom of the socioeconomic ladder. Thus while race was not *determinative* of socioeconomic position (many blacks were in a high position) it was *highly correlated* with it (most high positions were filled with light-skinned blacks or whites). Blocks to black mobility is what the immigrants expected to find in the United States—that while they *could* rise to the top, it would be more difficult, because whites were in control and would jealously guard their competitive position.

Although West Indians often criticized African-Americans for being too racial and reading race into situations where the immigrants did not see it, immigrant and native blacks shared the perception that structural racism existed and meant that whites tried to protect their control of the higher reaches of the socioeconomic structure of the society. For instance, these immigrants described blocked mobility for black people on the job, and the lengths to which whites would go to find a white person for a job when a qualified black was already on site:

> There's people working here for like excessive amount of years, OK, and they happen to be black. And a white person will come in here and the next thing you know, they're making X amount of money more than that person. There's a guy right here right now, he's white, he used to be in purchasing—he used to buy the foodstuffs. . . . Now he's been promoted to manager. He was just with the company for like two years. He's one of the managers. You got people here for like five, seven years. They didn't even ask you if you wanted to apply for it. And this guy have no experience whatsoever, you know, with food, because he just came off the streets, wherever he came from, he happened to know somebody here that hired him downstairs as a purchasing clerk, right? And then, he happened to know the executive chef, they were friends, because she's white too, they hang out together. She took a transfer to Florida. So she just give him a push. Which I think was totally wrong in front of everybody. I was made to understand, this is your boss. Now I can't figure it out. How could he be my boss if he can't even tell me, he can't even explain to me what is a tomato or a cauliflower? There's nothing that he can tell me that I can gain from. (Thirty-three-year-old Guyanese male supervisor, in United States nine years)

While the white managers believed charges of racism at American Food were unfounded, there was a widespread belief among the black immigrants and the black Americans that mobility beyond a certain point within the company was blocked for people with black skin—regardless of nativity. And this shared understanding of blocked social mobility due to discrimination based on race alone, not culture, provided the opportunity for West Indians and African-Americans to go to bat for each other and to see themselves as having common goals and experiences.

The achievement ideology of the West Indians prepares them to battle to succeed in the United States. They expect that it will be more difficult for blacks than for whites because they know that whites have more economic and political power in the United States than do blacks. The immigrants rationally conclude that whites will try to maintain that power and will resist attempts by blacks to enter the higher reaches of society. This is the immigrants' understanding of and experience of discrimination from back home. Their expectations match their experiences, and their interpretations of those experiences match the interpretations of their African-American coworkers and are at odds with the interpretations of their white American coworkers. But when it comes to interpersonal, not structural racism, the immigrants' expectations are in fact closer to those of white Americans, and very different from those of African-Americans, but their experiences are quite different from what they would have expected.

INTERPERSONAL RACISM. The *interpersonal* racism that the immigrants experience comes in two forms—old-fashioned racism and subtle racism. Old-fashioned racism consists of blatant acts of discrimination and prejudice such as being physically attacked or threatened, being insulted on the street, being denied housing or employment specifically for racial reasons, and being hassled or scared by the police. The stories of blatant discrimination told by these immigrants might very well shock Americans who believe that Jim Crow–style racism has been completely eradicated in 1990s America. But overt racism met these immigrants in housing, in employment, in police beatings of the Rodney King variety, on public transportation, and in the streets. This is a typical incident of blatant interpersonal racism; there are literally hundreds of similar incidents in my interview transcripts:

A: I had applied to get a condo—condominium—and I was told by this lady that they not going to take any niggers in this apartment.
Q: She said that to your face?
A: Yes. That turned me off right away. I said, well, I didn't, you know, I'm not going to give up, but still, same time I feel bad to say well, OK, I want to go into a nice decent area and the response that you get is that. (Twenty-nine-year-old Guyanese female worker, in United States nine years)

There is nothing subtle or open to other explanations about these experiences—they stem from racial prejudice, and the whites who perform these acts are up-front about their disdain for blacks—all blacks, including the foreign born. Immigrants who had lived in the United States for anything but a short period of time reported having experiences like these. The theme that appears over and over again in describing these encounters is surprise and shock that this could happen to them. Unlike blocked mobility at work, which they expected, these blatant acts of discrimination and raw interpersonal attacks are so disturbing because they are so unexpected.

Subtle racism includes the daily hassles, indignities, and "bad vibes" that black people experience constantly in interactions with whites. This includes being followed in stores because clerks believe you might shoplift, whites moving to the other side of the street and clutching their handbags when you walk by, taxis refusing to stop to pick you up, store clerks who refuse to put money in your hand because they do not want to touch your black skin, security guards asking for your ID when they let coworkers walk by unchallenged. Subtle racism also includes acts of omission as well as commission—never being invited to coworkers' homes, having wonderfully friendly relations with people on the phone and yet very cold relations when you meet them in person, professors in graduate school acting surprised when your work is excellent.

In subtle racial encounters the perpetrator can deny any racial animosity and claim their behaviors are due to other considerations. While working-class and middle-class blacks experience both forms of interpersonal racism, the middle class are more likely to experience subtle racism, and the working class are more likely to experience the more direct old-fashioned racism. The working-class immigrants were the ones who were traveling the subways when people yelled at them to stay out of their neighborhoods; the middle-class people try to get cabs and the cabs fail to stop. Both incidents are due to the race of the victim, yet in the case of the taxicabs, race is not the only possible explanation.

Many of the stories the middle class told us about discrimination involved people refusing to believe their middle-class status—thinking they could not afford things in the stores, for instance. The teachers felt acutely that they had a certain standing in the community back home that they did not have in the United States because the same amount of respect was not accorded to teachers and because race was such an overwhelming presence in American life. Many teachers were shocked by their experiences in graduate school as they came to realize that their professors did not expect them to do well academically because they were black. Most had received their undergraduate degrees at the University of the West Indies, where the vast majority of the students were black and professors did not differentiate students by race. In graduate school in the United States, all of a sudden they suspect their race is affecting how their professors respond to them. When immigrants notice discrimination in one area of their lives, they begin to see the subtle racism that exists in other areas:

I have felt it [racism]. Like the lecturers at City, they say "Oh, you write so well" or they meet you and they say, "Oh, you speak so well." Now I don't understand why they should single me out and say I speak so well. It's like it's not normal for that color skin to speak well. And because you have become sensitive to this thing now, you sort of sense it, you know. And at the school where I teach, sometimes you wonder whether it's because you are black that certain things are withheld from you, the whites are keeping all the little extra jobs in the school. They know about it, they put up an ad over the time clock and then you asked if it's been filled or something like that because they had picked out who was to do it already. My district is white and they do discriminate against blacks. . . . I often wonder too about some

ladies I work with that I often talk to, we are always together. I can get a lift
home if I don't have my car, and that sort of thing. And yet they would never
like invite you. They're going home for lunch, they're going to have lunch on
their back porch and they will not invite you. And you start thinking to yourself, how genuine are these people? What do they think you are going to do
if you come to their house? (Forty-one-year-old Jamaican female teacher, in
United States seven years)

The black Americans had the same litany of bad experiences based on race
that the middle-class immigrants described, including professors who doubted
their good performances in university, being passed over for promotions that
went to less qualified whites, being treated like a poor or criminal person just
because of the color of their skin. The teachers saw a great deal of intrenched
racism in the schools where they worked, and many were concerned that white
teachers had low expectations of their black students.

Many of the black American teachers compared race relations in present-
day New York with what they remembered from the South, most of them having come from there. Unlike the immigrants, they did not describe their original
home as a place where they did not experience racism—in fact, many told very
moving stories about their experiences with Jim Crow racism as young children.
Yet several of the teachers from the South suggested that it was easier to be
black in the South than in the North, because they had attended segregated
schools and lived their lives in such a way that they rarely encountered whites.
This was not possible in New York, especially as a middle-class person who
worked with whites; many of them lived in neighborhoods that were either integrated or were close to white neighborhoods. This nostalgia for the "power"
and "freedom" that segregation brought, especially in the schools, has been expressed by a number of black writers recently.[12] The parallels between the immigrants' discussions of the freedoms they felt coming from the majority-black
West Indies and the Southern blacks' remembrances of their home towns are
strong.

Interpersonal racism begins to undermine the immigrants' belief that they
can tell the difference between incidents that are racial in nature and those
that are not. Over time, the openness and willingness to respond to whites as
individuals who are not different because of skin color erodes. The suspicion
that any individual white you encounter might be about to treat you badly because of the color of your skin begins to shape every encounter between black
and white. Interpersonal racism ultimately erodes the ability of blacks and
whites to ever forget race. The ghosts of past bad encounters influence current encounters.

The experiences of Ginny, a twenty-nine-year-old Guyanese cafeteria cashier, and Charissa, a forty-one-year-old Jamaican teacher, illustrate this process. Ginny, like most other cafeteria workers, did not have very many areas of her life in which she interacted with whites, aside from work. Aside from fleeting encounters with whites in public arenas such as shopping, riding the train, in parks and beaches, and the like, most of her life was spent with other black people. Her friends, her neighbors, and many of her coworkers were either American or Caribbean blacks. Because of the high degree of racial segregation in housing and the ripple effects of that segregation on other institutions such as schools, churches, and parks, there are few areas other than work in which working-class immigrants have sustained contact with whites. Yet Ginny enjoyed very good relations with the whites she encountered on the job. This consisted of the back-and-forth banter she would have with the white office workers and executives who came through her line with their lunch every day. Her experiences had generally been quite positive and she had gotten to know many of her regular customers enough to ask about their vacations and their families, and they would also ask her about her family and her vacations. Some customers even asked a number of questions about what Guyana was like and why she had immigrated. Yet Ginny reports that her generally positive encounters with whites left her unprepared for and shocked by the negative encounter she had recently endured:

> The white people that come to my line, you know, they will greet me. They say, hello, morning, good afternoon. . . . But one day this guy, he came in my line and I was asking him what he have on his tray cause I couldn't see what he have, and he said "You can't see what I have on my tray? If you don't understand our language, why don't you go back to your country," and "I'm sick and tired of you black niggers—all you black people down here—all you niggers down here." That's what he said. And I went to get the manager and, you know, they told me the next time that he come back they going to talk to him. But he came like a lot of times and they never come and talk to him. And he was saying it loud and clear and the other whites that was behind him they was surprised to see how this man was going on. But—he acts like he has a problem or something, I don't know. But it was terrible that he said that, you know. *I feel bad because when one person mess up with you, well, everybody's the same thing.* (Twenty-nine-year-old Guyanese female worker, in United States nine years)

Of course on a cafeteria line, all service people will probably experience rude behavior and lack of respect from customers. But for Ginny and all of the other workers who witnessed this incident, the use of the term "nigger" and the racism it laid bare will affect future interpersonal encounters with whites. While most people getting their lunch on this cafeteria line are not likely to ever call anyone a nigger, that one encounter, as this worker clearly understands, will color her expectations and experiences with every white customer who approaches her cash register. Indeed, the story of how black immigrants come to terms with American racism really is more about how they see *interpersonal* racism, rather than *structural* racism. And this involves developing a sixth sense that picks up on whites' unspoken disdain, a sixth sense that notices the ways in which whites look at you. The immigrants have to learn for the first time that race in the United States is not just about intergroup conflict over societal rewards, which is what they had expected, but that many, many whites just do not see a black person as a human being.

Charissa, a forty-one-year-old Jamaican teacher, also had an experience that changed her expectations about race and its effects on her. While Ginny's experience was clear-cut and undeniably about race, Charissa's was more opaque and open to interpretation. But it also changed her expectations about interactions with whites. For most of her interview, Charissa was very concerned that she did not want to become racial in the United States, and is very concerned that her teenage children seem overly concerned with racial slights. She feels that black Americans are too concerned with their race:

> I can't help them [African-Americans] because they're so wrapped up in racism and they act it out so often, they interpret it as such so often that sometimes they are not even approachable. If they're going to teach anything and its not black, black, all black, they are not satisfied, you know. If they're going to teach poetry and it's not all written by blacks—it's strange that they think it should be so. Yes, we did black authors and black writers but certainly we did a lot of British. You know, for us that's not new. Sometimes I feel sorry for them, but you find that you just can't change their attitude because they just tell you that you don't understand. You weren't here to feel what we felt. (Forty-one-year-old Jamaican female teacher, in United States seven years)

Yet she had an experience that made her much more receptive to African-American friends' advice. She was attending graduate school to get a master's in education, and she had to take the national teachers' test to keep her position in the city schools. The forms you fill out for the test include a question on race. The first time she took the test she answered the race question by stating that she was black, and she was certain she had done very well on the test. But when she got the results she learned that she had failed the test. An African-American friend from one of her graduate classes told her that the test was rigged and that they purposely failed a certain number of blacks who took the test, and they let a larger number of whites pass. Charissa was very skeptical of this assertion at first, but the second time she took the test, she left the race question blank, and she passed the test. Since that time she has never put her race on any form that asks for it; and she really believes that many forms require information about race so that blacks can be discovered and discriminated against.

Whites Have a Comfort Factor

In his autobiography, Malcolm X wrote about why the white man hated the Negro:

> Do you know why the white man really hates you? It's because every time he sees your face, he sees a mirror of his crime—and his guilty conscience can't bear to face it. (Malcolm X 1964, 204)

West Indians provide a black face for whites to look into without seeing the sorry history of American race relations mirrored back. This puts whites at ease and a cycle of expectations gets created. West Indians expect good relations with whites, and vice versa. These expectations are often met and thus the race relations at an interpersonal level are smoother for whites and West Indian blacks than they are for whites and American blacks. The whites who worked at American Food and the white teachers we interviewed tended to see the immigrants as sharing an immigrant identity with them—because many of these whites are the descendants of European immigrants. Yet the relative warmth all of the whites we spoke with have toward West Indians as opposed to African-Americans goes beyond the basis of their shared immigration histories. Whites sense the lack of opposition in West Indians to their whiteness and report having far friendlier experiences with foreign-born blacks than with American blacks. For instance, this thirty-two-year-old white female supervisor senses exactly the difference that the West Indians describe in how they relate to her as a person who is in authority over them:

> Sometimes I feel that people who come from the islands are more appreciative of their jobs. They consider themselves fortunate. And sometimes I feel that the American [black] assistants feel that you owe it to them to keep them on when you have some problems. The island people are a little more open to white people than the American blacks who question authority more. And I don't know how to say it—the West Indians kind of accept the fact that even though you are white, it is not *because* you are white that you are dictating to them, but because you are the person in authority.

In a widely quoted popular article on relations among American whites, American blacks, and recent immigrants in *The Atlantic Monthly,* journalist Jack Miles argues that whites prefer to be with and deal with immigrants rather than American blacks. Speaking about race relations in Los Angeles, Miles notes that for Anglos, "Latinos, even when they are foreign, seem native and safe, while blacks, who are native, seem foreign and dangerous" (Miles 1992, 52). Miles describes this as the "comfort factor" and asserts that whites are more comfortable with black immigrants as well. He notes that when he was in college he had a Nigerian roommate whom he felt immediately comfortable with. The ease of his friendship with his Nigerian roommate showed him how deep an estrangement separated him from African-Americans (Miles 1992, 53).

Why did he feel such discomfort with black Americans? He notes that in the 1960s, when he was spending a great deal of time with American black people, he sensed how they were approaching their relationship with him:

[I]n the end I felt that even with me they were prepared at every moment, at every single moment, for the worst, braced as it were, for a blow. This is what slavery has done to us as a people, and I can scarcely think of it without tears. (Miles 1992, 53)

The comfort factor that whites felt toward West Indians and their discomfort with black Americans came through clearly in the interviews. A key difference that was cited over and over by the whites we interviewed was the sense of entitlement they felt among American blacks:

Q: What are the differences [between American blacks and West Indians] that you see?

A: From a working standpoint—work ethic? The willingness to work for a living—among some, as compared to American blacks. The willingness to be helpful. The chip isn't on the shoulder that you may get from an American black because they're black, and then a Jamaican person, you can go up to them—I'm willing to treat them same as me. He's no better than me, I'm no better than him. And I get that treatment all the time. And I treat that way.

Q: Where do you think this difference comes from?

A: Uh, their own cultures. I think—this is terrible, but I think American blacks sometimes think that they're owed something instead of working for it. (Forty-two-year-old white male manager)

Whites pointed to a difference between American blacks and foreign-born blacks in terms of the amount of anger and sense of entitlement they felt. For instance, this twenty-six-year-old white teacher was asked to describe what black Americans are like. She answered:

A: I think there's an evolving African-American character as differentiated from a black character. I think that has been around forever. I think that if it's going to be anything, if I could pick a word, I would say "angry."

Q: Really?

A: Yeah, because I think that there's this sense of "I want what I deserve" happening.

In contrast, the immigrants are described by the whites as being willing to work within the system, as not taking advantage of the system, as not feeling that they are owed something, and as not being angry and blaming whites for historical wrongs. So most whites reported that they felt more comfortable with foreign-born blacks than with American-born blacks.

Q: What about West Indians, or people from the islands? What characteristics come to mind when you think of West Indians?

A: Um, from my experience, I think for the most part, they're extremely friendly people. I mean, it just seems like they're friendly. They'll say hello to you, they smile, they wave. (Thirty-four-year-old white male manager)

At the same time, a significant number of the white managers describe the foreign born as being very outspoken, very aware of race, and very likely to be blunt about what they want. Yet this did not seem to dampen relations between whites and West Indians in the same way that it dampened relations between African-Americans and whites.

Q: Do you see ethnic differences between people from the islands and American blacks? Do you notice any distinctions there?

A: American blacks probably feel they, they probably feel that they wish—give more to them. You know what I'm saying? I don't know how to explain it. Whereas island blacks who come over, they're immigrant, they may not have such a good life where they are so they going to try to strive to better themselves, and I think there's a lot of American blacks out there who feel we owe them. And enough is enough already. You know, this is something that happened to their ancestors, not now. I mean, we've done so much for the black people in America now that it's time that they got off their butts.

Q: Do you think the immigrant blacks will end up doing better economically than the American blacks?

A: Sure. That's because I think they strive for it more. I think they've had, they—I don't think they feel we owe them a living. You know?

Q: But you get that sense from American blacks?

A: I get that sense, oh yeah. Yeah. (Thirty-three-year-old white female manager)

But the culture surrounding race that the immigrants bring with them has another component. In addition to the expectation of good, or at least neutral, interpersonal relations with whites, the immigrants are on the lookout for structural racism and the blocked mobility it entails. When they do encounter incidents of blatant racism on the job or structural incidents such as not being promoted or getting a raise, they become angry and militant about it, often raising quite a fuss. The immigrants are also likely to be angrier because injustice when first encountered and not expected is a different thing from long-simmering racial injustice that is always expected. The irony is that the black immigrants are perceived by the whites to be better workers because they are immigrants, nicer to be around most of the time because of their separation of hierarchy at work from racial hierarchy, and yet also very militant in a racial sense.

When promotions, raises, or special perks are discussed and disseminated at American Food, the whites notice that the West Indians become angry and militant, even more militant than the American blacks, whom the whites perceive to be always angry. The responses of whites to West Indians are thus complicated—they see the West Indians as more friendly, more approachable on an individual level, more cooperative, and at the same time, more aware of race, more likely to be angry and blunt about workplace race relations, and more demanding and arrogant than African-Americans.

Q: And you were saying that some groups were demanding?

A: Sure.

Q: Which ones were you thinking about?

A: It's like more of your island people. I mean, they come up with these like superior attitudes, like. You know, who-do-you-think-you're-talking-to-type attitude, you know. I'm their boss and yet I get this attitude. It's hard to describe it, but that's the way I feel. They think that because they're here working as a cook or a dishwasher or whatever they're doing that they should be paid for it. And every time they get reviewed they expect to get a raise and like, wait a minute, what did you do to earn that raise? It's like we should give it to you, and I don't like that. I did find that I have a hard time talking to them, to the—cause most of the people here are like, island people; Trinidad, Jamaica, Panama—you know, they're all island people. Sometimes you're almost afraid to say something because you don't know what's going to set them off.

Q: They get angry?

A: Yeah. They—it's like, angry and belligerent. . . . It seems that the American blacks are much more prejudiced than foreigners, yet sometimes I feel that some foreigners do really want to push it.

Q: Push being a foreigner, or push being black?

A: Black, being black. Mostly being black. (Thirty-three-year-old white female manager)

This seeming contradiction can be found in a number of studies of West Indians in the United States. They have been described as militant race leaders, with more advanced and confrontational racial ideologies and programs than American blacks. Yet they have also been seen as more conservative, less willing to challenge the rules of the game, easier to get along with.[13] This mix of confrontation and ambition at a structural level and openness and nonoppositional behaviors at an interpersonal level can lead to greater success in the economy, as well as the possibility of greater disappointment and rage about blocked mobility and racism if they do not achieve success in the labor market. By being friendly and open to whites they open themselves up to bitter disillusionment when the inevitable blatant racist comes along. However, because not everyone is racist, and because there are doors of opportunities open to blacks in American society, at the aggregate level there will be more West Indians who succeed in American life. So the strategy that opens each individual up to possible hurt furthers the overall success of the group.

Immigrants who expect structural racism and do not expect interpersonal racism will do very well in American workplaces. This is especially true in the service economy where taking orders and being pleasant is often part of the job. With affirmative action and corporate structures the way they are, a black person who aims high, challenges blocked mobility and missed promotions when they occur, and yet manages to maintain very friendly relations with whites and does not make them feel uncomfortable about issues of race can go very far. It is no accident that Colin Powell is the black person who has come closest to being accepted by a cross-section of whites for the highest office in America. His West Indian background gives him this particular set of skills— he is an ambitious man who aims high, who acknowledges the existence of racism and prejudice in American society and stands willing to challenge it when it affects him, yet a person whom whites of all backgrounds, particularly conservative whites, find comfortable. Indeed, Powell does not have a chip on his shoulder about race.

But what of the West Indian who does not achieve the social mobility of a Colin Powell? What of the person who has middle-class ambitions but does not have the degree of social mobility that cushions the inevitable encounters with old-fashioned and subtle racism? Louis Farrakhan is also a black American of West Indian background, and his fiery militance about racial matters also reflects the same mix of racial and socioeconomic expectations. He also reports never having experienced or expected the degree of interpersonal racism he first experienced when he traveled south for the first time as a young man. When West Indians experience blocked mobility that cannot be overcome through hard work and ambition, and when they experience interpersonal racism for which they are not prepared, they can become even more bitter and concerned with race than anyone—witness Marcus Garvey and Louis Farrakhan.

Change over Time

While I argue that there are cultural expectations about race that explain some of the dynamics of West Indian success in the service economy, I do not agree with the classic cultural explanations for West Indian success. The beliefs and practices I describe do not stem from historical differences generations ago, but rather from recent lived experiences in the Caribbean as well as from the immigration process itself. Indeed, the structural realities of American race relations quickly begin to change the beliefs and behaviors of immigrants and, most especially, their children (Waters 1994). The immigrants describe how the longer they are in the United States, the more they learn to see race operating in interactions that they would not have suspected were about race when they first arrived. The omnipresence of race in day-to-day interactions and the reality of subtle racial discrimination and prejudice mean that over time the immigrants become much less confident that they can tell when people are responding to their skin color and not some other characteristic or circumstance. In fact, when long-term immigrants are describing freshly arrived immigrants they comment on their inability to recognize the racism that is all around them:

> When the Guyanese come, and all the other foreigners first come, they come with the aim of succeeding. If they did not come to succeed, they would not have come. Therefore, they do not recognize the subtle signs of racism. They attribute racism to bad manners. (Forty-nine-year-old Guyanese female teacher, in United States nineteen years)

When the immigrants start to see subtle racism, it becomes much harder to maintain their initial militance—their pledge of always loudly challenging racial injustice and demanding proper treatment when they do encounter it. Over time you learn to pick your battles—expending energy and emotions on situations that you think you can change or that you know you cannot live with.

The reluctant acceptance that race affects the way whites respond to them, in both blatant and subtle ways, serves to undermine the approach immigrants initially adopt—to treat whites as individuals, not as representatives of their race. One Jamaican immigrant told me that he had experienced a lot of racial incidents, but he still tried to have an open mind.

> You might walk out there, something hit you in the face that this is racial. But if you didn't look for that, you safer to be naive. I don't go out and look for some white person to be mean to me. (Thirty-seven-year-old Jamaican female teacher, in United States seven years)

But if enough white people are mean to you, you can't help but learn to expect it. As Ginny, the cafeteria worker who was called a nigger by a customer, stated, "When one person mess up with you, well, everybody's the same thing." It may be *safer* to be naïve, but experience does destroy naïveté, and like it or not the stings of past racial experiences begin to color expectations of all personal encounters between black immigrants and white Americans.

So, as the immigrants spend more time in the United States, their expectations of interpersonal racism rise and they report more wariness in their encounters with whites. But no matter how many years West Indian immigrants spend in the United States, and however many negative encounters they have with whites, their interactions with whites generally produce better outcomes than black Americans' encounters with whites. Whites expect West Indians to be "better blacks"; they find common ground in the West Indians' immigrant experiences. West Indians have the immigrants' faith in the American dream, and their experiences growing up in a black-majority society inoculate them against a bitter attitude that turns off whites in interpersonal interactions (especially in the service industry, where many work).[14] At the same time their strong racial identity and experiences with blocked mobility for dark-skinned people at home inspire the militance and fiery attitudes that lead them to challenge injustice when they encounter it. Many of these characteristics might fade a little bit over time as the immigrants spend more time in a racist society. Yet most of these characteristics have shaped adults' characters and outlooks in a way that will change only slightly throughout their lives. It is in the second generation that this process of rapid cultural change is most evident. The children of these immigrants do grow up exhibiting the racialism their parents are concerned with preventing. Indeed, the rapidity of the change in attitudes about race between parents and children is quite dramatic.

All too often, cultural expectations of West Indian success appeal to whites because of their wish to believe that it is something in African-Americans' own behavior and beliefs that is responsible for their low status in American society. This is a preferable explanation for whites who do not believe that there are continuing prejudice and discrimination in American society. Whites who want blacks to forget about race and past injustice profess that if they do, and they shed their victim mentality, they will then do well. The experiences of the immigrants I describe here who fervently try to forget about race show a very small kernel of truth in that argument. A lack of expectation of interpersonal racism does make whites feel comfortable and does provide a small advantage in the workplace. But the weight of the evidence in this study leads to a very different overall conclusion. It is the continuing discrimination and prejudice of whites, and ongoing structural and interpersonal racism, that create an inability among American, and ultimately West Indian, blacks to ever forget about race. The behavior and beliefs about race among whites, and the culture of racist behaviors among whites, create the very expectations of discomfort that whites complain about in their dealings with their black neighbors, coworkers, and friends. That expectation is not some inexplicable holdover from the long-ago days of slavery, but rather a constantly re-created expectation of trouble, nourished by every taxi that does not stop and every casual or calculated white use of the word "nigger." If the West Indian experience teaches us anything about American race relations, it should refocus our attention on the destructive and everyday prejudice and discrimination whites are responsible for in our still chronically racist society.

Notes

This research was supported by grants from the Russell Sage Foundation and the John Simon Guggenheim Foundation. I am grateful for research assistance from Crystal Byndloss, Kayode Owens, Jimmy Phillipe, Tomni Dance, and Lisa Walke. I am also very grateful for comments on various drafts of this chapter by Michèle Lamont, James Jasper, Monica McDermot, and Peggy Levitt. I would also like to thank the people we interviewed for their time and their honesty.

1. Reid's work has been the only book-length comprehensive study of the black immigrant to date—and is a valuable and highly engaging study. However, the status of Reid's book as a classic should not lead to an unquestioning acceptance of his conclusions. He based a great deal of his book on entries by West Indians to a Life History Essay Prize Contest. Contestants entered essays about their experiences as immigrants, and described their reactions to specific situations, like employment and discrimination. People who enter an essay contest are a highly selected group and generalizations based on such a sample are highly suspect.

2. They also quoted from a novel about Barbadian immigrants in Brooklyn by Paule

Marshall. It is remarkable the number of people who use Marshall's fictionalized story of a Bajan family in Brooklyn as "social science" data about this group. Marshall herself describes how this use of her work has startled her. See Marshall 1987.

3. Smith (1985, 24) points to the economic vacuum created after slavery was abolished in the Caribbean that created opportunities for skilled black craftsmen and artisans. This did not happen in the American South because large numbers of poor whites were available to take those jobs and they created political and legal barriers to black advancement into those jobs in the form of the black codes and the like.

4. One study showed some distinct attitudes of West Indians that fit with cultural stereotypes, but it was based on a very small and nonrandom sample. Glantz (1978) compared the beliefs of West Indian students at Brooklyn College with white Catholics and Jews. He found that "the West Indian group expressed more trust in the responsiveness of the economic reward system, more faith in the value of hard work at school and in the value of hard work generally, and less negativism in their orientation toward the electoral system in the United States" (Glantz 1978, 200).

5. Roger Waldinger's (1996) book *Still the Promised City?* examines patterns of West Indian and black American employment and education in more detail and sheds some light on why the least educated West Indians are so much more likely to be in the labor force than the least educated African-Americans. He argues that patterns of network hiring led to the formation of racial and ethnic niches in employment—the concentration of racial and ethnic groups in industries or sectors of the economy beyond what one would expect given their proportions in the population.

He argues that West Indians have been able to expand their presence in New York's economy in recent decades while African-Americans' presence declined because the West Indians were poised to do well in New York's growing postindustrial service economy. In the 1970s and 1980s West Indians established strong concentrations in the expanding health care industry. By 1990 employment in the niches of hospitals, nursing homes, and health services provided employment to 22 percent of Caribbean New Yorkers. By contrast, African-Americans were concentrated in public-sector employment—an area that usually requires at least moderate levels of education.

Waldinger concludes that while employed skilled African-Americans are doing well in the niche of public-sector employment, with many of them employed in managerial or professional occupations, unskilled African-Americans have been locked out of the networks that provide entry to unskilled entry-level jobs. Those jobs have been taken over by immigrants—both black immigrants and others. Low-skilled West Indians have network ties that connect them to jobs in the lowest levels of the fast-growing service economy of New York.

6. Waldinger (1986, 9) makes the point that describing something as a cultural trait does not make it permanent. In fact, he argues that immigrants would be very likely to change their culture when the environment changes. "[J]ust as culture is learned through childhood and adult socialization so too are new cultural patterns learned and devised when the environment changes. Immigrants, after all, are unlikely to be the more traditional members of their original societies; rather they are more likely to stem from those sections of the population already most inclined toward adaptation and change."

7. Also see Fordham 1988 and Fordham and Ogbu 1986.

8. Many other researchers have noted this tendency to "forget" the discrimination and racism that did exist back home. See for example Holder 1980, 59; Lowenthal 1972, 227; Reid 1939. Hoetink (1967) notes that North American academics make this same mistake—viewing Caribbean society against the backdrop of the American one-drop rule and the starkness of American race relations leads the researcher to conclude race is not a major factor in Caribbean society (Hoetink 1967, 52).

9. See Hochschild 1995, 112–21, for a review of survey and anecdotal data of the difficulties faced by blacks. See also Feagin and Sikes 1994, Staples 1994, Fulwood 1996, and Williams 1991.

10. Holder 1980, 51; Hellwig 1978, 213; Reid 1939, 110.

11. Toney (1990, 12) argued that historically West Indians used an exit strategy at the individual level to deal with racism, but a voice strategy at the political level, where they felt they really could make a difference in American society. See also Vickerman 1994, 118.

12. See Fulwood 1996.

13. Forsythe (1976, 305) argues that West Indians exhibit both a radical streak in opposition to racial subjugation and a conservative base of conformism, legalism, and Anglophonism. Hellwig (1978, 212) notes that West Indians "readily expressed displeasure with any manifestation of discourtesy from whites. Often they applied for jobs which American custom designated as white." Patterson (1972, 59) discusses the rise of Marcus Garvey and his brand of radical black nationalism as stemming from the heightened racial consciousness of the West Indian peasant with a greater sense of racial and personal dignity being subjected to the starkness of American racial ghettos. Reid noted in 1939 that "the Pullman Company and certain railroads hesitated to employ West Indian Negroes as porters because of their rather vainglorious resentment exhibited when they felt that they had been insulted by passengers" (Reid 1939, 111).

14. Kasinitz (1988) suggests that because West Indians are concentrated in the service economy their interactions with whites are likely to develop these racial overtones.

References

Bryce-Laporte, Roy. 1972. "Black Immigrants: The Experience of Invisibility and Inequality." *Journal of Black Studies* 3:29–56.

Butcher, Kristin. 1994. "Black Immigrants in the United States: A Comparison with Native Blacks and Other Immigrants." *Industrial and Labor Relations Review* 47: 265–84.

Chiswick, Barry R. 1979. "The Economic Progress of Immigrants: Some Apparently Universal Patterns." In *Contemporary Economic Problems 1979*, edited by William Fellner. Washington: American Enterprise Institute for Public Policy Research.

Cornell, Stephen. 1999. "Ethnicity as Narrative: Identity Construction, Pan-ethnicity, and American Indian Supertribalism." In *We Are A People*, edited by Paul R. Spickard and W. Jeffrey Burroughs. Philadelphia: Temple University Press.

Farley, Reynolds, and Walter R. Allen. 1987. *The Color Line and the Quality of Life in America.* New York: Russell Sage.

Feagin, Joe R., and Melvin Sikes. 1994. *Living with Racism.* Boston: Beacon.

Foner, Nancy. 1987. "The Jamaicans: Race and Ethnicity among Migrants in New York City." In *New Immigrants in New York,* edited by Nancy Foner. New York: Columbia University Press.

Fordham, Signithia. 1988. "Racelessness as a Factor in Black Students' School Success: Pragmatic Strategy or Pyrrhic Victory?" *Harvard Education Review* 58:54–84.

Fordham, Signithia, and John Ogbu. 1986. "Black Students' School Success: Coping with the Burden of Acting White." *Urban Review* 18:176–206.

Forsythe, Dennis. 1975. "Black Immigrants and the American Ethos: Theories and Observations." In *Caribbean Migration to the United States,* edited by Roy Simon Bryce Laporte and D. M. Mortimer. Washington: Smithsonian.

———. 1976. "West Indian Radicalism in America: An Assessment of Ideologies." In *Ethnicity in the Americas,* edited by Frances Henry. Paris: Mouton.

Fulwood, Sam. *Waking from the Dream.* New York: Anchor.

Glantz, Oscar. 1978. "Native Sons and Immigrants: Some Beliefs and Values of American Born and West Indian Blacks at Brooklyn College." *Ethnicity* 5:189–202.

Glazer, Nathan, and Daniel Patrick Moynihan. 1963. *Beyond the Melting Pot.* Cambridge: MIT Press.

Hellwig, David J. 1978. "Black Meets Black: Afro-American Reactions to West Indian Immigrants in the 1920's." *South Atlantic Quarterly* 77:206–24.

Hochschild, Jennifer L. 1995. *Facing Up to the American Dream.* Princeton: Princeton University Press.

Hoetink, H. 1967. *The Two Variants in Caribbean Race Relations.* London: Oxford University Press.

Holder, Calvin B. 1980. "The Rise of the West Indian Politician in New York City, 1900–1952." *Afro Americans in New York Life and History.* January, 45–59.

Jencks, Christopher. 1992. *Rethinking Social Policy.* Cambridge: Harvard University Press.

Kalmijn, Matthijs. "The Socioeconomic Assimilation of Caribbean American Blacks." *Social Forces* 74:911–30.

Kasinitz, Philip. 1988. "From Ghetto Elite to Service Sector: A Comparison of the Role of Two Waves of West Indian Immigrants in New York City." *Ethnic Groups* 7:173–203.

Lowenthal, David. 1972. *West Indian Societies.* London: Oxford University Press.

Malcolm X. 1964. *The Autobiography of Malcolm X.* New York: Ballantine.

Marshall, Paule. 1987. "Black Immigrant Women in Brown Girl Brownstones." In *Caribbean Life in New York City,* edited by Constance Sutton and Elsa Chaney. New York: Center for Migration Studies.

Miles, Jack. 1992. "Blacks vs. Browns." *Atlantic Monthly,* October, 41–68.

Model, Suzanne. 1991. "Caribbean Immigrants: A Black Success Story?" *International Migration Review* 25:248–76.

———. 1995. "West Indian Prosperity: Fact or Fiction?" *Social Problems* 42:535–53.

Ogbu, John. 1978. *Minority Education and Caste.* New York: Academic.

———. 1990. "Minority Status and Literacy in Comparative Perspective." *Daedalus* 119:141–68.

Parris, D. Elliott. 1981. "The Contributions of the Caribbean Immigrant to the United States Society." *Journal of Caribbean Studies* 2:1–13.

Patterson, Orlando. 1972. "Toward a Future That Has No Past: Reflections on the Fate of Blacks in the Americas." *Public Interest*, no. 27: 25–62.

———. 1989. "Toward a Study of Black America: Notes on the Culture of Racism." *Dissent*, fall, 476–86.

Piore, Michael J. 1979. *Birds of Passage*. Cambridge: Cambridge University Press.

Portes, Alejandro. 1995. *The Economic Sociology of Immigration*. New York: Russell Sage.

Reid, Ira De. A. 1939. *The Negro Immigrant*. New York: Arno Press; New York Times.

Smith, J. Owens. 1985. "The Politics of Income and Education Differences between Blacks and West Indians." *Journal of Ethnic Studies* 13, no. 3: 17–30.

Sowell, Thomas. [1978]. *Essays and Data on American Ethnic Groups*. [Washington: Urban Institute].

Stafford, Susan Buchanan. 1987. "The Haitians: The Cultural Meaning of Race and Ethnicity." In *New Immigrants in New York*, edited by Nancy Foner. New York: Columbia University Press.

Staples, Brent. 1994. *Parallel Time*. New York: Pantheon.

Steinberg, Stephen. *The Ethnic Myth*. Updated and expanded ed. Boston: Beacon.

Sutton, Constance R., and Susan Makiesky-Barrow. 1987. "Migration and West Indian Racial and Ethnic Consciousness." In *Caribbean Life in New York City*, edited by Constance R. Sutton and Elsa M. Chaney. New York: Center for Migration Studies.

Tilly, Charles. 1990. "Transplanted Networks." In *Immigration Reconsidered*, edited by Virginia Yans-McLaughlin. New York: Oxford University Press.

Toney, Joyce Roberta. 1990. "A Minority within a Minority: West Indian American Response to Race and Ethnicity in New York City, 1900–1965." Paper presented at the annual meeting of the Organization of American Historians, March 22–25, Washington.

Vickerman, Milton. 1994. "The Responses of West Indians to African Americans: Distancing and Identification." *Research in Race and Ethnic Relations* 7:83–128.

Waldinger, Roger. 1986. *Through the Eye of the Needle*. New York: New York University Press.

———. 1996. *Still the Promised City?* Cambridge: Harvard University Press.

Waters, Mary C. 1994. "Ethnic and Racial Identities of Second Generation Black Immigrants in New York City." *International Migration Review* 28:795–820.

West, Cornel. 1991. "Nihilism in Black America." *Dissent*, spring, 221–27.

Williams, Patricia. 1991. *The Alchemy of Race and Rights*. Cambridge: Harvard University Press.

is racial oppression intrinsic to domestic work? the experiences of children's caregivers in contemporary america

julia wrigley

Domestic work intrigues researchers because it involves the forced intimacy of masters and servants across the social boundaries of class, race, or some combination of the two. There are almost two separate literatures on domestic work: European writers have focused on the class inequalities that created demand for servants and have explored the intricacies of stratified households (Gregson and Lowe 1994; Fairchilds 1984); American writers have focused more on the ways domestic work sprang from and reinforced racial hierarchies, with particular focus on black-white relations (Palmer 1989; Rollins 1985; Dill 1994). Behind all the individual variation in relations between employers and domestic workers, American writers have emphasized the racial dynamics that structured their interactions. When white women directed black women to clean their houses, they were not only acquiring a practical service, but also affirming the power of their own whiteness (Palmer 1989). Many authors have pointed to the relations between mistress and domestic as examples of the racial oppression that can underlie relations between women, arguing that white control over black women in the household renders universalistic notions of gender untenable (Collins 1997).

The racial focus of the American work has been reflected in the methodological specialization within the literature. Most researchers have studied only one racial or ethnic group. The largest number has studied black women's experience as domestic workers (Dill 1994; Palmer 1989; Rollins 1985; Gray 1993; Erickson 1996–97; Colen 1989; Clark-Lewis 1994;

Tucker 1988); others have studied Latinas (Romero 1992; Hondagneu-Sotelo 1994) and Asian-American women (Glenn 1986). The specialization arises partly because field researchers usually interview domestic workers of their own race. White domestic workers have received relatively little attention, but a contemporary study of children's caregivers conforms to the pattern of racial specialization, with the author analyzing only the experiences of white employees (Macdonald 1996).[1] The ethnically specialized literature on domestic workers contains much insightful analysis of the micropolitics of households, including domestics' strategies for resisting employers' demands. The lack of comparative focus, however, has hampered detailed understanding of how race plays itself out in domestic work.

Milkman, Reese, and Roth (1997) have argued that the (American) literature on domestic workers focuses so heavily on race that it has neglected the class inequalities that underlie domestic employment. They write that all too often the focus on race, ethnicity, and immigration obscures the enduring significance of social class in the employer-domestic relationship (p. 8). They try to right the balance by emphasizing income inequality as a key factor in determining the extent to which middle-class households hire domestic workers. In developing a macro explanation of variation in domestic employment, Milkman, Reese, and Roth move away from the social-psychological analyses of relations between women that have been an important part of the literature, arguing that it has slighted structural factors. They also strive to remove the mystique from domestic work, the sense that it exemplifies a microcosmic reflection of racial injury and subordination; instead, they treat it as one occupation among many in a class-divided, unequal society, with its own liabilities and advantages, all seen within the context of a general lack of control by workers compared to employers.

The emphasis on racial subordination within domestic work has led many authors to condemn this form of labor as exceptionally exploitative, although authors differ on whether and to what extent it can be reformed. The large-scale departure of African-American women from domestic work has been interpreted as liberation from a particularly negative and racially charged form of employment. Waldinger (1996) is one of the few authors to suggest that there may have been some costs to their departure from domestic work; he notes that abandoning this occupational niche to Caribbean immigrants, as has largely occurred in New York City, has reduced the employment prospects of African-American women.[2] With Milkman, Reese, and Roth (1997), Waldinger (1996) treats domestic work as a valid employment option, even if one at the low end of the scale, and thus to be analyzed in comparison to the alternatives rather than treated as intrinsically negative. If, though, the hiring of black domestic workers by white employers psychically affirms the employer's sense of racial superiority and subjects women of color to practical and emotional burdens far beyond those experienced by the relatively rare white women in the occupation, then the job indeed carries heavy costs.

The cross-currents within the literature on domestic workers, and the possibility that employment conditions have changed, raise the question of how race specifically affects the experience of domestic workers in the United States today. Most researchers have not distinguished between house cleaners and caregivers when they have studied domestic workers. This has meant that there has been little focus on those domestic workers—the caregivers—whose jobs are most structurally similar to those of domestics in traditional settings and whose personal characteristics, including their race, are likely to be of most interest to their employers. Caregivers are also of particular interest because their work is more emotionally charged than cleaning, involves more interaction across social boundaries of race and class, and entails more worker dependence on one employer (see Romero 1992 on how cleaners have transformed their occupation). Finally, substantial numbers of white, Latina, and black women all work as caregivers, and in many cities employers have some choice in the racial and ethnic traits of the workers they hire.[3]

As part of a broader study of children's cross-class socialization, I have interviewed a racially diverse group of children's caregivers in two cities, New York and Los Angeles, and have also interviewed employers and managers of domestic employment agencies in the two cities. Drawing on these interviews, I focus on the question of whether black caregivers experience different treatment from employers than do white workers. From a broader perspective, the essay aims to assess whether domestic work belongs in a distinct occupational category, standing as emblematic of outmoded forms of domination and oppression, or whether it should be understood more as an ordinary, if low-placed, job within the occupational hierarchy.

The Declining Significance of Race?

Historically, women of color have had different experiences with domestic work than have white women (Katzman 1981), but it is less clear whether the occupation's heritage of inequality necessarily carries forward into the contemporary era. For black women, in particular, confinement to domestic work was part and parcel of the racial caste system of the South (Jones 1985). Southern domestics, nearly all black, received wages so meager they were only half those of domestics in the North (Stigler 1946); in addition, they experienced constant reminders of their racial subordination, from employers' refusal to share bathrooms or tableware with them to their segregation in public facilities (Tucker 1988). Black women could not use domestic work as a temporary means of acculturation to urban living, as did many white immigrants. Instead, most stayed in the job for their working lives, perhaps switching to another form of domestic labor, laundry work, once they had children.

In the North, the caste system operated less strongly, but black workers competed directly with white immigrants for much of the twentieth century, and in the competition they got the hardest and lowest-paid jobs (Gray 1993; Erickson 1996–97). A review of *New York Times* classified advertisements for domestic workers in selected weeks from the 1920s through the 1960s demonstrates that race structured the matching of employers and employees, with many ads specifying whites only.[4] Only after World War II did racial specification decline. The classified advertisements show that black women had great difficulty competing with white women as children's caregivers, with these jobs particularly likely to be reserved for whites.

The history of domestic work in America led Du Bois to write that it had been done by slaves and then mainly by their descendants, thus adding a despised race to a despised calling (1996, 136). There are, however, reasons to expect that black and Latina women may no longer be as powerfully disadvantaged in domestic work as they were in earlier historical periods. Three factors may have improved their situation. First, the civil rights movement swept away key elements of the racial caste system, giving African-Americans access to a much wider range of occupations and making racial slurs socially unacceptable (Brown 1995, 209; Schuman et al. 1997, 306). Second, immigrants from Mexico, Central America, and the Caribbean predominate among domestic workers in cities such as Los Angeles or New York. These women stand somewhat outside the American racial system, as they come from countries with less polarized racial systems than the United States (Foner 1987). They do not necessarily associate domestic work with a heritage of slavery and oppression, and also face less stereotyping by employers than do African-American workers (Waters 1997). Immigrants usually have optimistic outlooks that may help them ride over racially negative situations they may encounter, which in turn may ease their relations with white employers. Third, with most parents who hire caregivers working, there are fewer occasions for the assertion of personal dominance. When mistress and servant shared the home, employee deference may have been at a premium; today, parents are likely to place greater value on employees' ability to provide quality child care (Wrigley 1995).

Despite these factors militating against racial oppression in domestic work, it remains an open question whether this occupation operates markedly differently than in the past. America continues to be a highly segregated society (Massey and Denton 1993) and race may indeed be a master status, which affects employer valuations of employees and their treatment of them once hired (Steinberg 1995; Carnoy 1994). Research has shown that there is substantial interpersonal awkwardness and discomfort across racial lines and that most whites want considerable social distance from blacks (Jaynes and Williams 1989, 151, 155). Employer-employee relationships generate their own tensions, and given the amount of racial friction in the society, it may be hard for people working together to avoid racial slights or misunderstandings. On a deeper level, when black women work for whites in their homes, the situation may evoke long-standing patterns of racial dominance and subordination.

The Study

My research assistants and I have conducted in-depth interviews with 166 employers and caregivers. Specifically, we interviewed 79 employers, all but two white, 41 Latina caregivers, 22 white caregivers, 19 Caribbean caregivers, and 5 African-Americans. Due to the informal and semiunderground nature of domestic work, it was not possible to randomly sample employers or employees. We concentrated employer interviews in two selected neighborhoods in the Los Angeles and New York areas[5] and found employers through snowball sampling, starting with lists of women doctors and lawyers supplied by professional associations and with personal contacts. We found caregivers through immigrant social-service agencies, personal contacts, and sometimes employers. In 24 cases, we interviewed employer-employee pairs, although always separately. We also approached caregivers in parks. Interviews were tape-recorded and usually lasted several hours.

The Latina caregivers interviewed mainly came from Mexico and Central America. The Caribbean immigrants came from Jamaica, Grenada, Barbados, Guyana, and Trinidad and Tobago. The small number of African-Americans reflects their declining numbers in domestic work, with most of those remaining in the occupation over forty years old (Milkman, Reese, and Roth 1997; Waldinger 1996). The white caregivers included young women from the American Midwest; au pairs, young women from Western Europe who work as caregivers for a year in exchange for modest wages and a chance to see America; college students, working part-time or taking a year off; and Irish or British immigrants. All the Latina women were interviewed in Spanish by Latina research assistants. Black caregivers were interviewed by an African-American research assistant and by me (a white woman).

We asked caregivers about their backgrounds, occupational histories, attitudes toward the children in their charge, and child-rearing values. We also asked about their degree of comfort in their employers' homes, any conflicts they had with employers, and their own children's care and academic or occupational success. We asked employers about their backgrounds, jobs, prior experiences (if any) with domestic workers, child-rearing styles and values, conflicts, and supervisory style. From both employers and employees we obtained detailed daily schedules.

Race and the Servant Role

Interviews with employers and heads of domestic employment agencies suggest that despite their highly visible presence as nannies, black workers can face problems in getting hired. Employers almost have to go out of their way not to hire them, but some do so. The head of a domestic employment agency in Manhattan said that black women had to be especially careful to present a low-key and unthreatening image when they went on job interviews. White employers in many lines of work have reservations about black workers, especially African-Americans (Waters 1997). Caribbean women benefit from greater employer acceptance, with their accent being a distinct asset. Employers see them as likely to be harder-working and less angry or bitter than African-American women. Despite this greater acceptance, some employers were candid about not wanting to hire a black woman. Sometimes they attribute this to the prejudices of the generation before them, their parents or in-laws. As a Los Angeles mother said, "I could tell she was black on the phone, I guess from her voice or her accent or whatever. And Bill [her husband] wasn't real big on interviewing this woman. The problem was that the woman was black. If his parents came to visit, they'd have a heart attack."

Other employers have a different fear. They worry that if they hire a black woman, it will inevitably create a servantlike relationship in their household. They don't want this, and have no sense that it could be avoided, so they hire an au pair or a Midwestern woman or perhaps an Irish or British immigrant. To these employers, race and hierarchy go hand in hand. This raises the question: Are these employers right? Is it possible for white employers to hire black workers and not create servantlike relationships, or are these inevitable in this personal-service occupation in what remains a racially divided society? What does a servantlike role consist of, and are black workers, in fact, much more likely to be in such roles than are white caregivers? While there is tremendous variability in employment relationships, some general patterns emerge. Relationships can be thought of on a continuum, with the most servantlike being at one end and the most egalitarian at the other. Key factors in defining relationships are the ratio of child care to housework; the extent to which stigmatized tasks or personal service are required of workers; and the level of social distance employers maintain between themselves and the caregiver.

HOUSEWORK. As a group, white caregivers can more successfully limit their tasks than can black or Latina workers. Sometimes parents make a hiring decision on this basis. If they want a lot of housework done, as well as child care, they opt for a black worker. When parents have had multiple caregivers, of different races, there is often a pattern of changing work assignments as well. At one extreme is the British nanny, who comes to the job with a strict definition of what she will and will not do. As the owner of one employment agency in Manhattan said, the type of parents who can afford this type of worker know in advance what she will do. They do not have to be told that she will do the child's laundry, keep the child's room in order, and prepare simple meals for the child, but will not do adult laundry, general cleaning, or meal preparation. Parents who can afford a British nanny hire other workers, usually black or Latina, to do these tasks. At the other extreme is the woman of all work, who does every facet of house cleaning as well as looking after the children. These workers are almost always black or Latina, the women who have the least ability to set a limit on their tasks. While white workers are allowed to specialize in child care, the part of the job that requires the most skill and judgment, most black and Latina workers do not have this choice.

Why don't they? First, there are some who do get jobs where they do only child care or perhaps a little cleaning on top of child care. Sometimes they are just lucky, accidentally meeting up with parents who mean it when they say child care is the first priority. A woman from Trinidad was walking in New York's Penn Station when a police officer approached her and asked if she was a nanny. "I was like, 'You know what? Let me try it.'" The officer hired her on the spot and she worked for three years looking after the family's young son. "Everyone was very nice to me. They're like a family to me. When they were eating, they wanted me to eat with them." She sometimes cleaned on her own initiative, to make life easier for her employers, but her employer would say, "Jennifer, that's not your job. You don't have to do it."

Aside from such accidental good fortune, caregivers' ability to limit their jobs depends partly on their having the resources to leave bad jobs. Many features of caregiving jobs are not evident before being hired; only once on the job are employers and caregivers able to adequately assess each other. Caregivers with resources who find themselves in bad situations leave if they don't like what they find. A white caregiver from Oklahoma who arranged a job in New Jersey through an agency had bad feelings when she first arrived at her employers' house. "When I got there I had this real sour feeling in my stomach." Her parents had accompanied her and told her that she did not have to stay. She also had an aunt in the area, quickly established herself in a local church group, and was in frequent phone contact with the head of the agency that had placed her. Unhappy in her new place, she knew that, if necessary, "I had the option of leaving. I had my own car." She soon had a disagreement with her employers and they ordered her to leave their house immediately. The agency head provided her with a place to stay while she looked for a new job. This woman had an extensive support network, allowing her to take the risk of being forced out of the place where she was both living and working.

Caregivers without support networks have less ability to confidently negotiate working conditions or to leave if they are unhappy in their jobs. They sometimes stay for years in jobs they hate, later asking themselves why they did not take the plunge of leaving sooner. They are, however, afraid that they will not do any better in the job market, or, worst of all, that they might be unemployed for a while, a particular problem for those women supporting children. This can lead some to accept the basic conditions of their jobs as they find them, including, sometimes, heavy workloads or distasteful personal relations.

While some black and Latina employees do not mind housework, those who are happy doing it usually feel they have some control over what they do and when they do it. A woman from Trinidad said that she didn't work for a "slave mistress" and could decide for herself if the books needed dusting or if she would skip housework altogether that day and just play with the kids. For many employees, though, housework involves a higher level of supervision than child care. Employers universally say that child care is the worker's first priority, but on returning home from career wars, parents want peace and order in their homes and many come to expect that the employee they are paying will provide them. They can see if the dishes are done and if the beds are made; they can't see if the worker read books with the child or listened to halting speech or allowed children to make time-consuming choices between red and blue cups. While they may say little, caregivers note the tightening of their lips or their frowns as they survey messy rooms, and the caregivers draw the appropriate conclusions. Middle-class families make enormous economic and emotional investments in their houses and want them to reflect their status (Argyle 1994, 114).

Parents can insist on their idiosyncratic ways of doing things, making lists for workers and establishing daily schedules. This type and level of supervision can make the workers who are subject to it feel that they have indeed entered a servant role, with the parents displaying a sense of superiority or being on a power trip. Detailed instructions undercut women's definitions of competence and can arouse irritation and resistance in employees. The control employers try to exert over house cleaning spills over into the general relationship between employer and employee. These parents might be equally controlling with white employees, but as white workers usually are allowed to concentrate primarily on child care, they more easily escape detailed supervision. Parents very rarely abandon child care when assigning it almost entirely to a domestic employee (although a few parents come close), but many abandon housework. This creates a stratification of jobs in the household, with only domestic employees doing housework; white workers more often have a sense of shared duties with parents, as they concentrate on a task the parents also centrally value and engage in themselves.

STIGMATIZED WORK. Racial elements enter still more profoundly when employers assign workers highly stigmatized types of work or polluted tasks. The most polluted tasks involve body secretions from adults, although some forms of animal care also involve polluted work. Interviews showed a clear racial difference in the assignment of such work. Black and Latina workers are assigned some types of work that white workers almost completely escape. There is a continuum of stigmatized tasks, with the least polluting involving adult laundry and making the parents' bed. Some white workers do these tasks, although those with the most status and power will not do them. They find the work itself demeaning. The couple's bed raises issues of sexuality and body discharges. In some countries local mores forbid domestic workers to enter the parents' bedroom, as Hansen (1989) reports in her study of domestic work in Zambia. In the United States, nearly all caregivers, black and white, feel uncomfortable in the parents' bedroom unless doing a specific task.

The most polluting tasks, from the workers' perspective, are those involving the parents' underwear.[6] Some black and Latina workers discussed their disgust at being asked to deal with underwear stained with menstrual blood or still containing sanitary pads. No white workers mentioned such a situation. A twenty-four-year-old from Barbados worked for a demanding family, looking after two children and doing housework. Being asked to do stigmatized work eventually involved her in an awkward incident with the father in the family.

> She [the mother] would leave her [sanitary pads] and other stuff and I would do her laundry, and I thought, "This is nasty. How could you leave this?" So, one time I took it out and put it in the garbage downstairs.

The father saw it and complained to his wife, who complained to the employee, who replied, "That's not mine, that's yours." This employee added, "Another thing I really hated was when I changed the sheets, there would be used condoms in the sheets and I don't feel that I should have to see that." She concluded that her employers were really nasty people. Cindy, from Tobago, had a similar experience. She was repulsed by the idea of dealing with her employer's underwear:

> I'm not working at picking up nobody's dirty underwear. When she has her period, she put all the pads in and if you tell her about it, she said she hired me to do a job. You either do it or leave.

Cindy angrily resisted, telling her employer, "I'm not going to wash out your panties because when I look at it, it makes me sick." She contrasted her employer's attitude with that of a black family she had previously worked for. In that family,

> I didn't have to do the woman's laundry or the man's, just for the kids. And eventually, when Andrea [the daughter] got a little older, I taught her how to use the laundry machine so she could do her laundry. But on Saturdays she had to wash her underwear in her hands. It was different doing that to coming to New York. This was a black family.

To Cindy, being asked to do demeaning work was tied to her race. "It's like, you know, forget it, I hate these whites, and I just leave [the job]."[7]

Domestic workers can also resent being asked to care for their employers' pets, partly because of the inconvenience and bother it occasions, but also because it can involve tasks they find stigmatizing. The employer of a caregiver from Barbados asked her to wash the dog once a week and then blow-dry the dog's hair. The employer took a picture of her blow-drying the dog, but said, "'Now we don't show people this picture. I don't want people to think this is what I had you doing.' I'm thinking, 'I'm doing it. What are you talking about?' I mean, here's the picture. I'm blow-drying this dog."

Some types of work do not involve human or animal pollution, but still are resented or refused because they entail a subordination workers find unacceptable. Here too there are echoes of long-standing racial issues. Latino farm workers used to be forced to work with a short hoe, despite their finding the bending it required painful and damaging. Similarly, black workers have histories of being ordered to scrub kitchen floors on their hands and knees (Tucker 1988). Requests from employers that evoke these cultural memories meet anger and resistance. Michelle's employer suggested she try scrubbing the grout in the tile floor of the kitchen with a toothbrush. Michelle, a Barbadian, replied, "'No, Jill, I don't think I want to try it.' She was very upset when I said that." The employer later brought Michelle a scrub brush to use on the floor. "When she brought me the brush, it didn't have a stick, it was just a brush. So I'm thinking she wants me to go down on my hands and knees and scrub this. I really hated doing this." Michelle took a stick off a broom and attached it to the scrub brush.

Black and Latina workers do not all experience demands that they do polluted or demeaning work. Many have to struggle with this issue, however, in ways they can find exhausting. They must be relentless in claiming boundaries for their jobs and then defending those boundaries. Open conflicts have costs, so workers sometimes do as Michelle did with the scrub brush, solving the problem by simply taking action on their own. Others try to forestall job definition problems by denying competence in certain tasks. Black workers who were interviewed told employers that they could not cook or could not drive, fearing that they would end up doing meals for the whole family or becoming chauffeurs for kids. Many black workers believe that the payoff for demonstrating skills is not sufficient to counterbalance the extra work entailed by their exercise. As a woman from Tobago said, "I wasn't driving because she was only talking about doing this, but she [the employer] didn't say whether she was going to increase the pay."

PERSONAL SERVICE. When caregivers are asked to provide personal services for employers, they can deeply resent the roles they are asked to play. Even mild-mannered women could become visibly angry when describing serving employers at the table or having to drop what they were doing to rush to an employer who called to them from different parts of the house. It was also notable that the situations that aroused the most anger often involved the parents' friends. They were occasions on which the parents were making an impression on guests; some caregivers said that they were showing off their command over their employees. A caregiver from Guyana commented on her employer's self-esteem problem. One described with distaste the way her employer always referred to her as "my housekeeper" in front of guests.

Others reacted still more adversely to situations where they felt they were treated in demeaning ways. Cindy, a twenty-four-year-old from Tobago, told her employer on first being hired that she did not want to do anything but everyday cleaning: "I even told her that I wasn't going to do what I don't do for myself." The mother, though, asked Cindy to work late one evening to serve friends. Cindy objected, "That's not my job." The employer insisted.

> Like she wanted you to make coffee or bring something to the table, and one of her friends, she never said hi, she just said, "Why don't you let the black girl do it?" I look at her and I said, "Excuse me, did you hire me?"

Cindy became so angered that she left the job and went to a new employer, where she had new problems. She refused to make the father's coffee in the morning and resented the mother demanding that she bring guests at a pool party drinks and towels. "And she had friends, it was like she was showing off." To Cindy, "It's just that, they want to work you as a slave."

When workers are asked to perform personal services, it increases their likelihood of seeing their employers as inconsiderate and selfish. Malinda, a thirty-nine-year-old woman from Guyana, said that her Manhattan employers invited friends over every Friday evening for dinner. After starting work at seven in the morning, she would do most of the cooking for the dinners and then would have to stay up until the guests left to clear the table and do the dishes. "At eleven o'clock you're still sitting there. She was very inconsiderate." She would ask herself, "Are they purposely doing this or what?" Finally, one evening she angrily cleared the table before the guests had left: "That was very rude, but I was that mad." The husband told her that she had a chip on her shoulder. She replied, "It's not a chip. It's a log."

Rarely do white workers provide personal service for employers, although I did interview several Irish workers who had worked in very formal households where they served employers' meals. They seldom stayed long in such jobs, not liking the coldness of the households or their own subordinate roles within them. Of course, many employers would find it embarrassing to have workers serve them; when they hire a caregiver, they want someone to look after their children, not someone to be a maid. Most mothers hire caregivers because they work outside the home, making them far more dependent on the women they hire than were their counterparts in previous eras. They also have far less occasion to ask for personal services, as their interactions with caregivers (at least live-out ones) are usually confined to a few moments at the beginning and end of each workday. Those employers who do want maids/caregivers, though, generally hire black or Latina workers and there are perhaps more such people than those in liberal professional circles realize.

SOCIAL DISTANCE. Servantlike relations have less chance to develop or are undercut when employers develop close or warm social ties with employees. There are some black and Latina workers who have such ties with their employers, most commonly when race differences are not combined with huge class gulfs. Some of the warmest relations between black caregivers and their employers occurred when the employers were on the lower end of the middle class. Often wealthy employers offer better working conditions and rooms for employees than those families that are only marginally able to afford a caregiver. Genuinely close relationships, however, appear most likely when workers and employers have some commonality in experience and education. A woman from Guyana, for example, greatly liked her New Jersey employers, who lived a simple life, and who shared conversation, meals, and daily activities with her. She found their simplicity and kindness offered some solace for her separation from her children.

Overall, though, black and Latina caregivers are not as integrated into their employers' lives and family activities as are white caregivers. They are more likely to eat alone or with the children, but not with the parents, and seldom accompany families on social outings. They talk to employers about the house and children but not about their own worlds and lives. This can make the caregivers feel that they exist for the parents only in their service capacity. A caregiver from Guyana working in Manhattan said that she [her employer] would never ask me about my kids. As far as she's concerned, only her kids are what matters. She didn't even know my daughter was graduating. I don't want them as my friends, but don't want to be treated like that. They don't know anything about me.

When employers hire black caregivers, they usually maintain clear lines of demarcation within the house. Live-in black and Latina employees often have rooms in remote parts of the house, such as basements, where they are unlikely to accidentally encounter family members in hallways. Black workers more often than white ones comment that they feel uncomfortable in the public rooms of the houses where they work. A woman from Trinidad said that it was impossible to feel at ease in her employer's house: "You're supposed to be at home, in your own place. I used to be happy for Friday evening just to get out. It's a whole different atmosphere." Another worker said she was comfortable only in the kitchen because that was where her work was. Sometimes caregivers were too uncomfortable even to accept overtures from parents, with one refusing to join the parents in the family room watching TV, instead watching from the kitchen door.

Isolated from their employers, even inside their own homes, caregivers' social position can cut them off from other people in their employers' neighborhoods. If there are no other caregivers nearby, their lives can become deeply lonely. A woman from Trinidad said of her loneliness in the evenings, "It was terrible. There was not much babysitters around there that I could have talked to. It was just the kids all the time, in the house, doing work." Another, a woman from Barbados, said, "I had no friends that I could see or anything like that. I didn't know anybody I could call up. And then, I couldn't use their phone." The lack of social ties can have deep effects. It removes the most socially isolated caregivers from the mainstream of society, making them feel that they have no identity beyond that of caregiver, no social existence that is acknowledged or accommodated. This reinforces servantlike roles, while white caregivers more often do the work temporarily while maintaining core identities elsewhere. When women do not have alternative identities, they can come to feel, as one expressed it, "like the help." They can feel employer slights acutely, reading them as messages, even if unconscious, that their needs do not matter. A young caregiver from Barbados served her two charges pizza one evening, putting out four slices for them and their two friends.

And then I remembered I left the iron plugged in and I ran downstairs and I came back upstairs and she [the mother] had asked the kids if they wanted more pizza. She gave each a second slice. I looked in the box and it was empty. She didn't even say, "Michelle, would you like a slice?" That brought tears to my eyes.

Intrusion of Racial Issues from outside the Household

Thus far I have suggested that servantlike roles are more common among black and Latina workers than among white caregivers. Most conflicts between employers and employees do not take on a distinctly racial tone, with race operating more as a background factor, affecting employers' views of how closely linked to their employee they want to be and what tasks it would be possible to assign.

This does not mean, however, that race does not figure directly in the experiences of black domestic workers. Most black and Latina domestics in New York and Los Angeles are immigrants and they must adjust to American racial attitudes, having come from countries with different racial dynamics. For black workers, in particular, American racial attitudes can come as a shock; in their home countries shade is more important and biological definitions of race are less important (Foner 1987). Some come from countries, such as Guyana or Trinidad, with complex racial groups and identities and polarized black/white identities are new to them. Waters (1997) reports that Caribbean immigrants adapt to American racial attitudes by gradually losing their optimistic expectations that whites will treat them as individuals. The reality of American racial boundaries strikes them and some can no longer maintain confidence that race will not affect their interactions with others. Having been raised in countries where race is not so pervasive a force, however, even as Caribbean immigrants become angrier, they do not entirely lose their ease in crossing racial boundaries, which makes white Americans more comfortable with them than with African-Americans.

The processes Waters describes can be observed in the experiences of Caribbean domestic workers in the United States. First, they almost invariably describe their shock at discovering just how strongly race defines Americans' experiences. They respond with varying amounts of dismay, anger, and resignation. A Jamaican caregiver said that she had learned, "This is a racist country. I see it all the time." When she first came to the United States, she did not think about race much, but gradually became aware that whites could be hostile to her, or even fearful, based on her race. She first noticed that store owners watched blacks more closely in stores.

> I didn't pay them any mind but then one night when I bought a new car I got lost in this white neighborhood. I was trying to get directions and approached this white woman and she flinched as I approached her. Then she started running across the street like I was trying to rob her or something. Then I asked another white person and the person said, "Get away from me, black bitch."

She added, "I was mad, sometimes I still get mad. It's sad, but I try not to let it get to me." A worker from Trinidad said with resignation, "Say you're black, whites just don't like blacks. That's the way all white people are. The younger ones, they're all right, they're more cool, down to earth. Not the older ones." Another Trinidadian described her surprise on finding how race conscious the United States was: "I never heard about it until I came up here to live. I never heard about it in Trinidad. Believe me. I was surprised." She, like most other caregivers, said that she tried to rise above it. "I adjust for it and you know, I don't really pay them no mind. I try not to let it bother me."

Some Caribbean immigrants emphasize that they do not share the racial anger they attribute to African-Americans. A caregiver from Guyana said:

I have a girlfriend who was living with an American guy and we used to have horrible fights. I used to say to him, "I cannot understand why everything is a black-or-white issue." I could not feel the way he was feeling because I don't know what slavery is. I mean, in 1962, when they were riding at the back of the bus, we already owned the buses in Guyana.

Even she, however, became more racially conscious after being in New York for some years. "You get to New York and then you realize, you were black all the time."

Rising above racial anger is made somewhat easier for Caribbean immigrants in domestic work because blacks have won some measure of social equality. Cindy, from Tobago, said that masters used to yell at slaves, who were unable to reply. "Today, it ain't nothing about slaves. Nobody's supposed to yell at you, or disrespect you. [If they do], you shouldn't take it. Today everybody should be outspoken." The average employer is quite aware that racial conflict in the household would be highly undesirable. This does not mean, though, that racial issues do not arise. Even if the employers have incentives to be careful, others around them may not feel the same pressure toward discretion.

Few employees mentioned any overtly racist comments on the part of employers. Sometimes they were bothered by employers' avoidance of contact. A caregiver said her employer put items directly into her daughter's hand, but pushed things at the caregiver. Domestic workers also resented it when employers brought up racially charged issues that put them on the spot. One father, for example, persisted in trying to speak with his employee about the O. J. Simpson case. "He would ask a question about the O. J. Simpson trial and all that stupidness and I would be like, 'I don't want to get into it with you.' He just wanted to bring up some racial garbage and then he would be like, 'Oh, I think he did it, what do you think?' And I was like, 'I won't comment on that.'" Her employers, she said, "talked to her as if they owned her, like white folks talk."

While caregivers sometimes found employer behavior and comments offensive, almost never did an employer offer any overt racial insult. Friends and relatives of employers sometimes did, however, presumably because they had less of a tie to the worker and felt less hesitation about expressing negative feelings. A twenty-five-year-old woman, Kern, from Trinidad said that she liked her employers very much and never thought they acted superior to her. The husband's father, however, didn't like blacks. Kern described him as obsessed with racial hatred. She endured several tirades from him, but her own employer apologized for his father's attitude.

Another worker had not thought of her employer as racist, but one time when carrying laundry up the stairs she overheard a discussion between the employer and a friend that changed her mind. The two were commenting on a story in the newspaper about a black high-school senior who was killed at a school dance when a chunk of the ceiling fell on her. The worker overheard the friend say, "Well, one less nigger." The mother said something in assent, then was beside herself when she realized the worker had overheard the exchange. Another worker left her job because her employer's friends angered her. "When they came over, they say, 'Why won't the black girl do this?' And I said, 'My name is not black girl.'"

In other situations, racial pressures from the larger society intrude on the worker while she is doing her job. Marilyn, an African-American, said that "the race issue surfaced more outside the home than in the home, when I had to interact with society." Black caregivers pushing white babies in strollers sometimes felt under surveillance from white passersby. They believed their identity was clear to all and that they were vulnerable to community judgment. Marilyn commented that "I felt I was being scrutinized closer than a white woman with a white child. I felt uncomfortable because I think that people were watching me, saying if this woman hurts this child, or if she doesn't watch the child correctly, they're going to report me to whomever."

Other workers reported that white people stared at them when they were out with the kids or that white parents in parks avoided talking to them. "Sometimes they just say hi to the kids and they look at you like, 'Who are you?'" One described an incident she witnessed at a park when a black caregiver kicked a white child. A white woman saw this and assailed the caregiver, saying "Why are you hitting her? They hire you not to hit. You black folks." The caregiver defended herself and the white woman then called the police (who took no action). The white community exerted far more surveillance in the era of the racial caste system, but even today black caregivers can feel subjected to a scrutiny that makes them feel onstage in the presence of whites. They recognize that in the public arena, they do not have a purely individual relationship with their employers and their charges, but one that potentially involves a larger, racially defined community. A black woman pushing a white baby in a stroller acquires a symbolic identity in American society and black women find that they are not free to discard this identity, with all its implications for how they are viewed or treated even by unknown whites.

In short, race helps structure the experiences of blacks and whites in domestic employment relationships. It tends to increase social distance between the parties, it is a factor in the greater assignment of housework to some workers rather than the others, with the creation of subsequent tensions over control of the work, and it can lead to black domestic workers experiencing incidents with racial overtones while on the job.

Conflicts and Conflict Management Strategies

Eaton reports that in the era of the racial caste system, black domestic workers were considered tractable by their employers. This docility had doubtless been developed by slavery, and it is not unlikely that it has been still further cultivated in these later days by their knowledge that losing their places in service may mean inability to get work of any kind for an indefinite period (1996, 481). The situation is considerably different today, although workers who are newly arrived in the country and very young workers are often particularly hesitant about resisting employee directives. They may stay with a first employer for several years, but gradually become aware that they could do better in the market. A young Barbadian caregiver worked for a demanding employer for three and a half years and commented on her own naïveté: "For some reason I felt that I had to do whatever she wanted. I don't know why. I guess maybe I was young and immature. I'm not going to do that again."

While young employees may not dare openly resist their employers, more experienced or bolder workers recognize that they have some cards to play. Some black employees recognize that white employers can be afraid of open anger from a black woman. Many whites fear violence from blacks (Bobo and Kluegel 1997, 118; Feagin and Vera 1995, 136, 152). Domestic workers themselves do not usually arouse anxieties about violence (although their husbands or boyfriends can), but some learn they can play on employers' fears by trying to intimidate them with firm or angry looks. A woman from Tobago, for example, said that if her employers asked her to do something she did not want to do, "I just look at them like this, in a mean kind of way." The employers usually retreat. Others also described using the look; no white or Latina workers mentioned this resistance technique, suggesting that it is most effective when it taps into a preexisting white fear. Looks, in fact, are a general means of intimidation across racial lines, often used by whites against blacks (Feagin 1991, 110).

A white employer on New York's Upper West Side described the impact of receiving the look. She and her husband had hired a Jamaican woman to look after their new baby and arranged with her that she would do some cleaning as well as child care. On the first day of her new job, the mother came home and noticed that no housework had been done. She commented on it to the care-giver, who fixed her with an angry stare. The mother quailed. The caregiver stayed on for seven years and never did any housework.

Some black caregivers described situations where they said they had the sud-den shock of realizing that their employers were afraid of them. An African-American woman worked for New York employers for several years and became deeply attached to their four-year-old son. The job came to an end one day when the boy was irritable and demanded that she iron a napkin for him; after she ironed it and thrust it at him, he told his mother that she had burned him. The mother would not listen to the caregiver's explanation and fired her on the spot. The mother told her to return that weekend to get her final check. When the caregiver appeared on the doorstep, the mother was momentarily startled to see her:

> She stood back from the door and she was scared of me. I did not show any rage in my face or anything. I was very passive on the outside but inside I was very angry. And that's the time it really kicked in. This woman is really scared of me because I am black.

Employers themselves sometimes mentioned fears that seemed race con-nected. One father who planned to hire from among a pool of Caribbean work-ers hired a private investigator to look into their backgrounds. He said that he worried a Caribbean woman might have brothers or uncles in Attica who could show up on his doorstep. While this father was unusual, a number of employers worried that an angry fired caregiver might take revenge on them. This fear was much more pronounced in regard to black workers than to white ones. It sometimes led employers to lie about their reasons for letting a worker go; even if they had evidence of malfeasance, they would try to arrange a more or less cordial parting, lying about the reason they no longer wanted the worker and offering severance pay.

To avoid situations of ill-will, employers sometimes consciously try to remain pleasant and to smile at their employees. Sometimes the employers' behavior is interpreted in racial terms. A black worker from Trinidad said that her employer always gave her a fake smile as she left. The interviewer asked, "What kind of smile?" and the worker replied, "You know how white people smile?"

In addition to trying, with mixed success, to minimize tension through smiles and small courtesies, employers and employees also reduce conflicts by lying to each other. Deception helps reduce open conflict, even when each side suspects the other of lying. Workers worry that employers are not honest about their plans to replace them. As one said, "No matter how nice they are to you, you always have to watch your back." A number of employers said that they thought it was best to line up a new employee before firing an old one. Workers have many reasons to lie to employers: They describe themselves as lying about why they cannot come in to work, with one routinely telling employers that her small daughter was in the hospital; they sometimes need a mega-lie, because employers pressure them to come in anyway if they give a lesser reason for being away. Sometimes lies can get workers into complicated situations. A young woman decided to use the occasion of a New York blizzard to avoid going into work, despite her employer's having given her detailed instructions on how to use the subways that were still running.

> I called her back on a pay phone, I lied to her, and I said, "I am stuck at Broadway and Nassau." I remember passing there years before. I said, "I am beside myself, I am upset, I've been out here all morning trying to get out there." So she was like, "Once you get home, I want you to call me and tell me exactly what trains you took and how'd you get there and what you did." This woman actually wants to know so she knows I wasn't lying. So I said, "OK, I'll fix her."

The caregiver went to a train station and studied the subway map, eventually coming up with a plausible account of her travel.

In African-American folklore, songs and stories celebrate triumphs won by cleverness or trickery (Levine 1977). As African-Americans gradually attained greater power, the folklore celebrated stories of direct confrontations as well as clever deceptions. The crucial change marking black folklore after emancipation was the development of a group of heroes who confronted power and authority directly, without guile and tricks (Levine 1977, 385). Black domestic workers do now confront employers; such confrontations occur over stigmatized work or over issues where racial respect appears at stake. In power struggles with employers when workers are not ready to risk being fired, or when the issue is not crucial, workers can find the best course of action is to do as they please with a cover (however thin it might sometimes be) of duty thwarted by untoward circumstances.

Because of mutual deception, unsatisfactory relationships can continue for some time without surface conflict. The worker's mode of exiting the job often provides a crucial clue about the quality of the relationship. When employees like their employers, they give notice or perhaps stay until their employers find a replacement. The caregiver from Trinidad employed by the police officer decided to leave her job because she needed more money, but did her best to make the transition easy for her employer:

> I gave her two weeks' notice. I told her that I can't do this job no more and I'm so sorry and I thanked her for everything. I was very comfortable there. That's why I put my cousin on the job. I didn't want to get anybody else because they were so sweet to me.

When they do not like their employers, workers sometimes maximize the inconvenience caused by their departure. One woman, a live-in employee, secretly took bits of clothing and personal articles away with her each weekend when she went to her room in the city. Finally, one Friday she packed up the last of her possessions and carried them away, with her employers none the wiser. She anticipated her employers' dismay as they fruitlessly awaited her return and then discovered her empty room. Another caregiver waited to leave until her employers told her that one Monday they both had exceptionally busy workdays. She left the Friday before with the certainty of knowing they would be frantic when she did not appear Monday morning.

Caregivers, Children, and Racial Consciousness

The white, black, and Latina caregivers interviewed for the larger project on the cross-class socialization of children varied greatly in how attached they were to the children in their charge. It was not simply a difference between caregivers, but in the attachment a particular caregiver felt to different children she had looked after. No caregivers interviewed disliked all the children they had ever cared for, but some were generally more open than others. In the case of black (and also Latina) caregivers, however, relations with employers' children can be complicated by racial matters. Caregivers can be critical of mothers for passing on the work of the household to them and see the employers' children as also being raised to expect others to do for them (Wrigley 1995). These issues are more pronounced with older than with younger children. In race-divided societies, caregivers can feel they are asked to give their all to children who may come to devalue them. In the South, black domestic workers had a saying, "I never met a white child over twelve that I liked" (Tucker 1988, 61). While no domestic worker interviewed made a similar statement, in some cases conflicts with children took on a racial aspect.

With young children, race is not an issue except in unusual circumstances. Most caregivers interviewed took pleasure in the young children's lack of racial consciousness. They enjoyed the children's innocence, their lack of understanding of the symbolic, socially created effects of being black in a white-dominated society. Two remarked on how their young charges had denied that the caregivers were black, telling them that they were brown. "We would be talking about something, and we'd be saying, 'Black people.' The kids would say, 'Mommy, not black, brown. They're brown people.' You know, this stuff is taught. These kids don't see us as black people, they see us as brown people."

In a few cases, racial issues intruded on relations between caregivers and children. A woman from Trinidad was hired to look after a baby whose mother had died in childbirth. There were four older children in the family, with the oldest being a boy of fourteen. Marcia disliked the older children, saying that "99 percent of the time, they were on my nerves." After a conflict with the eight-year-old girl, Marcia spoke harshly to her. "I get up and she started screaming because she think I'm black, and I shouldn't be speaking to her like that. The child said, 'You're not my mother. You got the wrong color.'" After a fight with the five-year-old boy, he called her a black bitch. These very bad relations between caregiver and children did not preclude occasional expressions of sympathy on her part for their predicament and for their widowed father, but most of the time Marcia felt too distant from the older children to make any effort to reach them, a feeling of distance that was increased by the interjection of race into their other conflicts.

Another caregiver also had a racial take on the children in her care. She deeply resented her employers, feeling that she was not treated with respect and that her employers acted as if they owned her. She did not like the five-year-old girl in her care, saying that she talked too much, and she described the eight-year-old boy as rude. "And the baby, the baby was nice, but I don't like white people. I don't like them."

Most caregivers do not develop a hard ideological view of racial issues, priding themselves rather on their ability to deal with people as individuals. The few who do can find their jobs exquisitely painful, and even their relations with the children in their charge can be affected. Many say they know that they could not handle the work if they allowed themselves to become depressed or angry about slights and some explicitly preach policies of forbearance. This orientation allows them to cope with a service occupation that inevitably exposes them to a range of racial attitudes, including some hostile ones. Domestic workers are not well insulated from attitudes of outsiders, as they do not control who enters their workplace, and their subordinate status makes it stressful or risky for them to call their employers' friends or relatives on racial slights. They do, though, risk challenges when their self-respect demands it or when they have the backing of their employers.

Conclusions

Is domestic work merely another occupation, low on the list but not qualitatively different from other occupations? Or does it carry a special racial charge?

There are no simple answers to this question, but interviews with children's caregivers and employers suggest two conclusions. First, black workers generally do not experience the occupation the same way as do white women. Second, despite this, racial oppression does not appear to be as central to the occupation as it was during the era of the racial caste system, when black women were funneled into domestic work and faced lifetimes of subordination. For immigrant black women, in particular, the job now serves more as it once did for white immigrants, as a readily available means of employment open to those without formal credentials, but entered with an expectation of something better, if not for themselves then certainly for their daughters. This outlook helps give caregivers the patience and discipline to at least tolerate their circumstances and the servantlike conditions their employment can entail.

While there are reasons to expect that this occupation has lost its racially oppressive heritage, black workers fall more readily into a servant role, pushed there by employer expectations but kept there by lack of resources, which keep them working for families even when they feel their situation is distasteful. In a stratified market, whites can more readily get the better jobs and, since job quality is hard to gauge in advance in the domestic market, can move on if they have made an error. The servantlike role has several aspects: on average, black and Latina workers do more housework, which not only increases the sheer amount of work and downgrades the part of it that requires the most judgment and skill, the child rearing, but involves workers in tighter supervision. They do more personal service and stigmatized tasks, which white workers almost entirely avoid, not so much because they refuse the tasks as because employers do not ask them to do them. And finally, occurring as both cause and effect of their more servantlike roles, they are overall treated with more social distance than are white employees.

It would be a mistake, however, to see domestic work as unchanged from its earlier history. Analysis of these women's experiences shows that they have not only inherited some of the problems of the African-Americans who long labored in the occupation before them, but also some of the victories of the civil rights struggles. They come into a political and economic system where to be black is to be, on average, poorer than whites; to be kept at a social remove from whites; to be subject to racial distrust and prejudice. Yet they also can claim the civil rights heritage and with it the idea, which white employers now also recognize, that to be black is not to be passively subordinate, but to be a person who can potentially raise a challenge. White fear of blacks stems partly from media portrayals of crime and violence and from the social realities of life in America's inner-city ghettos. It also, though, has a more positive root, a recognition that black workers, whether in factories, offices, or homes, will resist where they can. White employers of domestic workers know this too; many themselves applaud the changes brought by the civil rights revolution and even those who do not are usually careful not to openly insult the black women they hire. In this, they differ from their forebears, for whom expressions of racial superiority were not even considered insulting, but a simple statement of natural fact (Palmer 1989).

This, along with changed attitudes about racial issues, including much greater support for social equality, and employer vulnerability due to being out of the house all day, has led to changed power relations in private households and to greater employer caution. Even irritable or demanding employers usually maintain some awareness that their children could pay a price for their actions. When mothers stayed home, they could directly supervise domestic employees, but now they must depend on maintaining goodwill. In addition, deference requirements have diminished as parents concentrate more on securing child care than personal service. Domestic workers used to learn rituals of table service (Clark-Lewis 1994) and personal service was so important a part of their work that artists frequently depicted servants engaged in intimate acts of assistance to their mistresses (O'Leary 1996, 234–40). Employers today, however, dispense with ritualized meals in favor of the microwave and meals bought on the way home. They buy many services commercially rather than relying on domestic workers. Most employers and employees manage to work out at least passable relationships with each other and some are much better than passable, rising to genuine mutual liking and respect, but in a private household, with one adult the personal employee of another, and with the two of different races, there remain many opportunities for disagreements and misunderstandings.

It is striking that black workers presented a variety of ways race affected their working lives as caregivers, but few saw race as the defining element of their experiences. This was particularly true of the immigrants. Deeply pragmatic, most see their lives as containing numerous obstacles that they must overcome through hard work, self-restraint, and a refusal to allow themselves to be sidetracked by distress over racial slights. Focused on upward mobility, almost to a person they fiercely declare that their daughters will not do the work they are doing. As a thirty-four-year-old from Trinidad said, "I will work my way up, I'll make sure she [her daughter] gets a good education, so she won't have to be doing this." They feel that only circumstance accounts for them being one down and their employers being one up: A caregiver from Guyana said her employers, corporate lawyers, earned millions each year, but that "if I had had the opportunity Americans had, if I'd been born here, some of the employers might have been working for me."

It is a question whether immigrant caregivers will retain their optimism, which helps them see their jobs as stepping-stones to better lives. Without the optimism, the job's servantlike conditions could be an extraordinary oppression to the spirit, which undoubtedly accounts for African-Americans' massive abandonment of domestic work. Despite an apparent need to control as many occupational niches as possible, given high rates of unemployment, African-American women have made a collective judgment on domestic work. This type of highly personal service work is experienced differently by black and white women, and only black women who feel they have a future are likely to endure the job's costs. For those without such confidence, it is not an ordinary occupation, but a psychically costly one, even if the costs are borne more easily by those newly arrived in the United States.

Notes

I am indebted to Stephen Steinberg for stimulating discussions on race and domestic work, to Michèle Lamont for editorial and intellectual contributions, and to Linda Benbow and Robin Isserles for interviewing and research assistance.

1. Interestingly, while most research on domestic workers stresses the workers' subordination, the study of white caregivers takes a very different tack, arguing that these women can potentially present a competitive threat to the mothers who employ them. The implicit contrast with the rest of the literature is never developed, because, as with other studies, no comparative analysis of the experiences of different types of workers is presented.

2. Romero (1992) also emphasizes that the choice to do domestic work must be understood as offering women advantages compared to other kinds of work; specifically, those doing cleaning can control their hours better than workers with other employment. Unlike Waldinger, however, she also emphasizes the stigma associated with domestic work.

3. Census data show that whites are disproportionately represented as caregivers, compared to their overall numbers in domestic work, while black workers are relatively underrepresented in this sector of domestic work (Milkman, Reese, and Roth 1997).

4. All classified ads for domestic workers were collected for one week in January and one week in August for years in the midpoint of each decade from the 1920s through the 1960s. In addition, ads placed by domestic workers seeking positions were collected.

5. In the Los Angeles area, these were a middle-class area of Santa Monica and an upper-middle-class LA neighborhood just east of UCLA. In the New York area, they were a New Jersey suburb, Englewood, and the Upper West Side of Manhattan.

6. Some polluted tasks are not only distasteful, but activate deep cultural taboos. This is the case for Caribbean workers asked to deal with women's dirty underwear. Anderson (1991) reports that domestic workers in Jamaica are angered when they are asked to do work they consider unclean, too personal, or beyond the bounds of their agreements with their employers. Washing female underwear arouses the most disgust, far more than washing male underwear. Dealing with dirty female underwear "constitutes an area of greatest taboo in West Indian societies. The acceptance of this taboo is so widespread that it seldom becomes a matter for discussion, as little girls are taught

from the earliest possible age to wash their own panties, and female underwear is carefully separated from all other clothing and linen in the home" (1991, 22–23).

7. The importance of this issue can be seen in a comment by a third-generation African-American domestic worker. She told an interviewer that she fared better than her grandmother or mother had before her: "The greatest difference is in the way the work is done. Mama and Grandmama did more physical labor than I do." She continued that she only had to do laundry for the household, adding, "And one thing I like is they don't give me underwear with menstrual blood in it to wash" (quoted in Barnes 1993, 26).

References

Anderson, Patricia. 1991. "Protection and Oppression: A Case Study of Domestic Service in Jamaica." *Labour, Capital, and Society* 24(1) (April): 10–39.

Argyle, Michael. 1994. *The Psychology of Social Class.* London: Routledge.

Barnes, Annie J. 1993. "White Mistresses and African-American Domestic Workers: Ideals for Change." *Anthropological Quarterly* 66:22–36.

Bobo, Lawrence, and James R. Kluegel. 1997. "Status, Ideology, and Dimensions of Whites' Racial Beliefs and Attitudes: Progress and Stagnation." *Racial Attitudes in the 1990s: Continuity and Change,* edited by Steven A. Tuch and Jack K. Martin. Westport, Conn.: Praeger.

Brown, Rupert. 1995. *Prejudice.* Oxford: Blackwell.

Button, James W. 1989. *Blacks and Social Change.* Princeton: Princeton University Press.

Carnoy, Martin. 1994. *Faded Dreams.* New York: Cambridge University Press.

Clark-Lewis, Elizabeth. 1994. *Living In, Living Out.* Washington: Smithsonian Institute.

Colen, Shellee. 1989. "'Just a Little Respect': West Indian Domestic Workers in New York City." In *Muchachas No More: Household Workers in Latin America and the Caribbean,* edited by Elsa M. Chaney and Mary Garcia Castro. Philadelphia: Temple University Press.

Collins, Patricia Hill. 1997. "Defining Black Feminist Thought." In *The Second Wave: A Reader in Feminist Theory,* edited by Linda Nicholson. New York: Routledge.

Dill, Bonnie Thornton. 1994. *Across the Boundaries of Race and Class.* New York: Garland.

Du Bois, W. E. B. [1899] 1996. *The Philadelphia Negro.* Philadelphia: University of Pennsylvania Press.

Eaton, Isabel. [1899] 1996. *Special Report on Negro Domestic Service in the Seventh Ward Philadelphia.* In Du Bois 1996.

Erickson, Alana J. 1996–97. "'I Don't Want Her in My Home': Bias against African-American Domestic Servants, 1910–1980." *Race and Reason* 3:26–31.

Fairchilds, Cissie C. 1984. *Domestic Enemies.* Baltimore: Johns Hopkins University Press.

Feagin, Joe R. 1991. "The Continuing Significance of Race: Antiblack Discrimination in Public Places." *American Sociological Review* 56:101–16.

Feagin, Joe R., and Hernan Vera. 1995. *White Racism.* New York: Routledge.

Foner, Nancy. 1987. "The Jamaicans: Race and Ethnicity among Migrants in New York City." In *New Immigrants in New York,* edited by Nancy Foner. New York: Columbia University Press.

Glenn, Evelyn Nakano. 1986. *Issei, Nisei, War Bride.* Philadelphia: Temple University Press.

Gray, Brenda Clegg. 1993. *Black Female Domestics during the Depression in New York City, 1930–1940.* New York: Garland.

Gregson, Nicky, and Michelle Low. 1994. *Servicing the Middle Classes.* London: Routledge.

Hall, Stuart. 1996. "The New Ethnicities." In *Ethnicity,* edited by John Hutchinson and Anthony D. Smith. New York: Oxford University Press.

Hansen, Karen Tranberg. 1989. *Distant Companions.* Ithaca: Cornell University Press.

Hondagneu-Sotelo, Pierrette. 1994. "Regulating the Unregulated? Domestic Workers' Social Networks." *Social Problems* 41:50–64.

Hunter, Tera W. 1997. *To 'Joy My Freedom.* Cambridge: Harvard University Press.

Jaynes, Gerald David, and Robin M. Williams, Jr., eds. 1989. *A Common Destiny.* Washington: National Academy Press.

Jones, Jacqueline. 1985. *Labor of Love, Labor of Sorrow.* New York: Basic.

Katzman, David M. 1981. *Seven Days a Week.* Urbana: University of Illinois Press.

Levine, Lawrence W. 1977. *Black Culture and Consciousness.* Oxford: Oxford University Press.

Macdonald, Cameron Lynne. 1996. "Shadow Mothers: Nannies, *Au Pairs,* and Invisible Work." In *Working in the Service Society,* edited by Cameron Lynne Macdonald and Carmen Sirianni. Philadelphia: Temple University Press.

Massey, Douglas S., and Nancy A. Denton. 1993. *American Apartheid.* Cambridge: Harvard University Press.

McAll, Christopher. 1992. *Class, Ethnicity, and Social Inequality.* Montreal: McGill-Queen's University Press.

Milkman, Ruth, Ellen Reese, and Benita Roth. 1997. "The Macrosociology of Paid Domestic Labor." A revised version of a paper presented at the annual meeting of the American Sociological Association, New York, August 1996. Department of Sociology, UCLA.

O'Leary, Elizabeth L. 1996. *At Beck and Call.* Washington: Smithsonian.

Palmer, Phyllis. 1989. *Domesticity and Dirt.* Philadelphia: Temple University Press.

Rollins, Judith. 1985. *Between Women.* Philadelphia: Temple University Press.

Romero, Mary. 1992. *Maid in the U.S.A.* New York: Routledge.

Schuman, Howard, and Charlotte Steeh. 1996. "The Complexity of Racial Attitudes in America." In *Origins and Destinies: Immigration, Race, and Ethnicity in the United States,* edited by Sylvia Pedraza and Ruben G. Rumbaut. Belmont, Calif.: Wadsworth.

Schuman, Howard, Charlotte Steeh, Lawrence Bobo, and Maria Krysan. 1997. *Racial Attitudes.* Rev. ed. Cambridge: Harvard University Press.

Steinberg, Stephen. 1995. *Turning Back.* Boston: Beacon.

Stigler, George J. 1946. *Domestic Servants in the United States 1900–1940.* Occasional Paper no. 24. April. New York: National Bureau of Economic Research.

Tomaskovic-Devey, Donald. 1993. *Gender and Racial Inequality at Work.* Ithaca, N.Y.: ILR.

Tucker, Susan. 1988. *Telling Memories among Southern Women.* Baton Rouge: Louisiana State University Press.

Waldinger, Roger. 1996. *Still the Promised City?* Cambridge: Harvard University Press.

Waters, Mary C. 1997. *Ethnic Options.* Berkeley: University of California.

Wrigley, Julia. 1995. *Other People's Children.* New York: Basic.

part two
class and culture

above "people above"? status and worth among white and black workers

michèle lamont

How do black and white workingmen conceptualize the relationship between social status and worth? To what extent do they grant respect to others on the basis of their socioeconomic status? What other criteria do they use in their assessment of others? I explore these issues by analyzing how workingmen assess those that rank above them on the social-status scale—those they refer to as "the upper half," "professionals," "managers," "businessmen," "the rich," "the powerful," "the elite," "the upper class," or "the upper middle class." I am concerned with how workers evaluate these groups, as well as the traits, characteristics, and statuses associated with them.[1] Evidence presented herein suggests that while American workingmen identify with and positively evaluate the upper half, its positional attributes (particularly money), and cultural dispositions (particularly ambition), most also have at their disposal a set of standards for evaluating worth that is independent of social status. This alternative set of standards is highly moral and identifies worth not with the possession of positional goods (i.e., of scarce goods that can be the property of only a few, such as prestige, money, and power), but with goods (and attributes) that are available to all, such as rich interpersonal relations and sincerity.[2] While the Weberian theory of status posits that approvals and disapprovals are bases for social status (Milner 1993), American working-class men often explicitly refuse to associate one with the other. In other words, they evaluate worth on the basis of moral criteria, and give considerable weight to the latter in the evaluation of the status of a person, while dissociating status from socioeconomic status. The standards they use to evaluate worth allow them to locate themselves at the top of a hierarchy. This constitutes an interesting paradox from the perspective of sociological theory and suggests that (1) we need to rework our conceptualization of the relationship between status and socioeconomic status and (2) we need to be careful not to impute predefined conceptions of this relationship to others.

These findings also challenge the literature on the culture of the American working class that stresses the identification of this group with middle-class values.[3] They most starkly contrast with Richard Sennett and Jonathan Cobb's classic study, *The Hidden Injuries of Class* (1972), which argues that in the United States, the working man is deprived of dignity because it can be acquired only through upward mobility and the achievement of the American dream (p. 22). These findings also challenge Lillian B. Rubin's *Families on the Faultline* (1994), which presents workers as passive victims of broader social forces. By comparison, I show that workers find meaning, value, and worth in their own lives by downplaying the status criteria that are the dominant currency in the upper-middle-class world. While these discrepancies might be explained by time lag and differences in the socioeconomic status of interviewees, they are nevertheless worth exploring.[4]

Do black and white workers differ in this respect? I suggest that African-American workers more resemble the upper half than their white counterparts because they are more likely to define success in terms of economic success, to believe that their quality of life is inferior to that of the upper half, and that ambition is a positive characteristic. However, many blacks have very negative views of the moral character of the upper half and emphasize its exploitative nature. Their experience with racism makes them less likely to believe that upward mobility is an indicator of moral character. Hence, black men have more contradictory positions toward mainstream definitions of worth than white workers do. In the conclusion, I briefly sketch elements of multicausal explanations for these differences that take into consideration economic barriers that black and white workers meet as well as the cultural repertoires to which they have privileged access.[5]

This chapter draws on 75 in-depth interviews conducted with randomly sampled blue-collar workers and low-status white-collar workers living in the New York suburbs. This includes 30 African-American blue-collar workers, 30 Euro-American blue-collar workers, and 15 Euro-American white-collar workers (for details, see the methodological appendix). I focus on interracial differences and downplay differences between Euro-American blue-collar and low-status white-collar workers.[6] These interviews provide us with a glimpse into a world in which taken-for-granted measuring sticks and points of reference are often different from those that prevail in a middle-class world.

First, I describe Euro-American interviewees who have a positive view of the upper half and of its social and cultural attributes, particularly money, power, and ambition. Second, I discuss negative moral evaluations that white workingmen make of the moral character of "people above" and of their positional characteristics. Third, I consider the positive evaluations that workers make of their own moral worth and their discourse on egalitarianism and alternative definitions of success. These are used to justify positioning themselves above (and at times side to side with) middle-class people and to demonstrate that worth should not be equated with social status. In the last section, I address the cultural specificity of African-Americans, focusing on differences between black and white blue-collar workers.

White Workers Discuss Status and Worth

THE IMPORTANCE OF HIGH SOCIAL STATUS. Many Euro-American workers I talked to respect attributes that are hallmarks of "people above," namely money/wealth and authority.[7] As a mechanic puts it, "People are brought up in this society to respect money, power, and good looks. I think very close in that order too. Money, power, good looks. It's a role model. Mother Theresa is a role model only to certain categories of people. Not a general role model." These men attribute great legitimacy to wealth-producing activities, and they engage or hope to engage in such activities by acquiring real estate or getting involved in financial speculation and entrepreneurial risk taking. For instance, a policeman in his thirties explains that "by buying homes and renting them out, I'm a landlord and I get a positive cash flow. I get money I didn't physically go out and work for, which is what I like." He perceives himself as successful because his income gives him freedom, i.e., an ability to consume. He says, "I own three homes. I'll be living in a $300 thousand house when it's all said and done. I'm only thirty-four years old. . . . I got a boat, a jet ski, a motorcycle. I can pretty much do what I want to do, which a lot of people can't." Similarly, a worker explains that his daughter is successful because she is making $50 thousand a year. A third of the white interviewees mention economic status as a proof of success, which they may or may not equate with personal worth.

In an interesting twist, several individuals who have relatively low incomes also use financial status to show that they are successful. However, to do so, they redefine appropriate economic standards. For instance, an office clerk says that he is successful because "I can support myself, which is hard to do these days. I bought a brand-new car in June and I'm paying for that. It's not paid for but I am enjoying the new car and everything." Others describe themselves as middle class although they have relatively low incomes. One interviewee considers himself middle class because "I'm not out of work. I'm not to the point where I'm living in a cardboard box or living on welfare, food stamps, or you know. . . . I can take care of myself and my family." Still others explain that they would like to be part of the upper half to benefit from the advantages provided by a high income. It is notable in the case of a firefighter who says that in a next life, he would rather come back upper middle class "for the monetary reason. . . . I'd like to try upper class, sure . . . being able to join a country club, not having to go to the public golf course. Being able to afford a decent-size boat to fish salt water. Not having to worry about, you know, scraping up the pennies. Better house, whatever."[8]

These white working-class men put more emphasis on high income than education in evaluating peoples' worth, perhaps because they believe the former to be more within their reach than the latter. This is illustrated by a heating system specialist who says that "everybody thinks that a tradesman is stupid. . . . In a lifetime, it will be proven that a tradesman makes more money than someone who went to college—except for Yale or Harvard or something like that." By putting high income above education as a general criterion of evaluation, these men sustain the possibility of locating themselves higher than the college educated in the social hierarchy.

A few white workers also have a positive view of authority, another positional attribute of people above. They do not associate authority with domination or control. For instance, a broadcast worker says: "I don't think that for me, to show up five days a week and do certain things all the time in turn for them paying me to do this job [means that they are] controlling me. It's a contract that we have. I mean, I don't think it's wrong for me to expect certain things. . . . Because [people] pick up a check every two weeks you don't own these people . . . you don't control them." These interviewees attribute much legitimacy to authority if it is based on competence. This is illustrated by the receiving clerk who says of his boss: "I definitely recognize Jim as the boss. What he says goes. . . . You can see when you ask him a question, he is thinking about the options, the contingencies that are involved. He thinks before he comes to a conclusion." Such respondents value competence highly in part because they use this criterion to ground their self-worth.

Finally, a few workers I talked to put much emphasis on middle-class cultural orientations, such as ambition. It is notably the case of a pipe fitter who says that "everybody needs to have ambition. You have to want to make better of yourself because that's what America was founded on." Intelligence is at times equated with having ambition, as does this worker who explains how he judges differences: "Intelligence probably ranks high among that distinction. The fact that there are some people out there that could do better and don't try." Similarly, an insurance salesman says that he feels superior to people who are uneducated, by which he means not ambitious. He describes them as "people who

have no control over their lives. . . . It annoys me when people can't get it together." Many feel guilty for not being ambitious enough. That is the case for a
printer who says, "I like to see people exert themselves. I like to see people
show that they can leave a mark, and not just be lax and fall into a rut. I should
say that I see me lacking a bit in ambition lately. I want to be a little more
ambitious." Similarly, a laborer in his early forties says, "I was a little foolish
when I was younger, and I paid the price. It's like, guys were getting into the
electricians' union as apprentices, or a city job, sanitation, fire department, or
police department, and I let all that go by. They will all retire young, whereas
I'll be sixty-three when I retire."

Altogether, some 50 percent of the white blue-collar workers I talked to evaluate others largely in terms of financial success, authority, and ambition, and as
such can be described as "middle-class identified."[9] Half of these men have
a mixed position, being simultaneously middle-class identified and critical of
this group.

THE MORAL FLAWS OF "PEOPLE ABOVE." These positive evaluations of
the upper half, which tend to conflate social status and worth, tell only part of
the story. Indeed, 50 percent of the Euro-American blue-collar workers I talked
to find many flaws in the upper half, drawing strong boundaries against its members. Combined with the 25 percent who have a mixed position, the total of
white blue-collar workers who show some critical dispositions toward people
above comes to 75 percent of the sample. Hence, negative evaluations of the
upper half exceed positive ones.

Workers repeatedly argue that worth should not be judged on the basis of
social status, but on the basis of criteria such as the quality of interpersonal
relationships. The standards they use to evaluate worth allow them to locate
themselves at the top of a hierarchy and to promote criteria of evaluation available to all.

The white working-class men I talked to develop a sophisticated moral critique of people above.[10] They identify a number of moral flaws they consider
to be typical of this group. These flaws all point to the fact that workers rank
professionals and managers lower than themselves in terms of the quality of
their interpersonal relationships.

In the eyes of these workers, the main moral flaw of the upper half is that
they lack warmth and are domineering. They are described by a radio technician as "very cold, shallow people . . . concentrating a lot on finances and not
that much on personal needs." A train conductor concurs when he compares
himself to his "corporate" brother: "I feel that I'm more sensitive a person. He's
in a business atmosphere, a corporate atmosphere, where he has to be tough.
He acts sometimes, you know, 'corporate' when he's talking to me, so I get

upset. . . . He doesn't show any sensitivity to some things that I would like him to show." This man describes the images he associates with "corporate" as "domination, domination. . . . I have ten suits myself, but if a guy is wearing a suit and he has that attitude when he walks in a room, like 'I'm going to do this and this, and you are going to do this thing,' you have an attitude to back off and say 'Wait a minute!'"

In the eyes of these white interviewees, the upper half also lacks sincerity. A Jersey City fireman, who used to work in a bank in Manhattan, describes his former work environment as follows: "There's a lot of false stuff going on. A lot of people are 'How are you doing?' and they are smiling at you, and then you turn your back and they are like 'He's a jerk.' At least at the job in the firehouse, if you're a jerk, someone is going to tell you you're a jerk because there's no one there to tell them not to say it to you." A pipe fitter shares this view of the upper half as insincere. For him, the "shirt and ties types" engage in "too much politicking": "They are jockeying for jobs and worrying about whether they are making the right moves and stuff. I feel that I don't have to get involved in that. Their hair is turning gray, and they look older than I do. That's the way I would measure [my happiness], where I can come home and enjoy myself where they are sweating out things."

Another moral flaw of people above is their competitiveness. In the opinion of the same fireman, "I think professionals care more about showing off to other professionals. They have more of a contest with one another. I mean like you've got a Jaguar and you drive by to see your friends. . . . As for me, I couldn't care less what the other guy thinks of me. Because if I feel good about myself and my wife thinks good about me, and we're all happy, that's what matters to me. My family is what I center myself around. I'm not trying to keep a race with the Joneses, like that." Similarly, a mechanic who lives in Elizabeth, New Jersey, says of professionals: "They power-play people. They're better than them, or they're stronger than them. Strength goes in different ways, whether it's mentally or whether it's physically or whether it's a better job or they live in a better area. That's power play. . . . I have no time for it at all. A very big loss of time."

For many workers, this type of competitiveness generates dishonesty among people above. As a laborer puts it, "When you get that almighty dollar, you hate to lose it. So you step on somebody's feet, or somebody's hand, or somebody's head to make sure you stay on top, which is not the greatest thing in the world. . . . The lower-middle-class people, they got nothing to lose by being honest." A truck driver also ponders the moral character of rich people when he describes his cousin thus: "He always had everything he wanted and absolutely despised his parents. He had the best of everything: he went to college till he was thirty to do absolutely nothing, just to go into the family business. When his mother died, it didn't bother him a bit. The way he looked at it was: 'Great, my bank account is going up and I'm that much closer to the whole thing.' And he looked at his three brothers as if it was like a competition. . . . What the heck went wrong there? So you times that by every other rich person, how many percentages of them are like that?"

Finally, a third of the white workers I spoke to are somewhat critical of a crucial middle-class cultural disposition: ambition. Again, they point to moral flaws that often come with this trait. They believe that individuals who are too ambitious miss what is important in life. A bank supply salesman says that people who are too ambitious "have blinders on. You miss all of life. . . . A person that is totally ambitious and driven never sees anything except the spot they are aiming at." Similarly, an electronics technician defines overly ambitious people as "so self-assured, so self-intense that they don't really care about anyone else. . . . It's me, me, me, me, me. I'm not that kind of person at all, and that's probably why I don't like it."

Whether emphasizing the coldness of the upper half, its lack of sincerity, or its domineering tendencies, competitiveness, and ambition, white workers stress that high social status does not necessarily go hand in hand with moral worth. Workers also implicitly put morality and happiness above social status as criteria of evaluation, emphasizing standards that are available to all over positional goods. Most explicitly subordinate social status to what they perceive to be the "real" value of a person, and hence create the possibility of locating themselves at the top of the hierarchy they privilege.

A large number of white workers are as critical of the positional attributes of people above as they are of their moral character. They are particularly skeptical of the value of power and question whether income and education are proper measures of the worth of people. In the eyes of a fourth of the Euro-American blue-collar men I talked to, power impoverishes interpersonal relationships and hence is a basis for lower ranking on the scale of evaluation they privilege. While for a laborer, "power has no value in life," a mechanic who lives on Long Island says that people with power "have no time for anything but themselves. Unless you're someone that can make them powerful or something that they want as a toy, they would have no use for you. . . . What would you use power for? Manipulating people? To make people do something just for the fun of it? Stand on your head for half an hour and I'll give you $100? I think it's degrading to manipulate people just for the sake of manipulating them." Along the same lines, the Jersey City fireman explicitly distinguishes between power and worth: "I don't have to be in charge, you know, of a thousand people, to try to make them feel less. Power doesn't make a person. . . . I know a lot of people that give stuff away, just so they can feel more important, that they're better than you and then they kick you in the head."

A third of white interviewees emphasize that money and wealth are not indicators of worth, subordinating them to happiness. For a postal worker, rich people "are always like, out to get something, and they feel they haven't gotten to where they want to get. To me they're successful but to them they're not. They're always looking for something, trying to strive to get there and it seems that they never get there." Similarly, a tin factory foreman subordinates money to familial bliss when he says, "Money isn't a big thing in my life. I don't have to be a rich man, I have riches. As long as you have the love and a tight family and that my kids grew up good, I don't need a lot of money. For what? To spend it on this, spend it on that. How much money can you spend? . . . We just have this good thing going where we're close and we enjoy one another still." Finally, others stress that an individual's worth cannot be measured by level of education, as does this electronics technician when he says, "You don't have to be well educated to be likable. Education doesn't instill your values and your morals, and education doesn't make your personality."

THE MORAL SUPERIORITY OF THE WORKING CLASS. White workers also discuss the relative importance of various criteria for assessing worth when they evaluate themselves both as individuals and as members of groups they identify with. Here again, they mobilize various criteria that allow them to locate themselves "on top," whether they focus on work ethic, quality of life, or resilience.

A few of the men I talked to believe themselves to be better than people above because their work ethic is stronger. For a train conductor, "there is a difference between the corporate and the working class. Corporate is concerned with only dollars. The working class is concerned with doing the job right, the feel, and getting the job done. That's the satisfaction I get." For a storage worker, managers "don't work hard, physically hard." Also, a letter carrier is proud that instead of managing other people's money, he produces: "It's a service, it's actual production. . . . I get a sense of accomplishment out of something that I do everyday. It may be very boring and mundane, but I'm actually accomplishing something every day."

More than two-thirds of the white workers I talked to believe themselves to be better than the upper half because their quality of life is superior. A printer explains that whereas his yuppie brother always has financial problems on his mind, "What's on my mind is what am I going to do this weekend." Some interviewees say they have refused to be promoted because they wanted to "stay out of the corporate rat race . . . [the higher you go] the more aggravation you have." One interviewee compares himself with professionals and concludes: "My problems don't have the enormity that some of their problems have. I may even have more leisure time because I see a lot of professional people, especially wealthy people in powerful positions, they really don't have time for their own family." These men often attribute the superiority of their quality of life, compared to that of the upper half, to the fact that their environment is warmer. A police-man views upper-middle-class neighborhoods as unwelcoming "because people don't even come out of their houses over there. . . . Well, you can drive through that neighborhood and never see anybody. There's no activity. Everybody has their maid. They are not very social over there. . . . They are very professional, work too many hours, and are never home." Yet others characterize themselves and their own milieu as caring and genuine, as does this printer when he says, "I'm always after somebody, I try to have people rely on me a little bit. Get people to trust me. It's not really a social statement though. I'm not like the kind of person who goes out to theater and stuff like that. It's kind of like the working class, normal chump taking it up the street." Simplicity is taken to be tantamount to sincerity and to be scarcer in higher circles. While one worker states, "I don't have to live my life in a window. . . . I can pretty much do what I want. [I don't have to] maintain an image," a pipe fitter explains that "I'm happy with the people that I deal with. Not to say that I can't go to a function and get along and socialize and such, and enjoy myself, but I'd probably rather go next door and play cards and be with a bunch of beer-drinking guys [who are] just having a good time. That's me."

Finally, a few workers stress self-reliance to provide additional evidence of their moral superiority, implicitly drawing boundaries against those above, who have benefited from the help of their parents, and against the welfare dependent. For the same audio technician, "I'm more able to take care of myself because I'm working class. I don't really have to depend upon anyone else. I can support myself. I pay my own way." Moreover, a truck driver points to the practical intelligence and resilience that comes along with his working-class status. He explains that "I'm prepared for anything. There's absolutely no strain or crisis I can't handle, whereas there are a lot of things somebody from the middle class can't handle. They wouldn't be able to handle the simplest family crisis that comes up. If grandpa drops on the floor before them, it's 'What am I going to do?' Whereas I would know what to do. There are definite advantages." A mechanic concurs:

> Sometimes if you have people that are well educated, never picked up a tool, never cut their hands, were never cold and never hungry or uncomfortable, then they have no idea what it is to be those things and to get above them. . . . I think it's good for even the most wealthy children to go out and have a paper route, work in the rain. I think it teaches values, the values the country was founded on. . . . They have to learn how to be able to help themselves in an emergency. Many professional people fall apart in an emergency. I have my most respect for professionals that stay together in an emergency and know what to do. . . . *Respect has to be earned*." (my emphasis)

Finally, another truck driver says that professional people are not really superior because "if the impossible happened, . . . the technology trap sprung, no more electricity, nothing worked anymore, they'd be the first person to go in the bathroom and blow their brains out. . . . Without life's little pleasures they wouldn't have much to live for." Here again, working-class men put themselves above people above, mobilizing a range of moral evidences to support their claim.

EGALITARIANISM AND ALTERNATIVE DEFINITIONS OF SUCCESS. In their assessment of the worth of people, white workers downplay the importance of social status when they argue that people are fundamentally equal and when they promote definitions of success that are disentangled from socioeconomic achievement. For instance, a storage worker demonstrates equality between people by pointing out our common fate as human beings: "Everybody's born and everybody's gonna die. Nobody's any better or worse than I am. They may be better at certain things, but just because they have money, or they may have gone to school, or because they didn't go to school and they have been working since they were ten years old, or whatever, that's no reason to put me down. Everybody's got a different life." Similarly, an electrician explains that we are equal because we are different, putting education on the same plane as the courage of a fireman or the skills of a baseball coach: "Who's to say that I'm better than you or you're better than me? What makes you better than me or me better than you? Just because you may have a degree or maybe because I can go through a burning building or because I coach little league or you teach? Everyone has different values for what they want to do." An iron worker demonstrates equality by focusing on the universality of interdependence. He says that "It does not matter what people's political feelings are. It doesn't matter anything. Basically I think [what counts] is how we can interact together. You know, like, who can give what I need and who will accept what I have to give." The electrician quoted above grounds equality in self-esteem, as opposed to social position, when he says

there's nobody in this world better than me. You may have more money than me, more smarts than me, nicer clothes, better house, have less than me, but that doesn't make you any better than me, as far as I'm concerned. Bill Clinton is no better than me. . . . I don't mean to sound egotistical, but I feel very good about myself. I feel I have a lot to offer. I have enough smarts to sit there and handle the situation and maybe I don't have my degree and I don't have a lot of book knowledge, but I have mechanical ability. I have street smarts, and if I don't have the answer, well, I could look it up and find it for you, find somebody who does know the answer.

Hence, whether pointing to common fate, differences in skills and talents, the universality of human interdependence, or self-esteem as a criterion of evaluation, some interviewees use standards of evaluation that allow them to come up on top, or at least equal to others.

Many white workers also adopt alternative definitions of success that decouple social status and worth. Examples of this abound. Some define success, again, in terms of interpersonal relations and happiness. A foreman in a tin company says that he is successful because "I have the respect of people who know me. I'm cared for by a lot of people. My wife loves me a great deal and I love her a great deal, and we're very much in tune with each other. Our children are good children, so I have those kinds of things. I have a sense of self-worth." An electrician explains that "I'm successful because I'm me. I don't mean to sound egotistical, but I have a lot to offer the people. I'm a success. . . . I am well-known in this town, I can go down the street, everybody's like 'Hey, Rick, how you doing today?' Do I have a lot of money in the bank? No. I'm not successful in that way." A mechanic stresses interpersonal relationships less than "keeping it together" when he explains that for him, "rich" means:

> If I can sit here and survive through this whole rush around here, manage to keep paying my share without anybody coming around here and knocking on my door trying to take stuff away from me, and the kids making out all right without getting all wired out on dope, or you know, and getting in any sort of trouble, now that's rich! Nobody's hurt and you know, if they can live with themselves and not hurt other people to go ahead and make their living, that's surviving! That's rich!

Similarly, others define success by the mere fact of being stably employed, as does this postal worker when he explains that he is successful because "there is all these people out of work these days and I felt like I've gone the right route for me, you know with the choices I've made. I have a stable job."

These alternative definitions of success, along with the ideology of egalitarianism and workers' evaluations of the relative merits of their position and of that of people above, suggest again that a number of workers adopt criteria of evaluation of the worth of people that are relatively autonomous from traditional notions of socioeconomic status, and that they have access to an alternative system of evaluation that allows them to put themselves on top of (or side to side with) people above. Hence, a clerical worker believes that there is little class resentment in the American working class and that upward mobility is not valued by all. As he puts it, "An awful lot of the middle class and working people crave a whole lot to get out of that class. I really think inside, they don't. I think most people are happy being what they are in a class structure. . . . If I went to a working class or even a lower class, I don't think I'd be that much disappointed or unhappy. I think people in those classes are comfortable where they are. They're happy where they are."[11]

The Specificity of African-Americans

The attitudes of African-American workingmen toward the upper half are similar to those of white workers in many respects. Like whites, many black men I talked to measure success on the basis of income and value ambition, drawing boundaries against people who are not self-sufficient.[12] They value money in part because it acts as a racial equalizer and makes respect—as well as luxury— accessible to blacks.[13] They also acknowledge the importance of social status, as illustrated by this assistant cable splicer who says, "To me everyone is born equal. . . . You know, there are people who are equal out here: there are black doctors, lawyers, and politicians, the whole bit." In fact, a higher percentage of black interviewees than white interviewees can be described as middle-class identified: it is the case for 63 percent of them compared to roughly 50 percent of whites. Of these, slightly more whites than blacks—27 percent versus 20 percent—have contradictory positions, i.e., are simultaneously identified with the upper half and draw boundaries against it. Also, more whites than blacks are critical of the upper half without being identified with it (47 percent compared to 30 percent).

Overall, blacks are slightly more likely than whites to equate success with financial success (half of black workers compared to a third of white blue-collar workers)[14] and to praise ambition (a third of black workers compared to a fourth of whites). They are also more likely to believe that their quality of life is inferior to that of middle-class people. However, African-Americans I talked to also attribute less legitimacy to authority than whites do, being more likely to point to the exploitative and coercive dimensions of interclass relationships. They are less likely than whites to associate upward mobility with high moral character because of their own experience with racism. Like whites, they also point to the moral flaws of people above, but are much more vocal in denouncing their selfishness. Finally, they have a very negative view of power and also adopt alternative definitions of success. These differences suggest that paradoxically, proportionately fewer blacks than whites within our limited sample draw boundaries against the upper half, but those who do so draw stronger boundaries than whites do. More blacks also appear to identify more strongly with some middle-class standards of evaluation (such as money) than whites do. Due to space constraints, I focus on only a few differences between white and black workers.

African-American interviewees have a more conflictual view of class relations than white workers do, suggesting that they are more distant from the middle-class world. Indeed, exploitation is a recurrent theme in these interviews, as is the notion that profits come at the expense of workers. A production worker employed by a newspaper says about his bosses: "They don't really care about anyone anyway. They don't necessarily say, 'I'm paying you for your labor, so this is what you have to do, so sit there and do your job, don't get up.' No, it's not like that. . . . It's like sometimes they will do things that will remind you, 'Well, you're a commodity to us, and if we feel we're not getting anything out of you anymore, or we feel we can get more out of that person, you're out.'"[15] A number of interviewees echo this perspective. For a worker in the textile industry, "management is trying to squeeze us like a grape and get more, more, more, more," while for a fumigator "it could take five guys to do a job and you could get away with two, that's more money in your pocket. It's as simple as that." Similarly, for a sorter who works for UPS, "businessmen are only in business to make money. They don't want to be nobody's friend." And for a driver "anything they can beat you for, they are going to do it. . . . They hate when you go to the doctor. . . . They're crying poverty but they're always buying the machines and hiring people left and right."

Like the white workingmen I talked to, black workers are also very critical of the moral character of the members of the upper half. However, black workers more often describe them as selfish than white workers do.[16] For a maintenance worker, this trait is best exemplified by the Republican Party as representative of the interests of the rich and the middle class: "They look down on people, just like with Bush's trickle-down economics. . . . The rich get the money and then basically sometimes it would come back down to us and we'll help each other. That's the stupidest proposal to come out of his face because all he was doing is make the rich richer. And you know, if you're poor, the hell with you. . . . Republicans, they look down on people." Their experience with racial discrimination makes it more difficult for black workers to believe that social status signals moral character and that market position is a good indicator of people's ability. For a letter carrier, "There are so many advantages in being white, it's just so advantageous to be a member of the dominant group. . . . To me, there's no real reason for a white guy to be a failure. There's nothing that's not in his favor."

Interviewees stress time and time again that financial success is a worthy goal only if it is used to "give back to the community." They adopt various definitions of "giving back" and "community," but many agree that the upper half does not give back. As a recycling plant worker puts it, imagining his success, "When I get to that level, I'll know how to take it in stride. It wouldn't change me, or nothing like that. I'd change my living habits as far as that goes, according to how much money I get. But I will still always be the same person. And the people that don't have it, I would never turn my back on them, never. . . . I think people should come first. Peoples' heart should come first. [Don't] put money before people, or you know, use people to get money."

While African-American interviewees have positive views of some of the

main social and cultural attributes of the upper half, namely money and ambition, they are in large number very negative when probed on power. They do
not understand the latter as a tool for achieving common good; they view it as
arbitrary, associated with abuse, and based on violence. In the words of a hospital orderly, "Because some people get power, they want to be dominating, take
advantage, they mistreat people, step on you." Similarly, a driver says, "People
want power because they want to control people. When you want to control
people, it's because you feel inferior. You want to control people to bring people
down." Power is also associated with the underworld. For a worker in an X-ray
firm, "When I think powerful, I think someone's going to be corrupted, you're
going to buy someone and if that person doesn't do this as they're supposed to
do it, they get killed." A park maintenance worker describes the situation thus:

> How many powerful people do you know that ain't got shot, got assassinated,
> or whatever? What's the use of being powerful if you ain't going to be here
> so long? What's the use of being rich if you can't take it with you? So you
> should just survive and take care of yourself while you're here. . . . What's
> power going to do for you? . . . Power means nothing to me. . . . Power is
> something I would like to have only if I use it in the right way. . . . I'd use it
> in the way of helping people to do better.

The altruistic themes mentioned above remain salient, and more so than is the
case among white workingmen. This contradictory position toward money and
power might be accounted for by the fact that money is more impersonal than
power and as such might be easier to deal with in a situation of pervasive racism.
Furthermore, money can also generate self-sufficiency and create a buffer between one's family and a dangerous environment.

Black interviewees, like their white counterparts, often assess worth on the
basis of the quality of one's interpersonal relationships, which allows them to
put themselves above the upper half, at least in moral terms. Concurrently with
their critique of the exploitative nature of the upper half, they emphasize the
importance of sincerity and generosity. A phone technician describes the differences between workers and upper-middle-class people as follows:

> I think a distinction, from my own experience, between say a lower middle
> class and perhaps an upper middle class is the quality, the depth of the
> people. To use as an example, the guys on the job, they are more or less
> down to earth, you know, relate on eye level, more so than someone who is
> an upper middle class, a yuppie, or whatever the case may be. Mostly from
> what I see most of their friendships are kind of superficial. While the going
> is good, we are all peachy keen but then when something is bad, you get

fired from your job or something like that, all of a sudden your friends disappear. But more or less the people I associate with, they are always there. They don't change because something might happen. . . . These people are in the same class that I am, from the same background, the same kind of upbringing and the people in the upper class, I guess, there isn't so much depth to the friendship.

A maintenance worker makes a similar point when he explains that it is better to be friends with "a poor honest person because I know that in the long run if I get in a jam and he can help me he will. Where that guy that has all the money, he'll look back and go 'The hell with him, I ain't got no use for him.'"

The superior quality of interpersonal relationships among working people is also manifested in the fact that one finds more loneliness in the upper half. As a plumber puts it, "Some rich people . . . they can't live an average life. To me, it means driving around in a BMW, going to a big house in Sands Points and it being empty, [with] my cat Fluffy. Or having a boat with no one to be on it with. Or telling people where I've been and not being able to see or share it with some people."

Finally, like Euro-American workers, black workers also adopt alternative definitions of success that marginalize the importance of social success in their assessment of worth. In the words of a medical worker, "I believe everybody has an American dream, but everybody's dream is not the same." Their alternative definitions of success have slightly different emphases from those of whites, stressing more the importance of escaping the dangers of the environment in which they live. A sixty-year-old bindery worker considers himself successful "as far as being able to say that I have escaped the ways of the streets. . . . When I was a young man, heroin was the thing. I was successful in escaping that era. I was successful in that I was never a street walker or anything of that nature." Similarly, a photo technician who used to be a drug addict says, "I've graduated in lots of different things. . . . Just to come out of the drug world. I have come a long ways." Furthermore, like whites, many define success through good relations with their children and their environment. In fact, relationships with children often act as a source of alternative identities. It is also the case for white workers, although the latter more often discuss the quality of their relationship with their partner as an alternative source of identity.

In sum, the definitions of worth that black workers offer are paradoxical. On the one hand, they use financial success as a measure of worth and highly value ambition. On the other hand, they are particularly critical of the exploitative dimension of interclass relationships. They do not believe that social achievement correlates with moral character, in part due to their experience with racial discrimination. They are critical of the selfishness of the upper half and position themselves above it because of the quality of their interpersonal relationships. Finally, they are very critical of the effect of power on these relationships and adopt alternative definitions of success that leave room for noneconomic achievement.

Conclusion

Arguably, the main contribution of this chapter is to offer a glimpse at a world where points of comparison and measuring sticks used to assess the worth of people are different from those that prevail in the upper-middle-class environment. That survival and escaping drugs are taken to be measures of success is a particularly vivid example of such alternative measuring sticks. Only by exploring the cultural meanings that individuals attach to worth is it possible to document this type of qualitative difference. A survey could establish precisely the extent to which the differences that I have documented extend beyond the groups of East Coast men I talked to, and would allow us to tap into how criteria vary across ethnic groups and other demographic categories.[17] However, it would require a standardization of responses, i.e., a leveling of cultural differences, and hence not lead toward isolating many of the distinctive cultural meanings identified herein.[18]

More generally, this chapter provides evidence that the majority of the workingmen I talked to draw moral boundaries against the upper half, subordinating socioeconomic status to morality in their assessment of the worth of people. Seventy-five percent of the white interviewees and 50 percent of the black interviewees draw boundaries against the upper half. Among whites, more than half of those who adhere to middle-class criteria of worth also draw boundaries toward this group as do a third of blacks who adhere to middle-class criteria. Hence, whites are more frequently anti–middle class than blacks—although the difference is not a large one. As suggested above, blacks who draw boundaries against this group draw particularly strong boundaries, and as such, as a group, they can be described as having a more contradictory position than whites.

I have proposed that in emphasizing the importance of universally available goods, such as morality and good interpersonal relationships, over positional goods, workers locate themselves above (and in some cases, alongside) the upper half in a hierarchy that they privilege. Hence, they find dignity in a social environment where criteria of evaluation that favor the upper half predominate; they are not condemned to think of themselves as losers due to their failure to realize a materialist version of the American dream, as has been suggested by Sennett and Cobb (1972) and others.

In this process, the quality of interpersonal relations, particularly within the family, is crucial, as it serves as a refuge from the less satisfying spheres of life.

Through family and interpersonal relationships, one can develop and sustain an alternative identity as a decent, responsible, and honorable person.[19] Hence, we need to reassess the Weberian view of status, which unquestioningly links the latter to socioeconomic status, neglecting to take into consideration the ways in which individuals decouple status and worth from social position.

Some might object that this argument is built on a somewhat romantic view of the culture of American workingmen: instead of drawing on observed behavior, it discusses idealized a posteriori descriptions of criteria of evaluation provided in the context of an interview.[20] However, such descriptions are important templates of what individuals value and deserve to be treated seriously, as indicative of the self-image that they wish to project. Furthermore, drawing on interviews, as opposed to participant observations or surveys, makes it possible to maximize the number of cases under consideration while tapping qualitative differences in meanings. If interviews do not exhaust criteria of evaluations, they provide us with one detailed and significant expression of them.

How can we account for our main finding concerning racial differences, namely that African-Americans appear to be simultaneously more and less critical of the standards of worth valued in the upper half than whites, valuing middle-class criteria of worth while drawing strong boundaries toward people above? A multicausal explanation would take into consideration their interactions with middle-class people, the cultural repertoires made available to them via the entertainment and advertising industries, the educational system, and religious organizations—the supply side of culture—and their distinctive economic position. While space constraints prevent the development of a full multicausal model (an illustration is provided in Lamont 1992), a few factors should be mentioned here. First, blacks might be reacting to the repertoire of racist discourse they encounter on a daily basis that depicts them as lacking ambition and self-reliance, which discourse they might attempt to disprove by presenting themselves as valuing money and ambition as criteria of worth. Second, the vulnerability of their economic position might push them to want to identify more strongly with mainstream norms of success to maximize their chances of overcoming the numerous obstacles they encounter. However, their support for middle-class standards of worth might very well be mitigated by a perception that these are white standards. In other words, the moral boundaries they draw against the upper half are also boundaries drawn against whites, whom they associate with these middle-class norms (Fordham 1996). Finally, these findings can be accounted for as an artifact of the research: African-Americans who are most identified with middle-class values might be more likely to agree to be interviewed for a study conducted by a white academic. However, others might agree to be interviewed to display racial pride. The impact of such selection bias on our results cannot be readily assessed herein.

According to a pipe fitter quoted earlier, it is important for Americans to be ambitious because it is what this country is based on. Future research needs to explore how the criteria of worth, and particularly of moral worth, that workers value are articulated with their identity as Americans. Such an analysis might be particularly useful in revealing how the various political culture traditions that have shaped American society—including egalitarianism, individualism, and self-reliance—take different meanings for various groups. This would help us move away from a Tocquevillian view of American society that gives the culture of people above precedence over that of others, reinforcing among people below a self-concept that does not go beyond that of failing at the American dream.[21] Finally, future work should also compare our findings with the literature on how out-groups deal emotionally with their status.[22] Such a comparison would be conducive to a better understanding of what is distinctive in white and black relationships with people above.

Methodological Appendix

I draw on in-depth interviews to reconstruct the symbolic boundaries or mental maps through which individuals define *us* and *them,* simultaneously identifying the most salient principles of classification and identification that are operating behind these definitions, including race and class. I asked the men to describe their friends and foes, role models and heroes, and likes and dislikes.[23] In so doing, I tapped the criteria that are the basis of their evaluations and self-identity and reveal the natural order through which they hierarchize others when, for example, they declare that, of course, it is more important to be honest than refined or that money is not a good indicator of a person's value. The result is both a multifaceted theory of status that centers on the relationships among various standards of evaluation across populations, and a comparative sociology of models of inclusion/exclusion, that is, of the relative salience of various bases of societal segmentations across classes, races, and eventually, nations.

For this study, I talked with sixty stable blue-collar workers who have a high-school degree but not a college degree.[24] This includes thirty self-identified African-Americans and thirty self-identified Euro-Americans, who were, when possible, matched in terms of occupation and age.[25] I also talked with fifteen Euro-American low-status white-collar workers. They were randomly selected from phone books of working-class towns located in the New York suburbs, such as Elizabeth and Linden, in New Jersey, and Hempstead on Long Island.[26] This random selection and the relatively large number of respondents aimed not at building a representative sample, but at tapping a wide range of perspectives within a community of workers. Although produced in specifically structured interactional contexts, interviews can get at relatively stable aspects of identity by focusing on the respondents' taken-for-granted.

While the growing presence of women and immigrants has dramatically altered the character of the American working class,[27] the latter remains a highly gendered—masculine—cultural construct. I talked to nonimmigrant men only in order to minimize cultural variations unrelated to occupation and race/ethnicity—this choice is justified in part because the larger study within which this particular project takes place is concerned with cultural differentiation between college and non–college educated men, and not with the character of the American working class.

Notes

An early draft of this paper was presented at a special session at the Annual Meetings of the American Sociological Association, New York City, August 1996. This paper benefited from comments from the contributors to this volume, and from close readings by Jennifer Hochschild and Herbert Gans in particular. I also thank Nancy DiTomaso, Murray Milner, Richard Sennett, and Michael Wiseman for their comments. This research is supported by a grant from the National Science Foundation (#92-13363) and by fellowships from the German Marshall Funds of the United States, the Russell Sage Foundation, and the John Simon Guggenheim Memorial Foundation.

1. It is useful to analyze how workers assess members of these variously labeled groups, instead of focusing on their assessment of members of specific classes only, because, as shown by Burke (1995), Americans have been reluctant to use the language of class in classifying social groups, with the consequence that this language has been particularly unstable and contested throughout American history.

2. The notion of "positional good" is borrowed from Hirsch (1976). I use this notion to refer to resources that are distributed on a zero-sum basis. This contrasts with the use of the concept made by Frank (1985, 7) who defines positional goods as goods that are "sought after less because of any absolute property they possess than because they compare favorably with others in their own class. A 'good' school for example, is sought after less for its absolute quality than for its rank among schools in general."

3. This literature includes Chinoy's 1992 study, conducted in the fifties, which shows that American workers continue to believe in the American dream although they do not taste its promises. Similarly, using quantitative data, Coleman and Rainwater (1978, 220) argue that workers and middle-class people use economic standards to assess status. On this topic, see also Lipset 1996. However, works such as MacLeod 1987 emphasize cultural resistance of poor children, as expressed through a rejection of the achievement ideology model. Similarly, Vanneman and Cannon (1987) suggest that American workers manifest class consciousness through everyday resistance in the workplace. One of the most recent studies on attitudes toward the American dream, Hochschild 1995 compares the black and white middle class and the poor, but is not concerned with the attitudes of the working class toward the American dream.

4. Sennett and Cobb (1972) conducted their research in the Boston area in the early 1970s. Also, Rubin's (1994) respondents are poorer than the men considered in this chapter: their median family income was $31,500 in 1992 (p. 32) compared to $50,000 in the present study. For a discussion of the class status of my interviewees, see the methodological appendix.

5. The black/white comparison is important because these racial groups occupy polarized positions in American society, symbolically as well as economically. These groups often define themselves in opposition to one another, while taking into consideration other racial and ethnic groups in so doing. This chapter does not address the relevant literature on social-psychological processes that link self-evaluation, social identity, social comparison across groups, and social conflict. On this topic, see Tajfel and Turner 1986.

6. In the absence of African-American white-collar workers in the sample, the quantitative comparison of white and black workers excludes Euro-American white-collar workers. However, I quote members of this group in the narrative sections of the data analysis. Interviews reveal that Euro-American white-collar workers are more middle-class identified than Euro-American blue-collar workers. They also attach more importance to education, have a more positive view of power, attribute fewer moral flaws to the upper half, and are less likely to believe that they have a better quality of life than the upper half. Lamont (1997b) compares how French and American low-status white-collar workers evaluate worth and negotiate middle-class conceptions of worth.

7. Lamont (1992) documents the high-status signals valued by college-educated professionals, managers, and businessmen. The study finds that American upper-middle-class men living in the New York suburbs primarily use socioeconomic criteria to assess the worth of people (chap. 5).

8. The attitudes that workers have toward "people below" is also relevant to understanding their attitude toward money as a basis for evaluating worth (on this topic, see the chapter by Newman and Ellis in this volume). However, they will not be discussed because of space limitations. One should also analyze how the relationship of workers with money and socioeconomic achievement is expressed in their view of competing working-class lifestyles—that of the "respectable working class" versus that of the "hard-living working class," for instance.

9. In order to determine whether an interviewee is "middle-class identified," I compared his position and attitudes on (1) the attributes of the upper half (income as a criterion of success, power, education, ambition); (2) its moral character; and (3) an evaluation of its quality of life and advantages in contrast to those of the working class. Interviewees are classified "mixed," "middle-class identified," or "critical of the upper half" based on the distribution of their positions on twelve items included in these three categories.

10. There are similarities and differences in the moral criteria of worth most valued by American workers and upper-middle-class men I interviewed (Lamont 1992). Space limitations prevent a full discussion of this issue.

11. Similarly, Hyman (1966), who documents the "lower class value system," argues that the latter is also characterized by less emphasis upon the traditional success goals, including education. Whereas the middle class emphasizes career trajectory, the working class searches for stability and security. See also Willis 1977.

12. Along these lines, Gregory (1992) analyzes the boundaries that working-class homeowners draw against poor blacks.

13. For instance, Nightingale (1993) finds that although they are alienated from the American dream, poor black children embrace American consumer culture. He draws on participation observation conducted in Philadelphia.

14. A few have a fairly negative view of money, associating it with the difficulties of their lives. One defines happiness as being able to pay your bills, "having nobody crawling down my throat." Only the most religious respondents associate money with evil, while the majority of black interviewees use this standard to measure success.

15. One of the few ethnographic studies of the black American working class available, Williams 1987, 160, points out that black workers feel that foremen and supervisors lack the ability and desire to provide them with proper supervision and support and that they evaluate them harshly and show disrespect.

16. This is congruent with my findings that African-Americans have a more collectivist understanding of morality than whites do (Lamont 1997a).

17. Jackman (1994, 103) analyzes the results of a 1975 national probability survey that shows weaker negative working-class feelings toward the upper half than my findings suggest. She shows that: (1) 29 percent of the working class and 21 percent of the middle class have negative feelings toward the upper class; (2) 33 percent of the working class and 34 percent of the middle class have positive feelings toward the upper class; (3) 41 percent of the working class and 44 percent of the middle class have positive feelings toward the upper middle class. Jackman also shows that "Americans commonly believe that both intelligence and selfishness are found increasingly with ascending social class" (p. 334). The results in Halle 1984 are more compatible with mine. Halle's ethnography of workers living in Elizabeth, New Jersey, suggests that members of this group are middle-class identified in their private life and in their realm of consumption, but working-class identified at work. The types of data these studies draw on might account for the differences in findings.

18. Jackman (1994, 332) suggests that "traits and distinctions are drawn frequently between classes, especially between classes from opposite ends of the continuum, where distinctions are sometimes larger and more frequent than between race or gender. As with interclass feelings, the frequency and size of distinctions that are drawn between classes increase incrementally as one moves from adjacent classes to classes that are further apart. . . . The two highest social classes . . . are most likely to be described categorically."

19. On these issues, see also Anderson 1978, Duneier 1992, Gans 1962, and Kornblum 1974.

20. By using in-depth interviews instead of ethnographic observation, I sacrifice breadth to depth. While interviews cannot tap class consciousness "in action," they can tap broader cultural frameworks that are transportable from one context of action to another. For a study of working-class consciousness that is more context dependent, see Fantasia 1988.

21. Smith (1997) offers a provocative analysis of the relationships among the various traditions that shape this Tocquevillian view.

22. Sidanius (1993) reviews this literature, suggesting that out-groups can (1) defect;

(2) redefine key elements of social comparison; and (3) compete. Moreover, DiTomaso's (1997) theoretical essay discusses how the disadvantaged deal with conflict over self-esteem by focusing on comparison with "people like me."

23. Each interview lasted approximately two hours—long enough for me to develop a complex view of the ways in which these men understood the similarities and differences between themselves and others. I conducted all the interviews myself at a place these men chose. Respondents were asked to concretely and abstractly describe people with whom they prefer not to associate, those in relation to whom they feel superior and inferior, and those who evoke hostility, indifference, and sympathy. They were also asked to describe negative and positive traits in their coworkers and acquaintances, as well as their child-rearing values. The criteria of evaluation behind their responses were systematically compared to re-create a template of their mental map of their grammar of evaluation. Note that I did not ask respondents to define class, or to locate themselves within the class structure: their reactions to various categories of people, including "people above," are drawn from their answers to the general questions listed here.

24. These workers have been working full-time and steadily for at least five years. They do not supervise more than ten workers. I explicitly do not use income as a criterion of selection of respondents in order to include in the sample workers of various economic status. I consider the fact of not having a college degree as the most determinant of workers' life chances and privilege this criterion in creating the sample. Respectively 30 percent and 50 percent of white and black respondents have completed some college courses. Thirty-six percent of the African-American households make less than $40,000 a year compared to 24 percent of the Euro-American households. Thirty-nine percent of the African-American households have incomes from $40,000 to $60,000 a year compared to 36 percent of the Euro-American households. Finally, 13 percent of the African-American households have incomes above $60,000 compared to 40 percent of the Euro-American households (the data are not available for 12 percent of blacks). Half of both the white and black households are two-income households and 60 percent of the interviewees are married or cohabiting. African-Americans have more children; 33 percent of them have four or more children compared to only 10 percent of the Euro-American sample.

Although the income of the sample I interviewed is roughly equivalent to the median family income of the five New Jersey and New York State counties where I conducted interviews ($49,000 compared to $48,000 in 1989; data compiled from U.S. Bureau of the Census 1994), again, I consider them to be "below" by the fact that their life chances are severely limited by their lack of college degree. Also, many of them define themselves in opposition to the "upper half." Note that in this study the term "middle class" is equated with "upper middle class" and is used to refer to the top 20 percent of the population that has a college degree and works as professionals, managers, or entrepreneurs (see Lamont 1992).

25. Hundreds of letters were sent to potential respondents living in working-class suburbs in the New York area. In a follow-up phone interview, these men were asked to identify themselves racially; we chose interviewees who categorized themselves as black or white and who meet other criteria of selection pertaining to occupation, age, national-

ity, and level of education. I take the terms "black" and "white" to be moving categories that are the object of intersubjective negotiation within determined parameters.

26. In New Jersey, interviews were conducted in Bayonne, Elizabeth, Hillside, Irvington, Jersey City, Linden, Orange, Paterson, Rahway, Roselle, Roselle Park, South Orange, and Union. On Long Island, interviews were conducted in Hempstead and Uniondale.

27. Space limitations prevent me from dealing with the complexity of the changing social, occupational, and economic characteristics of the working class. On these issues, see Stacey 1989, chap. 11; Dudley 1994; and Rubin 1994.

References

Anderson, Elijah. 1978. *A Place in the Corner.* Chicago: University of Chicago Press.
Bureau of Labor Statistics. 1996. *Union Members in 1995.* [On-line news posting] URL http://stats.bls.gov/news.release/union2.toc.htm. February 9, GMT 10:00:00.
Burke, Martin J. 1995. *The Conundrum of Class.* Chicago. University of Chicago Press.
Chinoy, Eli. 1992. *Automobile Workers and the American Dream.* Urbana-Champaign: University of Illinois Press.
Coleman, Richard P., and Lee Rainwater. 1978. *Social Standing in America.* New York: Basic.
DiTomaso, Nancy. 1997. "The American Non-dilemma: The Dynamics of Privilege and Disadvantage." Unpublished manuscript, Rutgers Faculty of Management.
Dudley, Kathryn Marie. 1994. *The End of the Line.* Chicago: University of Chicago Press.
Duneier, Mitchell. 1992. *Slim's Table.* Chicago: University of Chicago Press.
Fantasia, Rick. 1988. *Cultures of Solidarity.* Berkeley: University of California Press.
Fordham, Signithia. 1996. *Blacked Out.* Chicago: University of Chicago Press.
Frank, Robert H. 1985. *Choosing the Right Pond.* New York: Oxford University Press.
Gans, Herbert. 1962. *The Urban Villagers.* New York: Free Press.
Gregory, Steven. 1992. "The Changing Significance of Race and Class in an African-American Community." *American Ethnologist* 19:255–74.
Halle, David. 1984. *America's Working Man.* Chicago: University of Chicago Press.
Hirsch, Fred. 1976. *The Social Limits to Growth.* Cambridge: Harvard University Press.
Hochschild, Jennifer L. 1995. *Facing Up to the American Dream.* Princeton: Princeton University Press.
Hyman, Herbert. 1966. "The Value Systems of Different Classes." In *Class, Status, and Power,* edited by Reinhard Bendix and Seymour Martin Lipset. New York: Free Press.
Jackman, Mary. 1994. *The Velvet Glove.* Berkeley: University of California Press.
Kornblum, William. 1974. *Blue Collar Community.* Chicago: University of Chicago Press.
Lamont, Michèle. 1992. *Money, Morals, and Manners.* Chicago: University of Chicago Press.
———. 1997a. "Colliding Moralities Between White and Black Workers." In *From Soci-*

ology to Cultural Studies, edited by Elizabeth Long. New York: Blackwell.

—————. 1997b. "The Meaning of Class and Race: French and American Workers Discuss Differences." In *Reworking Class,* edited by John A. Hall. Ithaca: Cornell University Press.

Lipset, Seymour Martin. 1996. *American Exceptionalism.* New York: Norton.

MacLeod, Jay. 1987. *Ain't No Making It.* Boulder, Colo.: Westview Press.

Miles, M. B., and A. M. Huberman. 1984. *Qualitative Data Analysis.* Beverly Hills: Sage.

Milner, Murray. 1993. *Status and Sacredness.* New York: Oxford University Press.

Nightingale, Carl Husemoller. 1993. *On the Edge.* New York: Basic.

Rubin, Lillian B. 1994. *Families on the Faultline.* New York: HarperCollins.

Sennett, Richard, and Jonathan Cobb. 1972. *The Hidden Injuries of Class.* New York: Vintage.

Sidanius, James. 1993. "The Psychology of Group Conflict and the Dynamics of Oppression: A Social Dominance Perspective." In *Explorations in Political Psychology,* edited by I. S. Iyengar and W. J. McGuire. Durham: Duke University Press.

Smith, Rogers M. 1997. *Civic Ideals.* New Haven, Conn.: Yale University Press.

Stacey, Judith. 1989. *Brave New Families.* New York: Basic.

Tajfel, Henri, and John C. Turner. 1986. "The Social Identity Theory of Intergroup Behavior." In *Psychology of Intergroup Relations,* edited by Stephen Worchel and William G. Austin. Chicago: Nelson-Hall.

United States Bureau of the Census. 1994. *County and City Data Book, 1994.* Washington: United States Government Printing Office.

Vanneman, Reeve, and Lynn Weber Cannon. 1987. *The American Perception of Class.* Philadelphia: Temple University Press.

Williams, Bruce. 1987. *Black Workers in an Industrial Suburb.* New Brunswick: Rutgers University Press.

Willis, Paul. 1977. *Learning to Labor.* New York: Columbia University Press.

"there's no shame in my game": status and stigma among harlem's working poor

katherine s. newman and catherine ellis

In the early 1990s, the McDonald's Corporation launched a television ad campaign featuring a young black man named Calvin, who was portrayed sitting atop a Brooklyn stoop in his golden-arches uniform while his friends passed by to hard-time him about holding down a "McJob." After brushing off their teasing with good humor, Calvin is approached furtively by one young black man who asks, sotto voce, whether Calvin might help him get a job. He allows that he too could use some earnings and that, despite the ragging he has just given Calvin, he thinks the uniform is really pretty cool—or at least that having a job is pretty cool.

Every fast-food worker we interviewed for this study knew the Calvin series by heart: Calvin on the job; Calvin in the streets; Calvin helping an elderly woman cross the street on his way to work; Calvin getting promoted to management. They knew what McDonald's was trying to communicate to young people by producing the series in the first place. Fast-food jobs are burdened by a lasting stigma, but one that can be overcome in time. Eventually, so the commercial suggests, the public "dissing" will give way to private admiration as the value of sticking with a job eclipses the stain of a burger flipper's lowly reputation.

One of the moral maxims of American culture is that work defines the person. We carry around in our heads a rough tally that tells us what kinds of jobs are worthy of respect or of disdain, a pyramid organized by the income attached to a particular job, the educational credentials it demands, and the social characteristics of an occupation's incumbents. We use this system of stratification (ruthlessly at times) to boost the status of some and humiliate others.[1]

Given our tradition of equating moral value with employment, it stands to reason that the most profound dividing line in our culture is that which separates the working person from the unemployed.[2] Only after this line has been crossed do we begin to make the finer gradations that distinguish a white-collar worker from his blue-collar counterpart, a CEO from a secretary. A whole host of moral virtues—discipline, personal responsibility, pragmatism—are ascribed to those who have found and kept a job, almost any job, while those who have not are dismissed in public discourse as slothful and irresponsible.[3]

We inhabit an unforgiving culture that fails to acknowledge the many reasons some people cross that employment barrier and others are left behind. We may remember, for a time, that unemployment rates are high; that particular industries have downsized millions of workers right out of their jobs; or that racial barriers or negative attitudes toward teenagers make it harder for some people to get jobs than others. Yet in the end American culture wipes out these background truths in favor of a simpler dichotomy: the worthy and the unworthy, the working folk and the lazy deadbeats.

For those on the positive side of the divide, those who work for a living, the rewards are far greater than a paycheck. The employed enter a social world in which their identities as mainstream Americans are shaped, structured, and reinforced. The workplace is the main institutional setting—and virtually the only one after one's school career is over—in which individuals become part of the collective American enterprise that lies at the heart of our culture: the market. We are so divided in other domains—race, geography, family organization, gender roles, and the like—that common ground along almost any other lines is difficult to achieve. For our diverse and divided society, participation in the world of work is the most powerful source of social integration.

It is in the workplace that we are most likely to mix with those who come from different backgrounds, are under the greatest pressure to subordinate individual idiosyncrasy to the requirements of an organization, and are called upon to contribute to goals that eclipse the personal. All workers have these experiences in common, even as segregation constrains the real mix of workers, conformity is imposed on some occupations more than others, and the goals to which we must subscribe are often elusive, unreachable, or at odds with personal desire.

The creation of a workplace identity is rarely the task of the self-directed individualist, moving along some preordained path. It is a miracle worked by organizations, firms, supervisors, fellow workers, and by the whole long search that leads from the desire to find a job to the endpoint of landing one. This transformation is particularly fraught for ghetto youth and adults, for they face a difficult job market, high hurdles in convincing employers to take a chance on them, and relatively poor rewards—from a financial point of view—for their successes. But the crafting of an identity is an important developmental process for them, just as it is for their more privileged counterparts.

Powerful forces work to exclude African-Americans, Latinos, and other minorities from full participation in American society. From the schools that provide a substandard education for millions of inner-city kids, to an employment system rife with discrimination, to a housing market that segregates minority families, there is almost no meaning to the notion that Americans all begin from the same starting line.[4] Precisely because this is the case, blasting one's way through the job barrier and starting down that road of acquiring a common identity as a mainstream worker is of the greatest importance for black and brown youth in segregated communities. It may be one of the few accessible pipelines into the core of American society and the one with the greatest payoff, symbolic and material.

This paper draws upon a two-year study of fast-food workers and job seekers in central and northern Harlem. Two hundred African-American and Latino workers participated in this study by participating in face-to-face interviews. Sixty of them completed extensive life histories, and a smaller group contributed yearlong personal diaries and permitted the members of our research group to spend extensive periods of time with them, their family members, and their friends. We draw upon all of these data here to explore the nature of values among the working poor in the inner city.

The Social Costs of Accepting Low-Wage Work

While the gainfully employed may be honored over those who stand outside the labor force, all jobs are not created equal. Fast-food jobs, in particular, are notoriously stigmatized and denigrated. "McJob" has become a common epithet meant to designate work without redeeming value. The reasons for this heavy valence are numerous and worthy of deconstruction, for the minority workers who figure in this study have a mountain of stigma to overcome if they are to maintain their self-respect. Indeed, this is one of the main goals of the organizational culture they join when they finally land a job in the restaurant chain we will call "Burger Barn."

Fast-food jobs epitomize the assembly line structure of deskilled service jobs: they are highly routinized, and appear to the untutored observer to be entirely lacking in discretion—almost military in their scripted nature. The symbolic capital of these routinized jobs can be measured in negative numbers. They represent the opposite of the autonomous entrepreneur who is lionized in popular culture (from *Business Week* to hip-hop).

Burger Barn workers are told that they must, at all cost to their own dignity, defer to the public. Customers can be unreasonably demanding, rude, and demeaning, and workers must count backwards from one hundred in an effort to stifle their outrage. Servicing the customer with a smile is music to management's ears because making money depends on keeping the clientele happy, but it can be an exercise in humiliation for inner-city teenagers. It is hard for them to refrain from reading this public nastiness as another instance of society's low estimation of their worth. But if they want to hold on to these minimum-wage jobs, they soon realize that they have to tolerate comments that would almost certainly provoke a fistfight outside the workplace.

It is well known among ghetto consumers that fast-food crew members have to put up with whatever verbiage comes across the counter. That knowledge occasionally prompts nasty exchanges designed explicitly to anger workers, to push them to retaliate verbally. Testing those limits is an outlet for customers down on their luck, and a favorite pastime of teenagers in particular. This may be the one opportunity they have to put someone else down in public, knowing there is little the worker can do in return.

It is bad enough to be on the receiving end of this kind of abuse from adults, especially white adults, for that has its own reading along race lines. It is, in some respects, even worse to have to contend with it from minority peers, for there is much more personal honor at stake, more pride to be lost, and an audience whose opinion matters more. This no doubt is why harassment is a continuous problem for fast-food workers. It hurts. Their peers, with plenty of anger bottled up for all kinds of reasons extraneous to the restaurant experience, find counterparts working the cash register convenient targets for venting.

Roberta Sampson[5] is a five-year veteran of Burger Barn who has worked her way up to management. A formidable African-American woman, Roberta has always prided herself on her ability to make it on her own. Most of Roberta's customers have been perfectly pleasant people; many have been long-time repeat visitors to her restaurant. But she has also encountered many who radiate disrespect.

Well, I had alcoholics, derelicts. People that are aggravated with life. I've had people that don't even have jobs curse me out. I've dealt with all kinds.

Sometimes it would get to me. If a person yelled out [in front of] a lobby full of people, "Bitch, that's why you work at Burger Barn," I would say [to myself], "I'm probably making more than you and your mother." It hurts when people don't even know what you're making and they say those things. Especially in Harlem, they do that to you. They call you all types of names and everything.

Natasha Robins is younger than Roberta and less practiced at these confrontations. But she has had to contend with them nevertheless, especially from agemates who are (or at least claim to be) higher up the status hierarchy than she is. Hard as she tries, Natasha cannot always control her temper and respond the way the firm wants her to:

> It's hard dealing with the public. There are good things, like old people. They sweet. But the younger people around my age are always snotty. Think they better than you because they not working at Burger Barn. They probably work at something better than you.

> *How do you deal with rude or unfriendly customers?* They told us that we just suppose to walk to the back and ignore it, but when they in your face like that, you get so upset that you have to say something. . . . I got threatened with a gun one time. 'Cause this customer had threw a piece of straw paper in the back and told me to pick it up like I'm a dog. I said, "No." And he cursed at me. I cursed at him back and he was like, "Yeah, next time you won't have nothing to say when I come back with my gun and shoot your ass." Oh, *excuse* me.

Ianna Bates, who had just turned sixteen the summer she found her first job at Burger Barn, has had many of the same kinds of problems Natasha Robins complains of. The customers who hard-time her are just looking for a place to vent their anger about things that have nothing to do with buying lunch. Ianna recognizes that this kind of thing could happen in any restaurant, but believes it is a special problem in Harlem, for ghetto residents have more to be angry about and fewer accessible targets for one-upmanship. Cashiers in fast-food shops catch the results:

> What I hate about Burger Barn is the customers, well, some of them that I can't stand. . . . I don't want to stereotype Harlem . . . , but since I only worked in Harlem that's all I can speak for. Some people have a chip on their shoulders. . . . Most of the people that come into the restaurant are black. Most of them have a lot of kids. It's in the ghetto. Maybe, you know, they are depressed about their lifestyles or whatever else that is going on in their lives and they just. . . . I don't know. They just are like *urff!*

> And no matter what you do you cannot please them. I'm not supposed to say anything to the customer, but that's not like me. I have a mouth and I don't take no short from nobody. I don't care who it is, don't take anybody's crap.

Despite this bravado, Ianna well knows that to use her mouth is to risk her job. She has had to work hard to find ways to cope with this frustration that do not get her into trouble with management:

> I don't say stuff to people most of the time. Mostly I just look at them like they stupid. Because my mother always told me that as long as you don't say nothin' to nobody, you can't never get in trouble. If you look at them stupid, what are they going to do? If you roll your eyes at somebody like that, I mean, that's really nothing [compared to] . . . cursing at them. Most of the time I try to walk away.

As Ianna observes, there is enough free-floating fury in Harlem to keep a steady supply of customer antagonism coming the way of service workers every day of their work lives. The problem is constant enough to warrant official company policies on how Burger Barn's crew members should respond to insults, what managers should do to help, and the evasive tactics that work best to quell an incendiary situation without losing business.[6] Management tries to minimize the likelihood of such incidents by placing girls on the registers rather than boys, in the apparent belief that young men will attract more abuse and find it harder to quash their reactions than their female counterparts.

Burger Barn does what it can to contend with these problems on the shop floor. But the neighborhood is beyond its reach and there too fast-food workers are often met with ridicule from the people they grew up with. They have to learn to defend themselves against the criticism that they have lowered themselves in taking these jobs coming from people they have known all their lives. Stephanie Harmon, who has worked at Burger Barn for over a year, explains that here too she leans on the divide between the worker and the do-nothing:

> People I hang out with, they know me since I was little. We all grew up together. When they see me comin', they laugh and say, "Here come Calvin, here come Calvin sister." I just laugh and keep on going. I say, "You're crazy. But that's OK cause I got a job and you all standing out here on the corner." Or I say, "This is my job, it's legal." Something like that. That Calvin commercial show you that even though his friends tease him and he just brushed them off, then he got a higher position. Then you see how they change toward him.

As Stephanie indicates, the snide remarks of peers and neighbors when a worker first dons a Burger Barn uniform are often replaced with requests for help in getting hired and a show of respect when that worker sticks with the job, shows up with money in her pockets and, best of all, moves into management. Still, the scorn is a burden to endure.

Tiffany Wilson, also a teen worker in a central Harlem Burger Barn, thinks she knows why kids in her community who don't work give her such a hard time. They don't want her to succeed because if no one is making it, then no one needs to feel bad about failing. But if someone claws their way up and looks like they have a chance to escape the syndrome of failure, it must mean everyone could, in theory, do so as well. The teasing, a thinly veiled attempt to enforce conformity, is designed to push would-be success stories back into the fold:

> What you will find in any situation, more so in the black community, is that if you are in the community and you try to excel, you will get ridicule from your own peers. It's like the "crab down" syndrome. . . . If you put a bunch of crabs in a big bucket and one crab tries to get out, what do you think the other crabs would do now? According to my thinking, they should pull him up or push him or help him get out. But the crabs pull him back in the barrel. That's just an analogy for what happens in the community a lot.

Keeping everyone down prevents any particular person from feeling that creeping sense of despair that comes from believing things could be otherwise but aren't.

Swallowing ridicule would be a hardship for almost anyone in this culture, but it is particularly hard on minority youth in the inner city. They have already logged several years' worth of interracial and cross-class friction by the time they climb behind a Burger Barn cash register. More likely than not, they have also learned from peers that no self-respecting person allows themselves to be "dissed" without striking back. Yet this is precisely what they must do if they are going to survive on the shop floor.

This is one of the main reasons why these jobs carry such a powerful stigma in American popular culture: they fly in the face of a national attraction to autonomy, independence, and the individualist's right to respond in kind when their dignity is threatened. In ghetto communities, this stigma is even more powerful because—ironically—it is in these enclaves that this mainstream value of independence is elaborated and embellished. Film characters—from the Superfly variety to the political version (e.g., Malcolm X)—rap stars, and local idols base their claims to notoriety on standing above the crowd, going their own way, being beyond the ties that bind ordinary mortals. There are white parallels, to be sure, but this is a powerful genre of icons in the black community, not because it is a disconnected subculture, but because it is an intensified version of a perfectly recognizable American middle- and working-class fixation.

It is therefore noteworthy that thousands upon thousands of minority teens, young adults, and even middle-aged adults line up for jobs that will subject them, at least potentially, to a kind of character assassination. They do so not because they start the job-hunting process with a different set of values, one that can withstand society's contempt for fast-food workers. They take these jobs because in so many inner-city communities, there is nothing better in the offing. In general, they have already tried to get better jobs and have failed, landing instead at the door of Burger Barn as a last resort.

The stigma of these jobs has other sources beyond the constraints of en-forced deference. Low pay and poor prospects for mobility matter as well. Fast-food jobs are invariably minimum-wage positions.[7] Salaries rise very little over time, even for first-line management. In ghetto areas, where jobs are scarce and the supply of would-be workers chasing them is relatively large, downward pressure keeps these jobs right down at the bottom of the wage scale.[8]

The public perception (fueled by knowledge of wage conditions) is that there is very little potential for improvement in status or responsibility either. Even though there are Horatio Algers in this industry, there are no myths to prop up a more glorified image. As a result, the epithet "McJob" develops out of the perception that a fast-food worker is not likely to end up in a prestigious posi-tion as a general manager or restaurant owner; she is going to spend her whole life flipping burgers.

As it happens, this is only half true. The fast-food industry is actually very good about internal promotion. Shop floor management is nearly always re-cruited from the ranks of entry-level workers. Carefully planned training pro-grams make it possible for people to move up, to acquire transferable skills, and to at least take a shot at entrepreneurial ownership. Industry leaders, like McDonald's, are proud of the fact that half of their present board of directors started out on the shop floor as crew members. One couldn't say as much for most other Fortune 500 firms.

Nevertheless, the vast majority of workers never even get close to manage-ment. The typical entry-level worker cycles through the job in short order, pro-ducing an industry average job tenure of less than six months. Since this is just an average, it suggests that a large number of employees are there and gone in a matter of weeks. It is this pattern, a planned operation built around low skills and high turnover, that has given fast-food jobs such a bad name. Although it is quite possible to rise above the fray and make a very respectable living in fast-food management, most crew members remain at the entry level and leave too soon to see much upward movement. Observing this pattern on such a large scale—in practically every town and city in the country—Americans naturally conclude that there is no real future in a job of this kind and that anyone with more on the ball wouldn't be caught dead working behind the counter.

The stigma also stems from the low socioeconomic status of the people who hold these jobs. This includes teenagers, immigrants who often speak halting English, those with little education, and (increasingly in affluent communities afflicted with labor shortages) the elderly. To the extent that the prestige of a job refracts the social characteristics of its average incumbents, fast-food jobs are hobbled by the perception that people with better choices would never purposively opt for a McJob. We argue that entry-level jobs of this kind don't merit this scorn: a lot more skill, discretion, and responsibility are locked up in a fast-food job than meets the public eye. But this truth hardly matters where public perception is concerned. There is no faster way to indicate that a person is barely deserving of notice than to point out that they hold a "chump change" job in Kentucky Fried Chicken or Burger King. We "know" this is the case just by looking at the age, skin color, or educational credentials of the people already on the job: the tautology has a staying power that even the most expensive public relations campaign cannot shake.

It is hard to know the extent to which this stigma discourages young people in places like central Harlem from knocking on the doors of fast-food restaurants in search of employment. It is clear that the other choices aren't much better and that necessity drives thousands, if not millions, of teens and older job seekers to repudiate the stigma associated with fast-food work or learn to live with it.[9] But no one comes into the central Harlem job market without having to contend with the social risks to their identity that come with approaching stigmatized ground.

Tiffany Wilson started working in the underground economy bagging groceries when she was little more than ten years old because her mother was having trouble supporting the family, "checks weren't coming in," and there was "really a need for food" in the family. She graduated to summer youth by the time she was fourteen and landed a job answering phones in a center that dealt with domestic violence cases, referring terrified women to shelters. By the time she was sixteen, Tiffany needed a real job that would last beyond the summertime, so she set about looking—everywhere. As a black teenager, she quickly discovered there wasn't a great deal open to her. Tiffany ended up at Burger Barn in the Bronx, a restaurant two blocks from her house and close enough to her high school to make after-school hours feasible.

The first Burger Barn I worked at was because nobody else would take me. It was a last resort. I didn't want to go to Burger Barn. You flip burgers. People would laugh at you. In high school, I didn't wanna be in that kind of environment. But lo and behold, after everything else failed, Martin Paints, other jobs, Burger Barn was welcoming me with open arms. So I started working there.

Tiffany moved to Harlem when she finished high school and found she couldn't commute back to the Bronx. Reluctant to return to the fast-food business, Tiffany tried her luck at moving up, into a service job with more of a white-collar flavor. She looked everywhere for a position in stores where the jobs are free of hamburger grease and hot oil for french fries, stores where clerks don't wear aprons or hair nets. Nothing panned out, despite her best efforts:

> I'm looking at Lerners and Plymouth [clothing stores] and going to all these stores and lo and behold Burger Barn is there with open arms because I had two years of experience by then.

The new Burger Barn franchise was right in the middle of Harlem, not far from the room she rents over a storefront church. It had the additional appeal of being a black-owned business, something that mattered to Tiffany in terms of the "more cultural reasons why [she] decided to work there." But she confesses to a degree of disappointment that she was not able to break free of entry-level fast-food jobs. With a high-school diploma in hand, Tiffany was hoping for something better.

William Johnson followed a similar pathway to Burger Barn, graduating from summer youth jobs in the middle of high school and looking for something that would help pay for his books and carfare. The Department of Labor gave him a referral to Burger Barn, but he was reluctant at first to pursue it:

> To go there and work for Burger Barn, that was one of those real cloak-and-dagger kinds of things. You'll be coming out [and your friends say], "Yo, where you going?" You be, "I'm going, don't worry about where I'm going." And you see your friends coming [to the restaurant] and see you working there and now you be [thinking], "No, the whole [housing] project gonna know I work in Burger Barn." It's not something I personally proclaim or pride and stuff. . . . If you are a crew member, you really aren't shit there. . . . You got nothing there, no benefits, nothing. It was like that [when I was younger] and it's like that now.

William tried every subterfuge he could think of to conceal his job from the kids he knew. He kept his uniform in a bag and put it on in the back of the restaurant so that it would never be visible on the street. He made up fake jobs to explain to his friends where his spending money was coming from. He took circuitous routes to the Barn and hid back by the gigantic freezer when he spotted a friend coming into the store. The last thing William wanted was to be publicly identified as a shift worker at Burger Barn.

In this, William was much like the other teen and young adult workers we encountered. They are very sensitive to stigma, to challenges to their status, and by taking low-wage jobs of this kind they have positioned themselves to receive exactly the kind of insults they most fear. But the fact is that they do take these risks and, in time, latch onto other "narratives" that undergird their legitimacy.

Breaking the Stigma

One of the chief challenges of an organization like Burger Barn is how to take people who have come to them on the defensive and turn them into workers who at least appear on the surface, if not deep in their souls, to enjoy their work. Customers have choices; they can vote with their feet. If ordering french fries at Burger Barn requires them to run a gauntlet of annoyance, rudeness, or diffidence from the person who takes their order, they can easily cross the street to a competitor the next time. It is clearly in the company's interest to find ways to turn the situation around. Ideally, from the industry's viewpoint, it would be best if the whole reputation of these jobs could be reversed. This is what McDonald's had in mind when it launched the Calvin series. But for all the reasons outlined earlier in this chapter, that is not likely to happen, for the conditions that give rise to the stigma in the first place—low wages, high turnover, enforced deference—are not likely to change. Beyond publicizing the opportunities that are within reach, much of which falls on deaf ears, there is little the industry can do to rehabilitate its workers in the eyes of the public and thereby dampen the tension across the counter.

Yet behind the scenes, managers and workers, and peers working together in restaurant crews, do build a moral defense of their work. They call upon timeless American values, values familiar to many, including conservatives, to undergird their respectability. Pointing to the essential virtues of the gainfully employed, Burger Barn workers align themselves with the great mass of men and women who work for a living. "We are like them," they declare, and in so doing separate themselves from the people in their midst who are not employed.

They have plenty of experience with individuals who don't work, often including members of their own families: beggars who come around the restaurants looking for handouts every day; fast-talkers who come into Burger Barn hoping for free food; and age-mates who prefer to deal drugs. In general, these low-wage workers are far less forgiving, and far less tolerant, of these people than are the liberals who champion the cause of the working poor. Since they hold hard, exhausting, poorly paid jobs, they see little reason why anyone ought to get a free ride. What the indigent should do, on this account, is to follow their example: get a job, any job.

Ianna Bates is an articulate case in point. She has had to confront the social degradation that comes from holding a "low job" and has developed a tough hide in response. Her dignity is underwritten by the critique she has absorbed about the "welfare dependent":

> I'm not ashamed because I have a job. Most people don't and I'm proud of myself that I decided to get up and do something at an early age. So as I look at it, I'm not on welfare. I'm doing something.
>
> I'm not knocking welfare, but I know people that are on it that can get up and work. There's nothing wrong with them. And they just choose not to. . . . They don't really need to be on [welfare]. They just want it because they can get away with it. I don't think it's right because that's my tax dollars going for somebody who is lazy, who don't wanna get up. I can see if a woman had three children, her husband left her and she don't have no job cause she was a housewife. OK. But after a while, you know, welfare will send you to school. Be a nurse assistant, a home attendant, something!
>
> Even if you were on welfare, it should be like, you see all these dirty streets we have? Why can't they go out and sweep the streets, clean up the parks. I mean, there is so much stuff that needs to be done in this city. They can do that and give them their money. Not just sit home and not do anything.

Patricia Hull, a mother of five children in her late thirties, couldn't agree more. Patty has worked at Burger Barn for five years now, having pulled herself off of welfare by the sheer determination to be a decent role model for her children. One might imagine that she would be more tolerant of AFDC recipients, since she has been there. She moved up to the Big Apple from Tennessee after her husband walked out on her, hoping to find more job opportunities than the few that were available in the rural South. It took a long time for her to get on her feet and even Patty would agree that without "aid" she would not have made it this far. Still, having finally taken the hard road to a real job, she sees no reason why anyone else should have an easier ride:

> There's so much in this city; it's always hiring. It may not be what you want. It may not be the pay you want. But you will always get a job. If I can work at Burger Barn all week and come home tired and then have to deal with the kids and all of that, and be happy with $125 a week, so can you. Why would I give quarters [to bums on the street]? My quarter is tax-free money for you! No way.

Or, in a variation on the same theme, Larry Peterson reminds us that any job is better than no job. The kids who would dare to hard-time Larry get nothing but a cold shoulder in return because Larry knows in his soul that he has something they don't have: work for which he gets paid.

> I don't care what other people think. You know, I just do not care. I have a job, you know. It's my job. You ain't puttin' *no* food on my table; you ain't puttin' *no* clothes on my back. I will walk tall with my Burger Barn uniform on. Be proud of it, you know.

These views could have come straight from the most conservative Republicans in the country, bent on justifying draconian cuts in the welfare budget. For they trade on a view held by many of the ghetto-based working poor: that work equals dignity and no one deserves a free ride. The difference between them is simply that the working poor know whereof they speak: they have toiled behind the hot grease pits of french-fry vats, they have stood on their feet for eight or nine hours at a stretch, all for the magnificent sum of $4.25 an hour. Virtually all they have to show for their trouble is the self-respect that comes from being on the right side of that gaping cavern that separates the deserving (read working) and the undeserving (read nonworking) poor (Katz 1989).

Other retorts to status insults emerge as well. Flaunting financial independence often provides a way of lashing back at acquaintances who dis young workers for taking Burger Barn jobs. Brian Gray, born in Jamaica but raised in one of Harlem's tougher neighborhoods, knows that his peers don't really think much of his job. "They just make fun," he says. "Ah, you flipping burgers. You gettin' paid $4.25. They'd go snickering down the street." But it wasn't long after Brian started working that he piled up some serious money, serious at least for a teenager in his neighborhood.

> What I did was made Sam [the general manager] save my money for me. Then I got the best of clothes and the best sneakers with my own money. Then I added two chains. Then [my friends] were like, "Where you selling drugs at?" And I'm like, "The same place you said making fun of me, flipping burgers. That's where I'm getting my money from. Now, where are you getting yours from?" They couldn't answer.

Contrary to public perception, most teenagers in Harlem are afraid of the drug trade and won't go near it. They know too many people who are six feet under, in jail, or permanently disabled by the ravages of drugs. If you aren't willing to join the underground economy, where are you going to get the money to dress yourself, go out on the town, and do the other things teens throughout the middle class do on Mom and Dad's sufferance? Most of Harlem's youth cannot rely on their parents' financial support to meet these needs. Indeed, this is one of the primary pressures that pushes young people out into the labor market in the first place, and at an early age. Most workers we interviewed had their first job by the age of fourteen.

What Brian does, then, is to best his mates at their own game by showing them that he has the wherewithal to be a consumer, based on his own earnings. He derives no small amount of pleasure from turning these tables, upending the status system by outdoing his friends on style grounds they value as much as he does.

It might be comforting to suggest that these hard-working low-wage workers were, from the very beginning, different from their nonworking counterparts, equipped somehow to withstand the gauntlet of criticism that comes their way when they start out on the bottom of the labor market. It would be comforting because we would then be able to sort the deserving, admirable poor (who recognize the fundamental value of work and are willing to ignore stigma) from the undeserving (who collapse in the face of peer pressure and therefore prefer to go on the dole). This is too simplistic. Burger Barn workers of all ages and colors fully admit that their employment is the butt of jokes and that it has subjected them to ridicule. Some, like Larry Peterson, argue that they don't care what other people think, but even these brave souls admit that it took a long time for them to build up this confidence.

Where, then, does the confidence come from? How do ghetto residents develop the rejoinders that make it possible to recapture their dignity in the face of peer disapproval? To some degree, they can call on widely accepted American values that honor working people, values that float in the culture at large.[10] But this is not enough to construct a positive identity when the reminders of low status—coming from customers, friends, and the media—are abundant. Something stronger is required: a workplace culture that actively works to overcome the negatives by reinforcing the value of the work ethic. Managers and veteran employees on the shop floor play a critical role in the reinforcement process by counseling new workers distressed by bad-mouthing.

Kimberly Sampson, a twenty-year-old African-American woman, began working at Burger Barn when she was sixteen and discovered firsthand how her "friends" would turn on her for taking a low-wage job. Fortunately, she found a good friend at work who steadied her with a piece of advice:

> Say it's a job. You are making money. Right? Don't care what nobody say. You know? If they don't like it, too bad. They sitting on the corner doing what they are doing. You got to work making money. You know? Don't bother with what anybody has to say about it.

Kim's advisor, a workplace veteran who had long since come to terms with the insults of his peers, called upon a general status hierarchy that places the working above the nonworking as a bulwark against the slights. His point was later echoed by Kim's manager in the course of a similar episode, as she explained:

> Kids come in here . . . they don't have enough money. I'll be like, "You don't have enough money; you can't get [the food you ordered]." One night this little boy came in there and cursed me out. He [said], "That's why you are working at Burger Barn. You can't get a better job. . . ."
>
> I was upset and everything. I started crying. [My manager] was like, "Kim, don't bother with him. I'm saying, *you got a job.* You know. It is a *job.*"

Absorbing this defensive culture is particularly important for immigrant workers in Harlem who often find fast-food jobs the first venue where they have sustained interaction with African-Americans who resent the fact that they have jobs at all, much less jobs in their community. Marisa Gonzalez, a native of Ecuador, had a very difficult time when she first began working as a hostess at Burger Barn. A pretty, petite nineteen-year-old, she was selected for the job because she has the kind of sparkle and vivaciousness that any restaurant would want customers to see. But some of her more antagonistic black customers saw her as an archetype: the immigrant who barely speaks a word of English who snaps up a job some native-born English speaker ought to have. Without the support of her bilingual, Latino manager, she would not have been able to pull herself together and get on with the work:

> I wasn't sent to the grill or the fries [where you don't need to communicate with customers]. I was sent to the cash register, even though the managers knew I couldn't speak English. That was only one week after my arrival in the United States! So I wasn't feeling very well at all. Three weeks later I met a manager who was Puerto Rican. He was my salvation. He told me, "Marisa, it's not that bad." He'd speak to me in English, even though he knows Spanish. He'd tell me, "Don't cry. Dry off those tears. You'll be all right, you'll make it." So he encouraged me like no other person in that Burger Barn, especially when the customers would curse at me for not knowing English. He gave me courage and after that it went much better.

Among the things this manager taught Marisa was that she should never listen to people who give her a hard time about holding a job at Burger Barn. Having been a white-collar clerical worker in her native country, it did bother Marisa that she had slipped down the status hierarchy—and it still does. She was grateful, nevertheless, to have a way to earn money and her family was desperate for her contribution. When customers would insult her, insinuating that someone who speaks limited English was of lowly status, she turned to management for help. And she found it in the form of fellow Latino bosses who told her to hold her head up because she was, after all, working, while her critics on the whole were not.

Once these general moral values are in place, many Burger Barn workers take the process one step further: they argue their jobs have hidden virtues that make them more valuable than most people credit. Tiffany Wilson, the young black woman who reluctantly settled for a Burger Barn job when none of the clothing stores she wanted to work for would take her, decided in the end that there was more substance to her job than she credited initially:

> When I got in there, I realized it's not what people think. It's a lot more to it than flipping burgers. It's a real system of business. That's when I really got to see a big corporation at play. I mean, one part of it, the foundation of it: cashiers, the store, how it's run. Production of food, crew workers, service. Things of that nature. That's when I really got into it and understood a lot more.

Americans tend to think of values as embedded in individuals, transmitted through families, and occasionally reinforced by media images or role models. We tend not to focus on the powerful contribution that institutions and organizations make to the creation and sustenance of beliefs. Yet it is clear that the workplace itself is a major force in the creation of a rebuttal culture among these workers. Without this line of defense it would be very hard for Burger Barn employees to retain their dignity. With the support of fellow workers, however, they are able to hold their heads up, not by defining themselves as separate from society, but by calling upon the values they hold in common with the rest of the working world.

This is but one of the reasons why exclusion from the society of the employed is such a devastating source of social isolation. We could hand people money, as various guaranteed income plans of the past thirty years have suggested. But we can't hand out honor. For a majority of Americans, honor comes from participation in this central setting in our culture and from the positive identity it confers.

Franklin Roosevelt understood this during the Great Depression and responded with the creation of thousands of publicly funded jobs designed to put people to work building the national parks, the railway stations, the great highways that criss-cross the country, and the murals that decorate public walls from San Francisco to New York. Social scientists studying the unemployed in the

1930s showed convincingly that people who held WPA jobs were far happier and healthier than those who were on the dole, even when their incomes did not differ significantly. WPA workers had their dignity in the midst of poverty; those on the dole were vilified and could not justify their existence or find an effective cultural rationale for the support they received.

This historical example has its powerful parallels in the present. Joining the workforce is a fundamental, transforming experience that moves people across barriers of subculture, race, gender, and class. It never completely eradicates these differences and in some divisive settings it may even reinforce consciousness of them—through glass ceilings, discriminatory promotion policies, and the like. But even in places where pernicious distinctions are maintained, there is another, overarching identity competing with forms that stress difference: a common bond within the organization and across the nation of fellow workers. This is what makes getting a job so much more than a means to a financial end. It becomes a crucial developmental hurdle, especially for people who have experienced exclusion before, including minorities, women, the elderly, and teenagers. Any experience that can speak back to the stigma that condemns burger flippers as the dregs, resurrecting them as exemplars of the American work ethic, has extraordinary power.

Never Enough Time

The acquisition of a mainstream identity as a working stiff is only one of the important changes that befalls an inner-city youth who remains committed to a job. He is also likely to experience a shortage of time. Hours that might once have been spent hanging out with friends, relaxing at home, doing schoolwork, or just doing nothing at all suddenly evaporate. Now he has to make priorities and face the fact that many pleasurable past times have to be sacrificed in favor of earning a living. For young people first joining the workforce, time binds of this magnitude are a new experience.

For workers with families, the conflict is even more extreme. Whatever time and energy they have left after the workday (or night shift) is over has to go into taking care of their own children and getting as much rest as they can steal (which is never enough). They too find they can no longer afford the time to hang out with friends and family who aren't working.

Latoya Dennis is a twenty-nine-year-old first-line manager at Burger Barn who has worked her way up from the shop floor over a six-year period. The mother of four kids, she has a sister and a cousin who work alongside her at the Barn. All three were known to be heavy party-goers before they started these jobs. These days, the parties are history. The work is too tiring:

My boyfriend thought I was joking. He was like, "Burger Barn—how could you be tired? They don't do nothing. All you do is flip burgers!" I'm like, "It's hard. It's really hard work." He sees that some days I come home from work, all I wanna do is just take my shoes off and get in the tub. I wind up sleeping in the tub and have to be woken up and he be like, "Get to bed."

So I don't hang out no more. I mean, before I was working I was like, "A party? I'm in there. We goin' to a club? I'm goin." Now they be like, "A party." I go to bed at eight o'clock. So [my friends] see that I'm really trying to get into work. So they be like, "Don't mention a party to Latoya. She don't wanna go. She's the working girl."

This is a common refrain among Burger Barn workers. They can no longer keep up with their friends who aren't on such tight schedules. They are too tired to stay up until 2 A.M. It doesn't take long before everyone in the neighborhood knows it and they find themselves subtracted from the party circles they used to run in. Whatever time they have left outside of their work hours is given over to school, to family obligations, or to blessed sleep.

Some youth, on the other hand, choose to work precisely to avoid a painful family situation or trouble in the streets. For those unhappy at home, and leery of the influence of street culture, the time constraints a job imposes are welcome. Jane Harris, a twenty-two-year-old manager, has worked at Burger Barn for four years. While at first reluctant to work there, she took the job to avoid spending time in her Bronx neighborhood. When she used to hang out on the block with her friends she'd get into fights, which she now considers too risky because the neighborhood has gotten so violent. When Jane began working, her friends noticed she hadn't been around the block much and told her she was working too hard and needed to take a vacation. These same friends are impressed now that Jane is a manager and has a diploma from the training she's received, as well as the promise of upward mobility.

Circles of Friends

The more workers withdraw from nonworking friends and neighbors, the greater the influence of more mainstream institutions on them. More and more of their waking hours are spent in structured activities that have real rewards and goals to work toward. But no one wants to be a work robot. Young people do find ways to have fun on the job, to gossip, flirt, and joke. However, if their social lives were entirely confined to these stolen moments, these jobs would hardly be worth the sacrifice. Some kind of extrawork social life has to be possible.

The pressures of work conspire to squeeze a worker's friendship circles, wringing out people in the neighborhood or passing acquaintances from school, in favor of fellow workers, especially people from the same shop floor. The time demands of the job push the same person into the arms of the organizational culture, or at least into the presence of fellow workers. And the similarity of workers' schedules and daily experiences creates a new, natural circle of friends. Over time, then, employees begin to spend much of the leisure time they have with one another. When they do go to the clubs, or to movies, or shopping, they are more likely to do so with someone they've come to know from Burger Barn.

Rosa Tampico is a Dominican student who works in a restaurant in the middle of a Latino neighborhood on Manhattan's far upper west side. She lives with her mother and some of her siblings; her father and the rest of the family are still in Santo Domingo, hoping to follow in their footsteps and emigrate in the next few years. Having had several jobs that involved a long commute, she eventually found one at a new Burger Barn that opened in her own neighborhood, thus eliminating the commute and putting her in the middle of a business where most of the other workers were Dominicans as well. Rosa found this a fine trolling ground for new friends, but it gradually put some distance between her and the kids she had been hanging out with before:

I like working at Burger Barn because I work with people of my own race. . . . You know, working there we always hang out, we go out together. . . . There is a sense of unity. When we go out, we go out together, the managers, the assistant manager, all of them.

Do you think your circle of friends has changed since you started working at Burger Barn? Yes, because I have three different kinds of friends. The friends in Santo Domingo. My friends of four years (since I arrived here). And since I started working at Burger Barn, I'm almost always with people from the restaurant. With the guys and the girls. I've neglected my other friends a little; they've gotten jealous.

They said something to you? Yes. They've told me, "Oh, because you're working there you've forgotten about us."

For Antonia Piento, who came to New York from Santo Domingo, the possibility of making a social circle out of people from work was a godsend. As a non–English speaker and a new immigrant, she had become quite isolated as a housewife. Few of her friends from the Dominican Republic had joined her. She knew almost no one and spent the whole day looking after her kids. But her sister and brother, both younger, finally landed jobs at Burger Barn and helped her in. That gave her a ready source of fellow Dominicans she could be-friend:

> I've been working at Burger Barn for a little more than a year now. . . . The best thing that's happened there is that almost all my friends—no, all my friends—are from work. Other than work, I don't have any more friends. I've met everyone I know there.

Tiffany Wilson is not one of those people who like their jobs. It is a dull, routine experience for her, more of a means to a financial end than anything else. But precisely because the job is no picnic, Tiffany looks to pass the time by having as much fun as she can with friends on the shop floor. Over time these joking relations have developed into friendships that transcend the job:

> When you get away from the hard, cold business ethic, that "Oh, we have to make money . . . ," we can just go with the flow and enjoy what we are doing. Then the job is fun, and you still make money. You make it fun for yourself. Most employees get together pretty often; we get along pretty good. People always have their cliques and remain in them. We do things for entertain-ment outside the restaurant. I've gone out shopping with some of the girls from the job. We spend time together, maybe a movie, clubs.

Why does the composition of young workers' friendship circles matter so much? It is important because as the proportion of time spent in the workplace increases, and the mix of their social acquaintances shifts toward other employ-ees, work culture comes to dominate their lives. The rhythm of the workday, the structure it imposes, the regularity of obligations and expectations become second nature. What recedes from view is the more irregular, episodic youth culture of the neighborhood and the streets. Working people gradually leave those less ordered worlds for the more predictable, demanding, and, in the long run, rewarding life of a wage earner. This is as true for the long-term fast-food worker as it is for the claims processor at an insurance company or an assistant nurse. There are, of course, more skills, greater future prospects, and certainly more money wrapped up in those other careers. But what all three jobs share is a regular structure, a structure that comes to set the parameters for most other aspects of life—including leisure, family, and time alone.

The dominance of work culture reinforces the division between the working-man and -woman and those among their acquaintances who do not work. It causes many to pull away from people who don't share their schedules, their problems, and in time, their way of looking at the world. Indeed, this separation can proceed to the point where workers in some of the most stigmatized occupations (like food service) identify more powerfully with other wage earners than they do with people they've known for years, people who live right next door, but who are not part of the labor force.

Tamara Jones provides a good example of the way in which working youth pull away from the bad apples in their environment as the grip of work culture tightens around them. Tamara grew up in a tough part of Harlem, surrounded by boarded-up row houses and broken glass on the sidewalk. Most of the folks in her neighborhood were looking for work, but relatively few had steady jobs. To have a regular job was to be an object of envy on Tamara's block:

> Everybody there, on the block, did not have a job. It was a big thing to have a job, you understand. People would look at me [when I started working at Burger Barn], "Oh! She's goin' out to work!" 'Cause everybody just sat and gossiped about everybody else.

Tammy was one of the lucky ones who did find work, due mostly to the divine intervention of her mother's best friend who was the manager of a Burger Barn in Harlem. Most people in Tamara's neighborhood didn't have these connections and didn't find it so simple to get a job.

Kids on her block looked up to people with money, people with cars and nice clothes, people with visible means. Some of those people happened to be drug dealers, while others came by their grandeur through legitimate means. Everyone on the block had to choose which of these means to glory was worthy of admiration. Tamara's role model was a generous man who earned a legitimate living and gave her a job too.

> Martin was one of the people in the neighborhood who had a good job. He owned the game room, owned the building it was in. He drove a nice car and he was building a Laundromat next to the game room. That's where I used to sell newspapers. Martin always gave to the block. We would come in there some time, the kids didn't have money, and he'd put quarters in for them. Or one day he'd say, "Giving out free cheeseburgers today." Yes! And you'd come in and get your cheeseburger. He always gave. All of us who grew up, all the girls around my age, he made sure nobody bothered us.
>
> There was also another guy on the block, [James], but he was selling drugs. He'd sell a lot of drugs, but he gave to the block too. I mean he gave free bus trips to Great Adventures and everything. He'd come into the game room and put quarters into the machine for everybody.
>
> Martin and James couldn't stand each other, 'cause one made his way of living selling drugs, but always gave to others and was never stingy with his

money. Martin was making it legally and he just gave, gave, gave. . . . They would try to outdo each other. People liked both of them, but James could do so much more.

Most kids look up to you and wanna be all under you when you have a lot of money. I tried to get under Martin because he was helping me out. James, I never tried to be up under him 'cause I knew, I . . . knew something was wrong. 'Cause it's not legal and you can get arrested for it. And I knew at that age. I always looked at him and I'd be like, "What's it like to have that much money?" But Martin would say, "He may have more money than me, but I make mine legally."

As Tamara's story illustrates, there is an ongoing debate among Harlem residents over the proper means of achieving honor, which draw on different aspects of mainstream conceptions of success. Those who choose to earn a living in the legitimate job market receive few material rewards for their effort, but they can claim moral legitimacy from the traditional American work ethic. They can't flash large rolls of cash before the eyes of their neighbors, but they can pride themselves on "doing the right thing," avoiding the dangers of the drug trade and the sloth of welfare recipients. While they understand that some people have a legitimate need to receive government assistance, they don't see the payoff of dealing drugs, and this is not an opinion they keep to themselves. Workers with friends or family in the drug trade often implore them to get out, warning them of the dangers, and reasoning that they each make about the same amount of money in a week, while the one involved with drugs has to work longer hours.

Nadine Stevens has worked at Burger Barn since graduating from high school five years ago. By all accounts she lives in one of the most dangerous neighborhoods in Harlem. Her apartment building is the home of an active drug trade and, indeed, the mailboxes were recently removed from the building by police because they were being used for drug transactions. She knows most of the drug dealers who sit on her stoop every day and night, having grown up with them. She and her mother and sister, whose ground-floor apartment faces the street, have seen many young women they know wasted by drugs, and young men killed in their hallway.

Nadine tries to convince the dealers she knows to get out of the trade, and to shoot for getting into management at Burger Barn. She and her sister, Rachael, with whom she works at Burger Barn, recently accosted a young teen they knew on the street whom they suspected of drug running. They told her that if she was desperate for money they'd get her a job at Burger Barn. Sensing the girl's reluctance, Nadine cried, "There's no shame in my game! Come work with me."

The dealers they know argue that the Burger Barn employee is working in a poorly paid, demeaning job and that, furthermore, they couldn't get hired there if they tried. Although their work is dangerous, illegal, and despised by neighbors, they brandish the accoutrements of success glorified in the United States: expensive cars, stylish clothes, and lots of cash. Their honor is measured in dollars, a common American standard that competes for the attention of people otherwise destined to earn little more than the minimum wage.

Anthony Vallo has had to choose on which side of the law to work and, once he secured his Burger Barn job, had to decide what to do about his friends and acquaintances who chose the wrong side. Two of his best friends are in jail. Another friend is dealing drugs and probably isn't far from a jail term himself. What Anthony does is try to maintain a cordial relationship with these guys, but to put as much distance between himself and them as he can without giving offense:

> This friend of mine is selling and stuff like that, but he's my friend. We used to go to school back then. He was like, "Damn, you still doin' that Burger Barn shit? I can get you a real job!" I think he respects me; at least he don't criticize me behind my back. But I try to avoid him, you know.

Drug dealers are not the only problem cases with which Harlem workers must contend. At least until welfare reform began to force women on AFDC back into the labor force, many young mothers working low-wage jobs were faced with the fork in the road that led either to a job at a place like Burger Barn or public assistance. Since most know a fair number of women who have elected, or had no choice but to opt for, the latter, it takes no small amount of fortitude to go for a minimum-wage job.[11] Indeed, given that AFDC offered greater financial benefits—when health coverage, food stamps, and subsidized housing are part of the package—than these jobs provide, it takes a strong attachment to the work ethic and a willingness to sacrifice elements of one's financial well-being in favor of the dignity that goes with holding a real job.

Patricia Hull has been on both sides of the fence. Her experience on the job convinced her that the honor gained has been worth the costs. But she has had to make the conscious choice to pull back from welfare:

> I tell the managers "I'm here 'cause I wanna be." I tell them, "This is no hobby; I'm your best employee." And I felt that way when I told them. I depend on this job. But a year ago, this was a hobby. I mean, I could've easily gone back to public assistance and got two hundred dollars more a month than working in Burger Barn. So I really wanted to be here.

Young people in Harlem are constantly faced with choices, presented with drastically different models of adulthood and asked to decide between them. What getting a job has done for the lucky ones like Tamara or Patty is to reinforce the right choice. For on the job, young workers are provided moral armor to be used in going "against the flow," opting for the legal, honorable, but generally poorly paid pathway in life. They join the fraternity of the minimum-wage worker, who sits at the very bottom of one pyramid—the status system that places professionals, white-collar workers, even sales people in Gap stores above them—and the very top of another—the world of people around them who may be dealing drugs, hanging on the street corner, or suffering the indignities and intrusions of the welfare bureaucracy. The more they adhere to the community of the workplace, the more they separate themselves from the irregular, the excluded, the demonized and cleave to the regular, accepted, but stigmatized.

They inhabit this strange "sandwich" world that denies them the prestige that more affluent and educated workers have, while according them the respect that working people give one another. They can look up at those who have so much more than they do and hope that by dint of their hard work, whatever education they can cobble together in the future, and the prospect of advancement at Burger Barn they might someday climb up that ladder. But most end up just staring up that tunnel because the deck is stacked against upward mobility. And they know that people located above them in the stacking order look down on them as drones who lack the brains to do any better.

Ianna Bates finds these attitudes a grind to endure. Even within Burger Barn, where she expects some regard, she often feels that she is deemed below notice:

> It's not that I'm conceited or anything. But I don't use my brain to the capacity I know it can hold, which is dumb. But I'm very smart and they ain't just gonna pay me enough money to do what I know needs to be done. They just couldn't do it. Cause, I mean, I'm a loyal worker. If you need me, I'll stay. I'll do anything. It's not so much the money; management just doesn't show the appreciation. . . . As soon as you display some kind of intelligence they look down upon you like, she doesn't know what she's talking about.

While some managers act as mentors to workers in whom they see potential leadership, others do not attempt to buffer them from customers' abuse and, indeed, belittle workers themselves. Employees are expected to defer not only to nasty customers, but to nasty managers, and conflicts with the latter are what often prompt them to quit. Ianna has had enough of being on the bottom of the deck and hopes to get a new job as a clerk with a city agency so that her occupation will garner her the kind of status and respect she thinks she deserves.

Frank Reynosa is a high-school senior whose family comes from a small town on the western side of Puerto Rico. Before finding his current job at Burger Barn, Frank worked as a youth counselor in a community center run by people from his hometown on the island. That job accorded with his sense of social position as a young man with promise; he finds Burger Barn a comedown—better than being unemployed, to be sure, but a lower-ranking status than he merits. "The workers are on the move all the time—you can never sit down," he complains, "and at the end they really don't get what they deserve out of it in terms of how they are regarded. There's people who do a lot less than what you are doing and get paid more." And those people also get more respect.

William Johnson knows just how much more respect because he used to have a white-collar job in a brokerage firm downtown. William manned the copy room, doing the photocopying for the lawyers and accountants. He was making good money, he wore a tie to work, and could hold his head up on his way down the street in Harlem. William moved from there to a big insurance firm where he worked as a filing clerk, handling the microfiche, supporting the investigative claims division. Both white-collar jobs paid well, but more than that, they were jobs that might have had a future. William made a lot of mistakes, though. He goofed off, flirted with the women on the job, and eventually lost what was then his best chance for a solid future in a decent job. "I was young and didn't realize what I had," he admits. "I had no plan, no sense of responsibility. I never looked at the job and asked where this job can honestly take me."

Moving down to Burger Barn has been a humbling experience. It has taught William that he is going to have to start all over again:

> Working at Burger Barn is like, "Yo, you gotta relearn all that stuff all over again." You gotta learn the value of a dollar, learn what it is to be responsible. Learn to appreciate what you got, not just look at it at face value.

It doesn't make William feel like cheering to know that he has tumbled down to the bottom of the employment system. Nobody hard-times him to his face, but he knows that he doesn't carry much weight as a burger flipper. And he feels like he blew it out of his own foolishness, pushed himself down a ladder that society has constructed, a status hierarchy of which he considers himself to be a part.

Although scraping the bottom of the employment barrel is no pleasure, Burger Barn workers can look down below to all the people who aren't even in the barrel—drug dealers, welfare recipients, the hustlers, the jailed, and the homeless—and feel superior to them. Working men and women, no matter how lowly their jobs, can hold their heads up in this company and know that American culture "validates" their claim to social rank above them.[12]

Indeed, some make active attempts to become role models for people in their community who have fallen by the wayside. Rather than leave these acquaintances in the dust, they try to exert some positive influence over them by showing them that there is another, more socially acceptable, way of living. Frank Reynosa selects his friends carefully, weeding out those people who are "goin' nowhere." But as Frank sees it, many of the young people around him seem destined for a life of hanging out. Because he can't completely isolate himself from them, and because he cares about them, he tries to use himself as an example of better values:

> Today, a friend of mine told me, "Yeah, I know you busted out on the report card," because they know that I be gettin' good grades and stuff. I told him, "Yeah, I got so-so grades." But I failed one. It was like, "Oh?" Like they'd be shocked. They'd be, "Wow, you didn't do good." And they'd be concerned with why. Because I usually show them [my report card]. I try to be a role model, let them know I'm trying, let them know I'd help them out. I'll say, "Look at my report card. . . . Where's yours? Why didn't you pass?" I don't say, "Yo, you should do this, you should do that." Because I don't wanna seem like I'm their mother or father.
>
> Like my friend. He used to be real good at school, when we was little, and stuff like that. He used to get awards. Not now, so I'll say, "What happened? You failed three classes. You dropping off. Not doing too good in school." He was, "Naw, it got harder." I was, "You better study you know. Do what you got to do just to get out." And I see him going now. He is going to summer school and stuff like that.

Larry Peterson plays a similar role in his friends' lives. He is struggling to work and finish high school, a combination that is never easy to manage. "Some of my friends think I should just go get my GED," Larry allows. "They think I should take the easy way out." But that is not what Larry has in mind. "I want to stick in there," he says with determination, "and go the whole nine yards." Larry's example has had its effect, though. His friends have started to look at him as the model to follow:

> Since they've been around me, they tend to look *my* way. They look for *my* advice, they look for *my* decisions. They look for what I want to go through so they can follow me.

Larry's determination to finish school and continue working has made an impression on his friends and boosted his currency in a neighborhood where many young people do neither. They can sense his resolve, the strength of his resolution and this they can respect.

Many young workers told similar stories. Their friends almost sheepishly admitted that it took guts to carry on in the face of so much criticism, that it was important to be persistent and hold a job, almost any job, for a long time. No small number would end up asking for help in finding the very same job they condemned a few months earlier.

Taking a fast-food job subjects inner-city dwellers to ridicule, but sticking with the same job can, in the end, earn them respect and even enhance their stature. For friends, neighbors, and family members understand that it takes real strength of character to stay with something—a job, school, a relationship, almost anything. Sheer duration, coupled with the willingness to buck the tide of local public opinion, conveys a kind of individualistic resolve that is valued.

Here too the power of mainstream ideals is clear. Americans value individualism, running against the tide, the square-jawed hero who stands against the crowd. This is not without ambiguity, for clearly we also place a value on conformity. But there is a cultural subtext to which people can refer with pride when they stand alone and fight the base morals of the group. Burger Barn workers can claim a whole new status: the individualist who stood against local pressure to conform in pursuit of widely respected purposes like working for a living.

Still, the ambiguous social position of the low-wage service worker does not completely satisfy anyone who partakes of it. Claiming a mainstream identity as gainfully employed certainly helps in warding off the stigma that customers, neighbors, age-mates, and society at large heap on people who earn very little and are under orders to be subservient. By linking one's claim to an honored status as a working person, the low-wage employee pushes back. But he can only push so far, for he soon hits the wall, knowing full well that people who wear white collars to work, who don't come home covered with grease, who hang diplomas on their doors, and who can count more zeros on their paychecks than any Burger Barn workers will ever see, barely rate them as in the same category. As Doug Carver, a particularly perceptive young black man at Burger Barn, put the matter:

> You accept the fact that you're not gonna get rich. You're working, man, but you're still struggling. You're not laid back. You're still humble . . . what makes it difficult is when you're smart. [Burger Barn] is not for anybody that has any type of brains. . . . You're being overworked and underpaid. You're making somebody else rich. So . . . you really got to brainwash yourself to

say, "Well, OK, I'm going to make this guy rich and I'm just happy to be making this little $5 an hour."

No one navigates this contradictory cultural maze alone, though. They can do so only in the company of others who are similarly positioned "betwixt and between." They learn the cultural defenses to the stigma heaped upon them in the workplace, from concerned managers and veteran workers who have already been there. The more they participate in this rebuttal culture, the more they are drawn into a social world that revolves around the work ethic, the company of fellow workers, and friendships that reinforce the defense of holding a fast-food job. Ultimately, being a member of this fraternity shifts their identities from kid in the neighborhood to worker on the shop floor, albeit a worker with a complex identity: part admired, part scorned.

The Importance of Going to Work

Although having a well-paid, respected career is prized above all else in the United States, our culture confers honor on those who hold down jobs of any kind over those who are outside of the labor force. Independence and self-sufficiency—these are virtues that have no equal in this society. But there are other reasons why we value workers besides the fact that their earnings keep them above water and therefore less in need of help from government, communities, or charities. We also value workers because they share certain common views, experiences, and expectations. The work ethic is more than an attitude toward earning money—it is a disciplined existence, a social life woven around the workplace.

For all the talk of "family values," we know that in the contemporary period, family often takes a backseat to the requirements of a job, even when the job involves flipping burgers. What we are supposed to orient toward primarily is the workplace and its demands. This point could not be made more forcefully than it is in the context of the welfare reform bills of 1996. Public policy in the late 1990s makes clear that poor women are now supposed to be employed even if they have young children.[13] With a majority of women with children, even those under a year of age, in the labor force, we are not prepared to cut much slack to those who have been on welfare. They can and should work like the rest of us, or so the policy mantra goes. This represents no small change in the space of a few decades in our views of what honorable women and mothers should do. But it also reflects the growing dominance of work in our understanding of adult priorities.

We could think of this increasingly work-centered view of life as a reflection of America's waning economic position, a pragmatic response to wage stagnation, downsizing, and international competition: we must work harder. And this it may be. But it is also part of a secular transformation that has been ongoing for decades as we've moved away from home-centered work lives in the agricultural world to employment-centered lives outside the domestic sphere altogether. The more work departs from home, the more it becomes a social system of its own, a primary form of integration that rivals the family as a source of identity, belonging, and friendship. Women like Antonia Piento are not content only to take care of children at home. They want a life that is adult centered, where they have peers they can talk to. Where they might once have found that company in the neighborhood, now they are more likely to find it on the shop floor. Those primary social ties are grounded in workplace relations, hence to be a worker is also to be integrated into a meaningful community of fellow workers, the community that increasingly becomes the source of personal friends, intimate relations, and the world view that comes with them.

Work is therefore much more than a means to a financial end. This is particularly the case when the work holds little intrinsic satisfaction. No one who gets paid for boiling french fries in hot oil thinks they are playing a world-shattering role. They know their jobs are poorly valued; they can see that in their paychecks, in the demeanor of the people whom they serve across the counter, even among some managers. But what they have that their nonworking counterparts lack is both the dignity of being employed and the opportunity to participate in a social life that increasingly defines their adult lives. This community gives their lives structure and purpose, humor and pleasure, support and understanding in hard times, and a backstop that extends beyond the instrumental purposes of a fast-food restaurant. It is the crucible of their values, values that we have argued here are decidedly mainstream.

The working poor sit at the bottom of the occupational structure and feel the weight of disapproval coming down upon their shoulders from better paid, more respectable employees. Yet they stand at the top of another pyramid and can look down the slope toward people they know well who have taken another pathway in the world.

Notes

The research for this chapter was made possible by generous grants from the Russell Sage, Ford, Rockefeller, Spencer, and William T. Grant Foundations. A revised version of this chapter appears in Newman 1999.

1. See Michèle Lamont's chapter in this volume for an analysis of the way working-class men bolster their self-worth by evaluating individuals according to moral criteria such as honesty and self-reliance rather than by socioeconomic characteristics like income and education. They may sit below the elite in this country based on standards of

wealth, power, and education, but they see themselves as sitting atop another hierarchy, a moral one, which they consider most important.

2. There are further shades of gray below the line of the employed that distinguish those who are searching for work and those who have accepted their fate as nonworkers, with the latter suffering the greatest stigma of all.

3. For more on the moral structure associated with work and achievement of the American dream, see Hochschild 1995.

4. See Wilson 1996, Massey and Denton 1993, Hacker 1992, and Urban Institute 1991.

5. All names and identifying information have been changed to protect confidentiality.

6. Hochschild 1983 documents similar attempts in the airline industry. One airline holds a mandatory seminar for flight attendants to teach them "anger-desensitization" when dealing with rude and demeaning customers.

7. In areas experiencing exceptionally tight labor markets—including much of the Midwest in the late 1990s—wages for these jobs are climbing above the minimum-wage line.

8. This is one of the many reasons why increasing the minimum wage is so important. Ghettos have such impoverished job bases to begin with that they are almost always characterized by slack labor markets. Only when the labor supply outside ghetto walls has tightened down to almost impossible levels do we begin to see this tide lift inner-city boats. Eventually employers do turn to the workers who are low on their preference queues (as we learned in the 1980s during the Massachusetts miracle), but these conditions are, sadly, rare and generally short-lived.

9. Indeed, over a five-month period in 1993 there were fourteen job applicants for every job opening at two different Burger Barns in Harlem (Newman and Lennon 1995).

10. The fact that Harlem residents rejected for these jobs hold these values is some evidence for the preexisting nature of this mind-set—although these rejects had already piled up work experience that may have contributed to the sharpening of this alternative critique.

11. It should be noted that women on welfare and women in low-wage jobs are not necessarily two distinct groups. Many women find it necessary to go back and forth between holding a low-wage job and relying solely on welfare, and many supplement one form of income with the other (not to mention other income from friends, family, and unreported work), since neither source alone provides enough money to support a family (see Edin 1994).

12. Elijah Anderson describes a similar phenomenon among the middle- and working-class African-Americans. The urban residents he writes about use the nearby underclass as "an important yardstick" that enables them to "compare themselves favorably with others they judge worse off, a social category stigmatized within the community" (Anderson 1990, 66). Likewise, Maureen Waller illuminates the way low-income single parents "endorse negative representations of the groups to which they belong,"

while distancing themselves, and other single parents they know personally, from such images, in order to view themselves as good parents (Waller 1996, 210).

13. As Jane Mansbridge mentions in her chapter discussing race, activism, and the evolution of feminist ideas in this volume, this expectation is nothing new for many black women. Julia Wrigley indicates the same thing in her discussion of the historic relationship between black domestic workers and white employers in this volume.

References

Anderson, Elijah. 1990. *Streetwise*. Chicago: University of Chicago Press.

Edin, Kathryn. 1994. "The Myths of Dependency and Self-Sufficiency: Women, Welfare, and Low-Wage Work." Unpublished paper. Department of Sociology and Center for Urban Policy Research, Rutgers University.

Hacker, Andrew. 1992. *Two Nations*. New York: Ballantine.

Hochschild, Arlie. 1983. *The Managed Heart*. Berkeley: University of California Press.

Hochschild, Jennifer L. 1995. *Facing Up to the American Dream*. Princeton: Princeton University Press.

Katz, Michael. 1989. *The Undeserving Poor*. New York: Pantheon.

Massey, Douglas S., and Nancy A. Denton. 1993. *American Apartheid*. Cambridge: Harvard University Press.

Newman, Katherine S. 1999. *No Shame in My Game: The Working Poor in the Inner City*. New York: Knopf/Russell Sage Foundation.

Newman, Katherine S., and Chauncy Lennon. 1995. "The Job Ghetto." *American Prospect*, summer, 66–67.

Urban Institute. 1991. *Opportunities Denied, Opportunities Diminished*. Report 91–9. Washington: Urban Institute Press.

Waller, Maureen. 1996. "Redefining Fatherhood: Paternal Involvement, Masculinity, and Responsibility in the 'Other America.'" Ph.D. diss, Princeton University.

Wilson, William Julius. 1996. *When Work Disappears*. New York: Knopf.

meanings and motives in new family stories: the separation of reproduction and marriage among low-income black and white parents

maureen r. waller

Close to one-third of births now occur to unmarried parents, up from about 10 percent in 1970 (U.S. Department of Health, Education, and Welfare 1975; U.S. Department of Health and Human Services 1994). Although this trend has generated a great deal of media and political attention, only a limited number of popular stories have been told to explain the separation of reproduction and marriage. In media and political accounts, African-American teenagers living in poor communities are the most familiar representatives of unwed motherhood. These young women are alternatively portrayed as rational maximizers who have children outside of marriage to receive welfare benefits, as products of an "underclass culture" that socializes children into patterns of early childbearing and state dependence, and as victims of their own ignorance about birth control and about the consequences of their actions (Luker 1996, 4). Stories about teenage pregnancy have also been expanded to include young African-American fathers who are portrayed as abandoning their economic responsibilities to their children and forcing them to rely on the welfare system for help.[1] More recently, a white, middle-class image of unmarried parenthood has also appeared in popular discourse. In these accounts, thirty- to forty-something middle-class "single mothers by choice" opt for careers over marriage, deciding to rear a child without the involvement of the father.[2]

Although these two stories have been told to make sense

of recent changes in the structure of American families, neither is adequate for capturing the experiences of a larger group of men and women who have children outside of marriage, many of whom look to public assistance for their support.[3] In this chapter, I explore the experiences of unmarried African-American and white parents who seem to be at the forefront of transformations occurring in families throughout American society but who appear less often in accounts of nonmarital childbearing.[4] Drawing on in-depth interviews with sixty-five unmarried mothers and fathers living in New Jersey, I investigate how parents with children receiving welfare explain decisions about reproduction and marriage.[5] This paper documents the responses of African-American and white parents to investigate both culturally shared and delineated meanings of nonmarital childbearing. It also focuses on adult parents, a group that is numerically larger but less frequently studied than adolescents (Moore 1995, xxi).[6] Finally, it includes the accounts of low-income, unmarried fathers, who have received relatively little scholarly attention.[7]

Based on parents' stories about the birth of their youngest child, the discussion begins with retrospective accounts about their expectations for parenthood and their options for responding to an unintended pregnancy.[8] It next examines how unmarried parents talk about marriage following an unexpected birth, why their relationship with the other parent ended, and the conditions under which marriage is regarded as an appropriate and viable option. When describing their expectations for becoming unmarried parents, I suggest that black mothers and fathers articulate a more consistent cultural script about these experiences than white parents and identify social and economic conditions that undermine marriage in their neighborhoods. At the same time, there is a significant amount of overlap between white and black parents' accounts. While many parents were open to having a child outside of marriage, about half of parents recalled feeling ambivalence or significant apprehension about the pregnancy. These parents typically characterized their decision to have a child as a moral or emotional response to an unintended situation. However, neither black or white parents I interviewed generally regard marriage as an appropriate way to resolve a nonmarital pregnancy, arguing that "rushed" or "forced" marriages are likely to fail. Instead, parents recount cultural explanations about the appropriate reasons to marry, which resemble those of other young men and women of their generation. In many situations, parents suggest marriage would be futile or risky and talk about their decisions in terms of minimizing the high likelihood of divorce. In particular, women with primary responsibility for children and African-American parents living in poor neighborhoods identified multiple risks associated with marriage. And, while many parents hope to marry, they suggest that they have more control over and confidence in their ability to be good parents than in the outcomes of their relationships.

Investigating New Family Patterns

Perhaps the most popular explanation of recent changes in family structure links increasing nonmarital birth rates to welfare receipt. Statistical research, however, generally fails to show a strong connection between state spending for welfare and births to unmarried parents (see Bane and Ellwood 1994, 109–12). Instead, social scientists point to a complex set of economic and cultural factors that have encouraged increases in nonmarital childbearing across social groups in the United States and in other industrialized countries. Some of these factors include a decline of men's earnings in relation to women's;[9] an increasing cultural acceptance of divorce, cohabitation, and sexuality outside of marriage; and changes in gender expectations.[10] Although researchers often disagree about why more men and women are deciding to have children outside of marriage, most agree that marital behavior is changing more than fertility behavior (e.g., Garfinkel and McLanahan 1986, 54).

In research that specifically examines nonmarital childbearing in poor, urban communities, social scientists often emphasize the negative impact of joblessness and falling wages on marriage among African-American families in the wake of deindustrialization (Wilson 1996, 1987). Researchers also suggest that white men at lower skill and educational levels may have become less "marriageable" in recent years, precipitating convergence in black and white family patterns (Luker 1996, 166–67).[11] While many writers agree on these structural factors associated with the decline in marriage, many of the most hotly contested questions in this literature address cultural factors or psychological motives underlying the decision to have a child outside of marriage.[12] However, much of this research focuses exclusively on the experiences of teenage parents. And while many social scientists situate their research within a macroeconomic context, they often do not explain low-income men and women's decision to become unmarried parents within a larger cultural context.

CULTURAL FRAMEWORK. To understand how low-income mothers and fathers make sense of their options and experiences as unmarried parents, I suggest that social scientists consider the ways of interpreting reproduction and marriage that single parents borrow from the "mainstream" American culture (including publicly available symbols disseminated through the educational system, popular culture, and media), from institutions, from parents' localized experiences in their families and communities, and from race, gender, generational, and class-based cultural conventions (Lamont 1992).[13] When considering the availability of discourses, however, I also take into account the unequal distribution of cultural resources that people have access to given their structural position in society and variations in actors' competence to use those resources

(Bourdieu 1984).[14] At the same time, I regard interpretations of marriage and reproduction that parents draw upon as polysemic (i.e., having multiple meanings). Therefore, they may appropriate ideas about reproduction and marriage (e.g., through popular culture) and "read" them differently from people in other social positions.[15] Because unmarried parents actively engage, reconstruct, and resist ideas that are made available to them, these explanatory frameworks may incorporate popular beliefs about family but offer culturally specified strategies for enacting them. And given their participation in various cultural groups, parents are able to invoke multiple explanations in their accounts.[16]

When examining accounts about reproduction and marriage in the larger culture, it is also important to note that this discourse is in flux following a series of cultural and economic changes that have occurred over the last few decades. Many low-income parents, particularly those in African-American communities, have been at the forefront of these changes. Moreover, African-American families have experienced nonmarital childbearing earlier and to a greater extent than white families (Morgan et al. 1993; Pagnini and Morgan 1996) and have historically "deviated" from the male breadwinner/female homemaker family pattern. Therefore, African-American families not only draw on available models, but have developed culturally innovative responses to them and to postindustrial economic and social conditions (Stacey 1991; Luker 1996).

NARRATIVE ANALYSIS. With the linguistic and interpretive turn in social theory, scholars in several disciplines began to focus on narrative as a way both research "subjects" and researchers themselves classify events to make them meaningful. When people's stories are the focus of analysis, it is possible to examine how they draw on available languages and conventions to construct a story, to explain their actions, to define their identities, and to persuade an audience. Researchers can also pay attention to why stories were told in some ways and not others (Riessman 1993). The analytical framework I use draws primarily on Burke's (1989) discussion of "dramatism," which examines how people select, define, and understand events through language (Gusfield 1989, 6). Burke observes that when actors make choices about how to tell stories in a way that will make sense to themselves and others, they offer particular interpretations of reality. As rhetorical constructs, narratives are typically devised retrospectively to organize a series of events that are complicated and disorganized in practice (Hopper 1993). Because actors order experience to make it comprehensible and because only a limited number of perceptual schemes are available, Burke suggests that linguistic representations of events are necessarily selective (Gusfield 1989).[17]

The attribution of motives is also central to Burke's discussion of narrative. In particular, Burke argues that when describing what actions are occurring and why they are occurring, people confer explanations of motives onto behavior. In a related discussion of "vocabularies of motive," Mills (1940) follows Burke in emphasizing the social character of motives which are drawn from an accessible repertoire of accounts and communicated to others.[18] According to Mills (1940, 905), motives are also words that "stand for anticipated situational consequences of questioned conduct. . . . Behind questions are possible alternative actions with terminal consequences." In this way, actors draw from available accounts to make sense of their experiences and to outline possible courses of action.[19]

The following discussion uses Burke's "pentad" as a framework to investigate how unmarried parents construct accounts of reproduction and marriage. In particular, I document how parents describe the "scene" (or circumstances in which decisions about reproduction and marriage are made), the "act" of having a child outside of marriage, the "agents" (or actors involved in responding to the pregnancy), the "purpose" (or why the actors made the choices they did), and their "agency" (or how the responses were carried out).[20] After looking at the accounts of two parents who tell different stories about their experiences of being unmarried mothers, the next section examines how parents explain their options for reproduction and marriage.

Data and Methods

The research for this study took place in central New Jersey, primarily in the city of Trenton and its suburbs.[21] This metropolitan area went through the type of deindustrialization process described by Wilson (1987, 1996), and it exhibits similar characteristics to some other northeastern cities, such as concentrated poverty and joblessness. Statistics reveal some of the problems that Trenton now experiences. In May 1995, Trenton had an unemployment rate of 11.6 percent as compared with the state level of about 6.7 percent (U.S. Bureau of Labor Statistics 1995). In 1993, per capita income in Trenton was about $11,000 (which is more than 40 percent below the state average), the high-school dropout rate was about 52 percent, and approximately 30 percent of the city was designated an urban enterprise zone (Gugliotta 1993). The Association for Children of New Jersey (1993) also reports that about 40 percent of children in Trenton live in single-parent households and about 27 percent of children live below the poverty line.[22] Though the cost of living in the northeast corridor between New York and Philadelphia is high, when the interviews were conducted the typical single mother with two children in Trenton could receive a maximum of $424 a month in AFDC benefits and $276 in food stamps. Furthermore, the New Jersey legislature had recently passed a "family cap" that denied additional cash benefits to women who have a child while receiving welfare.

My data are derived from in-depth interviews with 65 unmarried mothers

TABLE 1   SELECTED SAMPLE CHARACTERISTICS

	Black Women (n = 20)		Black Men (n = 20)	
	Percentage	*Average*	*Percentage*	*Average*
Age		24		26
Age of focal child[a]		2		3
Number of children		2		2
Received high school degree	45		45	
Received GED	10		15	
Currently working[b]	5		65	
	White Women (n = 16)		White Men (n = 9)	
	Percentage	*Average*	*Percentage*	*Average*
Age		26		31
Age of focal child[a]		3		6
Number of children		2		2
Received high school degree	56		56	
Received GED	6		22	
Currently working[b]	31		56	

[a]The parent's youngest child who has received welfare

[b]Full or part-time employment

and fathers (40 African-American parents and 25 white parents) who have a child receiving welfare. I contacted mothers through the Women, Infants and Children (WIC) program in Trenton and New Brunswick, New Jersey.[23] To schedule interviews, I talked to women informally at the clinics and provided informational flyers about the study. If a woman met my criteria and was interested in participating, we set up a time and place (usually her home) to meet for the interview. I also asked for referrals from respondents to create a snowball sample, but requested a maximum of four referrals from each respondent to ensure sampling from diverse networks. To interview African-American fathers, I established personal contacts in Trenton neighborhoods and was referred to fathers from each section of the city. I also walked around areas where young men in Trenton congregate (e.g., outside of housing projects, on street corners, on the stoops of houses, in front of stores, and in barber shops), passed out flyers, and discussed the project with them. When meeting fathers in their neighborhoods, I was always accompanied by a member of the community. Because unmarried, white fathers are not concentrated in particular neighborhoods, they were contacted through referrals from other interviewees and through a program for nonresidential fathers in Trenton.[24] Interviews with most fathers were conducted in fast-food restaurants.

While these groups were not randomly chosen, the sampling strategy allowed me to interview men and women who are typically not sampled or who are reluctant to speak openly with researchers. The sensitive nature of the questions asked in this study also demanded that I gain the trust of respondents through nonintrusive and often personal contacts and distance from child support and welfare agencies. Interviews ranged from ninety minutes to four hours, and all interviews were recorded and transcribed. Finally, I analyzed interviews using a qualitative software program (Ethnograph) and created a database to record demographic and other characteristics of respondents.

Considering Parenthood outside of Marriage

TWO STORIES

> [Having a] kid never crossed my mind before I was twenty-two, nope, never. Never even thought I had to worry about it. When I found out I was pregnant, you know, here I am in a relationship for a couple years and I thought it was everything it was supposed to be . . . and I was confused. And I kept it to myself because he took off on me, and then I was left in this little insecure ball. And I didn't tell anyone for months. I was about five months pregnant before I let my friends know. Which, at that time, you know, to look back from the outside was a mistake. I should have talked to people because I was very unprepared for everything. I really didn't know what was available, and I didn't even see a doctor until I was twenty-three weeks. You know, things like that. I just didn't know what to do because I was scared.

Julie, a twenty-five-year-old white mother who has made a successful transition off of welfare, tells me this story over Diet Cokes one evening when she has returned home from her new job. Her small one-bedroom apartment is located on the top floor of a row house in the Italian working-class section of Trenton. Julie's three-year-old daughter hides in a cardboard box that she uses as a playhouse, coming in and out of the room occasionally to inspect the stranger sitting on her couch. After describing the scene in which the pregnancy occurred, she continues the story by reconstructing her options at the time.

> And I didn't consider abortion. You know, I'm not against it. I'm not out there rallying, but for me it wasn't a choice. And I really considered having her adopted. I spent, up until like eight months I said I'm not ready for this.

I knew at twenty-two I was still immature, and I wasn't prepared to be a mother. I didn't think I was. And, almost last minute, I said no. I didn't go to any agency or anything, but I said, no, this is my responsibility and I'm going to regret it . . . so I just winged it.

In this account, Julie emphasizes her isolation and lack of preparation. However, motivated by feelings of responsibility and possible regret, she takes an active stance and resolves this conflict by becoming an unmarried mother.

Crystal, an African-American mother, who also became pregnant with her youngest child at the age of twenty-two, tells a different story about unwed motherhood. It is morning when I knock on the door of Crystal's apartment on the third floor of a low-rise housing project in Trenton. Although she had forgotten about the interview, Crystal, a mother of three who is currently two months pregnant, greets me warmly and asks me to sit down. Still wearing her robe, she instructs her two older children to play in their bedroom, while her one-year-old baby sleeps on the couch. Almost immediately, she launches into a narrative about her previous pregnancy:

I was surprised about being pregnant with him because I wasn't using no protection or nothing and it was like kind of shocking, because my daughter was four years old. And I was like, I was shocked, I couldn't believe it. I thought I couldn't make no more babies. It's not like you plan to have a baby, it just happens. But at that point it was my fault because I know, if you're not using no protection, there's a 100 percent chance that you can get pregnant again. And it happened again. It happened again. Mm mm. But you know, I'm dealing with it.

On the one hand, Crystal is surprised by the news of her pregnancy because she suspects that she is infertile. On the other hand, she is fully aware that pregnancy is the likely result of sex without birth control. Positioning herself as an active subject (she did not use birth control and therefore accepts responsibility), Crystal identifies her options for responding to the pregnancy.

And I never had an abortion. Never. I'd be kind of skeptical about doing that. I was kind of skeptical about [having] him because I wasn't with his father when we made him. We wasn't into a deep relationship. We were just seeing each other. And I was like, why should I have this baby? I'm not with him. But I had to think about it. My baby always going to be here. You have to think about the child first, before you think about the man. You got to think about: this child did not ask to be born. I did lay down and make it.

Crystal considers the situation in which the pregnancy occurred (i.e., a casual relationship with the baby's father) when deciding whether or not to keep the baby. But she explains that her reservations about abortion and feeling of responsibility led her to go through with the pregnancy. While both mothers cite a moral motivation in responding to an unintended pregnancy, Crystal, a more experienced mother, explains she "is dealing with it" while Julie "just winged it."

These women use different strategies for explaining unmarried motherhood because their families, friends, and communities may offer them different cultural resources to interpret their experiences. And although they have both received welfare, their general economic situations are very different. Perhaps more importantly, their accounts show some notable similarities. While both women struggle with their decisions to become mothers, later in the interview, both women reject the idea that marriage would have "resolved" their situations. They cite specific circumstances that prohibited marriage (i.e., the father of her child left her or the relationship was not serious enough for marriage), but, in principle, neither mother believes that pregnancy is a good enough reason to marry. At the same time, both mothers also express a desire to get married to their current boyfriends (who are not the natural fathers). They also identify potential risks associated with this option, but Julie is much more optimistic than Crystal about the likelihood of marriage.

These two stories point to the diversity among unmarried parents. In fact, I chose these examples to point to the differences rather than similarities in the explanations of white and black parents. More often, the accounts of white parents I interviewed resemble those of African-American parents in important ways and the dissimilarities that exist may largely reflect differences between black and white poverty.[25] While Crystal's story is shaped by collective accounts that more easily accommodate an unintended pregnancy, Julie has more economic resources available to support her child. For example, Julie lives in a working-class neighborhood and temporarily fell into poverty after becoming an unmarried mother. With only one child and financial help from family members, Julie was later able to go back to school and get a secretarial job that pays enough to cover their expenses. She also received child support payments for a period of time before requesting that the father be released from this financial obligation. In contrast, Crystal's mother and sister live in public housing. Without significant family economic resources to draw upon (she receives occasional help from her father) or financial support from her children's unemployed father, Crystal tries to maintain her family on her welfare check and plans to enter a job-training program.

The circumstances these two women face are not wholly representative of other mothers in the study (e.g., the typical mother in my sample has two children and was in a steady relationship when she got pregnant). However, their stories point to themes about parents' expectations, options, and responses to nonmarital pregnancy that emerge in other interviews. Some of these themes also appear in popular stories about unmarried mothers, but the narratives of parents I interviewed are more complex than accounts of black teenage mothers and white "single mothers by choice" suggest.

THE SCENE: EXPECTATIONS FOR PARENTHOOD. When parents give retrospective accounts about the timing and conditions under which they expected to become parents, they draw upon models of family available from their local contexts and the larger culture. The white mothers and fathers I sampled lived in more mixed-income neighborhoods than their black counterparts and had significantly less contact with other unmarried parents with children on welfare in their communities.[26] White parents also tended to be from higher-income families in which more of their siblings married. Furthermore, while all of the white parents I interviewed said their own parents were married when they were born, about 40 percent of African-American parents said their parents had never been married. As a result, black parents draw on a "cultural script" for becoming an unmarried parent available from their families and communities that represents nonmarital childbearing as commonplace (Furstenberg 1991, 134).

In general, African-American parents' accounts suggest they had anticipated becoming unmarried parents and tend to minimize any conflict this event may have caused within their family or community, particularly if they were adults when the pregnancy occurred. This is perhaps not surprising, given that about two-thirds of births to African-American women now occur outside of marriage and nonmarital birthrates are even higher in low-income communities. For example, although Alicia, a twenty-four-year-old black mother who lives with her parents, did not plan to have her son when she did or with his father, she did expect to be single when she had children. Alicia explains that her parents were

TABLE 2   FAMILY AND RESIDENTIAL CHARACTERISTICS (IN PERCENTAGES)

	Black Parents	White Parents
Ever married	0	25
Parents ever married	60	100
Lives in Trenton	85	25
Lives in Metro Trenton	15	50
Lives in Middlesex County	0	25

not disappointed in her when she became pregnant because she had finished high school and held a steady job.

> For me personally, I like this experience of raising a child on my own. 'Cause like I say, I don't see myself getting married or anything. I always pictured myself being a single mother anyway. It's just, I can never picture a man. You know how they draw the picture of Mommy and Daddy. I can't. There's a blank face there and I can't even get the face down as to who the man would be. He'd have to be a very strong man for me to marry him. I guess that's what it would have to be.

Despite Alicia's apparent resistance to marriage and willingness to embrace single motherhood, she acknowledges that she would be open to marriage if she met a man who was "strong," "educated," and shared her interests. She simply doubts this will happen in Trenton.

On the other hand, the accounts of white parents show less consistency in their expectations for becoming unmarried parents. Like the majority of African-American parents, many white parents I talked to framed nonmarital pregnancy as an everyday, relatively unproblematic event, often recognizing diverse family forms as legitimate. In contrast, other white parents described the birth of their youngest child as a more unusual, stigmatized, or socially complicated experience and attempted to explain why their experiences deviated from a two-parent family model.[27] Beth, a twenty-two-year-old white mother from a higher-income family, discusses her reaction to an unplanned pregnancy with a man she was not seriously involved with. Her description of the circumstances in which she became pregnant closely parallels Alicia's, but this event has a different meaning within her life.

> I thought I'd be like married in a house with kids and stuff. So, this is different than I expected. I *never* thought I'd have a child like this, in this situation, living with my parents.

Beth is like several other white parents I interviewed, who describe their lives as taking a different course than they had anticipated and making ad hoc adjustments to becoming parents. They describe the actual scene (unmarried, living with their parents) in sharp contrast to the ideal scene (married, living in a house with a husband and children). The stories of white parents also suggest that they faced more isolation and stigma after deciding to have children outside of marriage than black parents. They noted outside reactions to their marital status that ranged from "funny looks" to discrimination in finding a job. Two of the women I interviewed responded by wearing rings that resembled wedding bands and telling people they were married.

In contrast to the relative acceptance many parents felt for their decision to become unmarried parents, both African-American and white parents suggested that teenage pregnancies (particularly under age eighteen) elicited family and/or community disapproval. While all the parents I interviewed were adults, about 30 percent of African-American parents and 20 percent of white parents in this study had their first child when they were under the age of eighteen and faced varying degrees of support and disapproval for this decision.[28] Monica, a young white woman who lives in a suburban neighborhood outside of Trenton, says that her family "disowned" her when she became a mother at sixteen. She talks about her mother's reaction to the news of her pregnancy:

> I made the mistake of telling her in a moving car, and I was stuck in it. She was screaming. She was like, "You're going to have an abortion! I don't care if I have to hit you to have an abortion! I'm going to knock some sense into your brain!"

African-American parents often characterize nonmarital pregnancy as a crisis for young but not for older parents and suggest that parents experience stigma primarily on the basis of age rather than marital status.[29]

In general, the accounts of both black and white men suggest that they experienced less conflict associated with having children outside of marriage than women; those fathers who did face disapproval from their families were teenagers at the time their child was born. A few of the white men were able to avoid the possibility of upsetting their families by limiting contact with their child or by not telling their parents about the pregnancy. Because all of these fathers have lived apart from their children, they could choose whether or not to reveal their identities as fathers, in contrast to women, who do not have the option of concealing their pregnancies.

THE ACT, AGENTS, AND PURPOSE: PLANNING, OPENNESS, AND AMBIV-ALENCE. The way parents talked about their intention to have their youngest child was closely related to the way they described their general expectations for becoming unmarried parents. When characterizing their decision to have a child, 15 percent of the parents (i.e., 8 African-American parents and 2 white mothers) I spoke with spontaneously labeled their last pregnancy as "planned." All of the parents who talked about planning their children were involved in "steady" relationships or were living with the other parent at the time of the birth.[30] In contrast, parents more easily characterized their pregnancies as "wanted" than portrayed themselves as taking an active role in planning their pregnancies.[31]

The way Janet, a twenty-one-year-old black mother of three who was pregnant at the time of the interview, described her choice to have children outside of marriage suggests that she is aware that her pregnancies would be perceived as a deviation from a mainstream cultural model.

> Believe it or not, wasn't none of my children accidental. . . . All but that one, she wasn't a mistake, it just happened. But this one and my son and the one I'm carrying was planned. I, we sat down and we talked about it and it happened. So it wasn't like when I got pregnant, I was like "Oh my God, I'm pregnant again, oh my goodness." It wasn't like that. It was like, when I laid down, I knew what I was trying to do and he was trying to do. We was trying to make a baby. So you know, when it happened, I was like, "Well, you got your wish, I got my wish."

While Janet recognizes single-parent families as legitimate, this decision does not seem to represent a rejection of marriage. Janet said she would like to marry her current boyfriend, to have a nice apartment, good jobs, and a conventional family life but does not think this is likely.[32]

Overall, about one-third of African-American and white parents characterize themselves as accepting the pregnancy when it occurred rather than making a conscious decision to have a child outside of marriage. That is, they suggest they made themselves open to the idea of children or were pleased when they found out about the pregnancy, but they did not try to control the exact timing or the conditions under which it occurred. Like parents who "planned" their pregnancies, many of these parents also said they were in steady relationships when the pregnancy occurred and felt old enough to become parents. Yusef, a twenty-seven-year-old African-American father of one, said that a few of the women he had been involved with as a teenager had abortions. But he explains his decision to embrace fatherhood when he was older and living with his child's mother:

> I came to the age that I was in my twenties that I was ready to, that I wanted something, you know, everybody else around me have. And it happened where she got pregnant. It wasn't planned or nothing. And as soon as it happened I wasn't thinking about getting no abortion or nothing like that. I wanted to have it, you know, I was excited.

Yusef explains that the decision to have sex is also in some sense a decision to accept responsibility for a pregnancy if it occurs. Therefore, he does not make a moral distinction between sexuality and reproduction outside of marriage.

> See, the older the generation, the more they believe that [you shouldn't have a child outside of marriage]. The newer the generation would be like me: we

ain't got to be married. The older people be like . . . you should be married before you have sex. Sex is a beautiful thing if you don't abuse it. You know what I'm saying? So, I don't think you should be married to have sex. And you know what come along with having sex—children. You know, one day, one time, the woman gonna come up pregnant.

In contrast to these accounts, about half of parents interviewed (over half of African-American parents and about 40 percent of white parents) recalled feeling ambivalence or significant apprehension about the pregnancy.[33] Several of these parents considered abortion or adoption after finding out about the pregnancies. However, white parents more often characterized an unexpected pregnancy as an "accident" or crisis than black parents. Chastity, a white mother, recounts how she felt when she found out she was pregnant at age twenty-one:

At first, I was like, my life is over. That was my first like thought. Oh great, my life is over. I'm not gonna be able to do anything. I'm gonna sit home all the time. I'll have to stay home all the time, take care of my baby. I'm so young. I don't believe this. What am I doing?

In addition to the fact that fewer white parents said they expected to have a child outside of marriage, a convention for describing nonmarital pregnancies as planned may be less widely available to white parents. Therefore, they may be more likely than black parents to downplay their agency in becoming parents and to describe their pregnancies as unplanned or accidental. Alternatively, African-American parents more often emphasize that "a child is never a mistake" when they describe their experiences.

Gender also shapes which conventions parents use to describe a nonmarital birth. The fathers I spoke with were more likely than mothers to characterize the birth of their youngest child as unintended and less likely to label the pregnancy "planned."[34] When parents described the motive of the other parent, the accounts of a small minority of men also imply that the mother may have "trapped" them into becoming fathers.[35] However, the majority of mothers and fathers argue that men have an unconditional obligation to their children and those who did not want to become fathers should have used a condom or discussed abortion with their partner. In general, women do not portray themselves as being manipulated into pregnancy but strongly denounce men who are not involved with their children after they are born.[36]

PURPOSE AND AGENCY: ABORTION, ADOPTION, AND PARENTHOOD. Mothers and fathers who characterize their pregnancies as unexpected consistently represent their decision to become parents as an ethical and emotional resolution to their pregnancies, using therapeutic and religious discourses, collective stories, and popular wisdom to talk about this decision. In addition to having a nonmarital birth, parents identify abortion and adoption as two other options for resolving an unexpected pregnancy. Their explanations also connected these choices to anticipated consequences.[37] Overall, in accounts of their own experiences and in response to questions I asked about what advice they would give to other young couples who had an unintended pregnancy, African-American mothers and fathers sometimes considered abortion a viable (if morally ambiguous) response to an unexpected pregnancy, while white parents regarded both abortion and adoption as legitimate options.[38]

Parents' accounts were divided fairly evenly among those who opposed abortion in all cases, those who supported abortion, and those who supported abortion only in particular circumstances. Among the last group, parents made determinations about the appropriateness of abortion based on the circumstances and timing of the pregnancy. In particular, age was identified as perhaps the most important factor to be considered when deciding whether or not to carry a pregnancy to term. Because young teenagers are typically not thought to be emotionally and economically prepared to raise a child and because this often disrupts their education, many African-American parents point to the completion of high school or the age at which this would usually occur as a cutoff for deciding when abortion is or is not advisable. The decision to keep the pregnancy was more compelling for teenagers who had family support or adults who considered themselves capable of caring for a child. In fact, several mothers and fathers who said they or their partners had abortions as teenagers had decided to continue pregnancies as adults. Several of the women I interviewed said they considered abortion, but following a moral or emotional crisis decided to go through with their pregnancies. A small group of women who framed this as a moral decision also said that they chose not to have abortions against their parents' or partner's wishes.

Parents often framed their reluctance to have an abortion in moral terms, arguing that abortion destroys a human life. But some of the same parents who stated strong objections to abortion acknowledged that this choice was necessary in some circumstances. The majority of black parents in this study were raised in an Evangelical (e.g., Baptist or Pentecostal) church and the majority of white parents were raised Catholic. Based on these experiences, they often drew on religious discourses which oppose abortion.

> From my understanding, my belief, we are put here to replenish the world, not to destroy or not to stop kids from living. That's all life is about . . . in the books, in the Scriptures, it says we are put here to replenish the world, not to not replenish it. (Andre)

Using a religious framework to express opposition to abortion reflects not only an individual belief but sanctions that friends and family members impose on each other. One black father told me that he discouraged his partner from having an abortion after his mother "took him to the Bible" and talked to him about the immorality of taking a life. Discussing a conversation she had with a friend over an abortion she had previously had, Ishadeema says:

> Some people say [the baby] come back to you when you die, gonna be over you crying "Mommy." A lot of people say that. When I got rid of a baby she [her friend] used to always tell me God don't like murder. That's gonna get you or haunt you when you die. The baby gonna be over you singing.

Another common convention for opposing abortion emphasized the value of life and happiness derived from becoming a parent. Parents often counter abortion arguments with expressions that children are "precious" and "blessings from God" or that "life is beautiful" and should not be destroyed. Their accounts emphasize the high value placed on children and parenthood as a natural, human desire.

While many parents identified abortion as a viable response to an unplanned pregnancy, white parents were more likely than black parents to regard adoption as an emotionally and morally appropriate option.[39] Jean, a white mother of three, explains:

> Being a single mother's hard. 'Cause sometimes, you know, look, you got your kids. They were unplanned. You thought about what you were gonna do. Your parent's screaming adoption, your other parent's screaming abortion. Your other parent's screaming "You made your grave, you lay in it." I thought about all my choices. And if I could not keep my kids, like if I thought I'd be unfit, I would've put them up for adoption.

In contrast, black parents typically did not regard adoption as an option. As one African-American mother observed, "Being the fact that we young, black women, you don't hardly hear too much about adoptions." Black parents expressed a great deal of concern over where a child could be placed in an adoption.[40] Rather than characterizing adoption as a worthy decision, African-American parents sometimes drew moral boundaries against parents who have given their children up for adoption (see Lamont 1992).

> It's bad to have a baby and get an abortion, you know. Then it's bad to have a baby and give it up for adoption because you never know what kind of parents are gonna adopt the kid. You know, kill[ing] and the people these

days getting crazy. . . . It could go to a foster home. And how could you risk knowing you got a baby out there in the world [and] you don't know if he's being taken care of? (Mariah)

Considering Marriage Following Parenthood

Paralleling the analysis of parents' reproductive decisions, the following discussion examines how parents frame marital and relationship choices. In particular, it addresses how parents draw on collective discourses to make sense of their options and decisions about marriage and relationships (Swidler forthcoming). I look first at how unmarried parents talk about marriage following an unexpected birth; second, at explanations about why their relationships with the other parent ended; and finally, at conditions under which unmarried parents view marriage as an appropriate choice. In this discussion, I also explore how parents talk about options for marriage in relation to fertility.

THE ACT AND THE SCENE: ASSESSING THE RISKS OF MARRIAGE. Rather than viewing marriage as an option to resolve conflicts associated with a nonmarital pregnancy, more often, the parents I interviewed describe marriage as a decision that is separate from reproduction and invokes a different set of considerations. Furthermore, in scenarios in which I asked what advice they would give to young parents in an unstable economic position following an unexpected pregnancy, almost all parents said they would advise them against marriage. In the view of many parents, the average marriage is at a high risk for divorce, and marriages between young couples with marginal attachments to the labor force are even more likely to fail. The only respondents who thought marriage was a viable option added that the parents should wait until after the baby is born and parents feel economically and emotionally prepared to make this decision. Of course, I chose to interview unmarried parents whose views presumably differ from those of parents who married following a nonmarital pregnancy.[41] But their accounts also speak to the transformation that has occurred in family structure in recent years following complex cultural and economic changes. Three decades ago, if an unmarried woman got pregnant unexpectedly, a typical response was to marry the father of the child; today parents more often choose to stay single.[42]

Perhaps the majority of Americans would agree that teenagers or young couples should wait to marry.[43] When an unplanned pregnancy occurs to adults, why would they decide to remain single? Citing stories of failed marriages, parents suggest that exposure to divorce in their own families and in the larger society has made them approach this decision more cautiously. While parents point to advantages from marriage, particularly for children, they overwhelmingly argue that "forced" or "rushed" marriages should be avoided. For example, Sonny, a white father, warns, "Don't get married just for the kids. No, you'll be divorced just as fast. That's proven." Because parents can draw on personal anecdotes and publicly available information to identify the kind of marriages that will lead to divorce, they suggest it is futile, and perhaps irresponsible, to marry under many conditions. Overall, the dominant image of marriage in parents' accounts is one of risk and they typically frame the decision to marry in terms of minimizing the high likelihood of divorce.

From many parents' perspective, transforming a fragile relationship into an unstable marriage is unwise not only because of its likelihood of failure but also because of emotional turmoil that may be incurred in the process. These decisions are often framed as a choice between two alternatives and speak to the consequences of different courses of action (Mills 1940; Fraser 1989). For example, Julie, whose story appeared earlier, felt it would have been inappropriate to resolve her crisis through marriage. In fact, she suggests that having the child in the context of a conflictual marriage would have been worse (for all parties involved) than staying single. Julie's advice to other young couples in this situation would be:

> If they stay together, more power to them. But don't get married, because it's harder to undo than to do. There's time. Five, six years down the road when they're stable do it. There's no stopping you from getting married. The hard part is putting the child through a horrible marriage and getting out of it.

Describing her unhappy experience living with parents who fought constantly and later running away from home, she attributes many of her current economic and emotional problems to her volatile family life as a child. While she is considering marriage with her boyfriend, she explains that she wants to make sure the relationship will last before making her daughter emotionally vulnerable. In explaining this decision, she organizes her account around the strategies available to her, which include the ability to support herself and her daughter through employment.

When couples feel uncertain about their feelings, many take this as an indication of serious problems to follow. Because parents tend to characterize love as something that arises involuntarily, they suggest that it is difficult to control. At the same time, men and women suggest they calculate whether a relationship is strong enough to lead to a successful marriage.

> So she got a baby by you, things happen, OK. Then you got to think about, Is this the one you want to spend your life with, for the rest of your life?

You know what I'm saying? Marriage is forever, so that's something you gots to deal with everyday. You know, so it's good to stay single because you might marry her because she's your baby's mother, but is you happy? You know what I'm saying? Later on in life, is you still gonna want that same woman? ("G")

These views of marriage seem to invoke both "realist" and "idealist" ideas about relationships, which Illouz (1997) has identified as the two dominant models of love in contemporary American culture. According to Illouz, therapeutic and economic discourses that underlie the realist model suggest that love must develop over time after a process of information gathering and "work" on the relationship. This idea is frequently opposed to the idealist model, which represents love as an "all-consuming force." Because incompatible ideas about love are used simultaneously, she suggests that people are often frustrated in their attempts to bring them together into a single model (Illouz 1997, 77).

Parents' accounts also seem to draw from conflicting vocabularies about love and marriage that represent these decisions as both highly particularistic choices and as binding commitments (Hopper 1993; Swidler forthcoming). Both black and white parents emphasized the importance of selecting the "right" persons under the "right" conditions, arguing that a coerced or emotionally inauthentic marriage would self-destruct.[44] For example, Andre explains: "Marriage nowadays you can break up like a relationship. That's why, in a way, if I get married, it'll be for the right reasons. I mean, we ain't gonna be breaking up just like that." Rather than adopting a cavalier attitude toward marriage, parents suggest that choosing well is important precisely because of the seriousness of marriage and their anxiety about divorce.[45]

While many parents recognized the two-parent model as normative and often suggested it would be better for children to grow up in an "intact" family, they also pointed to many circumstances that prevent marriage. Joe, an African-American father, speaks directly to "mainstream" cultural expectations about marriage when he observes:

As a child, you want to be with your mommy and daddy. You want them to be married in a big house and a dog and all that. So, that just one step to getting that American dream, I guess. You know that dream you want fulfilled as a child.

In response to my question of why people are not getting married as much as they used to, he connects this more directly with economic problems facing families in his neighborhood:

That is a hard question. I do not know. It's like, well, see, times is just frustrating. Times is hard, and people aren't as happy as they used to be. So, I think basically that has a lot to do with it. I mean, if times wasn't so tough and people wasn't so aggravated and frustrated all the time, then people could be more loving.

Joe further explained these problems stem from a difficult job market and families' inability to "pull together" as they did in previous generations.

The accounts of many low-income parents suggest that economic uncertainty exacerbates emotional difficulties in relationships, such as distrust, failure to communicate, and incompatibility, that make marriage a worrisome enterprise for many men and women in contemporary society. In particular, the African-American parents I interviewed often pointed to problems associated with living in conditions of intense and concentrated poverty, such as incarceration, low wages, joblessness, and drug use, which make relationships more complex and difficult (Wilson 1987). For example, identifying problems that are "distracting" parents from marriage, Carl says, "The drugs, I hate them drugs. Them drugs tear up anything." To keep a marriage together in the face of these obstacles, he suggests that couples need to have an exceptional relationship and shared religious beliefs.

Like African-American parents, white parents also pointed to a general economic or cultural environment that discouraged marriage. However, white parents more often attributed their decision to remain single to a particular relationship that failed. Because the circumstances in which many white interviewees became parents diverged from their expectations, white parents also express more tension in reconciling their parental and marital statuses. Ashley, a white mother of one, contends that parents should be married when they have children, but when men decide to leave, women are often left to cope with the situation. Although she characterizes most men as "asses" and "immature," she suggests: "If the guy was really, if he was nothing like mine was, he would stick around, they'd get married. But, if they don't stick around, the hell with them. You don't need them." At the same time, Ashley wears a wedding ring she bought for herself and says she hopes that her daughter's father will leave his new wife to marry her.

The accounts of many African-American mothers also endorse essentialist ideas about gender that suggest men are "dogs" who cannot be trusted. But African-American women point to multiple risks associated with romantic involvement that have often been passed down from their female relatives and friends:

I want to get married, but if I can't find the right person, I ain't marrying him. I don't want no man that's gonna put his hands on me either. My grandma always told me, if he hits you, leave him. . . . 'Cause if he hit you one time, he'll do it again. . . . Not no drug dealer [either]. Next thing you know, he locked up in jail. See, I'm stuck. I'm on my own again. . . . I'm getting a divorce. (Evette)

The African-American women I talked to also tend to situate their choices within the social context of living in a poor neighborhood:

The only way I see marriage is like you're in college and you meet a guy in college. And after you get a career and he get a career and he find he love you then. But once they get a taste of the streets out here . . . you don't want to marry nobody like that. (Debra)

Intimate relationships may introduce additional concerns for women, particularly when they have sole responsibility for raising a child. In fact, almost 40 percent of women I interviewed spontaneously mentioned that abuse factored into their decision about relationships and marriage either directly, from experiences in their previous relationships, or indirectly, from awareness of abuse. Women also contend that in escaping abusive relationships, they protected their children from emotional and physical danger and from negative images of male-female relationships.[46]

PURPOSE, AGENTS, AND AGENCY: ENDING A RELATIONSHIP. In addition to looking at how parents assessed the "scene" for marriage, I examined more concrete reasons parents gave for why a romantic involvement with the other parent ended.[47] Specifically, I looked at explanations of who ended the relationship and why it ended in accounts of mothers and fathers who were no longer involved with their youngest child's parent. Some stories were also constructed to explain why they were not married to the other parent.[48]

When talking about the dissolution of relationships, I found more consistent patterns of responses across gender than across race groups. While about four-fifths of African-American and white women identified themselves as the party who initiated the breakup, only a minority of fathers suggested that they ended the relationship with their youngest child's mother. In addition to women claiming more agency in breaking off their romantic involvement with the father, women drew on a shared vocabulary of motives to explain or legitimate why the relationship ended. Importantly, women who ended their relationships cited abuse as one of the primary reasons for leaving their partners. Marie, a white mother of two, explains why she decided not to marry the father of her children.

I was always brought up to like, you get married, you have kids, and that's how it was. That's why . . . I was with their father 8½ years, but we never got married. But we tried to make it work. I mean, because I thought that, you know, that was the way it was supposed to be. But he had a problem with his hands, so eventually I just turned around and left. 'Cause he was an alcoholic and he beat me all the time. So, I just left him. But I tried to make it work . . . 'cause I guess that's just the way I was brought up, like you're supposed to have a little family and make it work. So, I tried, but it just did not work at all.

While portraying her situation as a deviation from a conventional family model, Marie, like other women I interviewed, is confident in explaining her motive for leaving the father: being a single mother is preferable to tolerating a partner's abuse and alcoholism. When discussing infidelity—another common explanation for their decision to end the relationship with the father—women also emphasize the need to remove themselves and their children from the destructive or disrespectful behavior of the father.

The majority of fathers who were in steady relationships also suggested that their child's mother broke things off, but they offered disparate explanations of the kind of problems they experienced and why their relationships ended. While a few men explained the end of their relationship in reference to their partner's infidelity or unwillingness to "settle down," others who initiated the breakup suggest that in some way they were not ready for the commitment. Jared, a white father, explains why he left his son's mother six months after he was born:

I guess it was the fact that I was young. Still wanted, you know, didn't want to get tied down too much. Still wanted to run around. And the fact that I was scared. You know, 'cause I had no clue about what to do. Had no clue of my responsibilities or nothing like that. Had no clue that the baby depended on me, and, you know, just didn't know. I was scared, so I ran.

Unmarried fathers often drew on a therapeutic discourse about emotional development to explain why their immaturity made it difficult to maintain a relationship.[49]

THE "RIGHT" CONCLUSION: MATURITY, ECONOMIC STABILITY, AND COMPATIBILITY. The preceding discussion suggests that the unmarried parents regard marrying as futile and risky in particular situations. Therefore, in order to avoid potentially painful and destructive relationships and to manage economic uncertainties, parents argue that men and women should evaluate whether the conditions, their relationship, and their partner are "right" for marriage. If parents emphasize the importance of selection and evaluating their own "readiness" to marry, in what circumstances do parents feel prepared to make this commitment? How do options for marriage compare to options for parenthood?

To explore how unmarried parents think about the relationship between marriage and reproduction, I asked them what advice they would give to other young couples about the appropriate timing of these events. Parents typically said these two decisions should ideally be timed together, suggesting that the transition to marriage and parenting should not occur until after finishing high school or securing stable employment (usually during their early to mid-twenties). However, the majority of parents did not report "planning" the exact timing or conditions of their pregnancy. Emphasizing that parents have an unconditional obligation to their child whether or not they feel emotionally ready for it, Carl, an African-American father, says, "Sometime it just happen, and when that time come, when you become a parent, you just got to rise to the occasion. Just take care of your responsibility. . . . No time's a good time to be a parent." In fact, the idea that there may be a good time economically to become a parent is related to the strategies of action men and women have available to them (Swidler 1986), and only young adults who have the hope of achieving significant economic mobility through higher education and employment may believe it is beneficial to delay parenthood.[50]

A smaller group of parents, most of whom were African-American, seemed to adopt a more calculated approach to reproduction and marriage, with several setting the appropriate age of reproduction earlier than that of marriage. And, in comparison to white parents, African-American parents more clearly articulated the rationale behind these decisions. Although they did not always notice they timed these events differently until I asked them to explain their responses, these accounts illustrate how parents come to decisions about reproduction and marriage through separate processes. For example, several African-American parents argued that mothers and fathers who were "too old" would have difficulty understanding and relating to their children. In their view, older parents would also have more trouble passing on cultural capital, such as knowledge of the streets. James, an African-American father, supports the decision to have children in his early twenties, saying, "I think you can more relate to them, because you understand a little bit about what they're going through right then. As you get up in age, you get stuck in your own ways." Another parent told me that he could spend more "quality time" raising a child in his twenties while he made money selling drugs. In his thirties, he imagined he would have a full-time job that would give him less time with his son. Several women also indicated that they had decided to have children as young adults and planned to return to school and/or find employment in their mid- to late twenties.

At the same time, African-American parents also drew a lower limit (around age eighteen) below which they believe it is too young to become parents.

Given this fairly narrow age range in which it is desirable to become a parent, they either open themselves up to the possibility of becoming parents during certain years or consciously plan to have children at this time. Again, as parents' accounts of reproduction suggest, this decision was typically made within the context of a steady relationship, but not necessarily one leading to marriage.

> When I was going to school, me and all my girlfriends always said we ain't never gonna have kids 'til we finish high school. 'Cause we don't never want to be a mother in school. Like some mothers go to school pregnant. We didn't want that when we was young . . . we always used to have fun. We never wanted kids. That was out. So I decided at twenty-two I wanted to have a baby before I turned twenty-five. I said if I was over twenty-five, I didn't want no kids. (Diamond)

According to Diamond, twenty-two was a "nice age" because she had been working for four years after high school and had saved up some money to buy things for her baby. She continues to live at home and, with the help of her family, plans to return to work next year.[51] Although the father of her child and his parents also help with child care, she explains that his immaturity and unwillingness to assume more economic responsibility make him a bad candidate for marriage at this time. And after watching her sisters' marriages end in divorce, she says she would prefer to wait.

> I'll say by thirty, I won't mind getting married when I'm thirty years old. I don't want to get married and next year I'm divorced. I'm not like that. I don't never want to rush into anything. Not me, never.

Yusef, an African-American father, offers a somewhat different rationale for the timing of these events. He suggests that the appropriate time to have children is in "[your] early to mid-twenties," cautioning:

> You don't want to get too old 'cause you want to experience things with your child, growing up with your child. See, I'll be like forty-something when my daughter graduates. I won't be too old and I'll be able to relate to her.

However, he explains that this may not be the right time to consider marriage:

> You still have that youngness in you that want to fool around and all that. It gets tiresome around my age, twenty-eight, twenty-nine. 'Cause you know you're tired of playing games, you're tired of playing the field and being single.

Like many parents, he also argues that couples should get to know each other well, and perhaps live together, before marriage. Mentioning that the relationship with his child's mother ended because of her crack addiction, Yusef suggests, "You need about three to five years under your belt before you even think about marriage."

While many young parents felt confident in their abilities as parents, they seemed less certain about entering a marriage before they or their partners were "ready." The contrast between their optimism about parenthood and skepticism of marriage points to how parents perceive the options available to them. When parents described their reproductive decisions, they typically suggested they felt competent to care for a child or had made a moral or emotional choice to continue an unintended pregnancy. Women, in particular, felt capable of loving and providing for a child alone, but most expect help from the child's father, regardless of whether or not they stay together. It should also be noted that parents talked about their fertility decision retrospectively. Therefore, many parents who said they were apprehensive about pregnancy now characterized their child as "wanted" and considered parenthood a positive experience. Overall, both mothers and fathers viewed the obligation to the children as unconditional and believed they could "rise to the occasion" and be good parents, even with limited economic resources (see Luker 1996). In contrast, they viewed romantic relationships as voluntaristic and often erratic. Therefore, while they generally believed they could control their behavior as parents through making an effort to love and provide for their children, they could not fully control the feelings or behavior of their partner or the course of the relationship. Precarious economic circumstances, abuse, drug addiction, infidelity, and the unpredictability of romantic love could all undermine relationships and marital stability. In that sense, parents could more easily choose to be good parents to their children than they could choose a stable relationship leading to a successful marriage. At the same time, the majority of parents hoped to marry.

For most parents, and for women in particular, this "choice" represented less a voluntary process of selecting from a range of partners than a decision to eliminate relationships they found untenable or detrimental. Moreover, parents suggested that their rejection of marriage was particular rather than general, and they hoped that a more appropriate partner would come along in the future; a minority of parents who were involved in relationships hoped they or their partners would become ready for marriage. According to parents' accounts, readiness demanded a certain level of personal maturity, and many suggested that young men were generally less mature and less able to make an emotional commitment than young women.[52] A twenty-two-year-old mother explains her decision to delay marriage:

My youngest son's father, he's talking about getting married. But I'd rather be in a better situation than I am now when I get married.

Why? I want to finish school, get certified [as a physical therapy assistant], get myself all situated, and have a lot more things than I do now. And for him too, I want him to get all his running and stuff out now before he really do that.

When asked to identify characteristics they value in a spouse, women also suggest that they would look for men who were supportive, understanding, caring, hardworking, trustworthy, and dependable. Men talked about similar qualities desirable in potential spouses but usually emphasized women's independence and ability to share financial burdens more than their reliability. Both men and women emphasized the importance of compatibility in a marriage: that is, they wanted a partner with whom they could share activities, interests, and responsibilities. And while the majority express a desire to marry, they suggest that things such as emotional maturity, economic stability, and compatibility are required to make a marriage work.

Again, African-American parents also point to social constraints that limit their options for marriage. In contrast to Wilson's (1987) account, both African-American men and women pointed to problems finding "marriageable," or employed, partners. While women supporting their families on a very limited welfare check may be afraid that taking an equally poor man into their households will threaten the delicate economic balance they have achieved, men also express reluctance about assuming financial responsibility for partners who do not have jobs or are not "trying to do anything for themselves." Furthermore, as women's accounts suggest, men are often considered unmarriageable if they are in jail, selling drugs, into the streets, or abusive.[53]

Because parents talk about marriage using both idealist and realist discourses about romantic love, they hope to find "Mr. Right" or the "perfect woman." But given the series of obstacles low-income couples face in trying to maintain a relationship, particularly African-American parents living in conditions of concentrated poverty, they also suggest that they cannot be sure about whether the person is right until they have seen their willingness to "be there" through difficult times.[54] In the following exchange, Crystal, the African-American mother whose story opened the discussion, describes her options for marriage in Trenton and the kind of husband she would choose.

I say out of a hundred, it's like 10 percent good dads because you can't find too many good fathers to be there. Most of the dads are in jail. Most of the dads are on drugs. Most of the dads are just not there period. There's not too much good dads. And then people wonder why would you want to have a baby from a guy like that. Why would you want to be involved with someone like that? Because at that point of time, that person was not like that. You don't really know a person till you get to know them. And then there's a big difference when you get pregnant with them. And then they start to acting stupid. Can't take the trials and tribulations and things like that. You never know who Mr. Right is until he put that ring on your finger and say I want to marry you. That's what I'm waiting for.

What kind of man would you want to marry? I don't know. I guess I'd have a storybook wedding. Sweep me off my feet. A good provider. Someone to love me the way I love him. I want us to be equal. I want us to be able to do things together, go places and experience things. A good father figure to my children. I want him to have a good job, a education. I want him to have money but . . . sometime you can't always get what you want. But that's what I would like.

As these accounts suggest, unmarried parents' decisions about marriage take place in a larger cultural context. And in addition to the minimal requirements for a "marriageable" partner, parents also point to other ideas that have become valued by men and women of their generation, such as companionship and equality in a relationship (Furstenberg 1988). As survey data suggest, young men and women now perceive fewer advantages to marriage, and the choice to remain single is increasingly viewed as legitimate by society (Thornton and Freedman 1982). Many couples today also seem to have greater difficulty fulfilling their economic and emotional expectations for marriage (Luker 1996, 159). In a context in which many unmarried parents face chronic economic instability and in which many unmarried mothers assume responsibility for their families' survival, parents express a desire to marry while at the same time believing marriage may be unattainable, risky, or futile.

Conclusion

When explaining their decisions about reproduction and marriage, low-income unmarried parents use culturally available ideas to describe personal and social contexts for their choices, to identify available options, and to motivate their responses. Overall, I find that there is a significant amount of overlap in unmarried parents' accounts with a few notable differences in African-American and white parents' stories. Black parents had more exposure to single-parent family models in their families and communities and seemed to draw on a common cultural script about their expectations for reproduction outside of marriage. The accounts of white parents were less uniform, with some white mothers describing unmarried parenthood as a socially difficult or isolating experience and others characterizing it as a more "normal" event. Though parents' expectations about becoming a single parent varied, many African-American and white parents suggested they did not plan the particular timing or conditions of their pregnancy but were open to the birth of their youngest child. However, about half of the parents I interviewed were ambivalent or apprehensive about the pregnancy and typically characterize their decision to have a child as a moral or emotional response to this unintended situation. At the same time, neither black nor white parents generally regard marriage as an appropriate way to resolve an unintended pregnancy. Instead, parents recount cultural explanations about the appropriate reasons to marry that resemble those of other young men and women of their generation.

Drawing from competing models of romantic love, parents argue that successful marriages are predicated on finding the right person and being ready to make this commitment. They also cite the high incidence of divorce in their families, communities, and the larger society when explaining why "forced" or "rushed" marriages fail. Often, parents characterize marriage as risky or futile and talk about their decisions in terms of minimizing the likelihood of divorce. In particular, women who often have primary responsibility for their children and African-American parents who live in impoverished neighborhoods refer to multiple risks associated with marriage. The majority of mothers I interviewed who were no longer involved with their child's father suggested that they ended the relationship, often due to abuse or infidelity. Both African-American and white parents also considered young men less emotionally ready for marriage than young women. In practice, women's "choice" to remain single usually represented a process of eliminating a harmful or untenable relationship, often with the hope that a more appropriate partner would come along in the future or that they or their own partner would become ready for marriage.

I have argued that variations in parents' stories about reproduction and marriage provide insight into the cultural resources available to different social groups to interpret their experiences. The majority of parents I interviewed hope to marry someday but express widely shared contemporary beliefs that emotional maturity, economic stability, and compatibility are required to make a marriage work. Given the options available to them, parents suggest they have more control over and confidence in their ability to "rise to the occasion" and be good parents than in the outcomes of their relationships. Despite these similarities in beliefs about marriage, African-Americans more often identified social and economic conditions that undermined marriage in their neighborhoods and articulated separate considerations for reproductive and marital decisions.

In contrast, unmarried white parents often had difficulty reconciling their parental and marital status. The low-income white parents I spoke with did not live in conditions of concentrated poverty and have more recently experienced increasing rates of nonmarital childbearing in their communities. Given these differences, the accounts of white parents suggest that they may have just begun thinking about separation between reproduction and marriage and are revising more conventional explanations to make sense of these experiences.

Notes

I would like to thank Frank Furstenberg, Hans Johnson, Michèle Lamont, Kristin Luker, Sara McLanahan, Belinda Reyes, and contributors to the volume for insightful comments on this chapter. This research was supported by the National Science Foundation, the Eastern Sociological Society (Orlandella/Whyte Urban Field Research Fellowship Award), the Woodrow Wilson Foundation (Princeton Society of Fellows), and the Center of Domestic and Comparative Policy Studies, Princeton University. An earlier version of this chapter was presented at the American Sociological Association annual meeting, New York, August 1996.

1. For example, this representation of young, unmarried fathers appeared in the Bill Moyers/CBS documentary entitled *The Vanishing Family: Crisis in Black America* (see Griswold 1993, 237).

2. In a book lamenting the cultural decline of fatherhood, David Blankenhorn (1995) echoes others in suggesting: "The daughter of the black teenage mother in the inner city and the child of TV's Murphy Brown are almost identical. What unites them is more important than the things that separate them." While at first glance, the Murphy Brown style of unmarried motherhood may appear to contrast sharply with the experiences of black teenage inner-city mothers on welfare, in fact, media reports often couple these two images in articles about nonmarital childbearing. Using a Lexis-Nexis search, I found 159 recent articles about unmarried parenthood that made reference to both Murphy Brown and teenage mothers. One of these articles (Healy 1996) compares the choice to become an unmarried mother of Alice McKinney, a forty-year-old white middle-class woman with that of Ra-Shonda Anderson, a seventeen-year-old black high-school student living in a low-income neighborhood. An excerpt from the article reads: "For both McKinney and Anderson, a baby would satisfy much the same urge. . . . But they have taken very different routes to their decision. For McKinney, the tick-tick-tick of her biological clock has set off an alarm. After years of graduate school, travel and a single life on the go, she has settled into the kind of stability she thinks is right for bringing up a child. . . . A husband—and a father for her child—would be nice, she says. But neither is in the picture, or even on the horizon. And neither, she has concluded, is indispensable. . . . Anderson, a shy teenager who has struggled through high school, has all the time in the world to have a child. But she sees little reason to wait. . . . She is about to move in with her 17-year-old boyfriend, Randy, who is all for having a baby. . . . While not pregnant, Anderson expects it could happen any day now. And she's doing nothing to prevent it."

3. Families headed by unmarried women now represent the poorest demographic group in the United States, and children born to unmarried women make up over half of the children receiving welfare (Ellwood 1988). Perhaps contrary to popular perceptions, about 70 percent of nonmarital births occur to women twenty years of age or older rather than to teenagers. Furthermore, although the proportion of black births that occur outside of marriage (68 percent) still greatly exceeds that of whites (23 percent), recent trends suggest that the rate of nonmarital childbearing is increasing more quickly among white than black women. About 60 percent of all nonmarital births now occur to white women (U.S. Department of Health and Human Services 1995).

4. Stacey (1991, 28) observes, "African-American women and white working-class women have been the genuine postmodern family pioneers, even though they also suffer from its most negative effects."

5. I interviewed low-income parents with children who currently or have recently received welfare. This research is part of a larger project that examines how unmarried parents interpret paternal responsibility and interact with the child support system (Waller 1996).

6. Although all were legal adults, about 11 percent of the parents I interviewed were eighteen or nineteen years old.

7. Unmarried, nonresidential fathers are often missing from national surveys either because they are not sampled (due to their loose attachments to households) or are included in the sample but do not acknowledge, or perhaps know, they have children. Therefore, the information we have about this group of men is limited and even such basic information as the size and economic characteristics is disputed (Garfinkel, McLanahan, and Hanson 1995).

8. I focus on parents' accounts about the birth of their youngest child to allow for comparability of information across interviews.

9. For example, between 1970 and 1990, the wages of women with a high-school degree declined by 2 percent while the wages of men with a high-school degree declined by 13 percent (McLanahan and Sandefur 1994, 142).

10. Over the last few decades, poll data suggest that nonmarital sexuality and cohabitation have become much more accepted among younger cohorts while marriage is viewed as less central to their lives (Thornton 1995). Some writers point to the importance of gender in explaining these changes. For example, women may be less willing to tolerate abusive or extremely hierarchical relationships (Stacey 1991; Luker 1996). As Ehrenreich (1983) suggests, a male revolt against commitment to family and children could perhaps have preceded women's resistance to an unequal gender bargain in marriage. In recent years, conservative writers have argued that the acceptance of divorce and nonmarital childbearing are part of a cultural shift toward selfishness and irresponsibility among younger generations of parents (Whitehead 1993; Blankenhorn 1995).

11. In light of these trends, Charles Murray (1993) has expressed concern over the emergence of a white "underclass."

12. Examples of research addressing cultural or psychological factors associated with these decisions include Dash 1989; Anderson 1989; Sullivan 1989; Burton 1990, 1995; Furstenberg 1991, 1992; Geronimous 1991, 1992; and Musick 1993.

13. This approach is influenced by Swidler's (1986, 273) discussion of culture as "a

'tool-kit' of symbols, stories, rituals, and world-views, which people may use in varying configurations to solve different kinds of problems."

14. In this chapter, I do not document discourses about reproduction and marriage directly but refer to them when interpreting parents' responses. For a longer discussion of how unmarried parents draw on available cultural discourses to frame their experiences, see Waller 1996.

15. In a discussion of how diverse audiences read fiction, Janice Radway (1991, 468) suggests readers actively engage texts and construct signifiers "as meaningful signs on the basis of previously learned interpretive procedures and interpretive codes." They read differently because they belong to "different interpretive communities" and have different purposes for reading.

16. My approach follows the work of writers in this field (Lawson 1992; Nightingale 1993; Hochschild 1995; Newman 1996) who argue that, rather than being radically isolated from mainstream culture, "underclass" families actively engage American culture.

17. Because the accounts I examine were solicited in interviews, I recognize them as explanations also constructed for me and the imagined reader. I consider the statements made in the interviews to be somewhere between "public" and "private" discourse for two reasons: First, they were made in the context of a private, one-on-one conversation but addressed to someone whom the interviewee did not know well. Second, while the confidential nature of the interview may have encouraged more openness, the content was also intended for a larger audience (Scott 1990). Although I attempted to create a trusting and egalitarian relationship with interviewees, they presumably responded to my race (white), gender (female), age (mid-late twenties), educational, and other identities when explaining their experiences (see Waller 1996, 68–117).

18. Following Burke 1989 and Mills 1940, this analysis does not attempt to tap into internal psychological states in order to uncover the motives for action but documents how actors impute motives to themselves or others to explain actions.

19. At the same time, as other writers observe, actors often tap into multiple discourses. Therefore, the ways in which they frame behavior may be inconsistent (Swidler forthcoming; Illouz 1997).

20. Drawing on Ginsburg's (1989) discussion of "procreation stories," I also consider to what extent the content of parents' accounts are framed in dialogue with the dominant cultural model of reproduction (i.e., a married two-parent family).

21. I also conducted six interviews in Middlesex County near the city of New Brunswick, New Jersey. Middlesex County is adjacent to Mercer County (where Trenton is located). I chose to sample white parents in suburban New Jersey as well as in Trenton because low-income white families in this region are not concentrated in inner-city communities.

22. In contrast, about 21 percent of the households in Mercer County as a whole and 14 percent in Middlesex County were headed by a single parent; respectively, 11 percent and 6 percent of children in the two counties were living below the poverty level (Association for Children of New Jersey 1993).

23. WIC is a federally funded program that provides nutritional supplements such as milk, cheese, and formula to infants, children under five, and pregnant or breastfeeding

women. I sampled from WIC because its clients match closely the total population of women on welfare.

24. This program was established as part of the 1988 Family Support Act to provide employment and training services to men with a child support obligation to the state.

25. Describing economic changes in the Northeast and the Midwest, Wilson (1987, 58) notes that poor whites rarely live in conditions of concentrated and extreme urban poverty. Because poor black families tend to live in different kinds of neighborhoods from poor white families, he suggests that economic and ecological differences between these communities underlie apparent cultural, attitudinal, and behavioral differences.

26. For example, because white mothers had different social networks from black mothers, few were able to give me referrals to other unmarried parents.

27. Among both black and white parents, when pregnancies were regarded as "normal" events, explanations of how other people reacted to their pregnancies were typically made in response to my questions, rather than being discussed spontaneously.

28. Black parents who had children as teenagers, for example, said that they were afraid of how their parents would react to the pregnancy, particularly when it threatened to interrupt their education. However, most black mothers said that while their parents initially disapproved of a young pregnancy, they later accepted it and offered support.

29. A few African-American mothers also described themselves as having consciously decided not to become teenage mothers, to have only one child, and to have their children in their early twenties after working for a few years and saving money. For example, Diamond, a black mother of one, says: "I just want one. . . . I don't want five kids without being married or nothing like that. I don't want a whole bunch of kids like that." Some mothers also drew moral boundaries (Lamont 1992) against unmarried women who had more children than they could support or had children with a number of different fathers.

30. Overall, about 3/4 of white parents and 2/3 of black parents characterized their relationships as steady or committed during the pregnancy. Furthermore, close to 1/2 of white parents and 1/3 of black parents cohabited with the other parent at some time. National data indicate that over 1/4 of nonmarital births between 1970 and 1984 occurred to cohabiting couples (Ventura et al. 1995, 4).

31. According to the 1988 National Survey of Family Growth, 88 percent of never-married mothers and 69 percent of formerly married mothers characterized their pregnancies as unintended. Similarly, 40 percent of married women indicated their pregnancies were unintended (Moore 1995, ix). However, as Luker (1996, 151–54) suggests, the meaning of survey reports about women's intention to become pregnant is often difficult to interpret.

32. In Janet's full narrative, she described being engaged to marry a man who was killed in a gang shooting.

33. These findings show some similarity with Frank Furstenberg's discussion of the fertility decisions of teenage parents. Furstenberg (1991, 134) writes, "[M]ost attempt contraception but practice it irregularly. As a result, many drift into parenthood as an unintended result of having sex." He also suggests that individuals may "misjudge or distort their chances of becoming pregnant in contrast to the chances of everyone else."

34. Six African-American mothers and two African-American fathers suggested that the birth of their youngest child was planned.

35. Five fathers said they were "trapped" because the mother either lied about contraception or took money from them for an abortion but later changed their minds.

36. Both mothers and fathers also made moral claims that men should try to prevent pregnancy when they do not want to accept responsibility for a child.

37. Because I chose to interview parents, by definition all respondents chose the first option with their youngest (or only) child. However, many seriously considered the other two options and some had previous abortions.

38. Some survey research suggests that African-Americans are less accepting of abortion than whites (see Thornton 1995).

39. Adoption has declined among both black and white parents. While 19 percent of white nonmarital births and 2 percent of black nonmarital births resulted in formal adoption between 1965 and 1972, these percentages dropped to 3 percent and 1 percent respectively between 1982 and 1988 (Ventura et al. 1995, 55).

40. Although there is a long history of informal adoption in black families, this option may be less available now than it was in the past, with more grandmothers and other female relatives in the labor market and fewer extended family resources to draw upon (Burton 1995).

41. It is also important to note that although none of the black parents I interviewed had ever been married, seven white parents had previously been married. Two of these fathers had brief marriages to "legitimate" an earlier unplanned pregnancy and one mother forged her mother's signature in an attempt to marry before she was legally permitted to do so. These parents may have revised their earlier ideas about marriage.

42. Between 1960 and 1964, about 61 percent of white women and 31 percent of black women who had a nonmarital pregnancy married before the birth of the child. Between 1985 and 1989, only about 34 percent of white women and 8 percent of black women married before the birth (U.S. Department of Health and Human Services 1995).

43. Survey data indicate that the age at which young people, particularly women, expect to marry has been rising (Thornton and Freedman 1982) and African-Americans want to marry later than whites (Thornton 1995). These attitudes toward marriage also correspond to changes in behavior (i.e., more young men and women are delaying marriage). In 1992, about 70 percent of black women and 76 percent of black men aged 20 to 29 had never been married, up from 33 percent and 43 percent in 1970. Among white women and men, 45 percent of women and 61 percent of men aged 20 to 29 had never been married in 1992, compared to 23 percent and 37 percent in 1970 (Ventura et al. 1995, 28).

44. The realist model of love also advocates "choice" and selection in order to bring love under rational control and to ensure the compatibility of couples (Illouz 1997).

45. Illouz (1997, 292–93) argues against critiques of "amoral relativism" launched at men and women in contemporary society suggesting that people are often forced to reconcile multiple and competing values that they are strongly committed to.

46. A recent study by Allard et al. (1997) suggests that an alarming 65 percent of

women receiving welfare in Massachusetts reported experiencing domestic violence by a boyfriend or husband at some time.

47. Joseph Hopper's (1993) study of divorce rhetoric reports that after one party has been identified as the initiator of the divorce, this person used socially sanctioned discourses to make his or her response appear legitimate. Hopper also finds that his respondents consistently used a vocabulary of individual needs (if they identified themselves as the initiator) or family commitment (if the other partner initiated). In contrast, not all of the men and women I interviewed identified who initiated the breakup or attempted to justify their responses, perhaps because breakups among unmarried couples are regarded as less momentous than those of married couples.

48. Close to one-third of the men and women I spoke with were still involved in relationships with their child's other parent, and some of these couples planned to marry.

49. About one-fifth of respondents suggested that they had not been in "steady" relationships with the parent of their youngest child. Parents who suggested that their relationships with the other parent at the time of the birth were casual or intermittent typically did not offer a detailed explanation of why the relationship ended.

50. Kristin Luker (1996, 170) observes:

[I]n the new global economy (and in the face of a declining middle class) the absence of a social structure that supports both work and motherhood has created a situation in which there is never a "good" time to have a baby. Thus, the birth patterns of poor and affluent women in the United States have begun to bifurcate, as each group tries to come to terms with the difficulties of having children in a country that provides so little support. Poor women continue the traditional American pattern of early childbearing, because in this way they can become mothers before they enter the paid labor force and while they can make moral claims on kinfolk who will help with childrearing. Affluent women, on the other hand, tend to wait until they are well established in the labor force before having a child.

51. Other mothers I interviewed adopted a different strategy, deciding to have their children as young adults and enter the labor force when their children begin school (see Luker 1996).

52. Drawing on his Chicago survey data, Wilson (1996, 101) suggests that the attitude of many young single black fathers is " 'I'll get married in the future when I am no longer having fun and when I get a job or a better job.' "

53. According to Wilson (1996, 104), his ethnographic data also show that "inner-city black males and females believe that since most marriages will eventually break up and since marriages no longer represent meaningful relationships, it is better to avoid the entanglements of wedlock altogether. For many single mothers in the inner city, nonmarriage makes more sense as a family formation strategy than does marriage. Single mothers who perceive the fathers of their children as unreliable or as having limited financial means will often—rationally—choose single parenthood."

54. This theme appears in what the *New York Times Magazine* dubbed the love song of the summer of 1995: "I'll Be There for You/You're All I Need to Get By" by popular hip-hop artists Method Man and Mary J. Blige (see Tatley 1995).

References

Allard, Mary Ann, Randy Albeda, Mary Ellen Colten, and Carol Cosenza. 1997. "In Harm's Way? Domestic Violence, AFDC Receipt, and Welfare Reform in Massachusetts." Research report, University of Massachusetts, Boston.

Anderson, Elijah. 1989. "Sex Codes and Family Life among Poor Inner-City Youths." *Annals of the American Academy of Political and Social Science* 501:59–78.

Association for Children of New Jersey. 1993. *Kids Count, New Jersey: State and County Profiles of Child Well-Being.* Newark: Association for Children of New Jersey.

Bane, Mary Jo, and David T. Ellwood. 1994. *Welfare Realities.* Cambridge: Harvard University Press.

Blankenhorn, David. 1995. *Fatherless Families.* New York: Basic.

Bourdieu, Pierre. 1984. *Distinction.* Cambridge: Harvard University Press.

Burke, Kenneth. 1989. *On Symbols and Society,* edited with an introduction by Joseph Gusfield. Chicago: University of Chicago Press.

Burton, Linda. 1990. "Teenage Childbearing as an Alternative Life-Course Strategy in Multigenerational Black Families." *Human Nature* 2:123–43.

———. 1995. "Family Structure and Nonmarital Fertility: Perspectives from Ethnographic Research." In U.S. Department of Health and Human Services 1995.

Dash, Leon. 1989. *When Children Want Children.* New York: Penguin.

Ehrenreich, Barbara. 1983. *The Hearts of Men.* Garden City, N.Y.: Anchor.

Ellwood, David. 1988. *Poor Support.* New York: Basic.

Fraser, Nancy. 1989. *Unruly Practices.* Minneapolis: University of Minnesota Press.

Furstenberg, Frank F. 1988. "Good Dads—Bad Dads: Two Faces of Fatherhood." In *The Changing American Family and Public Policy,* edited by Andrew Cherlin. Washington: Urban Institute Press.

———. 1991. "As the Pendulum Swings: Teenage Childbearing and Social Concern." *Family Relations* 40:127–38.

———. 1992. "Teenage Childbearing and Cultural Rationality: A Thesis in Search of Evidence." *Family Relations* 41:239–43.

Garfinkel, Irwin, Sara McLanahan, and Tom Hanson. 1995. "A Portrait of Nonresident Fathers." Paper presented at the Effects of Child Support Enforcement and Nonresident Fathers Conference, Princeton, N.J., September 1995.

Garfinkel, Irwin, and Sara S. McLanahan. 1986. *Single Mothers and Their Children.* Washington: Urban Institute Press.

Geronimus, Arline T. 1991. "Teenage Childbearing and Social and Reproductive Disadvantage: The Evolution of Complex Questions and the Demise of Simple Answers." *Family Relations* 40:463–71.

———. 1992. "Teenage Childbearing and Social Disadvantage: Unprotected Discourse." *Family Relations* 41:244–48.

Ginsburg, Faye D. 1989. *Contested Lives.* Berkeley: University of California Press.

Griswold, Robert L. 1993. *Fatherhood in America.* New York: Basic.

Gugliotta, Guy. 1993. "Cities Putting Enterprise Zones to Work with More Tax Breaks: Planners Turn Concept into Reality." *Washington Post,* June 1, A1.

Gusfield, Joseph. 1989. Introduction to Burke 1989.

Healy, Melissa. 1996. "Rethinking Murphy Brown/Unwed Motherhood: The Debate Now Includes the Financially Secure." *Newsday,* October 2, B4.

Hochschild, Jennifer L. 1995. *Facing Up to the American Dream.* Princeton: Princeton University Press.

Hopper, Joseph. 1993. "The Rhetoric of Motives in Divorce." *Journal of Marriage and the Family* 55:801–13.

Illouz, Eva. 1997. *Consuming the Romantic Utopia.* Berkeley: University of California Press.

Lamont, Michèle. 1992. *Money, Morals, and Manners.* Chicago: University of Chicago Press.

Lawson, Bill E., ed. 1992. *The Underclass Question.* Philadelphia: Temple University Press.

Luker, Kristin. 1996. *Dubious Conceptions.* Cambridge: Harvard University Press.

McLanahan, Sara, and Gary Sandefur. 1994. *Growing Up with a Single Parent.* Cambridge: Harvard University Press.

Mills, C. W. 1940. "Situated Actions and Vocabularies of Motive." *American Sociological Review* 6:904–13.

Moore, Kristin. 1995. "Executive Summary: Nonmarital Childbearing in the United States." In U.S. Department of Health and Human Services 1995.

Morgan, S. P., A. McDaniel, A. Miller, and S. Preston. 1993. "Racial Differences in Household and Family Structure at the Turn of the Century." *American Journal of Sociology* 98:798–828.

Murray, Charles. 1984. *Losing Ground.* New York: Basic.

———. 1993. "The Coming White Underclass." *Wall Street Journal,* October 29, A14.

Musick, Judith S. 1993. *Young, Poor, and Pregnant.* New Haven: Yale University Press.

Newman, Katherine. 1996. "Working Poor: Low Wage Employment in the Lives of Harlem Youth." In *Transitions through Adolescence: Interpersonal Domains and Context,* edited by J. Graber, J. Brooks-Gunn, and A. Peterson. Mahwah, N.J.: Erlbaum.

Nightingale, Karl Husemoller. 1993. *On the Edge.* New York: Basic.

Pagnini, Deanna L., and S. Philip Morgan. 1996. "Racial Differences in Marriage and Childbearing: Oral History Evidence from the South in the Early Twentieth Century." *American Journal of Sociology* 101:1694–718.

Radway, Janice. 1991. "Interpretive Communities and Variable Literacies: The Functions of Romance Reading." In *Rethinking Popular Culture,* edited by Chandra Mukerji and Michael Schudson. Berkeley: University of California Press.

Reissman, Catherine Kohler. 1993. *Narrative Analysis.* Newbury Park, Calif.: Sage.

Scott, James C. 1990. *Domination and the Arts of Resistance.* New Haven: Yale University Press.

Stacey, Judith. 1991. "Backward toward the Postmodern Family: Reflections on Gender, Kinship, and Class in the Silicon Valley." In *America at Century's End,* edited by Alan Wolfe. Berkeley: University of California Press.

Sullivan, Mercer L. 1989. "Absent Fathers in the Inner City." *Annals of the American Academy of Political and Social Science* 501:48–58.

Swidler, Ann. 1986. "Culture in Action: Symbols and Strategies." *American Sociological Review* 51:273–86.

———. Forthcoming. *Talk of Love: How Americans Use Their Culture.* Chicago: University of Chicago Press.

Tatley, Stephan. 1995. "The No. 1 Summer Song of Love." *New York Times Magazine,* August 13, 32.

Thornton, Arland. 1995. "Attitudes, Values and Norms Related to Nonmarital Fertility." In U.S. Department of Health and Human Services 1995.

Thornton, Arland, and Deborah Freedman. 1982. "Changing Attitudes toward Marriage and Single Life." *Family Planning Perspectives* 14:297–303.

United States Bureau of Labor Statistics. 1995. *Unemployment in States and Local Areas.* May. Microfiche.

United States Department of Health and Human Services. 1994. *Monthly Vital Statistics Report.* Vol. 43, No. 5(S).

———. 1995. *Report to Congress on Out-of-Wedlock Childbearing.* (PHS) 95–1257.

United States Department of Health, Education, and Welfare. 1975. *Vital Statistics of the United States, 1970.* (HRA) 75–1100.

Ventura, Stephanie, Christine Bachrach, Laura Hill, Kelleen Kaye, Pamela Halcomb, and Elisa Koff. 1995. "The Demography of Out-of-Wedlock Childbearing." In *Report to Congress on Out-of-Wedlock Childbearing,* 1–133.

Waller, Maureen R. 1996. "Redefining Fatherhood: Paternal Involvement, Masculinity, and Responsibility in the 'Other America.' " Ph.D. diss., Princeton University.

Whitehead, Barbara Defoe. 1993. "Dan Quayle Was Right." *Atlantic,* April, 47–84.

Wilson, William Julius. 1987. *The Truly Disadvantaged.* Chicago: University of Chicago Press.

———. 1996. *When Work Disappears.* New York: Knopf.

education and the
politics of race

friend and foe: boundary work and collective identity in the afrocentric and multicultural curriculum movements in american public education

amy binder

Suppose that in a nation that prides itself on its democratic principles there exists a large group of people that perceives that its intellectual history has been disregarded, at best, and systematically omitted, at worst, by the majority population's major institutions of learning and culture. Say, too, that this discontented population suffers from lower income, education, and occupation levels than do most other groups in society, not to mention a pervasive rage produced by daily indignities (Cose 1993; Feagin and Sikes 1994). How would members of this group seek to redress such wrongs done to them? Having experienced stalled gains over the past thirty years through legal measures such as civil rights legislation and by economic policies such as affirmative action, we might expect this group to "go cultural" with its sense of extraordinary disenfranchisement and to press for changes in their own and the majority population's acknowledgment of their contributions to world and national history.

The movement known as Afrocentrism—an intellectual movement that has grown in the nation's universities and a pedagogical reform movement that has taken place in many of the United States' predominantly black public school systems—can be thought of as just such a fight on the cultural front. It is a philosophy based on an essentialist conception of race that posits the cultural, behavioral, and lifestyle unity of all descendants of Africa, no matter where they have ended up following the black Diaspora (Lee forthcoming). In its practical application in public school curricula, Afrocentrism calls for an over-haul in the scholarly foundations of social studies and history instruction. In Winant's (1994) terms, Afrocentrism is a "racial project," insofar as it is an inter-pretation, representation, or explanation of racial dynamics and, at the same time, an effort to change the organization and distribution of resources along racial lines, in this case educational resources.[1] It has been waged by African-Americans who have been disappointed by the failures of their country to live up to its promise of inclusion and equal opportunity, who have become enraged by the closed access to its children of the American dream of social justice and mobility, and who have lost their faith in black and white political leadership to address their grievances (Marable and Mullings 1994).

The central concerns addressed by Afrocentrism—a sense of disappoint-ment and pessimism surrounding issues of mobility and respect—have been commonplace among many blacks in the past decade (Schuman, Steeh, and Bobo 1985; West 1992; Feagin and Sikes 1994). Yet Afrocentrism has not attracted overwhelming support among the majority of African-Americans (Adams 1995) and, in fact, has proved divisive within the African-American community wherever its tenets have been advocated.[2] Much like the black na-tionalist movement of the 1960s to which it is related, Afrocentrism erects sub-stantial boundaries around factions of the black community, particularly along class and cultural lines. These boundaries appeal to some and repel many others.

This boundary making—buffeted by a rhetoric of "real blackness" and "au-thenticity" as opposed to "selling out" and "assimilation" among blacks—can appear so intractable as to make the study of Afrocentrism interesting if only for the purpose of studying the divisions it creates within the African-American community. The presence of these cleavages is not the only reason to study the movement (there are many other aspects of Afrocentrism that prove interest-ing, primarily the nature of its struggle with public schools), but much of what is compelling about Afrocentrism is its unwitting ability to undermine the very concept it most seriously yearns to establish theoretically: that of a singular black people, or community. Ironically, while one of Afrocentrism's goals is to demonstrate the existence of an essentialized people called "Africans" who share with each other similar conceptual, interactional, and existential styles, the controversies Afrocentrism creates among blacks in fact produce significant divisions over identity within the black population.[3]

One of the best pieces of evidence undermining the notion of a like-minded, singular black identity is the fact that the Afrocentric movement was not the only attempt among black scholars and educators in the 1980s and 1990s to deal with the problems of black children's education and the obstructed mobility of much of black America. There were other African-American voices that also argued that a cultural corrective must be put in place to reverse racist historical wrongs, but these voices supported a distinctly *multicultural* form of instruction instead of an Afrocentric curriculum. Like proponents of Afrocentrism, multiculturalists fought textbook and curriculum content deemed Eurocentric and racist; unlike Afrocentrists, black multiculturalists made communion with other racial and ethnic groups (including whites) and demanded the inclusion of other minority groups' contributions in the classroom. The two agendas—Afrocentrism and multiculturalism—often were at odds in school districts across the country and created fissures among blacks fighting for reforms.

While the two groups advanced similar claims about the prevalence of biased, mainstream education and the harm such education visits upon children, they proposed quite different solutions to deal with this problem. It is important to ask why Afrocentrists and multiculturalists have taken different paths toward reform, to examine the basis of their different understandings of the cultural terrain, and to look at how each group has staked out its own logic in the education system. While there is considerable overlap between the two groups' rhetoric, there is also a discernible tension between the languages of Afrocentrists and multiculturalists, and in their racial projects as a whole. What are the sources of these tensions? To what extent do differences in racial identity and appeals to class play a role in articulating these conflicts? In large measure, Afrocentrists are unified in their agenda; multiculturalists represent a much more diversified group. In developing one's commitment to one or the other of these reform movements, who gets constructed as an enemy, and who gets considered an ally? Finally, what does the oft-strained relationship between these two groups tell us more generally about any assumed political cohesion of "black America"?

These are the questions this chapter seeks to answer. To address them I will look at how members of the Afrocentric and multicultural reform movements created collective identities for themselves vis-à-vis their adversaries, and how racial images played a role in those activities of identity construction. To think about identity construction in movements generally, I draw on theory from the social movements subfield of sociology. I then turn to work written by prominent black intellectuals who have defined the terms of the debate about *racial* collective identity particularly. After that, I outline the major premises of Afrocentrism and multiculturalism, and then proceed to an empirical analysis of the discourses present in three cases of Afrocentric reform challenges: in Atlanta, New York State, and Washington, D.C. I end with a comparison of the racial ideologies presented in the two movements.

Forging Racial Identity: African-American Intellectual Thought

COLLECTIVE IDENTITY. To begin, let's consider the primary social-psychological means by which individuals come to see themselves as belonging to one group and not to some other. *Collective identity* is a term used by scholars who study social movements to explore how individuals merge a sense of "who they are [as individuals] . . . with a definition shared by co-participants in some effort at social change—that is, who 'we' are" (Gamson 1992, 55). Creating a collective identity is an end in itself, insofar as it creates a sense of group identity that individuals are seeking as they join a movement. It is also a means to an end, insofar as the creation of this sense of being in a group of like-minded others helps movement members act in solidarity as they press their claims.

One way that collective identity and solidarity get created for a group is for members to have a clear understanding of the positions they are advocating; that is, which issues are included on their agenda, and which are excluded (Friedman and McAdam 1992). For the Afrocentric and multiculturalist movements, the question of inclusivity/exclusivity can be thought about in two ways. First is the question of the object itself: What kind of curriculum is being proposed by each group, what is the motivation of the scholarship that supports it, and who gets included in it? Are only Africans and African-Americans infused into the curriculum, or are all previously neglected racial/ethnic groups represented there, too? Does the scholarship celebrate the contributions of many cultures, or does it hark back to the traditions of one presumed people? Which students' needs are said to be addressed in the reformed curriculum: all children—including whites, Hispanics, Asians, and blacks—or primarily African-American children?

The second question about inclusivity/exclusivity and its relationship to collective identity concerns who the actual movement members are and just how restricted membership to the group is. In terms of each of these two intellectual movements: Is just one race represented among the activists in the movement? One social class? Or is there a cross-section of race and class representatives? These are foundational questions for insurgent movements because one of the primary means for creating collective identity is to cultivate for the group a firm sense of who one's enemies are; that is, who sits on the other side of the boundary marking "us" (Barth 1969; Gamson 1989; Taylor and Whittier 1992). Just as important as allies are for constructing one's identity, after all, are who one's adversaries happen to be.

But in the case of Afrocentrism and multiculturalism, "adversaries" and "allies" become tricky concepts. Because the two challengers end up competing, to some extent, against each other in the same market of curricular reform, and because each of the two challengers makes relatively similar claims about bias in the education system, the rhetoric of "enemy" is often applied not just to the system of Eurocentrism against which each is manifestly struggling, but to each other as well. This enemy talk provides Afrocentrists and multiculturalists with an effective means for differentiating their own project from the other and of consolidating an identity for each group's members within the universe of identities available to blacks (and others, in the case of multiculturalism) in this society.

DIVERSITY OF BLACK IDENTITIES. Which identities are available to blacks in the contemporary United States? For decades, African-American social scientists have explored the class and cultural politics that have divided and continue to divide the black community ideologically. In the terminology of the collective identity theorists laid out above, these divisions clarify who constitutes "us" and "them" both within the black population and with members of the dominant population. Perhaps most famously, these divisions were implicated in the conflict between W. E. B. Du Bois and Booker T. Washington over the appropriate stance of African-Americans toward white society and their own racial identity: whether aggressive protest for full legal rights and equality should be the primary fight, or whether economic improvement without an explicit political and racialized edge should be the path to peaceful coexistence. According to researchers who have studied these cleavages, such conflicts always play out at least partially along class lines.

Marable and Mullings (1994) give an overview of the modern-day dimensions of this enduring conflict about racial ideology within the American black community.[4] They argue that black intellectual thought has responded to issues of racial identity in three distinct ways: by using an integrationist/inclusionist rhetoric, a separatist rhetoric, or a transformationist discourse. The inclusionist vision "incorporates the traditional integrationist perspective of the earlier twentieth century, but also neo-liberal and pragmatic currents of the post–Civil Rights period" (Marable and Mullings 1994, 67). It disdains racial particularity and isolation, assumes that African-Americans should be considered "Americans who happen to be black," and opts to work within established institutions to affect public policy. It finds support among the black middle class, the professional and cultural elite, and public sector employees, who denounce "identity politics" as both demagogic and painfully divisive.

The separatist orientation encompasses black nationalism of years past as well as contemporary Afrocentrism. Its expressions include Marcus Garvey's Universal Negro Improvement Association of the 1920s and Elijah Muhammad's Nation of Islam in the 1960s. In its emphasis on race as a fixed category around which blacks must primarily define themselves, and in its deep skepticism about the willingness of the white power structure to ever relinquish its hegemonic position, it represents the opposite formulation to integrationism. It encourages retrenchment of identity into race alone, where race "remains the fundamental axis around which blacks need to be mobilized for liberation" (Dawson forthcoming). Its primary support derives from the marginalized

African-American working class, and it is most likely to gather force when African-Americans lag far behind others in society in economic gains, both major political parties reject calls to address racial inequality, the traditional black leadership is either unwilling or unable to articulate the grievances of the disaffected, and there is an acceptance by middle-class black leadership of the dominant cultural discourse within the social order (Marable and Mullings 1994, 69).

Marable and Mullings map out a third intellectual movement they call transformative, which centers on the eradication of all forms of inequality, not just racial inequality. It challenges the "institutions of power, privilege, and ownership patterns of the dominant society" (Marable and Mullings 1994, 69). Here, racism is understood to be an unequal relationship between social groups, based on power and violence, rather than as any sort of fixed reality of life. Support for the transformationist perspective, though relatively weak, is found most heavily in the "radicalized elements of the black intelligentsia, the more progressive elements of the black working class and middle class and also, to some degree, among marginalized youth" (Marable and Mullings 1994, 70).

Where Marable and Mullings advance the transformationist perspective as the preferred alternative to either integrationist or separatist racial ideology, Winant (1994) identifies another ideological route along which racial identity formation—particularly black identity—might travel. While not *ideal* in the same sense that the transformationist ideology is for Marable and Mullings, Winant's fourth path is also marked by resistance to the dominant racial ideology, insofar as it creates new identities more impervious to white society's intervention. He writes, "In terms of opposition, it is now possible to resist racial domination in entirely new ways, particularly by limiting the reach and penetration of the political system into everyday life, by generating new identities, new collectivities, new (imagined) communities. . . . Much of the rationale for Islamic currents among blacks in the United States, for the upsurge in black anti-Semitism, and to some extent for the Afrocentric phenomenon, can be found here" (Winant 1994, 19). In Winant's description of the fourth form of racial ideology we see heavy traces of separatism, but with a greater emphasis on strictly cultural forms of identity. The creation of Kwanzaa and the retelling of the legends of African kings and queens, for example, are meant to celebrate African history and to be kept within the black community, away from the consumption of whites.

We see from these descriptions that there are a variety of approaches to identifying as "African-American" in the United States, and that there are considerable historical roots of cleavage in the black community concerning racial self-definition. Any conversation about race identity in contemporary times must, therefore, be situated in this historical conversation. As we turn to two of the most current cultural expressions of racial identity—Afrocentrism and multiculturalism—we should bear these historical divisions in mind. It is pro-

ductive to think about how these two intellectual movements would be likely
to classify themselves according to a combined Marable-Mullings/Winant four-
way typology, and what the propensity of each might be for categorizing the
other. Surely, Afrocentrists both self-define, and are defined by multiculturalists, as "separatist" or "resistant." But what of the multiculturalists? Do they
view themselves as "transformationist," but get labeled "integrationist" by Afrocentrists? What do these definitions mean for black reform movements in the
United States?

Afrocentrism

Introduced in the early 1980s by Molefi Kete Asante of Temple University
(Thomas 1995), Afrocentrism has grown in black studies programs at universities around the nation as Maulana Karenga, Tsheloane Keto, Asa Hilliard
III, John Henrik Clarke, Leonard Jeffries, and others have pursued both the
intellectual bases of the project as well as its infusion into college, high-school,
and elementary school curricula. The intellectual project of Afrocentrism is
to "study African peoples from an Africa-centered prism" by placing the conti-
nent "at the center of any analysis of African history and culture, including
the African-American experience" (Oyebade 1990, 233). According to Mazrui
(1993) this perspective is a constructive response to the Eurocentric bias that
has pervaded intellectual thought and established European civilization as the
standard by which all other civilizations are judged. Afrocentrism "seeks to lib-
erate African studies from this Eurocentric monopoly on scholarship and thus
assert a valid worldview through which Africa can be studied objectively" (Oyebade 1990, 234).

The Afrocentric methodology rests on two primary assumptions. The first is
that analysis of any subject with roots in Africa must begin with "the primacy of
the classical African civilizations, namely Kemet (Egypt), Nubia, Axum, and
Meroe. . . . Adequate understanding of African phenomena cannot occur without a reference point in the classic and most documented African culture"
(Asante 1990, 14). Studies of African-American phenomena are no less tied
to this methodology than are studies of African phenomena, since Afrocentric
scholars view African-American experience as, first and foremost, a dimension
of African history and culture. Afrocentrism recognizes no division between
the African past and African-American history, and regards as "ahistorical" and
"mythical" any social science that does not trace these continuous African roots
(Oyebade 1990). So if, for example, a scholar sets out to study "Africans in the
inner cities of the Northeast United States, it must be done with the idea in the
back of the mind that one is studying African people, not 'made-in-America
Negroes' without historical depth" (Asante 1990, 15).

The second major premise upon which Afrocentrism is based is that all people of African descent possess essential cognitive, cultural, and aesthetic characteristics in common. Welsh-Asante (cited in Asante 1990), for example, argues that there is an African Aesthetic, which is "based on seven 'senses' shared by all Africa-descended people around the globe: polyrhythm, polycentrism, dimensional, repetition, curvilinear, epic memory, and wholism" (Asante 1990, 12). At its most controversial (and many Afrocentric scholars themselves reject such notions), this conception of race includes suggestions about personality based on melanin content and other genetic hardwiring. Whether at the extremes or not, however, defining the characteristics that are inherent in all black people is seen as "emphasiz[ing] the uniqueness of black folks' cultural truth" (Thomas 1995, 26) and creating cultural solidarity. In addition, by hailing to a pure African tradition that is said to antedate white civilization and contamination, "blacks become dominant by virtue of either biology or culture, [and] whites are allocated a subordinate role."

Combined, these two premises—that all African-American social phenomena can be traced to some degree or other back to Africa, and that all people of African descent share essential race characteristics—provide the foundations for Afrocentric curricula at the grade-school to high-school levels. Added to these foundational concepts in the curriculum are new, and often disputed, claims about African history and its influence on Western thought, as well as an emphasis on the contributions of African-Americans to the progress of the nation.

Mazrui[5] (1993) refers to this celebratory stream of scholarship in the Afrocentric literature as "Gloriana Afrocentricity," meaning that its emphasis is on kings and queens in ancient Egypt, and others who sat at the top of the cultural hierarchy. This stream he contrasts with "Proletariana Afrocentricity," which emphasizes the contributions of enslaved Africans to modern culture. Some of the most hotly disputed historical claims advanced by Gloriana Afrocentric scholars are that much of Western civilization—including theories attributed to Aristotle and many other Greek philosophers—were actually learned at the feet of ancient black Egyptians and stolen from them (James 1954); that ancient black Egyptians discovered the fundamentals of species evolution, astronomy, and human flight (Adams 1990; see also Ortiz de Montellano 1996 for a critique); and that Napoleon's army used the Sphinx's nose as target practice to eradicate evidence of its Negroid features and origins (Van Sertima 1990).

African essentialism and new historical scholarship—the bases of Afrocentric thought—are, then, designed to reverse the Eurocentric bias of traditional teaching and to generate interest and success among African-American students. How this agenda gets carried out across school districts and in individual classrooms varies, however. In one location, each day in the Afrocentric classroom begins with an "opening ritual," in which "children say affirmation, they hug each other, they sing, they dance." This practice has been implemented because "our people understood that we are spirits that have a body, not bodies that have spirits" (interview with Abena Walker, founder and principal of the African-Centered School in Washington, D.C.). Other programs focus much more attention on modified curriculum content, rather than on what are considered to be African-derived practices. In Atlanta, for example, Africanness does not appear to be expressed through ritual in the classroom. Instead, primary emphasis is placed on using supplementary materials (such as the controversial *African-American Baseline Essays* written for the Portland, Oregon, school district) to add information about African and African-American contributions to world history.

Afrocentrism versus Multiculturalism

Contrasted with Afrocentrism is multiculturalism, a movement whose exact definition is impossible to specify. As Austin (1995, 1) points out, people mean a great many things when they speak of multiculturalism, for its prescriptions range from "minor changes in English and history curricula to the restructuring of entire schools." At its most basic, however, multiculturalism's philosophical claim is that there should be a "parity of esteem of all cultures" (Mazrui 1993, 1); that "members of the different groups should appreciate and respect the other cultures in their society" (Raz 1994, 73); that while the world's cultures and societies may not be empirically equal (e.g., one society may be more democratic, richer, more troubled . . . than the next), they are all *morally* equal (Mazrui 1993). Thus, proponents of multiculturalism advocate a broadened curriculum that includes the contributions of all cultures to the making of the nation and the world. Such a curriculum is said to benefit society in a number of different ways: it introduces facts about America and the rest of the world hitherto neglected in textbooks, it promotes understanding among people of different ethnicities, it emphasizes the cultural interdependence of all people, and it prepares young people to more successfully navigate the global culture and economy that we now inhabit.

Proponents of multiculturalism come from a larger range of institutional and political positions than do Afrocentrists and are apt to have a variety of opinions concerning their more "radical" colleagues, Afrocentrists. Academic and policy notables who are commonly known as neoconservatives like Diane Ravitch, Arthur Schlesinger, and Nathan Glazer would be likely to regard themselves as multiculturalists who have little patience for the Afrocentric perspective. Their most plaintive protest against Afrocentrism concerns its trashing of a common culture and the attending loss of solidarity that occurs when each of society's racial and ethnic groups takes on a tribal mentality (see Giroux 1992 for a critique of the liberal-pluralist's "common culture" argument). Meanwhile, educators—including many African-American educators (school board members, midlevel administrators, superintendents, and members of teachers' unions)—generally distance themselves from the thinking of the neoconservatives, but also happily assume the multicultural mantle while eschewing the goals and scholarship of Afrocentrism (Moran 1996). Still others in the multicultural camp are friendlier to the claims of Afrocentrism, but withhold their support for practical or philosophical reasons.

Not surprisingly, Afrocentrists consider the ideology and reforms advocated by multiculturalists as woefully inadequate and ideologically suspect, even "integrationist," if they were to use Marable and Mullings's (1994) typology. Rather than placing a few sporadic and disconnected items about African-Americans or Hispanics, say, in the fundamentally biased curriculum, Afrocentrists argue that public school curricula must "undergo a thoroughgoing transformation" (Moran 1996, 1). The hallmarks of this transformation consist of the new scholarship to be infused into the curriculum, as described above: scholarship that talks entirely differently about the role of Africa and African-Americans in world culture. As the "antithesis" of Eurocentrism, Afrocentrism replaces multiculturalists' emphasis on pluralism and all cultures' interdependence, and stresses instead the uniqueness of African peoples, the impact of Africans on world civilization, and proposes that the ultimate "other" to white hegemony is Africanity (Mazrui 1993, 2). Afrocentrism's mission is felt to be revolutionary and, as such, is irreconcilable with the conventionally pluralist claims of multiculturalism.

Making such rigid distinctions between Afrocentrism and multiculturalism as have been drawn above serves to describe the *theoretical* divide that separates the two movements. And yet, on the ground level—e.g., in the school districts, where the real reform efforts take place—this division becomes much murkier. Before venturing into this practical terrain, it is important to clarify terminology. When I refer to *multiculturalists* I mean one thing only: advocates of a broadened curriculum that includes the contributions of all previously neglected races and ethnic groups. By *Afrocentrist*, on the other hand, I actually include two types of challenger. There is, first, the ideal typical advocate of Afrocentrism: the self-identified Afrocentrist who concentrates on the needs of the African-American student exclusively, not the Hispanic, Asian, Native American, etc., student population. The second type of Afrocentrist I refer to are those people who philosophically align themselves with the broader goals of multiculturalism, but who, because of the context they find themselves in (for example, a 90 percent–plus black school system), choose to champion the Afrocentric reforms being waged in their districts.

With that clarification made, we can examine the real-world reform activities of these two groups and the relationships that their ideologies have to each other. In the following sections, I use quotes from interviews that I conducted in the fall of 1995. I spoke with twenty people who had been active in Afrocentrism/multiculturalism reform debates in at least one of three locations: Atlanta, Washington, D.C., and New York State.[6] I chose these locations as comparative case studies because they represent three of the most visible sites of racial cultural challenge to public schools in the nation in the mid- to late 1980s and early 1990s. I determined that these were three of the nation's most important sites for Afrocentric reform in a variety of ways. First, when asked to comment on the crucial reform efforts around the country, my interviewees consistently mentioned these three. Among other locations cited by my interviewees (and in the media) were Portland, Oregon; Camden, New Jersey; Detroit; and Chicago.

Second, in its coverage of the Afrocentric reform movement nationwide, the *New York Times* (arguably the closest thing to a high-quality national newspaper) covered the events in Atlanta, Washington, and New York State more heavily than those elsewhere.

Finally, in selecting cases I looked at local media coverage of the efforts. For each of these cases I was able to collect nearly one hundred articles, both news stories and editorials. For the other cases that I might have selected, there was not as much local coverage. With the exception of Portland, Oregon, these three are the cases that attracted the most attention, both locally and nationally.

They also proved to be good comparative cases because they differed significantly in their processes of curriculum revision and in their outcomes. Although I do not use the cases as comparisons in this chapter but instead divide the interviewees across all cases into those who identify with Afrocentrism versus those who are multicultural, it is important to say something about these three sites. The three cases are ideal for comparison along a number of dimensions.

Of these three cases, the Atlanta curriculum reform effort ran into the least resistance from educators, parents, and community members. Because educators within the system (particularly the district superintendent, J. Jerome Harris) introduced the reforms, it faced the fewest obstacles to implementation. This is not to say that there were no barriers to its successful integration, however. The African-American Infusion Program eventually became a hot-button issue when it got enmeshed in the politics of the school district (board vs. superintendent) and when white and black media writers began questioning its ideological intentions.

In Washington, D.C., Afrocentrism had an entirely different debut, as community members and parents pushed a reluctant black superintendent into supporting an African-centered program. The most contentious battle was waged over a school-within-a-school program, which was directed by an African-centered educator named Abena Walker, whose credentials and curriculum designs were deemed incomplete and inadequate by district administrators and the media. Despite an enormous amount of negative press, the superintendent satisfied community proponents of Afrocentrism by allowing the program to go forward. At the same time, however, Superintendent Franklin Smith hastened to conceptualize and implement a separate multicultural curriculum that was said to differ dramatically from the African-centered program.

The New York case differs from Atlanta and Washington in several ways. First, the issue of Afrocentric reform was discussed in this case at the state level, not citywide. Second, the commissioner in place at the time, Thomas Sobol, was white, new to the job, and faced tremendous skepticism from minority interest groups. His appointment to the state's top education job had brought angry protests from minorities, particularly groups in New York City; to answer these protests, Sobol appointed a task force to examine equity in education across the state. Out of this task force was issued "A Curriculum of Inclusion," a report that was greatly influenced by Leonard Jeffries, then chairman of the department of black studies at the City College of New York and soon to become one of the nation's most controversial Afrocentric scholars. "A Curriculum of Inclusion," with its suggestion of the white school system's "deep-seated pathologies of racial hatred," set off a firestorm of protest in the media, and set in motion many years of subsequent commissions, reports, and damage control.

Within each case, I selected respondents based on a number of different criteria: I wanted my sample to capture the range of perspectives present in the debate (from strong pro-Afrocentric to strong anti-Afrocentric sentiment) and to represent a variety of institutional positions (superintendents, administrators, teachers, advisory members, media writers, academics, etc.). Each of my respondents played some kind of critical role in these public school challenges. I did not interview Afrocentric or multicultural scholars who kept their distance from the ground-level challenges, though I did read written commentary on these three Afrocentric challenges and others in scholarly journals and in the major newspapers for each location (the *Atlanta Journal and Constitution,* the *Washington Post,* and the *New York Times*). I draw on these written comments sparingly in this chapter and instead concentrate on responses to the questions I posed to my interviewees.[7]

Positing Problems and Identifying Solutions: Afrocentrism and Multiculturalism

As reported above, there are several important ideological and pedagogical differences separating Afrocentrism from multiculturalism, but there is also a fundamental commonality. The common ground is their specification of a root problem in public education: according to both Afrocentrists and multiculturalists, public-school curricula are deeply marred by a Eurocentric bias. Bias and its consequences are evident in many forms, but those most often cited by both camps (in order of macro to micro processes) are a culturewide system of discrimination that inevitably seeps into school instruction; the lack of information in the classroom on the contributions made to society by historically oppressed racial and ethnic groups; black and/or minority students' lack of interest and low achievement in school, which stem from not seeing "people like them" in the curriculum; administrators' reluctance to change the system in any meaningful way because change means more work for them; teachers who are uncomfortable with new forms of knowledge and, so, prefer to teach content as they traditionally have; white parents' discomfort with having history taught in any other form than what they learned in school. In short, the problems that Afrocentrists and multiculturalists identify in the education system are, by and large, the same.

But what of the concrete solutions they propose? Referring back to their more abstract theoretical discussions, we would guess that the two groups part ways over how to remedy these similarly specified problems. One theme that consistently runs through Afrocentrists' descriptions of their solution, but not through multiculturalists', is that a particularly African-American curriculum must replace the Eurocentric curriculum in black school districts because "that's who our clients are" (interview with Gladys Twyman, project coordinator of the African American Infusion Program for the Atlanta Public Schools). In predominantly black school districts like Atlanta's and Washington's, this opinion is expressed with little anticipation that refutation is even possible.

As Mae Kendall, director of program planning and curriculum development for the Atlanta Public Schools, told me, "The rationale behind starting with African and African-American history and culture here was that that was the population. The school district was at least 92 percent black, and it still is today. . . . For me, it's primarily *right now* about Afrocentric because we have so much catching up to do."

Thinking about the pressure that proponents of Afrocentrism placed on Washington's superintendent of schools, another of my interviewees, an administrator in the system, says:

> In the school system we *want* to have a curriculum that from beginning to end and from content to content, infuses the contributions of our students' cultures into everything they learn. . . . If you looked at our documents, you would eventually not get to see an African-centered curriculum, a Hispanic curriculum . . . , but you would get to see a curriculum that has all these elements built—fully integrated—into all of its components. And that's the thrust of our curriculum renewal.

But, at the same time having said that, the politics of the situation is that there is a significant and verbal enough component of our population to have us try and look at small situations—school-within-school situations—where we are going to focus on African-centered. (interview with Betty Topps, executive assistant to the superintendent, Washington)

And the Atlanta school administrator who speaks of "clients" expands on this point:

In a multicultural program you emphasize multi cultures, many cultures. And our thinking, in the Atlanta public schools, was that before you can know about other cultures, you should first know about yourself. "Know thyself" kind of thing. Know who you are and where you are coming from and what your place in the world is, and *then* you can start studying and appreciating other cultures. But first you've got to know who you are and appreciate yourself. (interview with Gladys Twyman, Atlanta)

In addition to teaching specifically African- and African-American-oriented content, some proponents of Afrocentrism speak of a particularly African methodology and ideology that must also be infused into the educational training of black children. Abena Walker, the director of the small, but much media-maligned, African-centered program in the Washington system, argues that such a methodology is derived from Africa, where "our people intuitively and through training came up with a system of parenting and teaching that the modern world still hasn't grasped" (interview with Abena Walker, Washington). This methodology proves beneficial to children of all races, she says, but if there is no political will to train all children with it, then at least black children ought to receive it:

The two most important aspects of education that we've updated from ancient Africa are the ideological concepts and the methodology. . . . OK, the ideologies are like educational concepts, the body of concepts makes your ideology. And the ideology of ancient Africa is almost the opposite of what we labor under today as Euro-American education. We're not saying everything African is good and everything Euro-American is bad. We're just saying it's time for a balance. . . .

The African ideology says that all adults are parents, whether they biologically produced children or not. . . . So, all adults are parents and, in turn, all parents are teachers. And are trained in the skills and competencies in traditional Africa that teachers were the parents, and everybody received an education. . . . So, our parents do come in, they observe what we're doing, they take some of the work home, they help create spirit journeys—that's what we call the homework. It's better than "homework." They say "spirit journeys." They still work, but these words are so important. Some words are just turnoffs: school, class, homework. So we call it spirit journeys.

So, one other ideological concept in the Euro-American education . . . [is] that children are like tabula rasa, a Latin word that means blank tablets, and that we kind of take these empty vessels and fill them up. John Holt[8] called it the assembly line approach, where our children are viewed as little cans or bottles on a conveyor belt, and teachers feverishly squirt in two years of math, two years of science. And of course the stuff is squirting all over the place. And when the children come out unfilled and unfulfilled, *they* are to blame, not this faulty system of squirting into these empty bottles.

So, out of that type of ideology you get methods that are very rigid, that are very teacher centered, that are very arrogant. They're mean-spirited, that's the word John Holt used. The system is very mean-spirited: good people learning to be mean. . . .

The African system says, no, children are not tabula rasa, actually they come in with all their knowledge and talents and skills intact. They are geniuses. And what the education must do is set up a system that receives them and gives them the freedom within the structure to share who they are, and then you build from that foundation. So then you can see from that ideology that your methods in the classroom would be more flexible, more child centered. More creative. (interview with Abena Walker, Washington)

An administrator in the Washington system also discusses the Afrocentric methodology, reporting that the system consults

with a university professor who has done a lot of study at Howard [University] around African-American children, and so she's linked herself to this notion that we ought to begin to restructure our curriculum so that it is consistent with the learning styles of our culture, which is collaborative. There's a notion that our kids don't learn as well because for years and generations it's been an independent approach to teaching and learning when our whole nature, coming from whatever, says that we are communal people. (interview with Betty Topps, Washington)

As these five quotes show, Afrocentric thought concerning curriculum reform is centered on two fundamental notions: that the contributions of Africans and African-Americans—and not of other groups—must be the primary change in curriculum, and that curriculum reform must also be accompanied by a change in teaching methods. These methods emphasize a more cooperative mode that coincides with a "natural" African learning style.

Multiculturalists' discourse on reform differs from Afrocentrists' on both of these points. On the first, while they agree with Afrocentrists that the curriculum is biased toward the accomplishments of whites and Europeans, as a revision, multiculturalists argue that the contributions of *all* groups must be integrated into the curriculum. Typical of this perspective are the thoughts of Linda Biemer, dean of the school of education at SUNY-Binghamton and a member of the social studies curriculum committee in New York:

> I agreed that the curriculum was pretty much Eurocentric; that there was not a lot of play given to people of other cultures. And this has been true pretty much in the teaching of social studies in New York. . . . Because I think that a lot of people who are teaching in New York State: they're white. I mean, the majority of the teachers in New York State are white, the majority of the history that they learned—and many of these teachers are in their forties, fifties, and sixties—what they learned was the sort of the standard Anglo-American history, Western European history.
>
> Even though, for many years, New York was one of only two states that even required that students study Africa and Asia. . . . But it was sort of treated as a novelty, you know? It was a separate thing: "Now we are going to learn about Asia and Africa." You know, it was almost the exoticness of it all. (interview with Linda Biemer)

On the second Afrocentric concern—implementing a new and more collaborative methodology for use with the revised curriculum—multiculturalists are largely silent. So, while each group describes the *problem* of Eurocentric education similarly (and its negative effects on minority children), Afrocentrists and multiculturalists part ways on the *solution* to this problem.

Constructing Enemies and, in the Process, Constructing Racial Identity

As some of these quotes suggest, both Afrocentrists and multiculturalists hold a white power structure accountable for the slanted instruction black and other minority children receive in U.S. public schools. In a word, it is white racism that is the enemy. In a caustic indictment of the white education system, Leonard Jeffries argues that the racist system is not prepared for significant curriculum reform:

> We expected [the "Curriculum of Inclusion" report] to be watered down because it was [to be used] for the general curriculum. An African-centered education curriculum couldn't be taught properly in the school system. You'd have to retrain the administrators and teachers. You *couldn't* have an African-centered curriculum. You *can* have it in an African school program that's planned for that. . . . But you can't get a white administrator trained in

the white system to administer an African-centered program. He's just not going to have the understanding to do it, no matter how much his heart may be moving in that direction. . . . White folks can't understand the black experience. . . .

This document, "A Curriculum of Inclusion," is very gentle. I was saying, "Let's balance Thomas Jefferson's good points with his negatives." But if you heard my analysis of T. J. today in [my City College] classroom: *that* was the African-centered analysis. That would never get through a committee put together by the commissioner. It would never get through a curriculum. But it is the *truth* of Thomas Jefferson: the ultimate contradiction in American society. . . . But that type of contradiction, we didn't weave into "A Curriculum of Inclusion." We just said, "Add some complementary facts." (interview with Leonard Jeffries, New York)

While this statement is identifiably Afrocentric, in most of my interviews, Afrocentrists' and multiculturalists' critiques of Eurocentrism and racism are virtually indistinguishable from each other. As examples:

We are trying to be intellectually honest in what is actually presented, and it is not to blame or put down any other group. It is to let people know that we are, for the first time, unearthing a lot of information sources that have not been considered because of the kind of entrenched racism that our academic institutions have been imbued with. (interview with Midge Sweet, member of the Atlanta school board; proponent of multiculturalism)

As a black American, what I am dealing with consistently is the fact that I opt to live just as a human being. And a citizen. But that is denied me because of my pigmentation. So often, I am viewed not firstly as a human being endowed with certain talents, certain characteristics. But I am seen firstly as a person of pigmentation, bringing along a long list of stereotypes.

Now, what this allows Americans to do—because the history is not known, and there is not the acceptance of a civilized, democratic society— it allows Americans to view me at best with ambiguity and at worst with hostility.

And so, I think if we can better educate this generation of students, maybe we can remove some of those things, and we can get a better idea of the reality of the evolution of the American republic. (interview with Walter Cooper, member of the New York State Board of Regents; proponent of multiculturalism)

My experience with [the superintendent, who advocated an African-centered curriculum] was major resistance by school board members, by parents. But primarily, I guess, more by Caucasian parents on the north side of town. (interview with Murdell McFarlin, former public information officer, superintendent's office, Atlanta Public Schools; proponent of Afrocentrism)

The *Washington Post* is very powerful and backed by the power structure. So they laid it on us.

[Asked what she thought the impetus was behind the negative treatment her program received in the *Post*:] Well, the good old *R* word: it's just a racist attempt to stop something that would help the black community. And whatever players played into it, black or white, it's just the way America goes. It's nothing new. It's nothing new, you know. (interview with Abena Walker, Washington; proponent of Afrocentrism)

If one were to attempt to pick out the proponents of Afrocentrism versus multiculturalism using just the quotes above, one would likely have a fairly low batting average. In their excoriation of white racism and the school system's resistance to change, the two groups sound remarkably similar.

But there is a second bastion of enemies that Afrocentrists point to that multiculturalists do not mention: these are African-Americans within the education system who are blamed for being sell-outs, assimilationists, and members of the middle class who are attached to the status quo. They are sometimes even accused of not being black enough. In other words, added to the baseline enemy of white racism—which is a kind of first-order system to be battled against by both Afrocentrists and multiculturalists—Afrocentrists also hold accountable those blacks they perceive to be beholden to that system. Several of my interviewees offer clear examples of this sentiment:

[African-centered education] shifted the social peer structure. And it put those who *had* been in charge of the educational system here on the back burner. *That* was the fight, *that* was the problem. And a lot of it was black on black.

[Asked who was previously in charge:] They were administrators. They were definitely principals. They were directors—curriculum directors—who had held those positions for many years. Really, they had done nothing. . . . I don't want to say that they had done *nothing*, but their levels of achievement were minimal in terms of outcomes, of what had been produced: low test scores, high drop-out rates. That kind of thing. It was all a self-fulfilling . . . I'm in this to see (a) how many Mercedes I can buy, (b) how many . . . And I am serious. When I came to the system, 90 percent of the focus was on what you looked like. What you wore. What car you drove.

Now, when I say 90 percent, I mean from your kindergarten teacher on up. . . . It's not good. It's a very sad commentary. And I feel very, very bad about it. Because (a) I'm black, (b) I work for the system, (c) I have children that finished this system, (d) my husband works for the system, (e) it's run by blacks. (interview with Murdell McFarlin, Atlanta)

Some proponents of Afrocentrism go even further in criticizing status quo black bureaucrats, intimating that they are less black than Afrocentrists:

I diplomatically say that part of the opposition to us was that people fear change. People just fear change. It's human nature, I guess. [Asked which people:] People, period. I would say the people that were fighting against us. . . . Some of the professors at Howard [University], the "house Negro" at the *Post*—and he's never even been here to visit our program. . . . I'm talking about those people that publicly denounced us. I say that, first of all, people fear change. Second of all, I'd say those people in the system that denounced us have bought into the system, so anything that threatens their position, their salary, their status quo, is a threat. (interview with Abena Walker, Washington)

Added to the charge that comfortable black professionals opposed Afrocentric education as a means of protecting their own positions in a reform-averse system was the unsubtle suggestion that blacks who opposed Afrocentric reforms were not as racially or ideologically pure as supporters were. Although I did not directly hear supporters of Afrocentrism make this charge—aside from Abena Walker's "house Negro" comment above—I did hear reports of such name-calling from those on the receiving end. A black New York State regent who voted against the recommendations of "A Curriculum of Inclusion" (the controversial report whose rhetoric was attributed largely to Leonard Jeffries), reports:

One of the things that happened when that report was delivered to the board of regents, and we determined that it was unacceptable for approval, one of the black members of the task force, Dr. Don Smith of Baruch College, made some rather impolite comments that he directed at me. He accused me of having betrayed my race for not having given assent to this document and being part of some unanimity of opinion. As if agreement over issues such as these were to be based on pigmentation and not on rational processes of determining one's own position on such questions!

[Asked how he responded to Smith's comments:] You don't get into great debates about these things. I have often run into this "blacker than thou" psychology, and it's better not to get into a debate about it. I just told him that this issue is a matter of opinion, and that this was my opinion. (interview with Walter Cooper, New York)

And Russell Adams, chair of Howard University's department of African-American studies (and the target of Abena Walker's "house Negro" accusation above), gives this trenchant analysis:

What happens in D.C. and in some other places—Atlanta, for example—is that there is a heavy class component to this within the black community. The more borderline economically, and blue collar and no-collar, so to speak [laughs], the stronger that notion of the "blackened" curriculum might be.

[Asked to explain:] It puts, ironically, some distance between—some distance they feel good about—between the haves and the have-nots in the black community. That *we* have kept the true faith, unbroken line, to ancient Africa. That *we* are black.

[Asked if this is an issue of "authenticity":] There is a sense of continuity, and hence, authenticity, that one should celebrate. And if you don't celebrate it, that's a sign that you've been captured by The Man [sotto voce]. Now, that plays out with these ideas getting the greatest push from the borderline and below the border between the two classes.

As you go to the middle class—if the middle class still has kids in the public schools—then there is less emphasis on that definition of purity. There is greater emphasis on either multicultural or the best parts of the curriculum that have been affected, whatever the contents are.... [The middle class] expect their sons and daughters to go on to college. And if they go to professional school, if they don't come to Howard, they will probably go to a place that's 98 percent white. And so, they are not, then, as trusting of this lower income group's version of authenticity. "So, all right, you're nice and black, but is it going to move you through the system, not only academically, but afterwards, economically?" And they tend to say no. (interview with Russell Adams, Washington)

As these four quotes demonstrate, supporters of Afrocentrism express skepticism directly (or are understood to be skeptical) about their black colleagues' commitment to the education of black children, and to the race more generally, and seem to be constructing their own identity as blacks in contradistinction to their "integrationist" counterparts. Instead of upholding the educational status quo and its accompanying material rewards (as they claim too many blacks employed by the system do), supporters of Afrocentrism see themselves breaking free from the system of nepotism to fight for the rights of young African-

Americans. Judging the actions of black superintendents, administrators, and school board members to be traitorous, Afrocentrism's advocates define themselves as keepers of the authentic race.

Interestingly, this language criticizing middle-class blacks often comes from people who are also established in the system: from professors and public school administrators, school board members and teachers. Although no data are available to give concrete support for this contention, at both an economic and institutional level, proponents of Afrocentrism and multiculturalism seem more or less to occupy similar class positions, in the strictest sense of the term "class." Afrocentric academics, in general, may not hold positions in institutions of as high status as multiculturalism's academic supporters, but they are likely to occupy the same income brackets and possess other similar class markings. So, when Afrocentrists use "middle class" and other such labels to deride multiculturalists and other blacks in the system, we should wonder what they mean. In this usage, it seems that "middle class" assumes a cultural connotation that is divorced from its strict economic meaning. It signifies a relationship to comfort, accommodation, and a dubious racial identity more than it does to a particular economic position. In other words, "middle class" multiculturalism means white and assimilationist, while an Afrocentric commitment signifies real African-Americanness. Class talk is used to differentiate between those who stop short of helping the race (putatively middle class, multiculturalist, and other more conservative blacks in the schools) and those who keep pushing for justice (Afrocentrists).

This Afrocentric vision of the racial terrain maps well onto Marable and Mullings's (1994) three-way typology of racial identity, where the relationship between the separatist and integrationist perspectives on race is described as a reverse mirror image. We see that this metaphor nicely captures the type of identity construction Afrocentrists engage in. By criticizing other blacks for being invested in the system and not sufficiently racially committed (that is, for being integrationist), Afrocentrists are definitively declaring what they, themselves, are *not*. Where integrationists protect their own material interests, Afrocentrists believe that they are looking out for the interests of black children. Where integrationists accommodate whites, Afrocentrists believe that they are true to their race. Even though there is no one exhaustive definition of what Afrocentrists believe or advocate (an absence that makes the term quite useful), there is a sense that Afrocentrism means *being black*, while multiculturalism does not.

How does the description of the mirror image work the other way: do multiculturalists construct *their* identity in counterpoint to the Afrocentrists as separatists? The answer appears to be yes. For even if multiculturalists are unwilling to define themselves as integrationist (in fact, they often argue that they are more radical and transformative in their vision than Afrocentrists are), they are clearly pushed into defending themselves against the integrationist, or apologist, label that the Afrocentric rhetoric casts upon them. This defense clearly emerges in the Cooper quote above when he resists entering into a blacker-than-thou competition with his accuser. But multiculturalists are likely to assert their mirror-image difference from Afrocentric separatism in their more affirmative statements of their project, as well. A Hispanic member of one of the New York commission task forces draws attention to the more sophisticated scholarship found in multiculturalism when she states:

> [The "Curriculum of Inclusion" report] did not include, according to my assessment, any notion of *interrelationship* among groups. Because you had four very distinct segments [in the report], as if they had never crossed each others' paths. . . . And we wanted to know—especially in a city and state like New York—what was happening at the intersections? How do you prepare people for the intersections? Certainly, the scholarship had to be inclusive and comparative and interdisciplinary. It had to be all of these things.
>
> And finally, there was absolutely no attention paid [in "Curriculum of Inclusion"] to gender, or working class. It was as if each of the cultures, or each of the groups being talked about, was monolithic. And was never going to change. But there is, in fact, an enormous amount of diversity within each of these groups. (interview with Virginia Sanchez-Korrol, chair of the Puerto Rican studies department, Brooklyn College, and member of the New York State Social Studies Review and Development Committee)

Like Sanchez-Korrol, Walter Cooper, regent for the state of New York and the person accused of betraying his race, draws a line between himself and Afrocentrism, even while being circumspect about criticizing Afrocentrists too harshly:

> Well, I think—this is my personal viewpoint—I think if you were looking for educational content that addressed the issues of something along the lines of "Who are we as a people and a nation?" and "What is the strength, or truth, of that society?" "What are some of the truths of our society, from a historical perspective?" then the "Curriculum of Inclusion" did not address those issues. I got the impression that it was more of a statement of ideology, more so than of having educational content. It might have satisfied some peculiar need of those who represented the task force, and I can't indict the task force. But in my opinion, it did not address the needs of this generation of students and future generations of students. . . .
>
> I view the business of really coming to grips with the problems confronting you here in the United States, it's out of the crucible of your *American*

experience that will enable you to solve the problems here in America. And it's not out of the African experience that you will be able to solve your problems. (interview with Walter Cooper)

How should we think about discourse like this as a construction of a multicultural identity? Perhaps we cannot expect advocates of multiculturalism to have as strong a commitment to their identities as "multiculturalist" as Afrocentrists have to their identity as "Afrocentric." After all, there is a great deal of variation and ambiguity among those ascribing to the multicultural label in what they mean by the term, much more so than among Afrocentrists. Since this is true, we should not suppose that the precision of specifying one's enemies and allies, the nature of relations to one's like-minded colleagues, the degree of commonality of dogma, and the degree to which their identity is organized around the ideology of multiculturalism to be commensurate with the more (though not totally) homogeneous Afrocentrist identity.[9]

Despite this, there are a few things we can say about how multiculturalists define themselves in contrast to an Afrocentric ideology, which they perceive as separatist. First, there is the notion that multiculturalism is a more cosmopolitan framework than the nationalistic Afrocentrism, insofar as it reaches outward toward the complexities of this world rather than backward toward a mythologized past. As Walter Cooper says in the quote above, multiculturalism is able to answer broader questions about us as a people; it is not confined, as Afrocentrism is, to addressing the particular needs of its architects. Second, multiculturalism is an ideology that allows proponents to conceive of themselves as global citizens, people who can work with others of different races and ethnicities to counteract centuries of harm done to all children—black, white, and other. In this, it is constructed as a decent and civic-minded agenda, and far more responsible than its brasher cousin, Afrocentrism. Finally, in their sense of responsibility, multiculturalists use the rhetoric of practicality to bolster their program: with the right appeals to fairness and pragmatism (such as training children to compete in a "global" culture), multiculturalism is a curriculum that can be made to fit into the institutional logic of the education system. In sum, advocates of multiculturalism represent their motivations as radical, while they speak of their solutions as rational, responsible, and workable. The importance of being "authentically" racial plays a minimal role in this identity.

Conclusion: Race, Class, and Culture

As a reform group, Afrocentrists in Atlanta, New York, and Washington faced a rather peculiar problem. Unlike other social movements or interest groups that just do battle with adversaries who reject any form of change that the movement is proposing, advocates of Afrocentrism had to wage battle on two fronts at once. Their first foe—which has been left virtually unmentioned here—was the conservative opponent who was opposed outright to all claims Afrocentrists made: those who argued that any change in public school curricula in the Afrocentric direction represented a scurrilous attack on the Anglo-European tradition. These traditionalist adversaries granted no credibility whatsoever to either the problems that the Afrocentric challenge sought to correct or to the solutions that they proposed. But few of this type of opponent showed up in the ground-level, intrainstitutional debates about curriculum. This steadfast opposition was best represented by commentators in the media, including such famous conservatives as Dinesh D'Souza and George Will. These opponents were uncomplicatedly called racists by both Afrocentrists and multiculturalists and were expected to react as such.

The other battlefront where Afrocentrists found themselves engaged was with people whose arguments sounded quite similar to their own: multiculturalists, who typify the majority perspective in public school administration. Afrocentrists' task in these battles was not so much to have the problems they cited taken seriously (because they already were) as it was to differentiate the solutions they offered from multiculturalists' proposals. In making these distinctions, Afrocentrists argued for their version of revisions using language that divided the black community into those who were tainted by middle-class, establishment interests and those who were ideologically purer. Issues of authenticity and loyalty to the race were clearly implicated. This kind of rhetoric, which is dependent on a process of differentiating "us" from "them," revisits a historic discourse that has long categorized African-American interests as accommodationist versus separatist.

In 1993, *The Black Scholar* published a collection of essays debating these same issues: African-American identity generally and intellectual movements like Afrocentrism and multiculturalism specifically. In his contribution to the forum, Molefi Kete Asante, a seminal theorist in the Afrocentric movement, encapsulates much of the discourse I heard among my Afrocentric respondents when he reflects on why so many black intellectuals seem interested in "leaving the race." He argues that upper-middle-class blacks fear strong racial identity—and Afrocentrism, in particular—because they are frightened of African agency, solidarity, and self-determination, and are unconnected to a black identity felt on the streets of the inner cities. Motivating this fear, he says, is middle-class blacks' careerist ambitions and, ultimately, their need for approval from whites. He ends his essay with a Ten Commandments–esque list that he claims is the accommodationist's guide to behavior. Because it states so clearly the criticisms some Afrocentrists make of other blacks in my cases, and because it infuriates so thoroughly those accused by it, I reproduce it here in full. For in its content lie many of the boundaries Afrocentrists use to distinguish themselves from other African-Americans:

> Thou shalt not accept an African origin
> Thou shalt not mock the white man
> Thou shalt not threaten the cultural imperialist
> Thou shalt not identify with Africans
> Thou shalt not despise the legacy of the white slave owner
> Thou shalt not speak evil of Thomas Jefferson and George Washington
> Thou shalt not praise other African men and women
> Thou shalt not seek to create values for African survival
> Thou shalt not work to develop an African identity
> Thou shalt not allow anyone to call you African (Asante 1993, 51)

For their part, multiculturalists are more diversified in their ideas about racial identity and curricular content. But a common strategy pursued by many multiculturalists is to clearly differentiate their goals from the Afrocentric project, at the same time that they also publicly recoil from the pro–Western culture ideology of the William Bennetts and Dinesh D'Souzas of the world. In the past decade, multiculturalism has become the standard position staked out by educators throughout the nation and is thus the legitimate curriculum against which Afrocentrists _and_ traditional-curriculum advocates now define themselves. While their location in the middle of the spectrum leads them to erect boundaries between "us" and "them," the rhetoric they use is considerably less racialized than the Afrocentrists'. Multiculturalists' strength is in numbers and in its diversity of races and ethnicities. Yet as their number and legitimacy in the educational arena increases, a consolidated definition of what constitutes "the multicultural perspective" becomes less attainable, and a unified definition of "us" and "them" becomes less possible to state with any authority. For this reason, the continued institutionalization of multiculturalism into educational curriculum may be inevitable, but it is apt to be broadsided again and again by movements with a stronger sense of who the enemy is.

Notes

1. Ebonics, a relatively recent initiative concerning the use of Black English in the instruction of students, can be thought of as another contemporary educational racial project.

2. Michael Dawson (personal communication) found that African-Americans are divided in their allegiance to black nationalism: approximately 50 percent of black respondents to a recent national survey supported a mild form of black nationalism, while about

25 percent could be considered hard-core supporters. Respondents were not questioned about Afrocentrism per se.

3. In its divisiveness. Afrocentrism is useful for questioning popular wisdom about America's black population. Despite reminders to the contrary (Du Bois 1970; Frazier 1957; Cruse 1967; Marable 1981; Winant 1994; Lee forthcoming; Dawson forthcoming), both the social science literature and the media frequently assume a monolithic "black identity," as well as "a black community" that holds the same political, social, economic, and cultural interests. The tensions that arise between Afrocentrists and other black intellectuals and reformers can be used as a strong indicator that assumptions of this sort ought to be discarded permanently.

4. Marable and Mullings's is just one possible categorization of extant black ideologies. Another approach is offered in Dawson forthcoming.

5. Ali Mazrui, professor of humanities at the State University of New York at Binghamton, has gone on record in support of multicultural revisions to curriculum, and not Afrocentrism. But his attitude toward Afrocentrism is deeply respectful in that he seeks a synthesis between what he sees as Afrocentrism's full-scale African assault on Eurocentrism and multiculturalism's broader emphasis on universal challenges to European hegemony.

6. Each interview was recorded and transcribed. With the exception of one person in Atlanta who wishes to remain anonymous, all other respondents consented to interviews for attribution.

7. This methodology differs from the strictly media-driven data I have used in earlier work on identity (Binder 1993). In the earlier work, I was primarily interested in how the media construct African-American and white identities for their readers. In this chapter, I am investigating African-Americans' constructions of their own identities in the service of some racial project.

8. John Holt is the author of *How Children Fail* (New York: Dell, 1964). Holt's work predates the Afrocentric and multicultural curriculum movements.

9. Personal communication with Arthur Stinchcombe.

References

Adams, Hunter Havelin, III. [1987] 1990. "African and African-American Contributions to Science and Technology." In *African-American Baseline Essays,* edited by Asa Hilliard III. Portland, Oreg.: Portland Public Schools.

Asante, Molefi Kete. 1990. *Kemet, Afrocentricity, and Knowledge.* Trenton, N.J.: Africa World Press.

———. 1993. "Racing to Leave the Race: Black Postmodernists Off-Track." *The Black Scholar* 23:50–51.

Austin, Algernon. 1995. "The Effect of Multicultural Education on the Academic Achievement of Black Students." Unpublished paper. Center for Urban Affairs and Policy Research, Northwestern University.

Barth, Frederick. 1969. Introduction to *Ethnic Groups and Boundaries,* edited by Frederick Barth. Boston: Little, Brown.

Binder, Amy. 1993. "Constructing Racial Rhetoric: Media Depictions of Harm in Heavy Metal and Rap Music." *American Sociological Review* 58:753–67.

Cose, Ellis. 1993. *The Rage of a Privileged Class.* New York: HarperCollins.

Cruse, Harold. 1967. *The Crisis of the Negro Intellectual.* New York: Morrow.

Dawson, Michael. Forthcoming. *Black Visions.* Chicago: University of Chicago Press.

Du Bois, W. E. B. [1933] 1970. "On Being Ashamed of Oneself." In *W. E. B. Du Bois: A Reader,* edited by Meyer Weinberg. New York: Harper and Row.

Feagin, Joe R., and Melvin Sikes. 1994. *Living with Racism.* Boston: Beacon.

Frazier, E. Franklin. 1957. *Black Bourgeoisie.* New York: Free Press.

Friedman, Debra, and Doug McAdam. 1992. "Collective Identity and Activism: Networks, Choices and the Life of a Social Movement." In *Frontiers in Social Movement Theory,* edited by Aldon Morris and Carol McClurg-Mueller. New Haven: Yale University Press.

Gamson, Josh. 1989. "Silence, Death, and the Invisible Enemy: AIDS Activism and Social Movement 'Newness.'" *Social Problems* 36:351–67.

Gamson, William. 1992. "The Social Psychology of Collective Action." In *Frontiers in Social Movement Theory,* edited by Aldon Morris and Carol McClurg-Mueller. New Haven: Yale University Press.

Giroux, Henry. 1992. "Post-colonial Ruptures and Democratic Possibilities: Multiculturalism as Anti-racist Pedagogy." *Cultural Critique,* no. 21 (spring): 5–39.

James, George. 1954. *Stolen Legacy.* New York: Philosophical Library.

Lee, Orville. Forthcoming. "Black Identity Politics and the Symbolic Economy of Race: On the Changing Structure of Racial Difference." *Cultural Critique.*

Marable, Manning. 1981. "On Being Black: The Burden of Race and Class." *Black Praxis,* No. 10.

Marable, Manning, and Leith Mullings. 1994. "The Divided Mind of Black America: Race, Ideology, and Politics in the Post Civil Rights Era." *Race and Class* 36:61–72.

Mazrui, Ali. 1993. "Afrocentricity versus Multiculturalism? A Dialectic in Search of a Synthesis." Presentation delivered to the University of California, Los Angeles, under the sponsorship of the James S. Coleman African Studies Center, May 5.

Moran, Rachel. 1996. "In the Multicultural Battle, Victory Is to the Weak." *Public Affairs Report* (Institute of Governmental Studies, University of California at Berkeley) 37 (January): 1, 14–16.

Ortiz de Montellano, Bernard. 1996. "Afrocentric Pseudoscience: The Miseducation of African Americans." In *The Flight from Science and Reason,* edited by Paul R. Gross, Norman Levitt, and Martin W. Lewis. New York: New York Academy of Sciences.

Oyebade, Bayo. 1990. "African Studies and the Afrocentric Paradigm: A Critique." *Journal of Black Studies* 21:233–38.

Raz, Joseph. 1994. "Multiculturalism: A Liberal Perspective." *Dissent* 41 (winter): 67–79.

Schuman, Howard, Charlotte Steeh, and Lawrence Bobo. 1985. *Racial Attitudes in America.* Cambridge: Harvard University Press.

Taylor, Verta, and Nancy Whittier. 1992. "Collective Identity in Social Movement Communities." In *Frontiers in Social Movement Theory,* edited by Aldon Morris and Carol McClurg-Mueller. New Haven: Yale University Press.

Thomas, Greg. 1995. "The Black Studies War: Multiculturalism versus Afrocentricity." *The Village Voice*, January 11–17, 23–29.

Van Sertima, Ivan. 1990. "Future Directions for African and African-American Content in the School Curriculum." In *Infusion of African and African American Content in the School Curriculum: Proceedings of the First National Conference,* edited by Asa Hilliard III, Lucretia Payton-Stewart, and Larry Obadele Williams. Chicago: Third World Press.

West, Cornel. 1992. "The Postmodern Crisis of Black Intellectuals." In *Cultural Studies,* edited by Lawrence Grossberg, Cary Nelson, and Paula Treichler. New York: Routledge.

Winant, Howard. 1994. *Racial Conditions.* Minneapolis: University of Minnesota Press.

multiculturalism as a moving moral boundary: literature professors redefine racism

bethany bryson

Introduction

In the early 1980s, the United States began to struggle openly with the question of cultural diversity. School board meetings attracted media attention when they erupted into major battles over the curriculum, and visibility continued to escalate to a high point in 1987, when Jesse Jackson joined a student rally against the "Western culture" curriculum at Stanford University. As the issue became more politically salient at the national level, the U.S. cultural elite began to face new questions and new political roles. Once charged only with the clerical mission of distributing consecrated knowledge, cultural professionals now perform an acknowledged role as policy makers who define appropriate reactions to cultural diversity—especially as it pertains to race.

In this chapter, I analyze the way debates over *multiculturalism* redefine morally legitimated behaviors, attitudes, and obligations regarding cultural differences among racial and ethnic groups. I reconceptualize "racism" as a socially constructed moral boundary rather than an individual attribute defined a priori by the researcher, and I show that this boundary distinguishes racists from nonracists on a moral basis (but it does so only to the extent that the indicators of racism are clearly defined and widely accepted within a given population). I argue that English professors are key actors in constructing and disseminating this boundary, and I draw on interviews with faculty in four English departments to examine the benefits of viewing racism as a symbolic boundary.

The most fruitful feature of a constructivist view on racism is that it high-lights changes in the meaning of the social category "racist." Racism constitutes a powerful moral boundary in our culture—a symbolic dividing line between the morally pure and those labeled racist. However, its meaning has changed so that people once considered solid liberals are now in danger of being labeled racist. Furthermore, the new definitions of racist attributes are not yet crystal-lized. Thus the boundary between the pure and the impure remains blurred, especially in elite universities. In the following pages, I will use evidence from elite universities to demonstrate these features of a constructivist view on rac-ism, but I add to this an analysis of the situation at nonelite universities and discover what the media have ignored: there are vast areas of agreement among nonelite faculty on how universities should address multiculturalism, and that agreement may be more important to American culture than the elite academic battles that attract the national limelight.

After introducing the theoretical and methodological background, I begin with an analysis of multiculturalism in elite universities. I first document how English professors connect their positions on multiculturalism and English lit-erary canons to charges of racism, and show that the racist label constitutes a symbolic boundary that operates to divide English professors from each other. Next, I discuss the factors that make this boundary particularly potent in struc-turing the relationships among English professors: the link to "traditional" understandings of racism and the *moral* nature of the boundary. Third, I de-termine the primary "problem" associated with the new boundary as it is ex-perienced in elite universities—that it is invisible.

In the second half of the analysis, I discuss the institutional differences be-tween elite and nonelite universities, and describe the process through which faculty in nonelite universities transform high theoretical canon debates into clear, institutionalized expectations for conveying a morally sensitive position on race and cultural differentiation—now called multiculturalism. It is particularly useful to compare how racism operates as a boundary in elite and nonelite uni-versities because we tend to focus our attention on the 2 percent of colleges and universities that house the most powerful scholars, and in so doing, we fail to understand the cultural power of nonelite college faculty. We have assumed that nonelite faculty merely distribute the work of elite scholars through the system of higher education. Instead, I find that nonelite faculty distribute inter-pretations and simplifications of that work. It is through this simplifying mecha-nism (at both the individual and the organizational level) that I find nonelite faculty to be the most influential in producing legitimate redefinitions of racism and the most likely to accept their role as cultural policy makers within their in-stitutions.

BACKGROUND. In this analysis, I will not discuss new versions of racism the way most cultural critics do. I will not deconstruct reactionary forces within higher education. Neither will I attempt to link syllabus content with any sort of racial equity in the academy (although much work remains to be done in this area). Rather, I focus on how specific forms of scholarship and teaching are labeled racist. I will show that racism marks an important moral boundary within academia, and that the location of that boundary is now contested and unstable. The relocation of this boundary is significant for two reasons. First, it reorders relationships and political orientations within American colleges and universities where important pieces of middle-class culture are created and distributed. Second, and by extension, these new definitions of racism are moving outside of higher education.

Multiculturalism and the redefinition of racism are phenomena that permeate many facets of contemporary American life from kindergarten to corporate culture, but the shift has been particularly apparent among English professors whose primary activity—the selection, distribution, and representation of cultural artifacts—has been identified as racially significant. Furthermore, because the work of English professors has been challenged on *moral* grounds, English departments have had to face these issues head-on before a national audience. At least one major survey has found that curriculum changes intended to address diversity have affected English more than any other discipline (Levine and Cureton 1992), and when media coverage of debates relating to race in the college curriculum focuses on a particular academic department, it is most often English and the alleged "canon" of literary works that "ought" to be assigned there. Although battles over multiculturalism have affected many academic disciplines, English professors are particularly prone to this boundary-drawing process because they produce and manage cultural representations that have become morally and politically charged. An important side effect of the resulting media spotlight is that English departments have gained equivalent attention for their *analyses* of the debates and the underlying theoretical and empirical questions—matters that might also be addressed by other disciplines.

I interviewed seventy-six English professors in four American universities to document the meaning and definition of multiculturalism in their work. In this analysis, I explore the role of racism in those definitions. Two of the research sites are prestigious universities with highly ranked English departments. In terms of political orientation, these departments are as far apart from each other as possible, given other constraints. These are the sort of departments that the press covers when there is a skirmish over curriculum or hiring decisions—names that a national audience would recognize. The other two departments are located in regional universities with less competitive admissions standards. They are also politically different from each other in mission and curriculum, but they represent an environment neglected by the press—the one most college students actually experience. All four universities are large, two are public, and each has approximately a 25 percent nonwhite student population. I conducted interviews that were recorded and lasted one to two hours. Transcripts from the audiotapes serve as evidence for the following discussion of the new racism in American English departments.

RACISM AND MULTICULTURALISM. I conceptualize multiculturalism as an attempt to address the inadequacies of our traditional definitions of racism. One English professor expressed that inadequacy this way:

> The day after Martin Luther King was assassinated, I walked into my classes, huhhhhh, and I read the funeral oration, and I still remember the looks on the faces of some of the white kids that day that said, without them having to put a syllable to their mouths, that they were glad the bastard was dead. [He says this in a heavy, bereaved whisper.] You know, I mean, things were more intense, they're more insidious now, perhaps. They were more intense then. I think we did a better job then, with it. I'm glad that we're reading African-American novelists. I never read a whole book—I haven't been teaching that class. Uh, I'm afraid that multiculturalism is something that we want to see, we'd like to encourage but we don't achieve.

Notice that this professor manages to convey his point without ever using the word *racism*. He doesn't appear to believe his white students today are any less racist than their sixties predecessors, but he does not know yet how to *name* their more subtle form of racism. He reaches for multiculturalism in an attempt to define the work that remains to be done.

The term "new racism" has been used to describe everything from a resurgence of sociobiology (Barker 1981) to affirmative action's "discrimination" against whites. The most useful developments, however, have come from the literature on *symbolic racism,* which argues that the traditional forms of racism that prevailed during the Jim Crow era were based on beliefs in genetic inferiority and that modern forms of racism are more culturally driven (Kinder and Sears 1981). The general application of those findings, however, is complicated by the fact that these opinion researchers often measured racism as a scale of attitudes toward public policy rather than a bias in affect. Other scholars have produced typologies of racism that generally move from essentialist to cultural (Frankenberg 1993; Winant 1992).

Rather than attempt to discover the true nature of racism, I view it as a social construction whose meaning is particularly flexible. As such, it is also a label that is used to designate an increasingly diverse set of attitudes. This approach reflects both the disagreement among social scientists and the frustration of social actors with respect to the appropriate definition of modern racism. It is particularly useful to focus our attention not only on attempts to define racism, but also on the social constructions promoted in attempts to combat racism. Here, social scientists agree there has been a shift from the rhetoric of cultural assimilation to cultural pluralism (Glazer and Moynihan 1970; Thompson 1989). The liberal position on antiracism revolves around these two poles, which are in conflict. Thus, while liberals once argued that traditional racism could be dissolved through cultural assimilation, the new antiracists have used multiculturalism to attack the assumption of cultural supremacy inherent in the position that minorities should assimilate to a dominant American culture. Just as Republicans were once the progressive force in American politics, assimilationists are increasingly considered a conservative—even "racist"—force in education.

It is not unusual to hear faculty and students refer privately to various teaching practices or scholarly work as, in effect, racist. Several authors have recounted their own experiences in which their open support for academic traditionalism resulted in claims of racism (D'Souza 1992; Hamilton 1995). A famous example is the 1987 draft of a report from the task force evaluating Stanford's Western culture requirement, which said:

> [C]ourses that do not acknowledge in some degree both the cultural diversity of Europe and the even greater diversity of our present American society have increasingly come to be seen as intellectually inadequate . . . [and] have been open to the charge of being socially irresponsible, however unintentionally and inadvertently, for they seem to perpetuate racist and sexist stereotypes and to reinforce notions of cultural superiority that are wounding to some and dangerous to all in a world of such evident diversity.

Not surprisingly, the statement above sparked a controversy that held a national spotlight for some time. While the statement expresses a commonly understood (if not agreed upon) aspect of contemporary academic life, such overt accusations of racism are rare precisely because they are so volatile. Eliasoph (1998) argues that Americans avoid controversial subjects even when the issue is crucial to civic life. In the case of new definitions of racism, an elaborate linguistic apparatus—an amalgamation of "political correctness," "awareness," "diversity," "sensitivity," and "multiculturalism"—allows members of college communities to talk about the racial implications of their actions without making specific claims about racism. Like a pearl forming around the tiniest grain of sand, our campus oyster has smoothed-over a painful word by transforming it into something hundreds of times its original size.

Elite Universities

In the late eighties, two controversies gained the attention of our national press. The first was a conflict over core curriculum requirements at Stanford University, where a task force had recommended expanding the required reading list of literary and philosophical works (Pratt 1992). The second controversy occurred at Duke University when the administration staged a coup in the English department by hiring Stanley Fish to chair the department, revise the curriculum, and attract a cluster of avant-garde scholars to the department (Heller 1987). These two battles attracted repeated attention from the press and some sociologists, both of which drew repeatedly on a common set of stories and sources to indicate a growing point of conflict on American campuses.

A survey of accredited colleges in the United States indicates that the vast majority (92 percent) of U.S. colleges have made curricular changes to address the diversity of American culture (El-Khawas and Knopp 1996). Furthermore, both the Stanford and the Duke conflicts have subsided, and reports indicate few or no smoldering antagonisms in either place. There is no reason to expect more conflicts to come and indeed, there were few conflicts in the departments I investigated. Where reports in the press might have suggested ideological splits, I found that professors' views of the situation are too complex to permit such divisions.

Nevertheless, the symbolic power of race was evident in both of my first research sites, the two elite departments. At the campus reputed to be more traditional, I passed a Confederate flag prominently displayed from a first-floor dormitory window on my way to the English department.[1] At the more avant-garde research site, I learned that English department offices would be closed on Martin Luther King Day although most of the university would be open. These events confirmed the salience of race in campus politics at each location, and they suggest that I was successful in selecting two sites at some distance from each other in that respect.

THE SHOCK: YESTERDAY'S PROGRESSIVES ARE TODAY'S "RACISTS." Herein I focus on the struggle between the proponents of the new definitions of racism and the people in danger of "becoming" racist if the definition is successfully altered. If a new definition of racism is taking hold in English departments as a boundary marker, we should see evidence of social exclusion associated with multiculturalism.

Most academics are aware that a new charge of racism is being leveled against academic "traditionalists." Their feeling of victimization became apparent to me while interviewing three distinguished literary scholars *in a row* who unexpectedly launched into monologues about their voting behavior and the racial composition of their friendship networks. They came to their professions as card-carrying liberals, defenders of human rights, and spokespeople for the disenfranchised. They have not done anything to *become* what one referred to as "Neanderthal conservatives." Rather, the moral high ground has moved from beneath their feet.

Surprisingly, many of this senior generation are what Kimball (1990) refers to as "tenured radicals." Several were involved in the introduction of some form of ethnic literature in their own departments and many supported increasing diversity—both academic and demographic. Yet they perceive themselves as victims of formal and informal political *struggles* to redefine racism. As I interviewed them, these men presented their liberal "credentials" before making the slightest critique of current literary trends, which I read as an indication that they anticipate being labeled racist. The last interview question on my survey was an open-ended one: "How do you feel about multiculturalism?" This professor begins his response but interrupts himself launching into an elaborate self-defense before returning to his point. Notice that the criticism he eventually makes is not particularly scathing. Nevertheless, this respondent reacted as though his concern for the canon might be interpreted as racist.

> The only thing that bothers me about multiculturalism—and I really— ah uh—One of my students is Hispanic-American and I love him I love his family . . . um. A couple of students who didn't actually do their work with me [clears throat] but whom I'm very close to, black people. I've always related very well to black people. The ones I know are people I relate to. I like their music, I talk to them, um, and we're friends. I have no problem with multiculturalism except that there's only so much time you can give to the study of literature in four years and if you're going to give time to the writers that in my terms are not very good writers at least not compared to Milton and Shakespeare and other people in the canon, then we're losing some of the canon.

I continue with this interviewee because his criticism and defense are so intricately woven. He begins with a critical reference to New Historicism, stammers a little, presents his liberal credentials, and ends by making an important connection between politicians and literary authors.[2]

> I try to make an effort to place these authors in the context of their times rather than trying to impose our expectations as post-1960 people—uh and

they're my expectations—I—my. . . . As I say, I'm sympathetic with them politically. I vote Democratic, I've never voted for anybody who wasn't a Democrat. Sometimes the Democrats are women; sometimes they're black; sometimes, for all I know, they're homosexuals. That doesn't figure into my appreciation of literature.

Another senior scholar responded in a similar pattern, interrupting his critique with self-defense:

No matter where a student comes from in the world, if he's going to live here and be here, those are the main [cultural] roots. It could work beautifully. The way we've integrated, in the past five years, Arabic materials so that the students don't think of them as rag heads, fundamentalists, and all that kind of thing. We [Europeans] were still practically swinging in trees when they were starting medical schools, beautiful architecture, elegant conversation, magnificent poetry, ice in the desert. They could make ice. It's amazing, you know. They just build a big wall that makes a shadow, and at night they flood it with layers of water which freezes, and then they store it underground. For thousands of years, the Arabs have had sherbets and things out in the desert and just about all they wanted, and air conditioning just using the wind itself.

While these individuals indirectly signal their concern with being perceived as racist, several faculty were more explicit, and in some cases, content with their marginalization. One drew connections between multiculturalism and literary theory to locate the source of his alienation. "I've been around long enough to see the fads come in, mellow out, and die, and I'm sure that all of the hermeneutic, poststructuralist, Lacanian, Derridian business will eventually subside. Uh, and I'll be glad to see a lot of it go. Because a lot of it is like sort of bigotry." Another cut right to the point: "I'm sort of on the fringe of my own department and that's fine with me."

THE CLINCHER: MORAL CLAIMS DEMAND ATTENTION. Disagreement and debate are integral parts of academic life, so it seems odd that tempers should flare so high over multiculturalism and curriculum decisions. Of seventy-six interview respondents, only three had real fears that English as a discipline would disappear, and a recent survey of English curricula found no evidence that standard texts are being taught any less than they were several years ago (Huber 1994). In all there is not much reason to believe that academics are fighting over significant material resources. What is at stake then? Moral character.

Substantive debates are frequent in academia. What distinguishes conflicts about multiculturalism is that they often take a personal tone. In a *New York Times Book Review* article, for instance, Henry Louis Gates said of two leading opponents of multiculturalism, "These two men symbolize for us the nostalgic return to what I think of as the 'ante-bellum aesthetic position,' when men were men and men were white." Similarly, Stanley Fish (1994, 12–13) writes, "What I find is a direct line between contemporary hostilities to black studies, ethnic studies, gay and lesbian studies, and so on and the anti-immigration, anti-Catholic, frankly racist writings of the late nineteenth and early twentieth century . . . although the language is softer . . . it still serves racist ends."

Based on interview data, Lamont (1992) divides symbolic boundaries into three types—socioeconomic, cultural, and moral—and she finds that moral boundaries have more cultural salience than the other types, especially in the United States. Debates over multiculturalism gain their social significance through the association between racism on the one hand and the moral purity of tolerance and justice on the other (Bryson 1996; DiMaggio and Bryson 1995). Because racism is already considered immoral, the push to redefine traditional scholarship as racist is a moral assertion. Claims that a body of work is out of line with current theoretical advances may be forgiven or ignored, but claims that it is racist move the discussion into a new arena. One respondent said of the word *multiculturalism:* "It seems to be the ultimate incarnation of doing right as opposed to doing wrong." Only a handful of respondents mentioned the moral nature of multiculturalism, but, as evidenced above, many scrambled for the other side of the boundary whenever they felt they risked being labeled racist.

Because it is the opposite of racism, and as such morally coded, multiculturalism has gained far more salience for both academics and the general public than it would have without the moral dimension. There are otherwise similar debates in the discipline about how the larger field ought to be divided (by genre, region, or historical period) and whether some periods, such as eighteenth-century British or seventeenth-century American literature ought to be considered to "exist." These debates have similar consequences in the allocation of resources and teaching assignments. They could even lead to the removal of whole categories of literature from a curriculum, but they do not attract the public attention and political heat that the debate over multiculturalism does because these issues do not make moral claims (except when they can be connected to multiculturalism). Regardless of one's position in the debate, shifting definitions of racism cannot easily be ignored.

THE PROBLEM: AMBIGUOUS BOUNDARIES CANNOT WORK EFFECTIVELY. The new definitions of racism can impose themselves, in part, because they are associated with moral impurity, but to be effective, a boundary must be widely accepted. In elite universities, the diffusion of new definitions fails on this point for two reasons. First, the research imperative at elite universities facilitates the emergence of more and more nuanced "understandings" of racism, which lead to more and more complex sets of indicators for racism (boundary markers). Second, in order to avoid being labeled racist, one must be able to recognize and avoid even the most recently identified indicators of racism, and that information is part of an elite body of knowledge that maintains its status and rarity, in part, through constant change that makes the knowledge even less accessible (Bourdieu 1984; Crane 1987).

The Research Imperative. Work by Bourdieu (1984) and Crane (1987) suggests that the pressure toward innovation in fields of cultural production increases the complexity and instability of avant-garde knowledge. Thus, to the extent that an important portion of literary scholarship seeks to enrich our understanding of the racial implications of human action, those scholars (like all others) are encouraged to continue making new discoveries in the field. With each new intellectual "advancement" in our understanding of racism, the boundary moves again. Staying on the nonracist side of the line requires sustained engagement with the current literature just to know where the boundary is located at any given point in time.

Thus, the incentive to avoid being labeled racist is connected to one's level of engagement with recent developments in the discipline. When I asked faculty to tell me their definition of a good professor, most began by saying that such a definition should be broad if it existed at all. The most common substantive response, however, centered around avoiding intellectual stagnation. According to these respondents, it is essential to follow major debates in the discipline. Being uninformed about the new set of indicators for racism not only risks crossing the moral boundary associated with traditional racism, it reveals a violation of what may be the most agreed-upon imperative for tenured professors in elite departments—staying current.

> It's easy to prepare a lecture and then use the same old yellow notes that they've been using for the last, you know, thirty years. . . . [A bad professor would be] somebody who puts in their three hours a week and then is gone, you never see them here except to get their salaries, and then they disappear.

This is not to say that there is no resistance to the pressure to read new work. The most common method of resistance is to claim that contemporary work evidences poor scholarship: "I love the English language. I get exquisite pleasure out of good writing and find it just a little bit short of excruciating torture to be asked to read bad prose, and there's a lot of bad prose coming out of these [multicultural] courses."

Nevertheless, even the staunchest critics of the new multicultural scholarship recognize the way increasing pressure to produce scholarly research shapes the discipline and antagonisms between two generations of academic culture. In fact the two respondents who produced the most critical reactions to multiculturalism (one in each elite department) also acknowledged one common source of the conflict—the pressure to produce work on the cutting edge. One said of the department's graduate students:

> So for me to say that they *should* be doing something—I think that's gotta be between them and their conscience. I—See, it's easy for me. I'm in my first year of phase retirement. I'm coming to the end of a very secure academic career. I've never had the worries these kids have, but I just think it's, it's, it's sad. I see something like this, to me, formative of my own character something that I regard as precious something that's given me much great pleasure—reading Shakespeare I love him, or even Pope, or even Wall or P. G. Wodehouse, Raymond Chandler, uh all these things, I love and what I'm afraid of is that they won't *love* literature. I don't know. I may be too— [trails off].

Scholarly expectations, then, have two effects on the dynamics of the racism boundary. First, the pressure to innovate helps encourage endless "discoveries" that constitute new indicators for marking the boundary that defines racism. Second, the expectation that faculty should follow major debates and developments in the discipline reinforces negative evaluation of those who indicate a lack of familiarity with recent changes. A professor who fails to use racially sensitive linguistic codes, for example, displays both an indifference to new expectations surrounding the discussion of race and a possible lack of familiarity with the body of work that explains the importance of the new conventions.

Poetry in Motion. A crucial difference between traditional racism based on genetic arguments and that rooted in cultural "bias" is that the latter attends to race-based cultural representation in the content of high-status culture. Multiculturalists advocate broadening the canonized elements of high culture, and they add new scholarly understandings of racism to that culture in the process. Hence, new definitions of racism are part of the elite conversation on literature. Like all elements of cultural capital (Bourdieu 1984), it is sufficiently dense, obscure, and vague to exclude uninitiated outsiders.

The vagueness of this new boundary has been used internally to claim academic turf for newcomers and exclude an older generation of English professors—those who now fear being defined as racist. This professor describes the role of obscurity in the context of his own marginality:

> They develop their own language which sounds like gibberish or jargon to the rest of us. And the rest of us are really in the minority now. Uh, I suppose we think of ourselves as humanists or something like that. We don't belong to the Modern Language Association any more. We belong to that other one whose name I can't remember right now, and we do pretty much hang out together. And most of those people are very senior—been around for thirty or thirty-five years.

Even faculty in the new generation find it difficult to keep up with the vagueness of shifting definitions of racism. One described the situation by saying this about multiculturalism:

> I think it is really unfortunate that we allow ourselves to be ruled by a word that remains so amorphous and yet seems to be invested with such heavy moral authority. . . . It reminds me of that episode of *The Twilight Zone* where the children can send their parents to the cornfield where they will vanish if the parents say the wrong thing, but the parents never know what the wrong thing will be.

Perhaps the best evidence that knowledge about these shifting definitions is part of high-status culture comes from the overall differences between the responses of professors in elite and nonelite universities to my question: "How do you feel about multiculturalism?" Transcripts of responses to this question in elite departments are usually one and a half to two pages long (or more), while faculty in the less prestigious departments tended to give short responses lasting no more than a paragraph or so. Faculty in elite departments produced complex responses and most denied having an entirely positive or negative reaction to the word. Faculty in nonelite departments provided clearer reactions almost overwhelmingly in favor of multiculturalism. Only three nonelite professors mentioned the names of major figures in the debate, and one of those was unable to fully recall the name he searched for in his head.

High culture, then, suffers an inherent contradiction between exclusiveness and legitimacy (DiMaggio 1982). On the one hand, the content of high culture must be sufficiently inaccessible to prevent outsiders from gaining easy access to it. On the other hand, high culture cannot convey status to an individual without a certain level of consensus on the question of what constitutes high culture. Shifting definitions of racism are, without a doubt, sufficiently obscure to be able to guard their gates. In order to gain currency as a real and valid extension of our understanding of racism, however, they must acquire legitimacy in the general population. In the following section, I discuss the reasons nonelite faculty do not experience many of the difficulties described above, and I discuss the implication of those differences for the future of legitimacy problems in the new definition of racism.

Nonelite Universities

I have argued that the primary barrier to widespread acceptance of multiculturalism as a new form of moral boundary is the ever-changing complexity of the ideas that inform current norms about race and culture. In this second half of the analysis, I will identify the factors that shape multiculturalism in the nonelite research sites—those that better represent a typical college English department.

EXCLUSION. Fourteen percent of faculty in the two elite departments I studied reported feeling excluded by advocates of multiculturalism even though only 25 percent of the faculty expressed clear support for multiculturalism. In nonelite departments, the situation is nearly reversed. Seventy-one percent said they support multiculturalism and *none* reported feeling excluded by those advocates.[3] Below, I describe a possible explanation for the stark contrast: different sources of individual power and prestige operate in elite versus nonelite institutions causing multiculturalism to interact with the distribution of power in two different ways.

Faculty in nonelite departments earn their power primarily through their position in the organization. They are likely to remain at their first job earning tenure and promotions by meeting internally defined goals of teaching, research, and service to the university. Faculty in elite departments, conversely, earn their prestige (and their promotions) primarily through external validation in the field of scholarly production. Therefore, a major shift in the value of one subfield relative to another can have far more serious effects on the power and prestige of faculty in elite departments because the value of a professor to the department is directly related to her or his value to the field. Reorderings in literary value have little effect on academic prestige in nonelite departments, where more weight is given to seniority in the establishment of local pecking orders.[4]

Furthermore, it might be useful to extend this explanation to another counterintuitive observation. Although none of the faculty in nonelite departments reported a sense of exclusion as a result of the movement toward multiculturalism, three respondents did report feelings of exclusion in general. In contrast to the group of white male respondents who reported exclusion in elite departments, members of the equivalent group in nonelite departments consisted of women from nondominant racial or ethnic backgrounds. Thus, it appears that environments where multiculturalism is accepted might be more hostile to minority faculty than environments where colleagues have critical orientations toward multiculturalism.

Again, the different sources of individual power in each type of department may provide at least a partial explanation. While all minority faculty face disparities in power and prestige relative to their white and male colleagues, those in elite departments (who specialize in ethnic or women's literature) are more likely than their nonelite counterparts to reap the benefits of disciplinary shifts in the value of their scholarly work. As a consequence nonelite faculty do not appear to benefit from the widespread acceptance of multiculturalism in their departments as much as we might have expected.

MORALITY. Are nonelite faculty immune to the moral claims of multiculturalism? Certainly not. However, nonelite faculty might feel less threatened by multiculturalism because their more formally structured institutional environment relieves a great deal of cultural uncertainty and absolves them of individual responsibility for learning ambiguous cultural codes. For example, faculty in the more progressive nonelite site often mentioned their *policy* on multiculturalism. In 1983, the faculty approved the following multiculturalism statement to be included on every syllabus:[5]

> We, the faculty of the [university name] English Department, in accord with our belief that literature and language both reflect and shape culture, affirm the importance of representing in our courses the complementary contributions of both sexes and also of diverse cultural representations.
> We, therefore, adopt the policy that:
> a) we will make a genuine effort to appropriately include both men and women, as creators and critics, in our course curricula;
> b) we will make a genuine effort to include works representing the various cultural perspectives appropriate to each course;
> c) we will make a genuine effort to heighten, in any works we teach, our students' awareness of tendencies to stereotype differences in culture, religious beliefs, gender, class, age, race and sexual orientation, and will at the same time encourage understanding of the above difference [*sic*].

This statement serves to clarify and define the academic responsibilities of faculty members with respect to multiculturalism. It does not reduce the moral strength of the boundaries that surround multiculturalism, but it eliminates the fear associated with uncertainty. In this progressive department, 64 percent of the faculty mentioned the policy when I asked how they felt about multiculturalism. Thus, the policy serves to define expectations for all members of the department and it even defines the word for many.

Elite faculty, on the other hand, encounter less formal regulation in their course construction. Greater emphasis on the application of individual expertise based on one's position in the disciplinary field results in a different approach to teaching decisions at elite universities. Although it is common for nonelite faculty to make formalized collective decisions about course content, elite faculty emphasize their autonomy in that respect.

The bureaucratic approach to nonelite departmental governance versus the elite assumptions of academic freedom and professional autonomy parallels elite-nonelite differences in power: bureaucratic seniority versus scholarly reputation.

AMBIGUITY. I have already shown that one source of ambiguity concerning shifting definitions of racism, scholarly progress, has less salience in nonelite than in elite departments. However, their connection to high culture (the second source of ambiguity) deserves further attention because it is different from that of elite faculty. That is, they may distribute knowledge about high-status culture, but they are less likely to perform the role of creating or consecrating high-status culture.

Faculty in all four departments expressed concern for enriching the intellectual lives of their students, but elite and nonelite departments assessed those needs differently. Faculty in elite departments stressed linguistic sophistication whereas the other faculty reported having to teach basic writing and comprehension in advanced English courses. One said:

> In an upper-level course you sincerely hope that they already know how to read, and you also would like to think that they already know how to write. Neither one of these hopes is particularly fruitful . . . they could not read *Melville*. They could not *decipher* the sentence structure. It wasn't the language [vocabulary]; it was the sentence structure . . . so we had to take it in terms of phrases and clauses. "See this punctuation mark? Let us read to there. Now what does that say?" You know? We had to decode a nineteenth-century American writer writing in basic English!

The extent to which the content of reading assignments can be lost in other goals is evident from the words of a professor in the more traditional nonelite department:

> When we were asked to survey our syllabi at my last institution . . . and to report how multicultural we were, I surveyed mine and discovered it was indeed over half women and nonwhite literature, and I reported this to my

students, who all sort of said they hadn't noticed . . . and I thought that was good. And then I thought maybe that wasn't good.

Three faculty in the progressive department are collectively teaching the undergraduate theory course for English majors. That course includes a section on multiculturalism. Given that they researched both multiculturalism and literary theory, one might expect these faculty to give responses about multiculturalism that resemble those of professors in the elite research sites. In fact they did mention many of the same ideas, but the message containing these references was one of clarity rather than ambiguity. I specifically avoid defining multiculturalism for respondents, but neither do I ask them for a definition. Nevertheless, one of these professors began his answer to the question, "How do you feel about multiculturalism?" by giving me a succinct definition: "Multiculturalism is theory of power and a theory of art that reflects where we are on this planet."

Compared to their elite counterparts, nonelite faculty are less likely to contribute to the diffusion of ever-changing definitions of what is appropriate (and what is racist) because they simplify complex elements of high culture in the process of teaching them. This simplifying mechanism, however, may turn out to be the linchpin for the generalized legitimacy of multiculturalism and new expectations with regard to race.

Conclusion

High culture can shape the habits of leaders and it can serve as a form of cultural exclusion (Bourdieu 1984; Lamont and Lareau 1988), but changing fashions of literary criticism do not have much direct effect on mainstream culture in the United States, and its political intentions cannot be realized until they are communicated to the general public in a simplified (i.e., transportable) form. Elite academics and public intellectuals are unable to perform that simplifying function because it would distort their own contributions beyond recognition and conflict with current academic standards that value complexity. The job of producing an externally legitimate redefinition of racism has, therefore, fallen to journalists, popular critics, and college teachers—who make these complicated issues clear and accessible to the college population, which includes nearly half of eighteen-year-olds in the United States every year.

Could academic debates about expanding a literary "canon" have any effect on traditional racism and racial politics in the United States? Absolutely. In elite corners of the academic world, traditionalist literary scholars have been fairly successful in maintaining that the shifting definitions of racism are illegitimate, but the tide is against them. Faculty in nonelite departments display far less resistance to multiculturalism than do their counterparts in elite universities.[6]

Once we expand the set of behaviors and opinions *legitimately* considered racist, the number of racist people in the United States increases. Remember that racism constitutes a moral boundary that people want to see as fairly sharp— i.e., without much gray area between racist and nonracist people.

New cultural boundaries lend themselves to new political boundaries, so I would expect to find, for example, that the backlash associated with new charges of racism might have been an important factor in the trend away from affirmative action. Moral boundaries are like the protective armor that arthropods must occasionally change. During transition from one shell to the next, the organism is vulnerable. As long as the definition of racism is contested, the moral force that has protected affirmative action and other such race-based policies is weakened.

Notes

For careful criticism, I owe thanks to Michèle Lamont, Paul DiMaggio, Robert Wuthnow, Hugh Louch, Sue E. Spivey, and participants in the Russell Sage Foundation conference for this volume. I am also grateful to the National Science Foundation, the Center for Domestic and Comparative Policy Studies, and Princeton University for research support.

1. Pratt (1992) suggests that multicultural education is a necessary step toward cultural competence in the United States by citing the example of some college students who performed a ritual resembling a Ku Klux Klan march and claimed they were unaware of the apparent similarities. My first impressions on each campus I visited tentatively support the position that the content of course materials has some relationship to racial politics in other arenas.

2. New Historicism is a theoretical approach to literary history in which the "ideological implications of the official American literature canon are exposed" (Graff 1987, 221). This respondent argues that the New Historicist approach is illegitimate because (in his view) the authors' intentions could not have been interpreted as ideological in their own period.

3. Two white male professors did, however, allude to the possibility of exclusion by explaining their method of avoiding it. One said he had rigorous training in the use of "sensitive" language in a previous position. The other credited hard-earned departmental cohesiveness and rule making.

4. To say that multiculturalism does not affect individual seniority is not to say that the movement has no effect on the demographics of faculty. Despite a few highly publicized claims of "reverse discrimination" in academe, none of the respondents in my study reported feeling that initiatives to diversify college faculty threatened their own chances of advancement. Some who had recent experience with the academic job market acknowledged a greater demand for nonwhite faculty, but this effect is believed to have negative effects only on white candidates who specialize in nonwhite literatures and nonwhite candidates who do not.

5. The statement was revised in 1989 to expand the list of groups included. It is unclear whether the statement was called "multicultural" in its first draft.

6. While the transcripts of my interviews indicate no resistance to multiculturalism on the part of traditionalists in nonelite departments, it would be an overstatement to suggest there is no opposition. Senior members of the faculty were more reluctant to agree to interviews and tended to require a longer warming-up period. Also, nonelite English departments experience greater pressure from university administration, which is pro-multicultural in all four cases.

References

Atlas, James. 1990. *The Battle of the Books.* New York: Norton.

Barker, Martin. 1981. *The New Racism.* Frederick, Md.: University Publications of America.

Blau, Peter. 1977. *Inequality and Heterogeneity.* New York: Free Press.

Bloom, Allan. 1987. *The Closing of the American Mind.* New York: Simon and Schuster.

Bourdieu, Pierre. 1984. *Distinction.* Cambridge: Harvard University Press.

Bryson, Bethany. 1996. "Anything but Heavy Metal: Symbolic Exclusion and Musical Dislikes." *American Sociological Review* 61:884–99.

Crane, Diana. 1987. *The Transformation of the Avant-Garde.* Chicago: University of Chicago Press.

DiMaggio, Paul. 1982. "Cultural Entrepreneurship in Nineteenth-Century Boston: The Creation of an Organizational Base for High Culture in America." *Media Culture and Society* 4:33–50.

DiMaggio, Paul, and Bethany Bryson. 1995. "Americans' Attitudes towards Cultural Diversity and Cultural Authority: Culture Wars, Social Closure or Multiple Dimensions." *General Social Survey Topical Report*, no. 27.

DiMaggio, Paul, John Evans, and Bethany Bryson. 1996. "Have Americans' Social Attitudes Become More Polarized?" *American Journal of Sociology* 102:690–755.

Douglas, Mary. 1966. *Purity and Danger.* New York: Routledge.

D'Souza, Dinesh. 1992. *Illiberal Education.* New York: Free Press.

Durkheim, Emile. [1912] 1965. *The Elementary Forms of Religious Life.* New York: Free Press.

Eliasoph, Nina. 1998. *Avoiding Politics.* New York: Cambridge University Press.

El-Khawas, Elaine, and Linda Knopp. 1996. *Campus Trends, 1996.* Higher Education Panel Report number 86. Washington: American Council on Education.

Fish, Stanley. 1994. *There's No Such Thing as Free Speech . . . and It's a Good Thing Too.* New York: Oxford University Press.

Frankenberg, Ruth. 1993. *The Social Construction of Whiteness.* Minneapolis: University of Minnesota Press.

Gates, Henry Louis, Jr. 1992. *Loose Canons.* New York: Oxford University Press.

Gieryn, Thomas F. 1983. "Boundary-Work and the Demarcation of Science from Nonscience: Strains and Interests in Professional Ideologies of Scientists." *American Sociological Review* 48:781–95.

Glazer, Nathan, and Daniel P. Moynihan. 1970. *Beyond the Melting Pot.* Cambridge: MIT Press.

Graff, Gerald. 1987. *Professing Literature.* Chicago: University of Chicago Press.

Guillory, John. 1993. *Cultural Capital.* Chicago: University of Chicago Press.

Hamilton, Neil. 1995. *Zealotry and Academic Freedom.* New Brunswick, N.J.: Transaction.

Heller, Scott. 1987. "A Constellation of Recently Hired Professors Illuminates the English Department at Duke." *Chronicle of Higher Education,* May 27, A12–A14.

Hirsch, E. D. 1987. *Cultural Literacy.* New York: Houghton Mifflin.

Huber, Bettina. 1994. "Recent Trends in the Modern Language Job Market." In *Profession '94.* Washington: Modern Language Association.

Kimball, Roger. 1990. *Tenured Radicals.* New York: Harper and Row.

Kinder, Donald R., and David O. Sears. 1981. "Prejudice and Politics: Symbolic Racism versus Racial Threats to the Good Life." *Journal of Personality and Social Psychology* 40:414–31.

Kuhn, Thomas. 1977. *The Essential Tension.* Chicago: University of Chicago Press.

Lamont, Michèle. 1992. *Money, Morals, and Manners.* Chicago: University of Chicago Press.

Lamont, Michèle, and Annette Lareau. 1988. "Cultural Capital: Allusions, Gaps, and Glissandos in Recent Theoretical Developments." *Sociological Theory* 6:153–68.

Levine, Arthur, and Jeanette Cureton. 1992. "The Quiet Revolution: Eleven Facts about Multiculturalism and the Curriculum." *Change,* January–February, 24–29, 42.

Lévi-Strauss, Claude. 1963. *Structural Anthropology.* New York: Basic.

Morrison, Toni. 1992. *Playing in the Dark.* Cambridge: Harvard University Press.

Ohmann, Richard. 1976. *English in America.* New York: Oxford University Press.

Pratt, Mary Louise. 1992. "Humanities for the Future: Reflections on the Western Culture Debate at Stanford." In *The Politics of Liberal Education,* edited by Darrel J. Gless and Barbara Herrnstein Smith. Durham: Duke University Press.

Rico, Barbara Roche. 1991. *American Mosaic.* Boston: Houghton Mifflin.

Simmel, Georg. 1908. *Conflict.* Translated by Kurt. H. Wolff and Reinhard Bendix. New York: Free Press.

Sniderman, Paul M., and Phillip E. Tetlock. 1986. "Symbolic Racism: Problems of Motive Attribution in Political Analysis." *Journal of Social Issues* 42:129–50.

Steeh, Charlotte, and Howard Schuman. 1992. "Young White Adults: Did Racial Attitudes Change in the 1980's?" *American Journal of Sociology* 948:340–67.

Strauss, Anselm, and Juliet Corbin. 1990. *Basics of Qualitative Research.* Newbury Park, Calif.: Sage.

Thompson, Richard. 1989. *Theories of Ethnicity.* New York: Greenwood.

Winant, Howard. 1992. "Postmodern Racial Politics." *Socialist Review* 20:121–47.

———. 1994. *Racial Conditions.* Minneapolis: University of Minnesota Press.

Wuthnow, Robert. 1987. *Meaning and Moral Order.* Berkeley: University of California Press.

Zerubavel, Eviatar. 1991. *The Fine Line.* New York: Free Press.

education and advancement: exploring the hopes and dreams of blacks and poor whites at the turn of the century

pamela barnhouse walters

In the late nineteenth and early twentieth centuries, three groups—northern urban immigrants, poor southern whites, and southern blacks—were each relatively poor and had been denied educational opportunities (albeit to varying degrees) within memory of contemporaries.[1] Our current understanding of the importance of education for mobility might lead us to expect that all three groups consciously used education to try to advance in American society, either collectively or individually. And there is ample evidence that elites at the time thought education could solve "the immigrant problem" or "the negro problem" or "the [white] southern problem." The issue I address here, however, is the place of education in the worldviews of immigrants, poor southern whites, and poor blacks themselves. I argue that there are more similarities than are generally assumed in these groups' pragmatic views concerning the usefulness of education for social advancement. I further argue that a full understanding of the role that education played in hopes and dreams for the future must be based on a distinction between the abstract, symbolic importance of the right of *access* to education and the pragmatic view of the ability to take advantage of that right, as well as the practical utility of doing so. There were important differences in the symbolic importance of education in the worldviews of blacks, immigrants, and poor southern whites.

Background

In the late nineteenth and early twentieth centuries, there were striking differences between the North and South in school enrollment rates and average educational attainments; large differences existed as well between subgroups within each region. In a nutshell, educational enrollments and attainments were higher in the North than the South, even when the comparison is limited to native-born whites in both regions. Within the North, native-born whites were better educated than immigrants, and within the South whites (virtually all of whom were native born) were better educated than blacks.

Why? It is tempting (and has proven all too tempting to social scientists) to conclude that those who were better educated *cared* more about education. This conclusion follows logically from a larger assumption that aggregate educational patterns (e.g., secular increases in school enrollments or attainments over time; differences between whites and immigrants in the North at a single point in time) vary largely because of changes in the *demand* for education, interpreted loosely as interest in and commitment to schooling. For example, much of the research on the growth of school enrollments in the United States focuses on factors that made children more likely to want to go to school (see, e.g., Fuller 1983; Meyer et al. 1979; Guest and Tolnay 1985). The finding, for example, that immigrants had lower school enrollments than native-born whites is implicitly interpreted as evidence that immigrants cared less about education. The residual approach has also been used to determine ethnic and racial differences in commitment to education: Any group differences that remain after economic and demographic differences are taken into account are attributed to "culture" (see, e.g., Perlmann 1988). Notably absent from these literatures is any theoretical discussion of the possibility that there were not enough schools or teachers to accommodate all would-be students. In other words, there has been little recognition that larger opportunity structures may stand between the desire for schooling and the behavior of actually going to school.

At the same time that racial and ethnic differences in educational enrollments and attainments existed, there were also striking differences in public clamor for education among these groups. Working-class immigrant groups in the North, for example, made frequent and noisy demands for more and better education in the late nineteenth and early twentieth centuries (see, e.g., Hogan 1985; Katznelson and Weir 1985; Raftery 1992; Ravitch 1974; Reese 1986; Wrigley 1982). Political disfranchisement and the enactment of a myriad of Jim Crow laws made it difficult and dangerous for southern blacks to make many public demands for more and better education, but within the limits imposed by segregation, subordination, and repression blacks did press for educational improvements and, in particular, access to public secondary schools (Anderson 1988; Bond 1934; Lieberson 1980; Margo 1990). Poor southern whites, in turn, were notably silent with respect to educational access and educational improvement. Public demands for better schooling for poor whites had to be made, in fact, by *other* groups speaking in the alleged interest of poor southern whites (Dabney 1936; Knight 1922; Leloudis 1996; Link 1986).

As with the racial and ethnic differences in school enrollments and attainments, one can ask *why* these racial and ethnic differences in public demands for education existed. Again, scholars have often reasoned backward from the outcome (in this case, public clamor) to draw inferences about group differences in cultural commitments to education. On the basis of this evidence, it is tempting to conclude the northern immigrants cared far more about education than either southern poor whites or blacks, and that poor southern blacks were more committed to education than poor southern whites. But the public positions about education adopted by leaders of racial or ethnic groups concerning educational opportunities are not necessarily accurate reflections of the sentiment of the rank and file.

Another barrier to our understanding of the place of education in groups' hopes and dreams for themselves, their children, and their communities is the common tendency to assume that the cultural interpretation of the importance of education that prevails today is historically invariant. In the contemporary United States, we "know" that education is one of the most important keys to personal advancement, and we caution young people that staying in school is vital to their own personal success. This belief is so thoroughly taken for granted that one seems silly for even thinking about challenging it. More important for my purposes, we often assume that this is the way it's always been, and we use the current cultural assumptions about education and mobility as a lens through which to interpret educational behavior in prior historical eras. It goes without saying that this is a serious methodological error.

I therefore argue that the three most common ways in which social scientists have attempted to get a handle on the cultural significance of education for whites and blacks in earlier historical eras—making backward inferences from individuals' educational choices, making backward inferences from leaders' public positions, and projecting contemporary cultural understandings backward in time—are inadequate. We must find more direct ways of gaining a window on the cultural significance of education and hopes for self and community wrapped up in education among ordinary folk in earlier periods. In the process, we will be in a better position to understand why there were racial and ethnic differences in the aggregate of individuals' educational choices and in the public demands concerning education made by ethnic and racial leaders.

Historical Change in the Concept of Education for Advancement

Why do people go to school? What does education mean to people? Why is it valued (or not)?

If these questions were put to a sample of Americans today, most would probably answer that the purpose of going to school is to get a good job. Examined more closely, two aspects of this taken-for-granted belief about the key purpose of education stand out: it argues educational benefits in individualistic terms, and it ties education to the economy—specifically, to the labor market. At present, then, education is tightly connected to the promise of upward social mobility. The American Dream, that amorphous but widely shared ideology, promises that "everyone, regardless of ascription or background, may reasonably seek success through actions and traits under their own control" (Hochschild 1995, 4). Public schools, in turn, occupy pride of place in this belief system, in part because public education is the institution in which, more than any other, individuals supposedly succeed on the basis of their own ability and effort rather than their race, gender, family background, or other accidents of birth. Success, in turn, is largely defined within the occupational and income structure. My own favorite example of the tight link between schooling and personal occupational success in American ideology is a bus poster that exhorts teenagers to "Stay in School; Get a Job."

This was not always the prevailing public vision of why schools were important. The architects of the common-school movement and their supporters through the early twentieth century justified schooling in terms of the benefits it provided to society as a whole (Dewey 1916; Jones 1952; Messerli 1972); claims concerning individual mobility via education were conspicuously absent from public discussion. The key purpose of public education was to safeguard democratic political culture and the democratic political system itself (Bailyn 1960; Cremin 1964; Kaestle 1983; Perkinson 1968). In short, schools were expected to create good *citizens*, not, as at present, good *workers*.

By the mid–twentieth century, the publicly agreed-upon political purposes of public education shifted in subtle but important ways. Greater emphasis began to be placed on the role of public education in providing an equal opportunity for all children to *succeed in life*. This was closely tied to American ideals of opportunity and meritocracy (Coleman 1968; Hallinan 1988) as well as fairness for individuals. Importantly, the "rational actor" belief about the key purpose of going to school—individual self-advancement in the labor market—did not emerge as a strong ideology in American culture until some time after World War II. Therefore, we should *not* uncritically assume that immigrants, poor southern whites, or southern blacks "knew" that they would realize tangible returns to investments they made in education (for an example of this mistaken interpretation, see Smith 1969, 1972).

Public Voices versus Private Interests

Most scholars who have tried to understand the educational views of groups in earlier periods have turned to sentiments expressed by relatively elite members of the groups, individuals who often claimed to speak for a large constituency. These, after all, are the people who made public statements and left behind other forms of written evidence (no small benefit when one is trying to understand the sentiments and views of groups that were, at best, semiliterate). In a word, scholars often look to the writings of relatively elite members of the black, poor white, and immigrant communities to gain an understanding of the educational commitments of blacks, poor whites, and immigrants.

I argue that there is no necessary one-to-one correspondence between the aggregate educational interests of a group (say, southern blacks) and the educational preferences publicly voiced by the group's leaders, even when those leaders claim to be speaking for their constituency. In addition to the problem that leaders may not correctly perceive or translate their constituency's interests, there is the considerable problem that some organizational mechanism needed to be in place for leaders to emerge and for leaders to have a platform from which to articulate public demands and interests with respect to education. In short, formal organizations may have been necessary for a group to successfully formulate and voice a set of educational interests,[2] and interests alone were not necessarily sufficient to create the organizational resources required to voice public interest.

Is it possible that differences by race and ethnicity and across regions in access to formal organizations explain differences in public educational demands among northern immigrants, poor southern whites, and southern blacks, net of any "real" differences among these groups in educational interests? Many accounts of northern school politics show that the working class made its educational claims *through* noneducational organizations: labor unions, the Catholic Church, and the Democratic Party, among others.[3] While historians of southern education find little evidence of educational claims made by poor whites, they fail to note that no organizational vehicle for expressing poor whites' interests existed. By the turn of the century, the planter class had virtually eliminated contending parties and purged challengers from the Democratic Party (Key 1949; Kousser 1974). There was no strong tradition of labor unions. No one Protestant denomination represented poor whites and, unlike in the North, the Catholic Church was not a strong presence. Without access to organizations, it is not surprising that poor whites failed to express an educational agenda.

Similarly, divergent interests are an insufficient explanation of differences in political voices between southern poor whites and blacks. Blacks' public voice was expressed largely through the black church[4] since blacks, like poor whites, generally lacked political parties and labor unions. A large part of the difference in public educational voice between blacks and whites may be due to the availability of an organizational vehicle for expressing interests for blacks and lack of one for whites.

Surprisingly (at least in the context of implicit assumptions that prevail in the literature), forms of evidence *other* than public voices depict more similarity than difference in educational interests among subordinate groups in the North and South. Social histories, oral histories, and turn-of-the-century investigations of reasons for low school attendance show that subordinate groups in both regions were unconvinced that education had much to offer. Poor parents often believed that education had little chance of paying off for their children and felt culturally alienated from the schools, and children often felt they were better treated at work. Underlying all this was poor families' reliance on child labor for sheer economic survival throughout the United States (Walters and O'Connell 1988). I return to this in a subsequent section.

In short, I believe that organizational voices were not simply an aggregation of private interests of constituents. Moreover, the organizational resources a group had for political mobilization had a great deal to do with whether they expressed a public voice. I believe that differences among subordinate groups in their expressed educational interests (their *public voices*) had less to do with differences in *private interests* than with differences in organizational resources for formulating and publicly voicing a set of interests.

Toward an Understanding of Private Interests

IMMIGRANT WORKING-CLASS WHITES. The late nineteenth and early twentieth centuries were, of course, a period of massive immigration to the United States. The social, cultural, and religious differences between these immigrants, many of whom were from Eastern and Southern Europe, and native-born Americans worried American elites. Much of the historical and sociological literature on immigrants and public education during this period focuses on how politicians and educators tried to use the schools to solve the social problems created by massive immigration, largely by Americanizing immigrant children and their parents and, in the process, bringing them into the mainstream political and social culture.

We also know that many groups that represented immigrants, or a particular ethnic group, or labor, often spoke on *behalf* of the immigrant working class. Unions, for example, argued for more high schools after the turn of the century, supported compulsory education and child labor legislation, and fought against an overvocationalization of the public-school curriculum (Curoe 1926; Reese 1986; Hogan 1985; Wrigley 1982; Katznelson and Weir 1985). The Catholic Church tried to fight the implicit Protestantism of the Americanization movement in public schools (Ravitch 1974) and, failing that, established a parallel system of parochial schools in parishes throughout the country (Baker 1992). Ethnic associations and some Protestant churches fought for what we would now call bilingual education in the public schools. In short, a range of corporate actors made demands on public-school officials for educational opportunities or changes that were supposedly in the interest of their constituencies, each of which constituted a portion of the urban working class.

Unfortunately, there has been less attention to the cultural understanding of the purpose of education on the part of immigrant groups themselves. As is the case with implicit comparisons often drawn between northern and southern whites, here too there has been a tendency to infer an ethnic group's interest in education on the basis of the group's school enrollment or attainment patterns. It is commonly assumed, for example, that a key reason that Jewish immigrant children were more highly schooled than Polish or Italian immigrant children is that education was more highly valued in Jewish culture (especially Russian Jewish culture). These differences are generally assumed to be located in the premigration cultures of the sending communities (see, e.g., Perlmann 1988; Sowell 1981; Olneck and Lazerson 1974). Others locate the cultural differences not so much in the specifics of different European contexts but rather in the general distinction between preindustrial peasant communities and industrial working-class settings (Gutman 1973).[5]

Scholars have been divided concerning how eagerly immigrants embraced education at the turn of the century. In one of the earliest treatments of the subject, historian Timothy Smith (1969) argues that Eastern and Southern European immigrants were extremely strong supporters of education, both for their communities as a whole and for their individual children. He attributes this high cultural commitment to education to the immigrants' belief that education was the key to personal economic advancement; he also argues, however, that immigrants thought education would make their children more familiar with their own cultural heritage and would help promote their ethnic group's social standing.

Other scholars, however, take issue with the picture that Smith paints. A series of social histories of specific ethnic communities, for example, shows that many new immigrants were highly distrustful of American schools. A key element was fear on the part of adults that American education would cause their children's loyalty to family, church, and community to weaken (see, e.g., Bodnar 1969; Morawska 1985). Morawska, for example, quotes an immigrant in Johnstown who reports that the older generation "deeply believed that in [public] schools the youth lose their religion and their faith weakens" (p. 132). Immigrant groups, especially those from Southern and Eastern Europe, are often depicted as being more oriented to the well-being of the family unit than to individual mobility, and little concerned with investing for the future (and hence less willing than native-born whites to sacrifice for their children's educations). In addition, many immigrants doubted that education would pay off for their children (i.e., they were painfully aware of the discrimination and other obstacles that immigrants and ethnics from Southern and Eastern Europe faced in the labor market) and they felt that the culture of the public school was alien to them (Bodnar 1982; Yans-McLaughlin 1977; Kessner 1977; Morawska 1985). Investigations of the children themselves revealed that many greatly preferred working to going to school—and not just for the money. They often felt better treated at work and liked their surroundings better (e.g., Todd 1913; Clopper 1912; Abbott and Breckinridge 1917).

Abbott and Breckinridge's (1917) investigations and long involvement with the Chicago immigrant community led them to believe that many immigrants had "high regard" for education, motivated largely by their desire to give their children something denied to them prior to migration (they note that education was generally unavailable to most peasants in the Eastern and Southern European countries of origin of Chicago immigrants early in this century). Their general commitment to education for their children, viewed as something to which their children should have access, was counterbalanced, however, by the families' needs for the children's incomes. As they explain the conundrum:

> The great majority of immigrants are eager to send their children to school, often more eager than many American families. The opportunity to give their children a chance at the education that they have missed has been one of the great factors inducing immigration to this country. It is clear, however, that with so many thousands of immigrants there must be a very considerable number of people who value the certain present earnings above the problematical future welfare of their children. (p. 268)

In the context of industrial America at the turn of the century, however, immigrants' faith in and hopes for education may be beside the point for purposes of understanding the actual educational choices they made. The key issue may be whether families could afford to allow their children to go to school, at least beyond the ages at which they could make substantial contributions to the family's economic well-being. The simple fact is that most urban immigrant families in this time period depended on the earnings or other economic contributions of multiple family members for sheer economic survival (see, e.g., Tilly and Scott 1978; Modell, Furstenberg, and Hershberg 1976; Hareven 1982; Pleck 1976; Goldin 1981). Urban working-class children labored in a variety of wage and nonwage settings to contribute to their families' survival (Brody 1980; Pleck 1979; Bodnar, Simon, and Weber 1982; Nasaw 1985).

I have argued elsewhere that one must situate the immigrant child in the context of the working-class family economy to understand his or her educational choices during this period, and that few immigrant families were in a position to *act* on whatever faith they may have had in education for collective or individual advancement (Walters and O'Connell 1988). This view asserts that the family rather than the individual is the basic decision-making unit that allocated the time of family members to various activities, including working and going to school, and that families could not afford to entertain any options that risked the short-term well-being of the family unit. In his studies of immigrant industrial workers in Pennsylvania, Bodnar (1982, 1977) clearly demonstrates that, while working-class families were aware of the middle-class ideology of individualism and material advancement through schooling, the pragmatic constraints of surviving from paycheck to paycheck and the need for multiple sources of income to provide any cushion against disaster oriented them toward the present and the family. The culture of the working-class family was guided by collective goals and needs, and the individualistic aspirations of children were subordinated to family demands (Weiss 1982; Yans-McLaughlin 1977; Pleck 1976). Most children from such families left school and went to work at an early age, often voluntarily, motivated by a desire to promote family interests. While such behavior appears "traditional" or "irrational" when viewed through the lens of contemporary understandings of the purpose of education, it was quite rational from the perspective of maximizing family survival. Taking children out of work and putting them into school would have posed a threat to short-term survival for many immigrant urban families (Hogan 1978). Moreover, the degree of discrimination they faced at school and in the labor market tempered their beliefs that education would make a major difference in their own opportunities for mobility.

POOR SOUTHERN WHITES. Unlike northern immigrants or southern blacks, poor whites in the South had little public voice, at least after the defeat of Populism and the enactment of disfranchising legislation that left many of them, along with virtually all blacks, without the vote and without influence in southern politics (Key 1949; Kousser 1974). And, very importantly, they had few organizations through which they could express their interests. They lost any voice they had had in political parties (which, as Link 1986 and Link 1946 show, had provided opportunities for them to press their educational interests prior to disfranchisement). There was no one Protestant denomination that was able to represent the interests of poor whites. Labor unions were few and far between in the South. In this context, it is not surprising that poor whites mounted no strong political campaign for more or better education in the South, or that no other public voices claiming to speak *for* poor whites were heard with educational demands.

I believe that if poor whites in the South had had the kind of organizational resources that were available to the urban immigrant working class in the North, or even the few organizational resources that were available to southern blacks (mostly the black church), they would have expressed a public commitment to education. I base this argument on what happened in brief historical moments when organizational resources were available. The most telling example is the support for education voiced by the Populist movement and the People's Party in the 1880s and 1890s. The writing on Populism as a national movement does not touch on education, dwelling instead on the economic reform agenda pushed by Populists. This is not surprising, however, given that education was not a *national* political issue—education was virtually entirely under the control of local and state government during this period. When one looks at the histories of Populism *within* states, the Populists' concern with education becomes apparent. Populists throughout the South voiced support for "popular education." A demand for better education was, for example, the first item in the constitution of the North Carolina Farmers' Alliance. But the same was true throughout the South. Link (1946, 174–78) shows, for example, that in Alabama in 1880 the Greenback-Labor Party's platform called for "adequate educational facilities"; in 1890 the Alliance in Tennessee and Georgia demanded "extension of the public school system"; and in 1892 the Populist platform in North Carolina included a call for "adequate aid to state educational institutions." When Populists gained power they implemented their agenda. The 1895 Fusion (Populist-Republican) legislature in North Carolina increased funding for public schools, for example. A frequent result of Populist agitation for education was increased emphasis on agricultural and vocational education in the public schools.

Labor unions were frequently used by immigrant whites in the North to express educational interests, but labor had little foothold in the South during the late nineteenth and early twentieth centuries. It is possible that our conclusions about poor southern whites' educational vision would be different had they had labor unions through which to express their interests. In at least some cases in which labor unions established a presence in the South, they voiced strong support for improved access to education for whites. One North Carolina union, for example, established a scholarship for workers' children to pay parents a sum equal to their child's forgone wages if the child stayed in school.

The evidence that is available about the educational hopes and dreams of poor southern whites comes largely from oral histories, social investigations, commentaries by elite contemporaries (including educational professionals), and the like. Elite contemporaries did not see any evidence of a groundswell of support for public education among poor whites. In fact, they mounted extensive propaganda campaigns to persuade the mass of white southerners to support public education. The clear image that emerges, then, is of an elite trying to convince a recalcitrant and unwilling mass of poor whites that education was beneficial to them (Dabney 1936; Knight 1922; Leloudis 1996; Link 1986; Maxcy 1981; Prather 1979).

When one turns to the voices of poor whites themselves, there is little evidence of a strong commitment to education, largely because the demands of surviving from day to day seemed to have allowed little opportunity to pursue an education. In addition, it is possible that poor southern whites saw even less of a purpose to going to school than northern immigrants. Many poor rural white parents believed that schooling beyond basic literacy was unnecessary, and the need for children to work simply reinforced this belief (Flynt 1985, 233). Newby (1989, 420) argues that poor whites "didn't believe in education," and that their hostility was entirely pragmatic.

> Schools did not teach children how to live or make a living; and after they learned to read and write or were big enough to work (at home or in the field or the mill), children were better off working. . . . To outsiders, "poor whites" and "lintheads" with the rudiments of literacy were still "trash"; and the prejudices of outsiders aside, plain folk did not center their lives on mobility and achievement.

Newby further argues that poor southern whites did not orient themselves to individualism and achievement, but instead they were "expected to learn what their parents knew and then duplicate their parents' lives" (p. 422). "Book learning" was not only unnecessary, but it could even be harmful if it alienated the child "from things that made accommodation, adaptation, and 'making do' easy" (p. 422). Tullos (1989, 185) echoes this theme with the comment that poor whites in mill towns thought that too much education would "cause children to 'rise above their raising,' becoming, in effect, strangers to their friends and families."

One study of cotton mill workers in the 1920s documents what the author refers to as a general "indifference" toward education on the part of children and their parents (Rhyne 1930, 201). Parents often felt that it was pointless to educate their children because "all they will ever be able to do is to work in the cotton mill anyway" (p. 202). They had little hope that an education would help their children improve their social or economic condition. In addition, of course, many parents relied on the children's incomes to make ends meet (also see Cook 1925; Hall et al. 1987).

SOUTHERN BLACKS. There is a fair amount of evidence in support of the argument that southern blacks, unlike southern whites, cared deeply about education and were strongly committed to improving educational opportunities for their children and their communities. This evidence falls into two general categories: statements by leaders and sustained efforts on the part of the southern black community to improve education.

The two best-known voices raised in support of education for African-Americans during this period were Booker T. Washington and W. E. B. Du Bois. Both were strong supporters of education and had large and loyal followings. They differed dramatically, however, in their visions of education. Washington supported vocational education for African-Americans, accommodating the prevailing sentiment in the white community about the kind of education that would be appropriate for black children. Du Bois supported classical education, and urged the black community to support particularly advanced education for the "Talented Tenth" to ensure the availability of an educated and trained leadership for the black community. Black religious leaders throughout the South championed the cause of greater educational access and improved education for black children (Anderson 1988; Bullock 1967; Dollard 1937; Du Bois 1898; Du Bois and Dill 1911; Higginbotham 1993). The black church, through separate denominations for black Baptists and Methodists (the National Baptists and African Methodist Episcopalians, respectively), was the major organizational voice that remained for southern African-Americans in the aftermath of disfranchisement and the enactment of Jim Crow laws.

In addition to the public pronouncements of black leaders and political demands they made for greater access to schooling and improvements in school quality, further evidence of black commitment to education comes in the form of a seeming groundswell of material support for establishing and sustaining schools for black children. In the eyes of many observers, the level of material support provided for schools by African-American communities went far beyond what one would expect on the basis of their general levels of poverty and want. In the immediate aftermath of slavery, for example, ex-slaves swamped the schools established by the federal Freedman's Bureau and established hundreds of schools on and of their own, despite their crushing poverty (Alvord 1866). One Georgia black teacher said that blacks begged for schooling (during Reconstruction, when education first became available to them in the South) "as a thirsty man would beg his neighbor or a friend for a drink of water" (quoted in Jones 1980, 59). Anderson (1988) documents the extensive financial contributions impoverished black communities made to establish and support "public" schools for black children until well into the twentieth century. The Rosenwald fund, for example, which was responsible for the construction of thousands of rural (public) schoolhouses for black children in the 1910s, 1920s, and 1930s, required a substantial contribution from the local community, much of which came from individual contributions of dozens of poor black families. A study of one rural community in North Carolina documents a wide range of efforts African-Americans undertook to try to improve the inadequately funded local public schools (Newman 1985, 449):

> 1916: Oak Grove Community parents cut logs to make timber for a new school; 1917: parents in Pine Hill Community, anxious for a new school, began raising money by having box parties and each pledged $10.00; 1918 was a good tobacco year, and parents built another room onto the school; 1921: patrons of Hillview got together and built a small room on their school.

Finally, one of the main motivations behind the Progressive Era campaign to improve public education in the South for white children was the fear that the black desire for education, demonstrated in these sorts of ways in various local communities, was outstripping white desire, and that poor white children might be left more poorly educated than black children. Clearly there was enough visible public clamor for education on the part of southern blacks to worry whites.

Why did poor blacks apparently value education more than poor southern whites? I believe that a large part of the answer lay in the symbolic importance of the availability of education within black culture. Reading and writing were seen as a "contradiction of oppression" and "a means to liberation and freedom" (Anderson 1988, 17); schooling was "an individual and collective defiance to white authority" (Jones 1980, 49). African-Americans' commitment to education must be seen in the context of the complete denial of educational opportunities during slavery. Based on his study of a community in the Alabama black belt circa 1930, for example, Johnson (1934) argues that poor blacks, even those who were themselves illiterate, maintain

> a firm belief in the mysterious power of education to accomplish fuller freedom for their children. For them writing is a vital symbol, and the ability to write a key to power. Sarah Key was one such person. She was positive that there was good in this form of knowledge, because white folks had been so particular to keep it away from Negroes. (p. 130)

The right of educational *access,* then, was extremely important to the black community in the South, perhaps because of the symbolic link between the right to education and freedom.

Toward the end of the nineteenth century, as the oppression of blacks deepened, racial uplift and the desire to prove worthiness to white society also emerged as strong motivations for blacks to seek education (the latter was part of the Booker T. Washington philosophy). The motto of the National Association of Colored Women, "lifting as we climb," could have been used to describe blacks' reasons for educational attainment. Describing black Baptists' attitudes toward education, Higginbotham (1993, 19) states that

> there was little doubt in their minds that education stood second only to religion in enabling their survival and salvation in America. . . . Despite the value of education to individual advancement, its larger, more lasting service was perceived in terms of collective empowerment. Education, especially higher education, was considered essential to the progress of African Americans as a group.

When one turns to social histories, social investigations, and other forms of direct evidence of how readily parents were able to permit their children to go to school, the picture that emerges of poor southern blacks is quite similar to what I have sketched above for poor southern whites and northern immigrants. In a word, economic hardship often prevented families from sending their children to school. Johnson (1934, 132) reports that middle-aged poor blacks in 1930 who were illiterate or barely literate told him that the need to work was the reason they had not gone to school. A WPA survey in the mid-1930s found that over half of the black children of school age who were not in school were absent because they were working (Holley, Winston, and Woofter 1940, 96). Unlike many urban children in northern industrial areas, poor southern black children were likely to be working in agriculture, and thus their work did not pull them out of school entirely. But it did cause lengthy absences from school, especially during the cotton-planting and -picking seasons, and high rates of "retardation" (being overage for one's grade level), which in turn contributed to dropping out of school for good. (Also see Woofter 1913; Bond 1934; Terrill and Hirsch 1978; Federal Writers' Project 1939; Dollard 1937.) As late as 1940, Johnson (1941, 109–14) finds that rural black youth, whatever their or their parents' desire for education, had to put schooling second to the family's need for their labor, especially during peak farming seasons. As Johnson put it, "Schooling for Negro youth is controlled by the exigencies of cotton" (p. 109). He goes on to cite examples of several families who deplored the need to compromise their children's educations but realized that they had to meet immediate economic demands of the family.

Conclusions

My purpose here has been to explore the similarities and differences in the cultural significance of schooling among northern urban immigrants, poor southern whites, and southern blacks in the late nineteenth and early twentieth centuries. How one sees these similarities and dissimilarities depends on the particular window through which one views the phenomena: from the perspective of public claims made about education by representatives of the group, from the perspective of rates of children's school enrollment and attainments, or on the basis of direct attempts to determine the attitudes and outlooks about education on the part of ordinary immigrants, poor whites, and blacks.

I have not tried to pick the "best" indicator of northern immigrants', poor southern whites', and southern blacks' understandings of the value of education and their commitment to it. My purpose is to use the differences between the impressions conveyed by public voices, by aggregate educational enrollments and attainments, and by more direct expressions of the meaning and significance of education to understand more fully the perceived importance of education in their lives.

Despite differences in aggregate rates of school enrollment and attendance and differences in educational attainment, and despite whatever differences may have existed in abstract hopes and dreams with respect to education, all three groups faced a similar set of pragmatic constraints when it came time to make choices about sending children to school. Many if not most families lived close to the edge of subsistence, and depended on children's labor contributions (paid or unpaid) for short-term survival. Hopes and dreams, then, often confronted the ugly reality that families could not afford to send their children to school for as long or as regularly as they might have liked.

In a more abstract sense, however, education was related to larger hopes and dreams in different ways for northern immigrants, poor southern whites, and southern blacks. The orientation toward education of southern blacks was more collectivist than for either of the other two groups. They looked to education to a large degree as a means of racial uplift; "advancement" was defined more in terms of advancement of the race than mobility for individuals. Poor southern whites, on the other hand, did not evince any sustained public passion for schooling; in fact, by some accounts poor whites had to be convinced by elites that school improvements and increased access to education were in their best interests during the southern progressive educational movement. This may be due to their position in southern society with respect to blacks: they did not need to rely on education to gain or maintain social and economic advantage over blacks. The racial caste system took care of that.

The evidence about northern immigrants' abstract commitments to education is more mixed. Some report that immigrants put great hope in education for personal and group advancement. Others argue that immigrant groups were cautious, even fearful, about the cultural influence that public schools would exert over their children, and worried about schooling creating too great a cultural and social distance between them and their children. I think we can understand this seeming contradiction if we make a distinction between commitment to the principle of the *right* to a public education, on the one hand, and the tensions associated with having one's children actually go to school, on the other. It seems to me that immigrants clearly wanted and appreciated the right of public education while at the same time they worried about whether their children would become alienated from family, church, and community if they became too assimilated into the culture of the public school.

That leads me to consider the similarities between northern immigrants and southern blacks in the importance they placed on the right of access to schooling. Again, this is a quite different issue from whether they wanted to, or were able to, send their own children to school. Both groups had had education largely denied to them in the previous generation or two. In that context, the symbolic importance of having access to something that had been denied to them makes a great deal of sense, even if poverty, a recognition of the real limitations on social mobility due to racial or ethnic discrimination, or alienation from the middle-class white Protestant culture of the public schools limited their interest in taking or ability to take advantage of the schooling opportunities available to them. For northern immigrants and southern blacks, the right of access to schooling seems to be linked to full personhood, to citizenship in a very broad sense (of entitlement, of social rights—see Walters, James, and McCammon 1997). For northern immigrants and, to an even larger degree, southern blacks, the right of access to public education was something to demand and fight for, part and parcel of full citizenship. Conversely, the denial of this basic educational right would have symbolized a lack of hope of social advancement for the collectivity. This importance of education in the abstract hopes and dreams coexisted, however, with severe limitations on the ability of individual immigrant and black families (and poor southern white families as well) to take full advantage of the social right they strongly desired.

Notes

1. Blacks, of course, were prohibited from any form of schooling—formal or informal—by law in slave states in the antebellum period. A large portion of the newly arriv-

ing immigrants in this period came from Southern and Eastern Europe, where education had been largely unavailable to peasants. Southern states did not establish systems of free public education until after the Civil War, and thus few poor whites had been educated in the antebellum South either.

2. This argument is similar to a point that is basic to the social movements (especially resource mobilization theory) literature: social movement organizations (SMOs) are crucial for advancing a movement's political agenda (e.g., McCarthy and Zald 1977).

3. Katznelson and Weir (1985) come the closest to making this claim, but they argue the point a little differently. They show that the northern working class never mobilized over educational issues *as a class*. Instead, they sometimes mobilized as labor (through labor unions) and sometimes as immigrants or ethnics (through ward politics). Nonetheless, they do not theorize the organizational means of translating private interests into public voices, nor do they question whether spokesmen's interests matched constituents' interests. Buechler's (1993, 228) criticism of resource mobilization theorists is similar: They often mistakenly assume "that the 'preference structures' of individual actors will simply be aggregated until . . . a group constituency is reached."

4. The three major black denominations were National Baptist, African Methodist Episcopal, and African Methodist Episcopal Zion (Lincoln and Mamiya 1990). The major white Protestant denominations in the South were Southern Baptists and Methodist Episcopal, South (Ayers 1992, 458). The white denominations included both elite and poor whites.

5. But see Cohen 1982 for an argument that differences between Jewish and Italian children's educational attainments in New York City were not due to cultural differences but instead to differences in the economic and social opportunity structures available to the two groups—differences that are not taken into account when one controls for family social and economic status and demographic factors.

References

Abbott, Edith, and Sophonisba P. Breckinridge. 1917. *Truancy and Non-attendance in the Chicago Schools*. Chicago: University of Chicago Press.

Alvord, J. W. 1866. *Fourth Semi-annual Report on Schools for Freedmen*. Bureau of Refugees, Freedmen, and Abandoned Lands. Washington: Government Printing Office.

Anderson, James D. 1988. *The Education of Blacks in the South, 1860–1935*. Chapel Hill: University of North Carolina Press.

Ayers, Edward L. 1992. *The Promise of the New South*. New York: Oxford University Press.

Bailyn, Bernard. 1960. *Education in the Forming of American Society*. Chapel Hill: University of North Carolina Press.

Baker, David P. 1992. "The Politics of American Catholic School Expansion, 1870–1930." In *The Political Construction of Education*, edited by Bruce Fuller and Richard Rubinson. New York: Praeger.

Bodnar, John. 1969. "Materialism and Morality: Slavic-American Immigrants and Education 1890–1940." *Journal of Ethnic Studies* 3:1–19.

————. 1977. *Immigration and Industrialization.* Pittsburgh: University of Pittsburgh Press.

————. 1982. *Workers' World.* Baltimore: Johns Hopkins University Press.

Bodnar, John, Roger Simon, and Michael P. Weber. 1982. *Lives of Their Own.* Urbana: University of Illinois Press.

Bond, Horace Mann. 1934. *The Education of the Negro in the American Social Order.* Englewood Cliffs, N.J.: Prentice-Hall.

Brody, David. 1980. *Workers in Industrial America.* New York: Oxford University Press.

Buechler, Steven M. 1993. "Beyond Resource Mobilization: Emerging Trends in Social Movement Theory." *Sociological Quarterly* 34:217–35.

Bullock, Henry Allen. 1967. *A History of Negro Education in the South from 1619 to the Present.* Cambridge: Harvard University Press.

Clopper, Edward N. 1912. *Child Labor in City Streets.* New York: Macmillan.

Cohen, Miriam. 1982. "Changing Education Strategies among Immigrant Generations: New York Italians in Comparative Perspective." *Journal of Social History* 15: 443–66.

Coleman, James S. 1968. "The Concept of Equality of Educational Opportunity." *Harvard Educational Review* 38:7–22.

Cook, John Harrison. [1925] 1972. *A Study of the Mill Schools of North Carolina.* New York: AMS Press.

Cremin, Lawrence A. 1964. *The Transformation of the School.* New York: Knopf.

Curoe, Philip R. V. [1926] 1972. *Educational Attitudes and Policies of Organized Labor in the United States.* New York: AMS Press.

Dabney, Charles William. 1936. *Universal Education in the South.* 2 vols. Chapel Hill: University of North Carolina Press.

Dewey, John. 1916. *Democracy and Education.* New York: Macmillan.

Dollard, John. [1937] 1988. *Class and Caste in a Southern Town.* Madison: University of Wisconsin Press.

Du Bois, W. E. B. 1898. *Some Efforts of American Negroes for Their Own Social Betterment.* Atlanta: Atlanta University Press.

Du Bois, W. E. Burghardt, and Augustus Granville Dill, eds. 1911. *The Common School and the Negro American.* Atlanta: Atlanta University Press.

Federal Writers' Project Works Progress Administration. 1939. *These Are Our Lives.* Chapel Hill: University of North Carolina Press.

Flynt, J. Wayne. 1985. "Folks Like Us: The Southern Poor White Family, 1865–1935." In *The Web of Southern Social Relations,* edited by Walters J. Fraser, Jr., R. Frank Saunders, Jr., and Jon L. Wakelyn. Athens: University of Georgia Press.

Fuller, Bruce. 1983. "Youth Job Structure and School Enrollment, 1890–1920." *Sociology of Education* 56:145–56.

Goldin, Claudia. 1981. "Family Strategies and the Family Economy in the Late Nineteenth Century: The Role of Secondary Workers." In *Philadelphia,* edited by Theodore Hershberg. New York: Oxford University Press.

Guest, Avery M., and Stewart E. Tolnay. 1985. "Agricultural Organization and Educational Consumption in the U.S. in 1900." *Sociology of Education* 58:201–12.

Gutman, Herbert. 1973. "Work, Culture, and Society in Industrializing America." *American Historical Review* 78:531–88.

Hall, Jacquelyn Dowd, James Leloudis, Robert Korstad, Mary Murphy, Lu Ann Jones, and Christopher B. Daly. 1987. *Like a Family.* Chapel Hill: University of North Carolina Press.

Hallinan, Maureen T. 1988. "Equality of Educational Opportunity." *Annual Review of Sociology* 14:249–68.

Hareven, Tamara. 1982. *Family Time and Industrial Time.* Cambridge: Cambridge University Press.

Higginbotham, Evelyn Brooks. 1993. *Righteous Discontent.* Cambridge: Harvard University Press.

Hochschild, Jennifer L. 1995. *Facing Up to the American Dream.* Princeton: Princeton University Press.

Hogan, David. 1978. "Education and the Making of the Chicago Working Class, 1880–1930." *History of Education Quarterly* 18:227–70.

———. 1985. *Class and Reform.* Philadelphia: University of Pennsylvania Press.

Holley, William C., Ellen Winston, and T. J. Woofter, Jr. [1940] 1971. *The Plantation South 1934–1937.* Freeport, N.Y.: Books for Libraries Press.

Johnson, Charles S. 1934. *Shadow of the Plantation.* Chicago: University of Chicago Press.

———. 1941. *Growing Up in the Black Belt.* Washington: American Council on Education.

Jones, H. M. 1952. "Horace Mann's Crusade." In *America in Crisis,* edited by Daniel Aaron. New York: Knopf.

Jones, Jacqueline. 1980. *Soldiers of Light and Love.* Chapel Hill: University of North Carolina Press.

Jones, Thomas Jesse. 1917. *Negro Education: A Study of the Private and Higher Schools for Colored People in the United States,* vols. 1 and 2. Bureau of Education, Bulletin no. 39. Washington: Government Printing Office.

Kaestle, Carl F. 1983. *Pillars of the Republic.* New York: Hill and Wang.

Katznelson, Ira, and Margaret Weir. 1985. *Schooling for All.* New York: Basic.

Kessner, Thomas. 1977. *The Golden Door.* New York: Oxford University Press.

Key, V. O., Jr. 1949. *Southern Politics.* New York: Vintage.

Knight, Edgar W. 1922. *Public Education in the South.* Boston: Ginn.

Kousser, J. Morgan. 1974. *The Shaping of Southern Politics.* New Haven: Yale University Press.

Leloudis, James L. 1996. *Schooling the New South.* Chapel Hill: University of North Carolina Press.

Lieberson, Stanley. 1980. *A Piece of the Pie.* Berkeley: University of California Press.

Lincoln, C. Eric, and Lawrence H. Mamiya. 1990. *The Black Church in the African American Experience.* Durham: Duke University Press.

Link, Arthur. 1946. "The Progressive Movement in the South, 1870–1914." *North Carolina Historical Review* 23:172–95.

Link, William A. 1986. *A Hard Country and a Lonely Place.* Chapel Hill: University of North Carolina Press.

Margo, Robert A. 1990. *Race and Schooling in the South, 1880–1950.* Chicago: University of Chicago Press.

Maxcy, Spencer J. 1981. "Progressivism and Rural Education in the Deep South, 1900–1950." In *Education and the Rise of the New South,* edited by Ronald K. Goodenow and Arthur O. White. Boston: Hall.

McCarthy, John D., and Mayer N. Zald. 1977. "Resource Mobilization and Social Movements." *American Journal of Sociology* 82:1212–41.

Messerli, Jonathan. 1972. *Horace Mann. A Biography.* New York: Knopf.

Meyer, John W., David Tyack, Joane Nagel, and Audri Gordon. 1979. "Public Education as Nation-Building in America: Enrollments and Bureaucratization in the American States, 1870–1930." *American Journal of Sociology* 85:591–613.

Mitchell, Theodore R. 1987. *Political Education in the Southern Farmers' Alliance, 1887–1900.* Madison: University of Wisconsin Press.

Modell, John, Frank Furstenberg, and Theodore Hershberg. 1976. "Social Change and the Transition to Adulthood in Historical Perspective." *Journal of Family History* 1(1):7–32.

Morawska, Ewa. 1985. *For Bread with Butter.* Cambridge: Cambridge University Press.

Nasaw, David. 1985. *Children of the City.* New York: Basic.

Newby, I. A. 1989. *Plain Folk in the New South.* Baton Rouge: Louisiana State University Press.

Newman, Dale. 1985. "Work and Community Life in a Southern Textile Town." In *The Labor History Reader,* edited by Daniel J. Leab. Champaign: University of Illinois Press.

Olneck, Michael, and Marvin Lazerson. 1974. "The School Achievement of Immigrant Children, 1900–1930." *History of Education Quarterly* 14:454–82.

Perkinson, Henry J. 1968. *The Imperfect Panacea.* New York: Random House.

Perlmann, Joel. 1988. *Ethnic Differences.* Cambridge: Cambridge University Press.

Pleck, Elizabeth H. 1976. "Two Worlds in One: Work and Family." *Journal of Social History* 10:178–83.

———. 1979. "A Mother's Wages: Income Earning among Married Italian and Black Women, 1896–1911." In *A Heritage of Her Own,* edited by Nancy F. Cott and Elizabeth H. Pleck. New York: Simon and Schuster.

Prather, H. Leon, Sr. 1979. *Resurgent Politics and Educational Progressivism in the New South.* Cranbury, N.J.: Associated University Presses.

Raftery, Judith Rosenberg. 1992. *Land of Fair Promise.* Stanford: Stanford University Press.

Ravitch, Diane. 1974. *The Great School Wars.* New York: Basic.

Reese, William. 1986. *The Power and the Promise of School Reform.* Boston: Routledge and Kegan Paul.

Rhyne, Jennings J. 1930. *Some Southern Cotton Mill Workers and Their Villages.* Chapel Hill: University of North Carolina Press.

Smith, Timothy. 1969. "Immigrant Social Aspirations and American Education, 1880–1930." *American Quarterly* 21:523–43.

———. 1972. "Native Blacks and Foreign Whites: Varying Responses to Educational Opportunity in America." *Perspectives in American History* 6:309–19.

Sowell, Thomas. 1981. *Ethnic America.* New York: Basic.

Terrill, Tom E., and Jerrold Hirsch, eds. 1978. *Such as Us.* Chapel Hill: University of North Carolina Press.

Tilly, Louise, and Joan Scott. 1978. *Women, Work, and Family.* New York: Holt, Rinehart and Winston.

Todd, Helen M. 1913. "Why Children Work, the Children's Answer." *McClure's Magazine,* April, 68–79.

Tullos, Allen. 1989. *Habits of Industry.* Chapel Hill: University of North Carolina Press.

Walters, Pamela Barnhouse, David R. James, and Holly J. McCammon. 1997. "Citizenship and Public Schools: Accounting for Racial Inequality in Education in the Pre- and Post-Disfranchisement South." *American Sociological Review* 62:34–52.

Walters, Pamela Barnhouse, and Philip J. O'Connell. 1988. "The Family Economy, Work, and Educational Participation in the United States, 1890–1940." *American Journal of Sociology* 93:1116–52.

Weiss, Bernard J. 1982. Introduction to *American Education and the European Immigrant: 1840–1940,* edited by Bernard J. Weiss. Urbana: University of Illinois Press.

Woofter, Thomas Jackson. 1913. *The Negroes of Athens, Georgia. Bulletin of the University of Georgia,* vol. 14, no. 4.

Wrigley, Julia. 1982. *Class Politics and Public Schools.* New Brunswick: Rutgers University Press.

Yans-McLaughlin, Virginia. 1977. *Family and Community.* Ithaca: Cornell University Press.

part four
ideology and the
politics of race

"you're too independent!": how gender, race, and class make many feminisms

jane j. mansbridge

Adherents of the feminist movement have learned, over time, that in a healthy movement many versions of feminism must compete and collaborate in an atmosphere of mutual challenge and synergy. In the United States, the movement has been refined, enlarged, and sometimes completely changed by the work of black feminist writers, the diverse experiences of black and other women-of-color activists, and the experiences of women of all races who are not activists. These groups have, for example, been responsible for the currently dominant conclusion that the plural *feminisms* rather than the singular *feminism* most accurately describes the varied lessons different groups and subgroups have drawn from their experiences challenging the inequalities between men and women.

Black and white women, activists and nonactivists do not always have the same trajectories regarding the interaction of race, gender, and feminist ideas. In the early days of the second wave of the feminist movement in the United States, from approximately 1964 to 1974, many political activists among black women rejected feminist ideas, as did many political activists among white women. Some commentators even concluded that "the Black woman" rejected the women's liberation movement.[1] By contrast, as we will see, nonactivist black women were more likely than whites to report on surveys that they supported both "the women's movement" and "feminism." Among activists and nonactivists, black women's support for feminism has almost always been combined with support for racially targeted causes, including in many cases explicit support for black men. Other issues relating to gender have also taken different modal trajectories by race.

In this chapter I discuss one example of an experience that seems to differ in its incidence by race, gender, and education. This is the likelihood of one's being told one is "too independent," with whatever connotations that charge might have in everyday life. I stumbled across this issue in the course of a series of relatively open-ended interviews with fifty low-income women in the United States. The interviews, with thirty-two white and eighteen black women, derived from a nonrepresentative, opportunistic sample of women whom I could meet through a mutual friend. From 1991 to 1994, I interviewed seven to nine women in each of several occupational categories: mothers receiving AFDC in Chicago, educational paraprofessionals in New York, secretaries in Missouri, minimum-wage workers in South Carolina, police officers in another large city (anonymous for confidentiality), and farm women in Kansas. In each case except the Kansas farm women (all white), the occupational categories had a mix of black and white members. Because of the nonrepresentative nature of the group I interviewed, I followed up the specific issue of being told one is "too independent" through two telephone surveys, in 1993 and 1994, of a representative sample of English-speaking residents of the Chicago area.[2]

Black Women Activists' Ambivalence Regarding the Feminist Movement, 1964–1974 and Beyond

Not long after the "second wave" of the women's movement developed its first formal organizations among primarily white and middle-class women in the late 1960s, politically active black women responded in at least two ways. As we will see, many avoided or condemned the women's movement as both not representing their concerns and having the potential to divide the black community. Others found issues of gender inequality a relatively high priority for them as black women.

Yet even those activist black women who were attracted to the women's movement soon began to point out the deeply embedded racism of some of the movement's positions and almost all of its organizations. Almost every distinguished black feminist writer has among her works at least one thoughtful and critical essay about the ways she and her interests were excluded or marginalized by the white middle-class feminist organizations she tried to join or the white middle-class feminists with whom she spoke. Writers as different in personality and political perspective as Michele Wallace ([1975] 1990), Audre Lorde ([1979] 1984a, [1980] 1984c), Alice Walker ([1979] 1983c), and bell hooks (1981) all report the effects of the conscious and unconscious racism they encountered in these organizations and encounters, including the short shrift given to their central concerns.[3] Indeed, for many black women today, the word *feminism* still connotes a movement that is white and middle-class, because white middle-class women have been the most visible and powerful actors in the movement. For these reasons, among others, Alice Walker in 1983 coined the term *womanist* for the convictions of black feminists, writing that "Womanist is to feminist as purple to lavender" (1983f, xii)—stronger, deeper, more vibrant, and in all ways less white. Most feminists now realize that feminist issues are often inextricably shot through with race. It is not possible to conceive of one without the other.

Consider women as sexual objects. White feminists have pointed out how ideals of femininity tend to subordinate women by, for example, encouraging high heels (e.g., Brownmiller 1984). Black feminists point out that most "feminine" images have a racial component as well: fair skin, blue eyes, blond hair. In fending off the destructive messages embodied in traditional femininity, black women must also fend off a deeply embodied racism. Michele Wallace writes:

> On rainy days my sister and I used to tie the short end of a scarf around our scrawny braids and let the rest of its silken mass trail to our waists. We'd pretend it was hair and that we were some lovely heroine that we'd seen in the movies. There was a time when I would have called that wanting to be white, yet the real point of the game was being feminine. Being feminine *meant* white to us. (1990, 18)[4]

Although the feminist quest for an ideal of beauty based on character rather than ascriptive traits can be shared by black and white women, for black women the struggle includes a struggle against racism in ways that white women rarely see so clearly.

Consider too the issue of violence against women. Black women show us that any extended feminist critique of rape, incest, and battering must include a critique and understanding of the processes that lie behind the lynchings of black men and white fears of black male sexuality.[5] Black women also confront a conflict when in response to domestic violence they call upon police forces that have historically been racist, targeting in particular young black men.[6]

Finally, on the issue that this chapter addresses, consider material, physical, and emotional independence. The southern cult of true womanhood equated femininity not only with whiteness but with weakness (Carby 1987, 20–39, 48–57, 66–69, 95–120). The delicate white woman, who needed a man to open a door for her or help her out of her chair, was contrasted explicitly with the strong black female slave, who could do as much work in the field as a man. After slavery, in contrast to the typical white woman, many black women worked in the paid labor force all their lives and were brought up to expect such work (Jones 1985). Today the image of "the strong black woman," who can support a household on her own, graduate from college at the same rate as black men, and deal with sexual harassment by giving as good as she gets, serves both as a source of pride for black women and as an overly demanding model that blames any weakness on the woman herself.[7] Here, as on almost all other central feminist issues, the experiences of women in the United States are intertwined with race and racial meanings.

Although the founding mothers of NOW at the highest levels included the Reverend Pauli Murray and Aileen Hernandez, although black women such as Florynce Kennedy, Frances Beal, Cellestine Ware, and Patricia Robinson were active in various ways in the early days of the women's liberation movement (Echols 1989, 291), and although that early women's movement addressed issues, such as abortion and child care, that affected all classes and races, neither NOW nor the "younger," more "radical" (Freeman 1975) branches of the women's movement developed these issues in ways that adequately captured the concerns of black women activists. In the case of abortion, for example, the movement did not develop a strong critique of the lack of consent or manipulated consent involved in the sterilization of poor and often black women. In the case of child care, most feminist analyses did not usually take into account the discomfort many black and working-class women had in leaving their children with nonrelatives. As a consequence of these and many other differences in sensitivity and orientation, the response of most black women activists to the emerging women's movement was mixed at best.

Some small part of that mixed response had its base in many white and black women's differing experiences with "independence" from men. Cynthia Washington, reflecting in 1977 on a conversation with Casey Hayden in 1964, a year before Hayden and Mary King's "a kind of memo" on the subordination of women in the civil rights movement, suggests how modal differences by race on the question of independence can affect politics:

> Certain differences result from the way in which black women grow up. We have been raised to function independently. . . . It seemed to many of us [black women in the civil rights movement] . . . that white women were demanding a chance to be independent while we needed help and assistance which was not always forthcoming. We definitely started from opposite ends of the spectrum. (Washington 1977, 14)

In 1971, Jean Cooper also concluded that the issue of independence affected black and white women differently. "The idea of liberation and independence of black women," she wrote, "is no less than a two edged sword and presents a real dilemma. Central to this dilemma is the strong role which economic and social conditions in the society have forced the black woman to play. . . . [I]n some respects black women have always been liberated, more so than they sought or desired" (1971, 522–23; see also Ladner [1971] 1995, 35, 283; also Echols 1989, 302 n. 28).

Diane Lewis explained what she considered a widespread "initial rejection . . . [of] the women's movement on the part of black women" by suggesting that until the black liberation movement had begun to generate important structural shifts in black-white relations in the 1960s, racism had to be the priority (Lewis 1977). When Gerda Lerner (1972) collected quotations from notable black women, none explicitly supported the newly developing women's movement and several implicitly or explicitly denounced it. In an interview with Lerner, Dara Abubakari, vice president, South, of the Republic of New Africa, produced a double-edged analysis. At first she stated bluntly:

> I feel that the role of black woman at this point in history is to give sustenance to the black man. . . . We cannot separate, and this is what I say to the Women's Lib movement. You cannot separate men from women when you're black. . . . The black woman is liberated in her own mind, because she has taken on responsibility for the family and she works. . . . The black woman is independent.

She then added:

> Now the black woman has been independent, but still she hasn't been able to make any decisions. She is liberated in her own mind, but the whole country still oppresses her as a woman. Women must be free to choose what they want. They should be free to decide if and when they want children. . . . Men shouldn't tell us. Nobody should tell us.[8]

Abubakari made it clear that on the question of independence many African-American women began in a different place from that of most white women. But the issue of independence did not thereby become irrelevant.

In the spring of 1973 Margaret Sloan (one of the founding editors of *Ms.* magazine) and Florynce Kennedy (an activist lawyer) brought together thirty black women to found the National Black Feminist Organization (NBFO). The NBFO organized a press conference in New York in August, getting over four hundred phone calls the next day, two hundred attendees for a meeting a week later, and four to five hundred for a conference two and a half months later. Chapters opened in city after city. Divisions within the organization—over the appropriate degree of radicalism versus liberalism, lesbian/straight conflicts, and strong opposition from women who saw the organization as undermining the solidarity necessary to the black power struggle—soon produced disintegration. But at its height the NBFO enlisted women such as Alice Walker and Michele Wallace, who rapidly established themselves as major black feminist writers.[9]

Spinning off from the NBFO's first eastern regional conference and distinguishing itself as more radical, the Combahee River Collective began meeting in Boston in 1974. In 1977 the collective issued its now-famous "Black Feminist Statement," defining oppressions of race, sex, and class as "interlocking." The statement came early in the first great surge of writings of black and women-of-color feminists, such as Ntozake Shange's *For Colored Girls Who Have Considered Suicide When the Rainbow is Enuf* in 1977, *Conditions 5: The Black Women's Issue* in 1979, works by Audre Lorde from 1978 on, bell hooks's *Ain't I a Woman* in 1981, Cherríe Moraga and Gloria Anzaldúa's edited volume in 1981, Gloria Hull, Patricia Scott, and Barbara Smith's volume in 1982, and Barbara Smith's edited volume in 1983. After that, the lid was off. The number of writings by feminists of color increased exponentially, clarifying the particular perspectives and needs of women of color in societies shaped by histories of domination and subordination based on race, gender, class, and sexuality.

One theme in these early writings on interlocking oppressions was that whereas white feminists often came to their understandings of the structured nature of their disadvantages through an intellectually and emotionally revelatory set of experiences (dubbed "the click" by Jane O'Reilly [(1972) 1980]),[10] black feminists had no such "surprise factor" (Smith and Smith [1980] 1983, 114). They did not need to find their independence or come to realize their oppression. Rather:

> There is virtually no Black person in this country who is surprised about oppression. Virtually not one. Because the thing is we have had it meted out to us from infancy on. . . . You're born into it and it's grinding.[11]

The feminist ideas that emerged from these discussions in the 1970s and 1980s required for their articulation a specifically African-American context. Whether the black feminists who were working out these ideas within the larger context of political activity both in the black community and nationwide were a smaller or larger percentage of their relevant activist communities than were white feminists in the communities of political activists that served as their reference group is an uncertain historical question. Although journalists and sociologists might generalize about "the black woman," no systematic data allow us to compare, within the activist population, the percentages of black and white women political activists who favored feminist ideas. The first available systematic evidence derives from a sample not of activists but of state legislators, more than ten years later. Among women state legislators surveyed in 1988, 55% of blacks said they identified with the label "feminist," compared to only 45% of whites.[12]

Black Women Nonactivists and the Feminist Movement, 1970–1996

We have more systematic evidence about black and white women in the general population than about activists. Among the general population (most of whom are not active in politics), black women were from the very beginning more likely than white women to support both feminism and the women's movement. Even before the formation of the National Black Feminist Organization in 1973, at a time when many black intellectuals and activists were concluding that black women rejected women's liberation,[13] black women were more likely than whites to support the women's movement. In the earliest survey on the women's movement, in 1971, 60% of a representative sample of black women in the general population told telephone interviewers that they supported "efforts to strengthen and change women's status in society." In the same survey, only 37% of white women expressed such support.[14] A year later, in the first survey ever to ask specifically about "women's liberation," 67% of black women said they were sympathetic to women's liberation groups, compared to only 35% of white women—almost double the support.[15]

A similar pattern emerged in 1986, in the first survey to ask women if they considered themselves "feminist." In this survey, a Gallup poll, question placement and wording caused an unusually high percentage of women (56%) to call themselves feminists.[16] Strikingly, 69% of black women responded that they considered themselves "feminist," compared to only 55% of white women. Indeed, 27% of black women said they considered themselves "strong feminists," compared to 8% of white women.[17] In the next year, 1987, Gallup developed a ten-point scale for regarding oneself as a feminist, on which "10" represented a "description that is perfect for you" and "1" a "description that is totally wrong for you." On this survey, 63% of black women put themselves at 6 or above on the scale, compared to 50% of white women, and 19% of black women gave themselves a "10" compared to 8% of white women.[18]

In 1989, the Yankelovich organization developed the first form of the question that has now become standard: "Do you consider yourself to be a feminist?" That year, 42% of black women said "yes," compared to 31% of white women.[19] The five surveys that asked a version of this question in the years 1991–92, when combined, show 35% of the black women saying they consider themselves feminist, compared to 28% of the white women.[20] Most recently, in the 1996 General Social Survey 27% of black women said they considered themselves feminists, compared to 26% of white women, and in a 1997 CBS News survey, 27% of both black and white women said they considered themselves feminists.[21]

Because the wording and question placement vary from survey to survey, and because the numbers of black women in many surveys are very small (for example, only 32 in the 1991 Gallup), it is not easy to track possible increases or declines in either the total percentage of women in the United States calling themselves "feminist" or the size of the differences between black and white women. The 1992 NES showed black women leading white by 11 percentage points, a gap nonsignificantly smaller than the 13 points in the first Gallup survey of 1986 and exactly the same as the gap in the first survey with comparable wording, by Yankelovich in 1989. The 1994 Princeton Survey Research showed black women leading white by 13 percentage points on feminist being "perfect for me," a gap nonsignificantly larger than the 11 points in 1987. But other measures seem to indicate a decreasing gap, including the 1992 Gallup, which shows a statistically insignificant reversal, the 1996 General Social Survey, which shows a statistically insignificant gap of only one point, and the 1997 CBS News Survey, which shows no gap at all.[22]

Moreover, these results must be interpreted with some caution. Even as late as 1994, a small percentage of women and men in the Chicago area interpreted the word "feminist" to mean either someone "who is very feminine" (5%)[23] or "who wants to keep—not change—traditional roles between men and women" (6%).[24] In my in-depth interviews, one woman identifying as a "strong feminist" revealed that she meant by this that she was both strong and feminist, not that she had strong feminist views or felt strongly about her feminism.

Yet in spite of these uncertainties about the meaning of the word "feminist" itself, the general pattern of greater historical support for the feminist movement by black than by white women can probably be trusted. In the earliest survey that asked about feminism in 1986, for example, the "women's movement" was probably a more familiar term than "feminism,"[25] and that survey also asked about the "women's movement." In 1986, more than twice the percentage of black women than white (39% compared to 18%) thought the women's movement had done very well in improving their "own" lives.[26] By 1996, white women seemed to have caught up, with 45% saying the women's movement had improved their own lives, compared to 49% of black women.[27] In the most recent survey to which I have access, a small CBS News survey from 1997 that tapped only 60 black women, 88% of the black women said they had a favorable opinion of the women's movement, compared to 64% of the white women, and 60% said the women's movement had achieved something that had made their lives better, compared to 42% of the white women.[28] Regarding women's organizations, 90% of black men and women gave the National Organization for Women a positive rating in 1989, compared to only 68% of whites.[29]

These survey data establish a firm pattern of greater support for the feminist movement among black women than among white in the years 1971 to 1992, and continuing support today. This pattern is, however, not well known. It was first reported by bell hooks in 1981 and is examined here for the first time in detail. The sentiments of the general population—primarily nonactivists— were probably not widely reported because in any one survey the numbers of black women were often too small to report, because racial patterns of support for feminism among nonactivists contradicted racial patterns of participation in the largest feminist organizations, because early in the movement black women activists sometimes denounced or were distinctly ambivalent toward the feminist movement, and because the media consistently portrayed feminism as predominantly white. Indeed, if recent data suggesting no current differences between black and white women in adopting the feminist label are accurate, one explanation for the convergence may be precisely the unrelenting media presentation of the movement as white for thirty years. In the early years the lead of black over white women in support for the movement was relatively robust. It appeared in many (although not all) surveys, and it has appeared no matter how the movement was labeled. It has appeared whether researchers asked about "efforts to strengthen and change women's status" (1970), "women's liberation" (1972), "feminism" (1986 to 1992), "the women's movement" (1986, 1997), or support for the National Organization for Women (1989).

Why, in these national surveys, have black women traditionally given more support than white to the feminist movement? There are at least two possible reasons.[30]

First, black women entered the paid labor force in large numbers earlier than white women. They were therefore the first to experience the "second shift" of responsibility for both home care and paid work. In the occupational "breakthrough" of the 1960s and 1970s, poorer black women moved overwhelmingly from domestic and agricultural to clerical work, leaving only 3% of all black women in domestic and agricultural work by 1988 (King 1993). This movement combined with increasing problems in employment for black men without high-school or college degrees to produce a situation in which poorer black women were often the primary breadwinners for their families, even though the low pay for this full-time work still often kept their families in poverty (Jones 1985). Among middle- and upper-class blacks, women by 1940 had become only slightly less likely than men to graduate from a four-year college, and had kept close to parity with men from then until 1990, in contrast to the far higher rates of male graduation among whites.[31] Yet their degrees did not bring black women parity with black men either in wages or in employment status. These experiences were likely to make black women of all classes sensitive to issues of gender equity.

Second, the experience of racial discrimination and the legacy of the civil rights movement gave both black men and black women a structural analysis of certain inequalities in the United States and an understanding of the need for collective action to combat those inequalities. Black men and women were, by and large, spared the kind of individualism that attributes every inequality to personal failures on the part of the less rewarded. Understanding the fact of racial discrimination helps one understand the fact of sex discrimination, and understanding the need for a civil rights movement helps one understand the need for a feminist movement. This is probably the reason that on surveys black men also tend to support the women's movement in higher percentages than white men.[32]

Although their experiences with gender as well as race discrimination probably predisposed black women toward supporting ideas that they concluded were "feminist," the context in which many black women came to their conclusions differed from that of many white women. That context included, among other things, the issue of independence.

Independence

In my fifth interview for the larger project from which this research derives, I was talking with a black woman in Chicago who had just left AFDC (Aid to Families with Dependent Children) about the closeness she had felt in her family of birth. I quote from that interview at length, partly because it alerted me to ask my later respondents about independence, but primarily because it raises most of the subthemes that surfaced later. As the mother described trying to pass on to her children the feeling of family closeness she herself had experienced, I asked how the men in her life might fit into this plan. She answered, in what seemed at first a non sequitur:

T: I don't know. I've been told I'm too independent. They say my attitude's too independent, but—

J: Do you think you're too independent?

T: I've been told.

J: You've been told you're too independent. Who has told you that you're too independent?

T: Oh, men friends.

J: Men friends have told you that you are too independent?

T: Yeah.

J: What do they mean by that?

T: I think more my attitude, my attitude. 'Cause a lot of times I, see, when I do things I like to do them and feel comfortable knowing, with knowing they're done already. I don't like to worry, you know. Instead of saying, "Well, you don't really need to pay it, you know, right now, you'll catch up with it," I don't do that. I don't do that. I pay it first, and then if something's left, or whatever, then, fine, we splurge. But, I just, 'cause I feel if I don't take care of it, then I'll do without. I'll come up short, you know. It's gonna cost me later on. I can't afford it, so I have to do it like that. I have to do it like that. So I've been told, you're too independent, your attitude is just—I can't help it.

J: So you think, you feel kind of, if you're taking care of it, you know that it's going to be taken care of?

T: Oh, yeah.

J: But if you're not taking care of it, someone else might not do it.

T: Exactly, exactly. I mean, you've got men that's responsible, but, so far, I haven't met one. I haven't met one that is. So—You know, to each his own. I don't mean nothing, you know, toward everybody, but, for me, personally, I like to do it alone.

J: So what, concretely, would you do that made somebody say you're too independent? What would be something you do, some statement you made, or something?

T: I'll just take charge. I'll do it myself.

J: And they'll say, "What are you doing that for?"

T: Because it needs to be done; it needs to be done. And I'm the person to do it. I think I know more about it, or I may know what it needs, or I may know where it has to go, or who gets it, you know. You know all these things, 'cause for me to sit down and just keep me explaining the same thing at bill time over and over again; I don't have to keep doing that. You know, I'd just rather just take charge and get it done. 'Cause I don't like to worry about it. Like, oh my goodness. I can't help it.

J: So, at work, in a job, or whatnot, have you ever had that independence, you know, and has anybody ever said "That's too independent" when you were at a work, at any kind of work?

T: No, no, no, no.

Two interviews later I drew consciously on these words, and specifically asked, "Has anybody ever called you 'too independent'?" Here is the response:

S: Yes, indeed.

J: What would be some examples, real examples?

S: My friend, my ex-boyfriend told me, he told me I should be the guy, 'cause I think I know everything, and "You think you could do everything."

J: He didn't like that?

S: I mean, 'cause I would, like, I would ask him to do something, and if it took him too long to do it, I'd get up and do it. And I might mess up halfway, but then he'd—and then I also tell him—I have a habit of telling him this—"I don't need you for nothing. I'm gonna take care of me, regardless. Whether you help me or not, I'm gonna get taken care of." And, you know, a lot of guys don't like that.

As I continued the interviews, I began to ask most of the women with whom I talked the question, "Has anybody ever called you 'too independent'?" As expected, I got very different responses from different people. But I also seemed to be picking up, I thought, something of a pattern among some of the black women I talked with.

When I asked the question of a young black teacher's assistant in New York City, she answered:

I get that all the time. . . . I live by myself. I support myself. I work, I go to school. Anything I need to do I do by myself. And in relationships I get it a lot. Like a lot, some of the guys I come across—"You're so damn independent." I say "Yes, I am." I say, "I don't need you. There's a difference between needing you and wanting you. I'm with you because I want to be, not because I need you." I said, "What do I need you for?"

. . .

[Regarding her last boyfriend] I said, "Why do I need to ask you? If I ask you, it's going to take forever to do it, so I might as well do it myself so I don't have a headache."

. . .

[W]hen I do ask, I expect to get it done. I don't expect to hear a story or reason why you can't do it now or when I ask you to do it. If you've got to give me a story, forget it, I'll do it myself. That's why—I know as a matter of fact—last year, one instance was my sister went to school upstate, to college. I had went up once and we went shopping and I bought a stereo upstate. At the time I didn't have a car to get up there and get it and my sister's car wasn't working too well to bring it down. So I asked my boyfriend, "Can you go with me one Saturday and pick the stereo up from my sister's room?" "Sure." I waited and I waited, and I said, "When are you going to do it? It's sitting in her room taking up space, she's in a dorm room." "Well, we can go maybe Sunday." Saturday I called my other girlfriend and I borrowed her car and went up and got my stereo. I brought it back and my brother helped me carry it upstairs and I put it in the apartment. He comes over and he sees it and he says, "Oh, you went and got the stereo." I said, "Yeah, waiting for you I couldn't leave it up there forever." Then he says, "Well, you don't need me for anything." I said, "No. That's not—if I'm going to ask you, then do it. Don't give me a story." If I get aggravated I'll do it myself.

A black woman police officer put it this way:

Let's say we're going on vacation or something—or let's say I'm going on vacation. And I would say, "Are you going to take me to the airport?—no, I'll take a cab. They do have cabs running." He'd say, "Oh, you're so independent." . . . [Then] when he sighed a little and clicked his teeth, I thought, "The hell with you. I don't need you." I'm always telling—they say I'm so independent, I don't give them a chance, or I never have to beg for nothing. You're damn right. Why should I have to beg? I don't beg anybody. I can take care of myself, not only financially, but other ways too. It's not just financially that I'm able to take care of myself. It's speaking up and not letting anyone run over me.

Another black woman police officer said that men tell her she's too independent "all the time." One told her:

"Well, you don't know how to ask for help. Why are you doing this yourself?" I said, "That's all right. I lose weight, I mow my lawn, I do what I have to do." . . . I don't feel that I should grovel. I can't do that.

A black secretary in Missouri told me:

I guess I was [told I was] too independent because I prefer to do things myself rather than wait. Maybe I wouldn't accomplish it, or fix it. I may have to eventually call somebody to fix it but I would try to do it myself.

Some of the same themes surfaced among the low-income white women I interviewed, but in most cases the contexts were slightly different. Only in one subgroup—of Kansas farm women—did a majority of white women answer affirmatively to the question "Has anybody ever called you 'too independent'?" Of the seven Kansas farm women whom I interviewed, all but one said that they had been told they were too independent—one by a father, irritated that his daughter had bought an '81 Mustang when he thought she should get something more sensible, one by a husband who wanted to be consulted on decisions in the house, one by a husband who was planning to open the door of the machine shed but on waiting a second too long found she had opened the door herself, and others by friends who thought their friend stayed home too much or by children whose friends did not have single mothers. The women told me that farm families are traditionally quite patriarchal, yet their reports also show that the lives of farm women are relatively autonomous. Perhaps this contrast produces high percentages of these women being told they are too independent. Yet, if their responses are at all typical, most of the reasons they offered differed from the reasons given by the black low-income women with whom I spoke.

The group of thirty-nine women, black and white, whom I happened to ask this question were in no way representative. They derived from various "snowball" samples that began with my own friends. In this nonrepresentative group, a pattern seemed to emerge that made me want to look at it with a more systematic sample. First, among the women with whom I talked, the overall incidence of this experience seemed to differ not only by farm-nonfarm experience but also by race: of the 13 black women I asked this question, 11 (85%) answered that someone had called them "too independent," but of the 26 white women, only 12 (46%) gave this answer. The pattern of reasons seemed to differ as well. Of the 11 black women who reported having been called too independent, 8 (73%) gave reasons related to not wanting to "wait." Of the 12 white women, 2 (17%) gave a reason related to waiting. I did not discern a dominant reason among any other subgroup. Among the black women, 9 (82%) of the 11 mentioned not needing a man, compared to 4 (33%) of the 12 white women.

Because my sample was not representative, I decided to put survey research to an unusual use—investigating the incidence of a phrase in everyday discourse. In 1993 and 1994, I put a question on the Northwestern University Chicago Area Survey, asking, "Has anyone ever called you 'Too independent'?" This survey taps a sample intended to be representative of the Chicago metropolitan area. The area has a socioeconomic distribution much like that of the United States, but is distinctly urban and suburban.

To my surprise, the responses to this question revealed no relationship with class. I had expected people with low educations and incomes to report more often than others having been told they were too independent. This was not the case. But there was a relationship with gender and race, and in one subgroup an interaction with education. In approximate terms, about 40% of white men reported being told they were too independent, 45% of black men, 50% of white women, and 65% of black women.[33] Among black women, those with more formal education were by far the most likely to report having been told they were too independent. Of the black women with a high school degree or less, only 55% reported that someone had told them they were too independent. With each increment of education the percentage went up, to the point at which 84% of black women with a college degree or more reported having been told they were too independent.[34] If the individuals in this sample are reporting their experiences accurately, for black women the modal experience is to have been told you are too independent, whereas for white and black men the modal experience is innocence of this charge. Moreover, for black women in particular, it is as if their education and perhaps the more assertive attitudes that come with education pose a particular problem for others they encounter.[35]

Zora Neale Hurston may have been reflecting her own experience as a highly educated black woman when she made Janie, the central character in *Their Eyes Were Watching God,* depend almost completely on her husband for material support, but establish mental independence through her proud spirit and words of defiance. The reaction of Janie's husband to that spirit was to berate her: "Youse powerful independent around here sometime considerin'" (Hurston [1937] 1990).[36]

I discovered these systematic differences in gender, race, and class in reports of being told one is too independent only after I had finished the in-depth interviews and could not probe the differences more deeply in the interviews themselves. I was, however, able to investigate the question a little more through the surveys, by looking at the relation of being told one was too independent to calling oneself a feminist, to being married or divorced, and to working full-time in the paid labor force versus working as a homemaker—all relationships mediated by race.

Racial differences shaped most prominently the interaction between considering oneself a feminist and being told one is "too independent." Among black women, those who called themselves feminist and those who did not were equally likely to report having been called "too independent" (65% of the feminists and 68% of the nonfeminists reported having been called "too independent"). Yet among white women, those who considered themselves feminists were noticeably more likely than the nonfeminists to report having been called "too independent" (60% vs. 45%).[37] Among white women, whatever goes into calling oneself a feminist makes one almost as likely as the average black woman to be called "too independent." These associations do not tell us whether among white women feminism caused the acts that resulted in being called too independent, whether having people think of one as too independent caused one to become a feminist, or whether a separately caused cluster of attitudes and actions made one more likely both to be called too independent and to become a feminist. Perhaps feminism makes white women act more like black women and get called too independent, while black women just act independently whether they think of themselves as feminist or not.

There seem to be parallel, but not so strong, racial differences in how marital status and employment related to being called too independent. Here too differences in status were more noticeably linked to differences in being called too independent among white women than among black. Married white women were considerably less likely than the divorced to have been told they were too independent (41% vs. 73%), with the widowed and never married falling somewhere in between (59% and 60%). Black women show a similar but less striking pattern. Married black women are somewhat less likely than the divorced to have been told they are too independent (70% vs. 83%), with the widowed and never married experiencing still lower rates (67% and 61%).[38] Divorced white women may have had experiences that make them look more like the average black woman and less like the average married white, whereas black women may be more likely to have had similar experiences no matter what their marital history.

The effects of paid employment may also be a little greater among white women, although here the differences among races were not great enough to be statistically significant. Of the white women who had full-time paid employment, 62% reported having been told that they were too independent, compared to only 31% of the part-time workers and 35% of the homemakers. The black women showed a similar pattern, with 77% of the full-time workers having been told that they were too independent, compared to 54% of part-time workers and 56% of homemakers. The small difference between the white and black women (a 29-point gap versus a 22-point gap), while not statistically significant, follows the pattern of the greater effects of marital status among white women.[39]

We cannot be sure of the direction of causality in any of these instances. Presuming that women are called too independent because they act more independently, we can conclude either that, among both whites and blacks, more independent women are less likely to get married and remain married, or that marriage reduces women's independence, or both (or that some third factor causes both effects). We can conclude either that more independent women are more likely to take on full-time paid jobs, or that holding a full-time job increases women's independence, or both (or that another factor causes both effects). Whatever the causality, we can expect the effects of these dynamics in the case of marital status to be greater for white women, though how those dynamics work out in practice may differ by race, class, region, religion, and a host of other factors.

Being told one is too independent thus serves as one of many instances in which particular cultural groups have experiences that, while similar in some ways, are differently inflected, have different incidences, have different relations with material positions such as marital status and employment, and have different relations with political stances such as feminism. Because of these differences, members of specific race, class, ethnic, regional, religious, and other cultural groups will often have specific issues relating to feminist analysis that they themselves are the most qualified to explore and that may pass completely unnoticed by others in the society.

The Emergence of "Feminisms"

From the 1970s to the 1990s, black feminist, womanist, and international feminist thinkers have helped the women's movement devolve into a plurality of "feminisms," each grounded in the experiences of members of different groups and subgroups. This chapter suggests that investigations of these experiences should focus on nonactivists as well as activists, because the two groups sometimes differ in their interpretations of the world around them.[40] It also suggests that some of these differences in experience can be captured by a combination of in-depth interviews and survey research, using the survey research unconventionally to measure everyday speech.

The survey question on being told one was too independent, measuring an experience that originally emerged from in-depth interviews, revealed that exposure to this charge varied by gender, race, and education. That variation in turn illuminates in a small way how each group of women, typically experiencing a particular constellation of structural forces, cultural patterns, and social supports, must craft from its experiences its own approach to gender equality. If white women are typically trying to become more independent while black women are trying to parse out the complex patterns leading to the charge of being too independent, the language in which members of each group discuss the problems relevant to them will not be the same. Differences of class and race, along with differences in sexuality and other orientations, will mandate different sensitivities and stances in the struggle against male dominance.

In the collective identification and naming of problems, and in the crafting of solutions, some issues can be analyzed best by mixed racial groups, but others require analysis primarily by women who have had similar experiences, talking with one another in the kinds of "safe spaces" that the original consciousness-raising groups of the women's movement often provided their members.[41] In the first decade of the second wave of the feminist movement, from 1964 to 1974, consciousness-raising groups brought the experience of deliberation in a safe space to many primarily white and middle-class women. That format was not useful for many black women, whose consciousnesses were already raised, who did not need the "click" experience, and who wanted to use what little time they could spare from their own and their families' struggles for survival to improve through concrete action their own lot and the lot of those with fewer privileges than they.

By 1999, black women's groups in the academy, organizations such as the National Political Congress of Black Women and the Black Women's Health Alliance, and journals such as *Sage* have provided formal organization around black women's issues, while informal discussions proceed apace, fueled by the explosion in black women's writing.

On a far less formal level, the world is changing as much through what women like those I interviewed do and say as through organizational activity and governmental enactment. The hundreds of millions of women's daily micro-negotiations—with husbands, bosses, lovers, and friends—work within the local environment and are based on local knowledge. But these small struggles are informed by, and themselves inform, the larger understandings of justice and injustice by which all members of a culture—black and white, male and female—regulate their lives. As each woman, for example, deals with being told that she is too independent, and finds a way to respond in word and action that keeps her dignity, upholds her spirit, and maintains the relations that she needs to survive, she shapes the normative world in which her daughters and sons will have to live. It is from that material that viable feminisms, with viable solutions to gender inequalities and gender tensions, will have to emerge.

Notes

I would like to thank Cathy Cohen of Yale University for insightful comments and colleagueship, and the participants in the Russell Sage Conference on Race, Class and Culture, December 16–17, 1996, New York, N.Y., for their helpful suggestions. This paper was completed while I was a Fellow at the Center for Advanced Study in the Behavioral Sciences; I am grateful for financial support provided by the National Science Foundation Grant #SBR-9601236.

1. Staples 1973 (168–69); see n. 7, below.

2. The larger research project, Everyday Feminism, which investigates the effects of nonactivists on the feminist movement, does not concentrate primarily on race. Like the current chapter, this project draws on in-depth interviews as well as on several questions inserted in the Northwestern University Chicago Metropolitan Area Surveys of 1993 and 1994 that were designed to measure the language used in common discourse about gender.

3. See also hooks 1984 (11–12); davenport 1983 (86–89); King 1990.

4. See also Collins 1990 (78 ff); Walker [1982] 1983e (295 ff.).

5. E.g., Walker 1981, 93. See also Richie 1996; Crenshaw 1991; Gilmore 1996, ch. 3. The strong sexual component of black/white relations, at least in the South, is evident from, among many other things, the punishments of black male slaves and postslavery lynchings, which were often accompanied by castration or genital mutilation even when the infractions had nothing to do with sexuality.

6. I thank Cathy Cohen for this point.

7. On the traditional "strong" black woman, see Ladner [1971] 1995, 35, 130–31, 285; McCray 1980, 69; Evans 1980; Coretta King, cited in Walker [1971] 1983a, 153; Zora Neale Hurston, cited in Walker [1982] 1983e, 306; Walker [1979] 1983d. For issues of sacrifice and strength in motherhood, see Collins 1990, ch. 6; hooks 1990, 45; Walker [1972] 1973, 13–14. For the myth of the strong black woman, see Wallace 1979 and Gillespie 1978. See also Collins 1990; June Jordan and Bernice Johnson Reagon 1981,

quoted in Smith 1983, xxvii; Dorothy Height, reported by Ferguson in Lerner [1970] 1972, 591; Tate 1992.

8. Dara Abubakari (Virginia E. Y. Collins), 1970, in Lerner 1972, 586. Robert Staples, generalizing from the activist to the nonactivist population, concluded: "At the root of the Black woman's rejection of the women's liberation movement are the different historical experiences she has encountered" (1973, 168–69). Frances Beal also concluded that "in all too many cases" "the women's liberation movement as a subversive phenomenon [is] in opposition to the interests of the black struggle as a whole" (1975, 8). See also Staples 1979 and Lorde's [1979] 1984a response.

9. On the NBFO, see Walker [1974] 1983b; Wallace [1975] 1990; Davis 1988; reports in *Ms.*, May 1974, 97 ff., and August 1974, 4 ff.; and *off our backs,* September 1973, 9, October 1973, 2 ff., December–January 1974, 2 ff., February 1974, 2 ff., and March 1974, 9 ff. A full history of this organization remains to be written, but for an impressive beginning, see Roberts 1996, from which I have drawn in this paragraph, and White 1999.

10. See, e.g., Shreve 1989, ch. 2 ("The Click").

11. See also hooks 1984, 10: "black women, as well as other groups of women who live daily in oppressive situations, often acquire an awareness of patriarchal politics from their lived experience, just as they develop strategies of resistance (even though they may not resist on a sustained or organized basis)." Dara Abubakari had much the same analysis in 1970: "There are only two kinds of oppressed people in this country, and that is black people and women. Still, the struggle of black women and white women is not the same. Because the white woman is oppressed and only now realizing her oppression" (in Lerner 1972, 586).

12. Center for the American Woman and Politics, Rutgers University, 1991. The survey question read, "I am going to read you a list of labels that some people reject, but others use to describe themselves. For each, we would like to know whether you do or do not identify with the label: . . . Feminist" white $n = 539$, black $n = 32$. I would like to thank Debra Dodson at the Center for the American Woman and Politics for providing these figures. The differences by race might well disappear after controlling for party identification and liberal-conservative ideology. Black women legislators are more likely to be Democrats and liberals, and legislators with these identifications are more likely to be feminist.

13. See sources collected in Lewis 1977, esp. 339 n. 2.

14. Harris and Associates 1972, 2 (survey described as "1971"; no exact dates or *n*s given). The next year, 1972 (survey described throughout as "1972," but actually done "at the close of 1971"; ibid., iii), the figures were 62% of black women ($n = 330$) and 45% of white ($n = 2,580$) ($p < .001$). In the 1972 survey black women were also more likely than white to "favor organizations to strengthen women's participation in politics" (63% vs. 50%, $p < .001$, p. 21) and to agree that "this country would be better off if women had more to say about politics" (73% vs. 54%, $p < .001$, p. 15). They were also more likely to have reported "frequently" thinking, "To get ahead in this world a woman has to be twice as good at what she does as a man is" (36% vs. 25%, $p < .001$, p. 9) and "If I had been a man, I would have gotten a lot further in this world" (17% vs. 8%, $p <$

.001, p. 9). Here and in subsequent analyses I report these percentages on a base that includes "don't know" responses. Eliminating don't-know responses would raise the "feminist" percentages overall and in most cases also increase the degree to which black women support the feminist movement and feminist positions more than whites.

15. Harris and Associates 1972, 4 ($p < .001$); also reported in hooks 1981, 148. Many activists, however, were not aware of or did not emphasize this support at the grass roots. From the perspective of an activist, as Barbara Smith reports, "In 1974, it took a great deal of courage for Black women to assert that they were Black feminists. Most African-Americans considered the mere act of addressing sexual politics to be divisive—an attack upon the Black community and especially upon Black men" (Smith 1993, 269; see also Cooper 1971, 521).

16. Gallup, February 5–11, 1986: women only, $n = 1,009$. The place in the interview schedule at which the question appeared undoubtedly helped raise the number of women who reported themselves as feminist. Before asking about feminism, the Gallup organization first asked four questions on issues that affect women: "Would you favor or oppose making it more difficult for women to get an abortion?" (favor 39%, oppose 53%, no opinion 8%); "Would you favor or oppose special efforts to hire and promote women because of past discrimination—even if it means putting them ahead of qualified men?" (favor 40%, oppose 55%, no opinion 5%); "Would you favor or oppose adding an Equal Rights Amendment to the U.S. Constitution which would prohibit discrimination on the basis of sex?" (favor 73%, oppose 21%, no opinion 6%); "Do you agree or disagree that sexually explicit movies, video cassettes, and books lead some people to lose respect for women?" (agree 77%, disagree 19%, no opinion 4%). Having thus procured the assent of 73% of the women being interviewed to at least one feminist policy, the interviewer then asked, "Next I would like to ask you some questions about the women's movement and feminism. . . . First, do you consider yourself to be a strong feminist, a feminist, not a feminist, or an anti-feminist?" Because they had just expressed a positive opinion on the ERA, a well-known feminist issue, some respondents may have felt tempted to align subsequently with the feminist label. The wording of the feminism question also undoubtedly helped raise the numbers reporting feminist. The set of proffered answers to this question has no neutral midpoint. "Not a feminist" appears on the "anti-feminist" side of the center, encouraging those respondents to choose "feminist" who otherwise might not spontaneously have adopted a "feminist" label for themselves but did not want to think of themselves as against feminism. Because these two factors encouraged respondents in the 1986 survey to identify themselves as feminists, this survey cannot be used as a first time point in comparison to later, differently worded, surveys such as that of Yankelovich Clancy Shulman, October 23–25, 1989 (contra, e.g., Faludi 1991, 465). When the Louis Harris survey organization used the same wording with no neutral midpoint in 1995, it produced a total of 51% "feminist" among women respondents.

17. Black women $n = 104$; white women $n = 876$. For 69% vs. 55%, $p < .01$; for 27% vs. 8%, $p < .001$.

18. Gallup, April 21, 1987; black women $n = 389$, white women $n = 1,693$. For 63% vs. 50%, $p < .001$; for 19% vs. 8%, $p < .001$. This question was repeated in 1989 and 1994. In 1989, 54% of black women vs. 48% of white women leaned toward feminism

(choosing 6 or above; not a statistically significant difference) and 28% of black women vs. 11% of white women chose "feminist" as a "perfect" description for them ($p < .001$; Princeton Survey Research Associates December 18–21, 1989; $n = 1,284$; black women weighted $n = 208$, white women weighted $n = 1,249$). In 1994, 51% of black women vs. 48% of whites leaned toward feminism (not statistically significant) and 22% of black women vs. 9% of white women chose "feminist" as a "perfect" description for them ($p < .01$; Princeton Survey Research Associates March 16–21, 1994; $n = 2,001$; black women $n = 95$, white women $n = 866$). In all three years, responses clumped at "5," suggesting that many respondents saw that as a halfway point between the two extremes. I thank Diane Colasanto of PSRA for making available the 1989 figures.

19. Yankelovich Clancy Shulman, October 23–25, 1989, women only; white women $n = 840$, black women $n = 99$, $p < .05$. On the same survey, 28% of black women called themselves a "strong supporter" of the "women's movement," compared to 16% of white women, $p < .01$.

20. Yankelovich Clancy Shulman, February 20, 1992, "Do you consider yourself to be a feminist?" black women $n = 68$ (29% feminist), white women $n = 498$ (29% feminist); Yankelovich Clancy Shulman, August 25–27, 1992, same wording, black women $n = 55$ (35% feminist), white women $n = 596$ (31% feminist); Gallup, October 10–11, 1991, "Do you consider yourself a feminist, or not?" black women $n = 32$ (47% feminist), white women $n = 308$ (33% feminist); Gallup, December 17–18, 1992, women only, same wording, black $n = 43$ (30% feminist), white $n = 673$ (33% feminist); National Election Study (NES) pre- and postelection survey 1992 (enhanced with 1990 and 1991 data), "Do you think of yourself as a feminist or not?" $n = 2,485$; black women $n = 193$ (35% feminist), white women $n = 1,092$ (22% feminist). Summed, these surveys yield a total of black women $n = 391$ (35% feminist) vs. white women $n = 3,167$ (28% feminist), $p < .01$. I am grateful to Keeting Holland of Yankelovich Clancy Shulman for making available figures from their 1992 survey.

21. General Social Survey, February 1–May 25, 1996, $n = $ c. 1,500, black women $n = 139$, white women $n = 645$, "Do you think of yourself as a feminist?" difference not statistically significant; CBS News, September 18–20, 1997, $n = 1,051$, black women $n = 60$, white women $n = 480$, "Do you consider yourself to be a feminist, or not?"

22. On a more regional level, the Chicago surveys from 1992, 1993, and 1994 showed fewer black women than white calling themselves feminist. This reversal remains unexplained, as other surveys do not show reversals or even decreases in the black-white gap in urban areas.

23. *Webster's Second New International Dictionary* (1935) gives as its first definition of *feminism:* "Feminine character or characteristics." King (1973) adopts this definition, using "non-feminist" as a synonym for "non-feminine."

24. The full question was worded as follows:

When you answered the previous question about being a feminist, did you have in mind that a feminist is someone

a) who is very feminine [5% answered in the affirmative]
b) who believes in equality between men and women [46%]

c) who wants to keep—not change—traditional roles between men and women [8%]

d) who is a radical, going overboard on the issues and trying to divide women from men [30%]

e) something else? [6%]

f) (volunteered) uncertain [5%]

Northwestern University Chicago Area Survey (CAS), May 2–June 16, 1993, $n = 1,053$ English-speaking residents of Cook, DuPage, and Lake Counties, Illinois; CAS April 24–June 5, 1994, $n = 1,111$. Black women were more likely than white to define feminism with definitions (a) and (c), but because those who gave definition (a) were *more* likely than others to consider themselves feminists and those who gave definition (c) were *less* likely to consider themselves feminists, these differences nearly canceled one another out. If we compare only those who defined a feminist as someone "who believes in equality between men and women" to the whole sample, the gap between black and white women in calling themselves feminist changes by only 3 percentage points.

25. Data collected by Dara Strolevich, with Jane Mansbridge and Leonie Huddy, from *off our backs,* a feminist journal operating continuously throughout this period, show that the word "feminist" or "feminism" appears first in 1970 and increases sharply in use after that date. Other sources, such as the names of women's collectives, also indicate 1970 for the introduction of the term.

26. Gallup, February 5–11, 1986: women only, black women $n = 89$, white women $n = 748$, $p < .001$. In the same survey, 44% of black women but only 20% of white women said they thought the women's movement had done "very well" in improving the lives of "working-class women" ($p < .001$). Differences in class followed a somewhat similar pattern. Women with high-school degrees or less ($n = 546$) were more likely than college-educated women ($n = 184$) to think that the women's movement had done "very well" in improving the lives of working-class women (30% vs. 11%, $p < .001$), and were as likely as the college educated to think that the women's movement had done very well in improving their own lives (20% vs. 21%).

27. In the 1996 GSS, the question was worded differently, eliminating the categories "very well, fairly well, or not well," which in the 1986 survey had seemed to encourage both black and white respondents to cluster in the middle category, and asking instead if the women's movement had "improved" one's life, made it "worse," or had "no effect." 1996 GSS: black women $n = 139$, white women $n = 645$, difference not statistically significant.

28. CBS News, September 18–20, 1997, $n = 1,051$, black women $n = 60$, white women $n = 480$. For 88% vs. 64%, $p < .001$; for 60% vs. 42%, $p < .01$.

29. Gallup February 28–March 2, 1989, no ns given. The 1989 Yankelovich Clancy Shulman survey also asked, "Do you have a favorable impression of the National Organization of [*sic*] Women, also known as NOW?" 54% of black women ($n = 99$) said yes vs. 67% of white women ($n = 839$), $p < .01$. When the same survey asked, "Tell me whether you think each of these groups is generally in touch or out of touch with the average American woman. . . . The National Organization of [*sic*] Women, NOW," 77% of black women ($n = 99$) considered NOW "in touch" vs. 64% of white women ($n = 840$), $p = < .01$.

30. One plausible reason might be simply that black women have traditionally been more liberal than white women, and more likely to belong to the Democratic Party. Liberals and Democrats are more likely to consider themselves feminist. Yet on the two surveys that have both enough cases and the appropriate questions, among Democratic women blacks were still more likely to consider themselves feminist than whites (Yankelovich Clancy Shulman 1989: black Democratic women 51% feminist [$n = 71$] vs. white Democratic women 36% [$n = 293$], $p < .05$; NES 1992: black Democratic women 46% feminist [$n = 72$] vs. white Democratic women 34% [$n = 210$], $p < .05$). Comparing only those who called themselves "liberals" does eliminate the gap (NES 1992: black liberal women 37% feminist [$n = 43$] vs. white liberal women 39% [$n = 225$]).

31. Rodgers-Rose 1980a, 33; see also for 1960, *Statistical Abstract of the United States* 1973, table 175, p. 115; for 1970 and 1990, *Statistical Abstract of the United States* 1992, table 220, p. 144. The reasons for the closer approach to gender parity among blacks include black women's expectation of greater labor force participation and black men's proportionally reduced returns to education compared to white men (until the 1970s, when the returns to schooling for black men became at least comparable to those of white men; see Smith and Welch 1989).

32. See, e.g., ABC/Washington Post, September 1986. More recently, on the 1996 General Social Survey black men were considerably more likely (40%, $n = 62$) than white men (25%, $n = 538$, $p < .05$) to say that the women's movement had "improved" their own lives. On the somewhat smaller 1997 CBS News survey, black men were also more likely than white to have a favorable opinion of the women's movement (black 91%, $n = 43$; white 64%, $n = 405$; difference not statistically significant). Black men are particularly more likely than white to think that women have been discriminated against in finding jobs (1997 CBS) or to think that employers should make special efforts to hire and promote qualified women (1996 GSS). When it comes to calling themselves "feminist," the differences are smaller and inconsistent (1997 CBS News: 23% of black men considered themselves feminists vs. 13% of white men; 1992 NES: 22% of black men [$n = 59$] vs. 17% of white men [$n = 485$]; 1996 GSS: 10% of black men [$n = 62$] and 12% of white men [$n = 538$], none of the differences being statistically significant). The difference between these results and other measures of support for the women's movement may be that the word "feminist" is often associated with being a woman as well as with supporting the feminist movement. For this reason, some surveys do not even ask men if they consider themselves feminist, but substitute a formulation such as "Do you support the women's movement?" (e.g., Gallup 1987).

33. The exact figures are (from 1993 and 1994 respectively) 40% and 39% of white men, 44% and 53% of black men, 52% and 51% of white women, and 67% and 65% of black women. The *n*s and significance for the following comparisons are: white women 411/white men 284 ($p < .01$); black women 144/black men 71 ($p < .01$); white women/ black women $p < .001$.

34. For 1993 and 1994, the percentages of black women with less than four years of high school are 48 and 59%, and for black women with a college degree 81 and 86%. Although the number of black women in the combined sample is small ($n = 144$), the association with education is strong enough to reach statistical significance at the .05 level.

35. A section in one of Donna Kate Rushin's poems (1983, 256) conveys one experience of the relation between education and having others consider one "too independent":

The Soc and Psych books say you're domineering
And you've been to enough
Sisters-Are-Not-Taking-Care-Of-Business discussions
To know where you went wrong
It's decided it had to be the day you decided to go to school.

36. Black female verbal defiance has produced a relevant folklore (see Jacobs [1861] 1988, 47, 61, 91–92, 115–16; Braxton 1989, 30 ff.; Carby 1987, 56). Mansbridge 1993a finds proverbs in many cultures denouncing women for talking too much, even though whenever quantitative studies have been conducted (all among whites in the United States) men dominated the conversation in mixed-gender groups. See also Joseph and Lewis 1981, 113, 123, on mothers warning their daughters to avoid depending on men, and Rodgers-Rose 1980b, 259, on black men valuing independence in women.

37. For 1993 and 1994 combined, black feminist $n = 112$, nonfeminist $n = 185$; white feminist $n = 328$, nonfeminist $n = 413$ ($p < .001$).

38. For 1993 and 1994 combined, married white women $n = 370$, divorced $n = 92$ ($p < .001$); married black women $n = 56$, divorced $n = 44$ (not statistically significant).

39. For 1993 and 1994 combined, full-time white women $n = 366$ vs. part-time $n = 123$ ($p < .001$), vs. homemaker $n = 101$ ($p < .001$); full-time black women $n = 141$ vs. part-time $n = 28$ ($p < .05$), vs. homemaker $n = 27$ ($p < .05$).

40. For the extensive literature on "elite-mass" differences, see the classic McClosky et al. 1960 and Converse 1964 and the more recent Miller and Jennings with Farah 1986.

41. See Mansbridge 1996 (and citations therein) on the functions and liabilities of safe spaces and political enclaves.

References

Beal, Frances M. 1975. "Slave of a Slave No More: Black Women in the Struggle." *The Black Scholar* 6, no. 6:2–10.

Braxton, Joanne M. 1989. *Black Women Writing Autobiography.* Philadelphia: Temple University Press.

Brownmiller, Susan. 1984. *Femininity.* New York: Fawcett Columbine.

Carby, Hazel. 1987. *Reconstructing Womanhood.* Oxford: Oxford University Press.

Collins, Patricia Hill. 1990. *Black Feminist Thought.* New York: Harper and Row.

Converse, Philip E. 1964. "The Nature of Belief Systems in Mass Publics." In *Ideology and Discontent,* edited by David E. Apter. New York: Free Press.

Cooper, Jean. 1971. "Women's Liberation and the Black Woman." *Journal of Home Economics* 63:521–23.

Crenshaw, Kimberle. 1991. "Mapping the Margins: Intersectionality, Identity Politics, and Violence against Women." *Stanford Law Review* 43:1241–99.

davenport, doris. 1983. "The Pathology of Racism." In *This Bridge Called My Back,* edited by Cherríe Moraga and Gloria Anzaldúa. New York: Kitchen Table/Women of Color Press.

Davis, Beverly. 1988. "To Seize the Moment: A Retrospective on the National Black Feminist Organization." *Sage* 5:43–47.

Echols, Alice. 1989. *Daring to Be Bad.* Minneapolis: University of Minnesota Press.

Evans, Mari. 1980. *I Am a Black Woman.* New York: Morrow.

Evans, Sara. 1979. *Personal Politics.* New York: Knopf.

Faludi, Susan. 1991. *Backlash.* New York: Crown.

Freeman, Jo. 1975. *The Politics of Women's Liberation.* New York: McKay.

Gillespie, Marcia Ann. 1978. "The Myth of the Strong Black Woman." In *Feminist Frameworks,* edited by Alison M. Jaggar and Paula S. Rothenberg. New York: McGraw-Hill.

Gilmore, Glenda Elizabeth. 1996. *Gender and Jim Crow.* Chapel Hill: University of North Carolina Press.

Harris, Louis, and Associates. 1972. *The 1972 Virginia Slims American Women's Opinion Poll.* New York: Louis Harris and Associates.

hooks, bell. 1981. "Racism and Feminism: The Issue of Accountability." In *Ain't I a Woman.* Boston: South End.

———. 1984. *Feminist Theory from Margin to Center.* Boston: South End.

———. 1990. *Yearning.* Boston: South End.

Hull, Gloria T., Patricia Bell Scott, and Barbara Smith. 1982. *All the Women Are White, All the Blacks Are Men, But Some of Us Are Brave.* Old Westbury, N.Y.: Feminist Press.

Hurston, Zora Neale. [1937] 1990. *Their Eyes Were Watching God.* New York: Harper and Row.

Jacobs, Harriet. [1861] 1988. *Incidents in the Life of a Slave Girl.* New York: Oxford University Press.

Jones, Jacqueline. 1985. *Labor of Love, Labor of Sorrow.* New York: Basic.

Jordan, June, and Bernice Johnson Reagon. 1981. "Oughta Be a Woman." In *Good News.* Chicago: Flying Fish Records, Songtalk Publishing Co.

Joseph, Gloria I., and Jill Lewis. 1981. *Common Differences.* Boston: South End.

King, Deborah K. [1988] 1990. "Multiple Jeopardy, Multiple Consciousness: The Context of a Black Feminist Ideology." In *Black Women in America,* edited by Micheline R. Malson, Elisabeth Mudimbe-Boyi, Jean F. O'Barr, and Mary Wyer. Chicago: University of Chicago Press.

King, Mae C. 1973. "The Politics of Sexual Stereotypes." *The Black Scholar* 4:12–23.

———. 1993. "Black Women's Breakthrough into Clerical Work: An Occupational Tipping Model." *Journal of Economic Issues* 27:1097–1125.

Ladner, Joyce A. [1971] 1995. *Tomorrow's Tomorrow.* Lincoln: University of Nebraska Press.

Lerner, Gerda, ed. 1972. *Black Women in White America: A Documentary History.* New York: Pantheon.

Lewis, Diane K. 1977. "A Response to Inequality: Black Women, Racism, and Sexism." *Signs* 3:339–61.

Lorde, Audre. [1979] 1984a. "Feminism and Black Liberation." In *Sister Outsider.* Freedom, Calif.: Crossing Press.

―――. [1979] 1984b. "The Master's Tools Will Never Dismantle the Master's House." In *Sister Outsider.* Freedom, Calif.: Crossing Press.

―――. [1980] 1984c. "Age, Race, Class and Sex: Women Redefining Difference." In *Sister Outsider.* Freedom, Calif.: Crossing Press.

Mansbridge, Jane. 1986. *Why We Lost the ERA.* Chicago: University of Chicago Press.

―――. 1993a. "Feminism and Democratic Community." In *Democratic Community: NOMOS XXXV,* edited by John W. Chapman and Ian Shapiro. New York: New York University Press.

―――. 1993b. "The Role of Discourse in the Feminist Movement." Paper presented at the annual meeting of the American Political Science Association, Washington, September.

―――. 1996. "Using Power/Fighting Power: The Polity." In *Democracy and Difference,* edited by Seyla Benhabib. Princeton: Princeton University Press.

Mansbridge, Jane, and Katherine Tate. 1992. "Race Trumps Gender: The Thomas Nomination in the Black Community." *P.S.: Political Science and Politics* 25:488–92.

McClosky, Herbert, et al. 1960. "Issue Conflict and Consensus Among Party Leaders and Followers." *American Political Science Review* 5:406–27.

McCray, Carrie Allen. 1980. "The Black Woman and Family Roles." In *The Black Woman,* edited by La Frances Rodgers-Rose. Beverly Hills: Sage.

Miller, Warren E., and M. Kent Jennings, with Barbara G. Farah. 1986. *Parties in Transition.* New York: Sage.

Moraga, Cherríe, and Gloria Anzaldúa. 1983. *This Bridge Called My Back: Writings of Radical Women of Color.* New York: Kitchen Table/Women of Color Press.

O'Reilly, Jane. [1972] 1980. "Click! The Housewife's Moment of Truth." In *The Girl I Left Behind.* New York: Macmillan.

Richie, Beth. 1996. *Compelled to Crime.* New York: Routledge.

Ried, Willie Mae. 1976. "Changing Attitudes Among Black Women." *Black Women's Struggle for Equality.* New York: Pathfinder. (Expanded from articles in *The International Socialist Review,* August 15, 1975, September 5, 1975, and April 30, 1976.)

Roberts, Tamara. 1996. "Lost to History: The Rise and Fall of the National Black Feminist Organization." Unpublished manuscript, Northwestern University.

Rodgers-Rose, La Frances. 1980a. "Some Demographic Characteristics of the Black Woman: 1940 to 1975." In *The Black Woman,* edited by La Frances Rodgers-Rose. Beverly Hills: Sage.

―――. 1980b. "Dialectics of Black Male-Female Relationships." In *The Black Woman,* edited by La Frances Rodgers-Rose. Beverly Hills: Sage.

Rushin, Donna Kate. 1983. "The Tired Poem: Last Letter from a Typical Unemployed Black Professional Woman." In *Home Girls: A Black Feminist Anthology,* edited by Barbara Smith. New York: Kitchen Table/Women of Color Press.

Shange, Ntozake. 1977. *For Colored Girls Who Have Considered Suicide When the Rainbow Is Enuf: A Choreopoem.* New York: Macmillan.

Shreve, Anita. 1989. *Women Together, Women Alone.* New York: Fawcett Columbine.

Smith, Barbara. 1983. Introduction to *Home Girls,* edited by Barbara Smith. New York: Kitchen Table/Women of Color Press.

———. 1993. "Combahee River Collective." In *Black Women in America: An Historical Encyclopedia,* vol. 1, edited by Darlene Clark Hine et al. New York: Carlson.

Smith, Barbara, and Beverly Smith. [1980] 1983. "Across the Kitchen Table: A Sister-to-Sister Dialogue." In *This Bridge Called My Back,* edited by Cherríe Moraga and Gloria Anzaldúa. New York: Kitchen Table/Women of Color Press.

Smith, James P., and Finis R. Welch. 1989. "Black Economic Progress after Myrdal." *Journal of Economic Literature* 27:519–64.

Staples, Robert. 1973. *The Black Woman in America.* Chicago: Nelson Hall.

———. 1979. "The Myth of Black Macho: A Response to Angry Black Feminists." *The Black Scholar* 10 (6–7): 24–32.

Tate, Katharine. 1992. "Invisible Woman." *The American Prospect,* winter, 74–81.

Walker, Alice. [1972] 1973. "Burial." In *Revolutionary Petunias and Other Poems.* New York: Harvest/Harcourt Brace Jovanovich.

———. 1981. "Advancing Luna—and Ida B. Wells." In *You Can't Keep a Good Woman Down.* New York: Harcourt Brace Jovanovich.

———. [1971] 1983a. "Coretta King Revisited." In *In Search of Our Mothers' Gardens.* New York: Harvest/Harcourt Brace Jovanovich.

———. [1974] 1983b. "A Letter to the Editor of *Ms.*" In *In Search of Our Mothers' Gardens.* New York: Harvest/Harcourt Brace Jovanovich.

———. [1979] 1983c. "One Child of One's Own: A Meaningful Digression Within the Work(s)." In *In Search of Our Mothers' Gardens.* New York: Harvest/Harcourt Brace Jovanovich.

———. [1979] 1983d. "To the *Black Scholar.*" In *In Search of Our Mothers' Gardens.* New York: Harvest/Harcourt Brace Jovanovich.

———. [1982] 1983e. "If the Present Looks Like the Past." In *In Search of Our Mothers' Gardens.* New York: Harvest/Harcourt Brace Jovanovich.

———. 1983f. "Womanist." In *In Search of Our Mothers' Gardens.* New York: Harvest/Harcourt Brace Jovanovich.

Wallace, Michele. 1979. *Black Macho and the Myth of the Superwoman.* New York: Dial.

———. [1975] 1990. "Anger in Isolation: A Black Feminist's Search for Sisterhood." In *Invisibility Blues.* New York: Verso.

Washington, Cynthia. 1977. "We Started from Different Ends of the Spectrum." *Southern Exposure,* winter, 14–18.

White, Deborah Gray. 1999. *Too Heavy a Load.* New York: Norton.

"dis beat disrupts": rap, ideology, and black political attitudes

michael c. dawson

This beat obstructs the justice of the peace
And the quiet in your neighborhood tonight.
GEORGE CLINTON

Introduction

Can a new black discourse, a new black center for critical debate over the future of the race be rebuilt on a new jack popular culture? Or is placing any political faith in this new culture
at best ridiculously naïve, perhaps even dangerous, as argue
the many critics of contemporary black popular culture? Certainly not all black popular culture is argued to be either the
potential site for political resistance or the most backward
and/or banal of black artistic endeavors. Black classical music,
or jazz, is popular among political activists of most persuasions
even if it doesn't now have the same political status as it did
during the civil rights and black power eras. During the 1960s,
however, writers such as Amiri Baraka (then known as the Pu-
litzer prize–winning author LeRoi Jones) claimed when talking about the new generation of jazz artists "there was a kind
of race pride or consciousness that animated the musicians
and their music," and Frank Kofsky could equally plausibly
argue, "Bebop can therefore be viewed in its social aspect as
a manifesto for rebellious black musicians unwilling to submit
to further exploitation" (Jones 1967, 209; Kofsky 1970, 57).
Cultural critics such as Tricia Rose believe that rap is this generation's answer to bebop. She argues that rap continues "the
long history of black cultural subversion and social critique in
music and performance" (Rose 1994, 99). For Rose, not only

does "dis beat disrupt," but rap represents "the central cultural vehicle for open social reflection on poverty, fear of adulthood, the desire for absent fathers, frustrations about black male sexism, female sexual desires, daily rituals of life as an unemployed teen hustler, safe sex, raw anger, violence, and childhood memories" (Rose 1994, 18). Rap provides a political outlet for the disenfranchised black inner-city and "alternative interpretations of key social events such as the Gulf War, the Los Angeles uprising, police brutality, censorship efforts, and community-based education" (Rose 1994, 18).

But great controversy surrounds the music, and detractors of the new black music abound. Adolph Reed starkly represents the point of view of the detractors of this artistic project when he bleakly argues that even the so-called political wing of hip-hop culture "spew garbled compounds of half-truth, distortion, Afrocentric drivel, and crackerbarrel wisdom, as often as not shot through with reactionary prejudices" (Reed 1992, 228). While Reed is generally suspicious of any claim that artistic production created for capitalist markets can play a progressive role, he says that the "black power consumerism" of the 1960s, while "parasitic" on black power ideology and the black power movement, was at least continually critiqued by both. The current black artistic consumerist fad, according to Reed, is neither critiqued nor influenced by a dynamic mass movement.

This view is not exactly compatible with that of Michael Dyson and other defenders of the more particularly political veins of rap. When discussing Public Enemy, the most famous/popular political rap group, Dyson proclaims, "PE has maintained its integrity and vision. . . . *It Takes a Nation of Millions to Hold Us Back* lunges far beyond anything in rap's past to help secure its future. . . . *It Takes a Nation* gave the genre ideological vitality" (Dyson 1996, 166). Houston Baker waxes equally poetic when he declares: "rappers had been prophetic with respect to tensions between black urban youth and metropolitan police authorities" (Baker 1993, 33–34). For these scholars, the new black culture represents the cutting edge of a rejuvenated critical black public sphere—a space that would provide black Americans not only the ability to critique the racist ills of American society, but also a social space that facilitates the process of consciousness raising necessary for rebuilding the black movement. For Baker, this is particularly true for black youth. He sees it as potentially the last "outpost of teenage redemption" (Baker 1993). Our youth may yet be saved by rap.[1]

A middle ground is taken by Ransby and Matthews in their essay "Black Popular Culture and the Transcendence of Patriarchal Illusions" (1993). They also caution us that even political rappers popularize backward points of view when they argue, "Even lyrical brews concocted with a distinctly militant flavour are frequently laced with enough counter-productive and counter-revolutionary messages, especially with regard to gender and the status of women, to dull their potentially radical edge" (Ransby and Matthews 1993). While they make the common and correct point that popular culture, whether it's in the form of wearing the "X" symbolizing Malcolm X or listening to the "undirected rage" of political rap, is no substitute for political action, they also point out that the vicious attacks on women have their roots not only in previous black cultural forms such as the blues and the toasts, but in American popular culture more generally. Such sentiments, including the less violent ones that attempt to relegate black women to a secondary role, they point out, potentially rob black mobilizations of half their potential force and leadership.

These visions of the relationship between rap and the black community are radically different from each other. Certainly the Dyson/Baker vision of rap as a site for contestation and black renewal clashes with Reed's view that any belief that rap can provide an impetus to political knowledge, let alone a guide to action, is fraudulent. In the remainder of this essay I outline and test several sets of assertions about the relationship rap music has to black political ideology (specifically to black nationalism and feminism) and to African-American political beliefs. The survey-based analyses demonstrate that both exposure to rap music and the belief that it constitutes an important resource of the black community directly and indirectly play a substantial role in shaping black political opinion. The normative and practical consequences of such a relationship are considered in the conclusion.

Why Rap?

Why focus on rap? Rap is certainly the most visible and debated black art form in contemporary America. Youth of all races have embraced rap and rap artists. It is easily accessible on radio and the television. Movie soundtracks routinely and prominently feature rap artists. Sports superstars cut rap records, including some Super Bowl–winning teams. Rap artists have become television and movie stars in their own right. Sadly, rap music has garnered even more attention in late 1996 and early 1997 due to the murders of two of the biggest gangsta rappers, Tupac Shakur and the Notorious B.I.G.

On the other hand, it is not just right-wing forces and the vice president's wife that attack rap as being detrimental to the black community. Religious leaders such as Calvin Butts have led protests against rap as a damaging force in the black community. Rappers themselves argue that they are both serious providers of needed knowledge for the black community and a source of inspiration for at least the young. Controversial and popular rapper Ice Cube describes the role of rappers: "We call ourselves underground street reporters. We just tell it how we see it, nothing more, nothing less" (Kelley 1994, 190).

In concentrating on rap there are four sets of claims that will be evaluated.

These claims add specificity to the disputes that we observed between a number of scholars of rap. Each set of claims is discussed before the results of the analyses are evaluated.

The first set of claims asserts that rappers are the new "griots" of contemporary African America.[2] As the "CNN" of the black community, rap music plays a vital role in rebuilding a dynamic black public sphere. One aspect of the functioning of a critical public sphere is providing the timely and accurate information necessary to make informed political decisions. From this perspective, rappers as modern griots would provide a "problack" source of information that in turn provides a necessary but not sufficient basis for forging a vibrant black civil society within which ideological debate would flourish and political mobilization proceed.

Second, it is claimed that rap music provides a contested, critical space that contributes to the political education of the black community. Further, rappers themselves are *ideological partisans* who attempt to persuade their audience, the black community (or at least the "righteous" sectors of the black community), to a "correct" ideological orientation. If the first set of claims at least implies neutrality (we're just "telling it like it is"), the second perspective requires a critical political viewpoint.

The third assertion is that the economics of the production and marketing of rap constricts the ability of rap artists to make a positive contribution to the black community. Others argue that the rap music provides the most "authentic" source of commentary on the economic devastation of the black community and its most disadvantaged residents.

Finally, it is claimed that the gender politics within rap, despite the presence of strong women rappers such as Queen Latifah, is overwhelmingly reactionary and contributes to the high level of misogyny, homophobia, and anti–black feminist sentiment within the black community. Some have argued that gangsta rap in particular contributes to both sexually oriented violence and generalized violence within the black community. Intracommunity violence, as well as misogyny and homophobia, is argued to do grave harm to the ability to build a black public sphere capable of including the viewpoints of the entire black community.

THE NEW GRIOTS? One claim that permeates the discourse about rap is that rappers are the new griots of inner-city America. Rap music is considered to be part of a long tradition of black music that features "the hip musician, the blowing trickster, [who] has learned many lessons, musical and otherwise, from [the] African god of interpretation" (Floyd 1995, 140). As observers of black culture from Malcolm X to Toni Morrison have observed, improvisation is a key aspect of this tradition. As is the case for much of black culture and art, race is "relentlessly foregrounded" in rap (Sexton 1995). Just as many jazz musicians during the black power era composed music that highlighted political events and figures (Mingus's "Fables of Faubus," Shepp's "Sing a Song of Songhai [My Lai]," and Hutcherson's composition dedicated to "Malcolm, Martin, and Marcus" provide excellent examples), a good number of rap artists focus some of their music on political figures and events from contemporary black politics. Just as Shepp argued that politically oriented jazz was influenced by the nationalist movement of the 1960s, rap is primarily influenced by contemporary nationalism, celebrating nationalist organizations such as the Nation of Islam and nationalist-sponsored events such as the Million Man March.

Like the griots, rappers and their supporters argue that they provide an alternative news tradition that tells those who would listen what *really* is happening in and to the black community. Chuck D of Public Enemy and Ice Cube both claim that "rap has done nothing but bring people together" (Ice Cube 1994, 159). Thus rap has become an integral part of a grapevine that is constantly critiquing the state of American race relations. Rap reveals what are seen as the vile and violent actions of the police and the behavior of corrupt politicians, black and white. It is an information network where CIA involvement in the ghetto drug trade is taken as a given, not as news that needs to be questioned. It is also an artistic medium that, much like earlier jazz styles such as bebop and avant-garde jazz, attempts to emphasize its black roots while resisting incorporation into what is seen as a banal mainstream (Kofsky 1970).

These griots, these "prophets of rage," are argued by their supporters not to equally represent the entire black community, but instead are particularly considered to be the voice of the most disadvantaged, downtrodden, and class-conscious segments of the black community (Dyson 1993; Rose 1994). Tricia Rose asserts that "rap music is a black cultural expression that prioritizes black voices from the margins of urban America" (Rose 1994, 2). The critics are wrong, she and others argue, when they state that rap is intended primarily for a white teenage middle-class suburban audience. The extreme emphasis on neighborhood authenticity, the large underground circulation of music, and pride in remaining true to one's roots are all signs that rap remains authentic black music despite the fact that rap like many other forms of black art has a large white audience (Baker 1993; Dyson 1993; Rose 1994, 1995).

The propensity of rap to challenge the boundaries not only of social and artistic acceptability but the political foundations of this nation's hegemonic discourse provides rap its cutting social edge. Rose, for example, argues that Public Enemy is politically so effective because "what makes them 'prophets with a difference' is their ability to retain the mass mediated spotlight on the popular cultural stage and at the same time function as a voice of social critique and criticism" (Rose 1994, 101).

Critics point out there are several dangers associated with this ghetto-based information superhighway. Rose herself points out that when rightists such as George Will decide that the "violent fantasies" depicted in much gangsta rap are accurate, they use the rappers' own material to call for increased militarization of the black community (Rose 1994). Another problem is that many rappers such as Ice Cube, the Geto Boys, X-Clan, and numerous others assert that they have a monopoly on authenticity so that those who disagree with their view on the Million Man March, the role of women in the black community, attitudes toward the black queer community, or interracial love should be, to use the "metaphor" from both the Geto Boys and Professor Grif, burned alive. These "griots" cannot be viewed as neutral information sources providing information for black political debate. Their news can restrict both the ideological space within which debate occurs and who is "allowed" into the debate.

At the same time, Malveaux (1992) points out that a problem with ghettocentric rap is that the emphases on "tales from the hood" can shroud the complex web of electoral politics, military spending, debates over balanced budgets, and corporate decisions about where to locate work that shape much of the devastation of the nation's inner cities. While both Kelley and Malveaux demonstrate the economic devastation that has led to the sense of inner-city alienation so poignantly captured by the best rap artists, very few of these artists point the way forward. This is not particularly the job of artists, as many rappers remind us, and many political leaders whose job it is are doing little better. Many rap artists argue that if they can provide a wake-up call for the black community in their role as griot, they are providing a needed service.

THE POLITICS OF RAP MUSIC. A stronger claim is that rap contributes to building a black counterpublic by directly influencing African-Americans' ideological orientations and political attitudes. Rap music becomes a critical instrument for both political education and commentary. Black artists have claimed this role before. Jazz saxophonist Archie Shepp described the relationship between the jazz artists of his era and black politics: "Some of us are more bitter about the way things are going. We are only an extension of that entire civil rights–black Muslims–black nationalist movement that is taking place in America" (Kofsky 1970, 63). In the absence of such a movement, rappers have associated themselves with a variety of political efforts. Some groups such as the Fugees have worked with music industry political initiatives such as the "Rock the Vote" voter registration drive. There is significant support for nationalist efforts such as the Million Man March on the part of other rappers. Michael Franti of the Disposable Heroes debated public policy with Bill Moyers on television while Paris writes policy essays for the op-ed page of the *Washington Post* (Paris 1995). By and large, however, rap music and rap artists are divorced from ongoing political organizing and mobilization.

Politically oriented rap artists often provide two critical political functions.

First, they provide what Rose calls "a contemporary stage for the theater of the powerless. On this stage, rappers act out inversions of status hierarchies, tell alternative stories of contact with police and the education process, and draw portraits of contact with dominant groups in which the hidden transcripts inverts/subverts [*sic*] the public dominant transcript" (Rose 1994, 101). By making hidden transcripts partially public, they provide a function of political education by allowing shared oppression and resistance to be commonly understood, discussed, and acted upon. The other major function rappers have taken on for themselves is to highlight causes and political messages with which they agree. The Geto Boys in "The Resurrection" highlight several snippets of an interview in which Chicago gang leader Larry Hoover says that "real gangsters go to the polls, . . . [we're] the sleeping giant, . . . we're the ones that make a difference." PE often uses samples from Malcolm X, Minister Farrakhan, and other prominent nationalists in its songs. There is a noticeable lack of diversity in which movements and ideologies are promoted; various forms of nationalism take center stage. But that rappers are performing a political function in popularizing a set of leaders, organizations, policies, and ideologies is hard to deny.

In doing so they must walk a tightrope. Rose describes the tension that many rappers face in trying to negotiate between the demands that record companies and major corporate players like MTV make about content, and a desire to remain true to their own artistic and political vision. This is a common theme in the rappers' commentary as well. Ice T and Ice Cube have both written about these pressures, and it is a theme that is present in many of the tracks of Paris's *Guerrilla Funk* (Ice T 1995; Ice Cube 1995).

Commentators such as Boyd argue that these pressures are so great that political rap reached its height in 1988 with PE's release of *It Takes a Nation of Millions* (Boyd 1994). He argues that only a few rappers remained "true to the game" while under considerable corporate and social pressure. Further, Boyd argues, gangsta rap represents an explicit rejection of politics, and that even politically oriented rap needs to be concerned with more than just racial justice but must also take into account concerns with class, misogyny, and homophobia.

The last caution is one that is at the center of much of Reed's criticism of contemporary black popular culture. Reed has argued at length that this generation's version of political art blurs the line between style and ideology, that the only ones who benefit are various corporate entities that garner massive profits from the commodification of the artistic product, and the rappers' ideologies and political standpoints lack any critical edge and are often reactionary in content (Reed 1992). Reed also severely critiques those he sees as rap's scholarly accomplices in the cultural studies movement. He claims they propagate the view that artistic endeavor can substitute for the blood, sweat, and tears that make up "real" organizing for political change. He sees the celebration of these artistic forms as nothing less than accommodation with the fact of the continued political defeat of progressive forces. He sees the entire crew of political rappers, the ones that are celebrated even by other critics such as Boyd, as being politically worthless. The critical question for this study is not whether rap influences African-Americans to adopt "good" or "bad" politics, but whether it influences black political opinions at all, and, if so, what the political domains are where rap has most influence.

GETTING PAID. Another set of claims about rap is that it accentuates class divisions between those who have work and those who are scraping desperately to survive. For Houston Baker this produces a theme that is antiwork and alienated from the structures of the modern, postindustrial American economy (Baker 1993). Baker continues by stating that this orientation toward work and the economy makes rappers dangerous in the eyes of society's elite and the media.

Rose agrees, and argues that the media elite are caught in a contradiction of their own. They want to both censor political rap due to its ability to "destabilize the appearance of unanimity" and at the same time to enjoy the profits that rap generates. Public Enemy, Rose argues, was a breakthrough group precisely because it was able to soar to the top of the charts while promoting a generally progressive political message (Rose 1994).

Many of the rappers themselves are worried, however, by the corrosive effect that "getting paid" has on the content of many rap artists. Songs by the Fugees attacked rappers who "forgot Harlem," Ice Cube often attacked his previous colleagues from NWA for selling out and gangsta rap in general as being influenced by the market and not what's best for blacks, while Paris rails against both the rappers and the record companies that "push that wannabe new gangsta of the week on the street but ain't got a clue." He goes on to denounce white-controlled record companies that promote gangsta "fantasies" of black-on-black violence while refusing to market or distribute positive politically oriented rap.

The cynicism and alienation that are the product of decades of inner-city economic devastation are one of the clearest themes in contemporary rap music. As Malveaux reminds us quoting Camus, "Without work all life is rotten" (Malveaux 1992, 204). What is sometimes forgotten is that many rappers' emphasis on "getting paid" results in an enormously individualistic celebration of some of the most brutal and naked forms of capitalistic entrepreneurship—the capitalism of the robber baron, the pusher, and the pimp. What is masked in the ghetto fantasy featuring yet another crack dealer blowing away his competition is that the financial rewards that flow to the best rappers are the result of years of gaining technical and artistic expertise. They are the result of years of hard study and years of hard work. The emphasis on a relatively narrow definition of "getting paid" in most of the music could well serve to undermine rap's critical message.

RAP, GENDER, AND RACE. Clearly the most controversial area of rap is contained in its attitudes toward women. Although Rose and many others point out that there are a number of vigorous women performers, many of whom provide a stark alternative to the brutal misogyny of much of rap, critics justifiably point out that when it comes to airtime, sales, and virtually any other measure of exposure, male performers dominate, and with them usually comes a view of gender relationships that even rap's supporters like Robin Kelley label "offensive and chilling" (Kelley 1994, 185).

As critics such as Kelley and Henry detail, there is a long tradition of black cultural forms such as the blues, toasts, and dozens that feature both the "bad nigger" and rampant sexism (Henry 1990; Kelley 1994). Henry elaborates this point: "It would be simplistic and a mistake to argue that the 'Bad nigger' offers blacks as a group a viable vision of the future. For example, the obvious sexism of the toasts presents a wholly male perspective on entertainment and survival" (Henry 1990, 58). I would go somewhat further: the rhetoric of the Panthers in the 1960s was not dissimilar to the rhetoric of the more political rap groups, particularly vis-à-vis the police. Just as the police used this rhetoric to launch a vicious wave of attacks and assassinations against the Panthers, the revolutionary fantasies promoted by some rap artists are not only entirely gendered (we must protect "our" sisters) but more likely to lead to bloody disaster than political progress.

The emphases on attacking the character of black women have led some in the black community to call for a boycott of the artistic efforts of rappers. Reverend Butts of New York has led such a movement. Others such as Rose denounce "the cowardly rappers" who are disturbed about the misogynist trend in rap, but refuse to criticize their colleagues. Until rappers take responsibility for their attitudes toward women, they remain vulnerable to attack from multiple quarters and risk having their entire message dismissed.

The Effects of Rap Music on Black Public Opinion

If Reed and like-minded critics are right, exposure to rap should have one of two effects on black political opinion and preferences. First, rap should have very little effect in politicizing blacks when it comes to mobilizations against the structures of power that progressive critics find oppressing. So for example, a positive cultural force would influence African-Americans to take a critical stance toward America's large multinational corporations. Second, and even more importantly, the critics argue, rap music encourages the rampant degradation of women, homophobia, and what we saw Reed characterize as "backward prejudices." Even Dyson agrees that the anti-Semitism of the most political of groups such as Public Enemy "marred their revolutionary agenda" (Dyson 1996). The basic set of predictions are that exposure and emphasis on rap leads to "negative" attitudes, but not to positive consciousness raising.

Those who see rap as playing a positive role would argue that the good outweighs the bad, that rap music provides a potential basis for political mobilization, political education, and progressive discourse. This set of predictions, particularly from radical and liberal defenders of rap, would be centered around a positive correlation between rap and a variety of political views consistent with a radical agenda. Nationalist defenders of rap, particularly the rappers themselves, would also argue that rap should be positively connected to building nationalist ideology among African-Americans. They also may argue, particularly to the degree that they're followers of the Nation of Islam, that promoting hostility toward gays, lesbians, and whites is healthy for the black community. In the next sections evidence will be considered about the degree to which these hypotheses are supported in contemporary black public-opinion data.

Data and Methodology

The analyses that follow use survey responses from the 1993–1994 National Black Politics Study (NBPS). The data for the NBPS were obtained from a probability sample of all black households; 1,206 telephone interviews were completed. Each interview was approximately forty-five minutes in length. To be eligible, respondents had to be both black and eighteen years or older. The survey was conducted between November 20, 1993, and February 20, 1994. The response rate was 65 percent.[3] The two main substantive foci of the study were providing instrumentation for the analysis of the relationships between black ideologies and their determinants and consequences and the relationship of black worship to black public opinion.

Table 1 displays simple bivariate relationships between both exposure to and evaluations of rap with a number of individuals' attitudes and beliefs. Males, the young, the more educated, the urban, and those who believe their fate linked to that of other African-Americans are more likely to have consistent exposure to rap music. Not surprisingly given the controversy over rap music in the mainstream media, those who perceive the survey interviewer to be white are less likely to report consistent exposure to rap. Gender, on the other hand, does not make a difference in whether blacks evaluate rap as a positive force. Age most decidedly does. There is over a 40 percentage point gap in the approval for rap voiced by young as opposed to older blacks. The only other significant and substantial relationship reported in table 1 is that blacks who believe they are

TABLE 1   DISTRIBUTION OF EXPOSURE AND SUPPORT FOR RAP MUSIC
ACCORDING TO SELECTED STRUCTURAL FACTORS

Variable	Percentage Exposed to Rap	Percentage Supporting Rap as a Positive Force
Gender		
• *male*	54.35	40.74
• *female*	44.05	38.20
	(11.72, 1, .001)	(.6054, 1, .437)
Age		
• *18–29*	78.39	70.48
• *30 & older*	38.10	28.55
	(134.02, 1, .000)	**(125.08, 1, .000)**
Education		
• *less than high school*	31.25	30.08
• *high-school degree*	46.01	35.12
• *some college*	58.49	49.58
• *college degree or greater*	47.11	39.36
	(32.66, 3, .000)	**(15.873, 3, .001)**
Urbanicity		
• *rural/county area*	47.92	34.15
• *small town*	41.57	35.21
• *small city*	55.09	39.85
• *suburb*	54.80	44.37
• *large city*	45.02	38.56
	(10.498, 4, .033)	(3.04, 4, .551)
Degree of linked fate		
• *none*	40.23	34.78
• *little*	46.43	37.36
• *some*	51.65	44.76
• *high*	51.57	40.12
	(10.199, 3, .017)	(5.3015, 3, .151)
Interviewer perceived as white		
• *yes*	39.84	29.56
• *no*	49.57	41.82
	(7.625, 1, .006)	**(10.074, 1, .002)**

SOURCE: 1993–1994 National Black Politics Study.

The parenthetical numbers on the last line of each cell are the c^2, the df, and the p-value. Boldface indicates statistical significance.

being interviewed by an African-American are over 10 percentage points more likely to voice their approval of rap.

The next step is to construct a multivariate model of the support for rap music. The following set of variables is used in all of the analyses. Two types of structural factors are included: social location and spatial situation. Social location is measured through indicators of gender, family income, education, and age. Spatial situation is represented through indicators of concentrated poverty and degree of neighborhood segregation. Also included are measures that tap the degree to which blacks believe that their fate is linked to that of other

TABLE 2   DETERMINANTS OF EXPOSURE TO RAP MUSIC

Variable	Coefficient (SE)
Do you think blacks are economically worse off than whites? (0 = no, 1 = yes)	—
Do you think your fate is linked to that of black people? (0 = no, 1 = yes)	.32 (1.69)
Gender (1 = woman, 0 = man)	−.30 (−2.02)
Family income (9 categories between 0 and 9 *1 < $10,000* *9 > $75,000)*	—
Age (years)	−4.40 (−11.41)
Education (number of years)	−1.42 (−2.25)
Census tract poverty (0 = less than 10% below poverty line, 1 = more than 31%)	—
Is interviewer perceived as white? (1 = yes, 0 = no)	—
Constant	1.98 (4.60)

SOURCE: 1993–1994 National Black Politics Study.

$n = 962$

Pseudo $R^2 = .14$

These are logit estimates. The figures in the parentheses are the ratio of the unstandardized coefficient to the standard error.

"—" denotes not statistically significant.

African-Americans and the degree to which whites are perceived to be faring economically better than blacks. I showed in detail elsewhere that blacks' belief that their fate is tied to each other serves as a powerful component of racial identity (Dawson 1994a). Further, I also argued that the historic economic subordination of African-Americans has helped to forge blacks' relative assessment of black/white economic status into another powerful influence on black public opinion. The perceptions that one's fate was linked to the race and that whites were faring better than blacks both had a radicalizing effect across a variety of domains. They are included here as general factors likely to shape black ideological orientations. Finally, Sanders (1995) has decisively shown that perception of the race of interviewer shapes how respondents filter and understand the political terrain of the interview process.

Results

This section attempts to address the effect that exposure to and support for rap music have on black public opinion. We start with the determinants of increased exposure to rap. The results are displayed in table 2.[4] Age is by far the strongest predictor of exposure to rap. Rap is the music of the young. At the ends of adult life, an eighteen-year-old is 76 percent more likely to have listened to rap than someone in their nineties.[5] Even a thirty-year-old is at least 20 percent more likely than a fifty-five-year-old African-American to have recently listened to rap. A few other indicators have modest effects on exposure to rap music. Women are 7 percent less likely than men to have listened to rap. Years of education is also negatively associated with likelihood of listening to rap. Those who believe their fate is linked to other blacks are slightly more likely to have listened to rap, although in this case the direction of causation is more difficult to pin down.

The next set of results illuminates the effects that both the exposure to and approval of rap have on the formation of black public opinion. One central question is whether rap promotes black nationalism. As discussed earlier, political rap in particular is often identified with black nationalism. First, we must answer the question, Do black nationalists seek out rap, does approval of rap make one more likely to adopt black nationalism, or do they simultaneously constitute each other?

The simultaneous equation analyses described in table 3 show convincingly that those that approve of rap are more likely to adopt community nationalism; however, those that uphold a nationalist ideology are no more likely to approve of rap than their nonnationalist cousins. This should not be a surprising result. While rap musicians such as Sister Souljah, Paris, X-Clan, PE, and Brand Nubian all consciously promote nationalism as an ideology, and artists such as Ice Cube implicitly advance nationalist sentiments, many nationalist activists and leaders have voiced strong criticism of rap music, particularly gangsta rap. Nationalist leaders and writers such as Minister Farrakhan of the Nation of Islam and Haki Madhubuti consistently argue that black men should show greater "respect" for black women (Farrakhan 1989, 1996; Madhubuti 1994). Indeed, Madhubuti makes a number of impassioned pleas that argue that men must be an integral part of building an antirape culture that combats the pervasive misogyny in the black community. Similarly, Bakari Kitwana worries that gangsta rap in particular not only promotes violence and disrespect toward black women, but can contribute to the genocidal levels of violence suffered by black men at each others' hands (Kitwana 1994). On the other hand, the relatively constant, if not consistent, message from numbers of rap songs that we should control "our thang" does seem to promote a modest increase in the probability of supporting community nationalism. Thus when we try to assess the effect of rap on black public opinion we can be confident that it is not an indirect proxy for support for community nationalism. As both many supporters confidently predicted and rap's detractors feared, appreciation for rap encourages support for black nationalism.

TABLE 3 BELIEF THAT RAP IS DESTRUCTIVE AND SUPPORT FOR BLACK NATIONALISM

	Ideological Orientation	
Variable	Nationalism Coefficient (SE)	Rap Coefficient (SE)
Do you think blacks are economically worse off than whites? *(0 = no, 1 = yes)*	.05 (2.00)	°
Do you think your fate is linked to that of black people? *(0 = no, 1 = yes)*	.03 (2.33)	°
Gender (1 = woman, 0 = man)	—	—
Family income (9 categories between 0–9 *1 < $10,000* *9 > $75,000)*	−.04 (−1.90)	—
Age (years)	−.001 (−2.52)	.04 (2.50)
Education (number of years)	—	—
Census tract poverty (0 = less than 10% below poverty line, 1 = more than 31%)	—	—
Exposed to rap music? (0 = yes, 1 = no)	°	−.36 (−8.67)
Is interviewer perceived as white? (1 = yes, 0 = no)	—	—
Constant	.62 (18.67)	.54 (1.83)

SOURCE: 1993–1994 National Black Politics Study.

These are two-stage least-squares estimates. The figures in the parentheses are the ratio of the unstandardized coefficient to the standard error.

"—" denotes not statistically significant.   ° denotes not included in equation.

The strongest predictor of belief that rap represents an important information source for the black community is, not surprisingly, exposure to rap. Those who have listened to the music are nearly 40 percent more likely to support the positive view of rap. The young are also, not surprisingly, more likely to reject the belief that rap represents a destructive force in the black community. Exposure and age are the only two significant predictors of approval of rap music. Rap is not particularly the music of an alienated middle class, nor the province of the most disadvantaged segments of the black community.

So does rap have an independent influence on black public opinion? Although the size of the effects are modest, the results displayed in table 4 demonstrate that the answer is decidedly and consistently yes. Critics of rap have fiercely argued that one of its most detrimental aspects is that it loudly, crudely, and constantly promotes violence against women and other forms of misogyny. Even politically oriented rap, it is argued, supports the patriarchal view of a subservient role of women in the struggle for black liberation espoused by many

TABLE 4A THE EFFECTS OF RAP ON SELECTED GENDER QUESTIONS

	Pro-choice? (0 = no)	Warmth for gays?	Warmth for lesbians?	Black women leaders troublemakers? (0 = yes)	Black feminists divide black community? (0 = no)
Rap a destructive force? (0 = no)	−.10 (−2.57)	−.04 (−1.90)	−.04 (−1.82)	—	.12* (3.04)

TABLE 4B THE EFFECTS OF RAP ON SELECTED INDICATORS OF BLACK NATIONALISM

	Warmth for whites?	Minister Farrakhan positive force? (0 = yes)	Blacks form own political party? (0 = yes)	Support community nationalism? (1 = yes)	Africa is a special homeland? (0 = yes)	Black children should study an African language? (0 = yes)	Support black male academies?
Rap a destructive force? (0 = no)	—	.16* (3.77)	.09 (2.44)	−.06 (−1.95)	—	.040 (1.93)	—

TABLE 4C THE EFFECTS OF RAP ON SELECTED INDICATORS OF ORIENTATIONS TOWARD AMERICAN SOCIETY

	American society unfair? (0 = no)	Large corporations unfair to blacks? (0 = no)	Problems of racism, poverty, and sexism are linked? (0 = yes)	Police contribute to problem of violence? (0 = no)
Rap a destructive force? (0 = no)	—	—	—	−.10* (−2.65)

SOURCE: Compiled by author from 1993–1994 National Black Politics Study.
"—" denotes coefficient was not statistically discernible from zero at the .10 level.

A set of basic measures is used to model the effects of rap on components of black public opinion. All of the right-hand-side variables used in table 4A are also used in this analysis. The "rap" variable is added to the sets of structural and racial identity variables used before. Instead of presenting the full results from each of the individual equations, these tables summarize the effects of rap on shaping various areas in black public opinion.

Each unstarred cell contains an unstandardized OLS coefficient. Starred cells contain probabilities derived from logit estimates. These probabilities represent the percentage change in probability as one moves from the view that rap is informative to the view that rap is a destructive force. In all cells, numbers within parentheses are the ratio of the unstandardized coefficient to the standard error.

nationalists. Frequent references to "ho," "bitches," "punks," and "faggots" do give a consistent misogynist and homophobic cast to rap that is not just confined to gangsta rap. Even given the crude measures we have available to us in this study, it is clear that we can detect a noticeable effect on questions of coldness toward gays and lesbians in the black community.

While there is very little rap that attacks gay bashing—The Disposable Heroes of Hiphoprisy song "Language of Violence" is an exception—there is a strong documented set of efforts by many women, and a few men rappers, to counteract the misogyny of rap. Queen Latifah has led the way not only in focusing her music toward critiques of the sexism in both everyday life in the black community and the music business, but also in providing a positive model of gender relations in the black community through her music. Consequently, the multiple messages on the role of women in the black community may counteract the dominance of the more brutal aspects of rap. Unfortunately, as expected, given the constant attacks against black gays and lesbians found within rap lyrics, both exposure to rap and the belief that rap provides a legitimate source of information within the black community contribute to negative attitudes toward gays and lesbians. Rap music contributes to black homophobia. While the size of the effects is relatively small, rap does significantly contribute to making black opinion toward the black queer community even more negative.

Rap music also has a discernible but mixed effect on attitudes toward black feminists and feminist issues. Those who appreciate rap are no less warm toward black feminists than other African-Americans. Indeed, when asked whether on one hand black feminists divided the black community or whether they made positive contributions to the black community, those that approve of rap were 12 percent more likely to answer that black feminists made positive contributions. Those who appreciate rap are no more or less likely to believe that controversial black women leaders such as Lani Guinier and Joycelyn Elders are troublemakers than other blacks. Supporters of rap are also equally likely to believe that the problems of racism, sexism, and poverty are linked, as many black feminists have argued. Exposure to rap (in an analysis not displayed in table 4) also does not contribute to the belief, held by one quarter of our sample of blacks, that the ravages of AIDS in the black community are the result of an antiblack conspiracy.[6] It is the case, however, that those who have a positive orientation toward rap are 10 percent more likely to oppose abortion under any circumstances than to support a woman's right to choose. Again consistent with black nationalist ideology, political rappers have with a very few exceptions been hostile to abortions within the black community.

I must point out that we don't have the best measures for assessing the effect of rap on attitudes toward black women; better measures to test this question would have included attitudes toward violence toward women, and whether women are less trustworthy than men. Both of these themes are often cited by the critics of rap as some of the most destructive themes within rap. But the results do suggest that rap does contribute toward black hostility to the black gay and lesbian community as predicted, thus contributing toward an increase in sexually oriented hostility within the black community.

Appreciation of rap increases support for a number of items that are correlated with support of black nationalism.[7] Rap artists such as Paris and Public Enemy sprinkle their cuts with praise for Louis Farrakhan. Farrakhan's speeches are often sampled for use in many groups' materials. Both exposure to and appreciation for rap increase the likelihood of supporting Farrakhan by 16 percent. Supporters of rap are also slightly more likely to support teaching black children African languages.

The great majority of the politically oriented rappers have very violent anti-police songs. Of course this theme is not confined to political rap; thus some on the border of political and gangsta rap such as Ice T, Ice Cube, Geto Boys, and the NWA all have had songs that show the most extreme contempt for the police. This theme transcends subgenre and is prevalent in the rap of artists such as LL Cool J who are not all that identified with gangsta rap (Rose 1994). Thus it is predictable that greater exposure to rap increases the probability by 10 percent that African-Americans believe that police are part of the problem of violence in the black community and not part of the solution. This is a result likely to reinforce the beliefs of both those who see rap as the authentic voice of the most disadvantaged and alienated segments of the black community that "tells it like it is," the CNN of the inner city to use Chuck D's phrase, as well as critics from the *right*, such as police organizations, and other government officials who worry that rap incites the black community to commit acts of violence against the police.

Those who believe that rap music provides an information source for the black community are also nearly 10 percent more likely to think it is necessary for blacks to form an independent political party than those who do not.[8] On the other hand (in analyses not displayed in table 4), neither approval of nor exposure to rap has an impact on the probability that blacks believe in a separate nation. Support for a separate black nation is confined to a sufficiently small proportion of the black community as to remain unaffected by rap, unlike other indicators correlated with support for black nationalism. Be that as it may, exposure to rap leads to a view of society where not only are the problems of Americans defined by race, but the solutions to these problems can be found within the ideology of black nationalism.

Finally, the results displayed in table 4 show that rap does not affect how blacks feel toward whites. As surprising, given the notoriety of lyrics such as Ice Cube's and Geto Boys' anti-Asian rhymes, rap also does not affect black attitudes toward immigrants except indirectly to the degree that it increases support for community nationalism (which does directly predict anti-immigrant attitudes). Similarly, exposure to rap music does not directly affect whether one believes that other people of color and poor people generally make suitable allies for African-Americans. There is a mixed message in much of rap concerning other people of color. Blacks and Latinos are often linked in descriptions of the unfairness and harshness of ghetto life, while Asians are routinely demonized as black oppressors only one step above the level of whites.

Less surprising, given that a large majority of blacks, without variation, believe that American society is unfair on matters of race, is the lack of effect that rap has on perception of the fairness of American society. Nor does rap affect whether one believes America's corporations aid or harm the black community. Adherents of rap are no more or less likely to believe that blacks have common interests or have too many social divisors for a common agenda. Rap has an effect in this realm of opinion only by influencing one's ideological orientation. Rap encourages nationalism, and nationalism heavily influences black public opinion across multiple domains (Dawson forthcoming).

Conclusion

Both exposure to and opinion of rap shape black public opinion. Even with crude measures, definite connections between rap on one hand and homophobia and black nationalism on the other were established. A direct relationship was found between rap and two of the four domains that were tested (ideology, sexism, homophobia, and general political attitudes). We do not know if rap has an influence in domains where we did not have direct measures on the attitudes. Thus, we do not know if rap encourages violence and other degradations against black women. There was no relationship between support for feminism, feminists, and feminist policy positions except for the significant increase in hostility toward pro-choice abortion stances. We also do not know if rap music is correlated with the type of violent outlook that has led to the devastating levels of black-on-black crime. This study suggests that research similar to that conducted here may help us more broadly understand rap's influence in the black community. On the other hand, there was no general connection between exposure to rap music and a more critical view of American society and its institutions. The strong connection, however, between rap and community nationalism means that rap actually has a modest but pervasive effect on black political preferences. As I show elsewhere, community nationalism has a dominating influence on black politics. Rap does have a substantial influence on black opinion, but its influence is mediated by ideology.

Art can influence political and social ideology and opinion, even in an era where there are minimal political organization, low levels of political mobilizations, and no active black social movement except in limited local areas. Consequently, artistic content is indeed an important site for *political* contestation. Art is ignored and dismissed by political activists at not only their peril, but also at the peril of the society. The best influence on rap musicians would be an active and progressive black social movement. The progressive movements of the 1960s had their own artistic wings that included such diverse artists as the church-inspired freedom singers of the civil rights movement, the *teatro*-based actresses and actors of the Chicano movement, and the R & B singers of the Black Panther group, The Lumpen. As importantly, these social movements directly influenced the mass consumer-oriented performers of that era. Even James Brown had a song or two that celebrated an unfocused black pride. Just one of the critical benefits of a revitalized progressive movement within the United States would be its eventual influence on performers who themselves are influential politically. Absent such a movement, the artists are themselves attempting to deal with these issues. Groups such as the Fugees and the Roots attempt to provide a critical political voice that is not only progressive and much less misogynist than others, but is also artistically successful, more identifiably tied to hip-hop roots than other political rappers, and commercially successful as well.

Elsewhere, I have discussed the feasibility and the desirability of rebuilding a black counterpublic (Dawson 1994b).[9] Popular culture, whether rap, jazz, theater, the visual arts, or novels, cannot provide the main site for such a reconstruction. Each has a role to play; popular art can incite, subvert, play with, and challenge the dominant hegemonic forces of a society that still systematically disadvantages entire populations along a variety of dimensions. Within the United States, racial stratification continues to severely and systematically disadvantage blacks in arenas ranging from daily encounters with the coercive mechanism of the state, particularly the police, in arenas such as the labor market, to the simple art of trying to buy clothing in a downtown store or boutique. Rap and black popular culture can help critique and expose the injustices of such systematic disadvantage. At its best, rap can inspire people to action. Buying a record, dancing to political music at a party, or reading a dynamite novel does not equal political commitment. Black popular culture, including rap, cannot substitute for the mobilization, organization building, and political, economic, and social struggle through which societies are transformed and social justice won.

Ideas *do* matter, though, and rap and other dynamic artistic endeavors can play an important role in the battle for the hearts and minds of society. Tricia Rose reminds us that rap music is part of the trench warfare of modern society in which one battles over the ideas of social legitimization that justify the hierarchies of power and stratification that leave entire groups disadvantaged. Dominant political and economic institutions need ideology to provide legitimacy and support for an unjust social and racial order (Dawson 1994a; Rose 1994). Rap can play either a positive or a negative role in such a battle. It can challenge dominant hierarchies and ideologies, while reinforcing critical ideologies, at the same time that it reinforces the most destructive aspects of violent, homophobic, misogynist hierarchies and ideologies. Rap can also glorify the most individually oriented celebration of naked violence in the name of getting paid. Many black teenagers in cities such as Chicago and Oakland believe that Tupac is alive, and not a victim of the "thug life" that was *not* part of his heritage, but was part of the devastating nefarious fantasy that he had created as part of a gangsta image. It is not automatic that the deaths of Tupac Shakur and the Notorious B.I.G. will teach the lesson that black violence is tearing apart the black community.[10] It is all too possible that many will either deny the reality of violent death that is part and parcel of the gangsta life, or continue to glorify living hard and dying young. The astronomic suicide rate found among young black men is a reflection of the deadliness of the message that young blacks are destined to die young.

Given the partial disintegration of the black counterpublic that I describe elsewhere (Dawson 1994b), rap music is more of a major force shaping African-American beliefs than it would have been a generation ago, particularly among the young. Key institutions such as the black church that are the sites of competing secular and political as well as sacred messages have less influence than they have had at any time in memory. Black political organizations, both the militant grassroots community organizations formed in this century and older electorally oriented black political organizations, are shadows of their former selves. There are not vibrant mass movements or organizing drives to attract young African-Americans as there have been during many periods of the twentieth century. The competing political, cultural, and social messages that were at the heart of the black public spheres of both the nineteenth and twentieth centuries are particularly poorly suited to reaching the alienated youth of black America, which is the core audience of rap music.

Robin Kelley reminds us in the shout out that concludes his piece on gangsta rap that the job of the MC is ultimately to entertain, to rock the house. But all of us, and rappers are no exception, certainly have a negative duty not to harm, and one would hope a positive desire to help. We all have a responsibility to act responsibly. This means minimally that we must be willing to take criticism when others believe that our actions harm the community. Beating black women because they criticize their raps, as Dr. Dre did, is wrong and we cannot minimize the destructiveness of these actions. The incidents of male rappers engaged in violence against women is hideous, although not surprising given the number of rap songs that took boxer Mike Tyson's side when he was sent to prison for rape.

We also should not minimize the destructiveness of MC's words when they call for the burning of one part of the black community that has friends and lovers outside of the black community. As we have seen, at least in one domain, exposure to rap further divides the black community. Rappers who have been repeatedly demonized by American society, as have young black people in general, should themselves refrain from demonizing groups of community residents and others who have done no harm other than being different from oneself. If rap can encourage, as Rose documents, everyday acts of resistance to injustice, then it does not take a huge leap of imagination to understand that reactionary rap can also encourage everyday acts of intolerance and brutality. That some rappers celebrate the "Thug Life" should be a matter of grief and anger for the rest of us.

But Kelley is also right when he says that the best of the rappers can indeed rock the house and along the way at their best the Fugees, PE, Paris, Kool Moe Dee, and many others shout their intention to educate at the same time that they're laying down fun dance tracks. In the context of a strong movement, or at least a strong public discourse on the future of black liberation and American society, art plays a valuable role in provoking political debate and reinforcing the values of a critical movement. In such an environment, we might see a hundred MCs grab the mike, and a thousand schools of (ideological) thought contend. As Hall (1992) suggests, there is a positive role for rap to play in subverting the racial hierarchies that dominate all aspects of American life, including its culture.

I agree with Dyson (1993) when he argues that an ethical perspective must be developed by rappers if they are to play such a positive role. I would go further than Dyson. Griots did not just describe life in African society, they also offered advice and provided a moral vision of the future. New jack griots must follow the lead of women rappers like Queen Latifah and develop an ethic that provides an inclusive vision of the future. Dyson is worried about the uncritical adoption of an old form of nationalism by political rappers. More problematic is the lack of other nonnationalist ideological perspectives in rap. There are only a handful of rappers like Latifah and the Disposable Heroes that present ideological alternatives to nationalism. Dyson argues that rap erases "cultural amnesia"; instead most rappers perpetuate political amnesia by presenting nationalism as the only authentic black ideological orientation. This hegemonic narrative erases the long history of nonnationalist, but struggle-oriented, alternatives such as those advanced by organizations as diverse as the SCLC during its heyday, the Black Workers Congress, which for a period could shut down Detroit's auto industry, or the black feminists of the Combahee River Collective as well as individuals such as Fannie Lou Hamer, Angela Davis, W. E. B. Du Bois, Ida B. Wells, A. Philip Randolph, and Ella Baker.

Unfortunately, rappers who some argue are exorcists, shamans who rid the community of demons, are more often guilty themselves of demonizing large segments of the black community. Vilifying critics of the Million Man March, as do the Geto Boys in their song "Niggas and Flies," retards the quest not only to rebuild the black public sphere, but also the overall quest for black justice. This does not have to be. There are commercially successful rappers who not only do no harm, but whose product is by and large positive. The inexorable pressures of the market, however, when combined with a contemporary cultural and political discourse that is dominated by patriarchal and often reactionary forces, ensure that the tendency of progressive political forces to dismiss rap artists and other contemporary cultural trends continues unabated. Ignoring rap, and the political discourse in the black community that it influences, is, however, profoundly dangerous.

Appendix

The comments that follow highlight some of the multivariate analyses that provided the foundation for the previous discussions. In all of the equations, the following variables were held constant. The text has the substantive justification for each, but as a reminder they were linked fate, respondents' comparison of black and white economic fortunes, age, gender, education, family income, race of interviewer, and the percent living in poverty in the respondent's census tract. All variables have been rescaled to lie in the 0–1 range.

A key concept in all of the equations is the idea that one either had a positive or negative orientation toward rap. This variable was based on a question where the respondent is asked to choose between the following two alternatives:

1) Rap music provides an important source of information about what's going on in the black community OR,
2) Rap music is a destructive force in the black community.

It should also be noted that table 4 displays selected results of the belief that rap is a positive force on various aspects of black public opinion. While only the coefficients and/or the probabilities on rap are reported, each cell represents a full multivariate regression equation with the same control variables displayed in table 2. Each unstarred cell contains an unstandardized OLS coefficient. Starred cells contain probabilities derived from logit estimates. Probabilities were generated using a program written in the Markov and Stata statistical languages. These probabilities represent the percentage change in probability as one moves from support for to opposition to rap. The program converts logit coefficients into probabilities across the range of an independent variable holding all other independent variables constant at the means. For discussion of this method and the formula used to calculate the probabilities, see King 1989. In all cells, numbers within parentheses are the ratio of the unstandardized coefficient to the standard error.

Notes

1. This belief that rap is a possible salvation for black youth leads Baker to not only attack critics of rap in print (see Baker 1993 for one of many examples). At a conference panel on race, gender, and culture at the University of Michigan, he replied to a question about whether politically oriented rappers should be criticized for their misogyny by stating that they should be nurtured and protected, not criticized given the magnitude of their contribution to black progress.

2. The term *griot* comes from the West African oral history tradition. Traditionally griots served the rulers of African empires such as that of historical Mali. They provided a record of the history of the kingdom and the ruling family, acted as advisers to the court, and were often accomplished musicians as well.

3. The principal investigators were Ronald Brown of Wayne State University and Michael Dawson of the University of Chicago. The study was administered through the University of Chicago. The Russell Sage Foundation provided a generous grant for the collection of the data. For information on obtaining the data set, contact the author.

4. More details on the estimation can be found in the appendix.

5. The percentages discussed in the text were obtained by converting logit coefficients to probabilities.

6. This is not quite accurate; exposure to rap contributes a small amount to the belief that the ravages of AIDS in the black community are the result of an antiblack conspiracy indirectly through the large effect that support for community nationalism has on that variable.

7. For more on the correlates of black nationalism in public opinion, see Dawson forthcoming, chap. 3. This chapter also describes many of the forms of nationalism that have played important roles in the history of black political discourse.

8. In all cases exposure to rap had similar effects on beliefs that rap played an important role as a communication medium in the black community. While the sizes of the effects were similar, it should be remembered that these are direct effects and do not take into account the indirect contribution that exposure to rap has, since it is also a predictor of the approval of rap.

9. For reasons I discuss in Dawson 1994b, I prefer the more accurate term *black counterpublic* to *black public sphere.*

10. Tupac Shakur and the Notorious B.I.G. were both popular rap artists who were shot to death in very public incidents. Both were very much identified with gangsta rap.

References

Baker, Houston A., Jr. 1993. *Black Studies, Rap, and the Academy.* Chicago: University of Chicago Press.

Boyd, Todd. 1994. "Check Yo Self, Before You Wrek Yo Self: Variations on a Political Theme in Rap Music and Popular Culture." *Public Culture* 7:289–312.

Butts, Calvin O., III. 1996. "Rolling Out an Agenda for Rap." In *Rap on Rap: Straight-Up Talk on Hip-Hop Culture,* edited by Adam Sexton. New York: Delta.

Combahee River Collective. [1977] 1981. "A Black Feminist Statement." In *This Bridge Called My Back: Writings by Radical Women of Color,* edited by Cherrie Moraga and Gloria Anzaldua. Watertown: Persephone.

Dawson, Michael C. 1994a. *Behind the Mule: Race, Class, and African American Politics.* Princeton: Princeton University Press.

———. 1994b. "A Black Counterpublic? Economic Earthquakes, Racial Agenda(s), and Black Politics." *Public Culture* 7:195–223.

———. Forthcoming. *Black Visions.* Chicago: University of Chicago Press.

Dyson, Michael Eric. 1993. *Reflecting Black.* Minneapolis: University of Minnesota Press.

———. 1996. *Between God and Gangsta Rap.* New York: Oxford University Press.

Farrakhan, Louis. 1989. *Back Where We Belong.* Philadelphia: PC International.

———. 1996. *Let Us Make Man.* New York: Uprising Communications.

Floyd, Samuel A., Jr. 1995. *The Power of Black Music.* New York: Oxford University Press.

Gold, Jonathan. 1996. "Why Rap Doesn't Cut It Live." In *Rap on Rap: Straight-Up Talk on Hip-Hop Culture,* edited by Adam Sexton. New York: Delta.

Hall, Stuart. 1992. "What Is This 'Black' in Black Popular Culture?" In *Black Popular Culture: A Project by Michele Wallace,* edited by Gina Dent. Seattle: Bay.

Henry, Charles P. 1990. *Culture and African American Politics.* Bloomington: Indiana University Press.

Ice Cube. 1996. "Black Culture Still Getting a Bum Rap." In *Rap on Rap: Straight-Up Talk on Hip-Hop Culture,* edited by Adam Sexton. New York: Delta.

Ice T. 1996. "The Controversy." In *Rap on Rap: Straight-Up Talk on Hip-Hop Culture,* edited by Adam Sexton. New York: Delta.

Jones, LeRoi. 1967. *Black Music.* New York: Morrow.

Kelley, Robin. 1994. *Race Rebels.* New York: Free Press.

King, Gary. 1989. *Unifying Political Methodology.* New York: Cambridge University Press.

Kitwana, Bakari. 1994. *The Rap on Gangsta Rap.* Chicago: Third World Press.

Kofsky, Frank. 1970. *Black Nationalism and the Revolution in Music.* New York: Pathfinder.

Madhubuti, Haki R. 1994. *Claiming Earth.* Chicago: Third World Press.

Malveaux, Julianne. 1992. "Popular Culture and the Economics of Alienation." In *Black Popular Culture: A Project by Michele Wallace,* edited by Gina Dent. Seattle: Bay.

Morgan, Joan. 1996. "The Nigga Ya Hate to Love." In *Rap on Rap: Straight-Up Talk on Hip-Hop Culture,* edited by Adam Sexton. New York: Delta.

Paris. 1995. "Yo! A Rapper's Domestic Policy Plan: How Clinton Can Bring Hope to Alienated Black America." In *Rap on Rap: Straight-Up Talk on Hip-Hop Culture,* edited by Adam Sexton. New York: Delta.

Ransby, Barbara, and Tracye Matthews. 1993. "Black Popular Culture and the Transcendence of Patriarchal Illusions." *Race and Class* 35:57–68.

Reed, Adolph, Jr. 1992. "The Allure of Malcolm X." In *Malcolm X: In Our Own Image,* edited by Joe Wood. New York: St. Martins.

Rose, Tricia. 1994. *Black Noise.* Hanover: Wesleyan University Press.

————. 1995. "Rhythmic Repetition, Industrial Forces, and Black Practice." In *Rap on Rap: Straight-Up Talk on Hip-Hop Culture*, edited by Adam Sexton. New York: Delta.

Sanders, Lynn M. 1995. "What Is Whiteness? Race of Interviewer Effects When All the Interviewers Are Black." Unpublished manuscript. University of Chicago.

Sexton, Adam. 1995. "Don't Believe the Hype: Why Isn't Hip-Hop Criticism Better?" In *Rap on Rap: Straight-Up Talk on Hip-Hop Culture*, edited by Adam Sexton. New York: Delta.

affirmative action as culture war

jennifer l. hochschild

If one examines any collection of books or syllabi on the subject of affirmative action over the past twenty-five years, one
observes two phenomena—a huge outpouring of legal and
philosophical analyses of its merits, and a paucity of empirical
examinations of its mechanisms and effects.[1] The legal and
philosophical analyses range from passionate assertions that
quotas are essential in order to mitigate American racism to
equally fervent arguments that any racial or gender-based
preference violates core American values of equality of personhood and opportunity. One can even find a few arguments
for carefully nuanced intermediate positions that subtly distinguish among recipients, procedures, triggering circumstances, and the like. Without denigrating the energy and cre-
ativity of many of these efforts, I believe it is fair to say that
the core legal and philosophical positions were laid out in the
first few years of this debate. With the exception of recent
claims about the intrinsic benefits of diversity for an organization, subsequent volumes have mostly developed or elaborated upon these original claims.[2]

What We Don't Know about Affirmative Action

There are, in contrast, huge holes in the corpus of what we
know about how affirmative action actually works in practice.[3]
For example, we know very little about just how people are
hired or admitted to universities. When is race (or gender)
a tiebreaker; when does minority status still count against
the applicant; when are less qualified African-Americans or
women hired/admitted over more qualified whites, Asians, or

men; when does the reverse occur? Do certain kinds of universities or firms consistently treat affirmative action in ways different from that of other kinds of universities or firms? I know of virtually no research within and across university admissions offices, corporate personnel offices, police or fire departments, etc., that carefully traces these processes and analyzes them comparatively or theoretically.[4]

What happens after a person is hired or admitted in circumstances where affirmative action is presumed to have played a role? Do blacks or white women feel stigmatized, inferior, insecure? If so, do they overcompensate by rigidity or racial paranoia or timidity? Do they feel any more insecure than, for example, alumni children admitted to universities as legacies, or white working-class athletes admitted to bolster Ivy League football teams, or the boss's nephew put in charge of the front office? Alternatively, if they do feel insecure or are stigmatized, are they able to overcome their initial obstacles and succeed at about the same rate as other workers or students? What are the processes by which people who are initially labeled as "affirmative action hires" move toward success or failure: do they have more to do with internal fortitude, organizational culture, structural opportunities, or what? Do some contexts facilitate success, or reify stigma, more than others? Again, there are very few careful and systematic studies of coworkers' interactions and corporate or university practices in which affirmative action is a central part of the organizational context.

Another set of questions: how many whites or men are told by admissions officers or personnel directors that they would have been hired/admitted if it were not for affirmative action pressures? After all, that is an easy and mutually gratifying response from a gatekeeper to an angry or disappointed candidate— and to many such candidates in a row, so long as each is addressed in the absence of the others. An example: one man recently reported on an e-mail list his stellar undergraduate record and his admission to several excellent law schools, but with little funding. "At least three admissions counselors stated outright, and others implied, that had I been anything but white male and had those numbers [GPA, LSAT scores, etc.], I would've been immediately full-ride plus living expenses" (Finley 1996). If his experience occurs frequently, that would explain why so many more whites than is arithmetically possible believe that they or someone they know about was denied a job or promotion because of affirmative action. (See my discussion of survey results below.) But to my knowledge, no one has conducted research on how affirmative action is presented to nonminorities denied jobs or admission or promotion.

We know very little about how minority set-asides for contracts work. Conventional wisdom holds that the process is corrupt, with the most common allegation being that an African-American (or woman of any race) is used as a "front" for predominantly white (or white male) owners of a firm (for example, see Oreskes 1984). How often does that occur? Why cannot those who grant contracts find out about it? Do they try? Conversely, how often do minority set-asides function as they were presumably intended to—giving a start to a firm headed by a woman and/or person of color who would not otherwise be able to find clients or win contracts due to racial or gender stereotypes? How and when does that more positive dynamic work, and what distinguishes successful from unsuccessful firms once set-asides are in place? Some analysts have begun to answer these questions, but the disproportion between assertion and knowledge is enormous (House Government Operations Committee 1994; Bates and Williams 1996; Enchautegui et al. 1996; Myers and Chan 1996; Rice and Mongkuo 1998).

Broader political research would also be useful. Why did affirmative action surface as an especially "hot" political issue in 1995, given that white men (and to a lesser degree, white women) have always disliked strong versions of it (Bennett et al. 1995, tables 2, 3)? Conversely, why haven't corporations, universities, most political candidates, and city governments jumped on the anti–affirmative action bandwagon? Do they see benefits in affirmative action policies that they would not be able to attain absent an apparently coercive governmental mandate? (An analogy here might be school superintendents who welcomed judicial decisions mandating desegregation because the mandate allowed them to make changes in the school system that were otherwise politically too difficult.)[5] Why was there an anti–affirmative action referendum in only one state (California) during the 1996 electoral season, and in one city (Houston) subsequently? How should we understand the conflicting views of affirmative action held by white women and Asians?[6]

Broader historical research would similarly be illuminating. In the 1960s, as Stephen Carter (1991) reminds us, some on the left saw affirmative action as an individualistic sellout. In their view, affirmative action encouraged personal mobility of the most energetic, articulate, and effective actors within a racial or gender group at the expense of structural transformation that would benefit the whole group. Regardless of whether it was right or wrong, what happened to that view? Why did support for affirmative action move from being a relatively right-wing position (President Nixon established the Philadelphia plan partly to give more blacks a stake in the extant economic system and endorsed set-asides in order to encourage black capitalism) to being a relatively left-wing position over the past thirty years?

I could list other arenas in which empirical research about the processes and effects of affirmative action are scarce or missing, but the point should be clear: Americans' elaborate and sophisticated legal and normative debate about the legitimacy, desirability, and impact of affirmative action has taken place in something close to a factual vacuum.

That might not be surprising in the political arena—after all, debates in Congress about welfare reform, illegal immigration, the effects of nuclear fallout, and other highly controversial issues often ignore what evidence exists or occur in the absence of much evidence at all. Such ignorance might not even be always inappropriate; elected officials and judges must sometimes make decisions regardless of whether they know enough about the choices confronting them. Similarly, the relative paucity of empirical knowledge might not be disconcerting among advocacy groups. Advocates of a particular policy position— whether support or opposition to affirmative action, welfare reform, nuclear disarmament, abortion rights, or something else—either are not primarily motivated by empirical considerations, or believe that they know enough facts or the right facts in order to espouse their position with confidence.

But the disproportion between legal and philosophical analysis on the one hand and empirical analysis on the other *is* inappropriate in the academy. Social scientists *do,* one normally assumes, believe that knowledge—about how processes work, what effects policy innovations have, how historical and institutional contexts affect behaviors and outcomes—matters. But except for crucial exceptions mostly buried in scholarly journals or legal briefs, they have not expended much effort on empirical analyses of affirmative action.[7] Why not? And what does the relative paucity of research compared with argumentation tell us about the policy of affirmative action, the cultural context of American racial and gender politics, and—most broadly—the ideology of the American dream?[8]

My argument, in brief, is the following: in the current American racial culture, affirmative action is more important to participants in the policy debate as a weapon with which to attack enemies in order to win some other battle than as an issue in and for itself. To be useful as a weapon, affirmative action must remain at the level of moral claims and single-dimensional outrage; the messy and complex realities that are likely to surface in careful empirical analyses do not help much in political and cultural warfare.[9] This phenomenon is as true in the university as in the explicitly political realm, because most scholars do not pursue the traditional objective of scholarly neutrality in the arena of racial politics and policy choices. To put it most succinctly, the debate over affirmative action is predominantly a culture war over what it means to be a good American, and only secondarily a dispute between political parties or policy analysts over how best to improve the status of African-Americans.

I do not make this assertion only to deplore it, although I will do some of that below. Nor do I claim that the culture war over affirmative action is unique; on issues ranging from a national bank in the 1830s to temperance in the 1890s to communists in the State Department in the 1950s, Americans have always become passionately concerned about social "crises" that in fact matter little to their daily lives.[10] Instead, I want to explore the culture war over affirmative action for a more analytic reason: comparing what we believe about affirmative action with what we know and what we have chosen not to find out tells us a great deal about Americans' hopes, fears, and self-images.

What Do We Know about Affirmative Action?

There has been, of course, some excellent empirical research on the subject of affirmative action (almost all of which has appeared only in esoteric professional journals or in unpublished legal briefs).[11] A review of what it tells us will begin to substantiate my claim about the symbolic functions of the debate over affirmative action.[12]

To begin with, a few solid historical analyses of the development and implementation of affirmative action policy have been published (Burstein 1985; Graham forthcoming; Skrentny 1996). With one clear exception (Skrentny), these analyses seldom address the issue of "why affirmative action?" and "why at a given historical moment?" Instead, their main burden has been to demonstrate that federal policy was in fact effective. That is, once federal officials, especially several presidents in a row beginning with Lyndon Johnson, decided to endorse affirmative action and develop an institutional structure to implement and enforce the policy, it happened. Graham (but not Burstein or Skrentny) even argues, roughly, that the federal government was *too* effective in the sense that affirmative action policy created an elaborate system of social regulation by bureaucrats and courts that is now unresponsive to public wishes, excessively interventionist, and counterproductive.

Thus affirmative action was encouraged, or at least not halted, by both conservative Republican presidents (Nixon, Reagan, Bush) and liberal Democratic ones (Johnson, Carter, Clinton). Federal laws and executive orders to foster or mandate affirmative action could have been reversed, but were not, when both houses of Congress were controlled by Republicans (or by Democrats); they could have been declared unconstitutional, but were not, when the Supreme Court was dominated by either liberal or conservative activists. The historical record is one of growth and persistence, with considerable trimming (especially of business set-asides) and usually more lip service than effort—but without rejection of its core mission—at the federal level (Rice and Mongkuo 1998; Leadership Conference on Civil Rights 1997, 2; Anderson 1996). Thus with rare exceptions, conservative opponents have not sought to eliminate affirmative action when they might have done so; that is the first suggestion of a gap between rhetoric and practice among policy actors and advocates purportedly on the same side of the issue.

A little research provides evidence about the economic effects of affirmative action policies on African-Americans (and/or white women) and on the corporations that hire them (Leonard 1984a, 1984b, 1986, 1990; Heckman and Wolpin 1976; Heckman and Payner 1989; Badgett and Hartmann 1995; Holzer and Neumark 1996; Holzer 1996; Rodgers and Spriggs 1996). Aggregate analyses of employment suggest that affirmative action did target blacks during the 1970s, and that it contributed to the creation of a substantial black middle class that has persisted over the succeeding three decades.[13] Thus federal regulations not only institutionalized the initial policy but also produced the desired outcomes, at least to some degree.[14] Affirmative action did not, moreover, target only those already well educated or in the middle income brackets; its initial effects were greatest for people in unskilled and semiskilled job categories.[15] There is no evidence that affirmative action policies have harmed productivity of participating firms (Leonard 1984c).[16]

The same story appears to hold for university admissions, "although there has been surprisingly little systematic effort to assess their [preferences'] impact." During the 1980s, the most selective four-year colleges were most likely to admit African-American and Latino students preferentially. In nonelite schools, which 80 percent of college students attend, students of different races with similar characteristics were admitted at essentially the same rate (Kane and Dickens 1996, 6). Elite colleges were not harmed by their energetic affirmative action practices; by the end of the decade, their tuition had risen disproportionately compared with other universities', as had the number of students applying for admission.[17]

For universities as for firms, individual participants as well as the institution appear to gain from being associated with affirmative action. Attending a high-quality school yields higher earnings in adulthood, even after controlling for family background and school achievement; one study even shows higher payoffs to blacks than to whites of attending an elite school (Brewer, Eide, and Ehrenberg 1996; Kane 1998; Daniel, Black, and Smith 1995). Thus affirmative action beneficiaries at elite universities did indeed benefit, to no apparent detriment to their white fellow students.[18]

Affirmative action was not, however, the most important factor in decreasing the racial wage gap between the 1960s and 1980s. Enforcement of laws against employment discrimination, as well as increasing educational attainment and achievement among blacks, did more (Heckman and Verkerke 1990; Leonard 1990; Smith and Welch 1984, 1989). During the 1980s, when enforcement of federal affirmative action regulations was all but halted and there was no demonstrable aggregate impact of affirmative action policy, the wage gap between fully employed blacks and whites fluctuated, but did not fundamentally change (Farley 1996, 249; see also Leonard 1986).

Thus analyses of firms and universities, while thin, suggest several results: when implemented with at least a little pressure for compliance, affirmative action has had slight positive effects on beneficiary groups and no discernible negative effects on employers or colleges. When all pressure for compliance disappears, affirmative action mostly disappears. Even at its strongest, affirmative action has had less impact on racial wage inequality than have the much less controversial policies of improving educational attainment and achievement and enforcing the law against employment discrimination.

Another small arena of empirical research encompasses psychological experiments (Clayton and Crosby 1992; Crocker et al. 1991; Steele forthcoming; Nacoste 1985, 1994; Blanchard and Crosby 1989; *Basic and Applied Social Psychology* 1994). Results from these experiments are important, but so far do not move much beyond a demonstration of common sense. If people are told that affirmative action has influenced their attainment of a position, they devalue the position or their performance—more so if they disapprove of affirmative action to begin with or if it was described as playing a central role, and less so if they see the apparent authority as racially biased. White women feel more demeaned by "unwarranted help" than do African-Americans, who are more likely to see affirmative action as an entitlement. Coworkers may change their initial judgment that a new black manager is incompetent if he demonstrates that he is not or if they want to help him succeed. African-Americans perform less well than they are capable of if they believe that they are underqualified compared with white students but must nevertheless uphold the honor of their race. In short, affirmative action may or may not have harmful psychological and interpersonal effects, depending on who is involved, how the policy is deployed, and the context within which it is deployed—extremely useful knowledge, but hardly grounds for passion in either defense or opposition.

Another arena of scattered but important research findings treats the organizational effects of affirmative action (Dobbin et al. 1993; Edelman 1990, 1992; Sutton et al. 1994; Konrad and Linnehan 1995). Since the laws and executive orders creating affirmative action did not detail concrete compliance mechanisms, managers have constructed a wide variety of practices and structures. "Personnel professionals, in particular, saw opportunities in these new areas of law and promoted responses that would expand their power and numbers" (Dobbin 1996, 2). The elaborate array of rules, offices, grievance procedures, plans, tests, and other mechanisms has come to have a life of its own; "over time, these structures, more than any particular substantive result, tend to be equated with compliance" (Edelman 1996, 2). Forms of affirmative action that comport with the economic goals of a corporation—such as "diversity" for certain firms or in certain markets—become part of the corporate culture and are thereby domesticated. They neither disrupt conventional practices of hiring and promotion very much, nor do they generate much opposition. If anything, many executives and managers strongly support affirmative action *as they understand it* for several reasons: they believe that they are doing something socially productive, they believe that if properly handled "diversity" can increase their profits, and they are not paying high costs for endorsing affirmative action (Thomas and Ely 1996; Cox and Blake 1991; Badgett 1995). Again, few grounds for intense defense or opposition here.

The very small amount of aggregate data available show no evidence that affirmative action creates a sense of stigma or inferiority in its recipients. African-Americans in firms that have affirmative action programs are at least as happy in their jobs as African-Americans in firms that do not. The former demonstrate greater occupational ambition and are more likely to believe that people are helpful than the latter (Taylor 1994; Blanchard and Crosby 1989). Blacks who believe that affirmative action played a part in their hiring or promotion have no less confidence in their ability to do their job than do other workers (Hochschild 1995, 98–102, 290–92).

Surveys of public opinion offer the most fully developed research arena (Kinder and Sanders 1996; Pettigrew and Martin 1987; Bobo and Kluegel 1993; Bobo and Smith 1994; Gamson and Modigliani 1987; Sniderman and Piazza 1993; Kluegel and Smith 1983; Schuman, Steeh, and Bobo 1988). Surveys provide several results crucial to my claim that the debate over affirmative action is more symbolic than substantive. About a third of white Americans cannot make any association with the phrase "affirmative action" (Steeh and Krysan 1996, 129).[19] Those who do have an opinion on the topic (most of whom presumably have some idea of what it means), produce more consensus than one would imagine possible if one listened solely to the political activists and news media.

Consider the following findings: although about three-fourths of white Americans consistently agree that blacks should "work their way up . . . without any special favors," so do about half of black Americans. Although 85 percent or more of whites endorse "ability" rather than "preferential treatment" to determine who gets jobs and college slots, so do about three-fifths of blacks. Conversely, fully seven in ten whites (compared with over eight in ten African-Americans) favor affirmative action programs "provided there are no rigid quotas." Solid majorities in both races endorse special job training and educational assistance for women and people of color, extra efforts to identify and recruit qualified minorities, redrawing of voting districts to ensure minority representation, and other "soft" forms of affirmative action (Steeh and Krysan 1996; see also Gallup Organization 1995). One quarter of those who voted for California's referendum banning affirmative action in 1996 would have preferred a "mend it, don't end it" option (Lempinen 1996).

If one can trust survey data, then, it seems possible to develop a workable political consensus around some "soft" affirmative action policies. African-

Americans and Latinos will always support these policies more strongly than will whites, and women will support them somewhat more strongly than will men. But that is no different from the pattern of support for any policy measure that benefits some citizens more than or at the expense of others. The likelihood of different levels of enthusiasm does not stop politicians and policy planners from initiating new laws and regulations, so long as they can forge a set of rules that some people strongly endorse and most can tolerate. There might be such a set of rules to be found within the wide range of possibilities for affirmative action policy, if the troops would declare a truce in the culture war long enough to move warily toward a no-man's-land in the center.

Other survey data, however, suggest caution; this no-man's-land will be safely occupied only if perceptions of affirmative action are brought more closely into line with its practice. Relatively few whites (under 10 percent) claim to have been harmed by the workings of affirmative action policy. Nevertheless, more (up to 20 percent) claim to know someone who has been so harmed, and still more (roughly 30 percent to 40 percent) claim to have heard about someone who was so harmed. Up to 80 percent of whites believe it likely that a white will lose a job or promotion to a less qualified black due to affirmative action. One third of whites think affirmative action programs frequently "deprive someone . . . of their rights," and half of white youth (compared with one-fifth of black youth) think that more whites lose out to blacks due to "special preference" than blacks lose to whites due to prejudice (Hochschild 1995, 144, 308; Steeh and Krysan 1996, 139–40).

Unless they define affirmative action as any situation in which an African-American bests a white, regardless of why, these survey respondents are wrong. In 1994, only 2 percent of 641 government contractors polled complained of quotas or reverse discrimination. Of the more than 3,000 discrimination cases to reach courts between 1990 and 1994, fewer than 100 charged reverse discrimination; most of those, like most claims about any kind of discrimination, were dismissed due to lack of merit (Stephanopoulos and Edley 1995, sec. 6.3; Blumrosen 1995). Possibly political correctness inhibits firms from complaining about quotas, and perhaps white men suffer under the same constraint when they consider bringing charges of reverse discrimination. But surely a strong legal case would sweep aside those hypothesized constraints. Thus it seems safe to conclude that many more people are exercised by fears of the policy of affirmative action than are harmed by its implementation. *If* views about affirmative action are subject to rational consideration (a large "if," and one that I dispute over the next few pages), then wide dissemination of information about who actually benefits from or is harmed by affirmative action would be an essential component of finding a workable middle position.

Affirmative Action as Cultural Warfare

Unfortunately, many people's views about affirmative action are not subject to rational consideration, any more than people could be persuaded to think coolly about the National Bank, temperance, or communism. If people did think about affirmative action by weighing its costs against its benefits, passions would not run so high. After all, the thin but illuminating research record gives warrant to neither the hopes of affirmative action's supporters nor the fears of its opponents. The policy has certainly aided specific individuals applying to elite colleges and professional schools or to middle-level public service jobs (Collins 1983, 1997). It has arguably harmed those who would have been admitted or hired absent affirmative action (Lynch 1989; Taylor 1991). It may even have simultaneously helped *and* harmed a few people (Carter 1991; Steele forthcoming; Clayton and Crosby 1992). It has had great impact on police and fire departments, on a few law and medical schools, and on the military. But compared to legislation and litigation against employment discrimination or barriers to voting and office holding or segregated schools, affirmative action has had relatively little aggregate impact. And it has, perhaps, benefited professional personnel officers and attorneys more than any other single group of people.

We face therefore two puzzles. Why are a lot of people so exercised over this particular policy, which distributes outcomes about as most other policies do and has done less to change American racial hierarchies than have a variety of other noncontroversial policies? And why is the empirical base for understanding the practice and effects of affirmative action so thin and publicly invisible, compared with the rich philosophical and legal arguments that the issue has evoked?

These two puzzles are both resolved by one answer: political actors find affirmative action an immensely valuable issue over which to debate, and therefore have little desire to figure out just how it operates. That is, affirmative action is too precious as a political weapon in a broader cultural war about what it means to be a good American to be blunted by attention to real-life complexities.

Many opponents of affirmative action are less concerned with the policy per se than with a wider assertion that racial (or gender) discrimination no longer exists, and that African-Americans' continued claims of its persistence are merely whining or self-seeking. At their crudest, opponents are racially hostile. Less crudely, they are unable or unwilling to see structural barriers or institutional advantages that are independent of individual intentions or awareness. The most sophisticated opponents are more concerned about class or individual, rather than racial or gender, barriers (Lind 1995; Woodson 1996), or they judge the costs of a continued focus on racial differences to be too great now that the black middle class is fairly well established (Sleeper 1997; Gitlin 1995), or they judge that laws and regulations against employment discrimination are strong enough to take care of the remaining racial bias in jobs (Heckman, personal communication, 1997). Alternatively, they espouse a principle of individual meritocracy that supersedes all caveats or shadings (Glazer 1975; Eastland 1996; Thernstrom and Thernstrom 1997).

Many proponents of affirmative action demonstrate an equal but opposite dynamic. They are less concerned with the policy per se than with a wider assertion that racial (or gender) discrimination is just as virulent as it has always been, and that whites' opposition is merely covert racism or inexcusable naïveté (Preston and Lai 1998). At their crudest, proponents are paranoid or self-seeking. Less crudely they believe, as one of my students recently put it, that blacks have just as much right to a class structure as whites do and just as much right to use all means legally available to reach the top of it. The most sophisticated proponents see affirmative action as a means for individual blacks to overcome persistent racism and attain resources that will help the African-American community and the nation as a whole to overcome its shameful past—Du Bois's talented tenth (Rosenfeld 1991). Alternatively, they see employment discrimination (or biases in universities' admissions policies) as sufficiently subtle as well as widespread that standard laws and litigation are insufficient. In this view, people of color and/or white women must be inserted into the core of the hiring/promotion/admissions processes in order to identify and bring to justice persistent hidden biases that work on behalf of white men (Bergmann 1996; Edley 1996; Gutmann's essay in Appiah and Gutmann 1996).

Political elites within these groups do not talk to one another and have no electoral, social, or organizational incentive to do so. Legally, they each have a rich set of court cases, laws, and regulations to bolster their claims. Normatively, each group has available to it more philosophical justifications for its position than anyone can possibly read or use. Historically, each group can point to its preferred victories and defeats. Politically, each group has a core constituency and a wider set of citizens to whom it can turn for occasional support. Organizationally, each group has well-established but complex and constantly renegotiated (thus energy-draining) internal ties of communication, bargaining, and resource extraction to maintain. Socially, members of the two groups seldom encounter one another outside of formal, scripted disputes. Neither group has, in short, much reason or incentive to question its own position or give serious consideration to the other's. (Skerry 1997 gives a somewhat similar analysis.)

Where does academic research fit into this picture? Not very clearly anywhere, which may explain why there has been so little of it compared with argumentation that is not empirically based. That is unfortunate for at least two reasons. First, some fascinating research questions are so far left untouched.

Second, in my view only reasonably dispassionate analyses could provide the possibility of intellectual space for people to separate their broad beliefs about being a good American from their particular judgments about the efficacy of affirmative action compared with other possible routes to racial equality. Only if there is a cohort of people who can persuasively say, "it works in this regard but not in that one" or "it works better than X but not as well as Y to achieve goal Z" have we as a nation any chance to get past the shouting.[20]

Why have advocates on all sides of the debate over American racial policy seized on affirmative action rather than, for example, wage discrimination or the quality of schooling in inner cities as the battleground for deciding what it means to be a good American? After all, affirmative action neither affects many whites nor comes close to solving the deepest problems of African-Americans. So why is it "the highest pole in the storm"?[21] Partly because opposition to affirmative action is one of the few remaining respectable vehicles for seeking to maintain white domination. No public figure can any longer argue, as one could fifty years ago, in favor of lesser schooling for black children or different wages for the same work based on one's gender and race.[22] In that sense, "ascriptive Americanism" lost the public debate to liberalism in the last third of the twentieth century (Smith 1997). But even if part of one's motivation is to resist black competitive success, one *can* oppose affirmative action in the name of values that all Americans publicly claim to share (see Hochschild 1995, chap. 7, on white opposition to black competitive success).

Opposition to affirmative action remains respectable because both sides to this dispute call on Americans' deepest and most cherished values (often the same value, in fact) and evoke the same cultural tropes to defend their position. That cultural construct can be characterized as the American dream. The ideology of the American dream is the promise that all Americans, regardless of their race, sex, or background, can reasonably anticipate the attainment of some success, if they use means under their own control such as talent, ambition, and hard work. The pursuit of success is associated with virtue, and so can legitimately be seen as noble and elevating, rather than merely materialistic or selfish (Hochschild 1995). More precisely, the ideology of the American dream implies a balanced contract between the public sector and private individuals. The government is expected to provide equality of opportunity—thus no discrimination by race, gender, class, or religion—and a structure that makes anticipation of success reasonable—thus a strong system of public education, a flourishing economy with plenty of jobs, physical security from enemies without and crime within the nation. Citizens, in turn, are expected to take care of themselves within the framework established by the government—to attain skills, support themselves and their families, refrain from discrimination or false claims of victimization, and follow a moral code.

Most Americans believe in each component of the American dream and most share an implicit conviction that the balance between governmental and personal responsibility is about right (Hochschild 1995, chap. 1). Hence the United States lacks strong libertarian and Marxist political parties, as well as widespread white racist or black nationalist social movements. But partly because that shared cultural construct is so strong, Americans contend fiercely over just how to translate its general guidelines into concrete practice.

To some, the culture evoked by the ideology of the American dream is irrevocably individualist. The ideology is intended to create a structure within which each person can rise or fall according to his or her merit alone. Some individualists reluctantly support affirmative action on the grounds that it is a necessary way station on the path from racial domination to race-blind individualism. But most see affirmative action as a denial of the deepest tenets of the American dream, since in their eyes it gives special privileges to some at the expense of others. The government formerly discriminated in favor of whites, and now it discriminates in favor of blacks—those are equal violations of the ideology of the American dream and they should be equally prohibited.

To others, the culture instantiated by the American dream is not necessarily individualist. The ideology can be just as well interpreted to mean that groups have the right to pursue success collectively. Until a group succeeds according to its own light, the individuals within it cannot attain their dreams (alternatively, the pursuit of group success shapes and directs individuals' dreams). In the eyes of those committed to group identity as a defining characteristic of social engagement, prior (or current) discrimination in favor of whites is not symmetrical with current proactive efforts to benefit blacks. Until the two races are equal in political power, economic means, social status, and cultural autonomy, equality of opportunity does not exist in the United States and calls for symmetry are a mere pretense for continued domination.

Just as principled opposition to affirmative action may reinforce or be a cover for a desire to retain white racial domination, principled support for affirmative action may similarly reinforce a desire to use public policies to benefit oneself or one's group. After all, Americans (like most other humans, probably) have historically shown themselves adept at making normative arguments that coincide with their self-interest. There is no reason to suppose that middle-class African-Americans are any different from European-Americans in this regard.

Thus some Americans see strong forms of affirmative action as violating the values of individualism, equal opportunity, and meritocracy that instantiate the American dream. Some of them may have less respectable grounds for opposition that merge with those values. Others see strong forms of affirmative action as the only lever available to pry open the hypocritical claim of purported equality but actual racial domination that characterizes "Amerikkka." Some of them too may have other, less publicly compelling, reasons for support that merge with their understanding of the American dream. Where self-interest and ideology coincide so powerfully and in two such directly opposed camps, nuanced skepticism or support do not flourish.

The clash between contending sets of interests and values is exacerbated by a growing perceptual gap between the races. On the one hand, the best-off African-Americans—those best poised to take advantage of the opportunities that affirmative action offers—increasingly distrust white Americans' racial values and practices. In the 1960s, poorly educated blacks were more likely than well-educated blacks to agree that "whites want to keep blacks down"; by the 1980s, the positions of the two groups were reversed (Hochschild 1995, 74). In 1990 and again in 1996, well-educated blacks agreed more than did poorly educated blacks that "the Government deliberately makes sure that drugs are easily available in poor black neighborhoods in order to harm black people" (Hochschild 1995, 74, and analyses of the *New York Times*/CBS News survey of October 13, 1996, in possession of author).[23] Given a perception of intransigent and even growing white racism in the United States, affirmative action becomes a crucial weapon in well-off African-Americans' arsenal (Hochschild 1995, chaps. 4–7; Bositis 1997; and Gallup Organization 1997).

On the other hand, whites are increasingly convinced that racial discrimination is declining, and that blacks no longer suffer much from the effects of previous discrimination. In 1995, 55 percent of whites (compared with 29 percent of blacks) mistakenly agreed that "the average African American" is as well off as or better off than "the average white person" in terms of jobs and education. Over 40 percent of whites (and about 20 percent of blacks) held the same mistaken view with regard to housing and income (Washington Post et al. 1995). By the 1990s a majority of whites typically agreed that blacks have equal or greater opportunities than do whites to get ahead generally, to attain an education, to be admitted to college, and to get a job (Hochschild 1995, 60–64, appendix B). They see the existence of the new black middle class as evidence to support that perception. And given that 15 percent of whites agree with the very strong statement that "almost all of the gains made by blacks in recent years have come at the expense of whites," it is especially striking that the "average American" estimates up to one-third of Americans to be black and one-fifth to be Latino (the real figures are 12 percent and 9 percent) (Hochschild 1995, 143; Gallup and Newport 1990; Nadeau, Niemi, and Levine 1993; Washington Post et al. 1995, table 1.1).

Thus for some whites as well as for some middle-class blacks, perceptions unite with interests and values to create passionate convictions about affirmative action, essentially regardless of whether it "works" or not. No wonder there is a culture war over an issue that directly affects only a small fraction of the American population.

Is There an Escape from the Impasse?

I noted earlier a broad band of rough consensus in the survey data—quotas or preferences are bad (the Supreme Court agrees) but extra efforts to identify and train people who have been disadvantaged by race or gender is good (again, the Supreme Court agrees). That is a workable starting point for designing a policy that could achieve many of the purposes of affirmative action without generating so much hostility—if people are susceptible to compromise on this issue.[24]

Even those who voted for California's Proposition 209 in the November 1996 election were not all strongly opposed to affirmative action, and even those who voted against it were not all strongly supportive. A Field Poll conducted several days after the vote found that fewer than half of those who opposed the proposition agreed that "affirmative action policies should not be changed." A third of the opponents further agreed that "affirmative action policies should be relaxed somewhat." Conversely, about a quarter of its supporters agreed that affirmative action policies should not be changed, or should be relaxed but not eliminated (Lempinen 1996). Some of these voters may simply have been confused about what they were voting for, but many apparently would have preferred a middle ground to the two stark alternatives they were offered. Similarly, 65 percent of respondents to a national survey the day of the 1996 presidential election hoped that President Clinton would "put more emphasis on affirmative action to improve educational and job opportunities for women and minorities" in a second term ("Clinton's Second Term" 1996, 1). In Houston, Texas, 55 percent of the voters in November 1997 rejected a proposition that would have banned "affirmative action" in city contracting and hiring (Verhovek 1997b).[25] In all of these cases, we see the glimmering of a political context in which citizens' opinions on affirmative action could come to stand for something other than racism or denial of meritocracy.

Similarly, many public officials and corporate officers seem wiser than either the activists or the academics. They focus more on the actual workings of affirmative action than the latter, and they find affirmative action more manipulable and less revolutionary (for better or for worse) than the former (Wolfe 1996). Local public officials find that appointing a few well-connected black advocates has symbolic as well as substantive payoffs in the next election. Corporate managers find that affirmative action has shifted from a pesky problem to a core management tool. A decade ago, problems of "equal employment opportunity" came in almost last (just above sexual harassment) on a list of executives' "human-resource management issues"; by 1992, "cultural diversity" led corporate executives' list of "workforce concerns." Almost two-thirds of companies surveyed by the Conference Board in 1991 offered diversity training to their employees, and most of the rest planned to do so soon (Schein 1986; Towers Perrin 1992, 3; Wheeler 1994, 9; Glater and Hamilton 1995). The Conference Board now promotes conferences and publishes reports on "managing diversity for sustaining competitiveness" (Conference Board 1997).

We have, then, an electorate and many public and private officials who apparently seek a middle ground of "extra help" but not "reverse discrimination," faced with a paired set of fiercely vocal activists who portray their opposites as either racist or un-American. For the former group, affirmative action is a policy with virtues and defects, appropriate interpretations and outrageous distortions—much like any other policy. Its members have little use for academic analyses of the policy, but for the same reason that they have little use for academic analyses of virtually all policies; scholars arc too slow, too methodologically driven, or too attuned to deep structures rather than useable facts. For the latter group, affirmative action is a symbol of deep racial claims and anxieties. Its members too have no use for empirical evidence, not because they find scholars irrelevant (often they are themselves scholars), but because the most careful analyses show that affirmative action seldom has dramatic impact, whether positive or negative, and that it frequently has unintended and ironic consequences.

At the most general level, affirmative action serves as a Rorschach test for anxieties about the meaning and validity of the American dream and the culture that it instantiates. Many African-Americans fear, perhaps rightly, that the American dream—and American society—was never meant to include them and can never be wrenched from its historical role of enabling some white men to legitimately dominate all other residents of the United States. In their eyes affirmative action puts into practice a new and more sympathetic interpretation of the nation's core ideology. It is also one of the only levers available to pry apart the tightly linked chains of meritocratic beliefs, personalistic practices, and structural biases in favor of the well-off. Many whites (especially but not only men) fear, perhaps rightly, that the American dream is losing its hold on Americans' moral imagination. They see affirmative action as the tempter leading people to believe that what they do does not matter as much as who they are. For both groups, the devil is at the gate, and affirmative action is implicated in the defense of the city. Under these circumstances, we should not be surprised that evidence on how it actually works is irrelevant to all except those who have to put the policy into practice, and live with it.

Notes

My thanks for comments on an earlier draft of this article to Amy Gutmann, Marianne Engelman Lado, Luke Harris, Ira Katznelson, Michèle Lamont, Dale Miller, John Skrentny, Alan Wolfe, and the participants in Princeton University seminars on Race, Culture, and Power, and in the Program in Ethics and Public Affairs.

1. For example, Edley's (1996) excellent book devotes 12 of its 280 text pages to "facts" about America's racial situation (and of them, only 3 pages address the effectiveness of affirmative action policies). A special issue on affirmative action of the *Issues Quarterly* of the National Council for Research on Women (1996) devotes 1 of its 12 substantive pages to "the evidence." One of the most sophisticated recent analyses of the meaning of race and racial policies is Appiah and Gutmann 1996.

2. The past decade has seen important judicial decisions on the extent of and reasons for affirmative action that are legally acceptable. These include *City of Richmond v. J. A. Croson Co.* (1989), *Adarand Constructors, Inc., v. Peña* (1995), and *Hopwood v. University of Texas* (1996). These decisions, however, did more to specify (mostly to narrow) the conditions under which affirmative action may be used and to define more precisely what the term itself may legitimately mean than to change the nature of the underlying debate over the need for affirmative action.

3. Note the obvious but important point that there is no single entity or process called "affirmative action"; the term is used to mean everything from efforts to ensure a broad applicant pool to strict quotas. Both proponents and opponents play verbal games with the term.

4. Another caveat: individual institutions and agencies sometimes analyze their own practices, and occasionally compare their own with similar institutions' practices. But these analyses are seldom made public, and by definition are not conducted by neutral evaluators. Policy analysts have known for decades that it is virtually impossible for an organization to evaluate its own practices in ways that are uncontaminated by internal politics or by the goals of the evaluators, no matter how hard they try. So even if these analyses exist, they do not count much against the claim in the text.

5. Many journalists have made some variant of this claim, but researchers have not investigated it carefully (Broder and Barnes 1995; Langfitt 1995; DelVecchio 1996; Pulley 1996; Kahlenberg 1996).

6. The *San Francisco Examiner* (Ness 1996) found that 50 percent of women (compared with 57 percent of men) and 45 percent of Asian-Americans (compared with 60 percent of whites, 26 percent of blacks, and 30 percent of Latinos) voted for Proposition 209 (the California Civil Rights Initiative) in November 1996. White men and women supported the anti–affirmative action proposition more strongly than did men or women of color. The *Los Angeles Times* ("State Propositions" 1996) reported essentially the same results from its own poll. Onishi (1996) provides a good analysis of the Asian-American college students' ambivalent views about affirmative action.

7. To give only one example of the many observations similar to my own: "Affirmative action's detractors have generally sidestepped time-consuming, substantive research to

verify their suppositions about who actually participates in or benefits from such programs. Even scholarly opponents of affirmative action have resorted to emotionally-charged rhetoric without offering clear evidence of their claims of reverse discrimination" (Washington State Commission on African American Affairs 1995a, 10). I would simply add that advocates have done little more.

8. The argument in this paper extends and develops my analysis in Hochschild 1995. That book eschewed discussion of specific policy or political issues, since it focused on variations within and across broad ideologies, especially the ideology of the American dream. Disputes over the meaning of the American dream, however, are often played out in the political and policy arena; I argue below that affirmative action is one of the most important sites for such a dispute. If Americans believed less intensely in those values that they hold in common, they might dispute less vigorously over how to translate those values into practice. That, at least, is one lesson of the culture war over affirmative action.

9. Holzer and Neumark (1996, 2) observe that "despite the intensity of the viewpoints held, the evidence to date on this issue [specifically, the underqualification of affirmative action beneficiaries] remains quite thin." I agree with them on the intensity and the thinness; in my view, however, the evidence is thin *because of* rather than *despite* the intensity of the viewpoints.

10. On the Bank War, see Meyers 1957; on temperance, see Gusfield 1986 and 1996; on McCarthyism, see Fried 1997 and Schrecker 1986. On the social construction of crises more generally, see Larana, Johnston, and Gusfield 1994 and Gamson 1990.

11. The best and most recent survey of empirical research on affirmative action is Reskin 1998. Readers of an earlier draft of this chapter pointed out that "much of the debate over affirmative action has taken place in the legal arena. . . . [Therefore] the lawyers and their experts build a record to support or oppose an affirmative action policy. . . . Moreover, . . . many public agencies and other organizations that receive federal assistance have conducted searching reviews of their affirmative action policies and extensive fact-finding" (personal communication from Marianne Engelman Lado and Luke Harris). They are, of course, correct, and this huge subterranean literature would be a gold mine for researchers seeking to make comparisons and draw generalizations about how and why affirmative action functions. But part of my point is the fact that researchers have seldom dug into this gold mine. And in any case each analysis in this literature is biased in favor of or against affirmative action since it was conducted by partisans in the middle of an active debate.

12. From here on, I will focus mostly on race-based rather than gender-based affirmative action, simply because I know more about the former than the latter. As I understand it, however, the evidence is roughly similar with regard to white women as it is for black women and men. However, the symbolic politics of affirmative action probably differ significantly between race and gender, and it would be illuminating to develop their differences in more detail.

13. For example, "between 1970 and 1990, the number of black electricians more than tripled (from 14,145 to 43,276) and the number of black police officers increased almost as rapidly (from 23,796 to 63,855)" (Karabel 1993, 159).

14. However, in Washington State "*whites* [including men as well as women] are the primary beneficiaries of the state's affirmative action program affecting hiring, . . . of special admissions programs at public institutions of higher learning, . . . [and] of programs designed to assist minority- and women-owned firms seeking to do business with the state" (Washington State Commission on African American Affairs, 1995a, 1; see also idem 1995b and 1995c). These and other possibly contradictory findings point up the need for more systematic research using a variety of methods, data, and analytic frameworks.

15. However, Holzer (1996, 21–23) finds "a strong *positive* correlation between education levels of hires and Affirmative Action." See also Holzer and Neumark 1996.

16. Echoing my complaint above, Holzer (1996, 29) points out that "we have little strong evidence to date on the efficiency effects of these programs, or on whether they generate any net new employment for less-educated workers." Firms subject to affirmative action regulations experience an increase of about 5 percent in labor costs compared with firms not so subject, according to the only set of scholars who have studied the issue (Griffin, Getis, and Griffin 1996, 39).

17. Average undergraduate tuition charges in private four-year colleges rose from under $4,000 in 1980 to almost $13,000 in 1996–97. Tuition charges in public four-year colleges rose during the same period from about $1,000 to $3,000 ("Tuition Trends" 1997; for more detail, see Clotfelter 1996).

18. Would-be students who are not admitted to elite universities have stronger grounds for opposing affirmative action. But their claim of harm or injustice is weak for two reasons. First, the overwhelming majority of applicants would not be admitted to Harvard or Princeton even if every beneficiary of affirmative action were denied a slot in the freshman class. (Fewer than 15 percent of those who apply to Princeton are admitted.) Second, no one has a right to admission to an elite private (or public) university or to a given job; one may be deeply disappointed by rejection, but one has no legitimate claim about unjust treatment.

19. Over four in ten Americans (41 percent of whites and Asians, 62 percent of blacks, and 57 percent of Latinos) perceive that "white men are generally covered under federal affirmative action" (Morin 1995). Legally speaking they are correct. But I think it fair to assume that in the context of public opinion surveys, this result indicates ignorance of how affirmative action normally operates rather than subtle knowledge of the law.

20. As President Clinton put it rather plaintively in his conversation with a group of racial conservatives, "I'd like to . . . hear from you . . . on the question of, 'Do you believe that race . . . is still a problem in some ways?' And if so, instead of our getting into a big fight about affirmative action. . . ." His plea was largely ignored; most responses to his and Vice President Gore's questions came back to a statement of opposition to preferences (Excerpts from Round Table 1997).

21. Comment by Christopher Edley, in Holmes 1997, 1. Edley goes on, as reported in the same article, to observe, "You can look at those figures [on how many are affected by federal contracts and elite college admissions] and ask, why are black folks making such a big deal out of affirmative action? That's the wrong question. The real question is why are white folks making such a big deal out of it?"

22. In 1942, only 32 percent of Americans agreed that white and black students should attend the same schools, and only 46 percent opposed "separate sections for Negroes in streetcars and buses." As late as 1963, fewer than half of Americans agreed that they would vote for a black presidential candidate of their political party even if he were qualified. Even more tellingly for this paper, in 1944 and again in 1946, fewer than half of Americans agreed that "Negroes should have as good a chance as white people to get any kind of job." The alternative response was "white people should have the first chance at any kind of job" (Schuman, Steeh, and Bobo 1988, 74; all responses are percentages of those giving a substantive answer).

23. The 1990 survey was of residents of New York City; the 1996 survey was a national random sample. My thanks to Michael Kagay of the *New York Times* for analyzing the data and discussing their interpretations with me.

24. If I were made race czar, I would work to strengthen at least the "soft" forms of affirmative action. In the long run, however, I would prefer for the state of California, among others, to engage in structural reforms of inner-city schools rather than merely allowing U.C. Berkeley to pick out the few black or Latino students who have somehow triumphed over the wasteland that has demoralized all of their fellow students. The university itself has taken tentative steps in that direction, in response to the brutal abolition of affirmative action through Proposition 209 (Tien forthcoming; Ponessa 1997).

25. Polls prior to the election showed that two-thirds of Houston's voters would have supported a proposition to "not discriminate against or grant preferential treatment to" any person or group based on race, sex, or ethnicity (Verhovek 1997a). The two propositions would have had identical effects; all the difference lay in the wording or, in my terms, in which variant of the American dream is invoked by the fluid concept of affirmative action.

References

Anderson, Bernard. 1996. "The Ebb and Flow of Enforcing Executive Order 11246." *American Economic Review* 86:298–301.

Appiah, K. Anthony, and Amy Gutmann. 1996. *Color Conscious.* Princeton: Princeton University Press.

Badgett, M. V. Lee. 1995. "Affirmative Action in a Changing Legal and Economic Environment." *Industrial Relations* 34:489–506.

Badgett, M. V. Lee, and Heidi Hartmann. 1995. *The Effectiveness of Equal Employment Opportunity Policies.* Washington: Joint Center for Political and Economic Research.

Basic and Applied Social Psychology. 1994. Special issue on affirmative action. Vol. 15, nos. 1 and 2.

Bates, Timothy, and Darrell Williams. 1996. "Do Preferential Procurement Programs Benefit Minority Businesses?" *Papers and Proceedings of the American Economic Association* 86:294–97.

Bennett, Stephen Earl, Alfred Tuchfarber, Andrew Smith, and Erick W. Rademacher. 1995. "Americans' Opinions of Affirmative Action." Unpublished paper. Institute for Policy Research, University of Cincinnati.

Bergmann, Barbara. 1996. *In Defense of Affirmative Action.* New York: Basic.

Blanchard, P. A., and Faye J. Crosby, eds. 1989. *Affirmative Action in Perspective.* New York: Springer-Verlag.

Blumrosen, Alfred W. 1995. "Draft Report on Reverse Discrimination Commissioned by Labor Department: How Courts Are Handling Reverse Discrimination Cases." *Daily Labor Report,* March 23. Washington: Bureau of National Affairs.

Bobo, Lawrence, and James R. Kluegel. 1993. "Opposition to Race Targeting." *American Sociological Review* 58:443–64.

Bobo, Lawrence, and Ryan A. Smith. 1994. "Antipoverty Policy, Affirmative Action, and Racial Attitudes." In *Confronting Poverty: Prescriptions for Change,* edited by Sheldon Danziger, Gary Sandefur, and Daniel Weinberg. New York: Russell Sage Foundation; Cambridge: Harvard University Press.

Bositis, David. 1997. *1997 National Opinion Poll: Race Relations.* Washington: Joint Center for Political and Economic Studies.

Brewer, Dominic, Eric Eide, and Ronald Ehrenberg. 1996. "Does It Pay to Attend an Elite Private College?" Working Paper 5613. National Bureau of Economic Research, Cambridge, Mass.

Broder, David, and Robert Barnes. 1995. "Few Governors Join Attack on Racial Policies." *Washington Post,* August 2, A01 ff.

Burstein, Paul. 1985. *Discrimination, Jobs, and Politics.* Chicago: University of Chicago Press.

Carter, Stephen L. 1991. *Reflections of an Affirmative Action Baby.* New York: Basic.

Clayton, Susan D., and Faye J. Crosby. 1992. *Justice, Gender, and Affirmative Action.* Ann Arbor: University of Michigan Press.

"Clinton's Second Term." 1996. *The Polling Report* 12 (November 18): 1, 6.

Clotfelter, Charles. 1996. *Buying the Best.* Princeton: Princeton University Press.

Collins, Sharon M. 1983. "The Making of the Black Middle Class." *Social Problems* 30:369–82.

———. 1997. *Black Corporate Executives.* Philadelphia: Temple University Press.

Conference Board. 1997. *Managing Diversity for Sustaining Competitiveness.* New York: Conference Board.

Cox, Taylor H., and Stacy Blake. 1991. "Managing Cultural Diversity: Implications for Organizational Competitiveness." *Academy of Management Executive* 5:45–56.

Crocker, Jennifer, Kristin Voellel, Maria Testa, and Brenda Major. 1991. "Social Stigma: The Affective Consequences of Attributional Ambiguity." *Journal of Personality and Social Psychology* 60:218–28.

Daniel, Kermit, Dan Black, and Jeffrey Smith. 1995. "College Quality and the Wages of Young Men." Unpublished paper. University of Pennsylvania, Wharton School.

DelVecchio, Rick. 1996. "Cities Trying to Detour Past Prop. 209," *San Francisco Chronicle,* November 25, A1 ff.

Dobbin, Frank. 1996. "Organizational Response to Affirmative Action and Equal Employment Law." Memo to Conference on Social Science Perspectives on Affirmative Action, American Sociological Association, Washington.

Dobbin, Frank, John Sutton, John Meyer, and W. R. Scott. 1993. "Equal Opportunity

Law and the Construction of Internal Labor Markets." *American Journal of Sociology* 99:396–427.

Eastland, Terry. 1996. *Ending Affirmative Action.* New York: Basic.

Edelman, Lauren. 1990. "Legal Environments and Organizational Governance: The Expansion of Due Process in the Workplace." *American Journal of Sociology* 95: 1401–40.

———. 1992. "Legal Ambiguity and Symbolic Structures: Organizational Mediation of Civil Rights Law." *American Journal of Sociology* 97:1531–76.

———. 1996. "Affirmative Action in Employment." Memo to Conference on Social Science Perspectives on Affirmative Action, American Sociological Association, Washington.

Edley, Christopher, Jr. 1996. *Not All Black and White.* New York: Hill and Wang.

Enchautegui, Maria, Michael Fix, Pamela Loprest, Sarah von der Lippe, and Douglas Wissoker. 1996. "Do Minority-Owned Businesses Get a Fair Share of Government Contracts?" *Policy and Research Report* (Urban Institute), summer/fall, 4–7.

"Excerpts from Round Table with Opponents of Racial Preferences." 1997. *New York Times,* December 22, A24.

Farley, Reynolds. 1996. *The New American Reality.* New York: Russell Sage Foundation.

Finley, Steve. 1996. "Re: Being a Privileged White Male." On Listserv Athena-discuss @info.harpercollins.com, June 5.

Fried, Albert. 1997. *McCarthyism.* New York: Oxford University Press.

Gallup, George, Jr., and Frank Newport. 1990. "Americans Ignorant of Basic Census Facts." *Gallup Poll Monthly,* no. 294:2–5.

Gallup Organization. 1995. *Affirmative Action.* Princeton: Gallup Organization.

———. 1997. *The Gallup Poll Social Audit on Black/White Relations in the United States.* Princeton: Gallup Organization.

Gamson, William. 1990. *The Strategy of Social Protest.* 2d ed. Belmont, Calif.: Wadsworth.

Gamson, William, and Andre Modigliani. 1987. "The Changing Culture of Affirmative Action." *Research in Political Sociology* 3:137–77.

Gitlin, Todd. 1995. *The Twilight of Common Dreams.* New York: Metropolitan.

Glater, Jonathan, and Martha Hamilton. 1995. "Affirmative Action's Corporate Converts." *Washington Post,* March 19, H1, H6.

Glazer, Nathan. 1975. *Affirmative Discrimination.* New York: Basic.

Graham, Hugh Davis. Forthcoming. "The Paradox of American Civil Rights Regulation, 1964–1994." In *Taking Stock: American Government in the Twentieth Century,* edited by Morton Keller and R. Shep Melnick. New York: Cambridge University Press.

Griffin, Peter, Arthus Getis, and Ernst Griffin. 1996. "Regional Patterns of Affirmative Action Compliance Costs." *Annals of Regional Science* 30:321–40.

Gusfield, Joseph. 1986. *Symbolic Crusade.* 2d ed. Urbana: University of Illinois Press.

———. 1996. *Contested Meanings.* Madison: University of Wisconsin Press.

Heckman, James, and Brook Payner. 1989. "Determining the Impact of Federal Antidiscrimination Policy on the Economic Status of Blacks: A Study of South Carolina." *American Economic Review* 79:138–77.

Heckman, James, and J. Hoult Verkerke. 1990. "Racial Disparity and Economic Discrimination Law: An Economic Perspective." *Yale Law and Policy Review* 8:276–98.

Heckman, James, and Kenneth Wolpin. 1976. "Does the Contract Compliance Program Work? An Analysis of Chicago Data." *Industrial and Labor Relations Review* 29: 544–64.

Hochschild, Jennifer L. 1995. *Facing Up to the American Dream.* Princeton: Princeton University Press.

Holmes, Steven. 1997. "Thinking about Race with a One-Track Mind." *New York Times,* December 21, sec. 4, p. 1.

Holzer, Harry. 1996. "Employer Hiring Decisions and Antidiscrimination Policy." Institute for Research on Poverty Discussion Paper no. 1085–96. University of Wisconsin, Madison.

Holzer, Harry, and David Neumark. 1996. "Are Affirmative Action Hires Less Qualified? Evidence from Employer-Employee Data on New Hires." Working Paper no. 5603. National Bureau of Economic Research, Cambridge, Mass.

House Government Operations Committee, U.S. Congress. 1994. *Problems Facing Minority and Women-Owned Small Business Including SBA Section 8(a) Firms in Procuring U.S. Government Contracts: An Interim Report.* HRPT. no. 103–870.

Kahlenberg, Richard. 1996. "Bob Dole's Colorblind Injustice." *Washington Post,* June 2, C1, C4.

Kane, Thomas. 1998. "Racial and Ethnic Preference in College Admissions." In *The Black-White Test Score Gap,* edited by Christopher Jencks and Meredith Phillips. Washington: Brookings Institution.

Kane, Thomas, and William Dickens. 1996. "Racial and Ethnic Preferences in College Admissions." Brookings Policy Brief no. 9. Washington: Brookings Institution.

Karabel, Jerome. 1993. "Berkeley and Beyond." *American Prospect* 12:156–60.

Kinder, Donald R., and Lynn M. Sanders. 1996. *Divided by Color.* Chicago: University of Chicago Press.

Kluegel, James R., and Eliot R. Smith. 1983. "Affirmative Action Attitudes: Effects of Self-interest, Racial Affect, and Stratification Beliefs on Whites' Views." *Social Forces* 61:797–825.

Konrad, Alison, and Frank Linnehan. 1995. "Formalized HRM Structures: Coordinating Equal Employment Opportunity or Concealing Organizational Practices?" *Academy of Management Journal* 38:787–820.

Langfitt, Frank. 1995. "GOP Abandons Effort on Minority Set-asides." *Baltimore Sun,* May 23, 1B.

Larana, Enrique, Hank Johnston, and Joseph Gusfield, eds. 1994. *New Social Movements.* Philadelphia: Temple University Press.

Leadership Conference on Civil Rights. 1997. *Affirmative Action for Women and Minorities.* Washington: Leadership Conference on Civil Rights.

Lempinen, Edward. 1996. "Affirmative Action Foes Span Spectrum." *San Francisco Chronicle,* November 22, B1 ff.

Leonard, Jonathan. 1984a. "The Impact of Affirmative Action on Employment." *Journal of Labor Economics* 2:439–63.

————. 1984b. "Employment and Occupational Advance under Affirmative Action." *Review of Economics and Statistics* 66:377–85.

————. 1984c. "Anti-discrimination or Reverse Discrimination: The Impact of Changing Demographics, Title VII, and Affirmative Action on Productivity." *Journal of Human Resources* 19:145–74.

————. 1986. "What Was Affirmative Action?" *American Economic Review* 76:359–63.

————. 1990. "The Impact of Affirmative Action Regulation and Equal Employment Law on Black Employment." *Journal of Economic Perspectives* 4:47–63.

————. 1996. "Wage Disparities and Affirmative Action in the 1980s." *Papers and Proceedings of the American Economic Association* 86:285–89.

Lind, Michael. 1995. *The Next American Nation.* New York: Free Press.

Lynch, Frederick R. 1989. *Invisible Victims.* New York: Greenwood.

Meyers, Marvin. 1957. *The Jacksonian Persuasion.* Stanford: Stanford University Press.

Morin, Richard. 1995. "Affirmative Action for White Guys?" *Washington Post,* October 22, C5.

Myers, Samuel, and Tsze Chan. 1996. "Who Benefits from Minority Business Set-Asides? The Case of New Jersey." *Journal of Policy Analysis and Management* 15:202–26.

Nacoste, Rupert. 1985. "Selection Procedure and Responses to Affirmative Action." *Law and Human Behavior* 9:225–42.

————. 1994. "If Empowerment Is the Goal . . . : Affirmative Action and Social Interaction." *Basic and Applied Social Psychology* 15:87–112.

Nadeau, Richard, Richard Niemi, and Jeffrey Levine. 1993. "Innumeracy about Minority Populations." *Public Opinion Quarterly* 57:332–47.

National Council for Research on Women. 1996. "Affirming Diversity: Building a National Community That Works." *Issues Quarterly* 1:1–28.

Ness, Carol. 1996. "Prop. 209 Wins, Heads for Courts." *San Francisco Examiner,* November 6, A1 ff.

Onishi, Norimitsu. 1996. "Affirmative Action: Choosing Sides." *New York Times,* section on "Education Life," March 31, 26–35.

Oreskes, Michael. 1984. "The Set-Aside Scam." *New Republic,* December 24, 17–20.

Pettigrew, Thomas, and Joanne Martin. 1987. "Shaping the Organizational Context for Black American Inclusion." *Journal of Social Issues* 43:41–78.

Ponessa, Jeanne. 1997. "Higher Ed. Outreach Plan Targets At-Risk Calif. Youths." *Education Week,* June 4, 5.

Preston, Michael, and James Lai. 1998. "The Symbolic Politics of Affirmative Action." In *Racial and Ethnic Politics in California,* vol. 2, edited by Michael Preston, Bruce Cain, and Sandra Bass. Berkeley: University of California, Institute of Governmental Studies Press.

Pulley, Brett. 1996. "Affirmative Action: Can Whitman Stand Firm?" *New York Times,* November 24, New Jersey section, p. 2.

Reskin, Barbara. 1998. *The Realities of Affirmative Action.* Washington: American Sociological Association.

Rice, Mitchell, and Maurice Mongkuo. 1998. "Did *Adarand* Kill Minority Set-Asides?" *Public Administration Review* 58:82–86.

Rodgers, William, III, and William Spriggs. 1996. "The Effect of Federal Contractor Status on Racial Differences in Establishment-Level Employment Shares: 1979–1992." *American Economic Review* 86:290–93.

Rosenfeld, Michel. 1991. *Affirmative Action and Justice.* New Haven: Yale University Press.

Schein, Lawrence. 1986. "Current Issues in Human-Resource Management." *Research Bulletin of the Conference Board,* no. 190.

Schrecker, Ellen. 1986. *No Ivory Tower.* New York: Oxford University Press.

Schuman, Howard, Charlotte Steeh, and Lawrence Bobo. 1988. *Racial Attitudes in America.* 2d ed. Cambridge: Harvard University Press.

Skerry, Peter. 1997. "The Strange Politics of Affirmative Action." *Wilson Quarterly* 21 (winter): 39–46.

Skrentny, John David. 1996. *The Ironies of Affirmative Action.* Chicago: University of Chicago Press.

Sleeper, Jim. 1997. *Liberal Racism.* New York: Viking Press.

Smith, James, and Finis Welch. 1984. "Affirmative Action and Labor Markets." *Journal of Labor Economics* 2:269–301.

———. 1989. "Black Economic Progress after Myrdal." *Journal of Economic Literature* 27:519–64.

Smith, Rogers. 1997. *Civic Ideals: Conflicting Visions of Citizenship in U.S. History.* New Haven: Yale University Press.

Sniderman, Paul M., and Thomas Piazza. 1993. *The Scar of Race.* Cambridge: Harvard University Press.

"State Propositions: A Snapshot of Voters." 1996. *Los Angeles Times,* November 7, A29.

Steeh, Charlotte, and Maria Krysan. 1996. "The Polls—Trends. Affirmative Action and the Public, 1970–1995." *Public Opinion Quarterly* 60:128–58.

Steele, Claude. Forthcoming. "A Threat in the Air: How Stereotypes Shape the Intellectual Identities and Performance of Women and African Americans." In *Pluralism and Diversity,* edited by Eugene Lowe, Jr. Princeton: Princeton University Press.

Stephanopoulos, George, and Christopher Edley, Jr. 1995. "Affirmative Action Review." Report to the President. Washington, D.C.

Sutton, John, Frank Dobbin, John Meyer, and W. Richard Scott. 1994. "The Legalization of the Workplace." *American Journal of Sociology* 99:944–71.

Taylor, Bron. 1991. *Affirmative Action at Work.* Pittsburgh: University of Pittsburgh Press.

Taylor, Marylee C. 1994. "Impact of Affirmative Action on Beneficiary Groups: Evidence from the 1990 General Social Survey." *Basic and Applied Social Psychology* 15:143–78.

Thernstrom, Stephan, and Abigail Thernstrom. 1997. *America in Black and White.* New York: Simon and Schuster.

Thomas, David, and Robin Ely. 1996. "Making Differences Matter: A New Paradigm for Managing Diversity." *Harvard Business Review,* September-October, 79–90.

Tien, Chang Lin. Forthcoming. Comments on paper by Neil Smelser. In *Pluralism and Diversity,* edited by Eugene Lowe Jr. Princeton: Princeton University Press.

Towers Perrin. 1992. *Workforce 2000 Today.* New York: Towers Perrin.

"Tuition Trends." 1997. *Chronicle of Higher Education,* May 30, A11.

Verhovek, Sam. 1997a. "Houston to Vote on Repeal of Affirmative Action." *New York Times,* November 2, 28.

———. 1997b. "Referendum in Houston Shows Complexity of Preferences Issue." *New York Times,* November 6, A1, A26.

Washington Post, Kaiser Family Foundation, Harvard University. 1995. *The Four Americas.* Washington: Washington Post.

Washington State Commission on African American Affairs. 1995a. *Affirmative Action: Who's Really Benefiting? Part I: State Employment.* Olympia: Washington State Commission on African American Affairs.

———. 1995b. *Affirmative Action: Who's Really Benefiting? Part II: Public Higher Education.* Olympia: Washington State Commission on African American Affairs.

———. 1995c. *Affirmative Action: Who's Really Benefiting? Part III: Contracting in State Government.* Olympia: Washington State Commission on African American Affairs.

Wheeler, Michael. 1994. *Diversity Training.* New York: Conference Board.

Wolfe, Alan. 1996. "Affirmative Action, Inc." *New Yorker,* November 25, 106–15.

Woodson, Robert. 1996. "Affirmative Action Is No Civil Right." *Harvard Journal of Law and Public Policy* 19:773–78.

the future of racial classification

the possibility of a new racial hierarchy in the twenty-first-century united states

herbert j. gans

Over the last decade, a number of social scientists writing on race and ethnicity have suggested that the country may be moving toward a new racial structure (Alba 1990; Sanjek 1994; Gitlin 1995). If current trends persist, today's multiracial hierarchy could be replaced by what I think of as a dual or bimodal one consisting of "nonblack" and "black" population categories, with a third, "residual," category for the groups that do not, or do not yet, fit into the basic dualism.[1]

More important, this hierarchy may be based not just on color or other visible bodily features, but also on a distinction between undeserving and deserving, or stigmatized and respectable, races.[2] The hierarchy is new only insofar as the old white-nonwhite dichotomy may be replaced by a nonblack-black one, but it is hardly new for blacks, who are likely to remain at the bottom once again. I fear this hierarchy could develop even if more blacks achieve educational mobility, obtain professional and managerial jobs, and gain access to middle-class incomes, wealth, and other "perks." Still, the hierarchy could also end, particularly if the black distribution of income and wealth resembles that of the then-dominant races, and if interracial marriage eliminates many of the visible bodily features by which Americans now define race.

Since no one can even guess much less model the many causal factors that will influence the future, the observations that follow are not intended to be read as a prediction but as an exercise in speculative analysis. The weakness of such an analysis is its empirical reliance on the extrapolation of too many current trends and the assumed persistence of too many current phenomena. The analysis becomes a justifiable exercise, however, because it aims only to speculate about what future "scenarios" are possible, and what variables might shape these.

Obviously, the observations about such a hierarchy are not meant to suggest that it is desirable. Indeed, I wrote the paper with the hope that if such a future threatens to become real, it can be prevented.

The remainder of this paper elaborates the basic scenario, adds a set of qualifications, and considers the variables and alternative scenarios now most likely to be significant for the future. The paper concludes with observations about the contemporary construction of race in the United States raised by my analysis about a possible future.

The Dual Racial Hierarchy

Before what is now described, somewhat incorrectly, as the post-1965 immigration, the United States was structured as a predominantly Caucasian, or white, society, with a limited number of numerically and otherwise inferior races, who were typically called Negroes, Orientals, and American Indians—or blacks, yellows, and reds to go with the pinkish-skinned people called whites. There was also a smattering of groups involving a huge number of people who were still described by their national or geographic origins rather than language, including Filipinos, Mexicans and Puerto Ricans, Cubans, etc.[3]

After 1965, when many other Central and Latin American countries began to send migrants, the Spanish-speaking groups were all recategorized by language and called Hispanics. Newcomers from Southeast Asia were classified by continental origin and called Asians, which meant that the later Indian, Pakistani, and Sri Lankan newcomers had to be distinguished regionally, and called South Asians.

At the end of the twentieth century, the country continues to be dominated by whites. Nevertheless, both the immigrants who started to arrive after the end of World War II and the political, cultural, and racial changes that took place in the wake of their arrival have further invalidated many old racial divisions and labels. They have also set into motion what may turn out to be significant transformations in at least part of the basic racial hierarchy.

These transformations are still in an early phase but one of the first has been the elevation of a significant, and mostly affluent, part of the Asian and Asian-American population into a "model minority" that also bids to eradicate many of the boundaries between it and whites. Upward socioeconomic mobility and increasing intermarriage with whites may even end up in eliminating the boundary that now constructs them as a separate race. Thus, one possible future trend may lead to all but poor Asians and Asian-Americans being perceived and even treated so much like whites that currently visible bodily differences will no longer be judged negatively or even noticed, except when and where Asians or Asian-Americans threaten white interests (e.g., Newman 1993). The same treatment as quasi whites may spread to other successfully mobile and inter-marrying immigrants and their descendants, for example Filipinos and white Hispanics.[4]

What these minorities have in common now with Asians, and might have in common even more in the future, is that they are all nonblack, although not as many are currently as affluent as Asians. Nonetheless, by the middle of the twenty-first century, as whites could perhaps become, or will worry about be-coming, a numerical minority in the country, they might cast about for political and cultural allies.[5] Their search for allies, which may not even be conscious or deliberate, could hasten the emergence of a new, nonblack racial category, whatever it is named, in which skin color, or in the case of "Hispanics," racially constructed ethnic differences, will be ignored, even if whites would probably remain the dominant subcategory.

The lower part of the emerging dual hierarchy will likely consist of people classified as blacks, including African-Americans, as well as Caribbean and other blacks, dark-skinned or black Hispanics, Native Americans, and anyone else who is dark skinned enough and/or possessed of visible bodily features and behavior patterns, actual or imagined, that remind nonblacks of blacks. Many of these people will also be poor, and if whites and other nonblacks continue to blame America's troubles on a low-status scapegoat, the new black category will be characterized as an undeserving race.

In effect, class will presumably play nearly as much of a role in the boundary changes as race, but with some important exceptions. For example, if a signifi-cant number of very poor whites remain as the twenty-first-century equivalent of today's "white trash," they will probably be viewed as less undeserving than equally poor blacks simply because they are whites.[6]

Furthermore, the limits of class are indicated, at least for today, by the con-tinued stigmatization of affluent and otherwise high-status blacks, who suffer some of the same indignities as poor blacks (Feagin and Sykes 1994).[7] So, of course, do moderate- and middle-income members of the working class, who constitute the majority of blacks in America even if whites do not know it. The high visibility of "black" or Negroid physical features renders class position in-visible to whites, so that even affluent blacks are suspected of criminal or patho-logical behavior that is actually found only among a minority of very poor blacks.

Despite continuing white hatreds and fears of blacks that continue almost 150 years after the Civil War, racial classification systems involving others have been more flexible. When the first Irish immigrants came to New York, they were so poor that they were perceived by Anglo-Saxon whites as the black Irish and often treated like blacks. Even so, it did not take the Irish long to separate themselves from blacks, and more important, to be so separated by the city's

Anglo-Saxons. A generation later, the Irish were whites (Roediger 1991; Ignatiev 1995).

Perhaps their new whiteness was reinforced by the arrival of the next set of newcomers: people from Eastern and Southern Europe who were often described as members of "swarthy races." Even though the word *race* was used the way we today use *ethnicity*, the newcomers were clearly not white in the Anglo-Saxon sense, and Southern Italians were sometimes called "guineas" because of their dark skin. Nonetheless, over time, they too became white, thanks in part to their acculturation, their integration into the mainstream economy, and after World War II, their entry into the middle class. Perhaps the disappearance of their swarthiness was also reinforced by the arrival in the cities of a new wave of Southern blacks during and after World War II.

A less typical racial transformation occurred about that time in Mississippi, where whites began to treat the Chinese merchants who provided stores for poor blacks as near whites. As Loewen (1988) tells the story, increased affluence and acculturation were again relevant factors. Although whites neither socialized nor intermarried with the Chinese, they accorded them greater social deference and political respect than when they had first arrived. They turned the Chinese into what I previously called a residual category, and in the process created an early version of the nonblack-black duality that may appear in the United States in the next century.

As the Mississippi example suggests, changes in racial classification schemes need not require racial or class equality, for as long as scarce resources or positions remain, justifications for discrimination also remain and physical features that are invisible in some social settings can still become visible in others. Glass ceilings supply the best example, because they seem to change more slowly than some other hierarchical boundaries. Even ceilings for Jews, non-Irish Catholics, and others long classified as whites are still lower than those for WASPs in the upper reaches of the class and prestige structures.

I should note that the racial hierarchy I have sketched here, together with the qualifications that follow, are described both from the perspective of the (overtly) detached social scientist, and also from the perspective of the populations that end up as dominant in the structure. A longer paper would analyze how very differently the people who are fitted into the lower or residual parts of the hierarchy see it.[8]

Qualifications to the Dual Hierarchy

Even if the country would someday replace its current set of racial classifications, the result would not be a simple dual structure, and this model needs to be qualified in at least three ways.

RESIDUALS. The first qualification is the near certainty of a residual or middle category that includes groups placed in a waiting position by the dominant population until it becomes clear whether they will be allowed to become nonblack, face the seemingly permanent inferiority that goes with being black, or become long-term residuals.

If such a structure were to develop in the near future, those likely to be placed in a residual category would include the less affluent members of today's Asian, Hispanic and Filipino, Central and South American Indian, and mixed Indian-Latino populations. The future of the dark-skinned members of the South Asian newcomers is harder to predict. Indeed, their treatment will become an important test of how whites deal with the race-class nexus when the people involved are very dark skinned but are not Negroid—and when their class position is so high that in 1990 it outranked that of all other immigrants (Rumbaut 1997, table 1.4).[9]

Who is classified as residual will, like all other categorizations, be shaped by both class and race. To borrow Milton Gordon's (1964) useful but too rarely used notion of "ethclass," what may be developing are "race-classes," with lower-class members of otherwise racially acceptable groups and higher-class members of racially inferior ones being placed in the residual category.

It is also possible for two or more residual categories to emerge, one for nonwhite and Hispanic populations of lower- and working-class position, and another for nonwhites and Hispanics of higher-class position, with the latter more likely to be eligible eventually to join whites in the nonblack portion of a dual hierarchy. Yet other variations are conceivable, however, for white America has not yet given any clues about how it will treat middle-class Latinos of various skin colors and other bodily features. Perhaps today's ad hoc solution, to treat nonblack Hispanics as a quasi-racial ethnic group that is neither white nor black, may survive for another generation or more, particularly if enough Hispanics remain poor or are falsely accused of rejecting linguistic Americanization.

Being placed in a residual classification means more than location in a middle analytic category; it is also a socially enforced, even if covert, category, and it will be accompanied by all the social, political, and emotional uncertainties that go with being placed in a holding pattern and all the pains these create (Marris 1996). True, residuals may not know they are waiting, but then the second-generation white ethnic "marginal men" identified by Stonequist (1937) did not know they were waiting for eventual acculturation and assimilation.

MULTIRACIALS. A second qualification to the dual model is created by the emergence of biracials or multiracials that result from the rising intermarriage rates among Asian, Hispanic, and black and white immigrants as well as black and white native-born Americans.[10] Interracial marriages increased from 1 percent of all marriages in 1960 to 3 percent in 1990 (Harrison and Bennett 1995, 165).[11] They are expected to increase much faster in the future, particularly Asian-white ones, since even now, about a third of all Asian marriages, and more than half of all Japanese ones, are intermarriages.[12] If Hispanic-white marriages were also counted, they would exceed all the rest in current number and expected growth, but these are usually treated as ethnic rather than racial intermarriages.

Another set of recruits for a residual position includes the light-skinned blacks, once called mulattos, who today dominate the African-American upper class, some of whom may be sufficiently elite and light-skinned to be viewed as nonblack. Even now, the most prominent among the light-skinned black-white biracials, including business and civic leaders, celebrities and entertainers, are already treated as honorary whites, although many refuse this option and take special pride in their blackness and become "race leaders."[13]

Meanwhile, "multiracial" is in the process of slowly becoming a public racial category, and someday it could become an official one codified by the U.S. Census.[14] At this writing, however, many people of mixed race are not ready to define themselves publicly as such, and those who can choose which racial origin to use are sometimes flexible on instrumental grounds, or may choose different racial origins on different occasions.[15] How people of various racial mixtures construct themselves in the longer run is impossible to tell, since issues of their identification and treatment by others, their own identity, and the social, occupational, financial, and political benefits and costs involved cannot be predicted either.

As far as the country's long-term future racial structure is concerned, however, what matters most is how whites will eventually view and treat multiracial people. This will be affected by the variations in class and visible physical features among multiracial people—for example, how closely they resemble whites or other deserving races. Another question is the future of the traditional identification of race with "blood," which counts all nonwhites in halves, quarters, or even eighths, depending on how many and which ancestors intermarried with whom.[16] If the late twentieth-century belief in the power of genes continues, blood might simply be replaced by genes someday.

Mixed race is a particularly complex category, for several reasons. In any racial intermarriage with more than one offspring, each sibling is likely to look somewhat different racially from the others, ranging from darker to lighter or more and less nonwhite. Thus, one black-white sibling could be viewed as black and another as nonblack—even before they decide how they view themselves. What happens in subsequent generations is virtually unimaginable, since even if mixed-race individuals marry others of the same mixture, their children will not resemble their grandparents and some may barely resemble their parents. Eventually, a rising number will be treated as, and will think of themselves as, white or nonblack, but this is possible only when people of multiracial origin can no longer bear children who resemble a black ancestor.

Empirical evidence about the effects of racial intermarriage from countries where it has taken place for a long time is unfortunately not very relevant. The closest case, the Caribbean islands, are for the most part, tiny. They are also former plantation societies, with a small number of white and light-skinned elites, and a large number of nonwhites—and a differential conception of white and nonwhite from island to island.[17] Caribbean nonwhites appear to intermarry fairly freely but skin color does count and the darkest-skinned peoples are invariably lowest in socioeconomic class and status (Mintz 1989; Rodriguez 1989).

The only large country, Brazil, also began as a plantation society, and it differs from the United States particularly in that the Brazilian state eschewed racial legislation. As a result, Brazil never passed Jim Crow laws, but as of this writing (January 1998) it has not passed civil rights legislation either. Racial stratification, as well as discrimination and segregation, has persisted nonetheless, but it has been maintained through the class system. Drastic class inequalities, including a high rate of illiteracy among the poor, have enabled whites to virtually monopolize the higher class and status positions.

The absence of state involvement has given Brazil an undeserved reputation as a society that encourages intermarriage but ignores racial differences, a reputation the state has publicized as "racial democracy." The reality is not very different from that of the United States, however, for while there has been more intermarriage, it appears to have taken place mainly among blacks and black-white biracials, who together make up about half the country's population. Moreover, biracials gain little socioeconomic advantage from their lighter skins, even as the darkest-skinned blacks are kept at the bottom, forced into slums and prisons as in the United States.[18]

In effect, the Brazilian experience would suggest an empirical precedent for my hypothesis that blacks will remain a separate, and discriminated-against, population in the United States of the future. Indeed, in just about every society in which blacks first arrived as slaves, they are still at the bottom, and the political, socioeconomic, and cultural mechanisms to keep them there remain in place. Although blacks obtain higher incomes and prestige than Asians or white Hispanics in a number of American communities, the descendants of nonblack immigrants are, with some notable exceptions, still able to overtake most blacks in the long run.

Since parts of the United States were also a plantation society in which the slaves were black, the leftovers of the racial stratification pattern will likely continue here as well. Thus, children of black-white intermarriages who turn out to be dark skinned are classified as blacks, even if the United States is on the whole kinder to light-skinned biracials than Brazil.

The future of Asian-white biracials remains more unpredictable, in part because no empirical data exist that can be used to shore up guesses about them. The same observation applies to the endless number of other multiracial combinations that will be created when the children of multiracial parents intermarry with yet other multiracials. There will be few limits to new variations in bodily features, though which will be visible or noticed, and which of the latter will be stigmatized or celebrated as exotic cannot be guessed now.[19] Most likely, however, the larger the number of multiracials and of multiracial variations, the more difficult it will be for nonblacks to define and enforce racial boundaries, or to figure out which of the many darker-skinned varieties of multiracials had black ancestors. In that case, an eventual end to racial discrimination is possible.

If future racial self-identification patterns will also resemble today's ethnic ones, the racial equivalent of today's voluntary white ethnicity and its associated lack of ethnic loyalty may mean that many future triracial, quadriracial, and other multiracial people may eventually know little, and care even less, about the various racial mixtures they have inherited. It is even conceivable that this change will extend to black multiracials, and should race become voluntary for them as well, the possibility of an end to racial discrimination will be increased. Unfortunately, at the moment such extrapolations are far closer to utopian thinking than to sociological speculation.

REGIONAL VARIATIONS. A third qualification to the dual model is that the portrait I have drawn is national, but given the regional variations in old racial groups and new immigrant populations, it fits no single U.S. region. Moreover, some parts of the country are now still so devoid of new immigrants, with the exception of the handful who come to establish "ethnic" restaurants, that the present racial hierarchies, categories, and attitudes, many of them based on stereotypes imported from elsewhere, could survive unchanged for quite a while in such areas. Furthermore, some areas that have experienced heavy immigration from Asia and Latin America are currently seeing an outmigration of whites, especially lower-income ones (Frey 1996). Thus, even current patterns in the racial makeup of U.S. regions could change fairly quickly.

In addition, regional differences remain in the demography of the lowest strata. The racial hierarchy of the Deep South will probably continue to bear many direct marks of slavery, although the de facto black experience elsewhere in the country has so far not been totally different. Moreover, in some regions, Latin American and other poor nonblack immigrants have already been able to jump over the poor black population economically and socially, partly because whites, including institutions such as banks, are less hostile—or less necessary—to them than they are to blacks.

In the Southwest, Mexicans and other Hispanics remain at the socioeconomic bottom, although in California, they may be joined by the Hmong, Laotians, and other very poor Asians. And Native Americans still occupy the lowest socioeconomic stratum in the handful of mostly rural parts of the country where they now live, although tribes with gambling casinos may be able to effect some changes in that pattern.

Even though some of the new immigrants can by now be found just about everywhere in America, the Los Angeles and New York City areas not only remain the major immigrant arrival centers but also contain the most diverse populations. As a result, a number of the issues discussed in this paper will be played out there, even as they are barely noticeable in the many smaller American cities that may have attracted only a handful of the newcomers. Since these two cities are also the country's prime creators of popular culture, however, their distinctive racial and ethnic characteristics will probably be diffused in subtle ways through the country as a whole.

Alternative Scenarios

Speculating about the future also requires some explicit consideration of the variables that could affect the guesses I have made here, which in turn could lead to alternative scenarios. Generally speaking these variables are macrosociological—major changes in the economy, demographic patterns including internal migration and immigration, as well as political realignments and racial divisions of labor, among others. These in turn can result in changes in racial and ethnic relations as well as in classification systems.

As noted earlier, dominant groups can alter racial categories and constructions. Model minorities are "chosen" by the dominant population precisely because they appear to share, and thereby to uphold, that population's behavior or values. If new behavior or values need to be upheld, new model minorities may be recruited. Scapegoats are populations that can be blamed for social problems, although the dominant populations choose, or even create, the social problems for which scapegoats will be blamed. Scapegoats, or targets for blame, generally come in two varieties: *higher* scapegoats, usually recruited from higher-status minority groups that can be blamed for obtaining too much economic or cultural power; and *lower* ones, typically the undeserving poor, who can be accused of deviant behavior or values said to hold back economic growth, require public expenditures that could bankrupt governmental budgets, threaten familial and sexual norms, or impair the moral fabric of the rest of society. Blaming both types of scapegoats is a politically easy way of responding to a crisis, particularly one for which immediate and feasible solutions are lacking.

During the long Cold War, the Soviets and other foreign scapegoats could be blamed for American problems, but now, domestic scapegoats have again become the primary target. While illegal and even legal American immigrants are once again joining poor blacks as the country's principal lower scapegoats, only a few states have sufficient immigrants to serve as targets for blame, which may help to explain why conservative politicians, particularly Republicans, have more often demonized poor blacks.

The most likely candidates for change in current racial categories, other than of model minorities, are the people whites now call Hispanics, as well as descendants of some now officially nonwhite populations in the new immigration. They will have to be allowed into the higher-status occupations in larger number if and when the supply of whites runs out, and in that case, today's forms of racial and ethnic discrimination against them, particularly those shaped by class considerations, would have to give way. In fact, by the middle of the twenty-first century, demographers and journalists may be amazed that fifty years earlier, whites expected to be swamped in 2050 by an aggregate of diverse peoples then all called Hispanics.

Two macrosocial factors are probably most important in thinking about alternative scenarios. One is the set of geopolitical and economic demographics that can be produced by cross-national population movements, including the one that has fueled the immigration from Central and Latin America, as well as Russia, Asia, and now Africa, during the last half century. These movements were controlled at least in part by U.S. government legislation, but world catastrophes could take place that could force even the United States to open its borders to much larger numbers of people who might alter the racial distribution significantly.

National demographics can also be changed by domestic political considerations, however, which could lead to a new search for white—and non-Hispanic—immigrants. The United States found its late-nineteenth-century industrial workforce in white Europe rather than among the newly freed slaves in the South. Likewise, Australia has recently looked for European immigrants to discourage the arrival of further Asians.

The second major factor is the state of the domestic economy. If late-twentieth-century trends in the world economy and on Wall Street continue in their present forms, the further disappearance of American firms, jobs, and high wages, as well as related changes in the country's economy, would persist too.

Suppose, for example, that unemployment, or the decline of real income, or both, worsened in the first quarter of the twenty-first century, and Americans in large numbers conclude that the country's economy can never again supply full-time jobs paying a living wage for everyone. While the descendants of the poorer immigrants would be the first to experience what I once called "second generation decline" (Gans 1992), other immigrants can also be dispatched into persistent poverty when not enough jobs are available, with the appropriate racial stereotypes invented or reinvented to justify their downward mobility. Even some middle-class descendants of Asian, Russian, and other newcomers could be transformed into lower scapegoats. Then, the dual racial hierarchy I have described would look very different or might not come to pass at all.

Should economic crises result in political crises as well, or raise religious and culture "wars" to more feverish pitches, the current movement toward a dual racial structure could also end quickly. Then, a modern version of the nineteenth-century American monoracial pattern might reappear, with the children of white newcomers joining older white ethnics and WASPs as the only acceptable race. Some members of the newly scapegoated races would probably react in turn, inaugurating political protest, intensifying identity politics and slowing down on intermarriage and other forms of acculturation and assimilation. Some descendants of today's newcomers might return to the old country.

What if a very different economic scenario were assumed, involving a return of old-style economic growth accompanied by a stronger U.S. position in the global economy, a shortage of domestic workers, and an upward trend in real income? In that case, the trend toward a dual structure might be hastened, and the erosion of perceived racial differences speeded up as well.

At that point, the now still visible bodily differences of Asian-Americans and their descendants might no longer be noticed, and these groups would repeat the post–World War II pattern by which Southern and Eastern European "races" were redefined as "ethnic groups." The reclassification of Hispanics, including the treatment of third-generation Central and Latin Americans, would probably move in the same direction.

The fate of blacks is more difficult to imagine. If the economy created a seller's market for people with job skills at all levels from blue collar to professional and managerial, all poverty would decline sharply, including that of blacks. Moreover, blacks would be able to enter the upper middle and middle classes in such numbers as to disturb white America's long association of poverty with blackness. Indeed, in an economy with enough decent jobs for all, private and public affirmative action policies to assure the spread of blacks at all levels of the occupational and socioeconomic structure would be likely as well.

Under such conditions, those aspects of white racism due to fear of and anger at black poverty would begin to decline, and if the federal government was committed to fight racial discrimination and segregation, so would the construction of blacks as an undeserving race. Black-white intermarriage rates might also rise more quickly.

If the prosperity were long term, and it as well as other events in the society and the world reduced the country's resort to domestic scapegoats, a dual racial hierarchy might be replaced by the beginnings of a multiracial structure in which the boundaries of all races would become fuzzier and weaker. Since now-stigmatized visible bodily differences would then lose their negative connotations, they might not only be ignored but even come to be celebrated as positive contributions to American diversity, just as current ethnic differences among Europeans provide the country with nonthreatening cultural diversities.

Prosperity alone does not necessarily solve a society's other problems, however, and political, cultural, and religious conflicts could remain, encouraging dominant groups to choose and stigmatize an undeserving race, even if it is not a poor one. Anti-Semitic activities, for example, have occurred in prosperous times and societies, and in nations with minuscule Jewish populations.

Likewise, more economic prosperity and other positive economic tendencies alone do not necessarily produce more acculturation and assimilation of immigrants. Even the acculturation of large numbers of immigrants and their descendants does not automatically preclude identity politics, for today's college and university campuses are rife with rapidly acculturating newcomers who nevertheless feel strongly enough about their racial identity to become active in identity politics.

It is even possible that in a multiracial America, some latter-day descendants of WASPs and white ethnics will resort to identity politics as an attempt to retain or restore their political and cultural dominance.[20] And if a global economy also produced pressures toward global cultural and political homogeneities, nation-states or their successors might develop now unimagined forms of national identity politics or cultural revivals to maintain some kind of national distinctiveness. Immigrants and their descendants might be victimized by such developments more than blacks, however.

Three Tendencies in the Contemporary Construction of Race

BIOLOGICAL CONSTRUCTIONS. The first tendency is the continuing construction of race from biological as well as social building blocks. Most scientific experts agree that there are no biologically definable races, and that race is therefore not a useful biological concept. The lay public, however, which is not ready to accept expert opinion, sees differences in visible bodily features, mostly facial, between people and treats them as racial differences caused by differences in "blood." People also racialize differences in personality traits such as "soul"—and national character in the case of immigrants.

The visible bodily differences are not imaginary, for people do differ by skin color, and the shapes or other characteristics of various body parts, including heads, eyelids, noses, hair, and others. To cite just a few examples, even in third-generation white ethnic America, one can find Irish and Welsh (or "Celtic") faces, southern Italian and Sicilian ones, and Slavic as well as Scandinavian ones.

What people notice are not scientifically defined races or subraces, but the descendants of once-isolated peoples who had been inbreeding for centuries.[21] Since most have now stopped doing so as a result of rural to urban and other migrations, their distinctiveness is disappearing with each new generation, but it has by no means disappeared.

Some of the variations in personality and social characteristics that laypeople correlate with race or "blood" can undoubtedly be traced in part to the societies and economies, as well as the racial hierarchies, in which these once-isolated peoples lived. The occupational and other social roles that immigrants play in their new societies also play a part, one reason why immigrant shopkeepers in "middlemen" roles are often seen as "clannish" by the populations they serve, for example.

Some visible bodily features that distinguish people are noticed and judged; some are noticed but not judged one way or another; and yet others are not even noticed, seeming to be virtually invisible. Although how features are judged can be traced in part to the popular Darwinisms of the last two centuries, in general, the bodily features of the most prestigious peoples are usually adopted as ideals of physical perfection, while features found among the lower social classes are judged pejoratively.[22]

Variations in skin color, as well as in head shapes, noses, eyes, lips, and hair, have been noticed in many societies, but differences in some bodily parts have been ignored, for example, the size of fingers and the shapes of ears and earlobes.[23] Yet other bodily features are not noticed because they are hidden by clothes; while a few are not noticed because people wear clothes to hide them. These often spur fantasies, for example about black penis size and other imagined racial differences in reproductive and other organs.[24]

A major ingredient of the social construction of race is the determination of which visible bodily features are noticed and used to delineate race and which remain unnoticed. In the process shaping that construction, various social constructors, including laypersons, experts, and, when relevant, commercial and political decision makers, take part. Unless explicit ideological, commercial, or political reasons are involved, the constructors may not be aware of the process in which they are involved, or the causes that shape the final determination. Usually, whites are the major constructors, but increasingly, representatives of the racial minorities to be constructed participate when they can politicize the process, or can frighten manufacturers or advertisers of national consumer goods.[25]

Strictly speaking, a biological construction should make racial characteristics and classifications relatively fixed, but lay biological construction is almost as flexible as social construction. The reason for the lack of fixity is not hard to find, for the choice of which visible bodily features are to be noticed has almost nothing to do with race and everything to do with stratification.

As the Brazilian and United States experiences indicate, the race of the lowest class became the lowest race because slaves were almost by definition the lowest class and race. That captured blacks were the only population economically and otherwise powerless to prevent their becoming enslaved in recent centuries led whites to use their distinguishable skin color and facial features to translate their class inferiority into a racial one (Fields 1990). Similarly, the stigmatization of "yellow" skin resulted from the serflike status of Chinese "coolies" on railroad construction gangs; the stigmatization of "swarthiness" followed from the low status of the Southern and Eastern European newcomers; and a century later, white Hispanic immigrants are sometimes called a race because of their low class position.[26] That the ancestors of now-respected Americans were once damned for their swarthy skins has been quietly forgotten, both among their descendants and among the peoples who "invented" the original stigma.

ETHNICITY AS RACIAL. The second, and related, tendency is the continuing lay practice of identifying ethnic and national differences as racial, particularly in private self-naming. Census analysts have discovered that in the 1990 census, respondents to open-ended questions claimed membership in nearly three hundred races or ethnic groups, including seventy Hispanic categories (Morganthau 1995, 64). In many instances, they equated their race with their nationality—or with their tribes in the case of Native Americans.[27] As Eleanor Gerber and Manuel de la Puente pointed out in reporting on a study of test questions for the 2000 census: "Most respondents recognized the term 'ethnic group' but . . . would indicate it was 'the same thing' as race . . . [and] often coined the term 'ethnic race' during our discussions" (Gerber and de la Puente 1996, 21).

The two Bureau of Census researchers suggest lack of education as the causal factor in this conflation, indicating that only the college educated could distinguish ethnic group from race. However, as long as Americans notice visible bodily differences among people of the same official race, they will hold on to *private* constructions of race that differ from the official definitions.[28] Even among the third- and fourth-generation white multiethnics whose "ethnic options" Mary Waters (1990) studied, some chose their ethnicities on the basis of racial conceptions of national origin.[29] In effect, ethnicity continues to be a matter of "blood."[30]

RACIAL TOLERANCE. The third and perhaps most important tendency is the apparently increasing white tolerance for racial differences, except with respect to blacks. At the same time, whites seem to use race less often as an indicator of class, except when they are considering poor blacks. This trend may become more widespread as racial intermarriage among people of similar class increases further. Today, class homogamy is apparently outranking racial homogamy among college-educated young people (Kalmijn 1991).

If this pattern spreads to other Americans of the same age and if it becomes permanent, and if whites were willing and able to see that their hatreds and fears of blacks and other very poor nonwhites are so often reactions to their extreme and persistent poverty rather than their race, class could become more important and more overt as a boundary and a principle of stratification in the future. If Americans could also realize that class is more than a matter of "life-style" differences among near equals, class stratification might someday become a matter of general public discussion. In that case, the myth of a classless America might eventually be laid to rest.[31]

Even a more modest increase in awareness of class would be desirable, because class is after all an achieved status, while race is not, even in its reasonably flexible lay construction. However, the shift from race to class would also require Americans to develop a more fundamental understanding of the United States and to invent a new conception of the American dream and its underlying myth to replace that of the classless society. So far, there is no indication of this happening.

In fact, it would probably not happen until events in the political economy make it possible to achieve a drastic reduction of joblessness and poverty, so that the correlation of poverty with blackness is significantly lowered. If and when blacks become roughly equal economically to nonblacks, blacks can no longer be treated as an undeserving race.

If poverty and inequality are not lessened, however, and if more poor blacks are condemned to work for nothing but their welfare benefits, they could be treated as an ever more undeserving race, and other populations who cannot enter, or stay in, the middle class, including poor Hispanics and Asians, might join them. In that case, the racial hierarchy of the next century's United States would look very different from the one I have sketched here.

Conclusion

A society's reconstruction of racial categories appears to require at least the following conditions: (1) an influx of immigrants who do not fit the existing racial categories and their associated class backgrounds; (2) a healthy economy with sufficient opportunity for upward mobility even for poorer immigrants; (3) a lack of demand for new lower (and higher) racial scapegoats; and (4) an at least temporary demand for model minorities.

If these conditions are met, existing racial definitions and categories will be

altered, sometimes even quickly if there is a proliferation of interracial marriages. However, in a society with a history of slavery, one possible effect is a
dual racial hierarchy, in which one part consists mostly of ex-slaves. However,
since even the effects of slavery should eventually be eliminated, at least in
theory, the United States could become a predominantly interracial or multiracial society someday.

Even then, the more prestigious racial mixtures are apt to remain somewhat
whiter for a while than the rest, and the less prestigious ones darker. But if the
country's racial mixing ever became so thorough that skin color and other currently used bodily features were sufficiently unrecognizable or no longer of sufficient interest to be noticed, race would no longer be associated with social
ranking. If Americans then still needed to rank each other, new criteria would
have to be found.

Notes

I am grateful for comments on earlier drafts of this paper from Margaret Chin, Jennifer Lee, an anonymous reviewer—and from my fellow authors in this volume.

1. These categories are constructions, but they also contain populations experiencing
all the pleasures and pains of being located in a hierarchy. And although I am often
discussing constructions, I will forgo the practice of putting all racial, national, and related names and labels between quotes, except for unusual racial stereotypes.

2. The two races may not be called that openly, but ambiguous pejoratives have long
been part of the American vocabulary, for example *underclass* now, and *pauper* a century
earlier (Gans 1995). Since races are social constructions, their names will depend in
large part on who does the naming—and whose names become dominant in the public
vocabulary.

3. Puerto Ricans are still often described as immigrants, even though they have been
American citizens for a long time and their move from the island to the mainland is a
form of interstate mobility. Racial, class, and linguistic considerations have undoubtedly
influenced this labeling.

The same dominant-race thinking led Irving Kristol and other neoconservatives to
argue in the 1960s that blacks were similar enough to the white European immigrants
to be able to adopt and act on immigrant values. They also assumed that blacks would
then assimilate like immigrants, ignoring such facts as that blacks had originally come as
slaves, not immigrants; had been here several centuries; and had not yet been allowed
by whites to assimilate. Thirty years later, many whites ignore the same facts to propose
the newest immigrants as role models for blacks.

4. Much less is said about black Hispanics, including Puerto Ricans, who suffer virtually all of the discriminatory and other injustices imposed on African-Americans.

5. Some highly placed whites are already worrying, for example in a *Time* cover story
by William Henry III (1990), but then similar whites worried a century earlier what the
then arriving Catholic and Jewish newcomers would do to *their* country. The current

worries are as meaningless as the old ones, since they are based on extrapolations of current patterns of immigration, not to mention current constructions of (nonwhite) race and (Hispanic) ethnicity.

6. Hacker (1996) notes, for example, that the term "white trash" is no longer in common use. Indeed, for reasons worth studying, the more popular term of the moment is "trailer trash," which nonetheless seems to be applied solely to poor whites.

7. In this respect, the United States differs from many other countries in the Western hemisphere, where blacks who have managed to become affluent are treated, within limits, as whites.

8. Not only might they perceive it more angrily than I am here doing, but they might be angrier about it than about the present hierarchy, simply because it is new but no great improvement. One result could be their constructions of new racial identities for themselves that depart drastically from the ones future nonblacks consider reasonable.

9. Being far fewer than Asians in number, South Asians are nationally not very visible now. Moreover, for religious and other reasons, South Asian immigrants have so far often been able to discourage their children from intermarrying.

10. My observations on multiracial constructions and people have benefited from many conversations with Valli Rajah.

11. Between 1970 and 1994, the number of people in interracial marriages grew from 676,000 to more than three million (Fletcher 1997). In 1990, biracial children made up 4 percent of all children, increasing from half a million in 1970 to about two million that year. The largest number were Asian-white children, followed by Native American–white and African American–white ones (Harrison and Bennett 1995).

12. Some observers currently estimate that 70 percent of all Japanese and Japanese-Americans are intermarried, mostly with whites. Since they came to the United States as families long before 1965, this estimate may supply a clue about what will happen to second-, third-, and later-generation descendants of other Asian-American populations.

13. Presumably class position will affect how other descendants of old Southern mulatto and creole populations (Dominguez 1986) will be classified.

14. In the political debates over the racial categories to be used in the Year 2000 Census, vocal multiracials preferred to be counted as and with various people of color. African-Americans and other officially recognized racial groups also indicated their opposition to a multiracial category, being reluctant to reduce the power of their numbers or the federal benefits that now go to racial minorities (e.g., Holmes 1996).

15. Kohne (1996) reports that light-skinned biracial Columbia University students who identify as whites also apply for scholarships as blacks. But then, four decades earlier, I met Italian-Americans in Boston's West End who took Irish names in order to obtain jobs in Irish-dominated city hall.

16. The practice of quantifying racial bloods has a long history in Europe and the United States, thanks to both eugenics and slavery. Perhaps it will disappear when enough people have to start counting three or more races. However, people also still use blood fractions when they marry across religions, so that the notion of racial, ethnic, or religious "blood" is by no means obsolete.

17. They are also different, for "one and the same person may be considered white

in the Dominican Republic or Puerto Rico . . . 'colored' in Jamaica, Martinique, or Curacao . . . [and] a 'Negro' in Georgia" (Hoetink 1967, xii).

18. This account is based mainly on the data summarized in Fiola 1990 and Skidmore 1992, the classic analysis of the Brazilian racial system in Skidmore 1993, Adamo's 1983 case study of race and class in Rio de Janeiro, and the sociopolitical analyses by Marx (1995, 1996). I am indebted to Anthony Marx for guiding me into the literature on Brazil, although there is still precious little social research, especially with current data, in English.

19. No one has so far paid much attention to who is constructed as exotic and why, except the multiracial people, mostly women, to whom it is applied. Some of them benefit because they are sought by industries that hire workers with exotic facial features; but women without these occupational interests resent such labeling because it turns them into sexual objects.

Industries that employ workers with exotic features, facial and otherwise, such as the fashion and entertainment industries, play an interesting, and probably unduly influential, role in the country's public racial construction.

20. Even now, at the close of the twentieth century, whites who argue that America is a "Christian" nation are pursuing a politics of identity as much as of religious dominance.

21. I am indebted to my Columbia University colleague, biologist Robert Pollack, for my understanding of this phenomenon.

22. Originally, people drew on nineteenth-century and earlier comparisons of apes and humans, with those determined to be closer to apes in facial appearance being thought inferior. Brain size was also used, at least until scientific research debunked its relevance, and the researchers also discovered that it did not correlate with status. The final blow was the discovery that the much maligned Neanderthalers had larger brains than *Homo sapiens.*

23. Ears have served mainly as anchors for adornment, although protruding ones have sometimes been brought surgically closer to the head.

24. Now that some young women show their navels or wear bathing suits with uncovered buttocks, these could become eligible for racial typing.

25. Constructionists in the social sciences and the humanities have so far mainly emphasized that races, like other human notions, are socially constructed, but social scientists have paid little attention to the actual construction process and its participants. What we know about that process comes mostly from scholars who analyze racial images over time, in literature or the popular culture, and have collected process information as part of their work.

26. Forced Chinese labor was also recruited for the cotton plantations, but the Chinese workers turned out to be inefficient cotton pickers and thus managed to avoid becoming slaves.

27. I am indebted to Roderick Harrison and especially Manuel de la Puente of the U.S. Bureau of the Census for materials that clarified this set of responses.

28. Social scientists on the staff of the Census Bureau and the Bureau of Labor Statistics spend part of their time analyzing the large number of private races that people supply in answer to open-ended questions to produce the small number of public ones reported by the federal government.

29. For some similar practices by Jews in post-Holocaust Germany, see Rapaport 1997, 166–67.

30. For example, one of Waters's respondents explained that she traced her bad moods to "the Irish in me," while "all of the good things" were Italian (Waters 1990, 25). Embryo clinics are asked by some of their customers to supply sperm and egg donors of similar ethnic origin, in one case to obtain an "Irish background, or at least light hair and light eyes" (Kolata 1997, 34). As a result, ethnicity may be so racialized that it is not very voluntary, although voluntary ethnicity may also be used to achieve voluntarily chosen racial features.

31. Needless to say, traumatic and long-lasting economic decline is a more likely cause for a public recognition of class in America.

References

Adamo, Samuel C. 1983. "The Broken Promise: Race, Health and Justice in Rio de Janeiro, 1890–1940." Ph.D. diss., University of New Mexico.

Alba, Richard D. 1990. *Ethnic Identity.* New Haven: Yale University Press.

Dominguez, Virginia R. 1986. *White by Definition.* New Brunswick: Rutgers University Press.

Feagin, Joe R., and Michael P. Sykes. 1994. *Living with Racism.* Boston: Beacon.

Fields, Barbara J. 1990. "Slavery, Race and Ideology in the United States of America." *New Left Review* 15:95–108.

Fiola, Jan. 1990. "Race Relations in Brazil: A Reassessment of the 'Racial Democracy' Thesis." Occasional Papers Series no. 34. University of Massachusetts Latin American Studies Program, Amherst.

Fletcher, Michael A. 1997. "More Than a Black-White Issue." *Washington Post National Weekly Edition,* May 26, 34.

Frey, William H. 1996. "Immigration, Domestic Migration and Demographic Balkanization in America." *Population and Development Review* 22:741–63.

Gans, Herbert J. 1992. "Second Generation Decline: Scenarios for the Economic and Ethnic Futures of the post-1965 American Immigrants." *Ethnic and Racial Studies* 15:173–92.

———. 1995. *The War against the Poor.* New York: Basic.

Gerber, Eleanor, and Manuel de la Puente. 1996. "The Development of and Cognitive Testing of Race and Ethnic Origin Questions for the Year 2000 Census." In Bureau of the Census, *1996 Annual Research Conference.* Washington: Government Printing Office.

Gitlin, Todd. 1995. *The Twilight of Common Dreams.* New York: Metropolitan.

Gordon, Milton M. 1964. *Assimilation in American Life.* New York: Oxford University Press.

Hacker, Andrew. 1996. Foreword to *The Coming Race War?* by Richard Delgado. New York: New York University Press.

Harrison, Roderick J., and Claudette Bennett. 1995. "Racial and Ethnic Diversity." In *State of the Union: America in the 1990s,* vol. 2, *Social Trends,* edited by Reynolds Farley. New York: Russell Sage Foundation.

Henry, William, III. 1990. "Beyond the Melting Pot." *Time,* April 9, 29–32.

Hoetink, Harry. 1967. *The Two Variants in Caribbean Race Relations.* London: Oxford University Press.

Holmes, Steven. 1996. "Census Tests New Category to Identify Racial Groups." *New York Times,* December 4, A25.

Ignatiev, Noel. 1995. *How the Irish Became White.* New York: Routledge.

Kalmijn, Matthijs. 1991. "Status Homogamy in the United States." *American Journal of Sociology* 93:496–523.

Kohne, Natasha G. 1996. "The Experience of Mixed-Race Women: Challenging Racial Boundaries." Unpublished senior thesis, department of sociology, Columbia University, New York.

Kolata, Gina. 1997. "Clinics Selling Embryos Made for 'Adoption.'" *New York Times,* November 23, 1, 34.

Loewen, James W. 1988. *The Mississippi Chinese.* 2d ed. Prospect Heights, Ill.: Waveland.

Marris, Peter. 1996. *The Politics of Uncertainty.* New York: Routledge.

Marx, Anthony W. 1995. "Contested Citizenship: The Dynamics of Racial Identity and Social Movements." *International Review of History* 40, supplement 3: 159–83.

———. 1996. "Race-Making and the Nation-State." *World Politics,* January, 180–208.

Mintz, Sidney W. 1989. *Caribbean Transformations.* New York: Columbia University Press.

Morganthau, Tom. 1995. "What Color Is Black?" *Newsweek,* February 12, 63–67.

Newman, Katherine. 1993. *Declining Fortunes.* New York: Basic.

Rapaport, Lynn. 1997. *Jews in Germany after the Holocaust.* Cambridge: Cambridge University Press.

Rodriguez, Clara E. 1989. *Puerto Ricans: Born in the U.S.A.* Boston: Unwin Hyman.

Roediger, David R. 1991. *Wages of Whiteness.* London: Verso.

Rumbaut, Ruben G. 1997. "Ties that Bind: Immigration and Immigrant Families in the United States." In *Immigration and the Family,* edited by Alan Booth, Ann C. Crouter, and Nancy Landale. Mahwah, N.J.: Erlbaum.

Sanjek, Roger. 1994. "Intermarriage and the Future of the Races in the United States." In *Race,* edited by Steven Gregory and Roger Sanjek. New Brunswick: Rutgers University Press.

Skidmore, Thomas L. 1992. "Fact and Myth: Discovering a Racial Problem in Brazil." Working paper 173. Helen Kellogg Institute for International Studies, University of Notre Dame.

———. 1993. *Black into White.* Durham: Duke University Press.

Stonequist, Everett V. 1937. *The Marginal Man.* New York: Scribner's.

Waters, Mary. 1990. *Ethnic Options: Choosing Identities in America.* Berkeley: University of California Press.

about the contributors

elijah anderson is the Charles and William L. Day Professor of the Social Sciences at the University of Pennsylvania. An expert on the sociology of black America, he is the author of *A Place on the Corner: A Study of Black Street Corner Men* (1978) and numerous articles on the black experience, including "Of Old Heads and Young Boys: Notes on the Urban Black Experience" (1986), commissioned by the National Research Council's Committee on the Status of Black Americans; "Sex Codes and Family Life among Inner-City Young" (1989); and "The Code of the Streets" (*The Atlantic Monthly,* May 1994). For his ethnographic study, *Streetwise: Race, Class and Change in an Urban Community* (1990), he was honored with the Robert E. Park Award of the American Sociological Association. Most recently, he wrote the introduction to the republication of *The Philadelphia Negro* by W. E. B. Du Bois (1996). He has also won the Lindback Award for Distinguished Teaching at Penn. Dr. Anderson is the director of the Philadelphia Ethnography Project, associate editor of *Qualitative Sociology,* and a member of the Board of Directors of the American Academy of Political and Social Science. He was a member of the National Research Council's Panel on the Understanding and Control of Violent Behavior, which published its report in 1993. Other topics with which he concerns himself are the social psychology of organizations, field methods of social research, social interaction, and social organization.

amy binder is Assistant Professor of Sociology at the University of Southern California, where she studies culture, race, education, and social movements. While a doctoral student at Northwestern University, she wrote an article that appeared in *American Sociological Review* (December 1993), which studied the media's construction of harm in two popular music genres: rap and heavy metal. She also coauthored an article with James Rosenbaum on employers' needs for young workers with academic skills, which appeared in *Sociology of Education* (January 1997). While in graduate school, Binder was the recipient of several teaching and research prizes, and she was awarded a dissertation year fellowship through Northwestern University for 1997–1998. She recently completed her dissertation, a comparison of two reform challenges (Afrocentrism and scientific creationism) to public school curricula, and the education system's responses to those challenges. The chapter appearing in this volume grows out of her dissertation research.

bethany bryson is Assistant Professor of Sociology at the University of Virginia. She has written on symbolic boundaries and sociocultural cleavages in "'Anything but Heavy Metal': Symbolic Exclusion and Musical Dislikes" (*American Sociological Review*, October 1996) and "Have Americans' Social Attitudes Become More Polarized?" (with Paul DiMaggio and John Evans; *American Journal of Sociology*, November 1996). She is currently working on a book that analyzes the emergence and institutionalization of multiculturalism in college English courses. This research is funded by the National Science Foundation and the Center for Domestic and Cultural Policy Studies.

michael c. dawson is Professor of Political Science at the University of Chicago and director of the new Center for the Study of Race, Politics, and Culture. Professor Dawson was co–principal investigator of the 1988 National Black Election Study and is principal investigator with Ronald Brown of the 1993–1994 National Black Politics Study. His research interests include the development of quantitative models of African-American political behavior and public opinion, the political effects of urban poverty, and African-American political ideology. Professor Dawson's book, *Behind the Mule: Race and Class in African-American Politics,* was published by Princeton University Press in 1994. Dawson is also the author of articles on African-American political behavior and race and American politics, which have appeared in *Public Culture, American Political Science Review, The National Review of Political Science,* and other publications. Currently his main project is *Black Visions: The Roots of Contemporary African American Mass Political Ideologies,* which examines the main historical trends in African-American political thought and the connections of black political thought to American political thought. This book also uses the survey generated by the 1993 National Black Politics Study to determine the degree to which these ideological tendencies are present in the African-American mass public.

catherine ellis is a Visiting Scholar at Radcliffe's Murray Center for the Study of Lives and a Ph.D. candidate in anthropology at Columbia University. Her dissertation examines the legacy of Jim Crow segregation in rural Louisiana, with a particular focus on how the racial attitudes of older whites and African-Americans in that area are linked to their memories of segregation. Previous published research includes an evaluation of "Managing Diversity" initiatives in several major U.S. corporations.

herbert j. gans is the Robert Lynd Professor of Sociology at Columbia University. Trained both as a sociologist and planner, he received his Ph.D. from the University of Pennsylvania. He has worked as a research planner for public and private agencies, and prior to coming to Columbia taught at the University of Pennsylvania, MIT, and Teachers College of Columbia University. His research and writing have been concentrated in urban sociology, poverty and antipoverty policy, stratification and equality, ethnicity, the news media, and popular culture. He is the author of nine books and over 160 articles; his first book was *The Urban Villagers* (Free Press, 1962); his latest are *War against the Poor* (Basic Books, 1995) and the forthcoming *Making Sense of America* (Rowman and Littlefield, 1999). He is now working on a book on the news media and citizen democracy. He is a past president of the Eastern Sociological Society and of the American Sociological Association.

jennifer l. hochschild is Professor of Politics and Public Affairs at Princeton University, with a joint appointment in the Department of Politics and the Woodrow Wilson School of Public and International Affairs. She has been a fellow at the Center for Advanced Study in the Behavioral Sciences, and was twice a Visitor at the Institute for Advanced Study. She has received awards or research support from the American Philosophical Society, the Spencer Foundation, the American Political Science Association, the Princeton University Research Board, and other organizations. She has also served as a consultant or expert witness in several school desegregation cases, most recently the ongoing case of *Yonkers Board of Education v. New York State*. She is the author of *Facing Up to the American Dream: Race, Class, and the Soul of the Nation* (Princeton University Press, 1995); *The New American Dilemma: Liberal Democracy and School Desegregation* (Yale University Press, 1984); and *What's Fair: American Beliefs about Distributive Justice* (Harvard University Press, 1981); and a coauthor of *Equalities* (Harvard University Press, 1981). She is a coeditor of *Social Policies for Children* (Brookings Institution Press, 1995). She has also written a variety of articles in the fields of political philosophy, American political thought, public opinion, and race in America. She is currently writing a book on lessons to be learned from the history of school and housing desegregation in Yonkers, New York. She is a Fellow of the American Academy of Arts and Sciences, a vice president of the American Political Science Association, and a member of the Board of Trustees of the Russell Sage Foundation.

michèle lamont teaches in the Department of Sociology at Princeton University. She has published broadly in the fields of cultural sociology, comparative sociology, inequality, sociological theory, and the sociology of knowledge. Her publications include *Money, Morals, and Manners: The Culture of the French and the American Upper-Middle Class* (University of Chicago Press, 1992), *Cultivating Differences: Symbolic Boundaries and the Making of Inequality* (coedited; University of Chicago Press, 1992), and *National Repertoires of Evaluation in France and the United States* (forthcoming, with Laurent Thévenot). In recent years, she has turned her attention to racial issues in *The World in Moral Order: Working Men Define the Boundaries of Race, Class, and Citizenship* (forthcoming). This work has received support from the German Marshall Funds of the United States, the Institute for Advanced Studies, the John Simon Guggenheim Memorial Foundation, the National Science Foundation, and the Russell Sage Foundation.

jane j. mansbridge is the Adams Professor of Political Leadership and Democratic Values at the Kennedy School of Government at Harvard University. She is the author of *Beyond Adversary Democracy* and *Why We Lost the ERA* (corecipient of the American Political Science Association's Kammerer Award in 1987 and its Schuck Award in 1988), editor of *Beyond Self-Interest,* and coeditor with Susan Moller Okin of *Feminism* (2 vols.). She has been involved with the women's movement from her first consciousness-raising group in 1969 and her coauthorship of the chapter on sexuality in the first edition of *Our Bodies, Ourselves.* She is currently working on *Everyday Feminism,* a book about the role of nonactivists in social movements, and with Aldon Morris on *Oppositional Consciousness,* an edited volume.

katherine s. newman is a cultural anthropologist and the Ford Foundation Professor of Urban Studies at Harvard University's John F. Kennedy School of Government. She is the author of several books on middle-class economic insecurity, including *Falling from Grace* (1988) and *Declining Fortunes* (1993). The chapter that appears in this volume is part of a longer study to be published in 1999, entitled *No Shame in My Game: The Working Poor in the Inner City* (Alfred Knopf/Russell Sage Foundation), which focuses on the job search strategies, work experiences, and family lives of African-Americans and Latinos living in Harlem. Newman's current work focuses on the career pathways of workers who enter the world of employment at the low-wage end and on the impact of welfare reform on the working poor.

maureen r. waller is a sociologist and a research fellow at the Public Policy Institute of California. Her research interests are in the areas of poverty, the family, social policy, and cultural sociology, and she is now working on a national study of unmarried parents and their children in collaboration with researchers at other institutions. Waller's previous work draws on in-depth interviews conducted in Trenton, New Jersey, to examine the meaning of fatherhood among poor, unmarried parents, and her current project uses both survey and qualitative methods to investigate the stability of relationships between unmarried parents living in Oakland, California. Waller's research has been supported by the Public Policy Institute of California, the National Science Foundation, the Woodrow Wilson Foundation, and Princeton University. In 1994, she received the Orlandella/Whyte Urban Field Research Fellowship Award from the Eastern Sociological Society.

pamela barnhouse walters is Professor of Sociology at Indiana University Bloomington. In her current research project, funded by the Spencer Foundation and the National Science Foundation, she is examining subordinate-group challenges to educational policy as attempts to secure greater educational social rights. In particular, she is comparing the strategies and tactics used by blacks in two southern states and working-class whites in two northern states to affect educational policy. Her prior research on school reform, on racial and class inequality in American education, and on school expansion has appeared in *American Sociological Review*, *Sociology of Education*, *American Journal of Sociology*, *Harvard Educational Review*, and *The Handbook of Sociology of Education*. She has received numerous grants for her research from the Spencer Foundation and from the National Science Foundation; she was the recipient of a Spencer Fellowship from the National Academy of Education in 1986; and she served as editor of *Sociology of Education* from 1994 to 1998.

mary c. waters is Professor of Sociology at Harvard University. She is the author of two books and numerous articles on racial and ethnic identity and immigrant assimilation. Her current research focuses on the racial and ethnic identities of Caribbean immigrants in the United States, patterns of assimilation among young adult children of immigrants from a wide variety of countries in New York City, and patterns of racial intermarriage and identity formation in the United States. She has consulted to the Census Bureau on issues of measurement of race and ethnicity, and was a member of the Panel on the Economic and Demographic Impacts of Immigration on the United States of the National Academy of Sciences. She has been a Guggenheim Fellow and a Visiting Scholar at the Russell Sage Foundation, and she is a member of the International Immigration Committee of the Social Science Research Council.

julia wrigley teaches in the Ph.D. Program in Sociology at the City University of New York Graduate Center. She studies class-based social conflicts and relationships, from those occurring at the political level (*Class Politics and Public Schools*) to those in households. Her book, *Other People's Children,* analyzes value differences between parents and their children's caregivers. With support from the Sloan Foundation, she is now exploring the emotional dynamics of cross-class relationships as experienced by children, parents, and caregivers. She edited *Sociology of Education* from 1991 to 1994.

alford a. young jr., Assistant Professor of Sociology and African American Studies at the University of Michigan, has done research and published in the area of race and urban poverty. His work focuses upon low-income black men in urban communities, and he is in the midst of writing a book entitled *The Minds of Black Men: Making Sense of Mobility, Opportunity, and Future Life Chances.* He has done additional work on how black men interpret municipal labor market opportunities. He also published work on the intellectual history of African-American sociology, and continues research on issues of identity, personal mission, and political engagement concerning African-American scholars.

index

Abbott, Edith, 275

abortion: objections to, 196–97; and race, 294; rap music in opposition to, 333, 335; unmarried parents on, 188, 189, 195, 196–97

Abubakari, Dara, 295, 309n.11

abusive relationships. *See* domestic abuse

"acting white," 69

Adams, Russell, 240

adoption: decline in, 214n.39; informal adoption in black families, 214n.40; unmarried parents on, 188, 195, 197–98

AFDC, 162, 173

affirmative action, 343–68; American dream violated by, 355; black executives on, 9, 13; in black middle class's expansion, 5, 25, 26, 348, 356, 360n.13; California Proposition 209, 6, 345, 350, 357, 359n.6, 362n.24; conflicting results of, 7, 352; conservatives and liberals supporting, 347; corporate support for, 349–50, 357–58; as cultural warfare, 352–57; economic effects of, 347–48; in elite universities, 348, 361n.18; empirical examinations lacking for, 343, 346, 347, 352, 360n.11; as entitlement to blacks, 349; escape from the impasse over, 357–58; harm claimed due to, 351, 361n.18; historical basis of, 4–8; as hot political issue from 1995, 345; as individualistic sellout, 345; and institutional racism, xvin.6; judicial decisions on, 359n.2; legal and philosophical analyses of, 343; new definitions of racism and backlash against, 265; as not a single entity or progress, 359n.3; opponents of, 352–53, 358; opposing as respectable, 354; organizational effects of, 349–50; Philadelphia plan, 345; placing premium on black skin color, 26; proponents of, 353, 358; psychological effects of, 349; reasons for contro-

versy over, 354–55, 361n.21; referenda on, 345, 357; as shifting from right-wing to left-wing position, 345; soft versions of, 350–51, 362n.24; as stigmatizing, 344, 350; strong versions of, 345, 355–56; as way station, 355; as weapon for attacking enemies in some other battle, 346, 352; what we do know about it, 347–51; what we don't know about it, 343–47; white backlash against, 6, 25–26, 265; whites as beneficiaries of, 361n.14

African American. *See under* black

African-American Baseline Essays, 229

African-American Infusion Program (Atlanta), 231, 233

African-Centered School (Washington, D.C.), 229, 231–32

Afrocentrism, 227–29; adversaries and allies for, 224–25; on African methods of education, 234–35; in Atlanta, 231; for black school districts, 233; class in acceptance, 222, 240–41; common ground with multiculturalism, 232–33, 236; conservative opposition to, 244; in the curriculum, 221–48; as divisive within African-American community, 222, 238–41, 244, 248n.3; emerging concern with difference, 8; essentialist conception of race of, 221–22, 228; fundamental notions about curriculum, 235; historical scholarship of, 228, 230; and inclusivity/exclusivity, 224; intellectual project of, 227; as meaning "being black," 241; versus multiculturalism, 223, 229–32, 243, 244; neoconservative criticism of, 229–30; in New York State, 232; opening ritual in Afrocentric classroom, 228–29; origins of, 227; primary assumptions of, 227–28; on problems and solutions in education, 232–35; as a racial project, 222; as revolution-

Afrocentrism (*continued*)
ary, 230; separatist orientation of, 225, 227,
241; two-front battle of, 243–44; two types of
Afrocentrist, 230; in Washington, D.C.,
231–32
AIDS, as antiblack conspiracy, 333, 340n.6
Allard, Mary Ann, 214n.46
ambition: black workers on, 143; in West In-
dian immigrants, 89; white workers on, 130–
31, 133; working class view on, 144
American Apartheid (Swidler), x
American dream, ideology of the, 354–56,
36on.8
American Indians, 372, 373, 378, 384
Americanization, 273, 274, 375
Anderson, Elijah, xii, 180n.12
Anderson, James D., 280
Anderson, Patricia, 120n.6
anti-Semitism: among black Americans, 226;
prosperity not necessarily mitigating, 382; in
rap music, 327
Anzaldúa, Gloria, 296
Asante, Molefi Kete, 227, 244–45
ascriptive Americanism, 354
Asians: and affirmative action, 343; in American racial structure before 1965, 372; Chinese, 374, 384, 388n.26; Filipinos, 372, 373,
375; as integrating with whites, 372–73; intermarriage with whites, 376, 378, 387n.11; Japanese, 376, 387n.12; as model minority, 372;
and multiracial individuals, 375; as nonblack,
373; rap music portrayal of, 334, 335; in residual racial category, 375; South Asians, 372,
375, 387n.9; women as domestic workers, 98
assimilation: Afrocentric criticism of, 222, 238;
as doubly threatening to involuntary minorities, 69–70; and emerging concern with difference, 8; and ethnic identity, x; of immigrants,
382; integrationist/inclusionist perspective,
225, 240–41; literature on, xvin.7; and residual racial category, 375; shift to pluralism
from, 253
athletics: in realizing racial constraint, 44–45;
in upward mobility, 35, 39, 59n.15
au pairs, 101
Austin, Algernon, 229
authenticity: in Afrocentrism/multiculturalism
debate, 222, 240–41, 243, 244; rap music emphasizing, 322, 323, 334

authority: black working class on, 138; white
working class on, 130
avoiding-oppression strategy, 51–54

"bad nigger," in black popular culture, 326
Baker, Ella, 338
Baker, Houston, 319, 320, 325, 340n.1
Baraka, Amiri, 318
Barbados, 71
Beal, Frances, 294, 309n.8
bebop, 318, 322
Bell Curve, The (Herrnstein and Murray), ix
Biemer, Linda, 236
bilingual education, 274
Binder, Amy, xiv
biracial individuals, 375–78, 387n.11
black capitalism, affirmative action for encouraging, 345
black church: decreasing influence of, 337; as
southern blacks' public voice, 273, 277, 279,
284n.4
Black English, 245n.1
black executives, 3–29; acceptable degree of
"whiteness" in, 15–16; on affirmative action,
9, 13; affirmative action in situation of, 4–8;
and black coworkers, 8, 11, 14; "code switching" by, 27; as communication links between
their community and the white firm, 18;
doing something for their people, 16; dress
of, 12, 17; as forming their own group, 8–19;
and lower-level black employees, 20; and
"normal" corporate employees, 23–25;
protégé-mentor relationships, 20–23; racial
solidarity among, 11, 15; reactions to presence of, 27; rising in the company, 14; sympathetic people in the organization, 18–23; two
groups of, 10; and whites, 8, 10, 11, 12, 13,
14; working to reshape corporate culture, 24
black feminism: black feminist writers, 296;
Combahee River Collective, 296, 338; formal
organizations of, 307; National Black Feminist Organization, 295–96, 309n.9; rap music's attitude toward, 321, 333, 335; womanism, 293, 307
"Black Feminist Statement" (Combahee River
Collective), 296
black lower class: black executives and lower-
level black employees, 20; black middle class
splitting from, 6–7; reproduction and mar-

riage separated in, 182–218; as scapegoats, 380; West Indian immigrants compared with, 93n.5; young black men getting ahead, 30–62
black men: advantages of, 49; black women as privileged compared with, 58n.11; dress of black executives, 12, 17; feminism supported by, 313n.32; finding marriageable partners, 207; increasing employment problems, 299; Million Man March, 322, 323, 338; public image of, 37, 46; rising age of marriage for, 214n.43; as "too independent," 304–5; unique constraints on, 37; and unmarried parenthood, 182–210; white fear of black male sexuality, 293, 308n.5; workers on the upper class, 138–42. *See also* young black men
black middle class: affirmative action in expansion of, 5, 25, 26, 348, 356, 360n.13; Afrocentrists on, 238; increasing distrust of whites in, 356; integrationist perspective of, 225, 240–41; in other countries, 387n.7; personal economic well-being as concern of, 26; splitting from black lower class, 6–7; as stigmatized, 373; strong racial identity feared by, 244–45; subtle racism experienced by, 81; on upward mobility, 32; women as college graduates, 299; young black men getting ahead, 30–62. *See also* black executives
black nationalism: African Americans as divided over, 245n.2; Afrocentrism compared with, 222, 225; black power movement, 26, 319, 322; and rap music, 322, 323, 324, 327, 330–31, 333–34, 335, 338; separatist perspective, 225–26, 241, 334
black-on-black violence. *See* violence within the black community
Black Panthers, 326, 336
black popular culture: the "bad nigger" in, 326; as blurring line between style and ideology, 324; jazz, 318, 322, 323; new jack popular culture, 318, 338; political uses of, xiv, 318, 320, 336. *See also* rap music
Black Power (Carmichael and Hamilton), xvin.6
black power movement, 26, 319, 322
blacks (African Americans): and affirmative action, 343–68; affirmative action in admission to elite universities, 348; affirmative action placing premium on black skin color, 26; AIDS seen as antiblack conspiracy, 333, 340n.6; in alternative racial scenarios,

381–82; in American racial structure before 1965, 372; anger of, 86–87; being black as not being white, 69; black existential angst, 74; boundaries among, 11–12; collective identity creation for, 223–27; collectivist understanding of morality, 147n.16; diversity of identities for, 225–27; European immigrants compared with, 70, 386n.3; as fast-food workers, 153–81; housing segregation, xviin.14; immigrants as jumping over, 378–79; informal adoption among, 214n.40; intermarriage with whites, 378, 381; job hierarchies seen as slavery by, 77; light-skinned blacks, 78, 376, 377, 387n.15; minority set-asides for contracts, 344–45; and multiracial individuals, 375–78; in new racial hierarchy of twenty-first century, 371–86; out-of-wedlock births among, 211n.3; payoffs for elite school attendance, 348; poverty associated with, 373, 381, 385; in public-sector employment, 93n.5; sense of entitlement, 86–88; sexual component of black/white relationships, 308n.5; the "Talented Tenth," 279, 353; on their fate as tied to each other, 329, 330; as too concerned about race, 75, 84; West Indian immigrants as more successful than American, 63–67, 93n.5; at white colleges and universities, 5; on whites as doing better than blacks, 329; whites fearing violence from, 113–14, 118; whites lumping all blacks together, 10, 18–19; whites wanting social distance from, 101. *See also* Afrocentrism; black church; black lower class; black men; black middle class; black nationalism; black popular culture; black upper class; black women; black working class; civil rights movement; slavery; southern blacks; violence within the black community
Black Scholar, The (journal), 244
black studies programs, 227
black upper class: light-skinned blacks in, 376; as stigmatized, 373; women college graduates in, 299. *See also* black executives
black women: abandoning domestic work, 98, 120, 299; activist women on feminism, 291, 292–97; black men as less privileged than, 58n.11; as children's caregivers, 99, 100, 102; as college graduates, 299; constraints on and advantages of, 37, 58n.11; as domestic work-

black women (*continued*)
ers, 97–120; dress of black executives, 12; finding marriageable partners, 207; independence from men, 294–95, 300–306; as liberals, 313n.30; "the look" for dealing with employers, 113–14; on men, 201–2; National Association of Colored Women, 281; nonactivist women on feminism, 297–300, 309n.14; occupational breakthrough for, 299; as primary breadwinners, 299; rap music's exposure among, 330; rising age of marriage for, 214n.43; social distance from domestic employers, 108–9; stigmatized housework by, 105–7, 121n.7; the "strong black woman," 293–94, 308n.7; surveillance when minding white children, 112–13; as "too independent," 300–306; unwed motherhood among, 182–210; verbal defiance of, 314n.36. *See also* black feminism

Black Workers Congress, 338
black working class: on authority, 138; middle-class orientation in, 138, 142, 143; separatist orientation of, 226; on status and worth, 127–50; as stigmatized, 373; success as defined by, 128, 138, 139, 141; on the upper class, 138–42; on upward mobility, 128, 138
blaming the victim, x, xi
Blankenhorn, David, 210n.2
Blumer, Herbert, 60n.19
Bodnar, John, 276
Bourdieu, Pierre, 32, 59n.17, 258
Boyd, Todd, 324
brain size, 388n.22
Brand Nubian (rap group), 330
Brazil, 377
Breckinridge, Sophonisba P., 275
British nannies, 103
Brown, James, 336
Brown, Ronald, 340n.3
Bryson, Bethany, xiv
Burke, Kenneth, 185–86
Burstein, Paul, 347
Bush, George, 5, 347
Butts, Calvin, 320, 326

California Civil Rights Initiative (Proposition 209), 6, 345, 350, 357, 359n.6, 362n.24
Cannon, Lynn Weber, 145n.3
canon, literary, 250, 251, 255, 264, 265n.2

Caribbean islands: class structure in, 66; inter-racial marriage in, 377; race relations in, 71–73; slavery in, 65. *See also* West Indian immigrants
Carmichael, Stokely, xvin.6, 64
Carter, Jimmy, 347
Carter, Stephen, 345
Catholic Church, 272, 274
Center for the American Woman and Politics (Rutgers University), 309n.12
Central and Latin American immigrants, 372, 375, 380, 381
child care: racial differences regarding, 294. *See also* children's caregivers
child labor, 273, 274, 276, 281
children's caregivers, 97–123; au pairs, 101; black and white women experiencing differently, 118; British nannies, 103; and the children in their care, 116–17; having resources to leave bad jobs, 103–4; house cleaners distinguished from, 99; housework done by, 102–5; personal service provided by, 107–8; racial issues from outside the household, 110–13; the servant role, 102–9; social distance from their employers, 108–9; social isolation of, 109; surveillance of black women minding white children, 112–13; white women as, 99, 100, 101, 103, 104, 109, 120nn. 1, 3
Chinese, 374, 384, 388n.26
Chinoy, Eli, 145n.3
Chiswick, Barry R., 65
Chuck D (rapper), 322, 334
church, black. *See* black church
civil rights movement: artistic wing of, 336; black inclusion resulting from, 4, 5; business and government responding to, 26; SCLC, 338; women as subordinated in, 294
Clarke, John Henrik, 227
class: as achieved status, 385; and Afrocentrism, 222, 240–41; Americans reluctant to use language of, 145n.1; and being called "too independent," 304; blacks as having right to a class structure, 353; black workers on class relations, 138–39; in Brazil, 377; in Caribbean cultures, 66; and culture, 125–218; in domestic work, 97, 98, 108; in emerging dual racial hierarchy, 373; and intermarriage, 385; and race, xiii, 36, 58n.10, 72–73,

385; rap music accentuating class distinctions, 325. *See also* low-income people; middle class; underclass; upper class; working class

Clinton, Bill, 347, 357, 361n.20

Clinton, George, 318

Cobb, Jonathan, 128, 142, 146n.4

"code switching," 27

Cohen, Miriam, 284n.5

Coleman, Richard P., 145n.3

collective identity: and the American dream, 355; defined, 224; diversity of black, 225–27; enemies in formation of, 224; forging a black identity, 223–27; and inclusivity/exclusivity, 224. *See also* ethnic identity; racial identity

Combahee River Collective, 296, 338

common culture, 229–30

common-school movement, 271

competitiveness, 25, 132

Conference Board, 358

consciousness-raising groups, 307

conservatism: affirmative action supported by, 347; Afrocentrism opposed by, 244; on gangsta rap, 323; of West Indian immigrants, 89, 94n.13. *See also* neoconservatism

contraception, by teenage parents, 213n.33

Cooper, Jean, 294

Cooper, Walter, 237, 240, 242–43

Cornell, Stephen, 71

"crab down" syndrome, 157

Crane, Diana, 258

Cubans, 372

cultural diversity. *See* diversity

cultural production, 258

culture: and class, 125–218; a common culture, 229–30; the culture West Indian immigrants bring with them, 73–78; high culture, 259–60, 263, 264; immigrant culture, 68–73; modern racism as culturally driven, 252, 259; and racial inequality, ix–xi; return to, x, xvin.8; as script, xi; as tool-kit, 211n.13; and West Indian immigrants' success, 63–66, 93n.4

"culture of poverty" thesis, x

culture wars: affirmative action in, 352–57; and alternative racial scenarios, 381

Cureton, Jeanette, 251

curriculum. *See* education

"Curriculum of Inclusion, A" (New York State), 232, 236–37, 239, 242–43

Davis, Angela, 338

Dawson, Michael C., xiv, 329, 340n.3

deindustrialization, 6, 7, 25, 184

de la Puente, Manuel, 384, 388n.27

Democratic Party, 272, 313n.30, 347

Denton, Nancy, x, xviin.14

discrimination. *See* racial discrimination; sex discrimination

Disposable Heroes of Hiphoprisy (rap group), 332, 338

DiTomaso, Nancy, 148n.22

diversity: affirmative action in increase in, 25; college curricular changes for addressing, 254; as corporate goal, 349, 350, 358; and "Curriculum of Inclusion" report, 242; of multiculturalism, 245. *See also* multiculturalism

divorce: as concern for unmarried parents, 198–99, 209; cultural acceptance of, 184; rhetoric of, 214n.47

domestic abuse: race as issue in, 293; single motherhood as preferable to, 203; of women on welfare, 214n.46; in women's decisions on relationships, 202, 207

domestic work, 97–123; advantages of, 120n.2; black women abandoning, 98, 120, 299; classified advertisements for, 100; conflicts and conflict management in, 113–16; declining significance of race in, 99–101; employers and employees lying to each other, 114–15; as exceptionally exploitative, 98; exiting the job, 115–16; forced intimacy of, 97; literatures on, 97–98; methodology of this study, 101–2; as one occupation among many, 98; racial issues from outside the household, 110–13; Southern versus Northern, 99–100; stigmatized tasks, 105–7. *See also* children's caregivers; house cleaning

downsizing, 6, 25

dozens, the, 326

Dr. Dre (rapper), 337

dramatism, 185

drug trade: dealers as role models, 171–72; dealers as unmarriageable, 207; fast-food work contrasted with, 172–73; government involvement alleged in, 322, 356; Harlem teenagers as afraid of, 163

drug use: Harlem teenagers as afraid of, 163; as obstacle to marriage, 201, 206

D'Souza, Dinesh, ix–x, 244
dual racial hierarchy, 372–75; alternative scenarios for, 379–82; and multiracial individuals, 375–78; as possibility for twenty-first century, 371, 386; qualifications to, 374–79; regional variation in, 378–79; the residuals, 371, 375
Du Bois, W. E. B., 13, 100, 225, 279, 338, 353
Duke University, 254
Dyson, Michael, 319, 320, 327, 338

Eastern and Southern European immigrants, 274, 275, 374, 381, 384
Eaton, Isabel, 113
Ebonics, 245n.1
Edley, Christopher, Jr., 359n.1, 361n.21
education: Afrocentric and multicultural curriculum movements in, 221–48; and being called "too independent," 304–5, 313n.34, 314n.35; black student success as "acting white," 69; the canon, 250, 251, 255, 264, 265n.2; cultural significance at turn of the century, 268–88; ethnic and racial differences in commitment to, 269–70; for getting a good job, 271; historical change in attitude toward, 271–72; identity politics in, xiv; in ideologies for personal mobility, 46–54; as key to personal advancement, 270; multiculturalism in university English departments, 249–65; North and South differing regarding, 269; opportunity structures for, 269, 284n.5; parochial schools, 274; and the politics of race, 219–88; Populism's concern with, 277; public education, 271, 354; racial inequality in, 38–39; rap music telling alternative stories of, 324; in realizing racial constraint, 38–46, 59n.16; in social and cultural reproduction, 55–56; and social mobility, 268, 270, 271; subtle racism in, 81–82; as symbol of citizenship, xiv, 280, 283; vocational education, 274, 279; "Western culture" curriculum, 249, 253; white workers as skeptical of, 133, 134; white workers emphasizing income over, 130. See also universities
egalitarianism: black working men on, 138; diversity as indicating, 25; equality of opportunity, 354, 355, 356, 357–58; white working men on, 136–38. See also income inequality

Ehrenreich, Barbara, 211n.10
Elders, Joycelyn, 333
Eliasoph, Nina, 253
elite universities: affirmative action in, 348, 361n.18; multiculturalism in English departments in, 250, 254–61, 263; research imperative in, 258
Ellis, Catherine, xiii
employment. See work
English professors: charges of racism dividing, 250; debates about dividing the discipline, 257; in elite universities, 254–61; on multiculturalism, 255–56, 259, 260, 264, 266n.6; multiculturalism as affecting, 249–67; in nonelite universities, 261–64; primary activity as racially significant, 251; standard texts still being taught, 256; yesterday's progressives are today's racists, 254–56
equality of opportunity, 354, 355, 356, 357–58
"ethclass," 375
ethnic identity: culture in, x; emerging concern with difference, 8; as a narrative, 71; as racial, 384, 389n.30; white ethnics in identity politics, 382
Eurocentrism: Afrocentric response to, 227, 230; Afrocentrism and multiculturalism opposing, 223, 224, 233, 237; multiculturalist response to, 236
European immigrants: blacks compared with, 70, 386n.3; from Eastern and Southern Europe, 274, 275, 374, 381, 384; Irish, 373–74, 389n.30
Everyday Feminism project, 308n.2

fair housing legislation, 25
family: Caribbean slaves' sense of, 65; in ideologies for personal mobility, 46–54; new patterns of, 184–86; in realizing racial constraint, 38–46, 59n.14; in social and cultural reproduction, 55–56; two-parent model of, 200; work taking precedence over, 178. See also marriage; unwed parenthood
Farrakhan, Louis, 90, 324, 330, 334
fast-food workers: ambiguous social position of, 177–78; assembly line work of, 153; breaking the stigma of, 161–67; circles of friends of, 168–78; competition for jobs, 180n.9; conflicts with managers, 174; deference toward

customers, 154; earning respect by sticking with the job, 177; harassment of, 154–56; immigrants as, 165–66; job tenure of, 158; low socioeconomic status of, 159; mainstream values of, 161, 164, 177; "McJobs" of, 153, 158; as never having enough time, 167–68; ridiculed by their peers, 156–57, 163–64; as role models for their community, 176–77; status and stigma among, 151–81; in the status system, 174; as stigmatized, 151, 153, 157, 159; upward mobility for, 158, 168, 174; wages of, 158; work culture of, 170–71; work ethic of, 164, 172, 173

femininity, race in ideal of, 293

feminism: activist black women on, 291, 292–97; and being called "too independent," 305; black men supporting, 313n.32; "the click" experience, 296, 307; consciousness-raising groups, 307; emergence of feminisms, 307–8; first survey to ask if women considered themselves feminist, 297, 310n.16; meanings of, 298, 311nn. 23, 24; National Organization for Women, 294, 298; nonactivist black women on, 297–300, 309n.14; race and plural feminisms, xiv, 291–317; racism in, 292–93; second wave feminism, 291, 292, 307; term replacing "women's movement," 298, 312n.25; white men supporting, 313n.32; women state legislators identifying with, 297. See also black feminism

Filipinos, 372, 373, 375

Fish, Stanley, 254, 257

Forsythe, Dennis, 65, 94n.13

Frank, Robert H., 145n.2

Franti, Michael, 323

Fugees (rap group), 323, 325, 336, 338

Furstenberg, Frank, 213n.33

Gamson, William, 224

gangsta rap: antipolice songs, 334; black nationalist criticism of, 330; as explicit rejection of politics, 324; homophobia in, 332; as market influenced, 325; rightist critics using its own material against it, 323; Shakur and Notorious B.I.G. murders, 320, 337, 340n.10; and violence within the black community, 321, 325, 335, 337

Gans, Herbert, xiv

Garvey, Marcus, 64, 71, 90, 94n.13, 225

Gates, Henry Louis, 257

gender: domestic work and universalistic notions of, 97; in rap music, 321, 326; working class as gendered cultural construct, 145. See also sex discrimination; sexism; women

Gerber, Eleanor, 384

Geto Boys (rap group), 323, 324, 334, 338

Ginsburg, Faye D., 212n.20

Glantz, Oscar, 93n.4

glass ceilings, 167, 374

Glazer, Nathan, 63, 64, 229

globalization, 7, 382

Gloriana Afrocentricity, 228

Goffman, Erving, xii, 7–8, 60n.19

Gordon, Milton, 375

Graham, Hugh Davis, 347

Guinier, Lani, 333

Guyana, 71

habitus, 32

Hall, Stuart, 58n.10, 338

Halle, David, 147n.18

Hamer, Fannie Lou, 338

Hamilton, Charles, xvin.6

Harris, J. Jerome, 231

Harrison, Roderick, 388n.27

Hayden, Casey, 294

Healy, Melissa, 210n.2

Hellwig, David J., 94n.13

Henry, Charles P., 326

Hernandez, Aileen, 294

Herrnstein, Richard J., ix

Higginbotham, Evelyn Brooks, 281

high culture, 259–60, 263, 264

Hilliard, Asa, III, 227

hip-hop. See rap music

Hirsch, Fred, 145n.2

Hispanics. See Latinos

Hochschild, Arlie, 180n.6

Hochschild, Jennifer L., xii, xv, 145n.2, 212n.16, 271, 360n.8

Hoetink, Harry, 94n.8

Holt, John, 235, 246n.8

Holzer, Harry, 360n.9, 361nn. 15, 16

homophobia, in rap music, 321, 327, 332, 333, 334

hooks, bell, 292, 296, 299, 309n.11

Hoover, Larry, 324

Hopper, Joseph, 215n.47

Horowitz, Ruth, 60n.24

house cleaning: children's caregivers doing, 102–5; children's caregiving distinguished from, 99; polluted tasks, 105–7, 120n.6; supervision of, 104, 118

Huddy, Leonie, 312n.25

Hull, Gloria, 296

Hurston, Zora Neale, 305

Hutcherson, 322

Hyman, Herbert, 146n.11

Ice Cube (rapper), 320, 322, 323, 324, 325, 330, 334

Ice T (rapper), 324, 334

identity: oppositional identity, 69, 85; scholarly attention to, ix; social construction of, x, xi; work in American, 152–53. *See also* collective identity; identity politics

identity politics: black middle class rejection of, 225; in educational system, xiv; immigrants in, 382; white ethnics in, 382, 388n.20

ideologies: of the American dream, 354–56, 360n.8; for personal mobility, 46–54; and the politics of race, 289–368

Illouz, Eva, 200, 214nn. 44, 45

immigrants: affirmative action benefiting, 5; Americanization, 273, 274, 375; assimilation and acculturation of, 382; blacks compared with European, 70, 386n.3; Central and Latin American, 372, 375, 380, 381; as clannish, 383; and competitiveness in the workplace, 25; culture associated with, 68–73; as domestic workers, 100; Eastern and Southern European, 274, 275, 374, 381, 384; economic decline affecting, 380–81; educational access as important to, 275, 283; educational opportunities for, 284n.1; education demanded by, 269, 273–76, 283; education in worldview of, 268–88; as fast-food workers, 165–66; the immigrant narrative, 71; Irish, 373–74, 389n.30; as jumping over blacks, 378–79; "new immigration" theory, x; public voices vs. private interests of, 272–73; racializing national characters of, 382; rap music and black attitude towards, 334; regional variation in settlement, 378–79; as scapegoats,

380; school enrollments of, 269; second generation decline, 381; selectivity of immigration, 66. *See also* West Indian immigrants

income inequality: affirmative action not decreasing, 348, 349; and variation in domestic employment, 98. *See also* class; poverty

individualism, 177, 300, 345, 355

inequality, racial. *See* racial inequality

infidelity, 203, 206

institutional racism, x, xvin.6

integrationist/inclusionist perspective, 225, 240–41

intermarriage: of Asians and whites, 372; of blacks and whites, 378, 381; in Brazil, 377; and class, 385; empirical evidence on, 377; increase in, 376, 387n.11; and multiracial individuals, 375–76; and new racial hierarchy of twenty-first century, 371; South Asians discouraging, 387n.9

interpersonal racism, 78, 80–85

interpersonal relationships: black workers on, 141, 142; white workers on, 131, 133, 137; working class emphasis on, 142–43. *See also* family; marriage

Irish domestic workers, 108

Irish immigrants, 373–74, 389n.30

Islam, 225, 226, 322, 327

Italians, Southern, 374

Jackman, Mary, 147nn. 17, 18, 148n.23

Jackson, Jesse, 249

Jamaica, 71, 72–73

Japanese, 376, 387n.12

jazz, 318, 322, 323

Jefferson, Thomas, 237

Jeffries, Leonard, 227, 232, 236–37, 239

Jencks, Christopher, 70

Jews: black executives helped by, 18; and the corporate norm, 24; education as valued by, 274, 284n.5; glass ceiling for, 374. *See also* anti-Semitism

Johnson, Charles S., 280–81

Johnson, Lyndon, 4, 7, 347

Jones, LeRoi, 318

Kalmijn, Matthijs, 65

Karenga, Maulana, 227

Kasinitz, Philip, 65, 94n.14

Katznelson, Ira, 284n.3
Kelley, Robin, 323, 326, 337, 338
Kendall, Mae, 233
Kennedy, Florynce, 294, 295
Kennedy, John F., 4
Keto, Tsheloane, 227
Kimball, Roger, 255
King, Mae C., 311n.23
King, Mary, 294
Kitwana, Bakari, 330
Kofsky, Frank, 318
Kohne, Natasha G., 387n.15
Kool Moe Dee (rapper), 338
Kristol, Irving, 386n.3
Kwanzaa, 226

labor unions, 272, 273–74, 277
Lamont, Michèle, xiii, 146nn. 6, 7, 147n.16,
    179n.1, 257
Latin and Central American immigrants, 372,
    375, 380, 381
Latinas: as children's caregivers, 99, 101; as do-
    mestic workers, 98, 100; social distance from
    domestic employers, 108–9; stigmatized
    housework by, 105–7
Latinos (Hispanics): affirmative action in ad-
    mission to elite universities, 348; affirmative
    action supported by, 351; black Hispanics,
    386n.4; and changing racial categories, 380;
    as fast-food workers, 153–81; intermarriage
    with whites, 376; Mexicans, 372, 379; and
    multiracial individuals, 375; as nonblack, 373;
    Puerto Ricans, 372, 386nn. 3, 4; as quasi-
    racial ethnic group, 375; as a race, 384; rap
    music portrayal of, 334–35; in recategoriza-
    tion of American racial hierarchy, 372; in re-
    sidual racial category, 375; in the Southwest,
    379; white fear of being swamped by, 380.
    See also Latinas
Lawson, Bill E., 212n.16
Lerner, Gerda, 295
Levine, Arthur, 251
Lewis, Diane, 295
liberalism: affirmative action supported by, 347;
    on antiracism, 253; ascriptive Americanism
    losing debate to, 354; black women as more
    liberal than white women, 313n.30; yester-
    day's progressives are today's racists, 254–56

light-skinned blacks, 78, 376, 377, 387n.15
Link, Arthur, 276, 277
literary canon, 250, 251, 255, 264, 265n.2
LL Cool J (rapper), 334
Loewen, James W., 374
long interview, 58n.8
Lorde, Audre, 292, 296
love, American models of, 200
lower class, black. See black lower class
low-income people: considering themselves
    middle class, 129–30, 146n.6; women as "too
    independent," 292, 304. See also black lower
    class; low-wage work; poverty
low-wage work: ambiguous social position of,
    177–78; breaking the stigma, 161–67; social
    costs of accepting, 153–61; status and stigma
    of, 151–81; welfare reform forcing women
    into, 173, 178, 180n.11; West Indian immi-
    grants accepting, 66; work culture in, 170–
    71; workers' circles of friends, 168–78; work-
    ers never having enough time, 167–68. See
    also domestic work; fast-food workers
Luker, Kristin, 213n.31, 215n.50

MacLeod, Jay, 30, 32–33, 56, 57n.5, 60n.23,
    145n.3
Madhubuti, Haki, 330
mainstream values: about marriage, 200; in
    fast-food workers, 161, 164, 177; single par-
    ents borrowing from, 184; in young black
    men, 46, 59n.18. See also middle-class values
Malcolm X, 64, 85, 157, 324
Malveaux, Julianne, 323, 325
Mansbridge, Jane, xiv, 181n.13, 312n.25,
    314n.36
Marable, Manning, 225–26, 341
marriage: considering after parenthood, 198–
    208; considering parenthood outside, 188–
    98; decline in, 184, 211n.10; "forced" or
    "rushed" marriages, 183, 199, 209; marital
    status and being called "too independent,"
    305–6; obstacles to, 201; realist and idealist
    ideas about, 200; reproduction separated
    from, 182–218; rising age of, 214n.43; as solu-
    tion to unintended pregnancy, 183, 198, 209.
    See also intermarriage
Marshall, Paule, 92n.2
Massey, Douglas, x, xviin.14

Matthews, Tracye, 319–20
Mazrui, Ali, 227, 228, 229, 246n.5
McDonald's Corporation, 151, 158, 161
McFarlin, Murdell, 238, 239
Mead, Lawrence, ix–x
men: affirmative action as harming, 344; characteristics valued in a spouse by, 207; earnings decline relative to women, 184, 211n.9; rising age of marriage for, 214n.43; "trapped" into becoming fathers, 195, 214n.35; unwed parenthood, 182–210. *See also* black men; white men
meritocracy: and affirmative action, 6; in the American dream, 355; and education, 271; young black men on, 36, 37
Mexicans, 372, 379
middle class: low-income workers considering themselves, 129–30, 146n.6; swarthy races entering, 374; white feminists as, 292–93. *See also* black middle class; middle-class values
middle-class values: in black workers, 138, 142, 143; in white workers, 130, 138, 142; working-class attitudes toward, xiii, 128, 146n.6. *See also* mainstream values
Miles, Jack, 86
Milkman, Ruth, 98
Million Man March, 322, 323, 338
Mills, C. Wright, 59n.13, 186
Mingus, Charlie, 322
minimum wage, 158, 180n.8
minority groups: and affirmative action, 5, 6, 343–68; and the corporate norm, 24; model minorities, 372, 379; voluntary versus involuntary minorities, 68–70; whites becoming a numerical minority, 373, 386n.5
minority set-asides for contracts, 344–45
misogyny: as pervasive in black community, 330; in rap music, 320, 321, 326, 330, 331–33, 340n.1
mixed-race individuals. *See* multiracial individuals
mobility, social. *See* social mobility
Model, Suzanne, 66
model minorities, 372, 379
Modern Language Association, 260
money: black workers on, 138, 140, 147n.14; as racial equalizer, 138; white workers on, 129, 133–34

Moraga, Cherríe, 296
moral value: employment equated with, 152; and social status, 131, 133, 136, 137; white workers on moral flaws of upper class, 131–34; white workers on moral superiority of working class, 134–36
Morawska, Ewa, 274–75
motives, attribution of, 185–86
Moynihan, Daniel Patrick, 63, 64
Moynihan report (1965), ix
Muhammad, Elijah, 225
mulattos, 376
Mullings, Leith, 225–26, 241
multiculturalism: adversaries and allies for, 224–25; African-American educators supporting, 230; versus Afrocentrism, 223, 229–32, 243, 244; basic philosophical claim of, 229; black supporters of, 223; common ground with Afrocentrism, 232–33, 236; as cosmopolitan, 243; in the curriculum, 221–48; diversity as strength of, 245; in elite universities, 254–61; in English departments, 249–67; English professors on, 255–56, 259, 260, 264, 266n.6; and exclusion within academia, xiv, 254–55, 259–60, 261–62, 265n.4; identity constructed by, 241–43; and inclusivity/exclusivity, 224; institutionalization of, 245; moral character of, 256–57; in nonelite universities, 261–64; personal tone of debates about, 257; pluralism of, 230; policies on, 262–63; practicality of, 243; on problems and solutions in education, 235–36; proponents of, 229; as response to inadequate definitions of racism, 252–54
multiracial individuals, 375–78; American society as multiracial, xii, 386; as Census category, 376, 387n.14; as exotic, 378, 388n.19; long-term prosperity affecting, 382
Murphy Brown (television show), 210n.2
Murray, Charles, ix, 211n.11
Murray, Pauli, 294

narrative analysis, 185–86
National Association of Colored Women, 281
National Black Feminist Organization (NBFO), 295–96, 309n.9
National Black Politics Study, 327, 340n.3
national identity, and postnational citizenship, x

nationalism, black. *See* black nationalism
National Organization for Women (NOW), 294, 298
Nation of Islam, 225, 322, 327
Native Americans, 372, 373, 378, 384
NBFO (National Black Feminist Organization), 295–96, 309n.9
Negroid physical features, 373, 375
Negro Immigrant, The: His Background Characteristics and Social Adjustment 1899–1937 (Reid), 64, 92n.1
neoconservatism: Afrocentrism criticized by, 229–30; on blacks adopting immigrant values, 386n.3; on racial inequality, ix–x
Neumark, David, 360n.9
Newby, I. A., 278
New Historicism, 255, 265n.2
"new immigration," x
new jack popular culture, 318, 338
Newman, Dale, 280
Newman, Katherine, xiii, 212n.16
"new racism," 252
Nightingale, Carl Husemoller, 147n.13, 212n.16
Nixon, Richard, 345, 347
nonelite universities: affirmative action in, 348; multiculturalism in English departments in, 250, 260, 261–64; seniority as emphasized in, 261
nonmarital births. *See* unwed parenthood
North Carolina Farmers' Alliance, 277
Northwestern University Chicago Area Survey, 304, 312n.24
Notorious B.I.G. (rapper), 320, 337, 340n.10
NWA (rap group), 325, 334

O'Connor, Carla, 60n.18
off our backs (journal), 312n.25
Ogbu, John, 68–70
opportunity, equality of, 354, 355, 356, 357–58
oppositional identity, 69, 85
O'Reilly, Jane, 296
out-groups, 144, 147n.22
out-of-wedlock births. *See* unwed parenthood

parenthood, marriage separated from, 182–218
Paris (rapper), 323, 324, 325, 330, 333, 338
parochial schools, 274
Patterson, Orlando, 73–74, 94n.13

PE (rap group). *See* Public Enemy
People's Party, 277
Philadelphia plan, 345
pluralism, 230, 253
police: affirmative action affecting, 352, 360n.13; black encounters with, 80, 336; in rap music, 324, 326, 334; and violence against black women, 243
political correctness, 253, 351
politically oriented rap music, 321, 323–25, 331, 333, 334
politics of identity. *See* identity politics
poor blacks. *See* black lower class
poor southern whites: educational access not demanded by, 270, 276–79, 282; educational opportunities for, 284n.1; education in worldview of, 268–88; public voices vs. private interests of, 272–73
poor whites: Caribbean islands lacking, 65; poor blacks contrasted with, 373; as "trailer trash," 387n.6. *See also* poor southern whites
popular culture. *See* black popular culture
Populism, 277
positional goods, 127, 145n.2
poverty: birth pattern affected by, 215n.50; blackness associated with, 373, 381, 385; among blacks and whites contrasted, 190, 213n.25; and child labor, 273; culture in persistence of, x; deserving versus undeserving poor, 164; in emerging dual racial hierarchy, 373; of families headed by unmarried women, 211n.3; the undeserving poor as scapegoats, 379. *See also* black lower class; low-wage work; poor whites
Powell, Colin, 64, 89–90
power: black workers on, 138, 140; white workers on, 129, 133
Pratt, Mary Louise, 265n.1
preferential treatment: in elite university admissions, 348; harm claimed due to, 351; opposition to, 6, 25, 343, 350, 357
pregnancy, unintended. *See* unwed parenthood
Professor Grif (rapper), 323
Proletariana Afrocentricity, 228
Proposition 209 (California Civil Rights Initiative), 6, 345, 350, 357, 359n.6, 362n.24
Protestant ethic. *See* work ethic
public education, 271, 354

Public Enemy (PE) (rap group): anti-Semitism of, 327; black nationalism promoted by, 324, 330, 333–34; as bringing people together, 322; as educating and entertaining, 338; political integrity of, 319, 325

Puerto Ricans, 372, 386nn. 3, 4

Queen Latifah (rapper), 321, 333, 338

quotas: government contractor complaints of, 351; legal and philosophical analyses of, 343; opposition to, 350, 357

race: and "blood," 376, 382, 387n.16; changing classification systems of, 373–74; and class, xiii, 36, 58n.10, 72–73, 385; comparison of apes and humans in construction of, 388n.22; as constraint for upward mobility, 36–38; deserving and undeserving races, 371, 373; and education, xiv, 219–88; ethnicity as racial, 384, 389n.30; family and schooling in realizing constraint of, 38–46; in feminine ideal, 293; and feminism, xiv, 291–317; the future of racial classification, 369–90; ideologies and the politics of, 289–368; money as racial equalizer, 138; a new racial hierarchy in the twenty-first century, 371–90; as not a biological category, 382; as not an achieved status, 385; polarization in United States, xii, 27; rap music as foregrounding, 321–22; scholarly attention to, ix; and the servant role, 102–9; social construction of, x, 382–85, 388n.25; swarthy races, 374, 384; visible bodily differences in, 372–73, 382–84; West Indian immigrants on American concern with, 75. *See also* dual racial hierarchy; intermarriage; multiracial individuals; racial discrimination; racial identity; racial inequality; racial solidarity; racism; skin color

"race-classes," 375

Race Matters (West), ix

racial discrimination: affirmative action as remedy for, 4, 5, 6, 343, 353; blacks and whites differing on extent of, 356; in black women's understanding of sex discrimination, 300; blatant acts of, 80; in Brazil, 377; as no longer respectable, 354, 362n.22; and relative lack of success of American blacks, 63; reverse discrimination, 6, 265n.4, 351, 358; and volun-

tary minorities, 69; against West Indian immigrants and American blacks compared, 67; West Indian immigrants on, 77–78

racial identity: boundaries of, xi–xii; forging a black identity, 223–27; middle class blacks fearing, 244–45; a new racial hierarchy for the twenty-first century, 371–90

racial inequality: affirmative action as remedy for, 4; black separatism as response to, 226; as continuing despite affirmative action, 6; cultural arguments regarding, ix–xi; and domestic work, 97–123; in education, 38–39; transformative approach to, 226. *See also* income inequality

racial insults (slurs), 100, 112

racialism, 72, 73, 75, 76, 84, 91

racial segregation: in Brazil, 377; fair housing legislation, 25; in housing, xviin.14; Northern racism versus Jim Crow South, 82; working-class immigrants' contact with whites limited by, 83

racial solidarity: assimilation as threat to, 70; among black executives, 11, 15; in involuntary minorities, 69

racial tolerance, 384–85

racism, 1–123; ambiguity in new definitions of, 257–61, 263–64; in Caribbean and United States compared, 73–74, 78; changing meaning of, 250, 251, 254–56; the experience of, xii; as explanation of black person's failure to succeed, 25, 63; in feminism, 292–93; as immoral, 257; institutional racism, x, xviin.6; interpersonal racism, 78, 80–85; liberal position on antiracism, 253; modern forms as culturally driven, 252, 259; as moving symbolic boundary, 249–67; multiculturalism as response to inadequate definitions of, 252–54; "new racism," 252; new sets of indicators for, 258–59; as socially constructed, 249–50, 252–53; structural racism, 78–80; symbolic racism, xvn.4, 252; systemic character of, xi; and voluntary minorities, 69; West Indian immigrants' attitudes changed by, 90–92; West Indian immigrants' reaction to, 73, 75–76, 88–89, 94n.13

Rainwater, Lee, 145n.3

Randolph, A. Philip, 338

Ransby, Barbara, 319–20

rap music, 318–42; abortion opposed in, 333, 335; age as factor in evaluation of, 327, 329–30; antipolice songs, 324, 326, 334; anti-Semitism in, 327; Asians as portrayed in, 334, 335; and attitudes toward whites, 334; authenticity emphasized in, 322, 323, 334; on black feminism, 321, 333, 335; and black nationalism, 322, 323, 324, 327, 330–31, 333–34, 335, 338; black public opinion affected by, 326–27; class distinctions accentuated by, 325; as CNN of black community, 320, 334; controversy surrounding political value of, 319–20; cultural studies movement on, 324; as damaging force in black community, 320; data and methodology of this study, 327–28; economics of, 321, 325–26; gender politics of, 321, 326, 331–33; ghettocentric rap, 323; homophobia in, 321, 327, 332, 333, 334; Latinos as portrayed in, 334–35; misogyny in, 320, 321, 326, 330, 331–33, 340n.1; politically oriented rap, 321, 323–25, 331, 333, 334; as political outlet for disenfranchised inner-city youth, 319; political wing of hip-hop culture, 319; race as foregrounded in, 321–22; rappers as new griots, 321–23, 338, 340n.2; rappers as standing above the crowd, 157; reasons for focusing on, 320–26; as this generation's answer to bebop, 318; violence against women as theme of, 333; and violence within the black community, 321, 325, 330, 335, 337; on work, 325; as youth music, 330; youth of all races embracing, 320. *See also* gangsta rap
Ravitch, Diane, 229
Raz, Joseph, 229
Reagan, Ronald, 5, 347
Reed, Adolph, Jr., 319, 320, 324–25, 326, 327
Reese, Ellen, 98
Reid, Ira, 63, 64, 65, 67, 74, 92n.1, 94n.13
relationships: dissolution of, 202–3. *See also* interpersonal relationships
reproduction. *See* parenthood
Republican Party, 139, 253, 347, 380
research imperative, 258
residual racial category, 371, 375
"Resurrection, The" (Geto Boys), 324
reverse discrimination, 6, 265n.4, 351, 358
Robinson, Patricia, 294

"Rock the Vote" voter registration drive, 323
Romero, Mary, 120n.2
Roosevelt, Franklin, 166
Rose, Tricia, 318–19, 322–23, 324, 325, 326, 336, 338
Rosenwald fund, 280
Roth, Benita, 98
Rubin, Lilian B., 128, 146n.4
Rushin, Donna Kate, 314n.35

Sanchez-Korrol, Virginia, 242
Sanders, Lynn M., 329
scapegoats, 379–82
Schlesinger, Arthur, 229
SCLC, 338
Scott, Patricia, 296
secondary cultural differences, 69
second generation decline, 381
second wave feminism, 291, 292, 307
segregation. *See* racial segregation
self-reliance: as American value, 178; black workers on, 143; white workers on, 134
Sennett, Richard, 128, 142, 146n.4
separatist perspective, 225–26, 241, 334
servant role: black workers falling more readily into, 118; race and the, 102–9
sex discrimination: affirmative action for, 343; in the civil rights movement, 294; understanding racial discrimination in understanding, 300
sexism: in rap music, 321, 326. *See also* misogyny; sex discrimination
Shakur, Tupac, 320, 337, 340n.10
Shange, Ntozake, 296
Shepp, Archie, 322, 323
Sidanius, James, 147n.22
Simpson, O. J., xii, 111
single parenthood. *See* unwed parenthood
Sister Souljah (rapper), 330
skin color: affirmative action placing premium on black, 26; black executives on, 9, 10, 12, 13, 15; in construction of race, 383, 384; light-skinned blacks, 78, 376, 377, 387n.15; and new nonblack racial category, 373; stereotypes associated with, 237; as stigma, 7–8; and subtle racism, 81–82; variations among blacks, 40, 78
Skrentny, John David, 347

slavery: in Caribbean and American South compared, 65, 73, 93n.3; descendants of slaves as still at the bottom, 377; domestic work as function of, 100; education prohibited for slaves, 280, 283n.1; eventual elimination of effects of, 386; female slave contrasted with delicate white woman, 293; job hierarchies seen as, 77; slaves as lowest class and race, 384; West Indian societies founded on, 68
Sloan, Margaret, 295
Smith, Barbara, 296, 310n.15
Smith, Don, 239
Smith, Franklin, 232
Smith, J. Owens, 93n.3
Smith, Rogers M., 147n.21
Smith, Timothy, 274
Sobol, Thomas, 232
social and cultural reproduction, 55–56
social constructionism, x, xi, xviin.12, 249–50, 252–53, 382–85, 388n.25
social distance: between servant and employer, 108–9; whites wanting social distance from blacks, 101
social mobility: education and, 268, 270; of first-generation immigrants, 68; for Southern and Eastern European immigrants, 275; structural racism affecting, 78–79; West Indian immigrants' reactions to blocked, 89–90. *See also* upward mobility
social movement organizations, 284n.2
social status: black workers on, 138, 139; and economic status, 127–28; of fast-food workers, 151–81; fast-food workers in the status system, 174; rap music inverting hierarchies of, 324; Weberian theory of, 127, 143; white and black workers on, 127–50; white workers on importance of high, 129–31; white workers on moral worth and, 131, 133, 136, 137. *See also* social mobility
solidarity, racial. *See* racial solidarity
"soul," 382
South Asians, 372, 375, 387n.9
Southern and Eastern European immigrants, 274, 275, 374, 381, 384
southern blacks: child labor among, 281; demanding better education, 269–70, 278–82; educational access as important to, 281, 283;

education in worldview of, 268–88; public voices vs. private interests of, 272–73
Southern Italians, 374
southern whites. *See* poor southern whites
Sowell, Thomas, ix, 63, 64
spirit journeys, 234–35
Stacey, Judith, 211n.4
standards, 24, 27
Stanford University, 249, 253, 254
Staples, Robert, 309n.8
status. *See* social status
Steinberg, Stephen, xvin.6, 63
stigma: of affirmative action, 344, 350; affluent blacks as stigmatized, 373; among fast-food workers, 151–81; of nonmarital pregnancy, 192; skin color as, 7–8; of swarthy races, 384; of teenage pregnancy, 193
Stonequist, Everett V., 375
strategic negotiation, 47–48
Strolevich, Dara, 312n.25
structural racism, 78–80
subtle racism, 80–82
swarthy races, 374, 384
Sweet, Midge, 237
Swidler, Ann, x, 211n.13
symbolic boundaries, 257
symbolic interaction, 42, 48–49
symbolic racism, xvn.4, 252
"system, the," 47

"Talented Tenth," 279, 353
"talking black," 11
teenage pregnancy, 193, 196, 213n.33
"tenured radicals," 255
Thomas, Greg, 228
toasts, 326
Tocqueville, Alexis de, 144, 147n.21
Toney, Joyce Roberta, 94n.11
Topps, Betty, 234, 235
"trailer trash," 387n.6
transformationist discourse, 225, 226
transnationalism, x
Trinidad, 71–72
true womanhood, 293
Tullos, Allen, 278
Twyman, Gladys, 233, 234
Tyson, Mike, 337

underclass: Murray on a white, 211n.11; as pejorative, 386n.2; and unwed motherhood, 182; working people measuring themselves against, 180n.12

unemployed, the, 152, 161–63, 180n.2

Universal Negro Improvement Association, 225

universities: affirmative action in admissions, 348; black students attending white, 5; "tenured radicals," 255. *See also* elite universities; nonelite universities

University of California Berkeley, 362n.24

unwed parenthood, 182–218; accepting the pregnancy, 194–95; apprehension about the pregnancy, 195; among blacks and whites compared, 211n.3; by choice, 182; in cohabiting couples, 213n.30; considering marriage after parenthood, 198–208; considering parenthood outside marriage, 188–98; ending the relationship, 202–3; expectations for parenthood, 191–93; marrying the father of the child, 198, 214n.42; as planned, 193–94; poverty and, 211n.3; the pregnancy as unplanned, 195, 213n.31; timing marriage and fertility, 203–8; and welfare, 182, 184

upper class: black workers on, 138–42; white workers on moral flaws of, 131–34; white workers on moral superiority of working class, 134–36. *See also* black upper class

upward mobility: affirmative action in black, 5; of Asians, 372; black middle class on, 32; black workers on, 128, 138; capital required for, 44, 55, 56; and education, 271; external constraints on, 32, 57n.3; family and education in realizing racial constraints on, 38–48; family and schooling in ideologies for, 46–54; for fast-food workers, 158, 168, 174; methodology and data set of this study, 33–35; race as constraint for, 36–38; as "rags-to-riches" phenomenon, 32–33; West Indian domestic workers seeking, 118, 119; white workers on, 137; in young black men, 30–62

value, moral. *See* moral value

values. *See* mainstream values; middle-class values

Vanneman, Reeve, 145n.3

violence against women: male rappers engaged in, 337; race in issues of, 293; as rap music theme, 333. *See also* domestic abuse

violence within the black community: in the drug trade, 172; gangsta rap as contributing to, 321, 325, 330, 335, 337

vocational education, 274, 279

wage gap. *See* income inequality

Waldinger, Roger, 93nn. 5, 6, 98

Walker, Abena, 229, 232, 234, 235, 238, 239, 240

Walker, Alice, 292, 293, 296

Wallace, Michele, 292, 293, 296

Waller, Maureen R., xiii, 180n.12

Walters, Pamela Barnhouse, xiv

Ware, Cellestine, 294

Washington, Booker T., 225, 279, 281

Washington, Cynthia, 294

Waters, Mary C., xi, xiii, 110, 384, 389n.30

Weber, Max, 127, 143

Weir, Margaret, 284n.3

welfare: abuse of women on, 214n.46; low-wage workers' view of, 162, 172; reform forcing women into low-wage work, 173, 178, 180n.11; unwed motherhood for receiving, 182, 184

Wells, Ida B., 338

Welsh-Asante, 228

West, Cornel, ix, 74

"Western culture" curriculum, 249, 253

West Indian immigrants, 63–96; on American concern with race, 75, 77; on black Americans, 74, 75, 77; British ties of, 76; as children's caregivers, 101, 102; conservatism of, 89, 94n.13; the culture associated with being an immigrant, 68–73; culture in success of, 63–66, 93n.4; the culture they bring with them, 73–78; discrimination in favor of the foreign-born, 67; on domestic work as stepping stone, 118, 119; as domestic workers, 98; in emerging dual racial hierarchy, 373; encountering American race relations, 78–85, 110–11; exit strategy of, 76, 94n.11; foreign status of, 70, 78; and interpersonal racism, 78, 80–85; low-wage work accepted by, 66; as more successful than American blacks, 63–

West Indian immigrants (*continued*)
67, 93n.5; networks of, 67, 93n.5; polluted
tasks done by, 120n.6; on race relations at
home, 71–72; on racial discrimination, 77–
78; racism changing attitudes of, 90–92; reaction to racism, 73, 75–76, 88–89, 94n.13; selectivity of immigration, 66; in service economy, 89, 91, 93n.5, 94n.13; structural
explanations of success of, 66–67; and structural racism, 78–80; study of New York,
87–88; as voluntary minority, 70, 77; and
whites, 70–71, 73, 77, 83–90, 91, 110; work
ethic of, 65, 77, 86
When Work Disappears (Wilson), x
white men: feminism supported by, 313n.32;
rising age of marriage for, 214n.43; strong affirmative action disliked by, 345; superior social position of, 37, 38; as "too independent,"
304–5; and unmarried parenthood, 182–210;
white workers on egalitarianism and success,
136–38; white workers on moral flaws of the
upper class, 131–34; white workers on moral
superiority of the working class, 134–36;
white workers on status and worth, 129–31
whites: affirmative action as harming, 344; affirmative action as not understood by, 350,
361n.19; affirmative action as threatening, 6;
as affirmative action beneficiaries, 361n.14;
in American racial structure before 1965,
372; Asians as integrating with, 372–73; becoming a numerical minority, 373, 386n.5;
and black executives, 8, 10, 11, 12, 13, 14;
blacks lumped together by, 10, 18–19; blacks
on whites as doing better than blacks, 329;
comfort factor for, 85–90; domestic workers
employed by, 97–123; ethnic features in, 383;
fearing violence from blacks, 113–14, 118; in
identity politics, 382, 388n.20; intermarriage
with Asians, 376, 378, 387n.11; intermarriage
with blacks, 378, 387; intermarriage with
Hispanics, 376; and interpersonal racism,
78, 80–85; Irish immigrants perceived as,
373–74; light-skinned blacks as honorary,
376; and multiracial individuals, 375–78; out-
of-wedlock births among, 211n.3; racial tolerance increasing in, 384–85; rap music and
black attitudes toward, 334; reproduction
and marriage separated among low-income,

182–218; sexual component of black/white
relationships, 308n.5; social distance from
blacks wanted by, 101; soft affirmative action
supported by, 350–51; and structural racism,
78–80; and West Indian immigrants, 70–71,
73, 77, 83–90, 91, 110; white minorities and
the corporate norm, 24. *See also* poor whites;
white men; white women; white working
class
"white trash," 373, 387n.6
white women: affirmative action benefiting, 6;
with black domestic workers, 97; black
women as more liberal than, 313n.30; as children's caregivers, 99, 100, 101, 103, 104, 109,
120nn. 1, 3; as domestic workers, 98; feminine ideal as white, 293; feminism as white
and middle class, 292–93; independence
from men, 294–95, 303–4, 305–6; nonactivist
women on feminism, 297–300, 309n.14; personal service for domestic employers, 108;
psychological effects of affirmative action in,
349; rising age of marriage for, 214n.43; social distance from domestic employers, 108;
in southern cult of true womanhood, 293;
stigmatized housework by, 105; strong affirmative action disliked by, 345; as "too independent," 303–4, 305–6; unwed motherhood
among, 182–210
white working class: on authority, 130; on egalitarianism and success, 136–38; on importance of high social status, 129–31; middle-
class orientation in, 130, 138, 142; on moral
flaws of the upper class, 131–34; on moral superiority of the working class, 134–36; on status and worth, 127–50; success as defined by,
131, 137
Will, George, 244, 323
Williams, Bruce, 147n.15
Wilson, William Julius, x, 207, 215nn. 52, 53
Winant, Howard, 222, 226
womanism, 293, 307
women: on abusive relationships, 202; and
affirmative action, 5, 343–68; black executives helped by, 18; characteristics valued in a
spouse by, 207; and the corporate norm, 24;
earnings increase relative to men, 184,
211n.9; minority set-asides for contracts,
344–45; multiracials as exotic, 388n.19; race

in ideal of femininity, 293; rising age of marriage for, 214n.43; southern cult of true womanhood, 293; as talking too much, 314n.36; unwed motherhood, 182–210; welfare reform forcing into low-wage work, 173, 178, 180n.11. *See also* black women; feminism; Latinas; misogyny; sexism; violence against women; white women

Women, Infants, and Children (WIC), 187, 212n.23

women's movement. *See* feminism

work (employment): affirmative action's economic effects, 348; in American identity, 152–53; and being called "too independent," 306; black American and West Indian immigrant compared, 93n.5; black women's occupational breakthrough, 299; deindustrialization, 6, 7, 25, 184; education for getting a good job, 271; glass ceilings in, 167, 374; job ceiling for blacks, 7; job hierarchies seen as slavery by blacks, 77; rap music as antiwork, 325; taking precedence over the family, 178; the unemployed, 152, 161–63, 180n.2; work-centered view of life, 178–79. *See also* work ethic; working class

work ethic: of fast-food workers, 164, 172, 173; as ideology for personal mobility, 49–51; as social life woven around the workplace, 178; of West Indian immigrants, 65, 77, 86; of white working class men, 134

working class: child labor in, 276; educational demands made through noneducational institutions, 272, 284n.3; as gendered cultural construct, 145; and middle-class values, xiii, 128, 146n.6; white and black workers on status and worth, 127–50. *See also* black working class; low-wage work; white working class

working poor. *See* low-wage work

WPA, 166–67

Wrigley, Julia, xiii, 181n.13

X-clan (rapper), 323, 330

Young, Alford, Jr., xii

young black men: family and education in realizing racial constraint, 38–48; family and schooling in ideologies for personal mobility, 46–54; getting ahead for, 30–62; methodology and data set of this study, 33–35; Protestant ethic of, 65; public image of, 37, 46, 59n.12; race as constraint on mobility of, 36–38; suicide among, 337